THE
CATHOLIC
TRADITION

THE
CATHOLIC
TRADITION

Thomas Langan

UNIVERSITY OF MISSOURI PRESS

Columbia and London

TO MY WIFE, JANINE

Copyright © 1998 by
The Curators of the University of Missouri
University of Missouri Press, Columbia, Missouri 65201
Printed and bound in the United States of America
All rights reserved
5 4 3 2 1   02 01 00 99 98

Library of Congress Cataloging-in-Publication Data

Langan, Thomas
    The Catholic tradition / Thomas Langan.
      p. cm.
    Includes index.
    ISBN 0-8262-1183-6 (alk. paper)
    1. Catholic Church—Doctrines.   2. Tradition (Theology)
    I. Title.
    BX1751.2.L336   1998
    230'.2—dc21   98-27053
                                                 CIP

♾™ This paper meets the requirements of the

American National Standard for Permanence of Paper
for Printed Library Materials, Z39.48, 1984.

Text design: Elizabeth K. Young
Jacket design: Stephanie Foley
Typesetter: Bookcomp, Inc.
Printer and binder: Thomson-Shore, Inc.
Typefaces: Palatino, Charlemagne

CONTENTS

THE
CATHOLIC
TRADITION

WHY AND HOW "APPROPRIATE ONE'S TRADITIONS"?

A Philosophical Foreword

THE NEED TODAY FOR METHODIC APPROPRIATION OF TRADITIONS

In *Tradition and Authenticity in the Search for Ecumenic Wisdom*, I argued the need in today's situation for personal, methodic appropriation of the traditions that have formed one.[1] Methodic appropriation entails a more explicit, more aware consciousness of the truth implications of the traditions that, in being formed by them, one has already in some less philosophical way appropriated—or, shall we say, been appropriated by them! This more critical reflection on who we are is demanded by our time, an epoch of unprecedented self-awareness, when nothing can be taken for granted, everything is in question, the most basic assumptions upon which a "commonsense" personal and social life could be based are under attack by some group. Moreover, encounters between peoples formed by the different great traditions are more intimate than ever before. The traditions challenge one another more insistently. A better grasp of why we believe what we do provides the security for letting the other be himself, a condition for any fruitful dialogue, while allowing one to respond in an enlightened fashion to the challenges of other visions, of foreign experience.

Many doubt that meaningful dialogue between traditions is possible. It is certainly already difficult—sometimes even more tense—between factions within a given tradition. A thoughtful friend said to me recently, "All we can do is better define different peoples' turf, and mediate political compromises to keep the peace." To be sure, Islam, for instance, can be ignored. For a while. And at our peril. Only through taking the great traditions seriously will we be able to cooperate at more than a superficial, pragmatic level with those of very different beliefs, and that goes, as I said, for those of different parties within our own traditions and institutions. The

---

1. Langan, *Tradition and Authenticity* (Columbia: University of Missouri Press, 1992). Hereinafter, *TA*.

appropriator will never take others seriously unless he comes to believe that they may offer insight into experiences foreign to him, which may be the basis of truths unifiable into an accumulating personal and communitarian wisdom. He is not likely to consider foreign experiences meaningful until he has probed a bit deeper than common sense into the significance of the things declared true by his own traditions.

My project of exploring how the many explicit traditions hand down (*tradere* means "to hand down," hence *traditio*) truths of many kinds is grounded in a particular sense of response-ability: How can we enhance our personal and collective abilities (and, just as important, *willingness*) to respond to the needs and possibilities of our situation in life and hence the needs and possibilities of one another? This particular sense is influenced by the Christian revelations about love—the key, I believe, to who we are. It is only the Christian-influenced traditions that are eager for dialogue.

The project of exploring what our planetary situation demands began with the just-mentioned programmatic introduction *Tradition and Authenticity in the Search for Ecumenic Wisdom.* That volume explained that different kinds of tradition pass on distinctive kinds of truth (a "true" work of art is something very different from a scientific principle, for example). It described the position of the main explicit traditions in the present world system, operating through their respective kinds of institutions, and expressing their distinctive kinds of truth through different sorts of symbol systems (musical notation is different from mathematical symbols, and English from Arabic).

While completing this programmatic introduction I was working on a first draft of my own effort to develop a method of critical appropriation, choosing the tradition that had most deeply formed me, Catholic Christianity. The two efforts were causing one another to be modified, and, as you might expect, I began to develop many urgent questions concerning knowledge and being. It became evident that yet another volume, one of what philosophers call "epistemology and ontology," would be an important part of this appropriative work. Over about ten years I was privileged to work with undergraduate and graduate students as I taught successive drafts of that text. It has now been published as the hefty tome *Being and Truth*.[2] That effort pointed the way toward a Christian anthropology. I was coming to see better what is demanded by focusing my own re-sponse[3] on what my life as a Christian holds as a personal mission. How am I called to move forward in my life, as a reflective intellectual who recognizes that any reflection is carried on within the context of daily challenges to live lovingly with others in a multilayered series of communities and institutions, while struggling to reach out to grasp the ultimate contexts within which that

---

2. Langan, *Being and Truth* (Columbia: University of Missouri Press, 1996). Hereinafter, *BT*.

3. *Spondeo* means "I commit."

action takes place?[4] I live in a family, city, university, nation, church, and the planetary high-tech "world wide web" as a Christian. What does that require of me?

The foundational question is what is this life to which I have been committed? Whence does it spring? What does it demand? Why do I see it as I do, and why and how do I try to live up to its challenges? The critical issue transfuses the whole enterprise: what evidence is there for my convictions about what reality demands of me?

STEPS ON THE WAY TO A METHOD

Now, helped not only by those previous general reflections in *Tradition and Authenticity* and *Being and Truth* but also by readers of two earlier drafts of my efforts at appropriation of mankind's oldest[5] tradition, I am beginning to understand what is involved in trying to wrap one's mind around thirty-five hundred years of history, carried forward by an institution—the Catholic Church—that claims a billion members. This involves situating it in relation to two other of the richest traditions of like ancestry, Judaism and Islam. It requires coming to terms with its ongoing tensions—within the Catholic Church, between Catholics of "different brands,"[6] and without— with a broad spectrum of kinds of Orthodox and Protestant Christians (perhaps seven hundred sects; no one can keep count), with all of whom I share fellowship in the One Jesus Christ. Just that obvious fact shows one cannot responsibly take for granted who that Jesus is, and that who He is is central to coming to grips with who I believe I am.

In wrestling with all these questions I have become clearer about dis- tinguishing what aspects of my own efforts might interest anyone else, hence what of these researches should be published, and for what potential audience.

In two monstrously long manuscripts I provided myself some necessary historical and theological education, on the way to understanding more clearly what are the essential issues for someone today confronting the mas- sive reality of this tradition and the Church that incarnates it. Now I can look back on what has proved profitable for me to research methodically and to write down as I pursue my own appropriative working through of this overwhelming tradition and distinguish in this research what might draw others into the conversation in a fruitful way. In *Tradition and Authenticity*, I suggested that without writing out one's research it is scarcely possible to reach the degree of explicitness called for by our critical, intellectual

---

4. *BT* describes the ultimate dimensions of being that furnish the largest contexts within which meaning occurs. See chapters 9 and 10.

5. If you count its Hebrew roots, without which much that is essential will be missing.

6. I recall testimony to an academic board in a Catholic college by fellow "practicing Catholics" announcing that they rejected "the Langans" brand of Catholicism. Recall Paul's First Letter to the Corinthians, perhaps the oldest Christian document, excoriating that primitive community for fighting over three brands of Christianity!

epoch. This also permits getting feedback from experts and helpful critics, which is vital, as one's own necessarily general efforts remain superficial, but they do not have to be wrong to boot. The experts—to whom I am most grateful—have helped me not foist the fruit of all this primitive research on an audience.

I confess there is a selfish reason for going to the considerable tedium of readying yet this, the third version, for publication: one spontaneously wants to share what he finds good, indeed the greatest Good. But in doing so I want to profit from the different experiences and reflections of others, hoping this will help me break out as much as is humanly possible from my own peculiar blind spots and those socially realized caducities of my Church, particularly the Church of "my brand."

This response on my part will, I am hopeful, seem more sincere once I have had a chance to explain that I believe *to cathalou*—the universal—is a welcoming open sense of truth conceived in a resolutely nonmythological and nonideological mode. Rightly understood it should protect your freedom to see and live the world differently, without the project of common wisdom having to be abandoned. I shall have a chance to explain how one might deal with the obvious fact that we hypocrites of all "brands" have rarely lived up to this vision,[7] and that no great tradition has produced nothing but saints, although Christianity is supposed to be about nothing else. (Making sense of Christ's command "Be ye perfect as your heavenly Father is perfect," given the society of hypocrites that is the sociological reality of the Church, is a central challenge of the present appropriation—a holy Church made up of sinners.) In the history of the Church we have produced betrayals à la Judas Iscariot in every generation, and continue to nurture genuinely ugly streaks in our Church, and debilitating mediocrity. The Church as the mystical Unspotted Bride of Christ is paradoxically not separable from the Church involved in St. Bartholomew's Day Defenestration of Protestants, nor dreary routinized liturgies. How ought one come to terms with that daily disturbing aspect of the divine-human paradox of the Incarnation? Certainly not by ceasing to be shocked by sin, especially not the Chinese water torture of carefully maintained mediocrity of daily life of those who proudly fly the flag of Jesus and maybe of the pope!

In the earlier versions, having plowed (in a very general way, hence superficially) through the whole history of the Church, I attempted a kind of résumé aimed at showing the intertwining of doctrinal, institutional, and cultural developments. Along with certifying that I had done some homework, this succeeded in producing good illustrations of how a living tradition must invent structures and express its growing experience in adequate symbols—institutions are great symbol factories (just look at

7. Last summer the pastor of the church in Dawson City, Yukon, said in a sermon that has marked my life that when he tried to bring his old friend John back to the Church, John shouted, "That church of yours is full of hypocrites, full I tell you!" The pastor replied, "That's all right, we always have room for one more!"

the U.S. federal tax code!). That work provided a feel for the daunting complexity of the Church's growth, and some support for my own version of what I came to consider the essence of the tradition and the reasons I accept its claims, in the form in which I understand them. Working through the materials methodically was necessary, because all the many aspects—doctrinal, liturgical, institutional, cultural—intertwine and interact, revealing the dynamic unfolding (and, in a sense to be explained, deepening). But the result was too long and demanding for a larger audience.

As I present now the essence of the tradition, while I cannot hope to satisfy experts in matters in which they spend their lives, I can provide for all a diachronic and synchronic context, historical and contemporary, while making the very notion of the essence of a tradition more meaningful. I do not pretend here to unfold horizon-opening new theology. But I do hope to find thoughtful, well-educated readers (many themselves expert in some part of this vast reality) who share my belief that it is vital to bring into relief the structure and overall sense of a tradition. (It is, for instance, useful to reflect on Hans Urs von Balthasar's contention that the basic institutional givens founded by Christ and elaborated in the early Church change very little, while dogma develops!) What I am pursuing here is a *philosophical* task, one a generalist can undertake meaningfully. Even the specialists profit from considering this tradition as a whole rather than being satisfied with a version they, once beyond their specializations, may have cobbled together out of haphazard impressions of Catholicism as a whole.

There is another, more pragmatic reason a broad audience should take this tradition seriously: Christianity has spawned institutions—the Roman Catholic, Orthodox, and Protestant Churches—that influence the lives of more than a quarter of mankind. And as this is the tradition that has begotten our own Occidental civilization out of which has grown the planetary high-technology phenomenon that is sweeping our time and transforming our lives, it affects everyone indirectly.[8]

To ignore those truth claims, or to refute only distorted disinformation versions of them, is to remain ignorant of oneself as a child of this civilization, and it is to miss the sense of a major struggle at the heart of our time. (Secularists are still having trouble understanding why the Polish pope played such a big role in bringing down "the Evil Empire." And they are puzzled, if they do not ignore it altogether, by his call for victory of "the civilization of life" over "the civilization of death.")

---

8. The "HTX" my research group calls it, because there is no word for what is neither a culture nor a civilization but a new kind of . . . "world wide web." What in *TA* was described as a "world system" (chaps. 6 and 7) has been subsequently seen to be only a part—albeit a major part—of the "HTX": the High-Tech Whatever. "The Web" interacts dialectically with most of the world's cultures and all its civilizations. New evangelization has to take place in this HTX planetary context. With a research group of my former philosophy students who have become "leading-edge techies," I have completed an analysis of our epochal situation tentatively titled *HTX: Learning to Survive in Virtual Reality.*

In seeking to illumine the sense of the central truth claims advanced today by this tradition, I shall be personal about my experience struggling to understand and to live them; I have discovered this is necessary because these truths are not principally theoretical; seeing (*theorein* means "seeing") their truth, and formulating it correctly, is of course essential (how else would one know what is expected of one?). But to be seen really for what they are these truths have to be lived out. (You can read *The Wine Spectator* for hours about the best California "cabs," but if you really want to know them, "then see and taste," as the Scripture says, "See and taste how the Lord is good!") The cardinal claim at the heart of the living tradition, one that can come to us only by revelation, is that God is love. Love can take place, and hence reveal itself, only in actions between persons freely offering themselves to one another. It is easier to theorize about love than to love.

I shall be trying to see my own loves better, and more critically (hence more honestly), and it is reflecting about them on that experiential level that the more theoretical formulations come to be understood and criticized. The critic, you the reader, will be hard-pressed to judge whether what I confess are my loves really are—"he is not my spiritual director, after all!" But you can legitimately build a case, when appropriate, that what I want is an illusion, inadequate, or inherently desirous, and/or maybe even good; or perhaps you will conclude that it sounds nice but just seems unconvincingly supported by the evidence. (After all this work, I am painfully aware that elements of my faith are still based in what is familiar, coupled with a defensive posture, more than in enlightenment from experience. The light well-disposed critics may throw on my situation, even when it illumines *a lack*, is an important part of what one seeks from a friend.)

Modern efforts to depersonalize truth do not work for the simple reason that truth is found and lived out only by persons, in intersubjective worlds. Now, the absolute claims made about Jesus Christ challenge the relativism that pervades today's academy.[9] Many in the academy have been busy since the Enlightenment trying to relativize those very claims, key to so much in Occidental society, but relativizing absolute claims distorts them out of existence. One may honestly reject them, but distorting them is a lie.

Anyone trying to return these absolute claims to the center of the debate appears to those who reject them as an enemy of modernity, or an ignoramus who has not grasped the thrust of "postmodernity" and "deconstruction."[10] This is not new. The same Jesus Christ who said, "My

9. The recently deceased grand theologian Hans Urs von Balthasar declares that the worst catastrophe that ever hit the Church was the professional separation, toward the end of the Middle Ages, of dogmatic and mystical theology. Before that, theology was written by saints as an expression of the love they had experienced in opening themselves to the life God poured out through them.

10. The university today is in the throes of a critical movement that is adept at showing the "vested interests" behind the necessarily finite horizons of interpretation of any exponent of any tradition. Nothing seems more ludicrous to the exponents of "deconstruction" than people who still cling to absolutes. The 367 pages of *BT* are

peace I leave you, my peace I give to you," and is called the Prince of Peace, is also found saying, "Unless you hate your mother and hate your brother, you cannot follow me" (Luke 14:26), "Let the dead bury the dead" (Matt. 8:22; Luke 9:60). The absolute claims made in His name are truly threatening of all tranquillity, dangerous to regimes of compromise and "muddling through," while at the same time these absolute claims pretend to hold out the only way to true peace.

People who make such wild claims are indeed dangerous! This is not the stuff of "working by compromise to define our different turfs," of which my friend spoke. I am being serious when I point to the danger. I do not blame in the least those who do not believe in Christianity for combating it with all their might: taken seriously, it undermines all other orders but its own, and it turns its back on the modern relativistic skepticisms. But—oh, paradox—Christians believe Christ alone founds adequately a space-time within which true freedom, respect for conscience, and for the otherness of the other can endure. The Enlightenment "Human Rights" tradition comes straight out of the claims of Christianity about the absolute dignity of every human person.

Each human being, from conception until death, and then into resurrected life everlasting, is infinitely precious? The finite is sort of infinite? Paradox . . . or just plain folly? Another gigantic, not evident claim, which, because it is at the center of my (paradoxical) faith, I shall try to support here.[11]

WHY SPORADIC, PIECEMEAL APPROPRIATION IS NOT ENOUGH

Tradition and Authenticity was not naive about the difficulties of getting anyone to appreciate a foreign perspective, or even of getting brothers and sisters to cooperate. Nor is *Being and Truth* Polyannaish about the difficulties of personal struggle to open up to every kind of truth. I promised there to explore more deeply, as part of developing my own Christian understanding of the dilemmas of the concrete human condition, the anthropological, psychological, ethical, and just plain practical grounds of the troubles we all have even *wanting* to live in the truth when it is hard (and why the truth, which "will make you free," is so hard). As a contribution I proposed to work on developing methods, first one for appropriating one of my own traditions, and then for the rather different task of appropriating explicit traditions foreign to one's experience. Obviously the challenge in each case is different.

---

the start of an argument against the deconstructionist and historical relativist forms of "postmodern" skepticism, though giving them their due.

11. That is what I did, but on a more epistemological-ontological, less revelational, level, in *BT*.

With one's own cherished tradition, which one lives out both because he loves it and because, being familiar, he has made it as comfortable as possible, the challenge is achieving more honesty. One must begin by getting some distance in order to objectivize it for reflection. The very possibility of being quite honest about our most cherished commitments—making them inevitably less comfortable—is part of what the deconstructionists are skeptical about. They are right in finding it difficult; indeed, achieving distance from one's own self is extremely challenging, as we shall see. Seeking to find and clarify the essence of a tradition within which we are deeply embedded, all the while trying to grasp better the meaning of the experiences that feed those deeply held beliefs, which we *desire* to believe, and love—sometimes with a pure love, sometimes with an impure or pseudolove, desires that are self-destructive because they are self-seeking—requires listening more sympathetically to those who disagree, who may even despise one's first loves. They may be pointing to our blinders, challenging sources of our comfort in unexamined routine. Much worse, pathological damage may even make the quest a nonstarter.

So the first experiment to evolve a method through intimate contact with the object, appropriating one's own tradition, requires somehow getting over defensiveness, out of love for the truth one professes—and struggles—to live.[12] The second, appropriating a foreign tradition,[13] demands another, related form of love: empathy for that which already stands over against one and is therefore already an object, and hence a challenge. The movement here is the opposite of the first kind of appropriation: the life of that other community has to be in some degree de-objectivized by getting somehow inside it, participating vicariously in its life to appreciate the different experiences that feed it.

Pride—and lack of imagination—keeps us humans from learning from the experiences of others. If we were to accept the skepticism of some of the postmodern deconstructionists, we could simply sigh and say, "You see the metaphysical myth of the unity of being is once and for all destroyed. People live in different and noncommunicating worlds, driven by conflicting interests. 'Ethnic cleansing' is a natural instinct." But as much of my two previous volumes was devoted to an anti-ideological refounding of the "metaphysical myth" of the unity of being in the face of contemporary nihilists, I shall have to continue, if I am not to become

12. More formal, methodic, written appropriation, which seeks to make the tradition's truths one's own by taking critical responsibility for what is claimed, can be found in accounts of "conversions" such as various *apologiae pro vita sua*, as Cardinal Newman titled his own appropriation, or in Albert Speer's *Inside the Third Reich: Memoirs* (trans. Richard and Clara Winston [New York: Macmillan, 1970]), fruit of twenty years' reflection in Spandau Prison. Critical distance, methodic consistency, ontological depth—striving to reach down to basic principle—and ecumenical sensitivity are demanded of good apologiae.

13. What is said here is also true of appropriating foreign subtraditions within one's own tradition, as the "conservative" Catholic ought to do for the "liberal," and vice versa.

a living witness to the anthropological error of the ontology defended there, to try to learn from others' traditions, starting with the scariest of all, the "heresies" of fellow Christians, and, worst of all, Catholics of other brands![14]

Being raised in a number of traditions, some more central to one's persona than others, one grows up accustomed to a pattern of activities, sharing communal experiences, and absorbing the language through which these get expressed, much of which is learned by imitation, including all the roles we are expected to play in different institutions. Such *implicit* tradition may be accompanied, as it is in the case of all the great traditions of revelation, as well as of philosophy and science, by *explicit* teaching. This *explicit* teaching includes the formulations in well-worked-out symbol systems—both doctrine and, in the case of religion, liturgy—of what the tradition claims to be true. This provides a skeleton of explanation for the sense of the experiences as well as an institutional framework, both shaped by and shaping the formulations—doctrine and rules providing guides for action. These explicit statements and explicit laws of organization, evolved and recorded over the centuries, offer a long-distance perspective one can never gain on a purely implicit (and hence unrecorded) tradition. This historical depth is indispensable if we are to avoid superficiality and parochialism in our embrace of what we believe to be the truths of the tradition. A good knowledge of that history is, then, necessary for responsible formal appropriation.

HOW TO START?

There exists no tradition for appropriating traditions methodically. To my knowledge, no one has ever examined various *apologiae pro vita sua* to see how the authors passed in critical review the process of their conversions and the rationale for their lives. At a time when one can receive training in the philosophical methods of particular schools, of how to analyze an

14. Of course, there are in each of us and in the world conflicting interests. Many of these interests are legitimate, but require limited resources (like *time!*) (the Church's teaching acknowledges this, and there can be no credible defense of human freedom without recognizing the legitimacy of differences, and the limits of resources, of all kinds). But there are also divisions nurtured by "bad faith." Yet, as a result of the exploration of *BT*, and eight years of teaching it to as "multicultural" a generation of students as you can find anywhere in the HTX, I am—surprise!—reassured about the commonality of human nature, and the ability to call on the goodwill that lodges in the hearts of most, to move forward toward mutual understanding. Further, and even more optimistically, I have been reassured by that effort that different experiences, when critically purified of elements of unnecessary blindness (bad faith, again, but sometimes just innocent ignorance), are somehow distinctive revelations of the same being, which, with much cooperative work, can be brought together critically and intelligibly—not eclectically ("eclectic" means just loosely thrown together without critical search for profound internal consistency, as well as conformity of experience)—in a collective wisdom. The purification of bad elements requires on the part of all some *con-versio*, a change of course, and that implies asking for, and offering, forgiveness.

engineering problem, and how to conduct microbiological research, the lack of even a sense that methodic appropriation of traditions is desirable is significant. It shows, I believe, how recently we have become aware of the ecumenical demands of the increasingly tight little world being woven by the emerging world system. Awareness of tradition as "a unit" that both is alongside and cuts across civilizations and cultures is itself new. The exploration of tradition in the way proposed in *Tradition and Authenticity* represents a new departure in the philosophy of history. The present study is an effort to show that such methodic appropriation of a tradition can be scientifically fruitful.[15]

The political philosopher Eric Voegelin has warned that method should not be developed apart from the actual research into the data being investigated. A dialectic develops between object and method.[16] I have heeded his warning: the method that is emerging here is a result of responding to the demands made upon me by the Catholic material. Its evoluative character was dictated as I worked through several drafts with somewhat different approaches. Central among those demands: the call to love truth, hence to drop all defenses. Has there been a little progress in this through the drafts? Has a methodological gimmick been found to ensure this (moral) progress? I am not sure. Surprises from the objects studied awaited me at every turn, not the least being discoveries about how and why we are so deeply defensive, and the particular ways I have found to build my own bastions.[17] Tearing them down has been neither easy, nor is it completed. I offer a few details now about my travails, to provide some insight into how a method for appropriating this tradition has evolved, hoping thereby to clarify the reasons for the method's present form.

Guided by a few principles developed in *Tradition and Authenticity*'s preliminary analysis of how in general explicit traditions unfold,[18] my first effort produced sixteen hundred pages divided into three books:

1. The Church's present authoritative (in the sense that the Roman Church has a very definite, explicit "teaching authority") understanding of the ideal as matured and developed over two millennia. This review of the authoritative ideal vision of the Church was built around a (tedious) condensation of the main documents

15. Its "interpersonal" nature does not make it unscientific, if phenomenological science can be permitted to invade the realm of history. Cultures and nature affect one another, a civilization develops many cultures, the civilization and the cultures mutually affect one another, the HTX penetrates, and is in turn affected by all civilizations of the world and almost all of their cultures. Don't kill the messenger: reality is not simple!

16. See previous note.

17. One of Balthasar's rare polemic texts, a remarkable little book published in 1952 attacking "integralism" (an intransigent conservatism) in the Church, is titled *Schleifung der Bastionen* (*Razing the Bastions: On the Church in This Age*, trans. Brian McNeil [San Francisco: Ignatius Press, 1993]). The present study is a reflection on how to be genuinely "open" without being empty.

18. *TA*, 51–88, 167–212.

of the Second Vatican Council,[19] which of course inevitably was my interpretation of the heart of the council's teaching, presented as faithfully as I was able.[20]

Because that council concerned itself primarily with ecclesiological issues and therefore did not much elaborate explicitly on the traditional understanding of the central figure, Jesus Christ,[21] I decided to recapitulate modern christological positions more methodically than it was by the council fathers, with the help of Walter Kasper's widely discussed postconciliar book, *Jesus the Christ.* Finally, to make sure every aspect of the present understanding of the essence of the Catholic vision had been covered, I worked my way through the great creeds, accompanied by the modern reading found in the sermons of Joseph Cardinal Ratzinger, collected under the title *Introduction to Christianity.*[22]

2. Thus, with some grasp of the present formulations of the Church's teaching, in the second book I went back through the two millennia of the history of the Church examining *the* crises (literally, "moments of decision") that shaped the current formulations of the ideal. To grasp the thrust of these formulations it proved necessary to know to what the fathers of the Church were responding throughout its history. The progressive historical elaborations of the seeds of what in *Tradition and Authenticity* is termed the original "founding vision" that developed the initial Privileged Experience of Being—the apostles' experience of the living, crucified, and resurrected Lord—into the rich elaborated ideals of the tradition was the goal of this exercise.

3. Finally, in this last book I unleashed completely my own critical powers of appropriation, which I had pretended to hold off until

19. The completion in the meantime of *The Universal Catechism* would have made that task much easier.

20. One of the great dramas in the Church today is the struggle between versions of "the spirit of the Council," as we shall see in the last chapter. A small (about eight) group of American bishops, led by Archbishop Rembert Weakland of Milwaukee, recently accused "the Roman curia" of "deliberately reinterpreting the Council" (*Inside the Vatican* [November 1995]). To be sure, the recently issued *Catechism of the Catholic Church* (London: Geoffrey Chapman, 1994), as well as a whole series of major encyclicals by Pope John Paul II, and major documents of the Sacred Congregation for the Doctrine of the Faith, headed by Joseph Cardinal Ratzinger, are intended to be authentic interpretations of the sense of the council. I am conscious of the fact that, of course, I too interpreted the council, but part of my way of trying to remain faithful to the rich, complex sense of its teachings of the several long conciliar documents is to display the fruits of that interpretation here, and then, as I said, listen carefully to detailed criticisms of any of my interpretations as too idiosyncratic, or just plain heretical.

21. Christological threads of course run through the council documents, but there is no christological treatise to be found among them.

22. Kasper, *Jesus the Christ,* trans. V. Green (New York: Paulist Press, 1976). Ratzinger's series of Lenten sermons given when he was archbishop of Munich in the late 1960s is marvelous for both its clarity and its profundity (*Introduction to Christianity,* trans. J. R. Foster [New York: Herder, 1970]).

then, thinking I would save until after a historical description of how the formulations and institutional forms developed my judgments of what in all this is true, and what is disputable, and why I believe what I do of what the tradition hands down. I was attempting to suspend the ultimate judgment of truth while addressing, in the light of the problems raised by the actual living (and hence ambiguous) experience of the real community, the tradition's development. *Tradition and Authenticity* had argued for the methodological desirability of first coming to understand a tradition in its own terms, as the people engaged in it experience it, with due attention to authoritative formulations, and only then, when such understanding has begun to be appreciated and enjoyed, addressing the critical question of subsuming the explicit truth claims into one's own global understanding of how it stands with reality as a whole.

Despite the labors on those three books constituting a large volume of sixteen hundred pages, which helped me identify themes, issues, and problems and to understand better the historical setting and meaning of many particular matters, observing them unfold over time, that approach actually did not work very well. Even the since-issued *Catechism of the Catholic Church*, with its clear overview in 2,865 paragraphs, almost all containing matters of import, will not solve the problem that emerged in the course of doing this work.

That problem is this: from the start I had to select and highlight, with no more authority than my own philosophical reflection upon the mass of information I had learned about the tradition,[23] guided by my own experience of living in the Church today, what I believe to be the irreducible, essential core of what the tradition has to pass on to us. With regard to the key dimensions, I was of course also judging how these themes developed over the centuries. The scholarly attitude, pretending to hold off the critical moment until the end, tended to disguise (rather thinly) this element of personal responsibility and indeed enthusiasm grounded in my own faith, which was inevitably active from the first moment of the written appropriating. It did succeed in delaying until the end a frank expression of the personal and communal experiences that all these complex symbols are meant to capture and without which they may seem a mere play of ideas.

Despite this disconcerting discovery that I was (unsuccessfully) hiding my own engagements, my own re-sponse, I still believe it is valid to try to withhold judgment as much as possible when approaching traditions

23. Cardinal Ratzinger and Archbishop Christoph Schönborn had international commissions and finally the 3,500 bishops and their theologians (who produced 25,000 suggestions for improvements to the penultimate draft!) to help them make their selection for the catechism. But then I am not writing a catechism. Indeed, my work is a philosophical document of deontic authority only; it is not about doctrine as such but about the life of a three-millennial tradition.

foreign to oneself, at least until the tradition's spokesmen have been permitted to communicate their experience and to make the best case possible for the validity of that experience. One should be aware that it is not because I have never enjoyed an experience personally that I need discredit the witness of those who testify that they have. At the critical moment, judging what one has himself never experienced is delicate. Offering some benefit of the doubt that there really is something worthwhile animating the lives of those who get their meaning from that foreign tradition may be wisest, and in fact most scientific!

But when one is not just appropriator but also, as in my case writing of the Catholic tradition, inevitably a (self-appointed) spokesman of the tradition under critical review, because it is, after all, what he lives and believes, I now see it is better to manifest frankly from the start one's enthusiasms in experiencing what one does, and dismay at experience of mediocre elements in the tradition (particularly those to which one himself contributes) that hide the splendor of the vision, and concerns with what is happening with one's tradition today—Catholicism in the midst of the most radical secularization ever seen—while trying to clarify for himself and his readers why he holds as true what he believes to be the reality manifest in these things.

So in the second version I decided to come clean from the start. One cannot present "realities" without confessing, at least implicitly, why one believes them worthy of mention, what one makes of them, one's adherence or rejection, and one's concerns for the future—which reveals one's loves and hates. That is why, at the start of *Being and Truth,* I laid my cards on the table by formulating an overview of my own "natural-faith" understanding of and position regarding the analogy of being and how we can attain any truth at all, and what, in the present work, I believe the essence of Catholicism to be. While I assumed responsibility for these judgments, my intention remained, in the case of appropriating Catholicism, to present the tradition itself, not an idiosyncratic view. That endeavor was an attempt to remain faithful[24] to the historic, sociological, and ecclesial reality of the tradition and the community that carries it on, as I believe it to be "in itself."[25]

I also thought I would have to show the reader how that reality effectively maintained itself over the centuries in mankind's oldest continual explicit tradition. But that generated the lengthy and tedious review of the history that, in the words of a friendly critic, "added little to the standard histories." So what I have done in the present version, after laying out my sense of

24. "Orthodox"? "Conservative"? "Reactionary"? Does that make him necessarily not "progressive"? Not "liberal"? Not "open"? The whole effect of my series of inquiries should be to carry us beyond all puerile labeling of one another. The reader who bails out at the first whiff of a tendency of which he does not approve will never be reached by appeals for the need for ecumenical dialogue.

25. The hermeneutic paradox is intended; that is what *BT* is all about, and that is why it developed in parallel with the different versions of the present appropriation.

the essential vision as it is promulgated by the Church today, is to single out certain key issues that remain centers of intense concern within and without the Church, and attempt to clarify my own stand regarding them, with the help of some pivotal moments in history.

What follows is, then, in no way a history of the Church, but *a reflection on the present life of the Church illumined through examination of moments in history that need to be known if present developments are to be evaluated.* This will give a sense of the intense life of the Church as it is presently struggling with the tensions and ambiguities of life in the HTX, while offering for all to see the strengths and limits of my own vision.

The word *sinner* will come up several times. Modernity would like to banish that term, but orthodox Christianity, for reasons to be explained, cannot. I will show why the term does not bother me. Christianity is about redemption, and I believe we need saving, and that only the Son of God can accomplish that for us. But what does bother me, and mightily—I tell you this now because this struggle has been going on throughout my appropriation—is the fact that "the Church of the saints" being made up only of sinners, Christ and Mary excepted, we are faced with this ghastly result: we Christians have deformed and continue to deform the truth, every day and in every sinful act, with awful effects on us and for those to whom we believe we are called to bring Christ's truth. Our sin hides the face of that God who chose to reveal Himself through human beings, made in His image but distorting the likeness. The great saints shine out, but in the midst of unacceptable mediocrity in the Church. This state of affairs requires, as the Church officially teaches, *constant reform*—indeed, conversion—of ourselves and of the Church *(ecclesia semper reformanda)*. Not lip service to reform but a mighty struggle to become a worthy witness. My present effort to be less defensive is part of a personal process of reform. With a Pauline-like modesty, I offer to all for imitation this fight against defensiveness, this personal effort to raze my own bastions! I just pray each of you will succeed better than I.[26]

---

26. The Catholic tradition, centered on the person of that Jesus Christ who claimed to be *the* way, *the* truth, and *the* life itself, has always stressed the need to present the *truth as a whole*—"the *catholica*"—thereby representing the divine integrity of Christ Himself, a perfect truth for all men. I therefore make every effort to present in harmonious form all that is essential in the teaching of the tradition. And while I renounce, as beyond my capabilities and as exceeding what one book could ever do, the effort to clarify its sense adequately from history (which would also mean plunging to the depths theologically—and even if I were a de Lubac or a Balthasar, it took the latter eighteen volumes of his unnamed trilogy to plumb those depths, inadequately, I am sure he would say!)—I shall place in a historical context adequate enough to furnish at least an introduction to the disputes my discussion of what I judge to be some particularly important "burning points" for the contemporary appropriator. This will prove helpful in understanding non-Catholic Christian traditions where they differ seriously from what others invariably term *Roman Catholicism,* but also the ongoing differences within the Catholic Church. (While the universal Church does indeed gather about the Chair of Peter, first bishop of Rome, if "Roman Catholic" hints at the slightest degree of

WHERE IS THE TRUE BEGINNING?

You may wonder why I do not begin by returning to the oldest texts of the tradition, most of which have been gathered together over time and in an obscure process "canonized" as the New Testament; or, as the coming of Christ founded a new tradition from out of an old Hebraic-Jewish one that prepared for it through millennia of experience, why I do not begin perhaps with the Old Testament. My crucial methodological decision not to do so is based in two convictions.

First, what is central to this tradition is not Holy Scripture, as vitally important—indeed, "normative," in a sense we shall discuss—as it is for the Church; rather, the tradition is centered in the Word of God incarnate in Jesus Christ who is found in living form in the whole life of the Church. Catholicism is not *el din al kitab* (a religion of the book) as is Islam, or as certain biblical fundamentalists try to make Christianity; Catholicism is religion centered in a person, whose presence among us continues ecclesiastically-sacramentally, as a unique, "mystical" kind of community gathered about the real presence of Jesus Christ in the Eucharist. That whole, which is the life of the community, includes not just the Church's tradition of teaching, which includes as the most important written source its active, ongoing interpretation of Scripture, but its sacramental and liturgical and institutional life; in short, the entire communal, anthropic, social pursuit of truth and holiness. It is out of that life, in the bosom of the whole unfolding tradition, that the New Testament Scriptures were formed in the first place (and at the start not yet even thought of as "Scriptures"—only the Old Testament enjoyed that status). It was the Church that gradually and eventually definitively decided what came to be included in the canon of what was later to be called the New Testament. The writing and the gradual formation of that canon (a word applied to the writings only in the mid-fourth century) was a prime work of the tradition.[27]

Second, I do not pretend to be able to present an independent interpretation of the gospel message as propounded in Scripture alone, and to situate it adequately in that long *preparatio evangelica* reported in the writings of the Old Testament that span fifteen hundred years of experience on the part

---

sectarianism or parochialism, then it is a misleading, even nonsensical, title, which goes against the central claim: to incarnate Christ, who is *the* truth.)

27. The great classic studies of this complex story are Adolf von Harnack, *The Origin of the New Testament and the Most Important Consequences of the New Creation*, trans. J. R. Wilkinson (New York: Macmillan, 1925); Theodor Zahn, *Forschungen zur Geschichte des neutestamentlichen Kanons und der altkirchlichen Literatur* (Leipzig: A. Leichert, 1903–1929); B. F. Westcott, *A General Survey of the History of the Canon of the New Testament*, 6th ed. (Cambridge: Macmillan, 1889); J. Leipoldt, *Geschichte des neutestamentlichen Kanons*, 2 vols. (Leipzig: Hinrich, 1907–1908); and two recent major studies: Robert Grant, *The Formation of the New Testament* (New York: Harper and Row, 1965); and Hans von Campenhausen, *The Formation of the Christian Bible* (Philadelphia: Fortress Press, 1972). For a recent summary see the short work by Harry Y. Gamble, *The New Testament Canon* (Philadelphia: Fortress Press, 1985).

of the Hebrew People of God. Therefore, since my understanding of the Holy Writ is so affected by my own experience of the tradition and all that I have been taught by the Church, it is with that whole that I must struggle in appropriation. Inevitably, I go to Scripture through the Church, not to the Church through Scripture.

In pursuing this point before I even begin I realize that I am already in hot debate, not only with fundamentalists within the Church, but also potentially with deconstructionists. The fundamentalist idea of *Scriptura sola* is an absolute nonstarter; with that the deconstructionists would agree. I would venture to say that most Scripture scholars today acknowledge the principle I confessed above, that what we call the New Testament is the fruit of the Church that produced and gathered these documents, and, coming to recognize them to be what God intended, eventually—after at least a century and a half—declared them inspired in a more explicit sense than the inspiration guiding all Christian saints. An evangelical, but nonfundamentalist, friend reacted thus to what I have just expressed:

> I certainly acknowledge the role of the "Church" here, yet I want to stress the primacy of "inspiration by the Holy Spirit" as the true "producer" of these documents, dual authorship, divine and human. The Church's role was to recognize these inspired documents which God intended to be in the canon, a very special providential role for the Church. But it is still secondary—the Church's role is always secondary to God's "first move."[28]

A difference in understanding what is meant here by "the Church" is evident. The Catholic would understand the Holy Spirit's inspiration of the human acts of writing down what Christ was seen to do and heard to say to be already and totally the work of the Church, not different from the Holy Spirit's guidance of those acts of discussion and eventual decision by which these works went through different redactions and finally found general ecclesial acceptance in the canon of the New Testament, and no different from the eventual acts of authority declaring the canon complete in the form to which it has come down to us, unaltered since probably the mid-second century. To be sure, the Holy Spirit takes initiatives all the time without first asking the permission of any Church authority. And it is indeed the charism of office in the Church to discern, eventually, the genuine from the in-genuine among claims—whether regarding powerful acts or doctrinal illuminations—presented as coming from the Holy Spirit.

Further, the Old Testament canon is also accepted by the Church, even though it is taught by the Church in the light of the Christ event as the Church lives it and carries its vision forward. This is a teaching that is enjoined by the tradition to be always respectful of the meaning clearly deposited in the ancient texts, but that develops, even as the Church's hermeneutics do—subtle from the earliest fathers, supersophisticated in

---

28. Private correspondence. Name withheld by request.

the thought of Augustine or of Maximus the Confessor,[29] but still evolving today, of course. Because the magisterium[30] of the Church today embraces many elements of recent historical-critical scholarship, the Church's interpretation manifests a renewed richness, and great nuance. As conciliar documents, papal encyclicals, and the recent *Catechism* have Scriptural texts woven throughout them, the Church's ongoing work of interpretation is obviously massive.

The Church, especially in and since the council, has ceaselessly stressed the importance of the written Word of God. The Bible is nothing less than *normative* for the Church in this precise sense: the living tradition feeds constantly from these texts, and is supposed to respect every iota of what is written there. The story of how each gospel came to be and that of the final establishment of the canon, of what among the early writings is to be honored as divinely inspired, is most complex, and new discoveries about it enter into the Church's interpretations. I decided not to go into it in the present volume, despite the fact that it presents a good example of the living tradition at work, because it would itself require a book. Rather, as disputed issues arise in the course of this appropriation, if differences in biblical interpretation are vital, I shall deal with them with as much attention to the relevant hermeneutical issues as is required. In fact, rarely throughout what follows are differences in interpreting the Bible in any narrow sense the issue.[31]

29. For some notion of the riches and subtlety of interpretation, see Henri de Lubac, *Exégèse médiéval: Les quatre sens de l'Écriture,* 4 vols. (Paris: Aubier, 1959–1964).

30. Meant here specifically is the special teaching authority of the Holy See. Two important documents on biblical interpretation have retained attention in recent years. The first is the highly authoritative document of the Second Vatican Council, "Dei Verbum, Dogmatic Constitution on Divine Revelation," in Walter M. Abbott, S.J., ed., *The Documents of the Vatican II* (New York: America Press, 1966), 111–28; the second is "The Interpretation of the Bible in the Church," Document of the Pontifical Biblical Commission, issued November 1993, available in *Catholic International,* Rome, March 1994, 109–47, which, as Cardinal Ratzinger points out in his preface, "is not an organ of the teaching office of the church" but a scholarly commission whose works have scientific value (110).

31. The following comment of a New Testament scholar introducing his book on the formation of the canon suggests the complexities that arise as one moves from a single phrase to the pericope, to the whole document, to comparison of the Gospels, to the all-embracing context of the whole canon: "the canon is a hermeneutical construct not only by circumstance but to some extent also by design. This design urges the coherence of the several collections [the four gospels, the letters, Revelations] within themselves and with each other and so promotes the interpretation of each text with a view to other texts. In this way, the import of single documents is qualified and revised by the larger whole, while at the same time the larger whole gives rise to new meanings through the textual configurations created by the canon. Thus the canon itself is a locus of meaning . . . the 'canonical sense' which arises through these juxtapositions is a dimension of meaning which belongs to the NT as such, that is, as canon" (Gamble, *The New Testament Canon,* 79). Indeed, the hermeneutical problems are endless, and exist on many levels. Harry Gamble summarizes these succinctly, and at the same time shows the importance of tradition in every moment: "The canonical sense of the texts

Here is a point stressed much more by Catholics than by most Protestants: from the start—before there was any New Testament and continuing once the canon settled into its definitive form—the Church has always taught more than what is explicitly stated in Scripture. The New Testament itself clearly authorizes this, both with Christ's charge of "I give to you the keys to the kingdom of heaven. . . . Whatsoever you shall bind on earth will be bound in heaven"[32] and with John's conclusion of his gospel with the words "There were many other things that Jesus did; if it all were written down, the world itself, I suppose, would not hold all the books that would have to be written" (John 21:25). One might add 2 Thess. 2:15, "Stand firm, then, brothers, and keep the traditions that we taught you, whether by word of mouth or by letter."

In struggling to make this appropriation *critical*, that is, to see the limits of the Catholic tradition as a human, historic reality, where the human obscures the divine, those limits manifested themselves in two forms:

1. Problems on the level of theory, including inadequate formulation. At the root of this tradition may be divine revelation, but this is received by sinful man, who, as Pope John Paul II reminds us, does not *possess* that mysterious truth, and whose theological efforts to understand it, despite the guidance of the Holy Spirit, to whom we never respond sinlessly, will always be inadequate.

2. Human disasters on the level of practice: the Inquisition, the Crusades, abuse of clerical power, everyday mediocrity, stultifying routinization of prayer and liturgy, pharisaism. But this tradition does claim of itself centrally that while it is "human, all too human," thus requiring that *ecclesia semper reformanda*, it is divine in its origins and has always been guided by the Holy Spirit of God in its struggle to transform a sinful world. We shall have much to say about the supernatural virtue of hope, and the evidence for the Spirit's transformative power within history, which helps animate faith in God as Himself faithful. But we do that gracious power no favor

---

is only one among other senses which have a different basis but belong equally to the canon. Each document in the canon draws upon and to some extent reproduces traditions, whether oral or written, which were in themselves authoritative for the Christian communities that cultivated them, and the meaning of these traditions had nothing to do with a larger literary context, still less with a canon of scripture. . . . Beyond this there is also an authorial level of meaning of such traditions as the author employed and from the significance of the author's work in its subsequent canonical setting. Yet another level of meaning is provided by the church's understanding of its scripture, and this ecclesiastical level is not necessarily to be identified with the traditional, authorial or canonical meanings which may be assigned to the canonical writings. Indeed, it is not in the canon in quite the same way, for it lies in the interaction between the canon of scripture and the ongoing life of the Christian community" (ibid., 81–82).

32. This power to forgive sins, and to "bind up the evil one" is divine, and implies a supreme power of discernment.

by averting our eyes from our failures, personal and ecclesial, to respond adequately.

A ready catalog of common grievances exists for every great tradition. Since all traditions show dangerous, even evil, ambiguities through the power represented in the world by the practices of their adherent communities, enemies and friends alike find much to worry about. In the case of Catholicism, the complaints are familiar; some are well founded, some suffer from disinformation: what about the deformation of the creed, adding *filioque;* the "dogmatization" of the religion, "closing the apophantic field"; the exaggerated weight given to papal prerogatives, which is often described as "creeping infallibility"; those terrible Crusades; the Inquisition; the martyrdom of science *(le cas Galileo);* abuse of authority, to the detriment of freedom of conscience; an inhuman sexual teaching; the oppression of women; is not Catholicism essentially undemocratic? And, above all, do not its claims to divinity breed an impossible arrogance, and prove a stumbling block to the New Age search for an ecumenical humanistic wisdom?

There is an issue looming in every one of these complaints, whether all their implications are just or not. Even though I personally believe the core of the tradition is divine, nothing is gained by trying to sweep the sins under the sanctuary carpet. I intend, using each serious complaint, to enhance my sense of the real difficulties presented by the "human, all too human" limits of this tradition. I have found this increases my appreciation for the contributions of other subtraditions of Christianity, the Protestant and Orthodox, as well as the contributions by certain post-Enlightenment (more or less) atheistic traditions. At the same time, honestly facing these difficulties is necessary for appropriation: separating, to the extent this is possible, what in the tradition is from Christ and hence ought to endure, from what is due to our sinfulness, and should be purged.

So, just as *Being and Truth* began with a straightforward confession of my "natural faith" about how it stands with Being, drawn from the totality of my lived experience, I shall start here with an overview of what I understand to be the core of the Catholic tradition's orthodox vision: a positive, indeed exalting vision of divine and human reality, offered at first uncritically, and without too many nuances. Later, I will elaborate on certain points as I listen to the major criticisms coming from within and from without the tradition, criticisms at the source of persisting tensions and with potential to force me beyond the limits of this more ideal formulation.

I do this from the perspective of a "natural faith" that includes much that is illumined by what I believe to be a *supernatural* faith, which Christians believe to be a gift of grace. That very notion must be irritating to a reader not convinced by the Christian claim that the religion of Christ is at its core a divinely revealed religion. In approaching any of the great traditions of revelation as a nonbeliever it is a struggle to understand how the matters portrayed must feel to someone who lives out the tradition because they do believe it is, at its core, the gracious work of the divinity.[33]

Any reader of the present work who believes such a faith is partly, even seriously, delusional in all that it claims comes from "God" will likely retain considerable skepticism about much that is recounted concerning what it is like "to encounter God in His Chosen People, Israel," or "to love Jesus Christ in His Church," or "to experience the glory and compassion of Allah in the reading of the Qur'an and living the life of the *umma*, guided by the example of the Prophet." Remember, I have the same problem in approaching, say, Islam, as the non-Christian reader has in approaching my text here. What the Jew, Christian, or Muslim experiences as God's initiative, as God bringing us into relationship with Himself, the skeptical reader will almost inevitably see as a mere human cultural, "mythological" element, perhaps a bit pathological around the edges. In *Being and Truth,* I explored the reasons the most intimate experiences of the human soul— love, for instance—can be witnessed to but not precisely communicated to one who does not share them.[34] It is no easy task to retain the deepest respect for people whose lives center around what we believe to be a delusion. Can we love the sinner while detesting the sin?

The atheist-humanist might think it a shame human history has worked out that way, and the sooner these particularist claims to catholicity—one Chosen People (to serve all), one *umma* of Islam into which we are all to be gathered, the fullness of Truth about the One God in His incarnate Son, the carpenter from Nazareth—get cleared away, the better, for then humanity can realize itself without transcendent claims, celebrating its own universal ultimacy.

Nonetheless, the presence of 2 billion Christians and Muslims, with both religions expanding (which is the case, despite media efforts to hide this fact), and the persisting, vibrant witness of 15 million Jews reminds us the New Age catholicity is not likely to prevail soon, despite the homogenizing effects of the HTX.

33. On the challenges posed by this kind of truth claim see the more extensive discussion in *TA*, 83–88.

34. *BT*, chapter 7, secs. F and G.

THE ESSENTIAL CATHOLIC VISION

A Contemporary View

SITUATING THE TRADITION

In terms of the different kinds of explicit traditions developed in *Tradition and Authenticity*,[1] Catholicism is a subtradition of the Christian subtradition of the Abrahamic trunk. There are, however, limits to looking at traditions in that genetic way, as though the breakthrough along its course was of secondary importance compared to the truths already contained in the previous tradition out of which the new tradition (or subtradition) originated. One particular text suffices to warn us pointedly about this: "I tell you most solemnly [it is Jesus who speaks], before Abraham was, I am" (John 8:58). The text goes on to remind us of the conflict that can separate subtraditions in the same great family of traditions: "At this, they [the Jews present] picked up stones to throw at him; but Jesus hid himself and left the temple" (John 8:59). This brings to mind another text: "And there is something greater than Solomon here" (Matt. 12:42; Luke 11:31).

What this carpenter's son Jesus claimed of Himself is so enormous, anyone approaching this tradition from the outside must at once acknowledge that here is something totally out of the ordinary. "He taught them as one having authority" (Matt. 7:29). This is not, to be sure, the first "son of god" to appear in religion, but it is the first where the historic figure was just a simple workman, as opposed to a Pharaoh or a King David, that is, a "son of God" as royal intermediary from heaven. (Mohammed, recall, vigorously repelled any effort to divinize the Prophet). This simple workman displays, through the texts, a complex self-awareness, and although His ways of relating to the Messianic expectations are cautious, and the "Son of Man" title He prefers also challenging for interpreters, the claims of divinity made in the Gospels transcend all others, in all traditions. They are not based on any office—"I run Egypt for God!"—but on the claim of having been sent as the unique Son of the Father who is in heaven, to be His perfect image, and to found a "Kingdom not of this world."

1. Cf. chapter 3 and appendix C.

It is fair to say that, if the staggering claim of this young man's divinity is believed, the Abrahamic trunk then gets its whole sense from this flowering. It is as though—if the metaphor can bear the weight—the fruit absorbs the tree into itself, roots and all, and all of Being with it.[2] For one who accepts the radical claim of Christ's divinity, *all else gets relativized:* human history, including the whole experience of "the Chosen People," and indeed all of natural cosmic development (and so all of science). All else becomes mere preparation for this event, and tools for grappling with it, and for carrying out Christ's project. Every other moment, before and after, gets its ultimate meaning through reference to the vertical in-breaking into the history of eternity in the Incarnation of the Source of the cosmos in this single, humble human being, who declares Himself *"the* Way, *the* Truth and *the* Life."

Such relativizing of all by such an absolute claim is more than dangerous. (You can see at once that His "Kingdom" and His community—His "Church"—would always have to be "countercultural"!) Consider this, for instance: if the central Christian claim is true, Mohammed cannot be, as all Muslims fervently believe, "the seal of the prophets," and Islam would be—to the extent it distracts from the central Christ-claim and despite its 900 million adherents—a deviation from the true Abrahamic, Mosaic, Prophetic Christian path. And Judaism, while God permits it to live, and indeed declares His faithful love to His "first chosen," would then be an enigma, surviving as a subtradition rooted in the same Abrahamic trunk as Christianity and Islam. If the enormous Christian claim is true, all other religious traditions and all atheistic traditions and all science and philosophy are missing the very center and meaning of history itself by ignoring His divinity.[3]

Such imperialistic claims, found in several of the great traditions, are especially off-putting to democratic people, educated to tolerate everything *except* claims of absoluteness. Democrats tend as naturally toward eclectic, universalistic vagueness, what these days is exemplified by the phrase "New Age," as readily as they are tempted to a mediocre egalitarianism. Christ, in exalting the very humblest, and attacking the self-content Pharisees, is a generator here too of the countercultural, being an upside-down elitist, the poorest will be the richest.

Non-Christians are not the only ones to find trouble with the Catholic notion of who this Jesus is and how His project is continued among us. Protestants, who embrace the core belief of Christ's divinity, often feel a bit cramped by Catholics, and frightened by outbreaks of Catholic excess,

2. Something similar happened in physics with Einstein's breakthrough. Neither relativity nor quantum mechanics can be treated as subtraditions of earlier physics. On the contrary, Newtonian mechanics now takes its place within the larger cosmic vision, while physics takes its place within the broader synthesis of a revelation-based theology.

3. This does not imply loss of autonomy for human rational inquiry, of course. Truth discovered through research is truth. Period. But both its ultimate significance and where and how individuals search for it is affected by the beliefs, personal and social, that establish ultimate context.

at least in the past. They agree that "the Risen Christ is among us, in the form of His Mystical Body, the Church." Further, most Christians—but not the evangelicals—will agree that every person of goodwill, insofar as he strives to do what is right (in religious language, "to do the will of God, in so far as it is known to him") is "in the Church." The evangelicals hold firm to Christ's word: "Unless you are baptized you will not enter into the Kingdom"; and Catholics insist: "The fullness of the revelation in Christ and the life in him, doing the will of the Father, is assured by the living, core teaching of the apostles he has chosen and ordained to continue the full 'sacramental presence.' " The Orthodox of the "Oriental Church" reply, "Amen!" The "Congregationalist" Protestant, however, complains, "What about the 'priesthood of all believers'?" The Catholic plows ahead: "And that is found fully only in the apostolic succession of the Bishops in union with the one Christ chose to head His Body, Peter and his successors." As a consequence of this position, the "imperialistic" Catholic has managed to lose the sympathy of both Protestants and the Orthodox, even appearing to some like a sectarian, representative of a narrowing subtradition among Christians.

But is that quite fair? We could conceive of the relationship between traditions another way, as a series of concentric circles each representing an ever more demanding "intellectual imperialism" while in some sense, paradoxically, becoming more "particularistic." For instance, first the Abrahamic tradition subordinates all other traditions of thought and belief with its claim, "All reality flows from one Source, knowing and free, who has revealed himself in all His glory to Abraham and His descendants; all owe that Source recognition and, indeed, praise and adoration"; then the Hebraic-Mosaic tradition adds, "And while this Source is the loving Father of all, he has chosen one people for the prophetic task of coming among the family of man to prepare and guide it, making demands upon us which we are called to heed"; next, the Christian tradition, "And that work of preparation has been completed, as the Source worked its most generous act, humbling its all-powerful, cosmos-creating Logos to come among us as a single human person, walk with us, teach us, demonstrate His authenticity and power with mighty works and words, using the full range of human capability as a 'language' to reveal the incomprehensible majesty of the Father and the Trinitarian life of God to us, and finally, taking on our sins, expiate them before the Father"; and most demanding of all, the Catholic claims: "And that continuing Christ-presence among us is a Eucharist, the sacramental presence of Christ in the Holy Spirit as the Church universal, founded and empowered by Jesus Christ, and centered in the descendants of the apostles, headed by Peter."

Paradoxically, the extreme particularism of this Catholic claim founds the strength of its universalism,[4] its character as the *catholica:* were this single

4. This claim to particularism can be summarized as follows: the Whole of reality is

human being, Jesus, truly the Christ, the incarnation of the divine Word itself, its very singularity—here, not there; male, not female; Jew, not Greek; then, and continued now in one unique way within our history, through a concrete handing down of authority—He would be the guarantee of its totality and availability for all (handed down concretely to all generations and spread to all nations). That is the supreme miracle, the divinization of matter, which from the atom on up always congregates into individuals, and in this one incarnate person is gathered up totally as the completion of creation in the Kingdom.

So the particularism is not narrowing: The Church is not founded by Christ to be one institution over against others, rather they all get their meaning from it; nor is it meant to stay stuck in the cultural confines of the Hebraic-Graeco-Roman-European tradition of its initial enfleshment. Rather, because it is founded in Him who is Truth itself, it is meant to be the beginning of the universal Kingdom of God, the gathering home of people of all cultures into the one absolutely universal human family, where what is good in all cultures is lovingly preserved, with no one and no thing and no iota of truth left out. That community is ordained by God as the one and only *catholica* belonging to all, including in itself all light: it is God's act of summing up His creation, which attains its summit in man, and all men in this perfect Man, in whose "Mystical Body" all come to dwell. It is undeniably in us human beings that the cosmos thinks itself, gets gathered up in thought. But it is in Christ that the depths of our humanity—its divinity—is revealed. This gathering then takes the form of the weaving of bonds of love between every human logos-center. It is an affirmation that being is one, and the cosmos has a sense: what pours from the Big Bang is not a series of senseless accidents. The Logos Himself is Alpha and Omega, the beginning and the end of this meaning-bestowing love; the Logos is "with God, and is God," and "God *is* love," giving Himself as the light that comes into the world with every human being, and the bond that ties them together in brotherhood.

I must admit, one thing I like about this tradition is that it does not fool around with modest claims! Here is a truly universal vision! If it is a fiction, it is no insignificant mistake; for then it would be so cosmically wrong that "we are indeed the most useless of peoples," as Paul said, when speaking about Christ's Resurrection, with his usual disturbing forcefulness (1 Cor. 15:19). It throws down the ultimate gauntlet: either the world makes sense, a complexity harmonized in its beginning and end that is located precisely

---

present in the one "fragment," the individual Jesus of Nazareth, and has been continued in His Church as gathered about that poor unique fragment, the Fisherman Peter, as well as in His chosen successors. I have deliberately echoed here the title of an astounding book by Hans Urs von Balthasar, *Das Ganze im Fragment* (The whole in the fragment) (Einsiedeln: Benzinger Verlag, 1963). The English translation abandons this wonderful title for the insipid *Man in History: A Theological Study*, trans. William Glen-Doepell (London: Sheed and Ward, 1968).

here, in Jesus Christ continuing in His community, or it is just running down to entropy.

If anyone were to become Catholic because he succumbed to a romantic temptation to leap into such an imperious belief, then he would be ignoring Christ Himself, who admonishes His followers, on the contrary, to be critical and to avoid fanaticism. He said, for instance, "Be as cunning as serpents and as harmless as doves" (Matt. 10:16); further, He tells us what to look for: "By their fruits you shall know them" (Matt. 7:20), and these are the fruits of love. (*Fruitfulness* is a key New Testament term.)[5] For, simply—and this is the very heart of what is revealed in Christ—the Source of all being, astonishingly, is love.

Christ's admonitions are extremely pertinent, for the history of the Catholic tradition is a jumble of both wonderful and poisonous fruits. Even the great saints most often have their dubious sides. Not everyone who has reservations about aspects of Augustine's spirituality or Thomas's rationalistic tendencies or who finds traces of fanaticism in Jerome and activism in Ignatius is being unfair. Indeed, the New Testament writers went out of their way to highlight the frailty and all too familiar sinful humanity of the apostles themselves. Statistically, the Church has never been as bad off as on the night of the Agony in the Garden and that Good Friday when all abandoned Christ except John, His mother, and maybe one or two of the other women. Indeed, the prince of the apostles, scared out of his wits, replied, "Jesus who? Never heard of him"—and not once, but three times. (And then the cock crowed.) Even Popes Julius II and Alexander VI Borgia never sank that low.

Nonetheless, here we have discovered one of the central themes of this entire tradition—again something unique, found only with true love: *forgiveness.* This is a tradition unapologetically about sinful human beings whom the Author of all reality knows well and to whom, astonishingly, He stays faithful; He has forgiven them every betrayal, every perversity, every abuse of His gifts, even before we commit them. He, we are assured, is patiently working to liberate each of His creatures from the self-enslavement of the crippling habits they have imposed on themselves and the unworthy desires, the addictions they have allowed to dominate. In keeping with His infinite freedom and our finite freedom (which we have damaged), He achieves the fulfillment of His plan, a *mysterion* (as Paul calls it in Ephesians, meaning a boundless being) known fully only to Him. Still, essential aspects of this *sophia* He has revealed to us, so far as we need to know them to carry out our cooperative roles—our *missio*—in building this liberating social structure, His "Kingdom" (Eph. 1:9).

The heart of this revelation about the Kingdom, then, is twofold: God's own revelation of what He wants His Kingdom to achieve, and what He tells us about the human instruments He has forged for carrying out this

---

5. See Balthasar, *New Elucidations,* trans. Mary Theresilde Skerry (San Francisco: Ignatius Press, 1986), 221–22.

work as He wants it carried out.[6] A possible misunderstanding should be cleared up at once. Are the Church and its tradition equivalent to that "Kingdom"? To the extent that members of the Church remain sinfully compromised by "this world," no, sin has no place in the Kingdom. To the extent that the Church is that communion of saints, yes, it gathers up all the good fruit out of historical time, saving it from what Augustine called "dead time" by uniting at the foot of God all that is worthy of preserving, this being possible because in His Christ God has broken into horizontal time.

How can we understand the human-fallible in its relation to the divine-infallible at work in it? Critical appreciation of our role is necessary, after all, for the ever needed reform to go forward. The tradition furnishes an answer as to how the believer is to distinguish the merely human, as it resists divinization: the key to everything lies in the correct, God-guided, "graced" discernment of the good, as He alone fully knows it. Only in the light of what He continues to teach us infallibly, authoritatively through His Church about the goodwill do we recognize what is "of the Kingdom" (the "good fruits": every genuinely good thought, desire, and act) and what is not (every impulse to "put down," to distort, and to destroy).

If, on the other hand, the appropriator is an unbeliever, the challenge this tradition poses is how to make sense out of the civilization-forming achievement (the Occidental reader's own civilization, after all!) of a tradition that is centered in such wild myths, the "divine" element then being the product of human imagination only. Nonetheless, he must still determine for himself, by the criteria furnished by his own natural faith, the good from the bad elements in the tradition: what may be absorbed into the perennial ecumenical wisdom of mankind, and what must be rooted out and discarded.

But at least he should acknowledge this about it: at its very heart, rightly understood, in its ideal this tradition is not in any way sectarian, it is in intent and in content truly universal. Every good for every person from every tradition is intended, in the end, to be gathered within it, nothing nor no one is despised, in their goodness. The claims it makes are put forth as expressive of the founding of all reality, and hence as absolutely valid for every human being at all times, because they are about the fulfillment of the ultimate potential of the entire creation, a potential that has been working itself among all peoples from the beginning. That good has always in every tradition been compromised by our perversity, from which Christ has come to save us. All good, wherever and whenever achieved—that is, all genuine being—is, therefore, redeemed and is to be taken up in our collective lives and further fructified, preserved in the tradition and offered back to its Source in loving praise and thanksgiving

6. The Christian tradition carries at its core its own anthropology, one revealed by the Author of human nature.

(eucharistia), in partial form now and in a Christ-forged perfection at the end time.[7]

Nor does the Church close her eyes to the danger of fanaticism or fundamentalism among those who, in the name of an ideology that purports to be scientific or religious, claim the right to impose on others their own concept of what is true and good. Christian truth is not of this kind. Since it is not an ideology (although its ideal has been a million times deformed into all manner of "Christian" ideologies), since Christians must not claim to *possess* the truth—the Christian does not have the living Word who is Jesus Christ in his pocket—Christian truth remains a faith, not an accomplishment; the Christian faith does not presume to imprison changing sociopolitical realities in a rigid schema but recognizes that human life is realized in history in conditions that are diverse and imperfect and "under way." Furthermore, in constantly reaffirming the transcendent dignity of the person, the Church's method is supposed to be always that of respect for freedom (as Pope John Paul II continually reminds us).

This said, contrary to Christ's command, and the pope's exhortations, sectarianism does creep into the tradition—*creep* is the word: Gnosticism in some form, present from the beginning, is like the serpent in Paradise or the creepy-crawler plants entwined in my garden. When exclusivity, power trips, the Inquisition, the smugness of pharisaism, and hatred in any form are to be found contaminating the tradition, as they do to some extent in every epoch (and in every human heart in its sinful imperfection), the tradition manifests, alas, its "human, all too human" dimension.[8] That is how that most paradoxical of realities—"Christian" ideologies—manage to pollute the universe. These evil things, explains the Christian, are of Satan and sinful man; they stem from finite freedom's ab-use, and therefore they are destined to be separated out "on the last day" and "thrown into the consuming fire," where their own disorder, defensiveness, and destructiveness will consume them from within. The vanity concealed in these things by perversely and cunningly using elements of the good, like diabolical parasites of the soul,[9] will be exposed by the Light as it reveals their ultimate nothingness. There is no greater triumph of Satan than when Catholics, who are supposedly recipients of the Good News of

7. We, the sinful members of the Church here and now, while guided in a sound direction by Christ, do not simply *possess* the truth, as Pope John Paul reminds all; we are, rather, unworthy keepers of the vision that illumines the continuing human struggles to know.

8. Nietzsche's wonderful phrase *menschlich, allzu menschlich*, applies to Christianity, which embraces the full human reality, in all its frailty, sinfulness, and perversion, which is precisely what is to be "redeemed"—saved from its own destructive self.

9. The word *diabolical* suggests leading astray, away from the truth, deceiving; *diabolein*, accuser, slanderer, transducer *(Oxford English Dictionary)*; literally, "to throw across." *Diabolus* was the Greek word used by the translators of the Septuagint for the Hebrew "Satan."

God's universal love, allow selections from their tradition to be turned into sectarianism and ideology.

A balanced history of the Church as human reality contains many chapters about just such perversions. In the appropriation of no other tradition does one encounter such a gulf between the divinely offered ideal and the everyday human reality that can sink to the level of the hesitation of Canadian bishops confronted with the embarrassment of a sex scandal at a boys orphanage and even to the torture rooms of the Spanish Inquisition. The vision is so vast and so demanding that the gap of discrepancy is indeed yawning. That gulf can be seen by the hater of the Church as the final evidence of the tradition's impossible (and wrongheaded) idealism, and by the believer as the mouth of hell itself. In any event, it is testimony to the reality and the resistance of our finite freedom.

Still, no fair person can fault this tradition for lack of grandeur, nor for that matter, great goodness—the saints, and not only the saints but also ordinary Catholics who are great lovers of God, though they are sinners too. For the believer, this scope of vision is a sign of the divine, just as was the incomprehensible humility and power of Mother Teresa. But the believer is inauthentic when he averts his regard from the depths to which the "human, all too human" in his tradition, as in every tradition and community, can sink. One advantage for those who believe, however, is that this tradition at least tries to offer a key to the undeniable mystery of evil present in all human affairs. Its central symbol is, after all, the God-man hanging on the cross, offering Himself for the forgiveness of the unforgivable. It must be left to each well-disposed nonbeliever to make out for himself what this reality of evil tells us about the human condition.

As I worked out the second version of this study, a surprising result of this research began to surface: What I was reflecting on was not just the relationship of Christology and ecclesiology, not just a theory of the incarnation of the Word, nor even the form the Church takes in the continuing incarnation through history. No, the surprise that surfaced, as I hinted a moment ago, was the centrality in all this of an *anthropology:* the Incarnation of Jesus is as much a revelation about the nature of man as it is a God-given glimpse of His own inner-Trinitarian life. I now believe we cannot know truly who we are except through this revelation from our Author. Indeed, we become so associated with the divine mission of Jesus that He calls us—and if He is God's Son, this must be the greatest shocker in history!—His friends and even His brothers.[10] Ultimately, this revelation points the way to the answer

10. As we shall see later, this is not a "politically incorrect" lapse. Just as we are all, without regard to sex, called to participate in Mary's nurturing role, so we are all called into union with Jesus Christ, regardless of sex, race, or earlier tradition. We are all brothers in being, one with Him and sharing in His male role of passing on the seed received from the Father. God uses human nature as the language of Revelation. The delicate weave of sexual symbolism used by Him to reveal His transcendent supersexual reality will be something we shall comment on as we see it unfold.

of the most important questions I can ask: Who concretely am I? To what am I called?

THE CHRISTIC CORE

The Starting Point: Experience

It might seem that the least demands would be put on the credulity of non-Christian readers were I to start this appropriation with the largest common denominator, the experiences that lead Catholics, along with all Christians, Jews, and Muslims, to accept the heart of the Abrahamic belief, a Creator-God, capable of revelation. There are, however, two problems with such a starting point.

First, with regard to a strategy to make this tradition at all interesting to nonbelievers: for many moderns, the notion that the world has been called into being intentionally by a Source that knew what He was doing and who looks providentially after the cosmic becoming is "mythological" and hence enough of a block to inhibit any sympathy for the various sub-Abrahamic traditions' historical claims of revelations. So anyone seeking to present a version of the Christian experience had best start with the undeniably enormous claims about Jesus Christ Himself, as they deepen and orchestrate the theme of creation. "Who has seen me has seen the Father" (John 13:9).

Second, I myself have not encountered my tradition and do not continue to experience it that way at all, as though one begins with the Creation and works down, so to speak, to Christ and His Church. I agree with Balthasar that man's unaided ability to reach up to the infinitely transcending God is shown by the results of all the natural religions and by the history of pre-Christian philosophy to be woefully inadequate to the task of knowing God as He has in fact revealed Himself.[11] Man's natural efforts to reach upward toward the infinite transcendent Source never got even near a beginning of insight into the true reality of God, that He is love.

So I, poor "practicing Catholic" that I am, look at the universe through the (imperfect) eyes of a Christ-and-his-Church-centered life. I have no experience of God, nor any knowledge of nature as, precisely, *creation* except as integrated in the Christic experience of the Church and the testimony of Jesus that is to be found there. I can indeed experience the Church, and through it Jesus Christ, but not the infinite transcending God directly, whom I only glimpse "darkly, as in a mirror," in His handiwork, nature. As a result of a life in Christ, I look at nature differently from a non-Christian,[12] including seeing its deformation by sinful man and its transformation by

11. Balthasar, *Love Alone: The Way of Revelation,* ed. Alexander Dru (London: Sheed and Ward, 1970), chapters 1 and 2; see also Balthasar, "Experience God?" in *New Elucidations,* 20–46.

12. In philosophic terms, the *Sein* of my world is Christo-centric. See *BT,* chapters 9 and 10. *Sein* here means the set of interpretative horizons forming a world of meaning. This is explained in *BT,* to which the philosophical reader is referred for more detail.

grace, "the Second Creation." For a Catholic who takes the challenges of his religion seriously, the cosmos has become first and foremost *a sacramental reality,* "God's body."[13]

The experience of the Hebrew people was a great beginning and preparation for this. It was through their unique encounter with the living God coming to them as a commanding presence and interacting with them in their history, forming and leading them, that they came to grasp His power as creator of nature. "The great psalm of nature" (Ps. 104) shows that Israel, banking on its historic experience of divine grace tangibly present in the prophets, can in joy and admiration interpret the whole cosmos as "a festive garment" of God (Ps. 104:1) and invite God Himself to rejoice in His works (Ps. 104:3).[14]

The whole magnificent cosmos is a less perfect icon of the infinite, transcending Source than the humble presence of God in the carpenter's son! (The non-Christian shocked at this should recall this truth of science: there is a complexity, a quality of "information," and a set of capabilities in a single living cell that exceeds the complexity and "information"—for there is none!—in the entire nonliving cosmos, even if it is 10^{40} larger.)[15] So there is something artificial, and perhaps even a bit false, about trying to untangle from an entire fabric of lived experiences an argument for creation, presented, as the starting point, without support of the whole weave of life, a Christian experience of which is animated by a daily thankful Christ-centered ecclesial-eucharistic experience of creation. To begin by trying to prove the existence of God from examining nature is something like being asked to situate your mother in the chain of evolution before continuing to love her. Your mother is more massively present, more real to you, than theoretical considerations about discoveries in natural history, however true they may prove to be. Anyway, they are finally most interesting because they have made it possible for your beloved mother to be! The revelation of that love may prove relevant for understanding the "mechanisms" of evolution itself.[16]

Christianity is like most of the world's great religions in holding up the person of the founder as center of its devotion: it looks as though a "cult of the personality" is natural for human beings. We do, after all, model ourselves on others, on our heroes. In each of these religions, the nature of

---

13. Balthasar, *Herrlichkeit: Eine theologische Ästhetik,* vol. 3, pt. 1 (The glory of the Lord: A theological aesthetics, trans. Erasmo Leiva-Merikakis, ed. Joseph Fessio and John Riches [San Francisco: Ignatius Press, 1983–]) (Einsiedeln: Johannes, 1961–1965). The quote is drawn from page 175 of the French translation of the work (*La gloire et la croix* [Paris: Aubier, 1975]). See also Pierre Teilhard de Chardin, *La messe sur le monde* (Paris: Desclée de Brouwer, 1962), first published as part 1 of *Hymne de l'univers* (Hymn of the universe, trans. Simon Bartholomew [London: Collins, 1965]) (Paris: Seuil, 1961).

14. Balthasar, *La gloire et la croix,* 175.

15. I have not calculated it; the figure I have chosen is rhetorical!

16. If this makes some readers think of the "anthropic principle," they may enjoy the reflections on this in *BT,* 290–93.

the devotion, however, is different in each tradition; it is even quite distinct as between the Mahayana and Hinayana traditions of Buddhism, the ways Gautama is revered being quite different. The Christian claim is that *imitatio Christi,* and being taken up eucharistically into the person of Christ, is not only something unique, but the divine revelation of personhood in and through Jesus Christ sets the standard by which every other "cult of the personality" should be judged. This is another illustration of just how large is the Christian claim. The proper modality, and the "ecclesial-sacramental" communitarian nature of such a "following of Christ" will be a central issue for the present appropriation.

For the Christian, everything—not just his understanding of the tradition, but his whole life—is centered in the person of Jesus Christ because He, the Word of God incarnate, is believed to be the fullness of God's revelation in His teaching and works, hence the key to who we are and what we are expected to be. Jesus' life and mission is my very personal guide: this is not a mission in general, but rather what God knows in His plan, from all eternity, only I can do. The Christian experiences this relationship, at its best, as a genuine love, an interpersonal, concrete reciprocal action, in which the Father's love flows to him through the Holy Spirit of the Risen Christ via the living social reality of His Mystical Body, the Church. Through the Church's teaching and living example I am offered guidance as to the good, the sacraments are always presented with the Word of God, and personal spiritual direction is available as a help in working out my own daily application of this light, all of this treasury undergirded by the concrete forgiveness of sins, so that this whole wealth may be given back as "a perfect offering" made by the Eternal Priest, Christ to His Father, fulfilling the whole loving purpose of creation. It is this same love, effective as the Holy Spirit, that, through the Logos of God, brought the universe into being, sustains it, and gives it its meaning, a meaning that, while animating all of human history, includes a place—a place of peace—just for little me and little you, a true home where there should be no occasion for loneliness.

Before any effort to discern whether this is a wonderful psychic fantasy Christians exploit to imagine for themselves some dignity or, on the contrary, a historically grounded and personally recoupable reality, we must struggle to get clear as concretely as possible just what it all means. Perhaps an illustration would help clarify the challenge. One evening I went to the memorial mass of a fifty-two-year-old former army sergeant killed by multiple sclerosis. Forty people of many religions (or none) who had been active in his care came to pray for him and to exchange experiences, as the priest said, "of ways in which Bob had changed [their] lives and has been a presence of God for [them]." Bob had not wanted a funeral, but he left a statement to be read, copied from something he had found in a paper, explaining how he hoped organs of his wasted body might be donated to help someone live. All present said they had found friends through Bob, that every time they visited him, they came away more alive, buoyed up by his corny jokes. The priest situated this as an "experience of Christ in the poorest of the poor": for ten years his dependence on others reminded the religious among us of our dependence on God. Powerless, Bob, unlike Christ on the cross,[17] and because of the grace flowing from that cross, was in fact never abandoned.

One does not have to be Christian to experience this transcendent dimension in the life-giving suffering of a great and simple person like Sgt. Bob Gilroy, "the saint with pinups on his fridge door." But knowing the life and teaching of Jesus gives it an expression, and through that an ultimate sense. The mystery of suffering turned into love is empirically encountered in the concrete fruits of the relationships built up in and through and about Bob Gilroy. The divine as fructifying love, which Christ preached and lived out through His sacrificial abandonment of everything on the cross, transforms what normally, for the world, would be a waste and a tragedy into a source of new life.

Through the Church one hears the Word of God taught, and one experiences it being lived out by at least some persons of charity who devote their entire being to witnessing; they are veritable "faces of Christ." When one sees the beautiful presence of the pope to the old and the handicapped, brought into the living room by television during his visit to Canada; when one met and heard Mother Teresa; when one reads Hans Urs von Balthasar meditating on what God has revealed about His own interior Trinitarian life, with heaven opening up to reveal innermost secrets of Being, one no longer allows oneself to be too depressed by one's own surprising mediocrity in prayer and lack of generosity and the sour fruits of groanings. This is not meant to constitute an "argument." Nonetheless it is important that for myself, the appropriator—and for the reader who, interested in finding out what is involved in life in such a tradition—I get as clear as possible about the basis for what I believe in experience, my connection to reality that, "internalized" and become attitude (Verhalten),[18] motivates my efforts to live a Christian life.

Balthasar's warning about experience must be heeded: experience is always an effort to grasp, hence in some sense to take control.[19] Obviously, finite human spirit cannot experience the God who is above all conceptualization, in transcendent majesty; we cannot control God. The question here is whether there is available to us a human experience that reverses the normal, controlling nature of knowledge, expropriating us from our debilitating limits, taking us out of ourselves, away from our desire to control, rather than our "appropriating" an object. Can there be an experience of a love that brings one out of oneself to devotion, to wanting to give himself over, opening him onto the transcendent majesty, before which one falls on his knees in adoration?

17. Whom the Father allowed to experience abandonment, as Christ took on the very dregs of our sinful existence.
18. See BT, chapter 10.
19. Balthasar, "Experience God?" in New Elucidations, 20–23.

As with all reports of experience, I have to try to capture it in symbols, here using traditional Christian symbols, but trying to translate them at least partially into more modern terms, closer to the reader's experience. There is an element of control in all that, trying to come to terms with the experience, but to the end of assessing the significance of an experience that challenges any tendency to settle down in a comfortable "natural faith."

How is what this experience allows me to see to be integrated with all I know? My natural faith is, after all, that overview of being that, while never demonstrable, serves as the ultimate context within which all my experience occurs, and gets judged by me. Thus, how am I to integrate this symbolic expression of my experience without succumbing to the temptation of letting that natural faith be just an idol, a comfortable world of meaning fashioned to make me feel good, rather than a step in opening out, giving over, growing toward . . . ?

The Symphonic Nature of Christian Experience

The Christian vision manifests an immense openness, but not a vagueness, an "anything goes" bonhomie, but rather an unfolding, demanding symphonic structure.[20] Each of its dimensions—cosmic, theophanic, prophetic-historic, Christ-centric, Catholic-ecclesial, final redemption (eschatological-[historico-]redemptive) in history—comes to us in different but related kinds of experiences; for example, it is one thing to experience a sunset, another to commune with God in the Eucharist; to experience Church unity in seeing a council at work, another to experience, as Moses did, a theophany on Sinai.

Although there are varying degrees of difficulty associated with understanding and accepting these themes, there is no hesitation where *the center* of this multifaceted symphonic vision lies: Jesus as the "Son of God." And if Jesus is Son of God, (whatever that key symbol means) then belief in the rest—the Creation revelation, God's Prophetic leadership of Israel, the supernatural reality of the Church, the struggle to redeem and sanctify man—each gets its sense from the Christ event. That is why the appropriator has to center his attention there. Once the enormous truth of the Incarnation has been embraced, and understood in some way, accepting these other dimensions of God's transcendence poses much less difficulty, and each gets its meaning from the Christic core of the tradition.

There is, in a sense, only one truth claim that ultimately matters; from one's stand toward this claim all else follows: the supreme mystery that Jesus Christ is "truly God and truly man." The essential and unique Trinitarian nature of this tradition is revealed in and flows from this truth.

There is, however, a corollary question of utmost practical importance, and this one, unfortunately, divides Christians who accept the divinity and

---

20. Balthasar titled a book *Die Wahrheit ist Symphonisch: Aspekte des christlichen Pluralismus* (Truth is symphonic: Aspects of Christian pluralism, trans. Graham Harrison [San Francisco: Ignatius Press, 1987] (Einsiedeln: Johannes Verlag, 1972).

the humanity of Jesus: how does Christ remain effectively among us—how are we enfolded in Him? This question, the ecclesiological dimension, is not whether He founded a Church—all Christians acknowledge that; rather, it asks about the nature of the authority and structure He intended for that Church. Beliefs about the nature of the authority and structure of the Church guide the development of the *communio* Christ intends and that is His life in us and ours in Him.

In this appropriation, discussion of the ecclesiological differences should follow review of the christological issues, for one's interpretation of "Who is this Jesus?" will influence one's view of His Church. True, the nature and experience of the church community in which one lives out one's life will influence one's beliefs about Jesus. But I shall begin by attempting to capture what motivates and orchestrates not just the Christian's belief in Jesus as Son of God, but His love for Him, and how that love is experienced, which, we shall see, is in the Church.

The basic proposition remains breathtaking, that the Source would so "empty itself out" as to become fully human:[21] first, a fertilized human egg, then the few cells of a unique, new human being at gestation, and finally, to follow the whole path of human development, ending at maturity in a criminal's violent death. Perhaps even more breathtaking is the revelation of the purpose of this incarnation: all in order to share our lives, teach us, take on Himself the destructiveness of our sins, conquer death, and put in place what mankind needs for redemption and fulfillment of God's plan, through our personal growth and the spread of His Kingdom.

Too good to be true! No Christian should ever be astonished that many just cannot imagine this could be true. I have known thoughtful persons who have testified that they would love to be able to embrace the central Christian claim (often because they admire, for instance, Thomas's philosophy, or Christian ethics), but they cannot bring themselves to accept that God so loves us that He would deign to be present to us as a simple human being. That the infinite majesty should be contained in a humble fragment!

But that is the right point at which to begin an appropriation of the Catholic tradition, with a consideration of the Incarnation, guided by these two questions: (1) *Cur Deus homo?* as Anselm put it; why did God become man? Based both on what Scripture reveals and on the subsequent history of God's interaction with mankind through the Church, what can we make out of the purpose of such an event? (2) *Qui est Christus?* How are we to grapple with this One who is "fully God and fully man," and moreover, through Him the Trinitarian reality of God's inner life as revealed in His life? This question is not only theoretical, but above all practical, for right "christological" understanding is the key to knowing what it means that He "calls us to a life in him." There is nothing easier than fabricating one's own "Christ," an idol built out of selected elements of the full and mysterious Jesus Christ of the New Testament, tailored to bring us comfort.

---

21. The language is from Paul; *kenosis* is the key Greek term.

The early Church struggled mightily to formulate its basic christological understanding beyond what was merely spontaneous for the community, and in a way that was not designed with comfort levels in mind. This right understanding is so critical for knowing the orthodox sense of the Church that we will later briefly review the complicated history of those ancient christological controversies.

Cur Deus Homo?

One way to approach this mystery would be to look back over the *results* of this sovereign and generous decision.[22] Christ taught His disciples, "By their fruits you shall know them," the actions of men. Several fruits of the centerpiece of God's creation, the Incarnation, spring to evidence:

1. The Logos' coming into human history made possible a complete revelation because God through Christ was able to teach us, in a way accessible to humans, all that we need to know for salvation and to demonstrate His power through "mighty works," themselves chosen—Scripture makes clear—for the further lessons they teach us.[23] By coming physically into history, the Logos used the whole vocabulary of symbols of all kinds, and every aspect of human action as a language to express the *mysterion* of God's infinite being. As Balthasar put it, "the whole in a fragment." Indeed; but a fragment—a man—an instance of the most complex reality ever created, leading us through Himself (as "way") to the Father.

2. Christ, working with chosen disciples, instituted for the benefit of all mankind *that way* that would allow Him to remain, mysteriously but effectively, among us as a *historical* reality until the end of time. His Church is therefore the ultimate community, continuing in eucharistic form the incarnate presence of the Son based in the revelation of the fatherhood of God. This makes every man not just a creation of God but through the Church an effective son, and hence all of us brothers. It is important to be clear here about the inclusive nature of this religious language, the Hebrew and Greek symbols as

22. *Mysterion* is a technical New Testament word signifying "the 'mystery' or secret of God that had now been revealed . . . ," "The idea of 'mystery' of wisdom . . . long hidden in God and now revealed. . . ." (*The New Jerusalem Bible,* at Col. 1:27, note "m"; Rom. 16:25, note "l"). In the New Testament it refers to something once hidden, now revealed, not that which is still hidden. When Gabriel Marcel distinguishes "problem" (in principle soluble) and "mystery" (the unfathomable depths of infinite being), his sense is certainly a valid idea in a New Testament perspective; but it is not what *mysterion* as a technical New Testament word signifies. In any event, the term has been cheapened through misuse in our language, and is still often confused with "problem."

23. For example, the multiplication of loaves and fishes as figure of and preparation for the institution of the Eucharist and the power of God over the wind and the waves provide a platform for understanding what He wants to teach us about the powerlessness demonstrated on the cross.

translated into modern English. The revelation of God as Father does not impute human masculine sexuality to the infinite (and therefore nonmaterial, nonorganic, nonsexual) Source of the universe. But to get across the sense that His powerful creative setting in place of the cosmos was a loving, caring initiative, He chose, among the things of human experience, this common experience of creative, selfless love, which is that of the good Father. So we are all sons and daughters. But the point is not here again our sexual-gender distinctiveness, so important in other contexts ("male and female He created them"): as children of God, we are all the same, we are all just men, in the root philological, all-inclusive sense the word has always had in Germanic languages until ideological feminists began to *reform* the language, with the resulting heightening of tensions and aesthetic deformation of the symbols. In the present context, it is better to say in English we are men and women equally, all sons, because we are all images of Christ, who is the image of the Father, the One who takes the initiative to send forth the Anointed One, His image, Jesus Christ, whom He chose to come among us as a male. But His receptive role here, like that of His Church, is "feminine," but as head of the Church also masculine, as He sends us all forth as His brothers, as "Christs," anointed in baptism to be a royal priesthood, and so on, providing through all Christian men and women a kind of masculine leadership, which will succeed only if we are as receptive of His Word—feminine—as was Mary. The total equality of men and women in all this is signaled by making no distinction: we are all sons, brothers, "Christs," and apostles, just as we are all, at the same time, like Mary, the ones who must say *Fiat!* and receive the seed of the Word, nurture it in the wombs of our humanity, and raise and nurture it in our families, as Joseph and Mary raised Jesus. We are all then "female" just as well in our function as "Church." (Hence, this corollary: the good qualities *we* call "feminine" and those we call "masculine" ought to be cultivated in each of us. This issue will be elaborated later.) This absolutely universal community, the only one founded by God Himself through Christ, was then conceived and structured to make possible such a gathering of people of all nations into a single, effective, loving family of God, the final work of sanctification. He provided the model of perfect humanity, the concrete ideal to guide, by imitation, all our actions and aspirations, as He showed us what it means to love. This human-divine reality dwelling in our midst is God present as someone to whom we can relate humanly, that is, personally, in a mode we fragile sons of Adam and Eve can give ourselves over to, in total love, without projecting an idol of our own. In so ennobling mankind by living our humanity with divine perfection, while, by virtue of being born into the human race, becoming our brother, thus making us also "sons of God," He challenges us to see Himself in the poorest of the poor (and the haughtiest of the haughty), and thus to learn a new love for all human life.[24]

3. This final, very "theological" point, is the hardest to grasp: by taking on our nature and thus participating directly in our history, God has *raised up* human nature so as to effect the creation of "the new man," as Paul preaches. Thus, when Jesus Christ took on the burden of our destructiveness, triumphed over this negativity, and rose transformed from the dead, He achieved, both as man as well as God, new *human* possibility as such. Here we have the foundation of a totally "other" (a countercultural) anthropology from the anthropology of death that holds materialistic society in its grip: *a Christic conception of man*, indeed of the new man, the "supra-man" (not "superman"!) with all the eschatological implications this entails, and all the new challenges as to how to live, in a con-verted way, contra the tendencies of all (sinful) cultures whatsoever. We can only learn from this new starting point who we are.

Let us reflect on each of these fruits—the revelation in Jesus, His founding the Church, and its sacramental character—looking for hints, not just with regard to why God became man, but also of the sense of the resulting reality, especially the implications for who we have now become.

The Revelation in Jesus

One might wonder, if it were just a matter of revelation, why God could not have been content simply to send yet another great prophet to gather a people to Himself. This is what Muslims believe did happen, both in Jesus, whom they see as only a prophet (albeit the greatest of the prophets, save only for Mohammed), and finally, supremely, in the angel Gabriel's dictation of the suras of the Qur'an to the ordinary human being who was called to achieve the seal of prophecies, the perfect form of the revelation already to be found, deformed by man, in the Bible. What then does the Christian perceive was accomplished *as revelation* through God's incarnation in Jesus that could not have been achieved by the much less startling act of inspiring a prophet? Jesus' founding of the Church: a new kind (and scope) of authority was established on earth and within history, on the basis of a new (and definitive) kind of divine presence, a "eucharistic (thanksgiving) presence."[25] Christ came to fulfill what man was originally made to do: to celebrate the Father, to give glory and praise

24. This is what Teilhard de Chardin, following Paul, expressed as the Omega drawing humanity into a loving unity, by attracting and guiding each "monad," each loving individual, along the Way, and situating each in the relationship with the others as He has planned it. Teilhard did not lose sight of the need for purification of the elements, inevitably painful . . . the haughty will be made humble and the poor rich.

25. This is explained by the key document of the Second Vatican Council, *Lumen Gentium.* I shall elaborate later.

and thanksgiving for the love He poured out in His creation; in brief, to return that love, which is what we do when we give thanks to another—"to give God back to God," as Balthasar expresses it. The redemptive act, from the founding of the Sacrament of the Eucharist in the offering of His own Body and Blood, which was to be offered "once and for all" in the supreme sacrifice, the total giving up of self on the cross, is all part of the ultimate act of rendering thanks. It redeems us by giving back to us the capacity to be thankful in the way God wants to be thanked, in a way that Adam and Eve rejected.

The Church's sacramental character: no Hebrew prophet nor the great Prophet of Islam ever pretended to be either sinless or the son of God, and, therefore, none could even think of restoring or creating anew mankind to replace what we had damaged. Without the new kind of authority, an unrestricted fullness and power of the divine Word, the new "sacramental" kind of divine presence could not have been instituted, would not have been believed, and therefore could not day in, day out effect its work of teaching us to love. Only because Christ achieved His powerful works and preached intensively to His little group and visited upon them divine-instituting power ("All power in heaven and on earth has been given to me . . ." [Matt. 28:18], "Whatsoever you shall bind on earth . . ." [Matt. 16:19]) were they prepared, when the Holy Spirit poured out his gifts, to begin to grasp this heightening and enrichment of God's historical presence with his people, and of their own human presence with Him, now that they had been exalted to "priest, king and prophet."

"From age to age you gather a people to yourself, so that from east to west a perfect offering may be made to the glory of your name," says the Third Eucharistic Prayer of the Mass; Christ is present in His Church as an active, attractive force and as a leaven raising all to God, con-secrating (making holy!) and healing mankind, as we are slowly molded into a cosmic force, strictly according to His plan. This task of rallying and uplifting, via the transformed intellect that can reach out to embrace the cosmos, centering and structuring the universe about the Logos as its Omega point, is a divine work of sanctifying the world that begins with "work of human hands," making the eucharistic bread and wine, as the prayer of the Offertory puts it.[26]

What energizes and holds together a people through two millennia and makes the Church the mother of civilizations is this central double reality:

1. The Word of God in a stronger and more concentrated sense than any Scripture can capture (it is beyond "the dead letter"), through the human presence of Christ personally choosing, instructing, and sending forth His apostles, to be guided through history by His Holy Spirit. This concrete presence gets continued in the *communio*

26. This then would be the "task of thinking" that Heidegger feared would be voided by "faith."

sanctorum through the Holy Spirit–inspired teaching *with authority* on the part of human beings in continual contact with one another, socially and in prayer, through the intercession of the saints in heaven. That *communio* is the Church. This teaching activity is effective, whether in the form of the most official pronouncements of popes and councils or at the lowest level of authority in parish catechism classes or parents teaching their children in the "domestic church," the home. This teaching continues down through the centuries, as the Church draws on the meditation, writings, and example of all the saints who have lived in every era and every social condition and who in heaven continue to be actively involved in the earthly Church's life, through their prayers and intercession for the presently "militant" members of the Church.

2. Of equal importance with that written word recording the fruits of the teaching efforts of the fathers, doctors, and saints down through the centuries is the living presence of Christ in the sacraments, especially the Eucharist, which is the gathering of a real people (*ekklesia* means "gathering," *Kirk* in Old German, from which our word *church* descends) into the timeless "Mystical Body of Christ." Thus conceived, the Eucharist is an act of love, for it is meant to flow out into all the corporeal and spiritual works of mercy, reaching out to the hurting and the poor. These are exteriorizations and manifestations building the Church as a real, supportive community, the Body of Christ in which the Lord comes to the partaker of this Sacrament, and through Him is taken actively to the workplace and the home, indeed, to all mankind, in ways that make not just a difference, but a progression toward a total transformation of humanity.

Incarnation, Eucharist, and Church are, therefore, inseparable. The Church demands for its institution not only divine authority but also divine action, for it is concerned with not just a set of ideas, a new philosophy, but, as Paul in his letter to the Ephesians says, "a new creation" (Eph. 4:24), which he also describes as a course to be run (1 Cor. 9:24).[27] The new order of reality brought by the Incarnation is one of incarnate grace that becomes visible in the Church, through the transformation of (human) nature, beginning with the forgiveness of sins and the restoration of friendship with God. As the progressive incarnation of Christ in human history, the people of Christ in human history, the Church is a form of what Hegel termed *objective spirit:* a visible transformation of matter, the concretion in our midst of gifts of opportunity for sanctification, handed down and made effective by the works of love of those who make it up, the communion

---

27. Paul's language is absolutely radical: "Your mind must be renewed in the spirit so that you can put on the new self that has been created in God's way, in the righteousness and holiness of the truth" (Eph. 4:24).

of saints. This body is built up not just as a treasure of illuminating and motivating symbols but finally as an accumulation of real virtues (that is, good habits) in real people. They are formed not only to lead good personal lives but also to play roles of charity and teaching with authority in the living institutional arrangements spawned by the Church. Founded in and by Christ's authority, these personal and institutional actions are carried out by sinful human beings striving for holiness. They have been "sent forth" *(apostolein)* by the Lord with the guarantee that, despite their extreme frailty and personal sins, the "gates of hell will not prevail" (Matt. 16:18) against His community. It will always, despite need for repeated reform, be able in the essential to serve as the Way.

This much is a fact of history: nothing like this sort of divine "presencing" and transformation was ever claimed before, and indeed, for all the ambiguities and failings that accompany the life of the Church, its transformation of history has been manifest, with unexcelled civilization-spawning results. Not until Christ's instruction and empowering of His apostles (as well as the sharing of His sacred Body and Blood with them) made it possible could such a spreading of "the people of God" beyond ethnic bloodlines to embrace potentially all humanity occur. Recall the unimaginable last words of the Gospel of Matthew: "All power in heaven and on earth has been given to me. Go, therefore, make disciples of all the nations" (Matt. 28:18).

It amazes me that Islam, which comes six centuries later and after the spread of Christianity even beyond the empire, remains, as Balthasar puts it, "essentially in the enclosure of the religion of Israel" and captures so little of this sense of a new kind of eucharistic-sacramental presence.[28] Christ did not function only as a prophet announcing what God wanted done. He "presenced" as Immanuel, "God with us," not only doing "the will of my Father who is in heaven," but also doing divine works: issuing vocational calls ("Sell all that you have and come follow me" [Luke 18:22]); reorienting lives (even to the point of changing names—Cephas to Peter— just as Yahweh had changed Abram to Abraham); casting out demons; commanding nature; extending divine law; establishing offices with divine authority ("I tell you, you are Peter and upon this Cephas [*petros* in Greek] I shall build my church"; "Whatsoever you shall bind on earth shall be bound in heaven" [Matt. 16:19]); and above all, doing what only God can do: forgiving sins ("Your sins are forgiven" [Mark 2:5]), at which point the Jews tore their garments and cried, "Blasphemy!" In a word, Christ Jesus established a new covenant between God and humanity ("This cup which is poured out for you is the new covenant of my blood" [Luke 22:20]). He thereby reordered how we should henceforth relate to God, transforming God's law, and even telling us how henceforth we should pray. He sealed all this with His total giving up of everything on the cross for the forgiveness of sins, His descent into hell, and His triumph over death on the third day.

28. Hans Urs von Balthasar, "A Résumé of My Thought," *Communio* 15 (winter 1988): 4.

That the Qur'an, after all this, reduces Jesus to the role of mere prophet, and Islam presents its own divine message as the greatest prophesy of all, the fullness of truth, but still only a prophesy, not an expiation, not a new creation, not the founding of a eucharist, is to me a bewildering historical regression.[29] (Adding to my bewilderment is the fact that a militant Arab Islam was successful in replacing a by then decadent Byzantine Christianity throughout the Middle East and a Roman Christianity, by then also in bed with the imperial power, throughout North Africa. That it could transform a tired pagan Persia, and inspire wild Afghans and Turks, and conquer vast territories in India and Indonesia poses no problem to me. But that Christians can allow their lands to become slack and later in modernity secularized has got to be for the believing Christian a shocking, disturbing enigma, the greatest obstacle for others to believe in Christianity. The disturbing effect of this is not sufficiently offset by Christendom's many victories repulsing the Turks, or by the fact of Christian renewal evident in all parts of the world. Large parts of the world, and vast segments of our own Western lands, never should have been lost to Christianity, given who we believe Jesus Christ to be. Sins may have been forgiven, but the fresh sinning of Christians has, since Judas's betrayal and Peter's denial of Christ, had dire consequences.)

The divinity of Christ is so clearly set out in the New Testament that efforts to reduce Christ to a merely human figure demand disregard for the Scriptures, and hence the denial of the historical witness, thereby deforming the tradition at its core.[30] The case for the merely human Christ must be built on some foundation other than the Christian revelation as the tradition has transmitted it to us, on a disbelief that has no choice but to regard the historical witness of Scripture as in part fraudulent, and the martyrdom of Christians and the devotion of saints as well-meant fanaticism.

Balthasar puts it bluntly: Anyone who consults the record will see that it compels this alternative, "either Son of God or else the hallucinatory invention of enthusiastic followers—God's Son or psychopath. Anyone who thinks 'religious genius' as a sufficient explanation has certainly not read the New Testament objectively."

Already Paul wrote eloquently of the human tendency to self-deception (Rom. 1:18), and Christ warned those Jews whose hypocrisy becomes a stumbling block, leading the innocent astray: "But anyone who is a stumbling block to bring down one of these little ones who has faith in me would be better drowned in the depths of the sea with a great millstone round his neck" (Matt. 18:6; Mark 9:42; Luke 17:2).[31] (This warning

29. The vision of the Islamic *umma al Kitab*, the People of the Book, falls far short of this vision.

30. Later we shall analyze one of the Gospels to establish this point.

31. For a complete biography of the astonishing amount of reflection that has been carried out on self-deception, see Greg L. Bahnsen, "The Crucial Concept of Self-Deception in Presuppositional Apologetic," *Westminster Theological Journal* 57:1 (spring 1995): 1–37.

obviously impressed the apostles—it is quoted almost unchanged in all three synoptic Gospels.) Ecumenism, indeed sustenance of a liberal society, becomes much more difficult if Christians doubt the sincerity of all dissenters in the Church, and of all secularized ex-Christians in their society who often seem to retain very little from their Christian heritage. It is not sufficient merely to invoke the great mystery of grace and freedom, which confronts everyone with very concrete practical dilemmas, as we shall see later.

Christ's Foundation of the Church

The institution established by Christ is obviously different from any social structure ever made. While we shall go into the nature of the Church more extensively later, when we reflect on the different ecclesiologies separating Catholics and Protestants, it would be appropriate to attempt now some description of that *ecclesia* founded by Christ, as it throws light on the intention and economy of the Incarnation itself. By reflecting on the marks by which this body has chosen to identify itself in the creed, "one, holy, catholic, and apostolic," we can acquire a preliminary idea of what the Church claims about itself.

The Church's oneness and catholicity are to be understood together. It is one, not only in the unity of all in Christ, but also in its human uniqueness: this social institution makes the ultimate "imperialistic" claim, that is, that God Himself has ordained that it alone be mankind's earthly and heavenly mansion. Only God Himself, present in history in Jesus Christ, could found one overarching and everlasting institution, established, alone of all societies, by contract between the divinity and man—the actualization of "the New and Everlasting Covenant" into which are gathered those living now and the saints who preceded us. Catholic in being for all peoples, it is catholic in its truth: the whole truth about Jesus Christ, who Himself is Truth, is handed on.

The Church alone is "apostolic," having been explicitly chosen, called, and sent forth into the world with God's authority to convert all: "Go, therefore, and make disciples of all the nations; baptize them in the name of the Father and of the Son and of the Holy Spirit, and teach them to observe all the commands I gave you" (Matt. 28:18–20). Its intentions and pretensions are from the start consciously divine.

The claim of its magisterium to be prophetic is also unique. Islam, too, believes it has received a divine mission to call all mankind to God through the way revealed to Mohammed and recorded in the Qur'an. But there is no Islamic Church, only a Scripture; it alone has divine authority, and all teaching authority is basically deontic, not ordained apostolic: the inspired Islamic teacher is the one who gradually comes to be recognized by the local community as best commenting upon the Qur'anic text (closer to the "Congregational" ecclesiology of the Anabaptists and comparable to rabbinic authority). In Islam, the hadith, traditions about the acts and sayings of the Prophet, are a source of guidance, but no institution is guardian of those traditions the way the Church can speak from out of the unwritten tradition, based on an authority believed to be derived from the present guidance of the Holy Spirit. The fatwa (the judgment or pronouncement) of the Imam has deontic, not express divine, apostolically passed down authority and is usually fairly local in impact.

Finally, holiness: only God is holy, for only He has integrity; only in Him are intellect and will completely one. Every creature fails to some degree to be what it is meant to be. All nevertheless are holy, in this sense: they all reflect the ultimate unshakable integrity of Being itself, but they are so only through participation, and hence imperfectly, to the extent each imitates the divine perfection.

Jesus Christ, however, present in His Church, is alone the unqualifiedly holy reality we can experience. The triumphant conclusion of the great opening prayer of praise of the Holy Mass, the Gloria, is "You alone are holy, you alone are the Lord, you alone are most high, Jesus Christ, together with God the Father in the unity of the Holy Spirit." The Church is the unique source of our experience of holiness, because it alone of all realities is divinely instituted to show forth God; through the Church, Christ lives in post-Resurrection form in the world, and into Him, living in His "ekklesia," is gathered every good act and every good thing.

Christ remains with us in the Church through His Holy Spirit, the soul of His Mystical Body. That is why, as Cardinal Ratzinger points out, in the Apostles' Creed the Spirit and the Church are proclaimed in almost the same breath, along with the communion of saints and the forgiveness of sins, founded in baptism and its extension, the sacrament of reconciliation.[32] Then all of these themes together are pointed toward their eschatological[33] fulfillment, the resurrection of the body and life everlasting. Thus, we have expressed in the creed: "I believe in Holy Spirit, the holy, catholic church, the communion of saints, the forgiveness of sins, the resurrection of the body and life everlasting."

In the earliest Greek formulation of the creed there is no article before "Holy Spirit," for, in Ratzinger's view, the creed is emphasizing less the third person of the Trinity than Spirit working in history through the Church. He sees the entire creed reproducing the eschatological movement from the creation by the Father, through the Son's sacrificial accomplishment of redemption, to the Spirit's fulfillment of the Father's and the Son's purposes, leading finally to resurrection, that is, transformation of *bios* into *zoe*, life everlasting.

---

32. Joseph Cardinal Ratzinger's reflection on the creed, published under the title *Introduction to Christianity* (1970), is about as good an introduction as one can find. I am indebted to this work for many formulations in the following pages, especially on the difficult matters of the descent into hell and the forty days after the Resurrection, where I virtually paraphrase Ratzinger.

33. From *eschaton*, having to do with the last things, that is, with the final fulfillment of God's plan.

All of this brings out the necessity for what Ratzinger calls "a theocentric ecclesiology," an understanding of the Church as the work of the Spirit, centered in the two great sacraments, baptism and the Eucharist. The work of the Church, then, is to proceed from God as the grace of the Spirit. This grace is offered most centrally through those sacraments in which all people are intended to be bound into one community. That community experiences the transforming power of God's own re-creative redemptive presence, including the transformation of matter, in the midst of human history, offering in return praise and thanksgiving to God for His having welcomed us back as friends. That is why the Church is essentially eucharistic.

The Sacramental Way to Holiness

Consequently, to grasp the essence of Catholicism, attention must be centered not on the details of institutional structure, nor on power struggles and every manner of admitted human failing that they display, nor on the tragicomic involvements of Church-state struggles, nor even on the glories of liturgy and architecture, but *only on the sacramental way to holiness*. This is the way in which God has ordained to pour His love into our lives through the Church's God-ordained ministering.

The political-social impact of the human institution, of course, remains important for human history, indeed for the lives of all of us. The effect of the mass of human beings who rally about this vision and are penetrated by it to whatever degree (from unimpressive, routinized fellow traveler to mystic transformed by the sacramental presence of Christ into an inspiring "face of Christ") has an immense influence on our civilization, and through it the whole world. What Henri-Bernard Vergote calls *la chrétienitude*, that set of European attitudes formed by *la chrétienité* and enduring even in a post-Christian and increasingly atheist Europe, much of it deformed as political correctness, retains its importance for any appropriator of the present world situation.[34] The historian should see that it draws its vigor, however remotely, from belief in the divine reality, and cannot be understood without confronting the sense of and the evidence for that supernatural core.

Armed with a notion of the Church's own self-understanding of its essence (Vergote's *chrétienité*), what the appropriator then makes of the evidence of concrete holiness, or lack of it, will depend on his own natural faith. Regarding the "sociological" evidence, this must be said: there is both too much and too little of it. The two thousand years of Christianity's existence is accessible to us in an overwhelming store of information involving every aspect of human existence. As with all the great traditions, reconstruction is inevitably highly selective. On the other hand, for the crucial apostolic and early-Church periods, there is often too little evidence, especially with regard to important points in the evolution of doctrine and institutional

34. Vergote, "Contrepoint du religieux au fanatisme religieux," *Cahiers universitaires catholiques*, no. 2 (November–December 1990): 23–29, esp. n. 9.

structure. This extends to the "archaeologists" an invitation to exercise their imaginations.[35]

In any event, for now let us concentrate on the core essential: the holiness of the Church consists in that power of sanctification that God exerts in it despite human sinfulness. In the new covenant in Christ, God has chosen to bind Himself to men, granting this new presence as a grace not dependent on man's faithfulness. Because of His love, God will not allow Himself to be definitively defeated by man's treachery but, loving Him as a good father would His prodigal child, will welcome Him back again and again, forgiving Him, slowly, painstakingly, and *realistically* (God alone knows the travails of our fallen nature) sanctifying Him.[36]

The interplay of God's loyalty and man's disloyalty that characterizes the structure of the Church (and is prefigured in the ups and downs of God's relationship with His faithless people in the Old Testament) is grace in *dramatic form.*[37] The reality of grace as the pardoning of those who are in themselves unworthy continually becomes visibly present in history, a history inspired and transformed by the Spirit's ingenious acts of bringing good out of mediocrity. One could say that in its paradoxical combination of holiness and unholiness the Church is in fact the shape taken by grace in this world.[38]

Despite much unholiness in the people of the Church, God is still prophetically and effectively present in the truth these poor souls manage to communicate through the divinely inspired symbols of the faith. (In the canon of the Mass all Catholics pray: "Regard not our sins but the faith of your Church.") The Church is holy because Christ present in the Eucharist is holy, and the face of Christ manifest in the saints is holy. The saint is a person who has allowed God to destroy the self-imposed bondages that keep the potential of the soul from being developed by grace. Saint Teresa of Avila expresses this experience of fatigue: "After all the kindness I had received

35. There is another kind of scarcity, too: that of reliable data of what really goes on in people's souls. Only in the case of some extraordinary recent saints are we privileged to witness in a rich and fairly direct way the fruits of their labors, while we know the more ancient fathers and doctors through their works, which bear good witness indeed. Even the life of a St. Francis is, however, embroidered (wonderfully, to be sure; but how much credence to put in the Fioretti?). Surely, joyous jewels though they are, they are generally not much to be believed. In both cases, for the periods of scarcity of information and for the periods of abundance, for figures sketchily known and, like (exceptionally) Augustine, St. François de Sales, Newman, or Teresa of Calcutta abundantly known, the clearer and more critical we are about the ruling assumptions guiding our own efforts, the easier it will be for us eventually to recognize the shortcomings and the strengths in our own reconstructions and interpretations.

36. The incomparable description of one such struggle that left God triumphant is known to all through Augustine's *Confessions.*

37. Joseph Cardinal Ratzinger, *Introduction to Christianity,* 221. The second part of Balthasar's great seventeen-volume trilogy is the seven-volume work *Theodramatik* (Theo-drama: Theological dramatic theory, trans. Graham Harrison, 5 vols. [San Francisco: Ignatius Press, 1988–]) (Einsiedeln: Johannes, 1973–1983).

38. Ratzinger, *Introduction to Christianity,* 221.

from you, my God, the hardness of my soul was almost unbelievable. I seem to have been almost totally powerless, as if bound by chains that were keeping me from making a total surrender to God. Then I began to understand that I wasn't living but wrestling with the shadow of death. My soul was utterly worn out; all it wanted was rest."[39]

If one dismisses the divine-human nature of the Church, then the following contention makes no sense: our acts and vices of unholiness are not of the Church, and hence are forces of destruction rather than of Being. Destructive acts have no future, and courses of destruction destroy themselves, eating themselves out by an interior fire.[40]

Still this fact remains: the radiance of God's glory, instead of shining forth for the earthly community as powerfully as God wants it to and it needs to, is tarnished and dimmed by us Christians in our evil. The redemptive act was the beginning of a revelation that is still being realized through the work of sanctification; but the slow working of the leaven in the midst of our confused and ponderous sinfulness can even seem, from our limited perspective, to slip into reverse, the heavy dough tending to sag down into nihilism.

One might worry that the claim that evil is not finally "of the Church" is an excuse that provides too easy rationalization for all the evil done in the name of Christ and His Church. Nothing could be further from Ratzinger's intention when he deals with the subject in his *Introduction to the Catholic Faith*. Not one single act of human treachery is acceptable, and every sinful act on a Christian's part is not only the cause of human suffering, but it also is made worse by being a block to God's grace.[41] Evil acts committed by agents of the Church add to their intrinsic perfidy that element of scandal that makes it better "for that man if he had not been born" (Mark 14:21). Yet here we encounter another incomprehensible mystery: so great is God's love for His creatures, He forgives us; indeed the Father has forgiven us in advance by accepting Christ's assuming our sins upon Himself on the cross.[42] He has pledged Himself to continue until the end to conspire for the salvation of each soul, and to plot the

39. St. Teresa of Avila, *The Book of Her Life,* in vol. 1 of *Collected Works,* trans. Kevin Kavanaugh and Otilio Rodriguez (Washington, D.C.: Institute of Carmelite Studies, 1976), 350.

40. As Balthasar shows us, the great novelist Bernanos demonstrates this in his literary phenomenology of evil. See Hans Urs von Balthasar, *Le chrétien Bernanos,* trans. Maurice de Gondillac (Paris: Éditions du Seuil, 1956), 354.

41. Imagine the destructive effect of the complicity of many Christians in the Holocaust of the Jews. How can one expect a Jew today to receive the message of Jesus Christ after that? Yet, miraculously, some do, knowing that acts like those of the Inquisition and the pogrom will continue until the end of time. So long as God allows human freedom to exist, the worst perversities can be expected.

42. Christ's abandonment on the cross, says Balthasar, is an arrow directed straight at the Father's heart, and from that divine heart flows out the answer: the grace flowing from the pierced heart of His Son (*Theodramatik,* 3:124).

ultimate redemption of His entire creation. If He did not, we all would have condemned ourselves.[43]

The Church is most present, then, not where organizing, reforming, and governing are going on, however indispensable to its earthly reality these things may be. Only one who has experienced how the Church raises men up, gives them a home and a hope, a home that is hope—the path to eternal life—only one who has experienced forgiveness of sins knows what the Church is, both in days gone by and now, regardless of the changes in her ministers and forms.[44]

Qui est Christus?
Christ as Model of Perfect Humanity

No other example of human existence lived in keeping with God's will compares with that of Christ.[45] The infinitely remote God sends His Son to take on the burdens and joys of our humanity. Better than merely restoring the noblest of God's creation to what it was before Adam's revolt, Christ reveals the source and the significance of our own personhood. He provides

43. Having just returned, as I write this, from backpacking high into the glacier-covered mountains of the Selkirk range in British Columbia, I am struck by a metaphor that expresses well my sentiment when I reflect on this Christian call to forebear one another, on the way to love. Descending eight thousand feet from the great Kokanee glacier into the sweltering humanity of Toronto's horrible Yonge Street strip, one still manages to remember that the mountain is really there in its glory. Such exceptional experiences remain with us, no matter how overwhelmed we may be by the vision of the skinheads, the child prostitutes, and the bikers who are also massively present in their own way. The fields ablaze with a million August wildflowers, the thrill of seeing the mother grizzly herding her baby and her two year old among the salmonberries, where the stupid refugees from Yonge Street had pitched our tents, and the refreshment of the frigid waters cascading from the glacier are meant to be brought back into the city to purify the urban dirt and clarify its noxious air. It is the same Church that gathers into one not-yet-purified human body both Mother Teresa and the pedophiliac priest from Newfoundland, Hans Urs von Balthasar and the Catholic father who abandons his wife and four children to go "find himself" with a young girl.

44. Ratzinger, *Introduction to Christianity*, 268.

45. Only one saint can even be mentioned in the same breath: Mary, associated so closely with the redemptive act that she, alone of all human beings since Adam and Eve's fall, was conceived in her mother's womb, teaches the Church, by normal paternal insemination but miraculously restored from the first instance to God's favor in a way enjoyed by no one since our first parents. Thus she, "the *Immaculata*," is not only, as the angel said at the moment he announced that she was to be the instrument of the Incarnation, "full of grace" but also spared the debilitating effects of a long human history of revolt and destruction. That is what is meant by the doctrine of "the Immaculate Conception of Mary." Balthasar points out that Mary is accorded this grace, fruit of the Resurrection by anticipation, before the historical fact of Christ's redemptive act and triumph over death, a reminder that eschatological events take place from all eternity, not according to human historical chronology (*Theodramatik*, 2:2:310–11). Balthasar cites Eph. 5:27, suggesting we apply to Mary what is there said of the Church as Christ's spouse. I shall return to this theme of Mary's role and status later.

us with a concrete guide for developing the unique role that each of us has been chosen to play, which is to follow Him by making our indispensable contribution to the building of the Kingdom.

The Muslim draws inspiration from the personal example of the Holy Prophet of God as retained and passed on in the hadith. The philosopher takes encouragement and guidance from the inspired behavior of Socrates, re-created for us in the *Apology*, and, more ambiguously, in other dialogues. The Buddhist emulates the great Siddhārtha Gautama. What, if anything, is different about *imitatio Christi*?

No Buddhist, no Muslim, no philosopher has ever claimed of their "Holy Man" what Christ claimed for Himself. Recall, for instance, a key text we have already seen: "All power in heaven and on earth has been given to me. Go, therefore, make disciples of all the nations; baptize them in the name of the Father and of the Son and of the Holy Spirit, and teach them to observe all the commands I gave you. And know that I am with you always; yes, to the end of time" (Matt. 28:18–20). The acceptance of such a claim would confer infinite value on every recorded gesture and word coming from such a perfect human being, the perfect image and likeness of God. This would give both an intensity and an unambiguousness to imitation that would leave behind all other instances, even that of the Buddha. Here would be a "cult of the personality" into which one can throw oneself with complete confidence, with the danger of fanaticism avoided so long as the imitation is faithful.

The Redemptive Climax and the Love of Christ

Plato suggests in the *Republic* what would be the inevitable lot of a perfectly just man: his open, generous life would constitute such an implied reproach to the rest of us, we would be unable to tolerate him. One should be cautious, warns Plato, not to appear too just. Plato's description of the fate of the just man, written four hundred years before the death of Christ, reads like a prophecy of Isaiah: "they will say that our just man will be scourged, racked, fettered, will have his eyes burnt out, and at last, after all manner of suffering, will be crucified."[46] In accepting to become man and to live among us as the just man, the Logos knew what we would do to Him. He knew that the bitter fruits of human social perversity would be visited upon Him and that He would taste the loneliness of biological death as man had degraded it, adding fear to the natural experience of the transition to a better life. When, on the night He was betrayed, He saw in the Agony in the Garden the full sweep of human degradation for the expiation of which He was to suffer, and in His humanity almost broke under the weight ("Father, let this cup pass from me . . ." [Matt. 26:39]), this was a suffering of unexcelled dimensions. It is echoed in His cry from the cross, the opening words of Ps. 22, "My God, my God, why hast thou

46. Plato *Republic* II.361E–362A, cited in Balthasar, *Herrlichkeit*, 3:1:161–65.

forsaken me?" (Ps. 22:1; Matt. 27:46). Every Jew, incidentally, knew that this great Psalm moves on from this cry of despair to assert the assurance of God's salvation. That is also part of its meaning here.[47] But, as we shall see later, the abandonment was real, for Christ suffered the total effect of our alienation from God, even to the point of descending with those sins into hell.

In tasting that ultimate loneliness, Jesus spans the distance separating the God of infinite openness and closed egocentric man, the one offering Himself totally, the other selfishly and destructively thinking only of himself. Christ spans this gap and breaks man out of His isolation through the gift of His taking on our life and death, and then showing us the way out of our self-imposed isolation.

This is why the cross is *the* Christian symbol. The sense of the cross as center point joining heaven and hell is wonderfully expressed by Jean Cardinal Daniélou:

> Our feeling of being torn asunder, which is a cross to us, this inability of our heart to carry within itself simultaneously love of the most holy Trinity and love of a world alienated from the Trinity, is precisely the death-agony of the only begotten Son, an agony which he calls on us to share. He who bore this division within himself in order to abolish it, was able to do so only because he had previously borne it within Himself. He stretches from one end to the other. Without leaving the bosom of the Trinity he stretches out to the ultimate limit of human misery and fills the whole space in between. This stretching-out of Christ, symbolized by the four directions of the cross, is the mysterious expression of our own dismemberment and makes us like him.[48]

Ratzinger's comment on this crucial passage—the cross being indeed "the crux of the matter"—is helpful to understanding of the Christian sense of existence: anyone who has stretched his existence so wide that he is simultaneously immersed in God and in the depths of the God-forsaken creature is bound to be torn asunder, as it were; such a one is truly "crucified." But this process of being torn apart is identical with love; it is its realization to the extreme (John 13:1) and the concrete expression of the breadth that it creates.[49]

47. "For He has not scorned him who is down-trodden, nor shrunk in loathing from his plight, nor hidden His face from him, but He has listened to his cry for help" (Ps. 22:24).

48. Daniélou, *Essai sur le mystère de l'histoire* (The Lord of history: Reflections on the inner meaning of history, trans. Nigel Abercrombie [London: Longmans, 1958]) (Paris: Seuil, 1953), cited without page reference by Ratzinger, *Introduction to Christianity*, 221.

49. Ratzinger, *Introduction to Christianity*, 235. These two texts from Daniélou and Ratzinger show that Christian wisdom, in this world, is no stoic, sublime, restful state, but a call to share in Christ's willfully accepted *kenosis*, emptying out, as only selflessly can we accept both the perfect God and His imperfect world. Something of that Christian angst before the imperfection of the world, which means above all our own personal mediocrity, shows up in my own text, especially in those passages where obviously I am haunted by the gulf separating the tawdry everyday face of the Church and its inherent sublime divinity.

Christ's sacrifice did not consist in the physical pain He endured. "Why should God take pleasure in the suffering of his creature, indeed his own Son, or even see in it the currency with which reconciliation has to be purchased from Him? The Bible and right Christian belief are far from such ideas." That pain was the destructive work of sinful man. No, it is not the pain that counts but the "breadth of love which spans existence so completely that it unites the distant and the near, bringing god-forsaken man into relation with God." Were it otherwise, then the executioners around the cross would have been the real priests. But if it is the inner center that bears and gives meaning to the pain, it is truly Jesus Himself who is the priest, He who "reunited the two separated ends of the world in his love."[50]

In the creed, the Passion is separated from the Resurrection by the declaration, "He descended into hell." What one makes of this mysterious phrase affects one's understanding of the Resurrection. I was disturbed by Walter Kasper's minimalist interpretation in his important work *Jesus the Christ*, and his suggestion that the three days is merely symbolic. Ratzinger, on the other hand, says that the Holy Saturday interval is experienced by modern man with particular intensity, for we have felt so strongly what it is for the world to live without God. The article about the Lord's descent into hell reminds us that not only God's speech but also His silence is part of the Christian revelation. God is not only the comprehensible word that comes to us, but He is also the silent, inaccessible, uncomprehended, and incomprehensible ground that eludes us.[51]

Jesus' descent into hell along with His cry, "My God, my God, why hast thou forsaken me?" mean that the Word in taking on humanity accepts as part of the human condition that otherness from God that makes possible ontologically the experience of God as inaccessible and of our being alienated.[52] With this descent it is humanity with all its troubles and low points that is being redeemed by Jesus. "Hell" is the state of radical loneliness of the soul that has refused God definitively. "Heaven," on the other hand, is that state in which the soul is allowed into such intimate company of God, and is so filled with His presence, that there is no longer any danger of its even wanting to reject Him.[53]

50. Ibid., 225. Compare the last quote with Eph. 2:13.

51. See also Balthasar, "The Absences of Jesus," in *New Elucidations*.

52. Ratzinger, *Introduction to Christianity*, 225. The scriptural passages referring to the descent into hell are all rather difficult: 1 Pet. 3:19, 4:6; Eph. 4:9; Rom. 10:7; Matt. 12:40; Acts 2:27, 2:31. But they reveal something important enough to have been included in the creed and hence to demand that the issue be faced as an important one.

53. Ratzinger and Kasper omit mention of the purgatorial dimension that might be thought to belong here. It is not in the creed, and while now part of the Church's essential teaching, it was not dogmatically defined until the Council of Lyons, 1274 (see H. Denzinger, *The Sources of Catholic Dogma*, trans. Roy J. Deferrari from the thirtieth edition of Denzinger's *Enchiridian Symbolorum* [St. Louis: Herder, 1957], 464). It is not appropriate to associate this teaching with the "descent into hell," which according to both Rahner and Balthasar, has to do with Christ's "touching the depths of human

Further, there remains an important insight in the traditional revelation that Christ descended to free the waiting souls in hell. The histories and the roles played by these souls are different from ours. "The just" of the Old Testament, the just among the Greek philosophers, and all just men in ancient civilizations are important to us living now, for their contributions in building the different cultures, the glories of which are aspects of what is to be redeemed, and, in the case of the just of Israel, in preparing the people who were to receive the Incarnation of God's Son. They have all worked to our benefit, and we pray for them, in gratitude; in their moment of glory, they will intercede for us. The point here is that "catholicity" is as much a universality in time as it is in space.

Following the deepest descent comes the great moment of triumph over sin: the resurrection from the dead. The concrete reality of the risen, glorified Body of Christ is emphasized because of its importance for the personal immortality of everyone. This is not to gainsay Cardinal Ratzinger's point that the risen Christ has not returned to the *bios* that ended on the cross but rather shows Himself to His disciples with His body transformed through being taken up into the everlasting *zoe* of life totally permeated and animated by love. This *zoe* is freed forever from the limits of earthly life. This difference commands what Ratzinger terms the *dialectical* nature of the biblical presentation of the event: because He rose to "the definitive life" no longer governed by chemical and biological laws, the risen Lord's encounters with the disciples are indeed "appearances": only when He opens their eyes are the disciples allowed to recognize Him. For the disciples on the way to Emmaus, who had sat with Him at the table three days before, He was unrecognizable, until He began explaining Scripture; He was then first recognized in the Word. It was not in the exposition of the Word, however, but in the giving thanks and breaking of the bread (eucharistically!) that they finally recognized Him. That is why it is so difficult, indeed absolutely impossible, for the Gospels to describe the encounter with the risen Christ; that is why they can only stammer when they speak of these meetings and seem to provide contradictory descriptions of them. In reality they are surprisingly unanimous in the dialectic of their statements: people recognize the Lord and then do not recognize Him again; people touch Him, yet He is untouchable; the crucified and the risen Christ are the same, and there is complete transformation. The dialectic is always the same; only the stylistic means by which it is expressed change.

The risen Christ is that Jesus who was born in Bethlehem, who died and who is risen, body and soul. But the risen body, which can be seen when Christ wills it to be seen and can be present in historical time-space, is nevertheless no longer subject to all the limiting conditions of biological

---

existence." The Eastern traditions have associated it with the redemption of those who died before Christ's coming, but this is not enthusiastically accepted as a correct meaning by most Western theologians. My thanks to Father Dan Donovan for his help in understanding this.

existence. Jesus can suddenly appear in the midst of His disciples who are locked in an upper chamber; and He can disappear just as suddenly. He can will to be present in a eucharistic fashion, under the appearance of bread and wine. But our belief in His eucharistic presence is founded in the disciples' witness to His physical appearing in His glorified body, after the Resurrection. The theologian should never lose sight of that.

For the same kind of reason, it is dangerous to tamper with the forty days Luke tells us separate Christ's Resurrection from His Ascension into Heaven. Granted, it is not absolutely necessary to think Luke means for the forty days, which recall the forty years the Chosen People wandered in the desert, to be taken literally and exactly (although Luke was a scrupulous historian, and not given to the kind of symbolism of John, so it could well have been forty days in fact). From the various scriptural accounts read together it is clear that over a period of some days the risen Christ appeared repeatedly to His disciples, shared meals, including the eucharistic meal, instructed them, and finally left them with essential, binding orders, before effecting a deliberate withdrawal into that sphere of everlasting life into which we can follow Him only after our own biological death. The loving preparation of the disciples for their immense mission before the Crucifixion evidently was not sufficient. A further time of instruction after the Resurrection was obviously deemed necessary by Christ. No doubt this post-Resurrection instruction emphasized the new state of affairs affected by the experience of the risen Lord, an experience that unquestionably expanded both the faith and the understanding of that bewildered though believing community; it is also likely that such instruction emphasized the founding of the Church and the significance of the Eucharist in its life.

The story recounted in the Gospels is through and through *eschatological*: it looks forward to the *eschaton*, the last end. Creation, rightly understood, is inseparable from eschatology: having created the world purposefully, God guides His world toward its fulfillment. God's preparation of mankind to grasp the sense of the world and to realize our role in its fulfillment has been going on since the beginning, and becomes historically visible in the call to Abraham. We have recently witnessed its latest chapter: the great Ecumenical Council's gathering up of all the teaching about the Church as God's eschatological instrument into the Dogmatic Constitution, *Lumen Gentium*.

In this effort to secure an overview of the issue *Cur Deus homo?* and seeking to get some feeling for the Christian sense of the Incarnation, I hope I did not leave the impression that the notion of the Incarnate God is itself fairly straightforward. Even a moment's pause shows that could hardly be so. In fact, whether one is inclined to be "Christian" in the manner of those who feel "Jesus is definitely extraordinary, but I'm not so sure about the divinity; I guess he's divine, so they say anyway, whatever that means," or in the way of devout and committed folk, who might say, "He's divine, no doubt about it; but honestly, I do not know how to begin to think what fully human and fully divine can mean and how they go together!" in either and all events wrestling with such a claim is obviously a mighty and treacherous challenge.

The early Church struggled to formulate its belief. Even a brief and necessarily superficial look at this is valuable: it can furnish us with some sense of what the Church has set as acceptable "orthodox" limits for all future Christology. But there is also much to be learned about this tradition from the way in which these matters were settled. Indispensable for any adequate understanding of Catholicism is its sense of how "dogma"—the matters to be believed—develops. There is no better or more crucial instance of this than the struggle to formulate christological dogma.

For these reasons, before moving to deepen further our understanding of the ecclesiological issues, I propose a historical excursus into the great christological controversies of the fourth century. I will also take a brief look at an attendant issue, raised in the virulent controversy of the seventh and eighth centuries: the advisability of representing Christ in icons, an issue that itself brings home essential points about the Church's understanding of who this Jesus Christ is.

WHO IS THIS JESUS?

A Deepening Understanding of Christ through the Christological and Iconoclastic Crises

CHRISTOLOGICAL CONTROVERSIES AND THE GREAT ECUMENICAL COUNCILS

The question "Who is this Jesus?" was of course present in some form from the beginning. Even the disciples who lived with Him for three years are portrayed in the Gospels as baffled by this greatest of all mysteries, until Christ sent His Holy Spirit on Pentecost to enlighten them. As we reflect on the experience of Christ and the development of doctrine we should keep that startling truth in mind: the apostles lived daily with Jesus, they were instructed by Him, they witnessed His powerful works, they committed their lives, but still, when His hour came, they abandoned the field—all but Mary and John. While the Holy Spirit was already inspiring them to commit their lives and to understand somewhat, the fullness of His gifts of illumination came only on Pentecost. Only with the Resurrection and the infusion of the Spirit at Pentecost are the new spiritual senses accorded. These realities are rife with implications about the nature of religious experience. The apostles are unique as witnesses to the historical reality of Christ, and to the eschatological reality of the Resurrection; both are essential to the objectivity of what the tradition claims. But the gift of faith and the infusion by the Holy Spirit of what the fathers would come to call "spiritual senses" are vital to the individual's response to the immense challenge all this poses and to living out this supernatural life.

But why did it take four centuries before the debates over the central reality of Christ's two natures became so passionate? It is not as though there were no doctrinal tensions in the Church before. These took precedence, often for practical reasons, over debate about Christ's two natures. Already the apostles themselves were in tremendous tension over the question of how "the New Israel" was to relate to the Old, a matter that required "the first Council," a meeting of the apostles in Jerusalem to adjudicate this issue, rife with implications for the spread of the faith and the everyday life of the Church. The first letter of Paul to the Corinthians and the Acts of the Apostles already evidence the existence of serious controversies between what was already, apparently, distinct parties. And from the time of the "Montanist" crisis of the second century, the Church had to confront divisions of belief in its ranks. As to the question of "Who is Christ?" almost every movement in the Church that had come to be seen by the prevailing main or "orthodox" current as "heterodox" or "heretical" had its own peculiar version of how the Christ event was to be understood. That is only to be expected, for this is the question par excellence for Christians, "softness" on the core doctrines about His divinity remaining to this day a hallmark of those the orthodox consider dubious Christians. But none of these crises had yet blown up into the full-scale uproar seen in the fourth century.

By that time, with the Church maturing into a major force within the Roman Empire, just about every possible speculation had been tried out. At the same time, the highest imaginable theological sophistication had been developed from intimacy with Greek philosophy. To be sure, with thinkers of the caliber of Irenaeus of Lyon this subtlety was visible already in the second century, not that enormous depth and richness of vision is not to be found in the Gospels, especially John's.[1] But in the fourth century, on the occasion of a period of sustained peace following Constantine's declaration of Christianity as *religio licita*, energies could be diverted into something other than the first reflection on the message, the initial work of apologetics and elementary building of the institution. The time had arrived to grapple more directly with increasingly virulent heretical challenges. Circumstances, as we shall see, left little alternative but to come to terms with a definitive formulation of the central dogma.

There are two reasons I am asking the reader to follow me through a rather detailed recounting of these controversies. First, there is the point already made: nothing is more important on the level of the vision than getting it right about who Jesus is. But, second, we shall see that the life of the Church reveals a dynamic between theoretical and institutional development. What may appear to the nonbeliever as the Church's genius for improvisation is seen through the eyes of faith as the Spirit-driven life, as "God continues to write straight with the crooked lines of our perversity."

The fact that one of the new fourth-century heresies, the Arian, assumed unprecedented influence of political proportions in the Church, truly threatening to split the community of Christians once and for all, and with it potentially the empire, made a new thinking through Christology practically urgent. This unhappy reality of an influence of matters of state on the development of doctrine—for the whole business turned political— would thereafter never be entirely absent from the life of the Church,

---

1. It is impressive how well worked out the Church's teaching was already by the second century. But then the Christology underlying Paul's letters and the Gospel of John is amazing, and these letters virtually form the beginning of the handing down. In Irenaeus it is well consolidated.

which lives always in an insufficiently Christianized world, subject to its tendencies to tear itself apart. (In our democratic times, divisive doctrinal disputes get aired in the *New York Times*. The Church still has much to learn in presenting itself in the new media of mass opinion.) Arianism had the potential in the fourth century of becoming the first permanent schism, tearing apart the empire, a challenge rather like that posed in the twelfth century by the revolt of the Cathari in southern France, which, too, posed an *affaire d'état*.

Very early, extreme positions about Christ's two natures appeared that to orthodox eyes were so obviously off-the-mark as to require no official conciliar condemnation: on the one hand, Docetism and various Gnostic positions denied Jesus' humanity in order to affirm His divinity; and on the other, Adoptionism denied His divinity, viewing Jesus as thoroughly and only human but only later (at His baptism or at the Resurrection) adopted as God's son. These firmly rejected extremes reemerge in modern times, in one form or another, particularly versions of Adoptionism (for example, the Jehovah's Witnesses), the humanitarian Jesus being seen as in some attenuated sense "divine" because of His goodness. Nonetheless, these were not the positions causing the main tensions in the great controversies.

In trying to put together Christ's humanity and His divinity without losing anything of the sense of either, the most seductive error has perennially proved to be some form of "subordinationism," claiming that while indeed the Son "proceeds from" He must therefore also be to some degree inferior to the Father. The classical and, in terms of a danger of splitting the Church, most serious instance of that began with Arius, a priest of Alexandria who died about A.D. 335, just ten years after Constantine's great victory at Chrysopolis.[2]

As with all subordinationists, Arius was preoccupied with preserving the transcendence of God. He did so by stressing (as the Gnostics had done) the exalted status of the Father, who was seen as the uncreated principle, remote from compromise with creation, that lowly seat of evil and death. To bridge the gap,[3] God's Word, the Logos, is said to be created by Him.[4] (Some subordinationists would have this be a creation from all eternity—but a creation nonetheless, and therefore clearly a subordination.) Through this subordinate, intermediary principle, all else comes into existence.[5] The Logos is clearly devalued in the process, for He is, in the words of Arius,

---

2. Jean Daniélou and H. I. Marrou, *Nouvelle histoire de l'Église,* vol. 1 of *Des origines à Saint Gregoire le Grand* (Paris: Seuil, 1963), and the *Encyclopaedia Britannica* both say Arius was a priest; W. H. C. Frend calls him "an ascetic layman" (*The Rise of Christianity* [London: Darton, Longman, and Todd, 1984], 134).

3. Here Arius took a leaf from the Neoplatonic philosophers.

4. Recall the beginning of the Gospel of John: in the beginning was the Word. We shall see later something of the sense of this revelation that the second person of the Blessed Trinity is not only Son but also Word, source of all intelligibility and structure in creation.

5. "All else" is, of course, in good Neoplatonic fashion, seen to be still more inferior.

"not eternal, not co-eternal with the Father, not like Him uncreated,[6] for it is from the Father that he has received both life and being."[7] Behind this refusal of full divinity to Christ lies a rejection of the goodness of the world, "that God so loved the world" He would come among us to share and completely redeem our created lives. A Puritan rejection of the fallen world, a hatred for the real world of our existence, a hatred rooted psychologically, some would say, in self-hatred, is a perennial temptation found throughout mankind. Orthodox Christianity fights against this more directly than any other tradition. Christ's power to forgive sins and our willingness to accept (and offer to others) forgiveness are all bound up with healing this festering hatred. Ask any psychiatrist about its corrosiveness, and consider Georges Bernanos's analysis in his powerful novels of the spiraling descent into self-destruction of those who have been damaged and thus start to hate themselves.

THE ARIAN HERESY PROVOKES A GREAT INNOVATION: THE ECUMENICAL COUNCILS

It is not altogether surprising that no "heresy" until the Protestant revolt of the sixteenth century so split Christianity as Arianism. (The intervening and gradual East-West Schism involved no heresy, except rejection of the Roman understanding of Petrine authority.) At one point it is thought that more than half the bishops were Arian. For some unclear reason, Arianism was especially successful among the newly converted, and vigorous, barbarians. The newcomers were perhaps seeking quick fixes and something easy to understand, rather than, as the orthodox would say, submitting patiently to the profound work of the Holy Spirit transforming us through our complete receptivity and obedience to experience the full *mysterion*, the "incomprehensible depths which now stand revealed" (Eph. 1:9).[8]

6. Literally, not engendered, not become, for Arius does not clearly distinguish between the participles coming from the different verbs, *gennaoo*, to engender, and *gignomai*, to become.

7. Letter of Arius to Alexander of Alexandria, quoted by Athanasius, *De Synodis*, 16.

8. Perhaps these vigorous pagan warriors were not practiced in patience and humility. Perhaps they too could suffer from self-doubts when confronted by the sophistication of Byzantine civilization. It is always tempting to speculate about what goes on in others' souls. A Catholic today observing the stream of new converts into Christianity from evangelical endeavors suffers some of the same consternation at the truncated "do it yourself" ecclesiology and the lack of roots in the old, rich, intellectually sophisticated traditions of Catholicism, East and West, of the new converts and many of the preachers who convert them with "enthusiasm." While the evangelical Christ is truly man and truly God, is He sufficiently sacramentally incarnate in Eucharist and ordained ministry and Petrine headship? The Catholic sees the wonderful vigor of new evangelical communities and watches Catholics going over to them. In many parts of the Catholic world this is a prod to sleepy Catholics, as the Arians challenged the Church to a new level of dogmatic formulation. In every era the diremptions in the body of Christ take new forms, providing new stimuli to its living more authentically.

Arianism was vigorously combated by the orthodox, and in a couple of centuries it died out with scarcely a trace remaining in the Middle Ages. That the Arian split did not remain permanent is a remarkable phenomenon, with lessons to teach us about how the central coherence of the tradition was maintained by a strongly structured Church, even in the face of a situation never seen before or since—defection of as many as half the bishops.[9]

But to return to the earlier phase of the story: Constantine became sole ruler of the empire in A.D. 324, only to find himself confronted with a politically destabilizing theological controversy racking Egypt and the Near East. He wrote to the two parties—that headed by Alexander, the bishop of Alexandria, and that of Arius, who had fled his enemies and taken refuge in Egypt—to tell them they were engaged in frivolous controversy and should bury their differences and live in harmony.[10] Instead, the parties moved rapidly toward yet more serious confrontation. In A.D. 325, Constantine took a fateful step for Church-state relations: he became the first civil authority to call into existence an ecumenical council.

Councils are a rather strange feature of Catholic institutional life. They occur seldom, and rather ad hoc; they are inspirations of the Holy Spirit, or, sometimes, so it seems, of high politics, an example of that "writing straight with crooked lines," at which God is adept! There had been councils before, the most significant being the first one, that of the apostles themselves in Jerusalem, when they resolved the question of whether newly baptized non-Jews would have to accept Jewish laws. Later, regional councils were called sporadically, but had not played an overwhelming role in forging doctrine or Church structures, and certainly none assumed the importance that Constantine's "ecumenical council"—the first ever so designated— was destined to have.[11]

The emperor chose Nicaea, a town about thirty miles from the capital, Nicomedia. The imperial post was put at the service of the fathers, about 250 to 300 of whom arrived to begin the council on May 20, 325.[12] We enjoy

9. Arianism advanced on the coattails of Constantius's imperial power, and its collapse followed the withdrawal of this power of the sword. Justinian defeated the Arian barbarians in Africa and Italy, the Frankish king Clovis's conversion eliminated Arianism from Gaul. It has reappeared in our time: "The Christology of Jehovah's Witnesses is a form of Arianism, Arius himself being regarded as a forerunner of C. T. Russell, the founder of the movement" (*Encyclopaedia Britannica*, 1966 ed., s.v. "Arianism," which is an excellent summing up of the history and doctrines of Arianism).

10. Eusebius, *Life of Constantine*, ed. I. Heikel (Leipzig: Hinrichs, 1902), 2:64–72.

11. In Greek, *Oecumene* means "the whole world."

12. Those who gathered at Nicaea—mostly from the East, only a few braving the distance from the West, although Pope Sylvester did send two deacons to represent him—felt that a new day was dawning as representatives came from as far as Persia and Mesopotamia, among them some of the confessors, still bearing the wounds of torture, the honored heroes of the last great persecutions. The missionary spirit of the Church was evident. I am following here Frend's *Rise of Christianity* for this historical information.

no record of the debates. But we have the result: several canons (or laws) touching the organization of the Church and the celebration of Easter, and the all-important creedal statement. At the key juncture in its formulation, the emperor himself put forward the accepted formulation: Jesus Christ is *homoousios*—"of one substance"—with the Father, a formula destined to stir profound resistance in due course, especially in Asia.

HOMOOUSIOS AND *SCRIPTURA SOLA:* THE CHURCH GUIDED BY THE HOLY SPIRIT . . . THROUGH THE EMPEROR?

The Role of the Emperor

This event set several precedents. First, the term *homoousios* appears nowhere in Scripture. This implies that the Church in council may teach regarding the heart of divine revelation beyond what is textually contained in the Bible, in this case taking from Greek philosophy certain concepts that were then used to express the core of the revelation. As all Protestants later accepted the creed, this implication causes difficulties, as we shall see, for those who adopt an extreme *Scriptura sola* position,[13] which Catholics would see as hemming in too much the necessary development of doctrine.[14]

The second and, from a Catholic perspective, less happy precedent was the role played by the emperor. In very short order, in fact within the century to follow, the whole question of the Church's relation to the state was posed in urgent new terms. With a Christian emperor beginning to make theological decisions, the different ways the Church-state relation would start to be considered in East and West were some of the factors increasing the division between the Eastern and Western Church.[15]

To this day, as Eric Voegelin points out, because of man's "in-between" nature, the tensions between the Church and whatever form the state takes in any epoch remain a (Voegelin says "the") "motor of history."[16] Whatever the problems raised by such imperial incursions, the resulting careful,

13. *Scriptura sola* is the position that rejects tradition as a font of revelation: if it is not written in the Bible, it is not revelation.

14. Protestant unhappiness with the formulation of the change in the Eucharist of the bread and wine into the body and blood of Jesus Christ as a "transubstantiation" is a rejection of this nonbiblical incursion of a philosophical term. But almost all Protestants accept this when it happened at the council.

15. We shall discuss this at length in the next chapter. At issue was the question of just how subordinate the Church was to be to the emperor. The Western Church, with its increasing emphasis on the supreme authority of the pope, would become the locus of a more independent Church, better able—the Catholic would contend—to rally, so important in our own time, a planetary community around itself. The orthodox contend that the purported subordination of the patriarchs to the emperor should not be exaggerated and point out that with the tenth-century emergence of autocephalous churches, and with the collapse of the empire in the fifteenth century, orthodoxy has managed to survive under the most difficult circumstances.

16. That is the gist of Eric Voegelin's *The New Science of Politics* (Chicago: University of Chicago Press, 1952), 162–63.

detailed definition by an unprecedented ecumenical council of imperial convocation enjoying papal participation should have put to rest, one would think, the christological controversies. For many reasons, some not easy to understand today, others undoubtedly reflective of the perennial blocks to adequately experiencing Christ, this was not to be. For another 125 years until the greatest council in antiquity, the Council of Chalcedon in A.D. 451, and even beyond, the battles raged despite the desire of most emperors to achieve peace and unity on the ecclesial front. (They had enough to do fighting Goths and Persians and holding two parts of an increasingly distinctive Latin West and Greek East Imperium together without having screaming crowds fighting over the *homoousios*.)

Some contend to this day that a terrible price was paid for the clear, rock-solid foundation for belief represented by the "dogmatically formulated" creeds of Nicaea and Chalcedon: a "hardening" of the tradition, a "narrowing of the theophanic field,"[17] in Eric Voegelin's words, a desensitizing of the central tradition to some dimensions of experience of the divine,[18] especially anything that might cause the orthodox symbols to be questioned. This complaint challenges the heart of what Catholics understand an orthodox tradition to be. Catholics (Eastern Orthodox as well as "Romans" and for that matter most Protestants) believe these special moments of the great ecumenical councils to be works of the Holy Spirit guiding Christ's Church, as Jesus promised it would, even writing straight with the crooked lines of the unsavory politics that accompany the process.

Although the danger insisted upon by Voegelin is real—that we stop at the words and that the apparent clarity of the formulations give the illusion of "Yes, that's it! We've got it!" dissipating the vital sense of bottomless depths of mystery—still I believe the tradition does benefit from these carefully honed formulations produced from conciliar debates. The Church is always trying to capture a living experience of Christ, an objective reality not to be separated from the event of the historical Jesus, but that opens to our experience the transcending majesty of the divine reality. By providing—in the light of excesses and infelicities that to all orthodox belief distort the objective historical and transcendental reality—

17. Meaning that opening "within the soul," within which God (*theos*) appears (*phanasthai*).

18. Cf. Voegelin, *The Ecumenic Age*, vol. 4 of *Order and History* (Baton Rouge: Louisiana State University Press, 1974), 48, 56–57. If one follows Voegelin in his tendency to reduce all difference between the "theophanic inspiration" of experience in the Metaxy—that "in between" nature and God that the human soul tensely occupies—enjoyed by the philosopher Plato and that occurring in the events on Sinai, then his complaints about all dogmatizing are valid. But Voegelin never accepted a Catholic sense of the Church as the unique and continuing presencing of Jesus Christ in his community; he never acknowledged anything like a divine teaching authority of the magisterium, and so he was never much tempted by Catholicism. Nor did he incline to that Catholic emphasis on the objectivity of prophetic events (for example, Sinai as an initiative of God confronting Moses "from outside," and Jesus Christ's power over nature in the miracles as events "outside the psyche"). More on that later.

certain cautious "signposts,"[19] the council fathers contributed to keeping all following generations on "the way." For example, someone today who calls himself a Christian yet reduces Jesus to a kind of good prophet has clearly distanced himself from the experience the orthodox tradition has struggled for two millennia to hand down whole and entire. The same would be said of a theologian trying some new version of a subordinationist solution to the issue of the two natures of Christ.

Dogmatic formulation does not imply that further innovative theological speculation is out of order. *An authoritative institution like the Catholic Church can afford to risk testing those limits, precisely because it can guard the integrity of those signposts jealously.* But we must never forget Christianity is not about the words: the very words of Scripture itself, as well as all dogmatic formulations, are meant to point toward the living reality of Jesus Christ. The Christian is supposed to open his heart to Christ through listening, entering into communication through self-offering in prayer, and obeying His commands, which are all about engaging in actual acts of love. By himself the Christian can do none of these things. Basically, what he can do is not interfere with the Holy Spirit's doing it in the Christian: "I live now not with my own life, but with the life of Christ who lives in me" (Gal. 2:20). As we shall see later, the Christian takes Paul literally. We can see the Father only through Christ, and we can see Christ only to the extent the Holy Spirit produces in us the spiritual senses for that experience *(Erfahrung)*. Balthasar reminds us that this experience is a journey *(fahren)* of love borne along by the Spirit, and through and through an ecclesial experience.[20] I just suggested that an authoritative Catholic Church can afford to risk testing the carefully formulated doctrinal limits, precisely because it can guard the integrity of these signposts jealously. Liberal theologians complain bitterly that the Roman authorities guard them much too jealously. The instances are legion where authorities' prudence became a frightened repression of what later became recognized as legitimate efforts to develop Catholic understanding in an orthodox spirit. In our own time, theologians who ultimately came to be accepted, such as Henri de Lubac, M.-D. Chenu, and Yves Congar, earlier had found themselves under a cloud. Since the divine authority of the Church is exercised by sinful human agents, the "how" of maintaining orthodoxy is always somewhat flawed, and not all that happens in the name of "guarding the truth" is genuinely of the Spirit. Ego can get into everything. But I ask myself whether—despite all the human errors and inconsiderations and downright repressions that occur (every such act to be condemned)—the truth is in the long run maintained or not. Since I believe the Holy Spirit has managed that feat, then, without

19. Limits marking out the points beyond which any theological speculation either ceases to share in the full central experience of the tradition, or interpretatively distorts it beyond recognition.

20. Balthasar, *The Glory of the Lord: A Theological Aesthetics*, trans. Erasmo Leiva-Merikakis, ed. Joseph Fessio and John Riches (San Francisco: Ignatius Press, 1983–), 228–29.

whitewashing any of the sad moments of the tale, I am inclined to turn my attention to the ongoing reforming, not just "due procedures," but above all the spirits of those in authority. "Insecurities you will have with you all days!" But insecurities have to be overcome, for they will always breed arrogance and repression.

One who does not believe the Church is guided by the Holy Spirit, especially if he doubts that the doctrine that has been integrally maintained is wholly true (or true at all), will be inclined to see the maintenance of orthodoxy simply as stifling. Those who believe the doctrine is true, and who are grateful therefore that it has been formulated and maintained, consider it inevitable, if regrettable, that a price has to be paid to preserve the integrity of the teaching, because the work of preservation, while essentially the contribution of saints, is also carried out by less holy people who can occupy the necessary offices, and even the saints can be sinful and unreasonable. If there is to be a Church at all, if truth is to be discovered in the founding experiences of a tradition, and handed down to be relived in every generation, this can be done only by sinners. There is no one else. I am not being facetious: this is a critical point. We shall explore these central matters from many perspectives in the coming chapters, as we unfold a picture of how the Church "works."

No one with a liberal bone in his body likes to see a theologian silenced.[21] But a theologian teaching in the name of the Church must teach what the Church believes. One who is open to experiencing the presence of the Spirit in the development of the Church's thought will see in its inexhaustible richness, and coupled with consistency, a divine fruit, but at the same time should admit the reality of the suffering, the bad fruit of human pride.

Already Bishop Irenaeus had insisted in the second century that all who were teaching in the name of the Church be sure that the whole truth of revelation, full and entire, was guarded intact as a single structure. The famous fourth-century statement of Vincent of Lerins comes to mind, that the *catholica* is to be seen in the fact that "we hold fast to that which was believed *everywhere, always, and by all*; for that is catholic in the true and proper sense."[22]

The creedal signposts, fruits of the great councils, are actually quite unique in the Church's long history. Only the addition gradually in the Middle Ages of the *filioque*—that the Holy Spirit proceeds from the Father *and the Son*, which we shall discuss later—and the papal definitions of the Immaculate Conception and the Assumption of Mary in the last

21. There are people with no liberal bones who delight in repressing. That is a sickness of the soul. The Church has to be vigilant not to allow such twisted people to occupy any position of authority in the Church. When they do, they wreak great damage, just as do those too pusillanimous to carry out their responsibilities of protecting the faithful from the injustice of someone in authority teaching "the little ones" error.

22. Quoted in Balthasar, *The Church's Confession of Faith: A Catholic Catechism for Adults,* trans. Stephen Wentworth Arndt, ed. Mark Jordan (San Francisco: Ignatius Press, 1987), 47.

hundred years have achieved such canonical status in all the time since the ecumenical councils.[23] The very enormity of the accomplishment of the council fathers will help us understand, when we consider it later, why the Orthodox feel so strongly about the gradual addition to the creed in the Middle Ages of that one word: *filioque*.

Eastern and Western Sociopolitical Directions Play into Theological Dialogue

The intense bitterness of the fights that swirled about these issues is appalling, even mystifying, although those were, admittedly, unusually troubled times. The radical change in the Church's status—from barely tolerated, often persecuted marginal oddity to imperially backed majority religion—was the greatest and most sudden revolution it had yet faced, comparable in its upsetting effect to the later diremption of the Protestant revolt and the destruction wrought by the French Revolution.

In human terms, the actors were now playing in a totally new game. Voegelin is surely right in seeing it as much less favorable to keeping the religion centered on God.[24] This was a sea change for which nothing prepared the bishops. Whereas before, being a bishop had meant one was a prime candidate for the lions at the next outburst of persecution, it quickly evolved into a position of considerable power, even civic power as the imperial authority became more remote, especially in the Far West.

The imperial authority was under even worse strains than the Church. For more than a century emperors had been military men, so exposed at the front as to give anyone in the job a short life expectancy. Newly converted to Christianity, and save for Julian the Apostate, not usually intellectual, Constantine and several emperors in his line still showed themselves, as we saw, willing and even, surprisingly, able to enter the subtle theological fray.[25]

23. So, in fact, very little has been dogmatically asserted as *de fidei* at this highest level of definition. It will be important to treat Voegelin's charge of "closing the apophantic field" both as a question in principle and in terms of the actual truth claims that have been set down in the specific dogmatic formulations. All of this then will have to be placed in the larger context of the questions of how and by what authority the Church teaches, as there are many other matters that are not thus once and for all precisely and dogmatically formulated—indeed, most of what constitutes essential parts of the Church's teaching is like that.

24. Voegelin, in *New Science of Politics*, speaks of an inevitable decline once the religion is open to the masses and becomes "the thing to do."

25. Was this out of sheer necessity, a desperate effort to hold the imperium together when theological warring could rip it asunder, or was there personal predilection for this sort of thing? It is not impossible that they may have been actually interested in the issues. After all, the question that Christ represents is the most important question a Christian can ponder. There has been much speculation about the sincerity of Constantine's conversion. It remains just that, speculation. We have no grounds for excluding the possibility that he personally considered the issue of *Qui est Christus?* of the greatest importance. Why not? Moreover, the Greek world's millennia-old passion for methodic philosophy had worked its way into the fabric of society and had been

The drifting apart of East and West posed another difficulty. This was a complex, gradual, dolorous process, caused in part by the inability of the great unifying power of the Roman Imperium to transform thoroughly the various civilizations (Greek, Persian, Egyptian) and dozens of cultures, many of them, like the Germanic, Slavic, and Arabian not much penetrated by any civilization, over which it extended its remarkable umbrella. Strains and antipathies between East and West were very old. Now, a language problem was growing increasingly serious. Latin had not succeeded in becoming the working language of the East—common *(koine)* Greek being the lingua franca in the Oriental provinces and beyond the eastern imperial boundary. In the late Republic and early days of the Augustine Empire, Greek was also the language of Western intellectuals, but by the end of the third century that was no longer the case. Increasingly, one found doctors of the West, like Augustine, who knew no Greek at all. This not only made mutual understanding harder, but it also contributed, along with many other factors, to producing two Christian worlds.

Differences in liturgy emerged early. Later, regional differences in theology began to assume importance. The christological approach of Origen, inspired by Neoplatonism, made a much greater impact in the East than in the West. After the Council of Nicaea in A.D. 325 the West became rather solidly Nicaean, while the Origen-influenced East remained wary of a lingering potential for a Sabellian (one divine substance but three modes of activity: Father, Son, Spirit) interpretation of the Nicaean homoousian formulation, that is, they feared that Christ would be seen as a mere mode of the Father rather than a truly distinct person. When the main seat of the empire shifted to the new capital in Byzantium, tellingly renamed Constantinople, there was a tendency in the East, strongly resisted in the West, to accede to the emperor's new role as virtual head of the Church. All of these differences became so many occasions for exaggerating sometimes subtle theological disagreements.

But in all this, and whatever the ravages of party politics, the sincerity of many great protagonists cannot be questioned. Critics have enjoyed making fun of the fact that the empire hung from an iota—the difference between the *homoousios* and *homoiousios* positions.[26] Such Voltairean historians do not care to appreciate the seriousness of the issues, and therefore do not understand that good men could be divided on what to any Christian is the most important of issues: the nature of Him, the God-man on whom our salvation depends.

Now that we see a little better what is at stake, and recognizing that it is enormous, not just for the future of the tradition, but because of the central

---

transformed with the advent of Christianity into a love for theological speculation. While the emperors were not intellectuals, those surrounding them were infected with the Greek passion for argument, and perhaps they passed on a bit of the malady to these sly statesmen-generals.

26. Was Christ of one and the same substance *(homoousios)* as the Father or only of like substance *(homoiousios)*?

truth claims involved, critical for all mankind, I propose to take a close look at the formulations of Nicaea and later of Chalcedon.

The Person and Natures of Jesus Christ as Formulated at Nicaea and Chalcedon

After a succinct affirmation of the Father's sovereignty and creative role ("We believe in one God, the Father Almighty, maker of all things visible and invisible"), the Nicaean creed passes at once to the Lord Jesus Christ, who is declared "one" (that is, Jesus and the Christ are not distinct, a blow to Adoptionism), as well as the Son of God (an appellation that Christ, according to Scripture, took on Himself, and the title Mark gives Him at the start of his gospel).[27]

Next the sense of that "Sonship" is explained: "begotten of the Father, only-begotten that is, of the substance of the Father *[ek tes ousias tou patros]*, God of God, Light of Light, true God of True God, begotten not made, of one substance *[homoousion tou patri]*." This affirms unequivocally the divinity of Jesus Christ, and, although proceeding from the Father, the sense of that proceeding is clarified to affirm His full participation in the divine Being. He is not conflated with the Father, but is distinguished from Him as He who proceeds or is begotten is distinguished from Him from whom He proceeds or who begets, a distinction of relationship. The further implications are spelled out in the next phrase: "through whom all things were made, whether in heaven or on earth." The creative activity of God the Father is mediated through the Son who shares fully the divinity of the Father in the Son's own cocreative activity.[28] It is this fully divine Son who "for us men and for our salvation came down and was made flesh and became man *[enanthropesanta]*, suffered, and rose on the third day, ascended into the heavens, is coming to judge the living and the dead."

The Nicaean creed says nothing, however, about how the divine and the human aspects, so firmly asserted, are related. That left room for every sort of speculation. Chalcedon closes the gap. The official text from the later council clarifies this as follows:

> Following therefore the Holy Fathers, we unanimously teach and confess one and the same Son, our Lord Jesus Christ, the same perfect in divinity and perfect in

27. Mark begins his gospel by calling Jesus Son of God; cf. also Luke 1:35. In John 10:36, Jesus acknowledges that He said "I am the Son of God." In that gospel He much more commonly refers to Himself as the "Son of man." This appellation, which goes back to the prophet Daniel, means that Jesus truly shares our humanity.

28. This was a central notion in Paul's thought and a key to the orthodox conviction that the perfect *imago Dei* is founded in the interior life of the Trinity: it is this Logos proceeding from the Father that becomes the perfect *ikon* of God dwelling among us in history. Man's being made in the image of God, as Genesis reveals, is then understood as brotherhood with Christ, approaching in sanctity His perfect imaging of the Father. See Hans Urs von Balthasar, *Theodramatik*, for a good synopsis of how the Fathers developed this notion ("Der Mensch in Gott" [Einsiedeln: Johannes, 1973–1983], 2:1:289–305).

humanity, the same truly God and truly man, composed of rational soul and body,[29] *homoousios* with the Father as to divinity and *homoousios* with us as to humanity, like unto us in all things but sin. The same was begotten from the Father before the ages as to the divinity and in the latter days for us from Mary the Virgin Mother of God [*Theotokos*].[30]

Concise and precise: the divinity, begotten before time, in other words, always existed in an internal procession from the Father; the humanity came into existence in time through the natural means of birth. The conception in Mary's womb itself is a meeting of the divine and the human, dramatized— with an effect on the later development of a theology of the role of Mary, by calling the Virgin *Theotokos*, Mother of God. The Chalcedonian fathers go on to spell out the relationship between the two natures:

> We confess that one and the same Lord Jesus Christ, the only-begotten Son, must be acknowledged in two natures, without confusion or change, without division or separation. The distinction between the two natures was never abolished by their union but rather the character proper to each of the two natures was preserved as they came together in one person [*prosopon*] and one *hypostasis*. He is not split into two persons but he is one and the same only-begotten, God the Word, the Lord Jesus Christ, as formerly the prophets and later Jesus Christ himself have taught us about him and as he has been handed down to us by the Symbol of our Fathers.[31]

It took all the skill of the imperial legates to win agreement on these formulations. J. N. D. Kelly points out that the final form is a mosaic of excerpts from the two letters of Cyril of Alexandria, Pope Leo's tome addressed to the council, the earlier profession of faith of Flavian drawn up at the Standing Synod, and the "Symbol of Union" contained in a letter sent after the Council of Ephesus in A.D. 431.[32] This is not to suggest that Catholic doctrine is a pastiche, but rather to show that this remarkable balancing of factors drew inspiration from widely divergent sources in the tradition, which shared the same basic intuitions.[33] "Its distinctive theology," says Kelly, "is to be seen in the equal recognition it accords both to the unity and to the duality of the God-man. We notice, in addition to the formula "one *prosopon* and one *hypostasis* [one person and one substance]," which comes straight from Flavian's profession, the monotonous repetition of the words "the same" and the insistence that, in spite of two natures, Christ remains "without division, without separation." Clearly, the divine Word is regarded as the unique subject of the Incarnate, a point further reinforced by the sanction given to the controverted title *Theotokos*.[34] The *Theotokos*

---

29. That precludes any talk of the human soul being replaced in Jesus by the Divine Spirit.

30. Quoted in Frend, *The Rise of Christianity*, 771.

31. Ibid.

32. Kelly, *Early Christian Doctrines* (New York: Harper and Row, 1978), 341.

33. The recent *Catechism of the Catholic Church* (London: Geoffrey Chapman, 1994) is effective in just that way.

34. Kelly, *Early Christian Doctrines*, 328; Jarsolav Pelikan, *The Spirit of Eastern Christendom (600–1700)*, vol. 2 of *The Christian Tradition: A History of the Development of Doctrine* (Chicago: University of Chicago Press, 1976), 122.

claim makes sense only if the human nature of Christ, born of the Virgin, is truly the human nature, the incarnation, of God Himself.

The West was fairly happy with Chalcedon. Some historians even see it as a Western triumph, although Kelly shows that it was a true balancing of the best theological instincts of Antioch, Alexandria, and Rome. In the East especially, Monophysitism (the doctrine of only one nature in Christ, a position still held by the Coptic Christians of Egypt) continued to spring up, particularly in reaction to a Nestorianism that exaggerated the distinctiveness of the two natures to the point of risking separating Christ into two persons. Despite the eventual East-West Schism and the Protestant revolt, Christians continued to unite around the careful formulations issued by the great ecumenical councils.

Is the Conciliar Creedal Position Faithful to the Biblical Accounts, and Why Do Catholics Hold on to Them?

A critical historical question remains: in going beyond Scripture, how faithful to the New Testament have the fathers in fact remained?

Here is one of the great advantages that explicit traditions enjoy over implicit ones: Because they have taken the pains to formulate their truth claims and have written them down, one can check formulations of one era with those of another, thus taking some measure of the development, and checking its fidelity to the earliest formulated vision.

That is what I am now going to do: I shall take the measure of the conciliar creed vis-à-vis the mind of the earliest church, which Christians believe to be "the mind of God" set down in Scripture in a unique and normative, that is, canonical, sense. How substantial is the development? Are there unresolved tensions?

Is the Biblical Account Ambiguous about Christ's Divinity? Is There an "Adoptionist" Strain?

"Who can this be? Even the wind and the sea obey him" (Mark 4:41). I had always been led to believe there was an "Adoptionist strain" in the New Testament, and hence that it must be somewhat ambiguous in its understanding of Jesus' divinity, and also that Jesus Himself as He appears in the Gospels was diffident about calling Himself "Son of God." So with understanding of the relationship between His human and divine natures sharpened by my examination of the great ecumenical councils, I went back to the New Testament as a whole rather excited to see what I would find from such an overview to be the New Testament writers' christological positions.

From Jarsolav Pelikan's recent *The Christian Tradition: A History of the Development of Doctrine*, I learned (and here he is drawing on the near classic work of Harnack) that only one document from the early Church was Adoptionist: *The Pastor of Hermes*, a text with no "canonical" status, but interesting nonetheless as evidence of an early current of thought. Of it, Pelikan judges, "The claim that *[The Shepherd]* was adoptionist in its doctrine is difficult to prove or disprove, because of the confusing language of the book and because of the literary problems of determining its origin and composition."[35] So I believe it prudent to leave *The Shepherd* aside.

In the canonically accepted texts—the New Testament—there are only two that could possibly lead to Adoptionist interpretation: a passage in the Acts of the Apostles quoting Peter, and then the more difficult issue of interpreting what happened at the moment of Jesus' baptism at the hands of John.

The passage in Acts is a report of the first Christian sermon in which Peter addressed the Jews assembled after they heard the roar of the wind on Pentecost. The part of the text that sounds most Adoptionist reads: "God raised this man Jesus to life, and all of us are witnesses to that. Now raised to the heights by God's right hand, he has received from the Father the Holy Spirit: the whole House of Israel can be certain that God has made this Jesus whom you crucified both Lord and Christ" (2:32–36).

The text does indeed have an Adoptionist ring. But given what will be argued below—that the entire remainder of the New Testament (including the Gospel according to Luke, author of Acts) is not—it seems to me reasonable to propose an explanation that will account for the anomaly.

Peter is addressing Jews who have just recently learned of the Crucifixion of the man Jesus of Nazareth. Peter is talking to them of this man, about whom they have all heard, with a view to convincing them that this individual, "whom you have crucified," is in fact *kyrios kai christos*, that is, somehow associated in a strong sense with the divinity and the anointed one of God, the Messiah, whom they have been awaiting. The sequence could be read in the sense of the Jews being brought progressively to understand who this man really is.

The expression is indeed Adoptionist: God reaches down to raise this man from the dead and to seat Him at His right side, making Him Lord and Christ. But perhaps Peter, in that first sermon, did not think his audience would understand that this Jesus is the Logos itself. As the rest of Luke, who wrote Acts as a continuation of the gospel, is non-Adoptionist and nothing else in Acts can be cited in support of such a position, this explanation is at least plausible.

The text can also be explained this way: as the enthronement of the Incarnate Son of God. That is, it is not that the eternal Son of God was ever not Lord; but the Jesus who became incarnate at a point in time, and was crucified in history, then "had to also become," as incarnate, "Lord and Messiah." God "made" Him such because God raised Him from the

35. Adolf von Harnack, *Lehrbuch der Dogmengeschichte* (History of dogma, trans. from the 3rd German ed. by Neil Buchanan [1931–1932; Gloucester, Mass.: P. Smith, 1976]). See Pelikan, *The Christian Tradition*, 1:175.

dead and seated Him at His right hand. This would accord with the New Testament use of Ps. 2:7: "You are my Son, today I have become your Father (begotten you)" (Acts 13:33), used with reference to the Resurrection (compare Rom. 1:4; Heb. 1:5).[36]

But what about the baptism in the Jordan? The heretical third-century bishop of Antioch, Paul of Samasota, considered the baptism "the decisive event in [Jesus'] divine sonship."[37] What does the purportedly "Adoptionist" description of the baptism in Luke 3:22 actually say?

When all the people had been baptized and while Jesus was at prayer after His baptism, heaven opened and the Holy Spirit descended on Him in bodily shape, like a dove. And a voice came from heaven, "You are my Son, the Beloved; my favor rests on you" (Matt. 3:16–17; Mark 1:11; Luke 3:22). If one takes the text by itself, it is not absurd to see in this descent of the Holy Spirit the beginning of a new status for Jesus. But if we examine all that has come before and the text that immediately follows, we see that this is more credibly interpreted as the sign of the beginning of Jesus' public mission. What follows is the affirmation that when Jesus began to teach He was about thirty, and then Luke gives one of the two genealogies of the New Testament,[38] this one reaching back to Adam, through David, Isaac, and Abraham,[39] intended to highlight a royal, prophetic, patriarchal descent. Everything from the beginning of the gospel to the baptism seems to be aimed at bringing out Jesus' divine Sonship. Take, for instance, only Luke's version of the Annunciation to Mary: "The Holy Spirit will come upon you, and the power of the Most High will cover you with its shadow. And so the child will be holy and will be called Son of God" (Luke 1:35).

Furthermore, both Paul's letters and the Gospel of John go to the greatest imaginable extremes not only to communicate the divinity of Jesus but also to develop fully a sense of the majestic implications of His divine "Sonship." And in this each of the three synoptic Gospels is also quite clear and strong.[40]

As it would be tedious to go through the entire New Testament citing every text, I shall make a collection of only the key points in the shortest and most "austere" of our sources, the Gospel of Mark, showing how the sense of Jesus' divinity is built up literally.

36. I am grateful to my evangelical friend for this latter suggestion.

37. Pelikan, *Christian Tradition*, 176.

38. These accounts do not agree: Luke emphasizes Mary's line, while Matthew emphasizes Joseph's.

39. If one thought to take it literally it would be quite unbelievable. Luke intends it symbolically, to say "this is the new Adam, this is the new David."

40. So called because the Gospels of Matthew, Mark, and Luke follow rather the same course in presenting the work and word of Jesus. Levantine documents (such as those that make up the Gospels) tend—whether secular or sacred—to operate on a number of levels of fact, allegory, symbol, and myth simultaneously. The Gospel according to John is organized differently and to different ends than the synoptics, but its principle of organization is also one that mixes fact, allegory, symbol, and myth, not a disregard of fact altogether, as the use of "synoptic" in some circles has tended to leave as an impression.

How Mark Invokes the Divinity of Jesus Christ

The survey of just this one gospel account, the Gospel of Mark, confirms my earlier conviction that for the primitive faith community there was no question of "Who is this Jesus?" Everything possible has been done to convey the sense of His divinity. Here in résumé is the catalog:[41]

1. He teaches "with authority."
2. He cures illnesses, physical and spiritual.
3. He calls men and changes their lives.
4. He forgives sins.
5. He overrides pharisaical understandings of the law as a higher authority as to its true meaning.
6. He has command over unclean spirits.
7. He has power over nature.
8. He has power even over death.
9. He respects human freedom.
10. He is glorified in the theophany of the Transfiguration.
11. He institutes the Eucharist, sharing in a divine way His body, *in-corporating* us all into His Mystical Body.
12. He founds the Church.
13. He sacrifices Himself for us, atoning for our sins as only God can do.

Of this we can say, with the centurion who pierced his heart with a lance, "This was indeed a Son of God" (Mark 15:39). But before I consider how well Chalcedon captured the sense of the central revelation, that this Jesus is the Son of God, whose dominion, as Paul says, is over all creation, and why, to what extent, and how justifiably in doing so the fathers went beyond the letter of Scripture, I believe it would be useful to pause now to consider how and why a modern person can believe such a staggering claim. The appropriator wants to get clear about the foundations of his own belief, and I am confident the reader will be curious to know how someone who strives to be thoughtful and critical experiences such an object. This will help us appreciate better the struggle of the fathers at Chalcedon to express this truth.

Why Believe Today That Jesus Is "Son of God"?

If Jesus were not what those early New Testament witnesses claim and the creed confirms, if, rather, He was merely some kind of extraordinary religious figure the purity and compassion of whose teaching impressed all who heard, and who, perhaps, through power of mass suggestion, affected a certain number of health "cures," then we should have to think that, after His innocent death, the grieving apostles, moved by their loss and by their love for Him, embellished His memory with powers of divinity such as

41. For the texts, see the appendix at the end of this chapter.

those we saw in our brief survey of the Gospel of Mark. In that case, the *authority* of this Jesus and of the community that follows His inspiration, "the Church," is really only "deontic," that is, persuasive, like that of the Buddha or any philosopher. That does not mean that Jesus has to be seen "to argue," but only that His "parables," when we take them to our experience of everyday life, illumine human reality, and woven together, provide a coherent and realizable pattern for existence.

This would be "Jesus, the gentle shepherd" of the modern liberal Protestant tradition. But such a view requires stripping away much of the New Testament, aimed as it is at presenting the humble man Jesus as Anointed One and Lord, "God of power and might." And it makes out of the faith, practice, and history of much of Christianity a misunderstanding, contaminated with illusion, requiring "demythologizing." However, if one embraces the Jesus *kyrios kai christos* (Acts 2:36) just as the gospel-rooted orthodox tradition presents Him, is one not throwing reason out the window, by rushing headlong into an absurdity that no post-Enlightenment person can be expected to respect?

I have never considered my faith something that can be so demonstrated, so laid out methodically before another, that, were he to follow the steps of the demonstration loyally, he would be required logically to assent. But then, as I suggested in *Being and Truth,* the basic natural faith of every human being is indemonstrable.[42] That does not mean, however, that one's basic beliefs are necessarily unreasonable, and, of course, I consider mine eminently reasonable, just as you do yours. But it will require an effort to render credible the validity of certain kinds of experience for one's faith to become at least respectable to others.

In *Being and Truth,* I devoted a chapter to the grounds for believing in a creating God, providentially caring for His creation; later in this appropriation I shall touch on it again. But for the moment I would like to assume a theistic framework and speak to the central Christian issue of why, within that, it is not so unthinkable that such a providential God would seek to enter into communion with us through an incarnation and that this Jesus could have been indeed *kyrios kai christos.*

Being is *"proved"* by living along with it; the German word for experience, *Erfahrung,* captures this sense of a voyaging along *(fahren).* Being shows itself *(monstrare,* as in *de-monstratio),* provided one elects to participate, that is to be opened up and to be present when being, in any of its forms, whether in science, in friendship, or in music, offers itself. Our freedom consists above all in our decision to be present or not, to attend when some aspect of being calls to us,[43] and then to re-spond (*spondeo* means "I commit"; *Ant-wort*

---

42. *BT,* chapter 2.

43. The reader can glimpse here the sense of an epistemology of service. As Balthasar shows so well, if knowledge is conceived as my need and emptiness reaching out to grasp *(begreifen)* and consume what I need, all objects are brought to serve me. If, on the other hand, we recognize that our knowledge capacity stands lovingly open to the

means "answer," a co-responding word) to what it demands, which calls us out of our old selves into something that is new for us.

What call do I hear, then? What do I see that convinces me to accept the claim that Jesus is Son of God in the strong sense put forward by the New Testament and confirmed in the creedal formulations?

First, the mysterious and great things I have seen happening down through the history of the people of God, from Sinai to the miracle of the great saints of our own time, harmonizing with the picture I see the New Testament painting of Jesus: the intellectual and spiritual greatness of the giant prophetic figures, from Moses, through the Elijahs, Jeremiahs, Isaiahs, and Daniels; the creative vision and the witness of the life of Paul; the missionary zeal and the martyrdom of the apostles; the profound vision of love in John; the early fathers, Irenaeus (whose work harmonizes so perfectly with the vision of orthodox Catholic theology today that it becomes for me a confirmation of the unity and consistency of the tradition) and Origen (whose ability to deepen the sense of what is taught through a deft employment of Greek philosophy appropriates, not flees, what is best in the contemporary culture); the sweep of the vision and the witness of the lives of the great fathers, Gregory of Nyssa, Basil the Great, John of Damascus, Augustine, Maximus the Confessor, each an ocean of wisdom and truth that could keep the ship of life afloat all by itself; the medieval doctors, from the ninth-century John Scotus Eriugena, through Anselm of Canterbury, Hugh of St. Victor, and the other "Victorines"—Thomas; Bonaventure; Duns Scotus; the unexcelled poetic vision of Dante Alighieri; the mystical visions of Bernard of Clairvaux, John of the Cross, Teresa of Avila (herself named "doctor of the Church"), Ignatius of Loyola. Is there

---

other as other, and is therefore at the service of the other in appreciation and admiration, then the sense of the world's calling me to a fulfillment in the midst of other centers that require fulfillment, and this together, co-operatively, something of this Christian sense of being stands a chance to emerge. I recall some months ago interrupting a young fellow passenger's viewing of an idiotic movie to point out to her the vast ice-filled canyons and cloud-swathed peaks of Greenland—one of the most incredible sights I have ever seen from a plane. After the most minimally polite, "Oh, interesting!" she plunged back into the film. How do you prove to someone totally ignorant of great music what awaits him at the heart of *Don Giovanni* or the last string quartets of Beethoven? One's decision to make the effort to get in touch involves, before the fruits begin to be accumulated, an act of confidence, and a humble attitude of service. (Faith is as much *con-fidence*, from *fides*, as it is the embracing of the content of what is witnessed—willingness to be open—and then loyalty, fidelity to what one has seen, both in remembering it and in acting in accordance to what has been discovered.) Responsibility—the capacity to respond—requires commitment, which is the sense of the Latin root *spondeo:* I promise or commit, that is, I agree to engage myself. The music analogy should not be pushed too far, however. Music is for enjoyment, for emotional uplift, and what it reveals about being is charmed precisely because it is (mysteriously) on a nonpropositional level. The claim "Jesus of Nazareth is Son of God," on the other hand, is thoroughly propositional, and someone confronted with such a claim has every right—indeed, a responsibility—to ask for reasons for assenting to it. 'Tis far from a mere matter of taste: it is a life-or-death proposition.

any point in continuing the list to today, to "le grand Newman," as de Lubac calls him, to "le grand de Lubac" himself, and to his great student and friend Hans Urs von Balthasar, to Karl Barth, Karl Rahner, Romano Guardini, and mystics such as Adrienne von Speyer, Marthe Robin, and so on, not to speak of all the witnessing through personal conversions, deathbed graces, and even those "private revelations," such as the extraordinary happenings in Lourdes, Fatima, and Medjugorje, which, however one judges them, are impressive through the undeniable effect they have had on tens of millions of lives?[44]

The point is, study of any and all of these great fathers and doctors and mystics confirms, over and over again, their total acceptance of the biblical vision of events and especially of who Jesus was, and their ability to plunge to the depths of the resulting vision and experience of life and to come up with infinite orchestrations that nevertheless remain entirely faithful and consistent with one another—symphonic—and hence with the whole tradition. One is nourished abundantly by the accumulated treasures of this life of the spirit. When I plunge into one of the profound and demanding tomes of Balthasar and participate in his wise appropriation of Maximus the Confessor and his illumination of the mystical meaning of Christ's abandonment on the cross as a revelation of love, the peace I find as this great vision opens up is difficult to describe. I know that the student of Talmud, the Hindu, and the Muslim, poring over the writings of Ghazālī and of the greatest (and most orthodox) of the Sufi mystics and the magnificent classical commentaries on the Qur'an, can testify to similar experience. And why not? I do not think God limits Himself to working in my Catholic tradition. But I do experience Him working there in this way of overwhelming richness of vision. Candidly, that is one source of my belief.

Neither my discovery of the consistency and richness of the orthodox tradition concerning the issue "Who is this Jesus?" nor the Muslim's sense of the lived consistency and richness of the orthodox Qur'anic tradition is an argument compelling for the non-Christian or the non-Muslim respectively; rather, it is the lived experience itself that reassures the believer in his faith in the orthodox tradition within which he lives, and it is his witnessing by living out this vision that attracts others.

An important part of the Catholic's experience is the sacramental life of the Church, which demands personal application in the form of a life of prayer, and the effort to struggle toward personal sanctification. Such a program of personal growth, based in an ancient and rich anthropology, a school of love, is a source of joy, especially as it is accompanied by God's forgiveness for one's stupid lapses, including the loving gift of the sacrament of reconciliation. It is often "tough love," which encourages one to avoid a proud self-satisfaction, and so to push on in the direction of that perfection

44. The question of private revelations and apparitions is covered in some detail in the final chapter.

Christ asked of all of us, in that startling command, "Be ye perfect as your heavenly Father is perfect!" (Matt. 5:48). Consider the alternatives: either a kind of flabby *laissez aller,* a self-indulgence, following the passions of the moment, which leads inevitably to nothing but conflicts between selfish egos; or, far nobler, the struggle to remain "ethical" (although without a well-grounded belief system it becomes ever more difficult in a dynamic and pluralistic society to discern the limits of the morally licit).[45]

As noble and difficult as the ethical way may be, the Christian struggle to love all, not just "one's own," whether the family or the group, but even your enemies, is a challenge to open with utmost generosity to the reality of the other *as other,* not just as mirror of me and me of him, to affirm therefore the infinite worth of all, to devote oneself to the maximal development of the other, with particular attention to those most in need, the poor. Just how hard this is comes across in Christ's command, "Love your enemies!" (Matt. 5:44; Luke 6:27), which is impossible without grace. (In a sense the "other" is always an enemy, to the extent that he is an obstacle to my egoistic agenda.) On this Christian road, the Church helps one along, through the nourishment offered by the sacraments, the inspiration offered by the Word of God, the exhortations of the (occasionally helpful) sermon and the (often superb) retreats, and the eucharistic example of those truly generous Christians one is privileged to know ("eucharistic" both because they are a cause of our thanksgiving and because they are nourished by Christ's sacramental Body and through their sanctity build up that body as Church).[46]

The belief-motivating role of the sacraments, especially the Eucharist, is hard to communicate to someone who does not accept the full Catholic sense of how Christ remains with His Church effectively and corporeally; this is at the heart of this most "incarnational" of religions. I shall come back to this when I have explained how the divine authority of Jesus Christ exercised within the Church serves as the framework for understanding this demanding reality.[47] But for now we should face the fact of what a demanding teaching this is.

45. That is why the West is becoming like Japan: the ethical is set uncritically by the group, which is very different from the articulated, explicit teaching of the great traditions.

46. This Christian way is shared intuitively by all the great religions and philosophies, because it corresponds to everyone's experience; only a tiny minority of cynics and soured skeptics will ever deny it in theory, although we all sin against it in practice.

47. It was when Jesus began to preach the coming institution of the Eucharist that the fascinated crowds turned away. The Eucharist demands that we be thankful, on God's terms, for reality as God intends it. "I tell you most solemnly, if you do not eat the flesh of the Son of Man and drink His blood, you will not have life in you" (John 6:53). He taught this doctrine in Capernaum, in the synagogue. After hearing it, many of His followers said, "this is intolerable language. How could anyone accept it?" Afterward, many of His disciples (in the broad sense) stopped going with Him (John 6:53, 59–60, 66.) The authors of the New Testament are at pains to bring out the centrality and enormity of the teaching.

One would not expect God's truth about the ultimate Source and meaning of all reality to be a small affair or easy to approach. On one level, the Eucharist can be approached simply, in simple faith. But if you stop to think about it—which the Church tries to get everyone to do, not just think theoretically but contemplate and adore—an abyss of possibility opens up. One possibility with which, as a believing Catholic, I of course have little sympathy is that Jesus may simply have been a religious genius who seized on this most primitive act of nourishment as a powerful symbol of the kind of communion that occurs about the dinner table and saw it as a good way to symbolize His remaining spiritually with His community after His death. But as mere symbol, it is no "hard teaching" (John 6:60),[48] so why did many of His close followers turn away when He announced it? They must have understood it in such a way that only divine authority on Jesus' part could found such a claim, and it was this they were unable to accept. This is why John sets the teaching of the "Bread of Life" in a context of authority: "No one can know the father unless through me"; and grace: "This is why I told you that no one can come to me unless it is granted him by the Father" (John 6:65). We see the rich young man turn away when Christ invites him to give up all he possesses and follow Him. Again it is the radicalness of demands such as "love your enemies" and "give up all you have to the poor" that shows Christ's claim to be nothing less than divinity, and requiring God's gift to be accepted.

But nothing centers our attention on the absoluteness of the basic claim better than the very *physicality* of that eucharistic presence as the Catholic tradition understands it. This is Spirit trans-forming (in a new creation) matter itself, resulting in a new kind of "presencing." Spirit is very much about being present. Spirit is also about creative spontaneity, yet here we encounter Spirit freely committed to entering into the finite form of the Church, Christ emptying Himself out so that He may be present to all of us until the end of time, in and through the institutionalized (and routinized!) sacramental forms of His Church.

What the doctrine of "the real presence of Christ in the Eucharist" affirms is nothing else but Christ's divinity, manifest in His power, not only over death, but also, as the creative Logos, over all matter. If God can will to be present initially in the form of the cosmos He creates for that purpose, and again in the form of the Son's Incarnation, so the Son, through the power of the Holy Spirit, can will to be present in a new creation, a heretofore unimaginable way, sacramentally in the bread and wine.

In every instance of being's presencing, the success of that *being present* requires a re-sponse from the one to whom it presences. Consider across the ages the variety of man's responses to God's gift of the Creation. Search the Scriptures for the variety of responses to the prophets, and finally in

48. The Jerusalem Bible translates *ho logos skleros* as "intolerable language." *Sclerotic,* "unbending," we might say.

His lifetime to Jesus Christ Himself. These forms of response range from completely ignoring God's initiatives, through revolt against them, to the saints' complete loving submission to the will of God implicit or explicit in every divine presencing.

The most perfect *ikon*, the Son incarnate, and especially its prolongation until the end of time in the eucharistic Church, requires our attentive hearing of the Word, through which alone we know of the efficacy of this new creation. The Incarnation employs matter in its noblest creative form, human cells, and in the Eucharist the much humbler organic matter of the bread and wine, but also the matter of the human beings called to minister and to enter into communion, receiving in essential co-operation with the redemptive act, the way Mary's consent was needed for the Incarnation. It gives the Christian worshiper, who is body as well as spirit, a palpable rallying place for his *communio*, the eucharistic community, with its unbroken physical continuity back to Jesus. This routinely repeated miraculous presence sums up the incarnational religion.

That nasty word *banally* hints at a central aspect of the sacramental-liturgical practice of the Church, the real, everyday Church I come into contact with concretely, that matter of average human beings we all find troublesome. Again and again, Jesus announced that He came to save, not the righteous, but sinners. The Pharisees are outraged with His sitting down to table with prostitutes and (worse!) tax collectors. Since there are no saints, in the sense of human beings requiring no salvation—indeed, as there are few persons in our experience (present company emphatically included) who do not need in the worst way to have their sins forgiven and to make progress toward sanctification—this is one of those evident truths it is well to keep in mind, as one slogs through the daily reality of routinized religion. It is easy to talk about sin; it is hard to put up with it in reality. Horrific sins have the merit of being dramatic, but most of the time the sins of the mediocre are just a frightful bore.[49]

To resist being worn down by mediocrity, my own especially, I try to keep three things in mind. First, how wonderful the few saints I do know really are; I am thinking of those who are not only trying to co-operate as much as they can with grace but also have been given the exceptional (judging by appearances) grace to shine out in the process as persons of utmost integrity, generosity, gentleness, and total gift of self. When I experience the light that shines from those exceptional individuals, I know that whatever animates them is a true source of life, and a way to follow. These Christian saints profess that they find this Source in Jesus Christ. When I experience the same radiance in a Jew and he testifies that he finds his life in the Torah given by God, I know that through that life of his people faithful to the

49. Albert Speer, reminiscing about the dinners with Hitler he was obliged to endure several times a week for ten years, found them, and especially the Führer's endless monologues, a crashing bore (*Inside the Third Reich: Memoirs,* trans. Richard and Clara Winston [New York: Macmillan, 1970]).

covenant, there is indeed reality to be found. That I also believe that this reality can be enfolded within the truth the Christian discovers in its fullness in Jesus Christ not only takes nothing away from the truth founding the Jew's saintliness but also in the eyes of my faith confirms it. I believe one can read something of this on the face of the Dalai Lama, whose gentleness and openness and generosity, which I have been privileged to see close-up, shines as a beacon. I do not hesitate to admit that I find him Christlike. That I find the most complete and rich revelation of what this Christlikeness is, not in the Way practiced by the Dalai Lama, nor any more in the Torah taken by itself, but in Christ Jesus, is no insult to any of the non-Christian saints I have known.[50] For my belief in a fullness of God's Trinitarian presence in Jesus takes nothing away from the love and fidelity of the unique Source they are allowing to flow through them, whenever they are open to the Light that comes from the common Father of all. They can be far more luminous "faces of Christ" than many small-minded grumblers "who never miss Mass on Sunday."

Some Christians have trouble understanding what I am saying here, because they do not reflect profoundly enough on the full sense of the revelation made in Jesus Christ. When John tells us that everything that was made has been created through the Logos, that it is this Logos, proceeding from the Creative Source who is the Father, and that this Logos is dwelling among us as the man Jesus, then it follows, with perfect logic, that the fullness of everything good, constructive, and desirable is found imaged in this perfect *ikon*. So what the good Muslim does in the name of Allah is a face of Christ and every good act is a moment of holiness, it is a working of the Holy Spirit—who is the Spirit of the Father and the Son, and the fruit of their mutual total love of one another—being that "salt" in the world that Christ called every one of us children of God to be (Mark 9:50). That the Jew or the Muslim or the honest secularist does not know it by this name of "Jesus Christ"—the name before which every power on heaven and earth bows its knee (Phil. 2:10)—is not here the issue, nor does this take away any of the importance of the question of why the Lord wants the fullness of the revelation of who He is made known to all.[51]

Second, perhaps without the liturgical and prayer life in which, seemingly routinely and uninspiringly, we, the mediocre, are engaging, we might all be worse. Certainly our lives would be much emptier. The point remains valid, even admitting how unsavory hypocrisy is, in whatever degree, and failing to fight mediocrity is for a Christian hypocrisy.

50. I am not being idiosyncratic here, and I am not leaving the Church behind. As we shall see later the Second Vatican Council reminds Catholics to find sanctity in all those who follow their best lights with integrity, and the present pope speaks of Protestants who died, often at the hands of Catholics, for what they believed, "martyrs of truth" (see the encyclical *Ut Unum Sint*, 1995).

51. There are indeed, as Rahner explained, "anonymous Christians," but as the German theologian also made clear, Christ calls Christians to see to it that He should not remain anonymous to them.

And last, one cannot legitimately judge, for you do not know what is going on really in the life of another, and not all that well in your own.[52] Christianity preaches that we are to learn to see Christ "in the little ones." We easily forget that the little ones very often wear not just the mask of dramatic tragedy, like the street people, but the uninspiring face of apparent mediocrity. Poverty takes many forms, including dearth of talent and "personality," a sad exterior that can hide interior spiritual riches we do not perceive in superficial contact.

Once again this may strike the reader as "rationalizing stultifying Catholic mediocrity." Actually, there is sound Christian teaching in what I am trying to express here. Nietzsche detested Christianity's having a place for the mediocre. He saw this as running against the force of life, which is cruel and efficient in its struggle upward to greatness. But just as the evolution of complexifying life runs counter to entropy, perhaps mercy and forgiveness of sins flows from a deeper source of life than Nietzsche was willing to admit, one that, if not against nature (indeed is the Author of nature itself), raises human nature to a new level of reality, a new creation, "not I live but Christ lives in me" (Gal. 2:20).[53] If Christ really was the Son of the Creator, a God of love and mercy, would this cocreating Son not love every one of God's own irreplaceable artifacts, and would He not be prepared to give up all that He has to save even one of these little ones? Christ spoke of the shepherd who left ninety-nine sheep to go after the one who was lost. That is precisely what the Jesus of the Gospels declares to be His love, and it is what He is shown doing.

And So Why Not "Anthropomorphic"?

The more I contemplate the whole of the gospel message the more I am consoled by it, but I am not insensitive to the disquietude of those who worry about its "anthropomorphism."

What both the Old and the New Testaments reveal is a universe that is far from being a cold and meaningless expansion and complexification of matter in the midst of which those finite intelligences that are, as Merleau-

---

52. Recently at an all-day conference, a blue-haired little old lady of unimpressive bearing, looking like all the other little old ladies I see at daily Mass, stood up to read a paper she had written in a generous hand on plain, ruled paper. Her voice too was unimpressive. But not what she said. It was overwhelming in its experience, compassion, and insight. The lady was Janet Summerhill, the founder of Birthright, an organization (with six hundred chapters worldwide) to help unwed pregnant girls and single mothers. Saints are not always flashy.

53. I believe one of the reasons that so many today walk out on their most solemn obligations, marriages, or perpetual religious vows is because they cannot accept that those to whom they have bound themselves turn out to be indeed really sinners, and that is, most likely, because they have not responded to the grace of humility to live with themselves as sinners. I have seen several Catholic marriages turn to dust just because each partner was simply bored with the other. Nothing very negative was happening. In fact, the problem was, nothing was happening!

Ponty has said, "thrown up in the foam of the great wave of being" are simply a kind of cosmic joke, left to fend for themselves, making what little bit of sense they can out of the fleeting moments of their lives. Rather, this world that has been willed into being is revealed to be an artifact conceived of within the interior life the Source reveals itself to possess, a life of love of which this creation is a fruit. This gives us a glimpse deeper than the mystery of the metals dug from a mine that were "cooked" billions of years ago in the heart of a now exploded star. This creation was begotten in the everlasting Spirit from all eternity but then was "made" at and with the beginning of time. The vision is that of a great wisdom unfolding before us in which man not only has a desired place but also is called to a cocreative partnership of highest nobility. It is good news, "too good to be true," as Balthasar says.[54] No wonder to me that nonbelievers see Christianity from without as an anthropomorphism, the fruit, as Nietzsche claims, of our "wishing it could be thus."

Man's role calls him to maximum self-development, but not of the "self-aggrandizing" yuppie sort, which, in addition to being a socially unlivable pattern, is plainly unaesthetic. Rather, man is called to that development of self that flows essentially from the love and generosity of others, and ultimately from the loving Source of the self. It is a development of *self for others*, a *missio* that we do not give ourselves but to which we are called by the divine Designer who calls us to participation in the incarnate personhood of His Son.[55] It is a participation that lovingly embraces nature, the given differences of man and woman, immediate source of new human life, the social nature of human beings, our dependency on physical-biological nature and on nature's source. This mature kind of self-development flows from a wisdom that views human wars not as part of nature's plan for "purification" (as Nietzsche contends), but as sin on the part of the aggressor, a revolt against God's loving plan. Man is called by God to rise above the collision of forces characteristic of the rest of nature and to use his God-given intelligence to move beyond zero-sum games toward social solidarity, permitting enhanced productivity and just distribution of the fruits of his labors and allowing the greatest development of the potential of all individuals.[56] We are to model our co-

54. "Its plausibility comes only from the form of the revelation itself" (Balthasar, *Love Alone*, 47).

55. This notion of *missio* as giving us our personhood when we co-operate with the life of the Holy Spirit, opening us to the service God intends for us, is a profoundly important and central notion of Christianity, to which we shall return.

56. There is an ontological link between a nihilist anthropology, a view of man as having to follow "iron laws of nature" seen as conflict and oppression (with the great mass of the defenseless triumphing by beating down the oppressive elite through a pitiless "dictatorship of the proletariat") and the socialist tendency to understand economic theory in zero-sum terms. Where emphasis is on the essential openness of creativity, love, and generosity, political economy is viewed as community, free election by all, and economics is seen as more creative: not "capitalism" if one understands that as raw competition, but entrepreneurship on a fair playing field with social net

operation on the complete devotion to one another in love of the persons of the Trinity.

Understood in this way, the anthropomorphism of which Christianity is accused is far more radical than anthropomorphic—it is anthropic: God did not take on the mere form *(morphos)* of a man; He assumed our entire condition, from the moment of lowering His cosmos-creating infinite majesty to dwell in a single fertilized cell, to the end, suffering the ultimate human pain of abandonment. Paul calls this God's "folly." No, not anthropomorphism, but the humanization of God, by God. "Too good to be true" is not an argument against it, but an ungrateful placing of limits on God's greatness, so powerful is He that He can show us the way to true power-love—by taking on our own powerlessness.

Another of the unique strengths of the biblical revelation for illumining human behavior is that far from sidestepping the mystery of evil, revelation unveils its origins and nature—the abuse of human freedom by our refusing to acknowledge our being as gift—and revelation tells how it is definitively (but again mysteriously) overcome, through the redemptive sacrifice of Christ. No other tradition approaches this one in the depth and comprehensiveness of its sense of freedom, love, and salvation, as well as their negations, evil, bondage, and loss of our lives. The humble Jew, Jesus, the Son of God, freely accepts that ultimate emptying—tasting the bitterest fruit of human perversity, even unto the experience of abandonment by all, even by the Father—in His supreme moment on the cross, expiating all evil through this divine participation in the human experience of "touching the bottom."

This expiation is the ultimate demonstration of God's love: His answer to our thankless revolt and self-destruction is to take the fruits of that destruction on Himself, the Son restoring friendship with the Father by making us His brothers caught up in the élan of His love.

The Crisis of the Icons: An Addendum to the Christological Crisis

Because I believe the historic transformative power of this redemptive act to be working itself through the life of the Church, which is the form the incarnate, eucharistic divine reality has chosen to continue its presence among us, I shall examine some of the critical issues causing perennial tensions in the tradition. This will help us to understand both what is at stake—what the options are in each of these critical issues within this paradoxical religion—and how the truths of the tradition develop in such an incarnational setting, amid the struggles of sinful men in whom the yeast

---

protection for those who are unable to compete, even with fair rules. The word *capitalism* can be recovered in a Christian context if *caput*, the head as source of inventiveness, is emphasized and used to achieve fairness as well as maximum efficiency. The support of dog-eat-dog competition, without rules to protect the legitimate interests of the less strong, is un-Christian, ignoring the reality of sin, and leads to monopoly.

of the redemption is managing to work its effect despite the resistance of the human matter.

One of these is an ancient battle, that over images, a tension no longer felt in Catholic or Orthodox milieus but still a difficulty between Catholic and Protestant Christians. (The more-Protestantizing Catholics, however, also like to throw out statues!) I pause to consider it in the context of our effort to understand something of the Christian sense of divine incarnation for two reasons. First, the iconoclastic struggle does indeed help to bring out the Catholic sense of divinity taking on human existence. But this controversy also illustrates well something of importance to understanding this tradition: theological issues have a sense in themselves, detachable from the complex political-social motives that account for the way in which they were used historically to attack or strengthen the imperial, patriarchal, episcopal, doctrinal, patristic, or popular authority.[57] When later we confront present Church crises, this separation between the truth of what is being put forward theologically and the hidden agenda of one group or another will prove important.[58]

The second lesson the icon controversy teaches is that the same basic tensions within Christianity cause new flare-ups from time to time in the course of the Church's history. The appeal to the tradition of the kind made by Catholics against Protestant iconoclasm already existed in the seventh century. John V, patriarch of Jerusalem in the eighth century, asked of the iconoclasts, who believed all efforts to represent holy personages a scandal, whether they were willing to claim, despite Christ's promise that the gates of hell would not prevail, that the Church had been in error for seven hundred years until they came along to enlighten it.[59] On the other hand, the defenders of icons had to admit that there was little written evidence, either in Scripture or in the earliest fathers, that is, before A.D. 300, for

---

57. I am aware that by insisting on theological truths having a sense in themselves that, while, to be sure, further illumined by the history surrounding their formulation do have a sense in themselves, I am flying in the face of the postmodern deconstructionists. If I appear to fall into an unreconstructed "metaphysics of identity" in here asserting that propositions can have objective referents, and that some of these objects stand in the light of the "vertical transcendence" of eternity that has broken successfully into history to offer everlasting truths, I would ask the reader to hear me out on the epistemological and ontological justification for such a position, as this study unfolds. Anyone seriously concerned with an effort to reconcile "historicity" and unity of truth may find *BT* a contribution.

58. When we sinful humans debate, we usually have something more in mind than a pure theoretical interest, utter devotion to the truth, as the deconstructionists, sensitive to the distorting effects of "vested interests," insist, something like gaining or consolidating power, or working out a psychological resentment. But the inherent meaning of the proposition within a context of theory that transcends the necessarily local interests of this or that temporarily socially coherent group can be of perennial significance. Icons, properly understood and used, for instance, can enjoy a fixed place in Christian worship, regardless of how they may have served one group in sixth- and seventh-century imperial Byzantium to beat another over the head.

59. Cited by Nicephorus, according to Pelikan, *Christian Tradition*, 123.

the practice of venerating icons. The partisans of images maintained that they were "supported by the simple faith and the unwritten tradition of the Catholic Church" and then argued that "unwritten tradition is most powerful of all."[60] Popular practice did win, after tumultuous struggles in the eighth and ninth centuries, but only with the support of powerful theological argument and, eventually, imperial authority.

What worried the iconoclasts? Essentially, that the veneration of icons would lead to idolatry. This legitimate concern was reinforced by a certain conception of Christ, who, as divine was the only adequate "image of God" and who, precisely because He was divine, could not be "circumscribed," that is, contained adequately in any man-made image. Arguing against reintroducing the danger of idolatry, which had been so vigorously combated by the Christians in opposing the early pagans, the iconoclasts cited the Old Testament proscriptions. The most powerful of these was Exod. 20:4, "You shall not make yourself a carved image or any likeness of anything in heaven or on earth beneath or in the waters under the earth; you shall not bow down to them or serve them." It is indeed categorical. The attack of monotheistic religion on idolatry follows from the sense of God's absolute transcendence, which comes with the breakthrough when God teaches us that the Source of all being is itself incomprehensible because it is a free source of all that is, not itself limited by creating nature. The effort of man to capture and magically manipulate this ultimate power by forging some kind of representation, a thing in which the divine power is supposed to dwell in a special (and manipulatable) way, is seen by monotheists (including Muslims today) as the most egregious antireligious error.

Iconoclasts admit that the coming of Christ, the Son as perfect image of the Father, introduces a radical new dimension into our relation to God. Christ is indeed an image of God, but one fashioned by God Himself. He is an "essential image," one in essence with that which is to be shown to us. But that is the rub: so perfect as to be unrepresentable in any meaningful way by some poor human icon.

One can glimpse the attitude behind this iconoclast position: it is the uncompromising position that things are either something, or they are nothing; if something is not fully what it represents, then it has no value at all; any partial manifestation is in the category *no-thing*; anything partial is bad, and should be altogether abolished. It is much the same attitude one finds in Parmenides, attenuated somewhat in Plato, but again shining bright in Descartes: the truth has to be true—period.[61] Only absolute certainty has any value. But what about valuing partial efforts as good as far as they go? Why is a partial, nonessential representation so bad? Such a pragmatic attitude has never appealed much to philosophical purists. But

60. John of Damascus, quoted in Pelikan, *Christian Tradition*, 122.
61. Parmenides was a sixth-century Ionian philosopher whose central insight was that "being is," hence anything short of absolute, timeless being simply "is not," hence all change and all finite things are illusions, rather like the Hindu notion of *maya*.

then perhaps philosophical purity is a trick of finite human reason trying to construct an absolute when in reality we cannot possess the absolute at all. The purist does not understand the need for *analogy*. He does not concede that we cannot bottle up life.

The iconoclast has another direction of attack: we do not need any other image but the one God Himself has given us. It is not as though Christ left us with no tangible representation of Himself. He left us Himself in the unsurpassable image of the Eucharist, again an "essential image" because in it we discover the real presence of Christ. Who needs the human images of Christ? What value could they have? They only distract us from the great gifts of God, the true images: Jesus Himself in His Word and His eucharistic presence.

The iconophiles respond by first agreeing with their opponents in the condemnation of idolatry. They point out that before the coming of Christ, the complete interdiction of all representations of God was absolutely correct. But they hasten to point out also that in the same book of Moses, a few chapters later, there is an account of his building a tabernacle with images of the cherubim, which, while not divine, are at least spiritual entities.[62] With the coming of Christ, a new representability of the divine becomes possible. The most enthusiastic defender of icons would agree that no manmade representation is a substitute for, or has the power of, the presence of God in Christ and of Christ in the Eucharist. But it is now appropriate to represent Christ in His humanity, as well as His saints, as aids to devotion.

The christological point here is this: just as God has made use of material objects, like the signs of language employed to speak to us through Scripture, so in becoming man God made use of our humanity in all of its corporeality to relate to us. In worshiping Christ, we adore God present in the divinized humanity of Jesus. Through the words of the evangelist or the form created by the artist, we are aided in our worship of God through His Son. We are aided first because the image is a memorial of the great event, of the Mother of God, or of the holy saint to whom we pray, asking for their intercession. Second, it not only helps us remember, but also aids us in concentrating our attention. The beauty of the image is in this regard important. Some would even say of the most inspired icons that they themselves become instruments of grace, incarnations of Spirit, showing forth in their beauty the *doxa*—the glory—of God.

Under the impulsion of the iconoclasts' attacks, the orthodox were motivated to define carefully the nature of images. With help from the emanative philosophy of Dionysius the Pseudo-Areopagite, John of Damascus (around 749) interpreted the universe as a graduated hierarchy of images.[63] The notion of image took on slightly different meanings, but in every case,

62. Pelikan, *Christian Tradition*, 122.

63. Dionysius the Pseudo-Areopagite was a Syrian monk—so it is thought—who lived about 500. His writing was influenced by the Neoplatonist Proclus, who lived

whatever the involvement between the image and the prototype, there was clear recognition of the essential difference: identical in what was represented, the image is simply not the imaged. The highest kind of image is that represented by the Son as image of the Father. The Son, an adequate image of the Father, is not Himself His Father. Then there is God's eternal will working itself out through images and paradigms that He creates, like those in the Old Testament. Among these creations are physical things, which are images of the divine prototypical ideas, and above all other created things, humans as creatures in the image of God, through whom are spoken the language-images we find in the Old Testament, like Shepherd, and the made things, like the temple or the priestly robes. Further, there are the Old Testament "types" that foreshadowed what was to come in the New Testament; there are images erected as memorials, such as an image on a grave, pointing backward as the Old Testament shadows pointed forward.[64]

In all of this, as with the emphasis on the role of the senses in worship, what the iconophiles were affirming is the role of the body in salvation: of the physical Body of Christ as the means of achieving it and of the physical body of every man as a participant in it, of course together with the soul. Hence, the important role of Mary for iconophiles: as the human being chosen by God to bear the Body of Christ, she, through her response, becomes not just a transitional figure, but the essential instrument of our salvation, the means through which our bodies become sanctified through the Body of Christ she bore, and because of the perfection of her "Yes!" the model for our own loving act of submission to God's will. It is proper to our own incarnate nature that we be led through corporeal things toward the spiritual reality of God. That is why there is a baptism in water as well as in spirit. John of Damascus puts it well: "Perhaps you are sublime and able to transcend what is material, but I, since I am a human being and bear a body, want to deal with holy things and behold them in a bodily manner." Jaroslav Pelikan comments: "The spiritualism of the iconoclasts seemed to put them in the same class with the ancient Gnostics, who claimed that the Body of Christ was not physical but heavenly, and who despised the physically-minded believers as less spiritual than they."[65] Such Gnostics, in every era, like the evangelicals today, downplay the Church as the real institutional body continuing the sacramental presence of Christ in favor of the immediate inspiration of the individual by the Holy Spirit. That we (mediocre) individuals *need* the ministering of those other (mediocre) individuals chosen by Christ, and that we have things He wants us to offer them, puts us all *very materially* together in the same boat—the bark of Peter!

To deny the representability of Christ in icons was to indulge in a kind of Docetism, a disrespect of the full humanity of the God-man. "Man has no

---

from about 410 to 485. His influence was great because he was taken to be that Dionysius who was with Paul when he addressed the Athenian philosophers (Acts 17:34).

64. Richard P. McBrien, *Catholicism* (Minneapolis: Winston Press, 1980), 361.

65. Quoted in Pelikan, *Christian Tradition*, 122.

characteristic more fundamental than this, that He can be represented in an image," John of Damascus reminds us. The incarnation was not debasing the Logos but rather honoring humanity.[66]

The central christological issue comes out in the iconoclasts' claim that it is impossible to draw a picture of one who is both God and man without either claiming to represent divine nature (which is blasphemy) or attempting to divide the natures and to portray only the human (which is heresy). They asked how the Absolute could be circumscribed. But to accept the humanity of that Christ whom the iconoclasts accept as image, and to accept the real presence of Christ in the Eucharist is in effect to accept that God did deign to work through the "circumscribed." So that cannot be the problem with images. What Christ did and said are an essential part of the redemptive act; His divinity shines through the humanity—every aspect of that (nonsinful) humanity—without its ceasing to be human. And so it is appropriate to represent that human presence of Christ among us whether in word or other form of depiction.

After the thorough victory of iconophilism, little more was heard of iconoclasm in either East or West throughout the entire Middle Ages. Its virulent reemergence in the sixteenth century, almost a half millennium later, proves, however, that it represents a perennial tension within Christianity. Anyone who has stood before one of the magnificent mutilated monuments of France, sadly observing the hammered heads and chiseled bodies of what were once glorious displays of Catholic imagery, can attest to the depth of the feelings on both sides of the images issue.[67]

CONCLUSION

In summing up the results of this initial reflection on the central question "Who is this Jesus?" and before proceeding to reflect on His redemptive reality working in the life of the Church, let us return once again for a moment to the formulas in which Nicaea and Chalcedon struggled to express the divine-human reality of the Christ, another form of "circumscription," and this time take more earnestly Voegelin's worry about such clear formalization "closing the apophantic field." Explicit traditions do that. Making anything explicit at the very least points a direction for the institution, which excludes other possible directions.[68]

In the final form of the creed Jesus is declared "Lord and Christ," the same terms used in Peter's sermon on Pentecost. As the Anointed One, He

66. Ibid. Think of the implications of this ontologically, for the full sense of "person," a notion developed in the heat of the christological controversies, and for the sense of the Absolute, of being itself, being able to be present in matter.

67. Again, there are Catholics today who experience these same feelings at the sight of their own churches' iconic art demolished or painted over, to be replaced by felt banners of simplistic design and ambiguous message, all in the name of "the spirit of Vatican II." It is not without reason that this type of action is considered by some within the Church to be evidence of the "Protestantization" of the Catholic Church.

68. See *TA*, chapter 3.

was sent forth into the world (*descendit de coelis*), born of a woman in virgin birth, and lived and died a human existence. As Lord, He was born of the Father, the unique progeny born before all ages, generated but not made, and—a key term, as we saw—*consubstantialem Patri, homoousios*, that is, of the very same being as the Father. His Incarnation through birth from a woman was made possible by an action of the Holy Spirit. The Trinitarian essential is there, and as clearly as one could ever hope such a supreme mystery to be formulated.

That is what some see to be the problem. Does not this "dogmatic formulating" then indeed "close the apophantic field"? Yes, but is that necessarily a bad thing? Every proposition in some sense closes the apophantic field. If I express the truth that "Thomas Langan has owned the house at 137 Strathallan Boulevard continually since 1968," that proposition leaves no room in the world of meaning for the possibility that from 1974 to 1976 he ceased for a while to own it. If I firmly held the proposition, as clearly formulated, to be true, then I would no longer be open to the proposition that "Langan did not own it from 1974 to 1976," unless and until some new evidence literally blasted its way into my awareness. "Look, I don't care what you say, here is a bill of sale, dated July 6, 1974, showing Langan sold 137 Strathallan." Stumbling upon this fact—a new experience—would demand a reopening of the field of consideration closed by the earlier proposition. If I have always been certain Langan continued to own the house, there would be resistance to accepting this new datum. I might stubbornly refuse even to consider it.

So of course the creedal formulations close the apophantic field to anyone who believes them. If one is convinced that it is true, for instance, that "Jesus was conceived by the Holy Spirit and born of the Virgin Mary," this excludes His being merely a human being at birth, who may have been adopted in some way later by the heavenly Father, calling Him to do His work. All possible Adoptionist explanations of "Who is this Jesus?" are closed off, deliberately and once and for all, for the council and with it the Church. The field of possibilities is closed off because His being *genitum* before all ages is declared to remain forever the sole and unique actuality.

This disturbs, among others, Voegelin because, as I see it, he does not in all sincerity believe Jesus was the "Son of God" in this sense of closing off possibilities. Close analysis of his text, especially of volume 4 of *Order and History*, called *The Ecumenic Age*, suggests that Voegelin believes some kind of theophanic event happened in Jesus, but in the sense it happened too in Isaiah and in Plato, a breakthrough deep within Jesus' soul to a sense of the transcendent majesty of God. I think many, including Voegelin's nemesis, Hegel, have believed this. Such an explanation of the Christ event removes a great stumbling block to ecumenical wisdom, as I explained at length in both *Tradition and Authenticity* and *Being and Truth*, as the way is opened to treating all kinds of "intuitions" or inspirations as events deep in the soul. The inconvenience with such deobjectification is that one then loads onto Saint Paul and Saint John the responsibility for falsifying the experience of

Jesus, and one finds oneself at odds with the sense of the Scripture, and so such an interpreter becomes opposed to the "orthodox" tradition of the Church.[69] The problem is not that the dogmatic formulations have closed the apophantic field; it is rather with a clash of faiths: Voegelin does not want the apophantic field closed this way, because he does not believe the key propositions are, in the final analysis (and taken as they seem intended to be taken), true.[70]

It is not a scandal that Voegelin or anyone else does not believe in the divine teaching authority of the Church. It is clear to me from his writings that he had little personal experience of the Church in the sense I have in this chapter barely begun to invoke. Many thinkers who take the figure of Jesus Christ seriously do not accept the orthodox belief in the divine teaching authority of the Church, and the orthodox tradition itself teaches that faith in the Church teaching is a gift. Is it unfair that many earnest and profound thinkers do not appear to have received or accepted that gift? If we, the Catholics, are simply deceived, then, no, they are the fortunate—or, as Paul already said, then we are the unfortunate for being taken in (1 Cor. 15:19).

But if it is true, what then? No point in assigning blame; we do not understand why some see the beauty and graciousness of this gift of teaching and sacramental presence of Christ in the Church and others do not. The Christian knows that he has been given the mission by Christ to see to it that "all nations" hear the fullness of "the Good News" and be baptized. As they have not, Christians sincerely blame our own lukewarmness and poor witness. I would fear that a great spirit like Voegelin may have been impressed by ugly faces of the Church that constituted impediments for his encountering Christ living in the communion of saints. What and who is incorporated in Christ, hence in the Church, is an issue of utmost importance to all, if there is a gram of truth in Christian claims about how God wants us united in His Son.

The history of that presencing of Christ among us in His Church is a story full of drama and mystery. In the following chapters I shall attempt to convey some sense of that experience of Immanuel (which means "God with us") as Church, with all its human-divine tensions and even ambiguities, reflecting on certain events that illumine what I believe are the most

69. Even Mark, so "unsophisticated" compared to John and Paul—Voegelin leaves Mark almost unnoticed—holds to the much more demanding sense of Jesus' divinity from before all ages, as we discovered in examining his gospel.

70. For those who do believe the creeds true as intended, this closing of the apophantic field by dogmatic formulation is welcome, as this truth is at the core of the Church teaching, and if the Church does teach with any God-given authority, then it is best that it co-operate with the Holy Spirit in expressing this truth as clearly as possible: all further reflection on the life and reality of Jesus Christ begins with, and always respects, the guidelines established by this millennial teaching. However ingenious a future theological speculation, if it has the effect of reopening the question of Christ's divinity in the sense captured by the great councils, then that reopening of the apophantic field should be rejected, because it is inconsonant with the truth always held by the Church and given a definitive formulation by the great councils.

essential and hence perennial tensions in this tradition that acknowledges itself to be one of paradox.[71]

APPENDIX: THE SIGNS OF CHRIST'S DIVINITY IN THE GOSPEL ACCORDING TO MARK

In just the first chapter Mark highlights four signs of Jesus' divinity. Mark's first line opens the challenge: "The beginning of the Good News about Jesus Christ, the Son of God." We already know by the end of this title line that Jesus is about Good News, and that He is "*Christos*—the Anointed one," the expected Messiah. Furthermore, the issue of His divine Sonship is set as squarely before us as possible.

Mark begins his account with the baptism in the Jordan. All four gospels mark this out as an important moment, all speak of the Holy Spirit descending, but in the Gospel of John it is the Baptist who witnesses to having seen it, while in Mark's and Matthew's it is Jesus who sees it, and Luke does not specify.

It is the Spirit that next drives Jesus into the desert, where He is tempted, but Mark, unlike Matthew and Luke, does not bother to offer any details. He does, however, tell us, "angels looked after Him" (1:13), suggestive of a royal court. Next Jesus is seen beginning His ministry with the announcement of the Kingdom, "The time has come [invoking that expected messianic eschatological "Day of the Lord," spoken of by the prophets], and the kingdom of God is close at hand. Repent, and believe the Good News" (1:15).

In the call to the fishermen Simon (Peter) and Andrew that follows next, and then a little later to James and John, there is something unnaturally authoritative in the way it is reported: no reasons are given, just the command and the promise, "I will make you into fishers of men" (1:16–20). The apostles' lack of hesitation has something eerie and impressive about it.

Mark then shows us Jesus teaching in the synagogue in Capernaum, with emphasis on everyone's being impressed "because he taught them with authority." As though to drive home the nature of this authority, Mark couples the event with Jesus' driving out an unclean spirit in one of the synagogue attendees. The demon shouts, "What do you want with us, Jesus of Nazareth? Have you come to destroy us? I know who you are: the Holy One of God." The incident so astonished the people that they began wondering what it all meant. "Here is a teaching which is new and with authority behind it: he gives orders to unclean spirits and even they obey him." His reputation, Mark tells us, spread rapidly through the Galilean countryside (1:21–28).

These then are the four signs of divinity already invoked in the first chapter:

71. Immanuel was the name announced to Mary by the archangel Gabriel at the moment of the divine child's conception by the Holy Spirit (Matt. 1:23).

1. Spirits, holy and unholy, acknowledge Him; the Holy Spirit guides Him; the angels minister to Him; the unclean spirits cannot resist Him and indeed, as Mark says in 3:11–12, wherever He went the unclean spirits would fall down before Him and shout, "You are the Son of God!" (divinity, then, is not just of this human world, but as we shall see below, it is about the power of the Kingdom of God, which as we shall also see is about "cleanliness of heart."
2. He teaches "with authority."
3. He cures illnesses, physical and spiritual.
4. He calls men and changes their lives.

Chapter 2 opens with a considerable escalation of the claim to divinity: it is the scene of Jesus healing the paralytic lowered through the roof into the crowded room. "Seeing their faith, Jesus said to the paralytic, 'My child, your sins are forgiven you.'" Mark makes sure the point is not missed: he tells us the scribes sitting there mumbled that he was blaspheming, as "who can forgive sins but God?" Then "to prove that the Son of Man has authority on earth to forgive sins, He said to the paralytic, 'I order you: get up, pick up your stretcher and go off home.'" The astounded crowd praised God saying, "We have never seen anything like this."

Next come a series of incidents in which Jesus shows His authority to override the law of Moses, simply because He is greater than that law (2:15–28, 3:1–6). That the Jews fully understood what was happening is shown by the concluding statement, "The Pharisees went out and at once began to plot with the Herodians against him, discussing how to destroy Him" (3:6).

The long series of parables about the Kingdom of God (4:1–32) can count in the same direction: again, Jesus discourses with authority about the innermost nature of the Kingdom, surely something only God Himself can do. As though to drive this home, Mark closes the series with the account of Jesus' miraculous command over nature, the calming of the storm, with the apostles exclaiming from their little threatened bark, "Who can this be? Even the wind and the sea obey him" (4:41).

One of the surprises that came from this rereading of the whole of Mark's gospels is to see the importance he gives to Jesus' command over the unclean spirits. The narrative comes across as a titanic struggle between the force of good coursing through Jesus and the forces of the "unclean."[72] (The relative unimportance of any "ethical" strain in this gospel—in the sense of prescriptions about how we are to conduct our lives—is surprising. The struggle between good and evil is placed rather on a transcosmic level, soaring far beyond the confines of natural ethical discourse.) That these tormenting spirits should be called upon again and again to witness who this is reminds us of Jesus saying to Peter when He acknowledges that He is the Son of God, "Flesh and blood have not revealed this to you, but my Father who is in heaven" (Matt. 16:17). So just after the impressive calming

---

72. I say "forces," because "a house divided cannot stand" (Matt. 12:25).

of the storm, Mark inserts the most dramatic incident with the unclean spirits in which Jesus drives out a host of them, allowing them to go into a herd of pigs, which then rush into the lake and drown (5:1–20). Again these spirits recognize Him explicitly, "Jesus, Son of the Most High God." Somewhat in the same vein of "spirituality," note that Mark invokes a sense of Christ's divinity as a kind of aura of sensibility surrounding Jesus. For instance, He knows what the scribes are thinking in their hearts (2:8), and He feels power going out of Him when the woman with a hemorrhage touches the hem of His garment; spirits seem able to sense this.

The greatest manifestations of Jesus' divinity have to do with His power over death, definitively shown in His own resurrection. To prepare us to accept this claim, all the evangelists show Jesus' raising people from death. Appropriately, the evangelists first prepare us for this great sign of raising others from the dead; it is described only after the "authority" with which He teaches and His power over unclean spirits, His ability to cure, and His power over the wind and the waves. In Mark, the raising of the daughter of the synagogue official does not come until the end of the fifth chapter (roughly the same position as in Matthew, while Luke places the raising of the son of the widow of Nain in his seventh chapter).

This divine power of Jesus, while irresistible by unclean spirits, seems unable to penetrate "the rocky soil" of obdurate human hearts. I see this as a variant on the underlying theme of the good struggling against evil, against the unclean. The point is, it is a real struggle: *the resistance is terrible.* Shortly after the first miracles and the gathering of the first crowds about Him, we are told even His relatives "thought he was crazy" (3:20–21). Even after calming the wind and showing power over life itself, Jesus is seen encountering a wall of incomprehension in His own hometown of Nazareth. "This is the carpenter, surely, the son of Mary" (6:3), and He could work no miracle there, though He cured a few sick people. Does Mark mean the really great miracle of conversion can be worked only when people freely decide to open their hearts? We touch here on the mystery Luther called "the bondage of the will," and we are reminded of the great challenges posed by the doctrine of "predestination."

In the next episode He sends out His apostles for the first time, after conferring on them the power to cast out unclean spirits and to heal the sick. "If any place does not welcome you, as you walk away shake the dust from under your feet as a sign to them" (6:11).

The spirits driven out were "unclean." There is "uncleanliness in our hearts" that Christ has come to purify. A significant conjunction of pericopes conveys a message of divinity being intimately related precisely to "cleanliness of heart." John the Baptist is invoked again, as the story of his beheading by Herod is recounted (with emphasis on the evil at the worldly court), recalling the prophet's role in "making the way straight for Jesus." Then as the apostles return from their mission, Jesus performs the first miracle of the loaves and fishes, a preparation for the Eucharist, which itself happens at the moment when He too, like John, must suffer death and replace His present corporeal presence with His eucharistic presence in the Church. This is followed immediately by another manifestation of His power over nature, explicitly linked to faith: Jesus walks on the water. Peter (whose simplicity always suggests lack of ego, a prime manifestation of impurity of heart, I would suggest) nevertheless can stay on the waves himself only so long as his faith does not waver. This suggests that faith is foundational to our participation in Christ's divinity. Then a dispute with the Pharisees, in which Jesus shows them that their unintelligent persistence in the letter of the law hides the uncleanliness in their hearts, whereupon He explains to them the nature of the true uncleanliness and that which makes the unclean spirits vulnerable: fornication, theft, murder, adultery, avarice, malice, deceit, and so on. "All these evil things come from within and make a man unclean" (7:22–23). Clearly, divinity is linked to the rectitude and cleanliness of the human heart, the issue lying behind all questions of ethics. More cures, and the second miracle of the loaves and fishes, followed by an astonishing event, which drives home magnificently the reality of the obduracy of the unclean heart: after all that, the Pharisees come up to Jesus and demand a sign from heaven (8:11–13). Jesus scornfully replies, "Why does this generation demand a sign? I tell you solemnly, no sign shall be given this generation." The irony is total: they ask for a sign, when the greatest sign God could ever give stands before them!

It is not only His enemies who do not see, but His friends, too. The apostles again find themselves with insufficient food, just one loaf. When Jesus, in the boat with them, suddenly warns, "Keep your eyes open; be on your guard against the yeast of the Pharisees and the yeast of Herod" (the leaven of iniquity, the unclean), they still understand nothing, thinking it is about food. Christ reminds them of the two miracles of the loaves and fishes, and then explodes in frustration at their lack of understanding. Implication: the hearts of the apostles, the men who will sleep through the Agony in the Garden, are not clean either. From accusing His closest friends of blindness, Jesus passes to a cure of physical blindness. The point is not subtle: the only serious, incurable blindness is known to God: blindness of the heart (5:22–26).

But all is not darkness surrounding Jesus. As the moment for His Passion approaches, signs of faith glitter here and there. Jesus asks His disciples what we in this appropriation have identified as the question "Who is this Jesus?" "Who do people say I am?" And they told Him, "John the Baptist," others said Elijah, others again said one of the prophets. "But you, who do you say that I am?" Significantly, it is as usual, Peter— the consistent spokesman in all the gospel accounts—who blurts out the sought-for answer: "You are the Christ." And He gave them strict orders not to tell anyone about him, for His "hour had not yet come" (8:28–30).

This faith of Peter, I said, flashes out at moments, but is inconstant. Immediately, the same Peter manifests complete incomprehension in the face of the first prophecy of the Passion. Christ rebukes him in the strongest terms, calling him by the name of the supremely unclean, "Get thee behind me, Satan! Because the way you think is not God's way but man's" (8:33).

This is followed by the most explicit statement of what is entailed in following Christ, the absoluteness of the divine demand daunting: "If anyone wants to follow me, let him renounce himself, take up his cross and follow me. For anyone who wants to save his life will lose it; but anyone who loses his life for my sake, and for the sake of the gospel, will save it. What gain is there to win the whole world and ruin one's life?" (Matt. 16:24–26).

This revelation is about life and death; it is absolutely crucial: the cross is indeed the crux. The promise is startling and unconditional: "I tell you solemnly, there are some standing here who will not taste death before they see the kingdom of God come with power" (9:1). This amazing statement is followed immediately by the most important theophanic moment of the gospel narrative, save only for the post-Resurrection appearances. "Six days later," Mark specifies, as though to emphasize this is a real event, no mere symbol, Jesus took the inner core of His fellowship—Peter, James, and the beloved disciple, John—up to a high mountain. There He was transfigured, His clothes becoming dazzling white, and Elijah and Moses appeared and were talking to him. The disciples were terrified, as a cloud covered Jesus and a voice spoke: "This is my Son, the Beloved. Listen to Him" (9:1–8).

And what do we find two paragraphs later? The disciples arguing among themselves about who will be the greater in the Kingdom! Jesus' response to this could be justifiably much angrier than it was. Instead, He took a little child to Himself and said, "Anyone who welcomes one of these little children in my name, welcomes me" (9:37).

Mark provides several incidents that add up to saying, as the Old Testament did when it showed that God was not in the great wind, or the earthquake, or the fire, but in the gentle breeze that passed before Elijah's cave, that the divine speaks softly, and to the childlike, to those who are "pure in heart" (the central point to which all of chapters 9 and 10 are devoted). The values here are exactly opposite to those of the "world," which aims for success. Jesus said, "Anyone who wants to become great among you must be your servant" (10:43). Such is the language of love. And, as John puts it in his first letter, God *is* love.[73]

Mark finishes this part of his narrative leading to his recounting of the story of the Passion and the Resurrection with sayings of Jesus of an eschatological nature. It is as though to announce: this end He will suffer reveals the ultimate end of all the creation, the end of the world; it is the fullness of good, the fulfillment of the world, the ultimate Epiphany of love. This preparation rises to a climax with the prophesy of the Parousia of the Son of Man "coming in the clouds with great power and glory, then He will send his angels to gather His chosen from the four winds" (13:27).

---

73. "Anyone who fails to love can never have known God, because God is love" (1 John 4:8).

The Crucifixion is presented, in conjunction with the inauguration of the Eucharist, as the great emptying out *(kenosis),* when God descends to the depths, to taste the dregs of that abandonment man has brought on himself through abuse of the freedom God has given him.

THE NATURE OF THE EARLY CHURCH

When inquiry into "Who is this Jesus?" carried us into the christological controversies of the fourth century, we witnessed the clarifying and consolidating role of the Church as institution, "teaching with authority." That role was exercised in uneasy cooperation with the imperial authority. That raises questions. Disagreements over the nature of the Church would eventually—sometime after the fourth century—begin to split the Christian tradition, contrary to Christ's explicit intention (John 10:10). The diverging ecclesiological conceptions partly responsible for the split are intimately related to differing notions—often nothing more than nuances—of how Christ works in the world, and in turn to nuances in anthropological faith, in what different Christian subtraditions come to believe about the nature of man, all fed by different spiritualities rooted in the distinctive cultures of the Latin West and the Greek East. These seemingly small differences of accent together led eventually to institutional splits of grave significance to the effectiveness of the Christian mission to the world.

That we project our experiences and beliefs about man onto our notions of God, and vice versa, and that what we come to believe about God illumines (to the extent those beliefs are true) our understanding of ourselves, none will deny. That both have implications for how religion is institutionalized is obvious. (In our own time, for instance, feminist issues—which are really issues about the nature of man—have arisen, with implications about power structures and so on, implying radical differences in understanding how God is present in the world, which clearly distinguish ecclesiological tendencies in the Church.)

In *Tradition and Authenticity*, I pointed out that two of the most visible elements in the dynamic essence of an explicit tradition are the evolving institutional structure (a kind of framework for concerted human action that is always being reformed) and moments of exceptional crisis (great events or concatenations of events that mark clear epochal change, often accompanied by drastic institutional restructuring).[1] The results of such change are reflected in the symbol systems, in the form of new texts of

1. A "crisis" is a moment of decision (*kritein* in Greek means "to decide") when those trying to live out a vision must make new determinations as to how they are going to organize themselves, in response to challenges that have arisen in the milieu.

"orthodox" (the mainline winners of the struggle) and "heretics" (one of the terms of endearment with which the winners endow the losers) alike. Those who succeed in retaining control of the old institution or in founding a breakaway institution (always presented as the true, pure ancient tradition recovered) endow their chief texts with some degree of canonical authority. For now I shall dwell more on the level of institutional structure than on the depths of the ultimate theological (swirling about the experience of Christ's eucharistic presence in His Church) and anthropological differences driving the divergences.

I shall now double back to the beginning, approaching the tradition somewhat as one would any other, looking historically at the greatest turning points in the institution's self-understanding as precipitated by crises that have marked the Church for all time. Later, we shall probe behind the institutional surface to recover the experience of the Church that these developments—ecclesial, doctrinal, anthropological, spiritual—reveal, with a view to understanding their implications for the tradition as it is lived today.

THE CRISIS OF AUTHORITY AND THE EMERGENCE OF A HIERARCHICAL STRUCTURE

From the earliest recorded experiences of the Church an ongoing tension between two tendencies is visible: one that in modern times would be called the evangelical, which emphasizes the charismatic individual or elect group directly inspired by the Holy Spirit, and the other, quite early called "catholic" (modern evangelicals often call it "sacerdotalist"),[2] which believes Christ established a line of continuing authority, ordained to interpret, develop, and hand on the tradition to everyone. Each of these tendencies appeals to different temperaments, satisfied by different spiritualities. But beyond this anthropological factor, both embrace both parts of the dogmatic truth, both agree that the Holy Spirit is not tied to the sacramental life, both agree that our salvation cannot be earned by us but comes from faith in Christ's salvific act, both believe that good works follow from this faith, when it is genuine, and both accept that a continuing struggle to accept sanctification requires the sacramental life, but they emphasize and interpret these dimensions differently. Mixed with the sad, sinful realities of pride and politics this historically has produced explosions.

In the early Church those of the charismatic mentality tended to expect that "the last days" meant the return of Christ was imminent. That was largely taken care of by events, as millenarian apocalyptics always will be, until the actual last days occur. When the "Second Coming" did not happen, the sense of the kingdom's being realized in a last era was retained, but now understood to be a long era, which called for the development of structures

2. See, for instance, Benjamin B. Warfield, *The Plan of Salvation* (Grand Rapids, Mich.: W. B. Eerdmans, 1975), 66.

of sacramental life and governance as the Church both settled down locally and spread internationally.[3]

So not only did the Church develop a highly articulated, hierarchical, monarchical governing structure (which has proved to be the longest-lasting aristocracy in the world, though it is an aristocracy of tailors' and bankers' sons), but also, from an early time, those in authority used their office to proclaim that they taught and ruled with supernatural power handed down to them from Christ through the apostles. The emperors of the cosmological empires had declared themselves to be "sons of God," privileged mediators between heaven and earth, by virtue of being themselves extraordinary individuals, called by birth, and above reproach. The apostles, on the other hand, present themselves as the most ordinary of men, even, left to themselves, losers, but called by the Holy Spirit to be servants of the servants of God. The fact that this extraordinary claim was made for two thousand years and is still accepted, wholeheartedly by some, partially by hundreds of millions, is a matter of historical record; the foundation of the claim, just what it means and whether it is true is another matter, one central to critical appropriation of the tradition. This is close to the spine of Catholicism. We shall return to the question of apostolic authority forthwith and in more detail than the first brief introduction of it.

Jesus Christ's Establishment of Petrine Office and Apostolic Authority

At the heart of the great diremptions of the tradition, the split between East and West, and between Protestants and Catholics, lie the disputes over the Petrine and apostolic-episcopal authority. Did Jesus give that authority? What is the nature of the authority He gave? If Peter was given by Christ the headship of His Church, how do we know this was meant to pass to his successors? And how does the Petrine office relate to the office of the bishops? How are we today to understand the mission of the papacy? Of the bishops?

Dilemma: I have before me a recent book, *The Shepherd and the Rock: Origins, Development, and Mission of the Papacy,* by J. Michael Miller, C.S.B., that sums up succinctly, from an orthodox Catholic perspective, the very issues we need to confront if the essence of the tradition is to be outlined.[4] Father Miller requires 370 closely written pages to accomplish the task. The reader will appreciate my sinking feeling as I attempt to lay out in a couple of dozen pages the heart of a Catholic vision of the papacy, an institution in evolution, based on principles, which, once adequately formulated, the orthodox Catholic considers rock solid (the pun is Christ's own), and then

---

3. To this day, charismatics still are often susceptible to predictions of the imminent arrival of end-of-the-world catastrophes. So strong is the psychological need in some to advance the hour, they ignore, despite their insistence on Scripture as the Word of God, Christ's clear warning: "But as for the day and hour, nobody knows it, neither the angels of heaven, nor the Son, no one but the Father only" (Matt. 24:36).

4. Miller, *Shepherd* (Huntington, Ind.: Our Sunday Visitor, 1995).

have to go on to discuss the papacy's relation to the evolving office of "bishop." In presenting my appropriation I am obliged to make many judgment calls as I further condense lengthy scholarly condensations (often based on hundreds of works) on various aspects of the subject. Such are the perils of any effort to present the overall vision of something so vast and complex as the Catholic tradition.

The Primacy of Peter

When John Henry Newman, leader of the Oxford movement in the Church of England, was reasoning his way into the Catholic Church, he argued roughly as follows about whether the papal office as it has evolved corresponds to Jesus' intention: If Jesus was the Son of God, He would have known that the Church He was founding would have to last a long time, and that maintaining its coherence and fidelity would be difficult. Under these circumstances would He not have been likely to foresee the need for a strong, visible center? Convinced that the only credible answer is, "Yes, He would," Newman then set out to search for evidence that Christ did found such an office and that in the early Church it evolved indeed into a strong center.[5] Let us now look for such evidence.

On three different occasions, Jesus picked out Simon Bar-Jonah alone and confided to him a unique role among His followers, recorded in the Petrine texts (Matt. 16:18–19, Luke 22:31–32, and John 21:15–17), each of which is without direct parallel in the other Gospels. The key text—and hence the passage subject to most intense criticism—is Matthew.

Now when Jesus came into the district of Caesarea Philippi, He asked His disciples, "Who do men say that the Son of man is?" And they said, "Some say John the Baptist, others say Elijah, and others Jeremiah or one of the prophets." He said to them, "But who do you say that I am?" Simon Peter replied, "You are the Christ, the Son of the living God." And Jesus answered him, "Blessed are you Simon Bar-Jonah! For flesh and blood has not revealed this to you, but my Father who is in heaven. And I tell you, you are Peter, and on this rock I will build my church, and the powers of death shall not prevail against it. I will give you the keys of the kingdom of heaven, and whatever you bind on earth shall be bound in heaven, and whatever you loose on earth will be loosed in heaven" (Matt. 16:18–19).

At one time those opposed to the papal claims insisted this text was a forgery inserted to boost the primacy of the bishop of Rome. But today most biblical scholars agree with the Lutheran-Catholic ecumenical study *Peter*

---

5. The doctrine of the papacy and the doctrine about Mary were the two great sticking points for Anglicans, the development of which Newman used as examples in working out his own theory of the development of doctrine, the work he was completing when he decided that Christ's Church is indeed centered in the papacy (cf. Thomas Norris, "The Development of Doctrine," *Communio: International Catholic Review* 22:3 [fall 1995]: 470–87).

in the New Testament in accepting its authenticity.[6] Miller points out: "Given the strongly Aramaic substructure of the passage, a convincing argument can be made that the early Christian community passed on its memory of this dialogue from original witnesses. . . . The play on words with 'rock' works perfectly in Aramaic, where *kepha* appears in both places. . . . Other Aramaicisms . . . include 'powers of death,' 'flesh and blood,' and 'Simon Bar-Jonah.' "[7]

Miller examines several other objections to the text, one of which seems particularly serious: why would Jesus who, these critics claim, expected the imminent coming of the reign of God speak of "his church"? Miller, after pointing out that Jesus' exact messianic expectations are not all that clear, replies, citing a work of Yves Congar, that most scholars today do not see a conflict between the idea of founding a messianic community even if the end is nigh, that the notion of founding such a community was familiar to Jewish thought of the time, and that, as Johann Auer points out, it would be understandable for Jesus to endow such a community with the office of a universal shepherd and the power to bind and loose.[8] (We shall see in a moment that the expectation that Christ would return soon, which Scripture at least suggests was present to some degree in the primitive community, probably slowed down somewhat the development of explicit thinking out of the nature and limits of the apostolic offices.)

But if one accepts the text as a genuine echo of Jesus' intention, there remains the task of determining just what that intention entails.[9] Changing Simon's name and calling him by a term that Scripture had used for God Himself—and given Peter's fickle and unsure but courageous nature, it would hardly be an appropriate nickname—is an affair of election and grace: Peter did not ask for it, the others did not designate him, it is entirely Jesus' doing. But could not that "rock" be precisely Peter's faith, not Peter the man, as Protestants have argued? As the Protestant theologian Oscar Cullmann says, the parallelism between "you are Rock" and "on this rock"

6. Raymond E. Brown, Karl P. Donfield, and John Reumann, eds., *Peter in the New Testament* (Minneapolis: Augsburg Publishing House, 1973), 85 n. 192. Any reader who wishes to base his own rejection of the Catholic position on the role of Peter on the old dispute about the authenticity of this text really owes it to himself to consult these excellent essays where the whole matter is laid out in complete detail.

7. Miller, *Shepherd*, 13–14.

8. Congar, "La Chiesa è apostolica," in *L'evento salvifico nella comunità di Gesù Cristo, Mysterium Salutis*, ed. Johannes Feiner and Magnus Löhrer (Brescia: Queriniana, 1972), 7:685; Auer, *The Church: The Universal Sacrament of Salvation*, trans. Michael Waldstein (Washington, D.C.: Catholic University of America Press, 1993), 8:242.

9. Avery Dulles points out in his recent study *The Catholicity of the Church* (Oxford: Clarendon Press, 1985) that the New Testament reveals Peter as "first of rank" among the apostles, in the spirit of the later institutional fact of papacy (140). The leadership of the See of Peter comes from Peter's role among the apostles. Jesus recognized this when He said, "You are Peter and on this rock I will build my Church" (Matt. 16:18). Even though James, the cousin of Jesus, was head of the prestigious Church of Jerusalem and clearly exercised much authority among the apostles, Peter is mentioned more than all the other apostles put together. And the "foundation text" in Matthew seems definitive.

shows that the second rock can be only the same as the first, and hence means the person.[10]

Peter was commissioned to provide the whole community with a stability that he derived by sharing in divine steadfastness. By giving the apostle a share in His own solidity, Jesus acted "like a man building a house, who dug deep, and laid the foundation upon rock" (Luke 6:48). Peter was made a solid rock by Christ who was "like a wise man who built his house upon the rock" (Matt. 7:42). As the rock foundation dependent upon Christ, Peter would guarantee the Church's endurance against the "powers of death" (Matt. 16:18).

The Gospels reveal not only that Peter was sometimes childishly impetuous (cf. John 13:9), lacking faith (cf. Matt. 14:28–31), and a self-confessed "sinful man" (Luke 5:8), but also that he failed, at least initially, to comprehend Jesus' identity. Only by divine Providence was Peter a solid rock. On his own he was an obstacle, a stumbling block, and a betrayer. Even so, Peter's personal weaknesses did not annul the ministry Christ assigned to him. Instead, they disclose that the apostle's role in the primitive Church was independent of the force of his personality or strength of his virtue. It was due to "a formal disposition by Christ," notes French theologian Louis Bouyer, "and therefore of an assured, unequaled, and corresponding charism." As in the case of Paul (cf. 2 Cor. 12:9), "grace is sufficient to Peter to achieve his fulfillment; the power of God is at its best in his weakness as a man." The shadows surrounding the Petrine texts vividly proclaim the mystery of grace that is the core of Christ's message and redemptive sacrifice.[11]

This very human Peter is given "the keys to the kingdom of heaven," and he is told by Jesus Christ that "whatsoever you bind on earth shall be bound in heaven, and whatsoever you loose on earth shall be loosed in heaven"; he is ordered to "strengthen your brethren" (Luke 22:32), and "to tend my lambs and to feed my sheep," (John 21:15–17), to take charge of Christ's entire flock, though it remains Christ's own flock.[12] To get some notion of how this authority was exercised and accepted in the apostolic community, we should see what Scripture has recorded about Peter's actual exercise of leadership.

Miller points out that the evangelists, while almost certainly influenced by later events and editorial concerns, nevertheless confirm that the apostle held a prominent position in the postapostolic community, the preferential treatment accorded him by the Risen Christ, preparing the way for his function in the post-Resurrection community. To start with, Peter is the

10. Cullmann, "Petros, Kephas," in *Theological Dictionary of the New Testament*, ed. Gerhard Friedrich (Grand Rapids, Mich.: Eerdmans Publishing, 1968), 6:105.

11. Bouyer, *The Church of God, Body of Christ, and Temple of the Spirit*, trans. Charles Underhill Quinn (Chicago: Franciscan Herald Press, 1982), 379; Max Thurian, "The Mystery of Unity of the Bishop of Rome to the Whole Church," *Bulletin/Centro Pro Unione* 29 (spring 1986): 10; Miller, *Shepherd*, 27.

12. Miller, *Shepherd*, 24.

first apostle to witness the Resurrection. In both Luke's (34:34) and Paul's accounts (1 Cor. 15:5), Christ appears first to Peter among all the apostles, and John (20:4–6) portrays the beloved young apostle dashing faster to the tomb, but then deferentially allowing Peter to enter first. Then in the Acts of the Apostles we are given many glimpses of Peter acting as head of the community. Among the apostles gathered in the upper room awaiting the coming of the Holy Spirit, Luke names Peter first (Acts 1:13). As Miller points out, this list follows the synoptic pattern cataloging the names of the Twelve, each of which mentions Peter first and Judas last; the remaining names are not in identical order (cf. Matt. 10:2–4; Mark 3:16–19; Luke 6:13–16).

We see him in action first *preaching,* with all the other apostles standing about him, the great Pentecost sermon, proclaiming on behalf of all the witnesses of the Resurrection, "this Jesus God raised up" (Acts 2:32).[13] Filled "with the Holy Spirit," he preached before the elders of the Jewish community that salvation comes only from Jesus (Acts 4:12). We see him again as spokesman before the authorities (Acts 4:19–20 and 5:29–32). Besides being shown as the most active in Jerusalem during the Church's first years, he is also shown to be at that period its greatest *missionary:* sent by the apostles to Samaria with John (8:14), to Lydia (9:32), and to Caesarea (10:1).[14] His ministry later extended beyond Palestine, including Antioch (Gal. 2:11) and Rome, probably Corinth, and possibly Asia Minor (1 Pet. 1:1, where he greets communities in Asia Minor). Paul refers in his letter to the Corinthians to a pro-Cephas party there (1 Cor. 1:12). And Paul simply assumes the Galatians, whom he himself has evangelized, know who Peter is. Miller comments, "Wherever Paul preached the gospel, Peter's role was part of the story."[15]

Peter is also the community's first *miracle worker,* the cure of the cripple showing this Petrine priority (Acts 3:1–10). Both in this miracle and in the raising of the dead girl Tabitha (9:36–41), Luke is at pains to draw parallels with similar miracles worked by Christ. The crowds seemed to expect miracles from him (5:15).

Luke shows Peter exercising initiative in resolving questions in the early Church. First, in the choice of Mathias to replace Judas: "In those days Peter stood up among the brethren . . . and said . . . 'So one of the men who accompanied us during all of the time the Lord Jesus went in and out among us, beginning from the baptism of John until the day he was taken up from us—one of those men must become with us a witness of the resurrection'" (Acts 1:15, 21). The apostles cast lots, and so Mathias was added to complete the initial Twelve, symbolic of the twelve tribes of Israel.

13. I am following here, without the rich details, the catalog of Peter's functions developed in ibid., 33–36.
14. A sign of the collective leadership of the apostles; we shall discuss below the relationship of Peter to the other eleven.
15. Ibid., 34. Miller cites Raymond E. Brown, *Biblical Reflections on Crises Facing the Church* (New York: Paulist Press, 1975), 69.

Luke provides us with a good example of Peter *exercising his power "to bind and to loose,"* as well as his *prophetic power:* With special insight he divined that the couple Ananias and Sapphira had held back some of the proceeds of land they had sold. "You have not lied to men but to God" (Acts 5:4). The couple dropped dead, which symbolizes, suggests Stanley Jaki, the supreme rule of the power of death outside the Kingdom of God whose keys Peter holds. Miller comments: "Such awesome authority would not be understandable if it did not derive from Christ." Miller states further, "Still more expressive of Peter's authority was his resolution to open the Church to the Gentiles. He was the first to baptize pagans without making them accept the Jewish law beforehand. . . . One day Peter had a vision of ritually impure food which he was three times told to eat (Acts 10:16). . . . The Spirit bade Peter to overcome his obedience to Jewish ritual prescriptions" (Acts 10:19–20). Peter was able to carry the whole Church with his decision. "It was not Paul, the great apostle to the gentiles, who began the mission to the pagans, but Peter, whose own evangelizing was confined mainly to the Jews."[16]

Later, some of the Judaizers continued to press against this decision. This led to the first council of the Church, that of Jerusalem, recounted in Acts. Peter was the first to speak, and his arguments prevailed: "his authority was crucial in resolving a question essential to the Church's development. . . . James, (the head of the local Church), the other apostles and the elders played a role in arriving at the decision. Together the assembly exhibited their 'one accord' " (Acts 15:25). James pronounced the decisive judgment (Acts 15:19–20), and the apostles and elders gave the sentence enforcing the decision (Acts 15:23).[17]

Peter's Relationship to the Other Apostles

Now that the biblical foundations of the primacy of Peter have been reviewed, the question naturally arises of his relationship to the other apostles, for all the Twelve are presented in Scripture as witnesses to the Resurrection, and they are shown in Acts as behaving collegially. As we saw earlier and shall discuss further in a moment, the question of the "apostolic succession" of the bishops is critical for the Catholic understanding of the Church. As Louis Bouyer sums up the issue, Peter "does not appear as a 'super-apostle,' but as the apostle in whom is found, personally reunited, everything that is shared or possessed in common with the whole apostolic college." Peter enjoys his particular ministry from within the apostolic college and as a member of it. But because of his singular call by Christ and the unique tasks he received, Peter shared in the authority belonging to the Messiah Himself. Within

16. Jaki, *The Keys of the Kingdom* (Chicago: Franciscan Herald Press, 1986), 49, cited in Miller, *Shepherd,* 35, 36.

17. Miller, *Shepherd,* 36.

the Twelve, he held "a special messianic vicariate." Peter received first, personally, and fully the mission and power that the other apostles received collectively.[18]

So Peter is first. But one of the Gospels, that of John, demonstrates another primacy, the primacy of love, found in "the beloved apostle" himself, who was always quicker to see, understand, and believe (cf. John 13:23–26, 18:15–16, 20:2–10, 21:1–23), something that in our time the theologian Hans Urs von Balthasar would take as a reminder that Peter's primacy of office, as vicar of Christ, must be balanced by the primacy of love shown forth by both John and Mary,[19] which primacy of love, Balthasar says, is the most important and alone will endure after the Parousia—the Second Coming of Christ. The Protestant theologian Oscar Cullmann concludes that "the special position of Peter is not contested [by John] . . . [and] proves how firm was the tradition about the precedence of Peter among the disciples." Brown thinks that the contrast between Peter and the beloved disciple is "a backhanded attestation to the importance of Peter as the apostolic witness best known among the disciples."[20]

Another great apostle looms large in the question of Peter's role. Much is made of Paul's rebuke of Peter for weakening in the issue of not requiring pagan converts to obey the old law. Reflection on this important incident is helpful for understanding the role of the papacy as it emerges.

To the Galatians, Paul wrote that "Before certain men came from James, he [Peter] ate with gentiles, but when they came he drew back and separated himself, fearing the circumcision party" (Gal. 2:12). Others, Paul says, also "acted insincerely" (Gal. 2:13). "This defection, even of Paul's companion, Barnabas, alludes to the high esteem in which Peter was held and how seriously his position was taken." Paul believed that Peter's action compromised "the truth of the gospel (Gal. 2:14). Significantly, he delivered his rebuke not to Barnabas, but only to Peter."[21] However great Peter's recognized authority, he, too, stood under the judgment of the gospel.[22] Miller adds:

> Scripture does not tell us why Peter acted as he did. It could be, as Otto Karrer suggests, that he wanted to keep the peace with the Jewish Christians, finding a way out of the problem they presented. After all, Paul himself had let Timothy be circumcised for a similar reason (cf. Acts 16:3), for the sake of peace. Paul did not wholly or relentlessly exclude every concession to those who continued to accept certain demands of the law. He had proclaimed that "to those under the law I became alone under the law" (1 Cor. 9:20). It is very possible that Peter, like Paul, had the best of intentions, trying as far as possible to avoid open conflict with the

18. Bouyer, *The Church of God,* 379, cited in Miller, *Shepherd,* 39.

19. This theme is found throughout Balthasar's work. But see especially *The Christian State of Life,* trans. Mary Frances McCarthy (San Francisco: Ignatius Press, 1983).

20. Cullmann, "Petros, Kephas," 6:102, cited in Miller, *Shepherd,* 39; Brown, *Biblical Reflections,* 75, cited in Miller, *Shepherd,* 39.

21. Miller, *Shepherd,* 42.

22. J. M. R. Tillard, *The Bishop of Rome,* trans. John de Satgé (Wilmington: Michael Glazier, 1983), 113, cited in Miller, *Shepherd,* 42.

Judaizers. When challenged by Paul, who thought his position was cowardly, Peter allowed his behavior to be corrected.[23]

Paul rebuked Peter because he wanted to correct a faltering brother, not because of a doctrinal divergence between them. "For if there is one thing that is certain in church history," contends William R. Farmer, "it is that in spite of any pig-headedness on the part of either or both of these great apostles, they did stand together on the fundamental theological basis of the faith." Paul's opposition to Peter centered "not on Cephas as a person claiming undue authority but on Cephas as acting without principle."[24]

Miller's summary comment reminds us of something that remains valid about all popes until the end of time: "Despite Peter's function as rock-apostle, he remained vulnerable to the personal weaknesses and temptations of Simon. The Apostle to the Gentiles reproved Peter's way of acting, but without questioning his leadership in the Church."[25] (Previously, Miller analyzed Paul's two earlier visits to Peter and the others in Jerusalem; of the second visit, Paul comments that he consulted "with those in repute . . . lest somehow I should be running or had run in vain" [Gal. 2:2].)

Succession to Peter's Ministry

The historical record is thin regarding the earliest stages of the development of the reality of bishops of Rome as successors of Peter. The evidence that Peter and Paul both went to Rome and were martyred there is fairly good,[26] but it depends more on the strength of the living tradition than upon documentary evidence. As Miller points out, the earliest extant list of Roman bishops distinguishes between Peter's function as the founder of the local church and Linus's function as bishop. Irenaeus notes, "the blessed apostles [Peter and Paul], having founded and built up the church [of Rome], they handed over the episcopate to Linus. . . . To him succeeded Anacletus; and after him, in the third place after the apostles, Clement was chosen for the episcopate."[27] What is quite clear is that by the beginning of the second century, the claim is being made that the bishops of Rome are Peter's successors, and there is good evidence of the claims generally being accepted. What is not clear, and what remains contested in parts of the Christian Church to this day, of course, is in what exactly consists the powers and prerogatives of the Petrine primacy adhering to this office. What is also clear is that the office of the bishop of Rome develops fairly early and ever stronger as a rallying point for and symbol of the unity of Christ's Church, and remains so to this day; but the very strength of the

23. Miller, *Shepherd*, 43.

24. William R. Farmer and Roch Kereszty, *Peter and Paul in the Church of Rome* (New York: Paulist Press, 1990), 49, cited in Miller, *Shepherd*, 43; Brown, Donfield, and Reumann, *Peter in the New Testament*, 30.

25. Miller, *Shepherd*, 43.

26. For details, see ibid., 50–54.

27. Irenaeus, *Against Heresies*, 3.3.3.

claim is dialectically related to later contests against it, first in the growing split of the Church between East and West and then with the fracturing off from Rome of the Protestants.

What makes this process, complex and obscure though it may be, so interesting, as one seeks to grasp the essence of a living tradition, is not only the extreme importance of the papal claims for understanding the teaching authority of the Church, but also the fact that the process is ongoing, the issues very alive. Most recently, in his encyclical letter on Christian unity, Pope John Paul II, after reaffirming the indispensable service of the papacy as symbol of unity, invited non-Catholic Christians to reflect on how this service could be rendered in a way they could accept.

> When addressing the Ecumenical Patriarch His Holiness Dimitrios I, I acknowledged my awareness that for a great variety of reasons, and against the will of all concerned, what should have been a service sometimes manifested itself in a very different light. But . . . it is out of a desire to obey the will of Christ that I recognize that as the Bishop of Rome I am called to exercise that ministry. . . . I insistently pray the Holy Spirit to shine his light upon us, enlightening all the Pastors and theologians of our Churches that we may seek—together, of course—the forms in which this ministry may accomplish a service of love recognized by all concerned.
>
> This is an immense task, which we cannot refuse and which I cannot carry out by myself. Could not the real but imperfect communion existing between us persuade Church leaders and their theologians to engage with me in a patient and fraternal dialogue on the subject, a dialogue in which, leaving useless controversies behind, we could listen to one another, keeping before us only the will of Christ for his Church and allowing ourselves to be deeply moved by his plea "that they may all be one . . . so that the world may believe that you have sent me" (John 17:21)?[28]

With the present pope's "watchdog of doctrine," Joseph Cardinal Ratzinger, prefect of the Sacred Congregation for the Doctrine of the Faith, warning that the Church, *semper reformanda,* must be prepared today to overhaul the old structures to meet the demands and possibilities of the times, we see that in reflecting on the almost two millennia of development of the papacy and its relations with the apostolic college of the bishops, we should be alert to find background that will point to possible ways forward.

The Apostolic Succession of the Bishops

As the claims of Petrine primacy became more explicit and more demanding, a key insistence of Rome that emerged—beginning to appear in the thin documentation rather early—concerns the Roman bishop's right as *primo inter pares* with the other bishops, president of their college, the one whose approval is essential for any council teachings to be accepted as valid for the whole Church. (Later we shall examine some of these developments at two of the most decisive points: at the emergence of "the New Rome," and the ecumenical councils, with new claims for the See of the ecumenical

---

28. Pope John Paul II, *Christian Unity. Ut Unum Sint* (1995): 106–7.

patriarch, and then at the time of the Protestant revolt, with the upsurgence of the Congregationalist model of the Church. Again, this critical issue of the pope's relations with the bishops, and of both with the laity, is ongoing.)

Since the Protestant revolt in the sixteenth century the question of apostolic authority has become perhaps the most critical issue separating these main traditions of Christianity. It is not a division between Catholics and Protestants, but between, on the one side, Catholics, Orthodox, Anglicans, and Lutherans, all of whom retain some sense of apostolic succession and apostolic charism, and, on the other side, the more "Congregationalist" Protestants. In other words, the divide separates those who accept the notion of a divinely instituted hierarchy, and those who espouse a model of the Church in which the Holy Spirit is seen working more "from below," in the mass of believers, with nothing special reserved for those the congregation elects to preside.[29] For Congregationalists the hierarchical notion is Gnostic—a kind of sacerdotalism, suggesting a noxious set of intermediaries between God and man:[30] the hierarchs insist that the priesthood of all the baptized is maintained, the Holy Spirit is held indeed to work in all, but to each He is believed to give a special role, and the role to which the ordained priests are called is that service of the Church that Christ instituted, that "over-seeing" (*episkopein*) of which Paul speaks, which we shall now consider.[31]

Several points seem fairly well established by the evidence: Jesus Himself—the unique apostle sent (*apostolein* means "to send") into this world by the Father—chose an inner group of disciples, the Twelve, most likely intended to symbolize, as John of Damascus said, the twelve tribes of Israel.[32] "As the Father has sent me so I send you" (John 20:21). Of these, Peter, James, and John appear to have constituted an inner core.[33] But little more is known of this. We have spoken of that other primacy—the all-

29. Many "evangelical" Protestants accept some form of Church office as part of the apostolic nature of the Church. But the power to call to office and to ordain resides in the Holy Spirit operating through the congregation as a whole. Many liberal Catholics today tend to this view, as often their sense of the special divine authority of the episcopate is undermined by their resentment of what they see to be all too human abuses of authority on the part of "clerics" (indeed, male clerics).

30. See, for instance, Warfield, *The Plan of Salvation*, 66.

31. The issue of a Congregationalist versus a hierarchical understanding of the Church will be taken up in more detail when we reach Chapters 8 and 9 on Protestantism and modernity.

32. Interestingly enough, this central symbol of the Twelve was not retained by the Church; there is no "Council of Twelve Patriarchs," or anything else of that sort. This shows that the living authority can drop as well as retain symbols and practices from tradition. The plurality of authority is of course retained: the college of bishops, over which the successor of Peter presides.

33. Because they were often taken aside, they alone were privileged to witness the raising of Jairus's daughter (Mark 5:37; Luke 8:51), the transfiguration of Jesus, when, shortly before His death, His divinity was allowed to shine forth in an overwhelming fashion (Mark 9, Matt. 17, Luke 9), and they went with Him (and fell asleep!) during Jesus' Agony in the Garden of Olives (Mark 14:33; Matt. 26:37).

important primacy of love John claims for himself, and we are also aware that James was head of the local Church of Jerusalem, the Mother Church of them all.

This emerging structure played a crucial role in two crises of the early Church, but meager sources prevent us from drawing firm conclusions from the incidents. One concerns the role of James, "the brother of the Lord," the powerful and prestigious head of the Church in Jerusalem. Some historians, especially Harnack, have tried to make a case for James's having attempted to establish a kind of "Caliphate of Jerusalem" based on heredity, as was earlier attempted in Islam, by the Party of Ali, the Prophet's son-in-law, proposing the head be chosen among the blood descendants of the Prophet. This project, so goes the theory, was ruined by the catastrophic weakening of the Church in Jerusalem after the Roman destruction of A.D. 70 and the subsequent decline of "Judeo-Christianity."[34]

There is more imagination than evidence behind this hypothesis. It does seem clear, however, that James was as powerful as any figure one finds in the scant pages of apostolic Church documents. We do not really know why he was in fact head of the Church in Jerusalem. Was it because he was "brother of the Lord," that is, a cousin according to the tradition that has since early times held that Mary remained "ever virgin," or, as some interpret the text, that he was literally son of the same mother? But why is that a reason? The blood relationship might support the "caliphate à la Shi'a Ali" suspicion,[35] but that possibility was definitely "not retained," nor is there evidence of the See of Jerusalem in later years laying claim to some sort of primacy, or of any kind of hereditary descent.

Jean Cardinal Daniélou has suggested that great apostolic figures emerged as the presidents (later, "bishops") of the council of twelve of important local churches, while other apostles like Thomas remained the heads of parallel missionary hierarchies. This makes good sense of what we do know from Acts and the Apostolic Letters.[36] If true, that would show a further flexibility in the early structure, as this rather important distinction disappeared when no longer relevant, just as the title *episcopus* (whence bishop, meaning "overseer") for the head of the local church came to prevail over early titles like elder or *Presbyteros.* What is not so clear is how and in what sense these overseers were considered descendants of the apostles.

Miller sums up clearly what little we do know about the transitional phase from the period of the apostles to the postapostolic emergence of bishops claiming succession to the Twelve. I shall follow here again his excellent summary. It shows just how thin the documentary evidence is.

34. W. H. C. Frend, *The Early Church* (Philadelphia: Fortress Press, 1965), 35–48.

35. I am alluding here to *the* major split in Islam, between those of the Party of Ali, who believed it was the Prophet's intention that Islam be presided over by a hereditary Caliphate (descended from the Prophet's family), and those of "the Way" *(Sunni),* who espoused the selection of a Caliph from among all Muslims.

36. Jean Daniélou and H. I. Marrou, *Nouvelle histoire de l'Église,* vol. 1 of *Des origines à Saint Gregoire le Grand* (Paris: Seuil, 1963), 43, 70–71.

During the lifetime of the Twelve, with whom Paul became identified, this original group soon chose certain men to be, as Vatican II states, "helpers in their ministry."[37] The Pastoral Letters contain evidence of the apostles' desire to preserve their mission through succession. Timothy and Titus, disciples and coworkers of Paul during his lifetime, both carried on his work after his death, having authority to "appoint elders in every town, in the way that I told you" (Titus 1:5). In the First Letter to Timothy, the author (whether it is Paul himself or someone who assumes his name and hence the mantle of his authority) gives a description of the kind of man who would be suitable to be appointed presiding elder, and the kind who would make good deacons (3:1–13). "Do not be too quick to lay hands on any man . . ." (5:22). A similar but shorter description of the ones to be chosen as elders appears in the Letter to Titus (1:5–9). That, through such choice by those chosen by the apostles, succession to the apostles occurred is indisputable. Just how it occurred throughout the Church remains obscure because of lack of documentation[38]—there is, says Louis Bouyer, "a kind of tunnel in which we are unable to discern the details of a transmission which may have been conducted in rather complex forms."[39] But by the mid-second century writers maintained that bishops succeeded to the place of the apostles. The earliest witness, from before the end of the first century, is Clement's First Letter to the Corinthians: "Our apostles knew through the Lord Jesus Christ that there would be strife for the office of bishop. For this reason, therefore, having received perfect foreknowledge, they appointed those who have already been mentioned, and afterwards added the further provision that, if they should die, other approved men should succeed to their ministry."[40]

Less than a century later, in order to preserve authentic teaching against the heresies of the Gnostics who claimed to possess private sources for their teaching, Irenaeus (who died in 200) formulated the classic statement on apostolic succession: "Those who wish to see the truth can observe in every church the tradition of the apostles made manifest in the whole world. We can enumerate those who were appointed bishops in the churches of the apostles, and their successors down to our day."[41] So by the second century, it seems quite clear that local churches everywhere were headed by a bishop, and that the notion of their authority descending from that of the apostles seemed widespread.

Miller offers an important warning: the bishops were not, however, considered apostles; they were not eyewitnesses to Revelation, as the Twelve were, but ministerial heads of communities who gave authoritative testimony to the deposit of faith that had already been formed. Only the

37. *Lumen Gentium*, 20.

38. Miller, *Shepherd*, 57.

39. Bouyer, *The Church of God*, 321.

40. Clement, *First Letter to the Corinthians*, 44, in *Die apostolischen Väter*, ed. K. Bihlmeyer (Tübingen, 1924).

41. Irenaeus, *Against Heresies*, 3.3.3, cited in Miller, *Shepherd*, 57–58.

original apostles are the Church's irreplaceable foundation (cf. Eph. 2:20), the foundation of the new Jerusalem (cf. Rev. 21:14). *Only their teaching constitutes the deposit of faith that later generations were to preserve.* Bishops are not vessels of revelation. And whereas the apostles individually possessed the charism of preaching the gospel without error, bishops possess this charism only as a collegial body. Finally, except for the pope, no bishop succeeds to a particular apostle, though he might succeed to an apostolic see. Instead, each bishop is accepted as a member of the episcopal college that succeeds as a body to the apostolic college.[42]

Developing Clarity on the Primacy of the Roman See

The need to fight the Montanist heresy in the second half of the second century strengthened the bishops' role. In the course of the struggle, the position of Rome seemed to become more clearly affirmed. Daniélou comments on this:

> In this setup the Church of Rome has a particular authority. Polycarp came to Rome in 155 to discuss a number of questions with Anicetus (the Bishop of Rome). Dionysius of Corinth writes to the Church of the Romans and to Soter. It is to the Bishop of Rome that Polycratus of Ephesus addresses his defence of the quatrodecimal usage, in the name of the bishops of Asia.[43] It is hard not to recognize in this collection of facts something more than the political and intellectual importance of the capital of the Empire. On the ecclesial level, Rome does not appear just to represent one of the diverse traditions inherited from the Apostles. Or rather it does indeed represent one of the traditions, that of Peter. But that tradition appears invested with a particular authority. That is what was recognized by Irenaeus, Bishop of Lyon, in his *Adversus Haereses,* despite his own Asiatic origin and his being a Gaul by adoption.[44]

The early Church historian Eusebius says that Peter went to Rome to combat the influence of Simon the Magician (cf. Acts 8:18–23) who had gone there, "the all gracious and kindly providence of the universe brought to Rome to deal with this terrible threat to the world, the strong and great apostle, chosen for his merits to be spokesman for all the others, Peter himself."[45] Athanasius (who died in 373) believed Peter's coming to Rome was the necessary fulfillment of God's plan.[46] Rome, of course, was the great center of the Mediterranean world, symbol of unity, and an excellent place from which to radiate the gospel.

Miller, in pointing out that "the evolution from Peter's original ministry to the pope's full claim to, and exercise of, primacy was slow," reminds us that the scriptural canon itself took several centuries to be officially

---

42. Congar, "La Chiesa è apostolica," cited in Miller, *Shepherd,* 58.
43. The quatrodecimal usage refers to the custom of those who celebrated Easter on the same day as Passover, that is, fourteen days after the first new moon of Nisan, as opposed to the majority usage of celebrating on the Sunday following Passover.
44. Daniélou and Marrou, *Nouvelle histoire,* 141.
45. Eusebius, *History of the Church* (London: Penguin Books, 1989), 2:14:49.
46. Miller, *Shepherd,* 64.

determined as such. "By comparison, the Roman church's role as the standard of the true apostolic faith is more ancient than the Church's recognizing the New Testament canon as sacred scripture."[47]

Other truths of faith were implicitly present in the Church's consciousness before they were explicitly professed. The christological and Trinitarian definitions of the early ecumenical councils, sacramental doctrine, and the Marian dogmas of the Immaculate Conception and the Assumption likewise point to doctrinal development. It took time for the Church to arrive at an adequate understanding of what Christ instituted and of what was contained in the deposit of faith.[48]

The implications of this developmental reality for our understanding of the Catholic tradition as a living, unfolding, complex interaction of divine and human initiatives—with the interplay of developing institutional self-understanding, the writing and codification of Scripture, and gradual, explicit dogmatic formulation all playing roles—are fundamental. Without attempting to sketch the whole course of the Church's history, I shall be looking at certain of the most important crisis points for glimpses of how the life of this social reality, which came to call itself "the Mystical Body of Christ," is lived out, with particular interest in how the Christian of today is guided by the light the tradition brings him through the working—the human-social dynamics—of this unique institution.

Until the first great tear in Christ's seamless garment—the East-West Schism, itself gradual and centuries in the making—the papal primacy was accepted by the Church as a whole, and today admitted in some form, as we shall see later, by both the Anglican–Roman Catholic International Commission and the Lutheran-Catholic Dialogues. Among many evangelicals, on the other hand, "popery" is roundly condemned.[49] Many liberal Catholics are more than nervous about the strong role the pope plays in today's Church. "The popes first acted in 'primatial' ways before explaining why, or on what grounds, they did so." This initial period of the papacy is marked by what Jesuit theologian Henri Cardinal de Lubac calls an "early sobriety."[50]

47. Miller cites Joseph Cardinal Ratzinger, "The Primacy of Peter," *L'Osservatore Romano* 27 (July 8, 1991): 8, in *Shepherd*, 72.

48. Ibid.

49. I heard it called that way one night, as one of the student leaders of the Inter-Varsity Christian Fellowship at the University of Toronto declared adherence to popery to be grounds for refusing a Christian platform to a Catholic speaker, namely me, even after the program had been advertised. (The other members of the executive committee present—two Anglicans, a member of the United Church of Canada, a Greek Orthodox, and a professor of medicine [an ardent Protestant Christian who said he had left the young man's church because of such narrowness]—lined up solidly against him. But the invitation to speak was not restored.) Some evangelical ministers are still preaching that the pope is the Antichrist.

50. De Lubac, *The Motherhood of the Church*, trans. Sergia Englund (San Francisco: Ignatius Press, 1982), 288, cited in Miller, *Shepherd*, 72.

The First Letter to the Corinthians, attributed by Eusebius to Pope Clement and written about A.D. 96, is the earliest example of a Roman intervention into the life of another Church.[51] In the throes of a revolt at Corinth, some duly selected presbyters had been deposed, which Rome judges "sedition, so alien and out of place in God's elect." The Corinthians are urged to restore peace and fervor. After setting out the principle of apostolic succession by tracing it back to Christ's will, the letter calls for the reinstatement of the expelled presbyters. The letter asks obedience "to the things which we have written through the Holy Spirit." The pope invokes the authority of the Roman Church: "But if any disobey the word spoken by Him [Christ] through us, let them know they will involve themselves in transgression and no small danger." Echoing, as Miller points out, the decree of the Council of Jerusalem (cf. Acts 15:28), the letter adds an admonition: "For you will give us joy and gladness if, obedient to what we have written through the Holy Spirit, you root out the lawless anger of your jealousy."[52]

It is almost a century before the sparse written record furnishes us with another example of vigorous Roman intervention, this time an effort by one of the more forceful second-century (from 189 to 199) popes, Victor, who was seeking to resolve the dispute about when Easter should be celebrated. Victor tried to get all the churches to celebrate Easter on the first Sunday following the Passover, not on the fourteenth of Nisan, thus keeping it on the original date of the Resurrection. At Victor's prompting, synods of bishops were held all over the Mediterranean world to discuss his proposal. Strengthened by the votes of the majority who sided with him, Victor threatened with excommunication any bishop who did not accept his ruling. The churches of Asia Minor, however, did not yield in face of his threat.[53]

> In response, Victor excommunicated those dissident churches. Eusebius records his reaction: "Thereupon Victor, head of the Roman church, attempted at one stroke to cut off from the common unity all the Asian dioceses, together with the neighboring churches, on the ground of heterodoxy, and pilloried them in letters in which he announced the total excommunication of his fellow Christians there." Irenaeus of Lyon (d. 200), for one, opposed Victor's action, begging that he allow the Eastern tradition of dating Easter to stand. Significantly, however, he did not question Victor's right to intervene.[54]

51. "Clement has left us one recognized epistle, long and wonderful, which he composed in the name of the church at Rome and sent to the church at Corinth" (Eusebius, *History of the Church*, 3:16:80). As Miller points out, the epistle itself does not mention Clement, and it is even possible that Clement was a presbyter charged with relations with other churches. But the fact remains of a Roman intervention (Miller, *Shepherd*, 74).

52. Clement, *First Letter to the Corinthians*, cited by Miller, *Shepherd*, 74.

53. J. N. D. Kelly, *The Oxford Dictionary of Popes* (London: Oxford University Press, 1992), 740.

54. Eusebius, *History of the Church*, cited in Miller, *Shepherd*, 75. We do not know whether Victor carried out the excommunications, but we do know that some churches

Miller comments on the significance of all this: "Before Victor's pontificate, bishops acting together in assemblies had expelled heretics from their own churches. Individual bishops had done likewise. Victor, however, maintained that his action served communion not just with the local church in Rome, but also with the other churches of the *koinonia*. His action was novel because he single-handedly excommunicated the whole church of another province."[55]

Documentation becomes more frequent from the beginning of the second century, and not one single source we possess, even when arguing that Rome was acting imprudently, disputes its right to provide pastoral care for churches other than its own. Interesting is the salutation Ignatius of Antioch uses in addressing the Romans, contrasting with the opening of the other six letters he sent the churches in Asia Minor: "To the church . . . which has the chief seat in the place of the district of the Romans, worthy of God, worthy of honor, worthy of congratulation, worthy of praise, worthy of success, worthy in purity, having the chief place in love." That last phrase about *agape* has attracted much attention. Most recently, John Paul II has said it expresses "the primacy in that communion of charity which is the Church, and necessarily the service of authority, the magisterium Petrinum." Miller adds: "Very free in offering advice to the other communities to whom he wrote, Ignatius, nonetheless, refrained from admonishing the church in Rome. According to him, while the Roman community could instruct other churches, it was not itself taught . . . 'You have never envied anyone; you have taught others, but I wish that what you enjoin in your teaching may endure.' "[56]

When Bishop Cyprian of Carthage (who died in 258) wrote to Pope Cornelius (pope from 251 to 253) that the Roman See was "the chair of Peter and . . . the principal church in which sacerdotal unity has its source," he recognized that Rome was the point of reference for orthodoxy of the entire Church.[57] The Synod of Sardica (which existed from 343 to 344), with an approximately equal number of bishops from East and West, held near what is today Sofia, decreed in its disciplinary canons that the Roman bishop was the legal court of appeal and recourse in disputes between churches.[58] As doctrinal disputes grew more serious, this authority soon extended to dogmatic issues. For example, Jerome (who died in 420) appealed to

---

continued the old date, and that not until the Council of Nicaea in 325 were the followers of the old date, "the Quatrodecimans," definitively excommunicated from the whole Church.

55. Miller, *Shepherd*, 75.

56. Ignatius, *Letter to the Romans*, introduction; John Paul II, Discourse, January 27, 1993, *L'Osservatore Romano* 5 (February 3, 1993), cited in Miller, *Shepherd*, 76; Ignatius, *Letter to the Romans*, 3, cited in Miller, *Shepherd*, 76.

57. Cyprian, Letter, 59:14.

58. Cf. Henry Denziger and Adolf Schönmetzer, eds., *Enchiridion symbolorum, definitionum de rebus fidei et morum*, 33rd ed. (Freiburg im Breisgau: Herder, 1964), 133–35, which is the standard source of documents important in the history of the Church.

Rome for an authoritative pronouncement on the meaning of the term *three hypostases,* used by the Cappadocian fathers to describe Father, Son, and Holy Spirit as distinct persons. Because Jerome translated the word as essence, it sounded to him as though the Cappadocians were tritheists. In desperation he appealed to Pope Damasus in 376: "Since the East, rent asunder by feuds of long standing, is tearing to shreds the seamless robe of the Lord . . . I think it my duty to consult the Chair of Peter. . . . As I follow no leader save Christ, so I communicate with none save your Beatitude; that is with the Chair of Peter. For this, I know, is the Rock on which the Church is built. This is Noah's ark, and he who is not found in it shall perish when the flood overwhelms all."[59]

THE STRUCTURE CLARIFIED UNDER FIRE: THE EARLIEST HERESY
The Montanist Heresy

The earliest heresy is instructive for grasping the Church's growing sense of its authority and structure, and for seeing the role of the Roman bishop as early made explicit. Montanism we might characterize as the charismatic gone wild—a perennial temptation, given the belief of all Christians that the Spirit is always at work in every person, hence the temptation to circumvent any churchly authority invested (by Christ, Catholics believe) in sinful humans. Tension existed already in Judaism between the charismatic outbursts of prophesy and the settled, regular operation of the community under the leadership of priest and rabbi. Evangelicals, always attentive to the Holy Spirit working directly within them, alone and gathered in His name, to this day condemn vigorously sacerdotalism, as I mentioned earlier. Now the newly born Christianity experiences the same tension as Judaism knew, one that will continue down through the ages with every "private revelation" and every claim to prophesy, many giving rise to sects that separate themselves from the main body of "the great church."

Prophets sprang up in the second half of the second century all over that part of Asia called Phrygia (modern Turkey) announcing that the time of the Paraclete[60] had come with the arrival of Montanus.[61] The New Jerusalem was about to be inaugurated for its millennial reign. To be ready, one must live continently, a trait shared with the Gnostics, and a Puritan consequence, to be sure, of rejection of this world, giving rise to an anthropology of disgust with the body (or bred by it?).

Montanus, a recent convert, was an exalted prophet, speaking in the name of the Paraclete. He was soon joined by two women prophets, Prisca and Maximilla. The movement was particularly strong in the rural districts

59. Jerome, Letter, 15.1–2, translated in *Documents Illustrating Papal Authority* A.D. *96–454,* ed. E. Giles (London: S.P.C.K., 1952), no. 117.
60. The Holy Spirit as advocate, pleading with the Father on our behalf.
61. Daniélou and Marrou, *Nouvelle histoire,* 133.

of Phrygia, where it endured for several centuries. (Frend suggests that such outbursts maintain themselves better in the countryside than in an urban setting, where the Church tends to more order and hierarchy. Phrygia had a long history of this kind of more magical religion.)[62]

Daniélou sees in Montanism an expression of Asiatic Christianity, and an exaggeration of the Johannine strain in early Christian experience.[63] (The later prophetic outburst of Islam has been seen by many as also typically Oriental.) The notion of the Paraclete comes to Montanus from the Gospel of John, and the millenarianism he espouses is to be found already in the Apocalypse.[64] The thirst for martyrdom, which is also one of the Montanist traits, likewise comes from the Apocalypse and from the apocryphal Acts of John. "Montanism," Frend sums up the matter, "blended the prophetic and orgiastic native Phrygian religion with exalted preaching about the approaching end. The orthodox clergy took fright."[65]

The paradoxical result of multiplication of sects was the strengthening of the role of the bishops. The issue posed by the appearance on the scene of more and more "do-it-yourself" religion, with any exalted individual arising to declare himself a prophet under direct guidance of the Holy Spirit, is then this: how to maintain the integrity of the Church with the fullness of truth, the Word as Christ revealed it in preaching and mighty act. The answer throughout the history of the Church has been the same, as here from the start: bishops united in regional synods to seek common solutions to problems raised by the sects. Patriarchs emerged who appear to exercise vast regional authority: Polycratus at Ephesus, Victor at Rome, Serapion at Jerusalem, and Palmas in the Hellespont stand out. Serapion of Antioch gathered signatures against the Montanists, Dionysius of Corinth wrote to the churches of Crete, and Nicomedia of Athens to those of the Hellespont.[66] Daniélou comments that we are struck by the difference in action between the founders of sects, which are personal in character and who seem like heads of schools, and the action of bishops, which is basically collective and seeks to disengage a common faith. Irenaeus of Lyon was describing the historic situation when he wrote: "The heretics are all later than the bishops, to whom the Apostles confided the churches, and the manifestations of their doctrine are different and form a veritable cacophony. *But the ways of those who are of the Church, circling the whole globe and holding firm to the tradition of the Apostles, show us, all of them, the same faith and the same form of organization.*"[67]

62. W. H. C. Frend, *The Rise of Christianity* (London: Darton, Longman, and Todd, 1984), 254.

63. Daniélou and Marrou, *Nouvelle histoire*, 133.

64. The anticipation of "the thousand years of peace" to be introduced by the return of the Messiah.

65. Frend, *The Early Church*, 69.

66. Eusebius, *The History of the Church*, 5:19:3.

67. *I. Apol.* 26.4, cited in Daniélou and Marrou, *Nouvelle histoire*, 141 (emphasis added).

An Early Father Leaves an Insight into How
the Authority Structure Was Understood

The work of one bishop, Irenaeus, sainted primate of Lyon, whom I have already cited several times, offers particularly precious insight into orthodox thinking in the second century.[68] He not only was in the middle of the fray, but also has left for us most interesting and significant accounts. When I looked at the evidence of how the Church in the second century conceived of the faith and how it experienced emerging Church structure, I was struck by the fullness of the vision to be found in what remains of Irenaeus's writings and by the consistency of what the Catholic Church teaches today with what was written eighteen hundred years ago. From this rich corpus I shall here cite only what this early father has to say about the significance of the "rule of faith" for understanding the nature of the Church.

Reflecting on the conflict between the various heterodox schools and the bishops, Irenaeus asks with what authority do these "heads of schools" teach? Their doctrine has no foundation other than their own imaginations. They preach *themselves!* They like to pretend at times to represent an esoteric tradition, but in fact they represent no tradition at all. They are themselves the origin of their own doctrine. However attractive their constructions, they are only products of the human mind.

In contrast, the authority of the bishops is not derived from personal attractiveness or their own account. They are invested with a charge: to transmit a doctrine that is anterior to themselves. That tradition comes from the apostles, who instituted the first bishops. To show this, Irenaeus establishes the details of the lines of succession of the three churches he knows well: Smyrna, which goes back to John; Ephesus, which goes back to Paul; and Rome, which goes back to Peter and Paul and for which alone he gives the complete succession.

Of course, the heretics appeal to the apostles as well. But they are without authority; they do not represent the *traditio ab apostolis* because their tradition does not rest on the institution and the legitimate transmission of authority.[69] The transmission of the teaching of the apostles is not left to individual initiative or to private teachers, claiming on their own witness to be imbued with divine authority. The apostles, acting on the authority Christ transmitted to them alone, established the organs of transmission through

---

68. Born at Smyrna about A.D. 115, Irenaeus as a young man had been initiated by the great Bishop Polycarp into the Johannine tradition. He seems to have spent some time in Rome, which may have influenced his favorable views toward the Roman See. By A.D. 177 he was a priest in Lyon (today France's second city), under the reign of Bishop Eleutherius. He wrote a capital book against the Gnostics, *Against Heresies,* in which he critically studied all the heterodox sects. Upon becoming bishop he summed up his teaching in a work that has come down to us, *A Demonstration of Apostolic Preaching* (Westminster, Md.: Ancient Christian Writers, 1996–).

69. Irenaeus, *Against Heresies,* 1.23.8; cf. Daniélou and Marrou, *Nouvelle histoire,* 143.

which they wanted their teaching to flow. These offices alone can provide the criteria for doctrines and guarantee their conformity with revelation.

The sign of this apostolic authority, says Irenaeus, is the uniformity of Catholic teaching, which is everywhere the same for all men, regardless of age, language, or degree of education (a blow at the elitism, secrecy, and exclusiveness and overemphasis on knowledge of the Gnostics of all stripes). This faith, as I have said, the Church, though scattered in the whole world, carefully preserves, as if living in one house. For the languages of the world are different but the meaning of the (Christian) tradition is the same.[70]

Frend points out that this was not strictly true, for the rule of faith in Egypt differed considerably from that professed in Lyon by Irenaeus. But, he adds, it is substantially true, as wide travelers such as Hegesippus the Palestinian or the Phrygian merchant Avircius Marcellus, circa A.D. 210, witness. Both had been impressed that everywhere they went Christians had the same organization and rites. "From the Rhône to the Euphrates the Faith ostensibly was one."[71]

In contrast, the Gnostic schools (and this will be valid for the other "heretics," Ebionites, Montanists, and all who come later) all contradicted one another; each was original and different. Daniélou comments that such was their diversity and their luxuriant growth—like the abundance of Protestant sects in America, which happens when emphasis is put on personal inspiration rather than office—and that the study of Gnostic schools is an almost inexhaustible subject, as would be the study of the luxuriant growth of the sects. "Over against them, there is the common teaching of the bishops contained in the symbol [the Apostles' Creed], in its simplicity and its unity."[72]

Of course, anyone today, with our highly developed sense of historicity, will wonder if and how this can be as Irenaeus envisioned: that an essence of true teaching can remain basically the same through thousands of years and despite translation into the language and meanings of many different cultures. The child of the present age of hermeneutics will worry that such a belief about the strong unity of truth risks stifling innovative and speculative thinking.[73] (Recall the comments earlier on "dogmatic formulation closing the apophantic field.")

The "orthodox" Christian, believing that the one unchanging God has revealed, once and for all, the redemptive Way in Jesus Christ, will want to defend this possibility of unchanging Truth, formulated in symbols that

70. Irenaeus, *Against Heresies*, 1.10.
71. Frend, *The Early Church*, 66.
72. Daniélou and Marrou, *Nouvelle histoire*, 143.
73. Hermeneutics is the theory of interpretation, which emphasizes how meaning changes with shifts in "horizons of interpretation," meaning contexts, and the understanding subjects bring to the interpreting.

retain lasting meaning, and are translatable.[74] Those, on the other hand, who do not believe in revelation in this "hard" sense will be tempted to treat every utterance as nothing more than a poetic symbol, seeking to fix a fleeting intuition into the chthonic layer of experience. They will emphasize how everything any Christian father writes seeking to formulate the fundamental truths is unwittingly a reproduction or slight development of common intuitions to be found in one form or another throughout ancient Middle Eastern religion (such as "the god-man" theme) or perhaps of "archetypes" deep in the human soul.

Balthasar is one among many distinguished contemporary voices who would defend the perennial worth of early formulations, for instance some of Irenaeus's casting of the symbols. He offers the following explanation for why the sainted bishop achieved such penetration. When Irenaeus set out to express the One Faith in all its splendor, he attained such a quality of discourse—a creative intuition plunging to the most incandescent center—because he was the first to have a personal adversary capable of bringing out the profundity of the Christian revelation to which he was formed solidly by the tradition and to which he willed, with all his being, to remain totally loyal. The pagan religion was too amorphous, the Jewish had to be treated with respect. But the Gnostics, helping themselves generously to the materials of the Bible, had constructed an absolutely non-Christian edifice of the highest intellectual and religious pretension. They had in this way attracted to themselves many Christians. Here was the adversary Christian thought needed in order to discover itself fully.[75]

When considering briefly the great christological councils we said a word about the possibility, strength, and limitations of dogmatic formulation, and its role in the life of the Church. We shall have further occasion to consider this capital issue more fundamentally, as it is so important for a concept of truth and tradition that can avoid the thinly veiled skepticism of historical relativism. In this chapter, we have made some progress in laying the foundation for understanding how an unfolding grasp by the Church of its authority and structure relates to its responsibility and its ability to formulate teaching.

---

74. On the problems of translation, see *TA*, chapter 8, "Can the Truths of the Various Traditions Be Translated into a Single Wisdom?" and *BT*, chapter 5, "The Possibility of a Single Wisdom."

75. Hans Urs von Balthasar, *La gloire et la croix: Les aspects esthétiques de la révélation* (originally, *Herrlichkeit*) (Paris: Aubier, 1968), 2:1:28.

THE EAST-WEST CRISIS

The Great Schism

Unlike the earlier crises, such as the Montanist and the christological controversies, which had a positive result in clarifying the Church's understanding of its nature and doctrine, the schism of East and West was basically a disaster for Christianity. For it did not challenge the Church basically, doctrinally, and hence ecclesiologically the way the sects did, but rather, it was a drifting apart resulting finally in splitting it, revealing that there had existed from the start a tension that grew into a gap right at its core. "The Church," says the present pontiff, "breathes with two lungs, East and West."[1] Yes, but if, as Catholics believe, the successor of Peter is the head of that body in its earthly existence, then the Oriental lung somehow has not been feeding the head fully, with bad results for the West's spirituality, nor has the life-giving pneuma of the Occidental lung via the head fed the other half of the body, which Catholics view as having become somewhat lethargic in its development. Lack of communication became particularly troublesome after the final catastrophe, which many date from the mutual anathemas of 1054. Dialogue is in only our time beginning again in a sustained fashion, and both sides are breathing better already.

By the onset of the "barbarian centuries," as they might be called in the West, so great had become the cultural and ecclesiastical differences separating Roman and Eastern Orthodox Catholics, their drifting apart institutionally would appear difficult to have avoided despite the continuation of almost complete agreement on creedal matters and adherence to one sacramental system. That the institution was not able to hold at the top stems in part from the fact that most in the East, while admitting a Roman primacy, conceived it differently from the doctrine of a stronger Petrine supremacy that was developing in the West. For many reasons, the Latin West had become more impregnated than the East with the Roman sense of an overarching unity, where the sense of the autonomy of the local Church—some of them founded by various apostles—remained dominant. (To this day, look at Islam in the Middle East, and at the governments of

---

1. Pope John Paul II, *Euntes in Mundum* (1988), 4.

Muslim countries: great diversity, little cooperation, no strength at all at the overarching umbrella level. "The Arab League"? It has always been largely a joke in Middle Eastern politics. The Islamic religious associations have little local clout.) The Greek fathers themselves admitted that the Orient was the seedbed of heresies; they admired Rome as a bastion of orthodoxy and would appeal when fighting heretics to the patriarch of Rome, "the first among equals," that is, among the five patriarchs of the apostolic churches.

The challenge facing the appropriator is, first, to understand Catholicism East and West, the unities and the differences, and the need of each for the other. But at the same time, if we aspire to understand better the situation of the Church in the present world, we should be aware of anything in this struggle that will help us see how the Church will always be working to penetrate distinctive civilizations, and with them, their many distinctive cultures. Like the HTX today, the Church brain must interact dialectically with all the civilizations and cultures (and beneath them, with nature itself). But whereas the HTX is driven by planetary-scale power and economic and scientific considerations, and can be very flexible, the Church, especially its Roman head, must at all times be faithful to the core vision given it by its divine head, to which the earthly vicar must be absolutely submitted.

There were repeated efforts along the slow course of devolution to patch things up, a desperate last effort as late as 1438, the Council of Florence, with the Turks at the door. But in time, the growing cultural and ecclesial differences bred theological differences too, although Catholics East and West to this day remain much closer to one another in their episcopal church structure, sacramental life, and general creedal understanding than are Catholics, Eastern and Western, close to almost all Protestant Christians.[2] (We shall consider the two great bones of contention: the Romans' addition of *filioque*—that the Holy Spirit descends from the Father and the Son—to the creed, an act of "papal arrogance" that leads to the second complaint, namely, the Roman "heresy" of contending that the pope has jurisdiction over all the churches rather than just a place of honor due to the heretofore good record of Rome as a seat of orthodoxy.)

Catholic spokesmen—such as Yves Congar, Henri de Lubac, Hans Urs von Balthasar, Pope John Paul II, indeed the Second Vatican Council— are eager to emphasize what still unites East and West and to downplay the gravity of what seems to them manageable doctrinal differences. The Catholic view is that Christianity has not entirely failed in Christ's call for a catholic people. After a thousand years of formal schism, the two traditions

2. I shall not here discuss the Eastern-rite Catholics who are in adherence with Rome. My repeated warnings about the misrepresentation of "Roman" in Catholicism should stand as evidence that I do not believe that only the "Latin"-rite Catholics exist, have standing, or are a superior type of Catholic. But the issue here is the split between "Constantinople" and "Rome."

have managed to "keep the faith" to the extent that their agreement on most essential points of dogma and practice is far more substantial than their disagreement. Father Yves Congar, a great ecumenist, argues that the two "sister Churches" are de facto and de jure one, despite differing theological interpretations (of a nonheretical sort, claims he) and Eastern refusal to accept the authority of the pope in the form demanded by the West, despite the East's acknowledgment historically that the Roman patriarch is first among equals. Congar is supported in this, to a certain extent, by the Second Vatican Council, which spells out the nature of the unity: "Although these Churches are separated from us, they possess true sacraments, above all—by apostolic succession—the priesthood and the Eucharist, whereby they are still joined to us in a very close relationship."[3] Because the Eastern Churches have remained validly episcopal, they remain substantially attached to the vine of Christ.

The less seraphic attitude within these sister Churches[4] sees the West as having drifted, from the time of Augustine, into too conceptualized a theology that opened the way for an oversharp distinction of a secular sphere, proper to man's mastery, and a spiritual sphere, into which God is, as it were, "kicked upstairs."[5] This led to a loss of the sacramental sense of everyday existence, and with it the growth of technological control and the extremes of secularization found in the West. Loss of the sense that the local church is a sacramental presence of Christ and His Holy Spirit, and that this spirit is what unites the Church—this loss is what led to a monarchical papacy. The austere, desacralized Western liturgy is a good sign of this impoverishment of daily life.[6] Some in the East worry that the West has gone so far that it could scarcely scratch its way back to the sphere of genuine spirituality, in which God permeates all.

As Robert Barringer, a Catholic priest who specializes in orthodox theology, points out, much more is at stake for the appropriator of the Catholic tradition in understanding the East-West Schism than simply preparing for reunification. The East holds up a mirror—distorted perhaps, but

3. *Decree on Ecumenism,* para. 15. While the comparison is not entirely valid, one could hazard the judgment that Eastern and Western Catholicism is at least as united in doctrine and practice as any two great families of Sunni Islam, say, Arab Maghrebian and Pakistani Islam. The wider separation of Catholics and Protestants is to some degree comparable to the split between Shiites and Sunnis.

4. This position is ably summed by Robert Barringer, "The Challenge of Eastern Theology to the Western Church," in *He Dwells in Our Midst: Reflections on Eastern Christianity,* ed. T. Lozynsky (St. Catherines, Ontario: St. Sophia Religious Society, 1988), 9–16.

5. We shall see better what this means in the last part of this chapter; the self-critical Catholic cannot just brush off this criticism.

6. Eastern-rite Catholics, which retain "Eastern" liturgies (for example, the Byzantine-rite Catholics who use the liturgy of Saint John Chrysostom as the root of their liturgy), do not, obviously, fall under this charge of desacralization. Many Roman-rite Catholics agree with the Orthodox that our liturgy has indeed become rather too austere. I shall reflect on this in the last section of the book.

precious—in which we in the West are invited to see ourselves and are urged to a radical critique of elements profoundly rooted in our civilization.

But the West holds up a mirror to the East, too. I was musing, as I considered these views, on the attendance at daily Mass—the most austere of liturgies—in our singularly cosmopolitan Toronto. I would venture the guess that it is negligible in the Orthodox churches but it is substantial in a very large number of Western churches. Of course, that reflects in part the fact that the Western Mass is less hieratic and hence awfully brief. But it also signals a devotion to the Eucharist that bears many fruits.

A hopeful view is to be found in a recent talk by the Russian Orthodox theologian John H. Erickson, in which he stresses both the gradual and highly political nature of the growing apart of the traditions and the fact that it is hard to assign a single date to the definitive schism. He concludes with these words:

> Some elements of communion have always remained between our churches, and daily we are growing closer to full communion, communion as deep and perfect as can be attained in this life. Already, agreement concerning the Holy Spirit is at hand; the question of Papal primacy is being discussed seriously, without all the rancor that characterized debates of the past. While I do wish Latin Catholics would use real bread in the Eucharist rather than those unleavened wafers, I do not believe this issue should divide us.[7] The schism of East and West is disappearing just as quietly and mysteriously as it developed. I have tried to show how difficult it is to say precisely when the schism occurred. Perhaps future ages will find it equally difficult to say when precisely the schism was healed. With Vatican II? With the reciprocal lifting of anathemas in 1965?[8] With the completion of the work of the Joint International Doctrinal Commission a few years from now? Or with gatherings such as this?[9]

Fortified by such a hopeful message, I approach my first task, understanding something of the processes by which these Catholic traditions grew apart, especially as this impacted the ways they came to conceive of themselves and their differences. Running at a basic level in all this are the deepest cultural differences.

Culture, ethnos, nation: these deep differences will always remain challenges to the ingathering of the people of God, for they are not only the source of human riches, but at the same time divisive influences. Awareness of this is now at a fever pitch; *inculturation* is a buzzword on the tongues of churchmen. The Word of God seeks to penetrate and transform cultures, but in the process is itself interpreted, and somewhat deformed, while being at the same time enriched. Hence, argue Roman Catholics, the need, foreseen by Christ, for a strong center to gather together and put into

7. In the full context of this speech, it is evident that this remark is made *in passim*, and tongue in cheek.

8. This act, by the ecumenical patriarch Athenagoras, and Pope Paul VI, was an event of utmost significance, the importance of which has yet to strike many ordinary Catholics, East and West.

9. Erickson refers here to the Michaelmas Conference at St. Michael's College in June 1990, which he was addressing. The excerpt is the conclusion to his paper.

communication those riches, to oversee the "translation" between cultures, and to counteract their tendency to become sources of division.[10]

When the innovative undergraduate Christian liberal-education program at St. Michael's College of the University of Toronto was named "Christianity and Culture," it was in recognition of this basic truth: that Christ's light is always penetrating and being refracted by the different cultures. Cultural differences played a role in influencing the fault lines along which the Western Church split in the Protestant Reformation, just as the Greek and Slavic cultural differences are significant in Orthodoxy. Understanding these matters can illumine in important ways our understanding of the Church, always moved along through these human, all too human cultural realities.

EAST IS EAST AND WEST IS WEST

The Church grew first on the fringes of the Roman Empire. For the "Orientals" themselves the eastern littoral of the Middle Sea was not, of course, experienced as a fringe but rather as the center of the world. For the Jews, Jerusalem was the *umbilicus mundi*—the "navel of the world"—and the gateway to heaven. For the Greeks, the center of the world was once Athens, then for a while it moved wherever Alexander moved, then for another while the world lacked a focus, only to find a properly Greek center again, with Constantine's founding at Byzantium of "the New Rome" in A.D. 330.

The people's sense of "the center of the world" is an influential dimension in the ontological space-time of their world. In each civilization, at each epoch, people look toward the center in distinctive ways, seeking different forms of inspiration and leadership. Think of all those pious Jews at the time of Christ trudging up to the temple in Jerusalem, every year, sometimes twice. Nor should one dismiss lightly the little arrow on the nightstand in the ultra-modern hotel in a Muslim land pointing exactly toward Mecca. In my book *HTX: Learning to Survive in Virtual Reality*,[11] the question of the world system's lack of a center, the dissolution into the "web," is shown to have great ontological and anthropological significance.

For much of the period of the early Church the world seemed pulled apart by the powerful attraction of two poles, Rome and the renascent Persian Empire. Christianity has evolved over two millennia by surviving the pull

10. The very homogenization of the planetary technological world system as it is formed by the highly secularized HTX techno-culture that has been generated by the "Christian" Occident is today, as it penetrates the civilizations and their underlying cultures from a strange new "overlay" of unprecedented kind, tending to form what is miscalled "the worldwide popular culture." It is too remote from nature to preserve much sense of *cultivare* (meaning "tending the fields"). This electrical phenomenon accounts for a new degree of contact between cultures, which offers new opportunities for communication, and may account in part for a new openness between contemporary Catholics and Orthodox.

11. Submitted for publication, 1998.

between a series of centers of the world, all of which seemed eternal at the time, until today the question becomes fascinating once again in a planetary epoch: how is the Church to navigate in the present economic-superpower bloc polarization, with a new power uniting Europe, replacing the old Eastern pole, the USSR, and a further new East-West polarity becoming daily more problematic as a massive China looms ever more menacing, and all being decentered by "the net"?

For the Catholic Church, the center is still Rome, a modern metropolis the Church is watching as it turns secularized on its doorstep, a Rome that weighs in no more heavily on the planetary scene than Chicago and less than Tokyo, with the great exceptions of the attraction of the papacy and the city's antiquity. For the Eastern Church, Istanbul is an honored, but not strong, source of leadership, located in the Turkish capital, which is slowly squeezing the life out of the tiny Christian community (eighteen hundred souls!) (the Russian patriarch was not hesitant to remind the ecumenical patriarch that Moscow claims 100 million souls under its jurisdiction!), nor is that lack of patriarchal authority experienced as a weakness by the autocephalous Churches,[12] proud of their distinctiveness within the one faith, and happy about the "flexibility" of this much looser Orthodox communion, more like the Anglican communion than the much more focused and centralized Roman authority.

Geopolitical considerations, while real for incarnate man, are not the heart of the truth of the Church's presence.[13] For the Catholic, the Church was present, full and entire, in that upper room in Jerusalem on Pentecost. And Christ is present, through His Holy Spirit, moving every good act, in every word of God meditated lovingly anywhere, and with a special eucharistic presence, in every tabernacle of every Catholic Church.[14] (The Orthodox are right to stress the divine indwelling in every church, and the importance of the bishop as center of the local Church.) Rome's importance is in the symbol of unity the successor to Peter represents, and in his witness to orthodoxy—all of that accepted by the Orthodox during the first millennium of the Church's life—but the Roman Catholic adds his teaching office and governing authority, which Catholics believe was established in Peter by Christ, and meant for his successors. Being a purely spiritual center, Rome is not meant to, and cannot, keep up in terms of cultural influence with the present-day capital of the Western "Empire."[15]

12. "Autocephalous" means literally, "having one's own head."

13. How vital is such a consideration as "the center of the world," at least religiously in this age of telecommunications? The fastest growing parts of the Church are in Africa, Korea, and Indonesia, the least European parts of the vast Church. The Holy See is a center, to be sure, but what is the significance of a center, residing in one man and his "bothersome" curia?

14. Each tabernacle is a center of the cosmos, for the Logos through whom it is created, dwells corporeally, mysteriously in that little ark.

15. That "capital," I suppose, is located (for the moment still and much contested, given the evidence of signs of decadence on its continent) where the Empire State

As troubling and unclear as all this kind of contemporary consideration may be, the history of the estrangement (the term is Congar's) within the one Church of Christ is fairly straightforward.[16] The gradual distancing is first of all rooted in cultural differences separating from the start the Greek East from the Latin West.[17]

The Roman roots of Roman Catholicism go back to the beginning. A strong Roman presence is visible already in the New Testament in the form of Roman officials who play key roles in the gospel story: Christ is judged by a Roman procurator of the troublesome Province of Judaea; there are Roman citizens among the early Christians in Acts (Paul was proud of his citizenship); and civil power is spoken of as "the things that are Caesar's." Yet, the early Christians thought of the community in terms of spiritual, not political, geography: Jews and Hellenes (that is, pagans), on the one side, "the saints" on the other, just as later Augustine would think of it as "the two cities," one squarely in this world, a city of changing empires, of shifting world centers, and one seated in both this and the world beyond and bound to endure in the everlasting center, the "Heavenly Jerusalem." "The two cities" constitute the ultimate and perennial superpower struggle for all Christians, with a very special kind of eschatological center transcending this world.

The "city of the saints," the "community" *(ekklesia)*, was organized in this sinful world about certain "great Churches" in cities of importance, founded by apostles: the Churches of Jerusalem, Smyrna, Ephesus, Corinth, Alexandria, and, after Peter moved there, the Church of Rome, enjoying, with Jerusalem, a place of honor.[18] It is probably fair to say that before the

---

(New York) is to be found, but drawing for "creative" talent on English hard rockers and rootless Central European geniuses, and on scientific and technical and financial talent from everywhere, while in the East, there is no pole of attraction left, the waning Moscovy, once pole of the northern Slavic Orthodox world, "the New Rome," and then of its bastard child, the Communist world, inspires no one anymore, and no longer serves even as common enemy for the Orthodox.

16. Yves Congar, *Neuf cents ans après: Notes sur le schisme oriental* (After nine hundred years: The background of the schism between the Eastern and Western Churches [1959; Westport, Conn.: Greenwood, 1978]) (Paris: Éditions de Chèvetogne, 1954). This small book was very helpful in preparing this section.

17. Will Christianity, which is being shaken by the galloping secularization brought on by the HTX, succeed in evangelizing the planetary, secular, high-technology urban culture now in the process of achieving at least a superficial pulling together of mankind? That is at present the central missionary issue for Christians. As we contemplate the earlier cultural growing apart, we should look at it with that question in mind.

18. The Orthodox developed, rather late, the idea of the five apostolic patriarchates. The idea of the Pentarchy, of "the five-fold strength of the Church," five patriarchates of apostolic foundation—Jerusalem, Antioch, Alexandria, and the two Romes—is traced by F. Dvornik in *The Idea of Apostolicity in Byzantium and the Legend of the Apostle Andrew* (Cambridge: Harvard University Press, 1958) to the laws of Justinian (266–67). According to George Every it was most clearly defined in the so-called Eighth Ecumenical Council in 869 (A. M. Allchin et al., eds., *Misunderstandings between East and West*, vol. 4 of *Ecumenical Studies in History* [London: Lutterworth Press, 1965], 54).

emergence of the full, clear sense of the role of Rome, recognized from the start as having some preeminence because of being the Church of Peter and Paul, the structure of the early Church rather resembled the later structure of the Constantinian orthodox East.[19]

Any effort to describe fundamental differences in mentality between the Romans and the biblical Orientals of what today we call "the Near East" risks reading later characteristics into people of earlier times. Suffice it to say that there were at least these clear important differences from the start: the Roman aptitude for administrative organization, law, and military technique eventually made its way into the Roman Church in the form of a strong tendency to centralized government, while an Oriental sense of the different nations (perhaps just a trace of tribalism remaining) affected the Eastern Churches, which emphasized and jealously guarded the autonomy of the local Church.[20] (The sense of a profound eucharistic *communio* [*sobornost*, as the Russian mystical writers would call it], a bond in the Holy Spirit working through the liturgical-eucharistic life of the Church, is a much later, post-sixteenth-century development within Orthodoxy.)

Further, as the Church grew up in the shadow of the pagan Roman Imperium, it developed the reflexes necessary to guard its distance from the state. So long as the government was hostile to the Church this was automatic. The problem of how the Church institution should relate to the secular power became acute only when Constantine decided "if you can't beat 'em, join 'em," intending to use the Church as an instrument of state power.[21] (The Church-state problem, as Eric Voegelin emphasized, will never be solved, but only redefined in every epoch, reflecting as it does man's situation in the metaxy, as Plato terms our being caught between nature and the transcending divine.)[22]

19. It is a curious fact that today, the Churches of the greatest Christian cities do not seem to weigh in heavily, at least not in our general consciousness. Some recognition comes in the Catholic Church in the form of awarding "the red hat" of cardinal almost certainly to the bishops of the greatest sees. And, especially when the cardinal sitting in the cathedral is a powerful and effective personality, certain great churches will assume an importance: the New York of O'Connor, the Paris of Lustiger, and perhaps the Cologne of Meissner overshadow even the Chicago of Bernadin and the Milan of Martini, at least in the sense of press coverage. And see what happened to the largest diocese in the world, São Paulo, which was recently broken up into four. Despite Rome's protestation to the contrary, the anti-Roman tendencies of Cardinal Evaristo Arns, almost everyone believes, was a factor.

20. In our time, the diaspora of so many peoples of Orthodox lands, due to Turkish and more recently Communist takeovers, has complicated enormously the now inter-national and dispersed structure of these national churches. With the fall of the Soviet Union, the resulting tensions are intensifying.

21. However sincere his personal conversion—that is impossible to judge.

22. Our nature forces Church-state problems upon us forever as surely as it opens es-chatological dimensions to our participation in Being. The Church-state metaxy tension provides, Voegelin claims, *the* prime motor of history. Only in today's secularized West is this elementary fact of human existence disguised through the apparent marginalization of religion. Closer scrutiny shows, however, in the virulence of debates over abortion

Until Constantine moved the capital to the East, the Oriental Churches enjoyed relative peace precisely because they were remote from the old center. But with a new Greek capital and the rising state-encouraged power of the ecumenical patriarch, the local churches of the East acquired an awareness of their status in relation to the new power in Constantinople. There began a long period of complex relationships, ecumenical patriarchs sometimes struggling to avoid suffocation by imperial power, sometimes giving in, and the other patriarchs struggling to keep their distance from Constantinople. The picture became further complicated in the seventh century, as Jerusalem, Antioch, and Alexandria fell to the Muslims and Constantinople's power became remote. Autonomy (more correctly, autocephaly) achieved a final fullness after the fall of Constantinople to the Turks in A.D. 1453.

STRENGTHENING OF ROMAN PRIMACY IN THE WEST, WEAKENING IT IN THE EAST

The situation for the Western Churches was quite different. Accustomed to a growing power of the Roman See, the Western Christians—as far as we can tell, the evidence is not compelling—appear to have experienced favorable protection from the heavy hand of the secular power offered by the strong bishops and the pope.[23] With Africa and the East, however, things were not always smooth for the Roman pontiff, but the evidence, such as it is, points to the acceptance of serious papal claims to authority.[24]

"rights," bishops' castigation of political leaders for their moral stands, control of education, and so on, that the issues of the meaning of life and of man's relationship to the ultimate source of the cosmos are just barely below the surface. Nevertheless, I hesitate to follow Voegelin so far as to say the Church-state tension is *the* motor of history, because, with secularization having gone so far, and the obsessive pursuit of control through technique proving so all absorbing and so (apparently) "successful," with the discussion of the criteria of success becoming so neglected, I am not sure Church-state tension is the great motor in the West at this point. Where does one see much effective resistance to the slide into power-brokered hedonism in our modern societies, apart from the increasingly private initiatives of relatively small groups? How nihilistic must society become before the evil fruits overwhelm us and force a new raising of sights, a regeneration of the Church to the point where it might again become an effective competitor to the ever mightier state?

23. As far as we can see, Western Christians appear not to have resisted very much the growth of papal prestige in the period of the Christianization of the empire. There was the schism of Hippolytus, who broke with Pope Zephyrinus (who was in power from around A.D. 199 to 217) over Trinitarian formulations, but it was not a challenge to papal authority but rather to Zephyrinus's orthodoxy and hence his right to exercise it. Setting himself up against Zephyrinus's successor, Hippolytus had the dubious distinction of becoming the first anti-pope. Fortunately, this event ended in reconciliation.

24. For the relevant texts on papal authority, see E. Giles, ed., *Documents Illustrating Papal Authority, A.D. 96–454* (London: S.P.C.K., 1952), and B. J. Kidd, *The Roman Primacy to A.D. 461* (London: S.P.C.K., 1936).

When the estrangement of East and West reached the point where papal authority was seriously challenged in the Orient, the Orthodox began to claim that Constantinople shared equal moral status with Rome (compare the canons of A.D. 381 and 451), and, eventually, as the Greeks came to charge the popes with "heretical innovations," the Greeks finally claimed for Constantinople a moral superiority. After introducing this fact of the New Rome and considering the role of the great ecumenical councils, and of the later councils, we shall return to the question of the papacy and its further consolidation in reaction to this new form of authority.

THE DECISIVE MOMENT: THE EMPEROR CONSIDERS HIMSELF "SERVANT OF THE HIGHEST DEITY," A.D. 313

All historians agree that this, with the Protestant revolt of the sixteenth century, is the most fateful moment of change in the history of the Church since Pentecost, and perhaps the Council of Jerusalem, which allowed equality to non-Jews in the Church. It would not be exaggerated to say that with this act of co-option began that overcozy condominium of state power and Church authority, however inevitable it may have been in those times of decaying empire and advancing hordes of barbarians. This rendered almost inevitable a great explosion—(over a millennium in the making) that in the event took the form of the Protestant revolt to shake the intertwined social, political, cultural, and religious structures at their foundations—to rattle the rock and the apostolic foundation stones of Christ's edifice. So severe was the shock that it split European civilization, facilitating secularization.[25]

Constantine conceived of his role in the Church as much like that of the popes.[26] He called himself "brother of the bishops" and "bishop of those outside," that is, in Frend's words, "a sort of universal herald and propagandist for his faith."[27] He created or modified ecclesiastical territories, called councils (especially the great anti-Arian council of Nicaea), supervised and closed debates (we saw in Chapter 3 how under his close

25. It took almost until World War I to divest the Catholic Church of the heavy moral baggage of the Constantinian co-opting of the Church for political purposes. As we shall consider later, we are privileged to live in a new era in which the Church stands freer of compromising involvement with the state than at any time since the fourth century. Persecution from secularists and from Marxist governments can be intense—not subtle in the hands of Communists, often insidiously so in the hands of secularist liberals, yet it is probably healthier from a Christian perspective than having the state, in any form, use the Church for its (always thoroughly "this worldly") ends. In terms of world evangelization, this new freedom from involvement with the state is a great positive factor. Today the church (at last!) understands the unacceptability of constrained conversions, so the new life coming into the Church through those the Holy Spirit leads to it is a stream of unusually pure, revivifying water.

26. Amédée Gasquet, *De l'authorité impériale en matière religieuse à Byzance* (Paris, 1879), 117.

27. W. H. C. Frend, *The Rise of Christianity* (London: Darton, Longman, and Todd, 1984), 501. Frend cites Eusebius, *Life of Constantine*, 2:69, 4:24.

supervision Nicaea hammered out the crucial creedal formulation and at his suggestion included the key non-Scriptural term *homoousios*, "of one substance"); in short, he exercised authority jointly with the bishops.

Frend's wry comment about this radical change from *religio illicita* to being the central part of the organizing force of the empire is a bit overstated, but too close for comfort: "The ancient world had exchanged the guardianship of one set of divine masters, capricious but generally benevolent, for another that would brook no opposition. There were already signs that the church which had suffered persecution for so long would soon be persecuting its opponents."[28]

THE POPES REACT, AND THE
BISHOPS REACT TO THE REACTION

As successive popes became aware of the implications of this rapidly evolving situation, they sought to consolidate their position by now defining it explicitly, in the terms in which it was generally understood, at least in the West. For instance, Pope Julius I got the Council of Sardica in A.D. 342 to acknowledge that it is within the power of the pope to annul any decision of a bishop, indeed even of the entire episcopate together. (Today, popes enjoy no greater power than that.) This council was boycotted by the Eastern bishops, who never accepted its canons. The popes seized occasions to show their authority over the East. For example, Pope Innocent I continued to support Saint John Chrysostom after he was deposed as patriarch by the emperor, and refused communion with his successor so long as John was alive.

With all these institutional developments, the bishops found themselves faced with three challenges to their autonomy: that of the new Christian emperors; later, especially from the sixth century when they became so powerful, the patriarchs of Constantinople; and that of the increasingly assertive pontiffs in Rome. It is not surprising that a kind of episcopal backlash occurred: the latent tendencies in Eastern ecclesiology toward local autonomy became perhaps more self-conscious, the importance of the five traditional patriarchs (with Rome still acknowledged first in place of honor) was affirmed, and the need for episcopal consensus at councils was brought to the fore.

The importance suddenly assumed by the ecumenical councils was itself a complex and ambiguous phenomenon, and confronts us with perhaps the most startling institutional development in the Church's long history. And remember their strange origin: the idea of ecumenical councils was an imperial initiative. The imperial role gave an excuse, perhaps even a certain responsibility, for the Christian *basileus* to look out for the well-being of the Church. As we saw in considering the christological controversies, the councils were not, however, just an arbitrary invention created uniquely

---

28. Frend, *Rise of Christianity*, 505.

to enhance imperial power. They furnished a focus of unity and a forum within which emerged the role of the great fathers.

How, given the seriousness of the christological controversy, could an institutional initiative have been avoided, as something was clearly needed to strengthen the Church's hold on its teaching—some definition of dogma being required to resist the inroads of menacing heresy, a way had to be found to achieve this thinking-through and formulating? "God writes straight with crooked lines": the historian Frend opines that, all things considered, the emperors did the Church a service by convoking and leading the ecumenical councils that led to the formulation of the creed, the · backbone of Christian orthodoxy through a millennium of doctrinal stress.

Recall that participation by Oriental bishops in the great councils was generally in large numbers, especially considering the rigor of travel. Legates from the pope, representing the Western Church, were treated mostly with great respect, but this should not be taken as any weakening of the bishops' awareness of their joint power to decide doctrinal matters for the whole Church. While such councils were a new governing feature of the Church (there were regional councils before, within the East and West), they played a key role for a restricted period of only about two centuries. No medieval council had the significance in forging the tradition that Nicaea and Chalcedon enjoyed.[29]

There are serious voices within the Church today who, in the interest of East-West reunification, would soften the Roman stand that its later great councils—sixteenth-century Trent and the two recent Vatican councils—are unqualifiedly ecumenical. When the Church again had recourse to the Great Council of Trent and the councils of 1870 and 1962, Vatican Councils I and II, it was, the Orthodox would say, the Roman Catholic Church that convoked them. Because the Roman pontiff claims to speak in the name of the Church universal, the "Roman Catholic Church" considers them not "Roman" in some restrictive sense but genuinely ecumenical. Representatives of the Eastern Orthodox Church were in attendance at Vatican II, but only as respected observers. Yet the fathers—Western bishops and a few "Uniate" Eastern-rite bishops—claimed to speak in the name of the whole Church.

While the Orthodox Churches could not accept that these councils were ecumenical, nevertheless out of the Second Vatican Council (with the East and the most important Protestant Churches at least represented by honored observers) came promising gestures of solidarity between Rome and Constantinople, culminating in an event that had not occurred since the Council of Florence in 1438: the meeting and praying together of the patriarch Athenagoras and Pope Paul VI on June 6, 1964, in Jerusalem, the one

29. Even the important Fourth Lateran Council of 1215 is no exception. While intended by Pope Innocent III to have ecumenical status, the fact that it lasted only three days during which the fathers could do little more than merely assent to a mass of legislation laid before them gave it little decisiveness in determining the course of the tradition. One matter, however, did have important doctrinal consequences: the definition of transubstantiation.

reading in Latin the other in Greek Jesus' prayer in John 17, and leading, in 1965, to the mutual lifting of "anathemas."[30] The patriarch generously expressed the hope that the day would come when pope and patriarch could concelebrate the Eucharist.[31]

Without a doubt, the earlier ecumenical councils played an important role in the clarification of structures and definition of roles within the Church, but the situation remains confusing. Two points are important regarding them. First, none of the great councils was *unqualifiedly* ecumenical. All were gatherings of significant numbers of bishops, sometimes several hundred. But no Eastern bishops came to Sardica because Athanasius was there, after being banned by a valid council (in A.D. 342–343); at all the others either only papal legates or at most eight or ten Western bishops were present.

Second, Rome often refused to accept administrative canons of these councils (and the East refused those of the "Western" Council of Sardica). But the creed and the christological formulations of Chalcedon in A.D. 451 were accepted as definitive and canonical by Rome and, once the Arians were defeated, by the entire Western Church.

Confusing indeed! East and West seemed agreed that ecumenical conciliar decisions were binding, but the West added after Sardica that the pope may override a council decision. Yet, it was not clear what constituted

30. Few Orthodox and Catholics seem to be aware that there no longer exists any mutual excommunications between the Eastern and Western Churches.

31. Fathers Louis Bouyer and Yves Congar, "ecumenists" both, believe that all great councils (West and East) held since the split should be considered general councils, not full-fledged ecumenical ones. Pope Paul VI himself used the expression "Sixth General Synod of the Western Church" apropos of the Second Council of Lyons in 1274. These general councils enjoy, in the view of Bouyer and Congar, great authority, and as the Churches come back to full union, each should accept provisionally the decisions of the other, approaching them with a positive disposition, but with the understanding that further defining will have to occur cooperatively, where necessary (Congar, *Diversités et communion* (Diversity and communion, trans. John Bowden [London: SCM, 1984]) (Paris: Cerf, 1982), 139–40. As things look now, I would opine that if ever there is to be union between the Orthodox and Rome, the positions outlined in the two Vatican councils will largely have to be accepted by all. If I am correct in this, then those councils will have proved binding on the whole Church. But who can tell whether, diplomatically, coming to treat them as "general synods of the Western Church," or whatever, will pave the way to such unification?

The Church, both Western and Eastern, has changed administrative structures—often dramatically—as demanded by differing epochal situations, without weakening its continuity as the catholic, apostolic Church. How does one today distinguish good change from bad—diremptive—change, unless he improves his understanding of what is mandated by Christ (and so should not be weakened), distinguishing this from what is subsequent fruit of experience and so may be prudently changed, and staying on the alert for changes that prove weakening to the Church's ability to penetrate whole cultures and offer to individuals the Christ-given means to sanctification. (In a later chapter, I shall cite in some detail the already mentioned recent speech of Cardinal Ratzinger in which he says this in clearest terms, and pleads for the need to clarify the essential and not hang on to outmoded structures.)

an ecumenical council, although East and West accepted some decisions of several councils that were dominated by the East. Later, at the Fourth Lateran (in 1215) and at Trent (from 1545 to 1563), and in recent times at the two Vatican councils, the popes convened them, and the councils themselves affirmed the popes' right to convene, preside over, and ratify councils—a position not accepted in the East. But that was long after the schism was complete.

And then there is another factor: the East has not attempted to mount an ecumenical council since the schism occurred, although some important regional councils have been convened. Generally, the Orthodox prefer to emphasize the ecumenical councils of the fifth to seventh centuries as the foundation of Orthodox doctrine and practice.[32]

Differences in the way the Church East and West was structured became more accentuated with time, especially the stress in the East on the autonomy of local Churches, coupled with the importance of synods, regional councils, and, later, ecumenical councils, and by contrast in the West the emphasis on authority descending from a strong center. Political differences were accentuated by the radically different experiences of the two empires. The East, embattled by a virulent Islam, succeeded in staying relatively culturally "pure" because Constantinople continued to enjoy continuity with classical civilization. In the West, absorption of Germanic tribes contributed to cultural decline. This was the beginning of those centuries of social and political dislocation later historians somewhat unfairly called the Dark Ages in which the papacy and bishops remained beacons of classical culture during a long period of difficult gestation that was to produce that Latino-Celtic-Germanic culture that later historians, again questionably, were to term the Middle Ages.

The rise of the patriarchate of the New Rome and its growing pretensions and close alliance with Eastern imperial power intensified the estrangement of Eastern and Western Churches. This is visible already in the texts of the First Council of Constantinople in 381 and then Chalcedon in 451. Canon 3 of Constantinople declares that the bishop of Constantinople has primacy of rank after the bishop of Rome, because Constantinople is the New Rome. Canon 28 of Chalcedon states:

> It is quite proper that the Fathers have, in effect, attributed to the see of the Old Rome the prerogatives which belong to it, because that city is where the basileus

32. Since the early 1970s, preparations, painfully slow and complex, for an ecumenical council bringing together all the Eastern churches has been under way. At this writing, it is impossible to say whether they will succeed within our lifetime in actually getting such a council together. In November 1995, however, the ecumenical patriarch did succeed in bringing together all the patriarchs, save one: the patriarch of Moscow, who boycotted the meeting because of his anger over the ecumenical patriarch's intervention in Estonia in favor of the Orthodox there who were resisting Moscow's authority. Indeed, for about three months Moscow was in open schism from Constantinople, the Russians refusing to pray for the ecumenical patriarch in the liturgy. At the present writing, that ban has been lifted and an uneasy peace restored.

reigns. Moved by the same consideration the hundred-fifty bishops who are God's friends have accorded equal prerogatives to the very holy see of New Rome, esteeming rightly that the city honored by the presence of the basileus and of the senate and enjoying equal prerogatives with those of the old imperial Rome should also ascend in ecclesiastical dignity, holding second place after old Rome.

In papal eyes this is a bad reason. Papal prerogatives stem not from the honor due Rome as an imperial city but from the succession of Peter, who settled in Rome.[33] The reaction of Pope Saint Leo to this twenty-eighth canon minced no words: *"In irritum mittimus et per autoritatem B. Petri apostoli, generali prorsus definitione cassamus,"* that is, "We make void and by the authority of the blessed Apostle Peter we annul by an absolutely universal definition." The pope vigorously attacked the principle associating ecclesial power with civil: "Nevertheless one reason has to do with worldly matters, the other with divine; except for that rock which the Lord has placed as a foundation, no building will be stable."[34]

Rome was never comfortable with the preeminent position of the ecumenical patriarch, second to only the pope, although basically it was grudgingly accepted, nor with the close alliance of the supreme ecclesiastical authority to the state. On the other hand, there is no evidence that the East accepted the strong Western sense of papal supremacy, or Western reasons for it. Peter's preeminence, the East would eventually argue, was due to his correct confession of Christ, and stemmed from Christ's recognition of his orthodoxy. Hence it is apostolic: "sent forth" are all those chosen and recognized by Christ as able to spread the true message. A certain preeminence came to be accorded Rome among the apostolic sees because it was the capital. Its bishops since Peter have been defenders of orthodoxy, and so deference was due them.[35] No great Eastern father expostulates on the Petrine claims. The East seems never to have conceived of Rome's position as anything stronger than that of "une première instance d'ordre ecclésiastique et canonique," a first instance of ecclesiastical and canonical order, as Congar expresses it. Monsignor Batiffol exclaims: "What a pity that so fundamental a point was not settled upon by a full discussion and an Ecumenical council during the centuries when one was still united!"[36]

In J. Michael Miller's recent study of the papacy, which was such help in an earlier chapter, a stronger sense of the appeal to Rome emerges, although

33. Catholics see no problem in papal succession because of the Avignon captivity, when for fifty years the popes were forced by the French kings to reside in Provence. If ever again the cardinals obliged to elect successors to Peter are forced to reside outside of Rome, the validity of the succession and the primacy of the See will not be at issue, it will be understood as "in exile."

34. *Epistle CV* to the Empress Pulcheria, 22 May 452 (PL 54:1000); *Epistle CIV* to the Emperor Marcian, 22 May 452 (PL 54:999–1000).

35. Pelikan, *The Christian Tradition: A History of the Development of Doctrine* (Chicago: University of Chicago Press, 1976), 147, 148–70.

36. Congar, *Diversités et communion*, 66; Batiffol, *Cathedra Petri (Unam Sanctam 4)* (Paris, 1938), 76.

Miller agrees with the Lutheran Pelikan that the East interpreted this not as jurisdictional supremacy but as exemplary orthodoxy on the part of Rome. "By the end of the fourth century many Byzantines admitted that the Roman bishop received from God the grace to uphold and pass on undefiled the truth of the gospel." Rome, therefore, enjoyed authority, "a weight of faith more than of powers," comments Tillard, "of example in witness more than jurisdiction." Due to dissension (on Trinitarian and christological matters), the leaders of both orthodox and heterodox factions sought the support and approbation of the Roman See. The advance of the Arian heresy in the fourth century led many Eastern theologians to take refuge in Roman orthodoxy. In desperation, bishops like Saint Basil (who died in 379) and Saint Gregory of Nazianzus (who died in 389) sent letters to Pope Damasus (pope from 366 to 384) acknowledging that God had given him an unswerving steadfastness in protecting the truth. They pleaded that he send envoys who would help them to restore orthodoxy and peace in the East. Later, Theoderet of Cyr (who died in 466) appealed to Pope Leo: "If Paul, the herald of truth, the trumpet of the Holy Spirit, had recourse to the great Peter in order to obtain a decision from him concerning those at Antioch (Acts 15:1–35), much more do we, small humble folk, run to the apostolic throne to get healing from you for the woes of the churches."[37]

Miller also recalls the *Libellus Hormisdae*, signed by the Eastern bishops to end the Acacian schism in 519.

> We cannot pass over in silence the affirmations of our Lord Jesus Christ, "You are Peter, and upon this Rock I will build my Church." . . . These words are verified by the facts. It is in the apostolic see that the Catholic religion has always been preserved without blemish. . . . That is why I hope I shall remain in communion with the apostolic see in which is found the whole, true and perfect stability of the Christian religion. (PG 63:460)[38]

In his dispute with the Monothelites, Saint Maximus the Confessor looked for help to the power of the keys of Peter (PG 63:460). Theodore of Studios wrote the emperor: "If there is anything in the Patriarch's reply about which you feel doubt or disbelief . . . you may ask the chief elder in Rome for clarification, as has been the practise from the beginning according to inherited tradition."[39] Later, Theodore wrote that the Roman See had been, "from the beginning until now, by the very Providence of God, the one and only help in recurrent crises . . . the pure and genuine source of orthodoxy . . . the distinct calm harbor for the whole church from every heretical storm" (PG 99:1159).

37. Basil, letter, 70, PG 32:433–36 (PG here and hereafter refers to *Patrilogia Graecorum*); Basil et al., letter, 92, PG 32:477–84; Basil, letter, 242, PG 32:900–901; Theoderet of Cyr's translation in Thomas Halton, *The Church: Message of the Fathers of the Church*, vol. 4 (Wilmington: Michael Glazier, 1985), 109.

38. Miller, *The Shepherd and the Rock: Origins, Development, and Mission of the Papacy* (Huntington, Ind.: Our Sunday Visitor, 1995), 126.

39. Quoted by Miller, *Shepherd*, 126.

The two parts managed to coexist for a long time, despite the East's not taking seriously the West's conviction about the supreme apostolic, jurisdictional power coming from Peter, and Western distrust of the Oriental tendency toward an imperial Church ruled by canonical devices more or less dependent on the *basileus*. As Congar says, "a modus vivendi was established." Part of this was a tacit acceptance of a tripartite exercise of papal power, as Monsignor Batiffol sees it:

1. the zone immediately subject to Rome *(une zone suburbicaire);*
2. the Occidental zone, beyond the part of Italy directly controlled by the Pope; and
3. the universal zone, which included the orient, in which Rome intervened only as arbiter of the universal communion and judge of Causae majores.[40]

Thus, the pope in Eastern eyes plays three complementary roles. He is bishop of Rome, patriarch of the Latin Church (with a hold over the West that rapidly grew to be much stronger than the patriarch in Constantinople ever had over the Eastern Churches), and successor to Peter, with a universal role, acknowledged everywhere in the East for a long period.

This coexistence lasted, with its ups and downs, through the early Middle Ages at least.[41] Could some sort of minimal unity have endured past the twelfth century, had there been more goodwill and understanding on each side? At that point—with the Western barbarians of the Fourth Crusade sacking Constantinople not helping much—the remaining unity all but evaporated in a volley of mutual excommunications (although the break was not definitively consummated, some argue, until the fall of Constantinople in 1453).[42] Given the differing interpretations of papal primacy that reach back to the time of Constantine, and the different nature of Church-state relations in East and West, it seems unlikely the split could have been avoided.

Before leaving the subject here, however, it would be a good idea for us Westerners to try to appreciate the strengths of the Eastern Church's much looser structure. We tend to think of it, without looking into it much, simply as a weakness. Pelikan analyzes the Eastern arrangement:

40. Congar, *Diversités et communion*, 55; Batiffol, *Cathedra Petri*, 41–59.

41. The powerful patriarch Photius, in the council of 861, appears to have understood Roman primacy in the terms of this modus vivendi: administrative and canonical autonomy of the local churches under regulation by the universal Church, ensured by the canonical primacy of Rome. This was exercised through appeals to Rome and judgment of the pope and his legates in canonical debates in the Orient. This is how Congar summarizes the analyses of Fr. Dvornik (cf. Congar, *Diversités et communion*, 68).

42. Some argue that a kind of remnant of unity, a sort of *laisser aller*, with Latin-rite churches being allowed to operate in Greek lands, and no definitive act of anathema having been taken, as the pope had died and the licence of the papal legates had expired, so their anathemas were not binding, lasted until the fall of Constantinople. This is argued, for instance, by Every (*Misunderstandings between East and West*, 54).

The relations of these autocephalous churches with each other are determined by a kind of hierarchy of honor, headed by the Ecumenical Patriarch of Constantinople as *primus inter pares*. This system has the great advantage of being elastic. It permits autocephalous churches to be founded, abolished, then re-established again in the course of history without affecting the entire organization of the Church. Moreover, the absence of any binding centralized authority permits the various hierarchies of the churches today to adopt different political attitudes without rupturing the doctrinal and sacramental bonds of unity. When conditions become more propitious, the leaders can once again establish more cordial relations, without too much difficulty. The disadvantages of the system, however, are equally obvious. Independent by right and in fact, the autocephalous churches are too inclined to live in isolation from each other, they are unable to take any common action effectively, and they lack a common system for the training of the clergy.[43]

DOCTRINAL DIFFERENCES

It is hard to separate the question of substantial doctrinal differences dividing the Eastern and Western Churches from differences in style of theologizing growing out of and reinforcing distinctive ecclesiological and cultural experience (political dimensions included).

When one listens today to the complaints of the most negative Orthodox critics of Western Christianity, such as Christos Yannaras, what one hears is something much more sweeping than complaints about Catholic theology.[44] It is, rather, a universal condemnation of Western society, rationalistic, technological, the anti-God secularization of which has its remotest roots, according to him, in theological errors already perpetrated by Augustine.

The Christians of the East find the essential of the true (the Orthodox) tradition in the fathers and the ecumenical councils. They tend to be leery of too much use of philosophy to draw new conclusions from the old doctrines.[45] Always aware of God's essential unknowability, they have a liking for "apophatasism," the negative way, the need to be ever aware that our theological constructions can never capture the unfathomable reality of God. "It is a thought more at ease in synthesis than analysis. Symbol plays a great role. Despite the excesses of Saint Augustine, in general the West

43. Pelikan, *Christian Tradition*, 2:169.

44. See, for instance, Yannaras, "Orthodoxy and the West," *Eastern Churches Review* 3 (1971): 286–300; and "Scholasticism and Technology," ibid., 6 (1974): 162–69. I am grateful to Rev. Robert Barringer, C.S.B., for these indications of modern Orthodox criticism of the Western Church.

45. Recall, however, that the fathers use philosophy extensively and the fathers of the great ecumenical councils did not hesitate to accept the emperor's suggestion of the use of a philosophical distinction to formulate the relation of the two natures of Christ. There may be truth in the accusation of a greater strain of rationalism in the West leading to its invention of the Western sciences and technology. But it is also the case that during the period of the most intense modernization in the West, the Orthodox lands lay under the dominance of either the Turks, or a tyrannical czar, or, later, Leninist communism. Finally, it should not be forgotten that this modernization did not bring only an exaggerated secularization but many advances in civic freedom and a more prosperous life.

theologized in much the same manner until the eleventh century (Gregorian reform—the first scholasticism being the big turning point)."[46]

There is no "magisterium" in the East, no collection of authoritative magisterial teaching, like Denziger, *Enchiridion Symbolorum—Manual of Creeds, Definitions and Declarations on Matters of Faith and Morals,* begun in 1854 and continuing today. Many Orthodox see in such a phenomenon a symptom at once of that overrationalization and tendency to impose systematically an exterior authority that they believe sins against the spirit and shows a lack of *sobornost.*[47]

In the pivotal issue of papal authority in the definition of doctrine, while the East, as we saw, tended for the first six hundred years to see the popes as bastions of orthodoxy during the theological controversies, they later considered Rome to be deviating. Earlier the only blemish was the naive monotheletism (the doctrine of but one will in Christ) of Pope Honorius that proved an embarrassment to those who hold papal infallibility.[48] Later, say by the twelfth century, as the *filioque* phrase crept into the credo in the West and was endorsed by popes, opponents of papal authority to define doctrine could point at last to that "innovation." Many in the East found such innovation fundamentally wrong.

The *Filioque* Dispute: The West's Version

The *filioque* dispute remains at the center of the East's theological objections to what the Western Church holds, not only because it is an addition to the otherwise universally accepted creed but also because, touching on the very nature of the Trinitarian life of God, it molds how one views the life of the Spirit in the Church.[49]

The Nicaean creed says the Spirit proceeds from the Father. The first Latin theologian of stature, Tertullian, had spoken of the Spirit as "from nowhere else than from the Father through the Son" and elsewhere of "the Spirit from God and the Son."[50] The theologian who made the issue prominent, quoted in Augustine's *De Trinitate,* was Hilary of Poitiers (who lived from around 315 to 367), who spoke of the Spirit as "proceeding from Father and Son."

The point was critical to Augustine's theory of the Trinity, since "the three persons are distinguished from one another solely through the functions that pertain to each in relation to the other two, the 'procession from the

46. Congar, *Diversités et communion,* 105–6.

47. *Communio,* as experienced among the Eastern Churches.

48. Pelikan, *Christian Tradition,* 150ff.

49. Many readers of this volume will be, I hope, neither theologians nor philosophers. As the next three sections are inevitably quite theological, they may want to skip them.

50. Tertullian, *Against Praxeas,* 4.1 (CCSL 2:1162), and 8.7 (CCSL 2:1168), quoted in Pelikan, *Christian Tradition,* 188. For a concise, insightful summary of the complex history of the *filioque* controversy from a "Roman" source, see Hans Urs von Balthasar, *Theologik III: Der Geist der Wahrheit* (Einsiedeln: Johannes Verlag, 1987), 189–91.

Father and the Son' is regarded by him as the specific property of the Holy Spirit within the immanent essence of God."[51] The Spirit is the *Spiritus* of the Son, Christ working in the world, just as much as He is Spirit of the Father. The West saw the procession from the Father and from (or through) the Son as both a protection against Adoptionism (if Christ, because of His love of the Father, is a source of the Spirit He cannot be reduced to a human divinized by the Spirit) and a way of explaining the unity of God, because it provided a functional relationship of the three hypostases within the one being of God.

The Setting of the East's Response: Eastern Spirituality

The East saw in the *filioque* a confusion between the theology of God and the economy of the coming into the world of Christ and the Spirit. The West confused, because of the imprecisions of Latin, the proceeding of the Spirit from the one Source with His being sent into the world. The latter does indeed occur through the Son.[52] There is a distinctive Eastern spirituality behind this insistence.

Contrasting (Complementary?) Spiritualities of East and West

It is difficult to capture in a few words some feeling for "the characteristic spirituality" of the East in contrast with that of the West. To begin with, there exists a multiplicity of traditions in the East as in the West, hence many spiritualities. But there are some generic traits. It is in any event hard to analyze something as living and synthesizing as a spirituality, and then to invoke poetically a feel for what one thinks he has found. Finally, each of these living traditions changes; for instance, charges brought against the "scholastic theology of the West" by the orthodox theologian Schmemann lose some of their force after the Second Vatican Council, which absorbed *la nouvelle théologie* with its profound *resourcement* from the Greek fathers.[53] The Catholic Church today is not nearly as "Neo-scholastic" as it was as recently as the 1950s. The problem comes to a head when one presents, as some writers do, late-medieval and even modern developments in one of these subtraditions as though they represented the very essence of *the*

---

51. K. F. Nösgen, *Geschichte der Lehre vom Heiligen Geiste* (Gütersloh, 1899), 87, quoted in Pelikan, *Christian Tradition,* 189.

52. Pelikan, *Christian Tradition,* 193.

53. See, for instance, Alexander Schmemann, *The Eucharist* (Crestwood, N.Y.: St. Vladimir's Seminary Press, 1988), 27–39. This great and deeply spiritual Orthodox theologian gives in this book almost no credit to the reforms leading up to and consolidated by the Second Vatican Council. I find this lack of generosity, bordering on distortion, a distressing sign of what strikes me often as almost a will to maintain separation by many Orthodox. While the Catholic Church may often prove insensitive to Eastern concerns and can run roughshod politically over their turf, I do not find hostility to Orthodox insight; on the contrary, there is a great awakening in the West, led by the present pope himself, to "the other lung by which the Church breathes."

West's or *the* East's spirituality. That is just what Vladimir Lossky, for instance, does. It is important to remember this when we avail ourselves of his brilliant little book. Recognizing that the spirituality of Saint Gregory Palamas, so influential on Lossky, dates from revival of his work in recent times more than it is an ongoing vast influence in Eastern traditions, we can still obtain some feel for the East-West difference from Lossky's brave effort to summarize.[54]

The East's concentration on the inexpressibility of the mystery of God, and the Oriental predilection for a "monarchic" and hence hierarchical sense of the Trinity, with descent from the Father overshadowing the reciprocity of relations, is why the East prefers the "apophantic" way, emphasizing the negation of the anthropomorphic qualities we predicate of God as well as the need for a complete "superlative" transformation of the ordinary sense of even our most sublime predicates. The internal, majestic, eternal life of God is not something we can ever spell out in clear philosophical terms—which is just what some modern Orthodox claim the Western fathers, notably Augustine and Thomas, attempted to do.[55]

The highest point of revelation, the dogma of the Holy Trinity, is, Lossky says, preeminently an antimony. To attain to the contemplation of this primordial reality in all its fullness, it is necessary to reach the goal that it set before us, to attain to the state of deification; for, in the words of Gregory Nazianzen, "they will be welcomed by the ineffable light, and the vision of the holy and sovereign Trinity uniting themselves wholly to the

---

54. Vladimir Lossky, *The Mystical Theology of the Eastern Church*, trans. from the French by members of the Fellowship of St. Alban and St. Sergius (Crestwood, N.Y.: St. Vladimir's Seminary Press, 1976). We should also remember that until the birth of ecumenical interests in the last decades, the East has been largely ignorant of the theology of the great Western fathers. Augustine, for instance, was first translated into Greek in only the fourteenth century, and was never much studied in the East. Augustine was translated by Demetrius Cydones, who also translated much of Thomas Aquinas (see G. Ostrogorsky, *History of the Byzantine State*, trans. from the German by Joan Hussey [Oxford: Blackwell, 1956], 421f).

55. Their defenders can show these saints were ever explicitly aware of God's majesty and transcendence. And with the *resourcement* of *la nouvelle théologie*, the return to the fathers, the sense of the transcendent majesty is reinforced. But at the same time, the West remains sensitive to the active presence of God in us through His love. The conclusion of Hans Urs von Balthasar's seventeen-volume trilogy shows how transcendence and immanence go together: he ends his long book on the Holy Spirit with two pages on "the invisible Father," and concludes his entire trilogy with this statement: " . . . *wir durch des Herrlichkeit des Sohnes hindurch den Abgrund der Liebesherrlichkeit des unsichtbaren Vaters erscheinen sehen, und dies in der Doppelgestalt des Heiligen Geistes der Liebe, indem wir, als aus dem Geist Geborene, im Feurer der Liebe existieren, in der Vater und Sohn sich begegnen, und damit, zusammen mit dem Geist, gleichzeitig auch die Zeugen und Verherrlicher dieser Liebe sind. . . .*" ("Through the glory of the Son we see shine forth the abyss of the Love-Glory of the invisible Father, and this in the two-fold form of the Holy Spirit of love, in whom we, as born out of the Spirit, existing in the fire of love, in the Father and Son encountering one another, are thereby, together with the Spirit, simultaneously the witnesses and the glorifiers of this love" [*Theologik III*, 410]).

whole Spirit; wherein alone and beyond all else I take it that the Kingdom of Heaven consists."[56]

The apophantic way, accessible only through personal sanctification, does not leave us in the meantime in an utter emptiness, for the unknowable God of the Christian is not the impersonal God of the philosophers. It leads to the Holy Trinity, "super-essential, more than divine and more than good." It is to this Trinity that the Author of the Mystical Theology commends Himself in entering upon the way that is to bring Him to a presence and a fullness that are without measure.[57] While I do not mean to erect Lossky as the spokesman for the East, I find his expression of the *filioque,* as the East understands it, the clearest I have found. Because we should hear this as an Easterner experiences it, I shall paraphrase him closely.

The position of the Greek fathers has always been that the Father is the unifying principle of the Trinity, Head and Source of the other two persons, of their generation and procession, and of the relations between them that uniquely characterize them. Hence, the *filioque* phrase causes one of two erroneous views of the Father: either that there are two principles of Godhead, the Father and the Son, or that the common nature of all three is responsible for the unity and relations. Either is contradictory to traditional Eastern belief. The Eastern sense is seen in Athanasius's discussion of a saying of Dionysus of Alexandria: we extend the monad indivisibly into the triad, and conversely we recapitulate the triad without diminution into the monad. And, there is a single principle of the Godhead, whence there is strictly a monarchy. The saying "a single God because a single Father" signifies the Eastern view that there is no priority of either persons or nature, but they are a whole, all possessing the Father's nature.[58]

In another place, Lossky expresses what may be his real grief with the Western approach—its "rationalism": By the dogma of the *filioque* the God of the philosophers and savants is introduced into the place of the Living God, and takes the place of the *"Deus Absconditus," qui ponit tenebras latibulum suum.* The Unknowable Essence of the Father, the Son and the Holy Spirit, receives positive qualifications. It becomes the subject of a natural theology, concerned with God in general, who may be the God of Descartes, or the God of Leibniz, or even perhaps, to some extent, the God of Voltaire. The manuals of theology will begin with a demonstration of His existence, thence to deduce, from the simplicity of His essence, the mode in which the perfections found in creation are to be attributed to this eminently simple essence. From His attributes they will go on to a discussion of what He can or cannot do, if He is not to contradict Himself, and is to remain true to His essential perfection. Later on, in a last chapter about the relation of the essence, which does not remove its simplicity, a fragile

56. Nazianzen, 1:1 (PG 3:997).
57. Lossky, *Mystical Theology,* 42–43 n. 241, 58–59.
58. *De setentiae Dionysii,* 17 (PG 25:505); *Contra Arianos,* Oratio 4.1 (PG 26:468); Lossky, *Mystical Theology,* 59.

bridge between the God of the philosophers and the God of revelation will be built.[59]

In the Orthodox view, according to Lossky, Christ is seen uniquely in and through the Church, and always in the fullness of Godhead, even in death, and in His emptying of Himself. To see this at all, one must be enabled by the Spirit. Christ has no other proper aspect than that of a person of the Trinity. The "historical Jesus," whom anyone may see, is not as full a revelation as the one who conquered death, rose again, and is now in heaven, and who could be seen by only those endowed with faith. The "cult of the humanity of Christ" lacks the full revelation of His deity as it was seen in the Transfiguration.[60] Hence, Easterners have not followed the way of "the imitation of Christ's humanity"; one is conformed to Christ by receiving the grace given by the Spirit, not by external imitation. So Eastern saints have never had stigmata,[61] but have frequently seemed "transfigured" by an inward light of grace.[62]

The accent in this spirituality then is *monastic:* the search for divinization, deification by bathing in the divine light. (We can see now why the Eastern liturgy, bathed in light, candles everywhere reflecting off the gold of the icons, with repeated chants for what seems like hours, strives for this feeling of transfiguration.) Christ is the "light that has come into the World." On the nature of God as light, Lossky refers to Saint Macarius of Egypt, who likens grace to a fire lit in Christian souls by the Spirit, visible to Jesus. This fire is given in proportion to the human will; so, some fires burn brightly, some faintly. It gives light to and tests souls. The apostles' experience at Pentecost, Paul's on the road to Damascus, Moses' with the burning bush, and Elijah's with the fiery chariot were all encounters with this light. This fire expels demons and destroys sin. It is the power of the Resurrection, the reality of eternal life, the enlightenment of holy souls, the strengthening of the rational powers.[63] "God is called light," says Saint Gregory Palamas, "not with reference to His essence, but to His energy," by which is meant His external activity on and in the world.[64] (There is no nature separate from grace; nature is redeemed, transformed Christic-eucharistic nature, as Schmemann would put it.)

In another passage, Lossky brings together his earlier reflections on the dogmatic difference over the procession of the divine persons with the

59. Lossky, *Mystical Theology,* 59.

60. Western theologians will certainly take issue with this. For a von Balthasar, for instance, in the human being Jesus of Nazareth we have before us the perfect *Imago et Similtudo Dei,* because this Jesus is, from His conception, fully God, and hence the full Word of God, inexhaustible icon.

61. Stigmata are the marks of the wounds of Jesus Christ. The most famous saint to receive this mysterious mark was Francis of Assisi.

62. John Meyendorff, *The Orthodox Church: Its Past and Its Role in the World Today* (New York: Pantheon, 1962), 144–45.

63. Saint Macarius of Egypt, *Spiritual Homilies,* 5.8, 12.14, 15.9, 15.10 (PG 32:513, 565, 673).

64. Palamas, *Contra Akindynum* (PG 150:823); Lossky, *Mystical Theology,* 219–20.

christological difference, capturing the overall sense of what separates the two spiritualities: "The Western is more engaged in the world, and hence suffers from the world's lack of sanctification, the Eastern goes more directly for the transfiguring Light of divinity. Both the heroic attitude of the great saints of Christendom, a prey to the sorrow of a tragic separation from God, and the dark night of the soul considered as a way, a spiritual necessity, are unknown in the spirituality of the Eastern Church."[65]

Just how differently do East and West view the Spirit, source of holiness? According to Lossky, the two conceptions correspond to two different experiences of sanctification, the West's arising through fidelity to the darkness of Gethsemane, the East's through union with God in the Transfiguration. This simple distinction blurs the subtlety both ways can evince, Lossky warns, and the existence in both traditions of saints who cannot be thus characterized—for example, Saint Bernard in the West, and Saint Tikhon Zadonsky from the eighteenth century in the East—is a warning to us not to oversimplify or not to harden the difference too much.[66]

Another influential Orthodox theologian, Alexander Schmemann, points, as a protection against a Western tendency to explain mysteries too rationalistically, to the need for a profound sense of symbol in the Orthodox tradition:

> In the final analysis the true and original symbol is inseparable from faith, for faith is "the evidence of things unseen" (Heb. 11:1), the knowledge that there is another reality different from the "empirical" one, and that this reality can be entered, can be communicated, can in truth become "the most real of realities." Therefore, if the symbol presupposes faith, faith of necessity requires the symbol. For, unlike "convictions," philosophical "points of view," etc., faith certainly is contact and a thirst for contact, embodiment and a thirst for embodiment: it is the manifestation, the presence, the operation of one reality within the other. All of this is the symbol (from *sumballo*, "unite," "hold together"). In it—unlike the simple "illustration," simple sign, and even in the sacrament in its scholastic-rationalistic "reduction"—the empirical (or "visible") and the spiritual (or "invisible") are united not logically (this "stands for" that), nor analogically (this "illustrates" that), but epiphanically *(epiphaino)* and communicates the other, but—and this is immensely important—only to the degree to which the symbol itself is a participant in the spiritual reality, but not everything pertaining to the spiritual reality appears embodied in the symbol. The symbol is always partial, imperfect: "for our knowledge is imperfect and our prophesy is imperfect" (1 Cor. 13:9). By its very nature the symbol unites disparate realities, the relation of the one to the other always remaining "absolutely other." However real a symbol may be [as for instance the real presence in the Eucharist], however successfully it may communicate to us the other reality, its function is not to quench our thirst but to intensify it: "Grant us that we may more perfectly partake of Thee in the never ending day of Thy Kingdom." It is not that this or that part of "this world"—space, time, or matter—be made sacred, but rather that everything in it be seen and comprehended as expectation and thirst for its complete spiritualization: "that God

---

65. Lossky, *Mystical Theology*, 226. This view of Lossky's has been contested by Hausherr. For my part, I simply do not have the knowledge to comment.

66. Ibid., 227, cites N. Gorodetsky, "St. Tikhon Zadonsky." For my part, I remain leery of drawing any such distinction at all.

may be all in all. . . ." Christian worship is symbolic not because it contains various "symbolical" depictions. . . . Christian worship is symbolic because, first of all, the world itself, God's own creation, is symbolic, is sacramental, and second of all, because it is the Church's nature, her task in "this world," to fulfill this symbol, to realize it as the "most real of realities." We can therefore say that the symbol reveals the world, mankind, and all creation as the "matter" of a single, all-embracing sacrament.[67]

The Western Catholic can embrace this spirituality, and agree with every word of Schmemann's beautiful statement. But it is true that in general Western anthropology is more engagé in the world, hence more in the body, the Eastern more spiritual and monastic. Strange, then, that the West embraces the monastic discipline of celibacy for all priests (only the Eastern rites being excepted). Just this anomaly suffices to warn us to be cautious: matters are more complex, as Lossky warns. As he further hints, these differently accented spiritualities may be capable of accommodation within one united Christian fellowship, although at times he, like many Orthodox, seems to despair of such an eventuality, and even to hint that things have gone so far as to make such an accommodation fundamentally undesirable.[68]

I believe that a contemporary "Western" theology of the Trinity, of the sort expounded by de Lubac and Balthasar, bound up with a certain theology of love, and developing a deeper, less rationalistic anthropology, recuperates well the vision of the Greek fathers. I tried to reflect something of that in the christological chapter above. Because of this, I tend to be more hopeful with Erickson, and while Father Barringer is right to point out strong currents of wanting to remain separate among many Orthodox, all Christians must constantly recall the will of Our Lord: "that they be one."

---

67. Schmemann, *The Eucharist,* 39f.

68. Robert Barringer recently warned of the need to face the fact that many among even the moderate Orthodox theologians remain convinced that the West has wandered so far astray there may be (now) no hope of straightening out the "schismatics" (that is, the Catholics) sufficiently to make full union with them possible. So distinctive have the traditions become that Christos Yannaras "hints strongly at mutual incompatibility" (Barringer, "The Challenge of Eastern Theology to the Western Church," talk given to the Michaelmas Conference, St. Michael's College, June 1990).

THE WESTERN CHURCH'S
SEARCH FOR A NEW SYNTHESIS

THE RISE AND DECLINE OF CHRISTIAN EUROPE

While Byzantium struggled to hold off Arab Muslim and later Turkish invaders, Rome could not hold off and the Western Church had to absorb "barbarian" peoples and assimilate them into what evolved into a new Christian civilization, Roman, Celtic, German. This European Christendom was forged not only with the guidance of light from classical civilization, and by the breath of the Holy Spirit, but, alas, as it was also the work of sinful human beings, with clanging iron and bloody, forced conversions. What emerged has been called the product of "a second childhood," so distinctive some philosophers of history like Oswald Spengler and Lawrence E. Brown exaggerate, treating the result as a new religion, no longer "Levantine" in character.

With all its human ambiguities, this formative half millennium (from A.D. 500 to 1000) of struggle in Europe brought about, if not a new religion, a new Europe, with the Church playing both a fatherly and a motherly role in this new birth: fatherly, as the commanding hierarchy gave firm direction to the development of this emerging Christendom; motherly, by receiving these rough people into the home of its well-developed synthesis of the light of Christ with the wisdom of late antiquity.

The resulting Western European Christian civilization reached a flourishing adulthood in what is usually called, rather inappropriately, the High Middle Ages. Some of the cultural, theological, philosophical, artistic, and institutional fruits of this creativity remain perennial aspects of the Catholic tradition. (That means the appropriator ought to consider those medieval elements—if he can identify them—for the truth challenges they pose: are they good things to be retained in the living tradition to the extent we can mold its future?)

But then, softened by success, and racked in the fourteenth century by a series of devastating plagues, "the Black Death," this European body suffered a premature senescence. It sprang up from its deathbed with a new vigor in the fifteenth century, still very Catholic, only to suffer soon afterward a hideous nervous breakdown (midlife crisis of this *nouvel enfant*?) as the accumulated effects of long-accelerating strains in the social, economic, political organism at the most basic level produced the split personality of Western Europe. Whereas the Protestant Reformation and the Catholic Counter Reformation both introduced positive elements into the Christian tradition, the Protestant *revolt* and the violent Catholic counterattack, accompanied by a disastrous Thirty Years' European civil war, were virtually the suicide of Christian Europe. It may have taken until the catastrophes of 1914–1919 and 1939–1945 for its full death potential to be realized, but there is no question: what became a Protestant-Catholic bloody struggle in the sixteenth century evolved into a secularized Europe with a remaining, still vital Christian element in the midst of a larger devastation of *de-Christianization,* helped mightily by the materialism induced by the unprecedented wealth poured out by the industrial cornucopia.

European Christianity has gone through great spurts of religious renewal since the vicious Thirty Years' War, but that catastrophe so scandalized masses of people, producing both skeptical intellectuals and de-Christianized countrysides, that breeding grounds for a series of increasingly disastrous revolutions were formed—the 1792 perversion of the élan of 1789 was a ferocious fruit of this, since exceeded in murderous results by the Bolshevik uprising of 1917 perverting a bourgeois revolution and the fascist seizures of power (Mussolini at the heart of Roman Christianity, Hitler by democratic election in the midst of the decadent Weimar Republic followed by a plebiscite, Franco in the midst of the destruction of Catholic Spain by socialists) leading to the greatest of all wars, the horrible HTX paroxysm of 1939–1945 that left 65 million dead and all of Eastern Europe in Stalin's hands. So relentless was the sustained attack of Christian upon Christian from the sixteenth century on, it is no wonder so many, from the subjectivist turn of Descartes through the Enlightenment, turned away from faith to find a new "rational" or, later, voluntaristic base for civil society. Intellectually this base, alas, was a narrow scientific rationalism, which remains a fundamental and thoroughly antireligious dimension of our own HTX epoch, the aridity of which has helped provoke the voluntaristic outbursts, from the romantics and Nietzsche to the base rantings of Hitler, and the cold efficient murder machines of the SS and Stalin's gulags. Institutionally, Europe has become first and foremost the interacting financial, manufacturing, transportation, and governmental arrangements we call the Industrial Revolution, which have survived the paroxysms of fascism and communism now to be transformed in the information age into a part of the planetary-scale HTX, the most dynamic social development in all history, but one menaced by decline into mediocre consumerist materialism.

The spectacular secularizing forces of a "modernity" preoccupied with creating and managing a dynamic, wealthy, planetary-scale society form the most severe threat ever in history to the underlying sense of the sacred. If the sense of the sacred is overwhelmed by the flashy creations of the

Disney Company, interest in a serious relationship with a transcendent God fades away, to be replaced by playing around with every manner of do-it-yourself cult and New Age spirituality responding to man's natural hunger the way Doritos do.

A materialistic society with an ever weaker moral foundation is sliding toward catastrophic nihilism. The effects even among active Catholics can be felt in many ways, including in some an individualistic pseudodemocratic revolt against the very idea of divine authority operative in the Church. (There is circulating a petition to the pope for local election of bishops, ordination of women, and an end to obligatory celibacy, signed by 2.5 million German Catholics, after the pope declared that he had no authority to change the male nature of the ordained priesthood, and that this is final.) Remnants of the old pagan fascination with the chthonic dimensions of nature in the form today of a planet-conscious "ecological" religion emerge in the place of true transcendence revealed by God's own gracious gift of Himself. This ecological religion is accompanied by fanatic "multicultural" thought-control efforts—dubbed "political correctness"—fueled by the ever resentful of an increasingly spoiled society of the rich who believe they are poor.[1] But New Age and politically correct ideas are no help for the good life, as they are themselves pathological deformations of otherwise sound insights drawn from Christian humanism. These ideas reveal the bankruptcy of a false positivistic kind of "reason," and are an emotional revolt against it.

With the gloom of that estimate of the present situation hanging over me, I went to look at the Middle Ages for help in understanding how we got into such an impasse, and to see in what ways those "Catholic centuries" offer help in discerning the way forward. My goal in working this out was both positive and negative: I was asking about the good perennial contributions of both medieval intellectual accomplishments and institutional innovations, and at the same time cocking a critical eye at whatever contribution that half millennium has made to the present slide into nihilism.

This required the synthesizing of an overview of the Occidental medieval "second childhood's" understanding of the essential matters, interpreted, of course, as this struggling Christian, your author, sees them: of the world as the God-created stage for the dramatic interaction of the infinite divine and the finite created human freedoms; of that drama itself as the perfecting of nature by grace, with attention to the medieval sense of the role of reason, understood as a summit of nature, and guide to our action.

1. I do not mean to demean the suffering of those who cannot find a job or are mentally or physically unable to cope. On the other hand, society loses all perspective when it fails to see that a single mother of two in Toronto receives from the government real buying power exceeding that of a highly skilled worker in Russia, even under Brezhnev when the Soviet state still paid workers regularly.

I believe this so important because the great medieval doctors' pursuit of reasoned thought at once fed—deformed, the defenders of the medieval doctors would say—the current of civilization that became modernity and also provided some perennial elements for later Catholic intellectual syntheses. I have not forgotten the Eastern complaint about Western "rationalism," an alleged failure to see that nature without grace is hopeless. In short, Catholics today remain as seized as were our medieval forebears by *the need to keep working on the development of a proper sense of reason,* purified of Enlightenment, Hegelian, and positivist excesses, and saved from deconstructionist and nihilistic attacks; a reason grounded in and illumined by faith. We must get clearer about reason's relation, through "experience," to all reality, which means the properly Christian sense of experience has to be a central concern of the appropriating Catholic.

What I sought to pull together here are a few glimpses of a medieval *vision,* hence a few glimmers of an ideational construction. As it both grew out of a historic social, political, economic, and spiritual situation and served to guide and form the institutionalized realities of everyday life, this vision evolved, we now know looking back after the event, in the direction of that terrible explosion I have called "the civil war of European Christendom." This dialectic of influence from the high intellectual through the cultural into the social, political, and economic sphere of everyday life and back again to the evolving vision requires analysis first largely on the plane of ideas (the ideational world enjoys some autonomy, after all—even the Marxists admit that!), then analysis on the plane of daily action, and finally a look at how they interact. That is the plan I shall follow.

As desirable as it would be as part of methodical appropriation of a great tradition, even a minimal synthesis of the great medieval vision requires an important part of a life's work by a devoted specialist, and could be expressed in only a great volume, like Étienne Gilson's *Christian Philosophy of the Middle Ages* or his classic, reedited and expanded in seven or eight editions, *Le Thomisme.* As I was getting clear for myself what is needed to grapple with the present situation of the Church, I became more aware of the limits of my own knowledge of this vast, rich period. In assessing the limits of my 1950s education in Thomistic philosophy I must tell the reader that my understanding of Thomas is filtered through Gilson filtered through his students who taught me at St. Louis University.

So all I can offer here are a few personal "takes." This is no scholarly presentation of what was really happening in the bottomless cauldron of brilliant, bubbling medieval thought. It is beyond the limits of the modest place accorded each critical epoch in this long tradition to offer a balanced assessment of the thought of Thomas, let alone a penetrating history of the Augustinianism of the Middle Ages, Thomas's revolution in introducing Aristotle, and the developments and deformations of the great interacting syntheses of the thirteenth century—the Bonaventurian-Augustinian and the Thomistic-Aristotelian-Augustinian—not even an appreciation of the giant John Duns Scotus will be found in these few pages. I am simply trying to arm myself with some sense of *aspects* of our medieval roots that may help throw light on major concerns about the present. (An advantage of written appropriation, recall, is that the experts can correct the worst distortions of my impressions.) As I reflected on my ideas about the Middle Ages, it helped to bring my current concerns, of which I see principally three, into focus.

The first is about "routinized Roman Catholicism" continuing to contribute to the loss of many from the new generation. Calling it "Roman Catholic" points to the narrowness of mediocre Catholicism. This routinization contrasts with "charismatic" spiritualities in all their forms, within and without the Catholic Church, and among the orthodox and evangelicals.[2] To what extent is a certain deadness of routine, and a lack of depth in penetrating to the heart of the reality that God is the transcendent *mysterium tremendum et fascinans* and Jesus Christ is truly present in us as divine life, caused by *a taking for granted* of institutional and pious forms forged long ago, which, while they can be instrumental in handing on God's grace, also perhaps somewhat anesthetize us to the mystery? What have we Catholics inherited from the Middle Ages that still needs, if not to be overcome, at least recharged with *fresh thinking founded in sound experience, accepting of grace?*

My second concern stems from another effect of this routinization: the failure on the part of many Catholics to appreciate the earth-shaking discoveries of the modern age, of science and technology, of *historicity* and a contemporary Christian synthesis.[3] Among the other bad effects of this is that it hampers Catholic thought about many of the technological, social, political, and economic phenomena of our wild times.

2. The "charismatics" present, of course, their own dangers, especially the perils of generating an *immediacy of religious experiences,* which can be mindless in its own way when rooted in the hysterical rather than the genuinely pneumatic. There are lurking in the background of this *inquietude* those basic questions about the nature of genuine Christian experience I just mentioned and catechistic issues of how it is to be handed on. See the classic by Jean Mouroux, *L'expérience chrétienne* (Paris: Aubier, 1954), and the section on "The Experience of Faith" in the first volume of Balthasar's *The Glory of the Lord: A Theological Aesthetics,* trans. Erasmo Leiva-Merikakis, ed. Joseph Fessio and John Riches (San Francisco: Ignatius Press, 1983–). The uniqueness of the apostolic witness to the historic and risen Christ, how that witness is passed down and graspable by the spiritual sense that is animated by the gift of faith, and the relation of both to mystical experience is a central question in the Catholic tradition. These issues will be discussed later.

3. "Historicity" translates the Heideggerian barbarism *Geschichtlichkeit.* It means that sense in an ontology of the development of meaning over time, and that how we interpret reality from within such a historical meaning-setting is essential to the coming to be of being. Chapters 9 and 10 of *Being and Truth* are devoted to explaining this key notion, vital to contemporary thinking, and as yet not well integrated into Catholic thinking.

I believe that modern ideologized synthesis of certain medieval thought has contributed greatly to this block in the thinking of some serious Catholics. In the 1950s my Catholic higher education consisted of taking three degrees in Thomistic philosophy—yes, "philosophy," and inclining in a rationalistic direction at that, although Thomas was a theologian, and not a rationalist.[4] The fathers and doctors did think of their syntheses as "the completion of true philosophy." But they knew that the Greek philosophers were pursuing *theo-logia*, their thought rooted in the sense that all is founded in God. By the twentieth century the sense of philosophy as somehow only an affair of reason had infiltrated Western consciousness widely. Neither as an undergraduate and master's student at a Jesuit university nor as a doctoral candidate at the Institut Catholique de Paris was I ever led to read one line of Thomas's (or anybody else's) fertile commentaries on Holy Scripture! Nor was I ever led to understand that Christian thinking must grow out of adoration and prayer as condition for the possibility of sound thinking! The "autonomy" of reason, and reason reduced to logical argument, was in the air.

To this day I see thoughtful converts returning to the powerful vision of Thomas Aquinas especially, looking for guidance in the intellectual and moral struggles of our day. But few of them are being taught by the remaining Thomists a living theology, and they are not being prepared at all to absorb into their Catholic wisdom the discoveries of the last hundred years. I do not see many of them reading Blondel or Bergson or Newman or Teilhard de Chardin, indeed the latter is presented as deformed by New Age. Fortunately, some do also read Augustine seriously.[5] More positively, many are at last discovering the fertile work of *la nouvelle théologie* and are venturing into the immense synthesis of Hans Urs von Balthasar. But while Balthasar thought it vital to integrate the discoveries of science, and for that matter the earthquakes of contemporary societal developments into Christian wisdom, he left much of the work

4. I do not mean to accuse my good Gilsonian teachers of Enlightenment narrowness, but they showed little of the poetic magic of their master, Étienne Gilson, and even less sense of "symbol" and beauty, with faith and prayer taking less of a place in their pedagogy than *demonstratio*. (Well, this is philosophy, you know! My reply: Excuse me? Are you sons of Ignatius not running a Catholic university? Have you not a responsibility for the development of Christian, not just "scientific," souls?) I exempt my nonphilosophical master Maurice McNamee, S.J., head of the English Department, founder of the Art Department, and director of the Honors Program at St. Louis University, a poet and lover of beauty. When I returned to Saint Louis after my Paris-contracted infection with phenomenology, my old philosophy masters (excepting James Collins, the great historian) were totally hostile to my efforts to introduce the ambiguities and dynamism of historical reality into my teaching. This autobiographical note is included here so that the reader may better understand the animus hidden in my wide-sweeping synthesis.

5. One cannot blame them for their allergy to the more hazardous innovations of Karl Rahner, or—worse yet—liberation theology and New Age misappropriation of Teilhard. But so many seem oblivious to all the salvageable, and I believe true, discoveries of the kind of phenomenology developed in fidelity to Catholic thought by Gabriel Marcel.

of doing this to the present generation of thinkers formed by *la nouvelle théologie*.[6]

My third worry: too many "faithful Catholics" dream of a bygone day when a Catholic Europe lived under a sacred order. How, or whether, Western medieval theologizing may have opened the way, as the Orthodox claim, to the drastic secularization from which we now suffer, which invites such flight into fantasy, they do not consider, but we should. The lasting and perhaps still enhanceable good effects of medieval civilization on the Church need to be properly appreciated and thoughtfully incorporated into genuine efforts to create new community. But only those spending their lives trying to reconstruct a reliable view, rather than a naive dream of what went on in the Middle Ages, can contribute much that is solid to such speculation.

As I look in a broad way for certain common denominators in medieval Western thought relevant to my questions, I shall assume, without being able to spend here the considerable space necessary to defend such a hypothesis, that at its best, medieval theology achieves a balance between, on the one hand, a sense of mystery, and, on the other hand, the advocacy of the use of reason. On the mystery side: I see in Anselm, Bernard, Albert, Thomas, Bonaventure, and Scotus an essential Christian sense that grace is indeed a gift that, while absolutely necessary for man's fulfillment, is not "due" us—God's love is not to be earned. And on the side of reason, the best of the medieval thinkers embrace a kind of adoring reason, guided by faith. This reason is clearly distinguishable from what I shall argue later are the deformations of Enlightenment rationalistic thought. Let us now see some grounds for such a positive reading.

CREATION, THEO-DRAMA, AND REASON

The revelation of creation, central to all that sets the Hebrews apart from the Greeks, demands a different sense of reason from that developed by the philosophers.[7]

While, because of its finitude, creation is incomparably inferior to God, it nonetheless exists because God loves it, wills it into being, and sustains it.[8]

6. The legitimate discoveries of phenomenology and the post-Kantian "transcendental" perspective Balthasar himself has appropriated, duly purified by criticism, and integrated with his own profound thinking through the analogy of being. In a small early work, *The God Question and Modern Man*, trans. Hilda Graef (New York: Seabury Press, 1967), Balthasar shows what he would be capable of in the area of integrating modern science and technology into Christian wisdom; but he spent most of his life making available in a profound way the incandescent, revealed core of the tradition from its earliest biblical traces.

7. Even in that summit of Greek thought, Plato's myth in the *Timaeus* of the *Demiurgos* fashioning the cosmos out of matter, Greek philosophy did not attain anything near the Genesis sense of the world as an act of loving divine design that involves God in the very fabric of His creation.

8. Plato's *Demiurgos* appears more an impersonal and necessary force.

And this sustaining God reveals Himself as no battleground of caprice and envy, like Zeus and his court, but rather as a loving father engaged with His children. As the Greek fathers would say, God's *energeia* constantly illumines mankind, so that creation is not only intelligible but also loved. But a father must guide his children, and this Father in heaven is active in history as a leader of a people He has chosen for Himself, as He works with them throughout history to bring them to their fulfillment.

In his "natural religions" and "philosophy," man gropingly reaches up by use of his natural faculties of reason and mytho-poetic imagination toward the Source.[9] But once the truth about God is revealed by the Source's reaching across the infinite gap, faith then understands that man by himself can never arrive at the ultimate truth about God and the world: now it stands revealed that the issue is more a mysterious drama between the infinite divine initiative and man's finite (and often destructive) freedom than it is a task of human intellectual construction. The base issue is a practical one: our being open to His call, faith as the obedient listening, responding, hence not blocking (by perverse finite will) the divine power from flowing into us, that power that keeps all from falling back into chaos. At stake, given our refusal to listen, hence our sins, is *redemption:* repairing the break we introduced into our relationship with God, causing cosmic disorder, so that now we must cooperate in the creative restoration.

Every trace of ancient fatalism, all sense of blind necessity, all feeling of being trapped in this mortal world is banished by God's revelation that His energy is unleashed benevolently, that we have spurned His friendship, and that He has restored it, indeed more than restored: He has called us to divinization.

The Orthodox are right: any diminishing of the sense of God's loving presence in all of nature, and especially as crucial to all we do, is a falling away from that revealed vision, and a failure to understand the true freedom that it is about. The *dynamic reason of a theo-drama* between God and man must replace the determined necessities of a Greek-idealist construction.

But does not such emphasis on love as source of all install a kind of voluntaristic irrationalism at the core of the tradition, in place of a structural, natural, reason-founding necessity as the Greeks grasped it? Is not God's will itself then a kind of unintelligible force? Is the Apollonian not abandoned to the Dionysian, the chthonic given free reign?

On the contrary, Catholic thinkers would respond, the whole sense of the Revelation points to the opposite of a Bacchanal.[10] To be sure, "God's ways are not man's ways," but His will is never arbitrary: because He *is* Truth and

---

9. For the limits shown by these efforts throughout history see the dense pages of the two short first chapters of Balthasar's *Love Alone: The Way of Revelation,* ed. Alexander Dru (London: Sheed and Ward, 1968).

10. There is a strain in Protestantism, reaching a summit in the great Kierkegaard, reacting to Hegelian rationalism, that emphasizes the utter freedom of God in a way that tends to confound our inability "to know His ways" with a sense that they are

Goodness itself (see the Psalms), His willing of creation was not a caprice, but a *natural*, free outpouring of His infinite necessary nature, which of itself is giving; because "God is love," His giving is of a *dynamic* order, an *ordo* (a favorite word of Augustine, dear to the Middle Ages). What God created is no whimsical fantasy. It is as it had to be to express, in the way He chose out of an infinity of possible ways, the Being that He Himself is.

That is an important point for appreciating any genuinely Christian sense of reason: there is "out there" an objective world, created by the same God who made our intellects to be capable of knowing it, a real intelligible order. Faith in the loving, creating God grounds a realism at the base of every form of Catholic reason.

And what is that Being? Study of this creation in the light of Revelation does not permit us to know perfectly, but always, as we adoringly reflect on His Word, ever more profoundly. The self-revealing God has unveiled this much to us of His plan: the cosmos was meant to be an order that could answer (*re-spond*) to the love that brought it into being by a returning act of love. This "loving back" (*re-spondeo*) would be the highest fulfillment of the possibilities of His finite creatures.[11]

God willed creation, then, as "nature," choosing to create an *ordo* that is not just a set of counterbalancing blind forces, as the Greek understood it, but a more complex, unfolding dynamism, more like Augustine's sense of "the seminal reasons,"[12] which includes the human faculties, intellect and will, and is intended to flower in love. Think of this *ordo* as a scheme more like a history than a pyramid of ideas, in which things manifest structures and capabilities of their own, including those singular points of initiative— human wills—and stand in relationship to other things according to a plan, as freedoms interact. It is revealed to be a *providentia* flowing from love, not, as contemporary nihilists believe, a jumble of accidental relationships that just happen to sustain life for a while.

The builders of the Romanesque churches of the late eleventh century sought out and found (as their Greek predecessors, the architects of the great Doric temples) the *scala aurea*—the golden scale of cosmic harmonies operating in all things, and built their churches incorporating its proportions.[13] But whereas the Greek builders sought to find the formula for ultimate repose in those naturally given proportions, the Romanesque and later the Gothic master masons combined the harmony of a well-seated basic

---

inherently inscrutable, even to Him. Ultimately, of course, Kierkegaard would not deny that God knows what He is doing.

11. Recall that *spondeo* means "I commit."

12. But we shall see a Greek tendency to "freeze" natures, putting too much emphasis upon the eternity of formal intelligibilities. This creeps into the tradition from Greek philosophy, too.

13. Take a stalk of wheat, break it at its joints, and lay them out: the ratio of the Greek lyre, the *scala aurea*. With the recent discovery of fractals—the branches of a stream, of a river system, and of the cardiovascular system in man are strikingly similar—something of this same sense of repeated basic harmonies in nature reappears on the scene.

structure with the upward thrust of a development reaching toward its Omega point in heaven.[14] Western medieval society, inspired both by Roman law and by what was perceived as the order of creation, sought to incorporate social order through charters and law codes, banding together in evangelically inspired corporations intended to bring to society a rational *ordo* of enduring significance, but one that sought to enhance and protect community freedoms, and educate for love. Pragmatism and relativism, so characteristic of post-Enlightenment modernity, had no more place than pagan fatalism. Nor despite the high degree of technical expertise they developed was this codification "technological" thinking: far from treating nature as an instrument for man's use, medieval thinkers and practical men alike sought in nature always keys to God's will, as expressed in that given, objective *ordo*, to which they thought they were called to conform their own initiatives.[15]

RELATING NATURE AND GRACE

The Greek philosophers, while lacking the revelation of creation, nevertheless did discover that being, truth, and goodness are "convertible": things are what they are (being), we are made to know (truth) and desire them (the good), including to know and to desire the fulfillment of our own natures. The knowing-loving activity of our being Aristotle and the Stoics considered the attainment of wisdom. Since things are intelligible (true) it is vital and good to know them, our actions toward them, and toward ourselves, need to be based on sound knowledge. The philosophers' moves toward a rational study of the cosmos, and the things in it for their own sakes as well as for their utility, constituted a first step in separating science from religion, a first move toward secularization. The gods shrink—not everything is the result of their caprice anymore—to make place for the effectiveness of the things' own natures, rooted in a supreme transcendent Intelligibility, known naturally by the human intellect, fruit of man's hard work of "dialectic."

14. Consider the Abbey of Tournus, Burgundy, built in the eleventh century, where a constructural breakthrough was initiated: the barrel vault was sliced into sections and turned ninety degrees, so that a series of them shoulder one another. This distributes the weight of the vaults so as to permit their being carried on relatively thin, round columns. The much later Gothic (more properly, "ogival") sense of height and light is fully present. Or, look at the tendency to soar of Cluny, and its reduced, feminized sister model, Paray-la-Moniale.

15. Being sinners, hubris was not absent among them, of course. Beauvais Cathedral strikes us as built as much *ad majorem hominis gloriam* as *ad majorem Dei gloriam;* and the military field excursions of rough feudal lords, whether on "crusade" in Christ's name or putting down rebellious barons in their own name, were no more angelic than the Milkens and Boeskys of our time. But at least they admitted their sins. It was a civilization secure enough in its beliefs still to be able to say mea culpa. Ours, more prevaricative because of its perpetual adolescent "identity crises," always has to try to make sin seem like virtue.

There is, of course, a danger that this sense of inherent necessity in things when taken up in a Christian synthesis might tend to separate grace—that freely given *energeia* poured out by God's love—from nature, with grace becoming something added to an undisturbed natural order. That would have the consequence of marginalizing the Fall as a phenomenon of the human soul only. The Hebrew sense of contingency and of God's spontaneity, and hence of the dynamism and dependency of all of creation, could fall victim to the Parmenidean, Platonic, Aristotelian sense of the necessary intelligibility of being; where is there space for the ever renewing creativity of love? Is not love the dynamic Dionysian and hence anti-Apollonian? Is not the charismatic-Protestant in tension with the Catholic Apollonian, with its emphasis on a hierarchical *ordo*?[16] Might feudal hierarchical social structures not get frozen in time?

Medieval thought would be much less interesting (and contemporary Orthodox critique much more devastating and evangelical immediacy more attractive) if the Christian thinkers of the twelfth and thirteen centuries had merely succumbed to this Greek sense of necessity, leaving the Catholic tradition too intellectualized, too static. But the "Scholastic" doctors were all disciples of that great Neoplatonist who was also a Christian "existentialist," Augustine, the greatest poet of love since Paul and John. More important, most of the great theologians—Anselm, Bernard, Albert, Bonaventure, Thomas, Duns Scotus—were men of exceptional Christian spiritual experience and depth, inflamed by love of God, *mysterium tremendum et fascinans*, sensitive to His lively presence, not only as the source of the soul's abilities to know and love, but also as Providence working even in the regular realm of nature.[17]

It is clear to the medieval doctors therefore where the basic priority ought to lie in the Christian's "reasoned" search for understanding. The adoring thinker begins with the gift of faith, "con-fidence" in what has been revealed, obedience (from *audire*, meaning "to hear") to what God teaches; his thought is *fides quaerens intellectum*, faith seeking insight, in the treasures of the tradition, in Holy Scripture, in the living authoritative teaching of the Church. The fathers and doctors of the Church all embraced Paul who, in Ephesians, revealed that through Christ, faith brings an understanding

16. The drama of history inevitably gets played down when the Apollonian-Parmenidean is too much to the fore. The tendency then is to a necessitarian sense of reason, precisely the recent Orthodox critics' worry about the medieval turn. (Irony! The Orthodox are saying the Catholic West is too Greek! Yet it is today in the Catholic West, rather than the Orthodox East, or in the chaos of the Protestant charismatic, that the deepest sense of a dynamic historicity—of growth and continuity in time—is to be found. Obviously, this demands more probing on our part.)

17. They did not lose sight of the theo-drama: there is no *fatum*—the tragic is replaced by the *Divina Commedia* behind the scenario of which stands the ordering, loving intelligence of the Father, and at the center of the stage, the Incarnation of the Word. His ultimate offering on the cross wiped out the disaster of our revolt and conquered death—a supreme victory over a fallen nature, now being (painstakingly) reformed through our life in the Church.

of the *mysterion* beyond anything of which philosophy as unaided reason could dream.

In a word, such a faith will first and last seek God. That does not imply any anti-intellectualism in the medieval doctors. We are made by God to love Him, and for that we must know Him. Man always wants to know more of what he loves. Faith puts us on the right path to that knowledge, which will be complete only in the life beyond. (Christ said, I am that path, hence the truth that is life.)

The Monk's Dilemma

But there is in all this what I shall call "the monk's dilemma": If knowledge of God is the goal, what point is there, beyond the need to solve practical problems, in pursuing knowledge—theoretical knowledge—of the things of this world? Should we not concentrate on what brings us as directly as possible to God?

For Augustine and for some of the Augustinians the things of this world are interesting only to the extent they bring us closer to God; they become damnable temptations when they distract us from our one true destination. Augustine states: "I desire to know God and the soul. Nothing more? Nothing whatever." He prays: "O God, who are ever the same, let me know myself and thee."[18] Of all the things accessible to our experience, the self is the knowing, loving soul that most resembles God—that is the imago Dei. The Augustinian does not altogether forget the body, but the divine in us is reflected above all in the intellect and will—and the soul is our medium for reaching toward Him. If the unique reason for our existence is to know, love, and praise God, then distraction by the world, which keeps us from turning to the depths of the soul to find Him, is the ultimate disaster, as Pascal will later insist, and our Orthodox critics tirelessly repeat—on this point showing themselves good Augustinians (who largely ignore Augustine!).[19]

---

18. *Soliloquia*, 1.2.7 (PL 32:872); ibid., 2.1.1 (PL 32:885).

19. Granted, we can be brought to wonder at God's beauty and wisdom when we know more about His creation, but given our limited time on earth, the monk's dilemma may still seem compelling: why not go the most direct route, through contemplation of His revealed Word, through disposing ourselves interiorly to receive His special favors, becoming as close to the inner secrets of His being as He allows us to? Something like this has been the path followed by the monastic-mystical Eastern Churches. Are they perhaps, Christianly viewed, not right? The roads of Thérèse of Lisieux and of Louis Pasteur do not seem to converge. Even the great scientist-mathematician Blaise Pascal would seem to split the ways: *ésprit de géométrie, ésprit de finesse; le coeur a ses raisons que l'ésprit ne connaît point.* The spirit of subtlety and the clarity of the spirit of geometry do not meet. As to "the heart having its reasons which the spirit cannot know at all," well, the division Pascal makes does seem extreme! The great challenge of Teilhard de Chardin, as we shall see, lies in his insistence that these ways to God do rejoin. Balthasar, while failing to emphasize natural science as a way to God, is so conscious of Jesus, the Incarnate Christ, as the perfect imago of God, His chosen

Why Then Did Mathematical Physics Arise in This Christian Milieu?

If something approximating what I have called the monk's response was prevalent among the greatest thinkers in the Middle Ages, one may wonder why a secular science should have arisen at all in a Christian milieu (and, not incidentally, *only there!*).[20] With the revival of urban culture, from the time of the true "renaissance" of learning, beginning in the twelfth century, the effort was renewed to find a balance, not only between legitimate concerns of this life and the overriding imperative of moving toward God, but also between a more mystical access to God and appreciation of Him in the beauty and intelligibility of His handiwork.

The pioneering physics of the thirteenth century was not the work of monks, but nevertheless of religious, members of the new urban-based so-called mendicant orders: Robert Grosseteste (who lived from 1175 to 1253) and Roger Bacon (who lived from 1214 to 1294) were Franciscan friars, and Albert of Cologne (who lived from around 1200 to 1280), in his lifetime dubbed "the Great," was a Dominican.[21]

At the Cathedral School of Chartres—late-twelfth-century precursor of the universities—an interest in nature was already manifest: the quadrivium was emphasized and anatomy and physiology studied. A serious interest in the things of this world for the sake of their own being and intelligibility began to manifest itself unequivocally,[22] however in only the

---

revelation of the whole in the fragment, that He will emphasize the need to know this world in order to sanctify it (which is the title of an important work of Balthasar's, *Das Ganze im Fragment*). But his reticence toward Teilhard's efforts goes beyond defensible hesitations about some of Teilhard's emphases. I am tempted to think Balthasar just does not believe that particle physics, cosmogenesis, and theories of the development of organic life and how it works contribute much to the most important knowledge: a deepening in that Christic discernment that comes when "not I live but Christ lives in me." More on this later.

20. Stanley Jaki, the contemporary Benedictine monk-physicist and historian of science, carefully documents the influence of the belief in Creation on the medieval search for the meaning of nature, the greatest impetus to the rise of modern science, from Robert Grosseteste and Roger Bacon in the thirteenth century to Galileo and Newton in the seventeenth. But Neoplatonic belief in the perfect (stable) intelligibility of numbers was at the base of the thirteenth-century Oxford Franciscans looking for the ratios in the heavens. Isaac Newton still produces an ungenetic mechanics (Jaki, *Science and Creation: From Eternal Cycles to an Oscillating Universe* (New York: Science History Publications, 1974). The sense of a dramatic explosion and unfolding of a creation, fortunately, was still present in the spirits of some of the late-nineteenth-century greats, like Clerk Maxwell, who tells us he discovered field theory while contemplating the sustaining work of the Holy Spirit; without it, would the dynamism of quantum mechanics ever have emerged?)

21. All three are roughly contemporaries of Saint Thomas (who lived from 1225 to 1274), and Albert of Cologne was his teacher.

22. There is evident among the theologians of the twelfth century, heavily Augustinian, and the great Augustinians of the thirteenth, like Saint Bonaventure, a sense of the freedom of creation and hence a concern to avoid a Neoplatonic necessary emanationism, as though being had to shine forth from the divine One directly and could not be reflected from things. (It is also at this time that the condemnation of the

first half of the thirteenth century, and then in Dominican circles, with Albert, and in Franciscan, with Grosseteste and Bacon. The Franciscans were Augustinians, concerned to find the ratios in the perfect movement of the stars.[23]

Magister Albertus offered theoretical, theological justification for so much interest in the things of this world. Yet, for the good Dominican friar, what is most interesting still comes from beyond. Despite his use of Aristotelian terms, his view of the soul (and therefore of human knowledge) is also still Augustinian: While we can know external things only with the help of the senses, it is by the interior route of illumination from God that the soul knows itself. Through degrees of illumination, that is, various gifts of God, the soul can come to know Him. As Armand Maurer sums up Albert's position: knowledge by abstraction is a lower form of knowledge preparing the way for divine illumination, but even abstraction is impossible without the illuminating help of God. Our "agent intellect"—the active source of insight—must be brightened by God's own light, or by the combined light of the angels and God, "as the sun's light is added to that of a star." Albert calls this divine illumination a grace in the broad sense, for it is a gift added to our natural endowments, but it is not a supernatural grace on the level of faith or the light of glory.[24] As has been perceptively observed more than once, Meister Eckhart, the mystic, and not William of Occam, the hard-nosed nominalist, is the true descendant of Albert the theologian.

THE BALANCE ACHIEVED: SAINT THOMAS AQUINAS

The great Albert, an avid observer of nature, prepared his brilliant student well. Now it is Thomas who achieves at last a satisfactory theological justification for serious interest in the things of this world, for that "secondary created order," endowed by God with an intelligibility genuinely

---

earlier work of John Scotus Eriugena occurred. Strong arguments can be mounted that the charges brought against Eriugena's thought miss the point of his work. But the coincidence in time is indicative of the concerns of the thirteenth-century Augustinians and Neoplatonists of the schools.) Emanationism obscures the status of Creation as having a reality of its own given it by God. It is not as clear as it should be that Creation, as being, is intrinsically intelligible and desirable, able to operate and make sense in the sphere God has allotted it. Emanationists tend to distinguish between the body's sensible contact with external things and the soul's interior grasp, in the roots of its own being, of the transcendent God's active presence, and then to emphasize the latter. For those who emphasize the inherent intelligibility of the world, interest and concern is centered, too, on the interior way of the *itinererium mentis ad Deum,* as the title of a major work by the greatest Augustinian in the next century, the Franciscan Bonaventure, puts it. But at the same time, the goodness and reality of the external world is affirmed, as Bonaventure's spiritual father, Francis, himself did in his evident love for God's little natural creatures.

23. Jaki, *Science and Creation,* 226–28.

24. Albertus Magnus, *Commentary on the Sentences,* 1.2.5, cited by Maurer, *Medieval Philosophy* (New York: Random House, 1962), 159; also Albertus Magnus, *Summa Theologiae,* 1.15.3.

built into it. His emphasis on the intrinsic interest of the "secondary order" marks an ontological shift away from Augustinian interiority.

But there is a shadow: why then did Thomas's magnificent balanced synthesis, with its generous openness to the exterior world, fail to get history back at the center of his thought? For all the hesitations a good Thomist might have about Augustine's turn deep into the soul, it has to be said: Augustine possessed a better feel for the theo-drama, with its historical dimensions, than Thomas, even, as I shall suggest below, the "existentialized Thomas" of Gilson's presentation.

Insisting on the substantial unity of man, Thomas solved the problem of how the intellectual soul, able to survive the death of the individual through the separation of soul and body, could nevertheless be truly the form of the body, hence the animating source of its ability to know, with the material things of the exterior world constituting the human being's "proper object." The great risk Thomas took was to embrace the new science of the time—actually a thirteen-hundred-year-old science newly rediscovered, Aristotle's analysis—modified by lights from Revelation. He used it to argue the case for the uniqueness of human nature as a kind of thing, meant by God to know and act in its own peculiar way, which was that of an intellectually informed material being, master of this world, and God-ordained instrument of the world's sanctification.

In embarking on this course, Thomas broke in one central way with the whole history of Christian thought from the fathers to his own day, a break not with revealed matters of faith, but with the approach heretofore taken in seeking philosophical understanding of them. If contemporary Orthodox critics want to find the person responsible for the change of direction that, taken to extremes, may have contributed to modernity's secularizing, they should look, in my view, less to Augustine and more to Thomas.[25] I shall argue, however, that for our exaggerated modern desanctification of the world, Thomas is simply not guilty. But, despite his great innovations in elevating existence above essence, which we shall discuss, his Aristotelianism proved a block to his developing the proper historicity necessary to integrate the theo-drama dynamically enough into his synthesis so that human freedom, as he understands it, is not shown as pro-jective, interpretive of reality. To what extent is the relative lack of such a dimension in Thomas, less lacking in Augustine, an unwitting con-

25. I can see an advantage for those Orthodox commentators who may be more interested in polemics than in healing the rift to push the start of the trouble as far back as possible. Given that Augustine's Trinitarian theology undoubtedly contributed to the West's eventually embracing the *filioque*, and as he coincides roughly with the Constantinian bipolarization of the empire, it would be neat to hang everything on the complexities of Augustinian theology, even problems with nature and grace. But to make Augustine responsible for a desacralizing of the world, as it began in the later Middle Ages and accelerated under the shock of the Protestant revolt, is not credible. Hanging some of the blame on the Aristotelian Thomas is less incredible.

tributor to the later development of an unsound, subjectivistic, relativistic historicity?

It is of singular significance to us today to see that within the mainline Catholic tradition such a radical revolution of thought as that introduced by Thomas can take place and be tolerated,[26] that it need not destroy the balance that retains a proper—an overriding—sense of the sacred while acknowledging the role of human freedom and human reason in the fulfillment of sacred intentions in the created order. It was not just a daring innovation on Thomas's part, after a thousand years of seeking understanding of Revelation through modified Neoplatonic ways of thinking, to adopt a quite different philosophical science as part of the basis of one's approach. Just as Teilhard de Chardin would, in our time, take on the challenge of having to overcome the apparent materialism of contemporary science in using some of its categories and insights to help understand the world in the light of Revelation more profoundly and more relevantly (more in relation to the truths recent science had unearthed), so Thomas took up the challenge of accepting man's embodiment as central, and with it he sought to appreciate this created world as endowed with a status and significance of its own, within God's plan.[27]

Why was this a needed development? Such revolutions—whether it be the fathers' adoption of Neoplatonism to think Revelation, or Thomas's adoption of Aristotle, or the Cartesians' "new beginning," or Newman's notion of development of doctrine, or Teilhard de Chardin's taking evolution seriously—are never without their problems, and indeed those problems can be severe.

THE PERENNIAL CHALLENGE: ADAPTING CONTEMPORARY SCIENCE AND CONTEMPORARY EXPERIENCE TO THE UNDERSTANDING OF REVELATION

Thomas sided squarely with Aristotle in insisting that everything man can know must first come to him through the senses. What is first in the senses has, of course, to be raised to the level of insight *(intellectus)*, that is, penetration by the mind to the meaning of what is superficially (but really) presented in the senses. Only the human soul, by virtue of its spirituality,

26. Not without a fight: many propositions of Thomas were condemned in 1276 by Étienne Tempier, archbishop of Paris. Thomas's posthumous defense was taken up by his brother Dominicans, just as Jesuits, like Cardinal de Lubac and René d'Ouince have taken up the defense, in our own day, of their brother Jesuit revolutionary Pierre Teilhard de Chardin.

27. As he had to be attentive to the authority of the fathers who preceded him, especially Augustine, and of course of Holy Scripture itself, Thomas was obliged to build up a thought structure of vast synthesis, the most complete and overarching ever achieved, matched by only that of Augustine, *"the maximum differentiation,"* in the words of Eric Voegelin (see *BT*, chapter 5, for an explanation and discussion of this important claim on Voegelin's part).

can do this. The forms of things are knowable through the things' own sensible data revealing their structure, which the intellect is able to grasp as stable forms.

That this shift in understanding being was a further step toward secularization, just as Greek science had been, cannot be denied. That is one reason among others that this secularization becomes more visible in the fourteenth century, as other thinkers, not all as orthodox as Thomas,[28] took up neo-Aristotelianism. But so to agree is not to damn Thomas. Secularization is not an easy notion, indeed it is an ambiguous affair. If by secularization nothing more is meant than according to this world the status and intelligibility with which God endowed it, what Thomas achieved, seen with Christian eyes, would be progress. If, however, one means the gradual diminution in this world of concern for, and all sense of the centrality of its Author, then every step in that direction is antireligious and fraught with danger. Whatever the later deformities, the step Thomas took was vital.

A SHIFT IN NATURAL FAITH PROVOKED BY GENERAL SOCIAL CHANGE

It would be altogether unjust and misleading to suggest that Albert and Thomas alone, or in cahoots with Aristotle, account for the revolutionary shift in the focus of intellectual interest we observe in some quarters as we pass from the thirteenth into the fourteenth century, just as it would be wrong to suggest that enthusiasm for such a shift was universal; there were, in fact, vigorous reactions against it, including the formidable opposition of Bonaventure, Thomas's fellow master of theology at Paris and later for eighteen years superior-general of the Franciscans. But an interacting constellation of intellectual, spiritual, sociological, and economic factors was at work, shifting for some influential thinkers the whole sense of our position in the world, what we are doing here, what it is fruitful to be interested in. Just as one cannot reasonably blame the Second Vatican Council's openness to "Teilhardian" pleas for coming to terms with the new truths of science for the great shift and resulting debacle of the crazy sixties and seventies of this century, so we must see the shift in the natural faith of most of the society as something much broader than any cautious developments of a Christian reason and a sharply modified anthropology by Thomas. Christianity had become the "civic theology"[29] of a remarkably (but of

---

28. Think of the notorious Siger of Brabant (who lived from 1240 to 1284) as a worse-case example. Étienne Tempier, who condemned his heterodox theses in 1270, is the condemner of Thomas that I mentioned previously.

29. By this rather difficult notion is meant the ruling assumptions in a society about the "sense of it all," which govern the general acceptability of practices touching ultimate matters, including the always difficult relations of Church and state, and what is allowed in the debates taking place in "the public square." I am aware that this notion is anything but clear, and it should be used with caution.

course not perfectly) united Western Christendom, and hence since the fall of the Roman Empire ever more implicated in "secular" affairs. Shifts in the secular world brought new pressures to bear on the intellectual life.

This medieval Christendom was not a foretaste of the "heavenly Jerusalem" but a political economy well installed in this world, as full of sinners as any other, and hence, alongside its own peculiar accomplishments, displaying its own peculiar forms of injustice. As we have seen, from the middle of the twelfth century well into the fourteenth, wealth, city life, and a sense of well-being were all expanding together. The following factors contributed to the revision in Europe's natural faith: city life's distancing from the natural rhythms of agricultural life; growing affluence due to commerce; the leisure provided by wealth (not to be confused with the *chronic underemployment* that characterizes low-productivity agriculture); spreading education beyond the clergy to men of the world; rapid population growth, demanding job creation and producing roving, unattached bands of "students"; wide travel, begun by the Crusades and pilgrimages, reinforced by booming international commercial life (discovery of other customs invites questioning one's own); the growth of vigorous intellectual establishments, especially those "corporations of masters," prominent among them those corporations called "universities of study." In contrast, the weakening spiritual hold of a corrupt clergy, in tension with an increasingly efficient Church bureaucracy, both somewhat offset by the engagé life of the urban-oriented mendicant orders; the intellectual demands posed by administration of a great international church and the emerging central nation-states; and growing awareness of the need to solve problems of navigation, architecture, and engineering.[30] All these factors and more were interacting with one another to contribute to a very basic change of mentality, producing yet more elements of "modernity," arousing a proud, activistic sense ("Faustian," in Spengler's term), long-term preparation for today's HTX.[31]

Yes, Christians were beginning to feel comfortably installed in a world that seemed to be unfolding in a favorable way. Visible progress, by anyone's definition of the term, was being made in every department of life (not spectacular in medicine, however, which did nothing to ward off the great shock of the bubonic plague), and in a more harmonious way than at any time since the heyday of the Roman Republic. Dangerously, this sense, despite setbacks, was carried over into the invisible realm: the feeling of an eschatological age of fulfillment starting to take place was more widespread than just in the rather extreme speculations of the infamous Joachim of

30. The increasingly successful harnessing of water and wind power were impressive, as was the engineering of the great cathedrals.

31. May we not see in the great cathedrals, monuments of unprecedented splendor that began to rise in the late twelfth century not only an outpouring of devotion and piety, which touches us still, but also—dare I suggest it?—a touch of "triumphalism," capable of overwhelming even twentieth-century men accustomed to eighty-story monuments of bankers' hubris? (My thirteen-year-old grandson upon entering the cathedral St. Étienne de Bourges, the first he had seen, said, "WOW!")

Flore, the prophetic figure who declared that "the Third Age," that of the Holy Spirit, had begun with the birth of Francis.[32]

Add to all this a weakening of respect for the papacy. Whereas in the Gregorian reform, the papacy emerged strong against the increasingly powerful emperors and kings, by the fourteenth century the papacy had fallen on hard times: the "Babylonian captivity"[33] and the great schism hurt its prestige. The excesses of the Renaissance popes—symbolized by the names Borghese and Borgia—reduced the papacy as a spiritual force able to offer the whole Church direction in a time of profound and rapid change.

M.-D. Chenu comments on the fact that, interior to the Church itself, "in the limits of its orthodoxy as in those of its authentic regime, this balance [of a "proper secularism"][34] has proven variable, and as though malleable to fit the temporal situations of humanity."[35] All the factors mentioned played a role in bringing about such a shift, which the Church did, after all, achieve without volatilizing, despite the disastrous split of Christendom—it is still with us, vigorous in the most secular of ages, despite the ongoing siege!

THE BALANCE OF SAINT THOMAS

But this is getting ahead of the story. Let us consider in some detail the balance maintained by Thomas as he achieved his great philosophical shift, for it contributed substantially to the survival of the Catholic vision.[36]

32. Joachim's speculations launched a long and tragic history of efforts to drag the *eschaton* from the supernatural into the natural-cultural realm of human history. Through degrees of secularization, this finally issues forth in the thoroughly atheistic forms of national and international socialism, that is, Marxism-Leninism, fascism, and the many forms of "national socialism" found in the Third World. All of these are efforts to bring about, by human will, the eschatological fulfillment of "the Third Age" (or the "New Age") as an earthly utopia. On this important theme in the philosophy of history see three remarkable works: Henri de Lubac, *La postérité spirituelle de Joachim de Flore*, 2 vols. (Paris: Lethielleux, 1978–1980); Étienne Gilson, *Les métamorphoses de la cité de Dieu* (Louvain: Publications Universitaires de Louvain, 1952); and Eric Voegelin, *The New Science of Politics* (Chicago: University of Chicago Press, 1952).

33. From 1309 to 1377 the popes were forced by the French kings to reside in Avignon. While recognized as bishops of Rome and successors of Peter, they were nevertheless dominated by the French throne. Following this, from 1378 to 1417, the great Western schism saw three pope pretenders contesting the authority of the papal see. This was resolved by an ecumenical council, amid a resurgence of claims that councils were superior to the pope. Once reestablished on firm grounds, the papacy successfully rejected this claim.

34. Which is not just one between faith and reason, but more profoundly between nature and grace.

35. Chenu, *La théologie au douzième siècle* (Paris: J. Vrin, 1957), 244.

36. Chenu is right to remind us that "The economy of salvation is not defined just in the reflective and reasoning intelligence of a few acknowledged thinkers, but also in concrete decisions, in the ways of life that are adopted, in the ideals of holiness, in evangelical work which the Church, in its head and in its members, approves, arouses, promotes or defines" (ibid., 225). But the lucid synthesis of Thomas served many actors in many periods as a precious road map to their action.

Consider the implications, for those who want to take more seriously the intelligibility in themselves of the things of this world, of Thomas's Aristotelian convictions about knowledge.

Thomas's insistence on the natural capacity of the intellect to know the things proportioned to its nature (material things and human beings) does not mean that Thomas eliminates the role of special illumination by grace—he has not ceased for a moment to be a theologian of Christian redemption, guided by Revelation, and seeking God above all else. First, we must remember that we humans have corrupted ourselves through sin and need the healing effect of grace. Second, only by grace—the creative source of new being ("Not I live but Christ lives in me")—can we know things higher than our own being or beyond the natural capacity of our intelligence.[37] But by separating out and insisting upon the undestroyed capability of our naturally given knowing faculties, Thomas encouraged confidence in the scientific use of reason. M.-D. Chenu has caught the spirit of the transformation that occurred when reason was thus accorded the fullest possible place within Christian thought: it was no longer a question of merely commenting on the sacred texts, of explaining them in homilies, catechesis, and glosses, of ordering them in a rational coherence that would make the *sacra historia* intelligible; nor even, as they did at Saint Victor,[38] of building on the foundation of that history an edifice of allegory doubling as a typological interpretation of the sacred events of the past. From now on the faith wants, in its light and with full possession of what has been divinely revealed, to construct from within and to think humanly the Word of God. Incarnating the divine truth in the very tissue of our spirit, it is not an extraordinary charism that its transcendence would hold beyond our human mode of thinking; it puts into action the various resources of reason, which are thus introduced into the mystery of God. By engendering a theology, it is in the very logic of its perfection.[39]

But Chenu knows well such faith in human reason can lead to exaggeration. He reminds us that conservative advocates of the old "monastic theology" at the Lateran Council of 1215 were right to recall that the dissimilitude between God and creature is greater than the similitude. Chenu comments:

> The scientific function is necessary for the spiritual and temporal architecture of a Christendom: thus it triumphed in the XIII century; *but it can only achieve solid results if it remains evangelical,* always bearing the Word of God as a message, assiduously frequenting the ancient witnesses, *resisting the temptation to objectify the mystery in an unconscious scientism,* conserving the free intimacy of the faith in the midst of the most rigorous explanations.[40]

37. See, for instance, *Summa Theologia,* IaIIæ, 109.1.
38. The Victorines were a school of twelfth-century Augustinians of considerable influence, with Hughes and Thierry being the most famous.
39. Chenu, *La théologie,* 249.
40. Ibid., emphasis added.

Thomas achieves a sense of the interrelationship of God's activity as creator and font of all graces, with us, struggling to make our contribution through the use of the faculties God has given us. His concept of humanity as naturally sound but partially corrupted by sin, needing God's grace to guide our natural faculties to the required fullness of truth, retains, I believe, a defensible orthodox balance.

I would add, however, that the Augustinian insistence on the centrality of the interior life is a protection against the temptation, following from an overly empiricist reading of Thomas, of becoming fascinated with the intelligibility of this world, just as Thomas is protection against exaggerated Augustinian otherworldliness. Both Thomas and Augustine enjoy a good balance, but with different accents. There is a danger in Thomas's leaving nature itself uncorrupted by man's revolt against God, with his failure to emphasize enough that the redemption affects the whole of the cosmos, and not just man; through God's becoming man, all of the cosmos is put back on the godly path to soundness. Reflecting on the thought of both of these architects of the tradition can be the soundest pedagogy for our own efforts to maintain ourselves today in an equivalently balanced way within the whole wisdom.

PLATONIC HIERARCHY OF FORMS AND ARISTOTELIAN FORM-MATTER AS PROBLEMS FOR CONTEMPORARY THINKING

But the greatest medieval syntheses inevitably suffer the limits of their underlying ontology. This theology, great as it is, remember, is not infallible divine revelation. The limits of mainstream medieval theology of course contributed to the tensions that led to the blowup of Christendom. If one asks oneself what is (inherently?) limiting in the medieval ontology, what at the core causes serious problems for later thinkers who must achieve the syntheses of their own thought by including truths discovered by modern science, I would zero in on the theory of the forms. Indeed, it is hard to say which causes more problems, the Neoplatonic sense of a hierarchy of forms descending from, and ever more remote from, the Creator, or the very fixity of the forms themselves.[41] And as if that were not bad enough, along with this Platonic heritage comes the complication of thinking of change in terms of Aristotelian "matter and form," "act and potency." While still useful categories in a commonsense context, these Aristotelian notions pose problems when brought into the world of

41. *Being and Truth* explores at length the problem of describing the form-process relationship adequately. Permanence in the midst of transforming energy is a reality that requires explanation in ways that take into account what we now know is true about "matter and energy" as described by physics, while making sense of our common experience that things change at vastly different rates, and from "temporary permanencies" of finite form we can abstract lasting intelligibilities—"concepts" (see especially chapters 4, 6, 7).

evolutionary science and quantum mechanics.[42] And analysis of man in terms of faculties tends to obscure the truth of the total interpenetration of human spiritual activities; the dependence on and transcendence from the physiology of the body of the higher, more spiritual activities; and it distracts from the sense of the historicity of human operations: that the past not only is deposited as habit but also is present in historically formed horizons of interpretation.[43]

Perhaps what is most at odds with contemporary thinking is the Greek sense of form. That theory grows so naturally out of common experience, and it has so permeated Christian thought, it is so central to a way of thinking that has proved an obstacle for developing an adequate theory of truth unfolding in history—for an adequate theory of "historicity," a central challenge for all thought today—it behooves us to pause right here to consider how the mind comes to think "form" spontaneously and to clarify its significance for premodern scientific thinking.

At the risk of gross oversimplification, consider the classical Christian view of the hierarchy of forms. The source of the forms is found in the never changing, infinitely perfect divine ideas. Among the infinity of these is one chosen freely by the Creator, the overall idea in keeping with which He creates this present cosmos. The overall idea of the world in turn contains a hierarchical set of forms, the natures of all created things, reaching in a gapless chain, a gradation of forms from the splendid, purely spiritual forms of the highest "separated substances" (roughly, angels) down to the lowest dirt clods. Each of these natures has its place within the perfection of the overall idea, and is simply and eternally, ideationally, if I may so put it, just that which it is.

This is a rather static, abstract notion of form. Why from earliest philosophy does a quite static sense of form have such a hold on the human mind? Its origin, psychically, as I pointed out in *Being and Truth*'s discussion of

---

42. The great difference between modern Western science and other cultures' scientific efforts has come about through the Western move to the concept of "operational causality," that is, that the efficient cause is to be decomposed reductively into lower-level efficient causes. But, as Aristotle noted, there comes a point beyond which one cannot further ask why. At that "lowest level," the efficient cause must be "grammatical" in nature, meaning the cause is named but not decomposed. The fourfold causality of Aristotle and Thomas collapses the operational question, and gives a "grammatical" reply to efficient causes ab initio. As the other causes—material, formal, and final—are not operationally decomposable in the manner efficient causation is, the modern prejudice against their explanatory role that has developed is understandable: rather than recognizing that an "analysis of elements" (operational reduction) is an *enhancement* of the core "analysis of principles" (grammatical explanation), modern thought has chosen instead to pit one type of analysis against another. For more on this see Lawrence Brown, *The Might of the West* (Washington, D.C.: Binns, 1963), 48–80; and Kenneth Schmitz, "Analysis by Principles and Analysis by Elements," in *Graceful Reason: Essays in Ancient and Medieval Philosophy Presented to Joseph Owens, CSSF*, ed. L. Gerson (Toronto: Pontifical Institute of Medieval Studies, 1983), 315–30.

43. See *BT*, chapters 4, 6, 7.

insight,[44] lies in the formal, intelligible necessity produced by an insight into either a brute *perceptum* (such as the color red) or a structure (such as this house)—the grasp that *something simply is what it is,* resulting in the formation of a universal concept (that is, "redness," "houseness"). This ability to grasp and abstract an intelligibility—without a doubt one of the great manifestations of human spirituality—so impressed Plato that it became for him the very paradigm of what it is *to be.* Formal insight is like that, it carries a taste of the absolute: once the mind has "seen" the distinctiveness of a color or number or the sense (the meaningful way in which the parts belong together) of a structure, such an insight has formal validity—the concept is abstracted from the circumstances of its first discovery, and will forever mean what it means—without reference to time or place, or whether any actual exemplar exists or not. This *absoluteness of formal insight* has not lost its attraction: it so impressed the twentieth-century mathematician Edmund Husserl, it led to his founding of an idealistic "eidetic" philosophy he called "eidetic phenomenology."[45] The very man who discoursed on "inner-time consciousness" was (rightly) fascinated by formal absoluteness!

Idealists tend not to emphasize the fact that this mysterious ability of the mind to understand is founded on the things of our experience manifesting different kinds of permanence that give rise to the very possibility of true formal insight. Aristotle and Thomas saw the importance of this. Things show themselves to be in themselves[46] of distinctive kinds or as being structured, that is, organized in such a way that our understanding them both as having a certain endurance and as exemplars of kinds of "whatnesses" is a true experience of them.[47] The mind's ability to relate them, which is often founded in apparent similarities, can also be founded in objective causality accounting for these similarities.[48]

If this is so, what is wrong then in saying of the things of our everyday experience that they manifest themselves as having forms? Nothing at all, or a great deal, depending on how "form" is understood. Thomas, like

44. Ibid., chapter 4, paras. A and F.

45. Étienne Gilson, Thomas Langan, and Armand Maurer, *Recent Philosophy* (New York: Random House, 1962), chapter 3; cf. *BT*, chapter 4.

46. I am so aware of the anti-Kantian thrust of this claim, I had to expend literally hundreds of pages in *BT* trying to make it credible—you talk about "countercultural"!

47. For example, we now know that the color red is the perception by the human optical-nervous system of a certain band of frequencies of electromagnetic radiation. Two permanencies are required for a given "red" to exist: a steady radiation of photons within that band and the continued existence of a human organism with healthy sight. From such a perception we can abstract the form, the meaning on a certain level of consideration, of the "color red" as a universal concept, a general possibility. So not only do the concepts that we form enjoy eternal intrinsic intelligibility, but they also are useful for knowing the world: they reflect the actual "natures" of things, referring to the particular entities that have this nature and come into and go out of existence.

48. Sometimes the comparison is based on superficial resemblance only, without causal foundation.

Aristotle before him, most emphatically objected to the Platonic notion of what it is to have a form: for Plato, the idea of the thing, properly speaking, exists absolutely apart from all exemplars in a higher ontological realm—a world of ideas—separate from, and superior to, the experienced world of time and space. Indeed, the things of this world enjoy whatever organization and intelligibility they may temporarily have as they go on their changing way, through "participation" in the unchanging Ideas. It is the "Ideas" that count, this is where Being resides, and individuals—far less *being*—just come and go. Aristotle and Thomas insisted that, no, the organization and intelligibility of the things of our experience come from their actually being these kinds of things, as the result of their truly having been caused to have their own forms, their real internal organization, so to speak, that has been passed on to them through the efficient causality of real agents acting in time and space.

Here is where Thomas's distinction of existence and essence—unknown to Aristotle, introduced because of insight that comes from the revelation of Creation—can be not just helpful, but for a Christian, *vital*. There is much to defend in the Thomistic notion of a distinction between that which makes something what it is, its essence (form and matter), and the principle that makes it actually exist, its *"to be" (esse)*. After all, the concept of a thing can be abstracted then to exist in the mind after the thing has ceased to exist, or, in the case of an imaginary object, without its ever having existed at all.[49] Moreover, an actual essence as type can be enjoyed by many individuals of the same species,[50] but each individual has its own unique act of "to be,"[51] its own dynamic hold on cosmic time-space, the inflowing of the ontological reality from its efficient causal source.

So far so good. Neither common experience nor even the most sophisticated scientist ought to object to the considerations we have just been discussing. The problem is, however, that this way of expressing the entity's being tends, paradoxically, to distract attention from the dynamic becoming of the thing. Attention to form draws away attention from *esse*, the act of existence. As a deployment of finite energy, finite existence, you would expect, is always in a state of becoming. But if one concentrates on the stability of essence, through insisting on the intelligibility of form, with the dynamism inherent in the very notion of "potentiality" somehow tending

49. That concept is derived either from knowledge of the essence as actually structuring the concrete thing while it enjoys existence, or from its having been dreamed up in the imagination, creatively composed out of the debris of things known, and may never come to actual existence.

50. The mechanism of the efficient causality accounting for the many similar nails or the many oaks of the same species can be explained.

51. It is important always to bear in mind that the limiting potentiality, the "whatness," and the energizing actualizer, the existence, constitute a whole, indeed the essence only is through the actualizing effect of the existence that has been given by the efficient cause, and the act of existence is what it is because limited by (and formed by) this essence to be the existence of a tree, for instance, rather than a cat. The concept, without a real act of existence, is only a "mental being," just that—an idea.

to get lost to view, a vision of the world as much more stable than we now know it to be tends to emerge.

In the case of an organism, it is of course perfectly correct to say that the form[52] is actively guiding the push of existence to develop the mature entity—the "end" predetermined by the form—and one has no great difficulty in understanding as natural the decline into old age and finally death. However, as one tends to think of form in terms of the full reality of the thing, and one tends to abstract it, one has to be careful to remember that the acorn is already the oak in seed, just as the senile old man who recognizes no one still is essentially the same human person, but in terminal natural decline.[53]

The modern materialist does not work from completed, intelligible, stable form downward, but rather seeks to understand how more complex entities are built out of the building blocks provided by less complex ones. In the process, he discovers new and useful information. He brings us to

52. However this active regulative principle may be explained—as genetic information encoded in the DNA we would say today. The maintenance of any organism's integrity in the midsts of the energy flows within and between it and its environment is infinitely more complex than what just the role (itself already incredibly complex) of the DNA and RNA of the cells can explain. This is discussed in some detail in *BT*, chapter 7.

53. The challenge is to name as unmisleadingly as possible the regulative principle governing the "substance" as it maintains its identity in the midst of change; "form" does not say very much (but with its long history, maybe too much?). It is unfortunate for the advance of knowledge if the thinker tends to be satisfied with that symbol as some kind of an answer to the mystery of consistency in the midst of restless change, rather than undertaking the arduous research to understand how, for instance, in the development of a complex organism the genetic information carries out its regulatory tasks, helping the organism know what it can absorb and what it has to reject and how it is to order the assimilated atoms into its life-preserving proteins, for the constant renewal of cells. Even in the case of a granite boulder, the "form" way of looking at things plays to the limits of common experience: the boulder, on the scale of everyday human activity, is, for all practical purposes, static and "forever." When instead of thinking of it in terms of its "having the form of a granite rock" we approach it as having a certain crystalline molecular structure, we are more inclined to insert it cognitively into the larger dynamic context of its formation and to wonder how something so "electric" as its whirling atoms can be held temporarily (but by human measure for a very long *tempus*) in such stability. Consider again the note above about "operational causality." Each reduction in operational causality allows for a new explanation by principles to be advanced suited for its level. The use of principled explanation at lower levels also affords an opportunity to deal more effectively with agglomerations, heaps, and so on, than Aristotle or Thomas were able to, as well as dealing with artifacts and the like, that is, "created forms." We seek then to understand it as a phenomenon changing more slowly than many of the things around it, but still a long moment between solidification of the molten magma until its final erosion into sand. (Even without outside forces of erosion, atoms will continuously escape—at a slow rate by our human scale—so that eventually the boulder will "evaporate"! That fact, startling to common sense, escapes everyday observation.) It is more informative to describe the grains of sand as small crystalline clumps with the same structure as the boulder than it is to think of them as entities with different forms from that of granite boulders. Both are, to be sure, workable descriptions, but the molecular is potentially less misleading, given all that we now know.

puzzle over the more startling moments of transition as we follow up the ladder of being (instead of assuming, on the basis of a poetic intuition, a great descending "chain of being," or, ideologically assuming an evolution with no breaks or leaps, which ideology weakens the will to acknowledge the mystery of every higher form of organization). So we are encouraged to search harder for the details of the binding forces that structure the more complex entity, and for the mechanisms that could account for their having come to be in the first place, and for their continued transmission from generation to generation. (Think how long it took for something like present genetics to come to the fore, and remember how long has been the gap since Gregor Mendel's first inklings, around 1860.)

Recalling what was said above about the difficulty of reconciling the dynamism of the *sacra historia* with the stability of a hierarchy of forms, the reader now enjoys a hint of the advantage the modern perspective has furnished a Teilhard de Chardin, as well as a suspicion of the unresolved problems it brings with it.

SAINT THOMAS'S EXISTENTIALIST REVOLUTION

I do not mean to diminish the importance of the revolution introduced by Thomas in what Étienne Gilson considers Thomas's most original breakthrough: the reality ascribed to the ultimate act of existence, or *esse*.[54]

No Greek philosopher understood that in every created thing "what it is" and "that it is" are distinct. That is because the very notion of creation, of the world's being brought into existence from nothing, of its receiving existence and hence its dependence on God for its *esse,* was not revealed to them, and so they tended to locate ultimate reality in that which made things intelligible, their essences.

Gilson is right that the full implications of Thomas's existentialism were not grasped by his contemporaries, or, indeed by his followers.[55] Indeed, not until the neo-Thomistic revival in this century did the radical nature of the breakthrough become clear. This for the very reason I have been invoking: the human intellect seeks repose in the abstractions of the understanding, in its grasp of intelligible forms; they are something clear one can hang onto, they give an illusion of one kind of control, just as materialism, with the idea that one can find the ultimate building blocks and the final laws of their combination and thus build "a final theory of Everything," feeds the illusion of a control "from below." Instead, one should return with the clarifications introduced by abstract analysis to the inexhaustible reality of the concrete beings, directly experienced and never exhaustible, never perfectly under our control. These acts of existence overflow the limits

54. Along with Jacques Maritain, Étienne Gilson was the principal commentator on the writings of Thomas of the last generation.

55. This is the argument of the whole of Gilson's *Being and Some Philosophers,* 2nd ed. (Toronto: Pontifical Institute of Medieval Studies, 1952).

of essence, which is what Thomas meant by saying "the individual thing is ineffable."[56]

Gilson's recovery of this fundamental new insight into the nature of existence as the irreversible, unique act that gives each thing its status as this entity, along with the theory of causality and the implications regarding the nature of God, was ingenious. Gilson claimed that Thomas had shifted the emphasis in Greek philosophy from essence, universality, and intelligibility to existence, uniqueness, and dynamism, and thus opened a place for the importance of individual history. I would add, this dynamism is more faithful to that experience of life that is central to a Christian "eucharistic" appreciation of God's creation, to the notion of the dignity of the person, with emphasis on the unique and irreplaceable contribution of each individual to the Mystical Body of Christ.

Thomas himself was not always faithful to the full implications of his own radical discovery. He could on occasion, according to Gilson, "receive into his work, on its margins, already sclerotic essences without always taking the time, or perhaps even feeling the need, to rejuvenate them through contact with existence."[57] As Gilson sees it, the dynamics of Thomas's thought transcend the limits of classical ontology, even though Thomas may not in every instance draw full advantage from his own existentialism. Gilson might respond to the modern Orthodox critics that one reason the modern West slipped away into excesses of rationalism was precisely the inability of Thomas's predecessors to grasp profoundly enough the existential revolution he had launched. In its effect on the intellectual landscape, Thomistic existentialism à la Gilson belongs not to the Middle Ages but to the contemporary period. But even then it was not able, in my judgment, to open an adequate place for history.

OPENING A PLACE FOR HISTORY

It is vital to the larger discussion that follows of where an adequately conceived Catholicism would fit into the intellectual landscape today to raise the question of the difficulties of opening a place for history within the still heavily Greek-influenced structures of medieval thought. If even the Thomistic existentialism developed by Gilson, lacking a phenomenological analysis of human consciousness as "interpretative," that is, opening a time-space world of meaning, has difficulty making a central place for human history, the development of culture, the continuity of tradition, how then is Catholic thought to do so, without slipping into historical relativism, which is just skepticism about truth?

56. Étienne Gilson, *Le Thomisme*, 6th ed. (Paris: J. Vrin, 1979), 455. I sought in *BT* to explore phenomenologically the evidence for just such a realistic existentialism. See especially chapters 2 and 4.
57. Gilson, *Le Thomisme*, 451.

Why is this such a serious problem for the Catholic tradition? Greek thought, as "essentialist," lacked completely the sense, which the Hebrews have enjoyed since Moses' encounter with Yahweh on Sinai, that mankind, endowed by its Creator with a destiny, is under way, following a particular, unique, and *personal* path to redemptive fulfillment. Medieval thought, struggling to unify a wisdom out of its twin origins, Hebrew revelation introducing a linear and personal sense of time, an instinctive "existentialism," and Greek cyclical thinking and formalism never succeeded in coming to terms perfectly with the Bible's implications for historicity.[58] This leaves an immense intellectual challenge for today's Christian thinkers who, since John Henry Newman (who lived from 1801 to 1890) with his reflections on the development of doctrine and Maurice Blondel (who lived from 1861 to 1949), have begun to struggle with the task of producing a thought of "the Way" centered in the gestalt of a single human existent, Jesus of Nazareth.[59]

Speaking of the theology of the fourth-century Neoplatonist Dionysius, whose thought was so influential,[60] M.-D. Chenu is severe in regard to the effects of such formalism: "The *anagogia* of Dionysios develops in a metaphysical order and in a symbolic play, from which *historia* is *completely eliminated and looked down on*, including the *sacra historia*, the goal of which is no longer to teach us a recital of facts but 'to initiate' us through the symbols into the *teleiosis* (the fullness) of the Divine Life."[61]

Over against such a static, hierarchical view of reality Étienne Gilson would place the sense of the *sacra historia*, the belief that a providential God interacts with the individual human beings in creation to bring out of history a fulfillment through a long struggle, a gradual, progressive construction of a social (but not all "this worldly") reality, the divine *civitas*.[62]

58. For a discussion of this issue, see my Presidential Address to the American Catholic Philosophical Association, "Historicity and Metaphysics," in *Proceedings of the ACPA*, volume 48 (1974): 1–13.

59. There are several excellent articles on Newman's role in developing such a historicity in the fall 1995 issue of *Communio: International Catholic Review*. I especially recommend the article of Thomas Norris, "The Development of Doctrine: 'A Remarkable Philosophical Phenomenon,' " 470–87.

60. He was presented to the late twelfth and early thirteenth centuries as Saint Paul's Athenian Convert (hence his present-day soubriquet, "Dionysios, the pseudo-Areopagite").

61. Chenu, *La théologie*, 133 (emphasis added).

62. This theme runs throughout many works of Gilson, including, prominently, *Les métamorphoses de la cité de Dieu*, *The Unity of Philosophical Experience*, and *Being and Some Philosophers*. But his fear of the subjectivist turn taken by Descartes, and growing out of it, the transcendental turn, which reaches a summit in Kant, Hegel, and Husserl, prevented him from integrating adequately into his epistemology the sense of historical continuity in consciousness, the building (*bilden*) of culture. That it is difficult to integrate an objectivistic metaphysics of *esse* with a phenomenology of historical consciousness I can attest, having attempted it in *BT*. On the question of achieving an adequate theology

The Christian sense of history and Providence, if it is faithful to Revelation, should be a far cry, on the one hand, from a free existentialism of
arbitrary liberty, and, on the other, any form of determinism of massive
social structures, like that of Marx.[63]

The contemporary atheist existentialist finds the medieval attitude to
Providence and the idea of a Benign Supreme Intelligence participating
in perfecting the world to be an "escape" from our responsibility. To be
fair, it should be recalled that medieval man was not in a good position
to be as Pelagian as modern man: lacking modern medicine, the high-tech
means of production, and, for the most part, even literacy, and hence much
information, he was spontaneously inclined to be more the passive victim of
circumstances than are the citizens of developed countries today. So it was
natural for medieval man to be inclined to deliver himself more willingly
into God's hands, just as villagers in poor countries still are so inclined
today more than the job-jumping yuppies who can live in the virtual
reality of television, dash away in fast motorcars, and have their hearts
electrically zapped back into sinus rhythm. Even many modern Christians
judge harshly what we have termed above the "monastic temptation":
seeing this world as a hindrance in our search for God rather than as the
Creator's first love that He came to redeem and He intended as the pathway
to heaven.[64]

A medieval thinker, living with poverty, so with a short life expectancy,
and equipped with a formalistic notion of a fixed, rather than an evolving,
creation, and hence little sense of history unfolding, would have found
it next to impossible to rise to the heights of a Teilhard de Chardin in
developing the Paulinian notion of the cosmic Christ taking up historically
into Himself all of reality, through a God-directed human transforming
work. The Eastern fathers, living in an aristocratic milieu at the end of high
Hellenistic culture were more inclined to emphasize Christ as *Pantocrator*,
the Word of the Father through whom all is created, and thus with their
view descending from on high, to see the cosmos as a kind of radiation

---

of history today, nothing is better than the rich work of Hans Urs von Balthasar, *Das
Ganze im Fragment*.

63. Marx insisted that the Feuerbachian atheist revolution was essential before
mankind would feel free to seize control of its destiny, but then he seems to many of his
critics to surrender that freedom to the heavy and necessary movement of the laws of
social conflict. I raise this here under the "balance" banner: to show how difficult it is to
strike a balance in which a sense of genuine individual freedom is preserved, but along
with it the realization that there are ponderous realities at work in the larger structures
of nature and human nature—the sense, in other words, that our freedom is finite and
operating in a context with meaning not created by human will, and by meaning created
by human will but no longer subject to easy change by the lonely individual.

64. The monastic temptation here again refers to a certain conception of the role of
this world in the redemptive scheme. We are not commenting here on the monastic life
of contemplation as a vocation of some who pray for all and give witness to God's gifts,
that few who pursue the contemplative life to the full, anticipating in this world what
we shall enjoy in heaven. We shall return to this question later.

from God. The medieval Augustinians shared some of that sense. A mystical thinker like Bonaventure definitely managed to penetrate to some sense of this. In his *Itinerarium mentis ad Deum*, we glimpse that the world as a whole is offered to the Father through Christ. But a contemporary soteriological ontology like that of Teilhard is bound to be different.[65] It does not descend from either Eastern or Bonaventurian-Augustinian mysticism, despite some resemblances: rather, it is hard-won from the Jesuit scientist's trying to think through a new discovery, *evolution*, in the light of the revealed role of Christ.[66] He thus appreciates this world, with man at the summit, truly as the Mystical Body of Christ, as the way of redemption. He reads the history of the evolving "hominization" of the cosmos christologically, and he observes the grand historical transformation of the planet and of our grasp of the cosmos. Created being is envisioned then as a continuum evolving under the push and pull of the Creator as beginning and end, Alpha and Omega, rising to consciousness in man. This is a consciousness centered in the Christ revelation and destined to cast a dense weave of Christ-centered intelligence (the Christianized noosphere) around the whole of creation, integrating it into a lasting, adoring community. But Teilhard de Chardin understands this integration to be grace-led hard work, pushing against the resistance of matter and death, and the perversity introduced by the abuse of freedom. The noosphere can yet produce "the great Molloch" of collectivism, becoming a final trap for mankind. The *civitas Dei* is painfully but ultimately joyously forged by God's creative impulse, through and with and in the Christ, working through human intelligence and human hands, out of the stuff—material, first living, now human—of this created cosmos.[67] Christ will triumph, if we cooperate.

How did the Western Catholic tradition get from medieval thought's relative failure to accommodate the historical and even to discover the evolutionary, to something as radically different (and indeed perhaps extreme) as Teilhard's synthesis? Many moderns would see the Protestant Reformation and the Enlightenment as necessary steps in freeing individual creative energy and scientific push in large masses of people, a condition for reaching a society of free association of self-standing individuals— Hegel's *gute bürgerliche Gesellschaft*, the good bourgeois society. Medieval corporatism, goes this criticism, was too hierarchical and elitist, and too static, education too limited and concentrated in a few at the top of the

65. *Soter* means "savior," in Greek.

66. What "evolution" means is of course the subject of raging debate since the introduction of the notion. My own efforts to forge an ontology that integrates what has been discovered in recent science about the unfolding-complexifying of created being occupies much of chapter 6 in *BT*. We shall discuss something of this in chapter 9, section D, on Teilhard.

67. We shall return to a more extensive discussion of Père Pierre Teilhard de Chardin and his contribution to Christian philosophy in a later chapter, so I postpone until then discussion of the difficulties that his synthesis raises.

intellectual pyramid,[68] and dominated by ecclesial dogmatism, to allow a sense of society as a whole moving and developing; the free potential of the individual, in such circumstances, was far from being realized.

There is more than a grain of truth in the Saint Simonian-Marxist observation that a man has to eat (and be educated) to be able to think properly. For my part, I have never been tempted to spend much time in nostalgic glances over admittedly attractive aspects of medieval corporatist society, for I believe there is little in what was genuinely achieved in "Christendom," when it still flourished, that can today be restored. We shall consider in the next chapter what that society still has to offer us.

THE LIMITS OF MEDIEVAL ONTOLOGY

As the above rather negative remarks about the medievals' ability to synthesize history into their wisdom hint, I think it is misleading to suggest that the medieval synthesis was ideal, as though the Protestant revolt and the more wrenching aspects of the rise of modernity were simply the work of so many perverse acts on the part of big egos, destroying without any justification a perfect balance.

If the medieval syntheses were so perfect, why did there grow in the late Middle Ages and early modern times a strong feeling of revolt against the refined and elegant but perhaps all too complete structures of "scholastic" thought? Paradoxically, with the ever more elaborate and subtle structures of late-medieval thought there came a growing feeling of a need to free a space for fresh experimentation and observation, for a new approach especially to the material world. (This reached an extreme in the seventeenth century with Galileo's attack on the whole Aristotelian edifice, as he struggled to blast open a space for a new physics.) Meanwhile, much earlier others sought a fresh return to the interior life (experiments range from the Rhineland mystics, the Dutch lay confraternities, to the great mystics of Spain in the sixteenth century).

Coupled with this intellectual and spiritual dissatisfaction came a growing social malaise, especially in the burgeoning bourgeois class, cramped by the aging and ponderous structures of late feudalism, and now wanting somehow to open a space for more political and social freedom for themselves.

68. It is important, however, to distinguish between the learned and the educated. The broadening availability of knowledge through schooling that we think of as education is necessarily "behind the times." Communities of learning—what the university was meant to be but seldom if ever is now—are up-to-date both with the "leading edge" of thought in disciplines, and in the interrelationships of that across disciplines, in other words, *uni-veritas*, one truth. After the Black Death, the loss of the learned led to a broadening of education to provide clerical replacements (creating the "lessened knowledge" the Renaissance has mythologized into the common view of the Middle Ages); the rise of the technocracy in our own century has fractured learning with the specialization of disciplines and the attendant unwillingness to surmount this specialization found on today's *multi-versity* campuses.

Some of the intellectuals sought inspiration (and distance) in pagan classical texts (the so-called humanists); others favored closer attention to the inspired word of Scripture, but read in full context—a characteristic not only of the Protestant reformers but also of orthodox Catholic "Christian humanists," such as Erasmus of Rotterdam. Such a sound return to the Scriptures was not new to the fifteenth-century Renaissance, but was a perennial experience since at least the time of "the apostolic revival" of the twelfth century, flowering in earlier centuries in the return to Scripture and lay preaching of the confraternities.[69]

There are many angles to this struggle to move beyond the mental world of the medieval Occidental Christian synthesis. Some will come up later, but here, before looking more deeply into the social legacy of the Middle Ages, I want to sum up something of the central intellectual legacy. It has left the intellectuals who still follow the Way with essential inspirations but also with formidable tasks of thinking. Here I want to emphasize the positive.

CONCLUSIONS

A number of conclusions from this brief reflection on the medieval synthesis will be a guide as I undertake to define and criticize modernity, the setting within which the tradition now has to make its way, providing the englobing context within which our thinking must go forward.

First, the Western medieval understanding of faith and reason, and nature and grace, far from being catastrophically deficient, as the Orthodox critics suggest, achieved, in my view, an admirable, although not perfect, balance: reason, guided by the grace of Revelation and whatever interior mystical illumination God may offer, must do its task of continual investigation of and reflection on nature and the societal experience of mankind. But this should be done without hubris, always recognizing that the Holy Spirit is trying to work through our reason, if we are attentive to its teaching (in the Church).

Second, without grace there is no salvation; without grace, reason will not be directed on the true way. Through Jesus Christ as center passes the whole history of mankind.

Third, supernatural saving grace elevates nature but builds on the inherent intelligibility of the natures of things as God has created them, or, put in more modern terms that have emerged from the evolutionary process, created and guided by God; rather, grace espouses the providential vectors and brings the humanizing processes to fulfillment.

Fourth, the challenge of integrating history into the synthesis of a wisdom demands constant attention to the (always surprising) revealed givens of the *sacra historia* and to the increasing experience of mankind.

---

69. These confraternities, which played in many countries a big role in the life of the Church, are reminiscent of the vast lay movements of renewal in the present Church. On the latter see the last chapter of this book.

Fifth, for this an ontology is needed capable of making sense of permanence in the midst of change and encouraging investigations of foundational phenomena, an ontology that neither denies lasting intelligibilities nor mistakenly erects concepts in the place of developments, and can give the intelligibility of history its due place.

Sixth, there is potential for Thomistic existentialism, as Gilson has elaborated it, to contribute to such an ontology. But at the same time, one must beware the limits of medieval thought, even that of the great Thomas. The effort to "blast out" of a too static notion of form led to the excesses of nominalism, empiricism, and with them, voluntarism, all of which have infected modernity. For none of these is Thomas responsible, but they might have been forestalled if a more adequate Christian notion of historicity could have been developed. Like their great medieval forebears, today's Christian thinkers must respond to the challenge of integrating into our wisdom the truths of the sciences of our time, including the dynamism revealed in them, but without destroying the evidence of the permanence that common experience, at the human scale, reveals. (By and large our Orthodox critics have underestimated the importance of this challenge, reflecting a different view on their part of nature and grace. This has left them marginalized in the great ontological and epistemological debates of our time.)

One should not allow repugnance at Marx's exaggeration of the foundational character of material conditions to dissuade him from considering the interaction between the social, political, and economic conditions of an epoch and the intellectual visions that develop. For my part, I try not to fall either into a Heideggerian *Seinsdeterminismus*,[70] by putting too much emphasis on the epochal mode of thinking, nor into a neo-Marxist socioeconomic determinism that fails to accord to the realm of thought enough autonomy and underplays thought's influence on the course of events. (Can anyone deny that a philosophy—Marxism-Leninism—changed the course of history?) Theologians, mystics, and scientists are, after all, interested in the truth of what they directly observe, contemplate, and live. And while they may show their epoch's limits of conception, to be sure, if they were not able, with the tools provided them by society, to learn something about God, nature, and themselves, then no civilization would move forward, impelled by breakthroughs to reality. And they inspire their students to put their theoretical visions into practice.

So in due course, when I have reviewed the events of the Protestant revolt, I shall have to see what these socioecclesial developments brought

70. By this I mean a sense of Being as a kind of mysterious all-organizing illuminating light, giving life to a set of horizons of interpretation, which establishes the essence of an epoch without due consideration to the ontic-factual givens of the situation. It is true, there is an uncanny harmony between ways of thinking, of art, of means of organizing economy and politics characteristic of each great epoch; but the task of the thinker is to research the sense of this, alert to the autonomy of regions of being, the inconsistencies, the pluralism of communities and traditions and subtraditions that influence each other only very slightly. See *BT*, chapters 7, 10, and especially 9, for a discussion of these issues.

in their wake in the way of important philosophical developments that in turn have much shaped the modern history of the Catholic tradition.

But for now I must finish the other side of this brief review of medieval Catholicism, as I seek to capture some sense of corporate spirit achieved by that most incarnational religion.

MEDIEVAL CATHOLICISM

An Incarnational Religion

WAYS OF LIVING OUT "EMMANUEL": THE THEOLOGY OF INCARNATION INFORMING A SOCIETY

In our effort to understand Catholicism as an incarnational religion, knowledge of Church life in the Middle Ages can help, indeed is indispensable for adequate understanding of this tradition. By observing the multitude of ways in which the Catholic sense of *Emmanuel*—of God with us—was actually interwoven into the lives of Frankish and Gothic and Celtic and English peoples in the society that came closest of all to becoming Christian, we can attain a feel for what it would mean to aspire to a Christ-centered society. We shall observe this massive "inculturation" process, and see how the dialectic between the cultures and the revealed Word of God is handed down by the Church and constantly illumined by the Holy Spirit. We will see also how this interaction produces that ever strange mixture of saint and sinner in the real world we call "Christendom," and, surviving it, the Church.

Medieval society was by no means unqualifiedly Christian. No society en masse has ever been, or ever will be, as Cardinal de Lubac reminds us.[1] So forget nostalgic trips back into an imaginary Christian Middle Ages as a way of dreaming of instituting the Kingdom of God on earth. Nevertheless, many of the Christian social, ecclesial, and aesthetic forms developed at that time have remained—despite the assaults of Protestantism and modernity upon them, and despite the subsequent destruction of broader social underpinnings for them—an integral part of Catholic life, and often a very good part. On the other hand, some of the limitations of medieval life and understanding have left a legacy the Church has had to struggle hard to overcome—a struggle helped, paradoxically, by the Protestant revolt and the subsequent "Enlightenment."[2]

---

1. De Lubac notes: "A perfect Christian civilization, or even a rather imperfect one, has never existed in history and never will" (*A Brief Cathechesis on Nature and Grace* [1980; reprint, San Francisco: Ignatius Press, 1984], 88).

2. Both Protestantism and the Enlightenment have also played a bad role, not only in their contributions to exaggerated individualism and extreme secularization, but

176

In the Middle Ages a sustained effort to realize a kind of incorporation of the divine in the human followed from a sense of Christ's God-given authority and the conviction that God has indeed come to dwell among us to transform society through its sanctification, the Church being the overriding divine instrument created by Christ to that end. Worldly improvement is per se a good thing and would follow from the conversion of individual hearts—"good works" flow from faith. But Augustine, for one, certainly never thought that the "city of this world" would become a peaceful dwelling place, our final home; nor did Thomas with his balanced view of nature and grace, *gratia perficit naturam*. The resistance of finite freedom—of a self-damaged *natura*—to God's love is never lost to sight by the Angelic Doctor. Nor by any of the great Franciscans and the later Spanish mystics, who strove to intensify the experience of Christ's divine presence, stressing the centrality of charity but with no thought of social engineering capable of removal of the great "sinful structures" of society.

Without believing in any utopia, then, orthodox medieval Catholics[3] worked to put into practice their belief in this revelation of God as love, as individuals and entire religious communities and lay confraternities struggled to become an effective divinizing presence in society, but with a realistic emphasis on personal relationships, not on utopian social engineering. The large structures of society were taken for granted, indeed they were accepted as descending from God's authority. Not even the powerful nobles fighting to expand their immediate control thought it possible or advisable to dream of refashioning society. Only the fringe Gnostic heretics, and that dangerous dreamer Joachim of Flore, thought of that. They could get dangerous once they threatened to become more than a marginal phenomenon. These predecessors of the modern Gnostic social dreamers will be treated later.

Within this great mass of social considerations, I want to take a moment to present those elements that contrast most starkly with the later Protestant and post-Protestant modern development. Protestantism grew in a climate of more bourgeois individualism than could be found even in the cities of the eleventh to fourteenth centuries, and in reaction to certain obvious medieval excesses. Some strains of the Reform (particularly the Anabaptist and Calvinist) were "tailor-made" for the new individualism, local control of small communities replacing hierarchical authority descending from on high. Modern Catholicism has learned lessons from Protestant experience, and has absorbed some individualism, especially its foundation in the doctrine of the liberty of conscience, and a renewal of the sense of the role

also by their proponents' propagation to this day of disinformation about Catholicism and the Church, as though medieval forms of thought control, which reached their nadir in "inquisition," in any way characterize the Church's authentic teaching today on freedom of conscience and political liberty.

3. The qualifier is intended to exclude the likes of Joachim of Flore who preached that history has, with Francis, entered the final age, the age of the Spirit, touched with a bit of millenarian perfectionism.

of the laity. As Catholics, too, became more "bourgeois," corporate life has been de-emphasized and the search for physical presence of Christ has been toned down. In the process the Catholic Church itself has tended to "Protestantize" in ways that both purified feudal excesses and opened new possibilities of, for instance, individual freedom and a sense of self-direction.

But this "Protestantizing" also risks loss of some of the old sense of objectivity and authority. As relativism gains ground in modern society—"I have my truth, and you have your truth"—the seriousness of the challenge of possessing and incarnating the truth collapses. Paradoxically, this opens the way for the deformation of the notion of the Kingdom of God into a blueprint for an earthly utopia, because the realization that only God can finally transform sinful structures through a conversion of individual hearts is lost sight of by those who become materialistic. Ecclesial authority, devoted to leading mankind to eternal life, gives way to political authority seeking to forge arbitrarily a socialist paradise on earth.

The great strength of Catholic Christianity lies in its ability to develop, based on the revelation of the Man-God, a sense of mediation between our lowliness and the untouchable, remote, and overpowering splendor of the Most High. When it is at its best, it has been able to do this without either diluting the sense of the divine—revealed as infinite transcendent love that is also immanent to us in the depths of the soul—or tying it to a narrow ethos, the tight limits of a particular race of people (as happened with the Jews and the Anabaptist "remnant," such as the Mennonites). It thus avoids an exaggerated humanism, as though fallen man were, after all, the measure of all things and not God. Rather, it holds fast the revelation that *man in Jesus Christ*, and only in Him, is that measure. Observing what happened in modern "mainline" Protestant Christianity, we can see now how easily this "incarnational" religion can slip into this humanistic exaggeration, with Christ Himself becoming so humanized His very miracles, showing the creational power the Father has given Him, are explained away in purely human, do-good terms, with results disastrous for preserving the sense of God's transcendence and power.[4]

Medieval Christianity permeated the daily life of many races, uniting people in international community and avoiding much parochialism (all the more remarkable when one remembers how difficult were communications then). It was able (and modern Catholicism remains able) to do this because of a strong sense of universal mission, of reaching out to the whole world, united in the divine personhood of Jesus Christ. So like those other great traditions, Islam and Buddhism, it became an international transformer of peoples, as communism (another brotherhood inspired, as was Islam, by the Christian *catholica*) was later to become. But Christianity

4. The day before writing this I heard a sermon in our Catholic parish explaining that what really happened in the miracle of the multiplication of the loaves and fish was that Jesus touched the "generosity" of those present, so those who had hidden a little bread (no mention of hiding a fish!) under their cloaks brought them out and shared!

(and later Islam) pursued this earthly transformation without losing the hieratic sense of God's transcendence, which Marxism denounced.[5]

A good symbol of this international yet incarnating character of Catholicism was the thirteenth-century Sorbonne.[6] Students from as far northeast as Krakow studied with masters from as far south as Sicily (Thomas came from south of Naples) and lived together there, not without national rivalries, to be sure, but still with a sense of catholicity. As at the Kahbah, a truly international culture was in evidence, but lived intensely, daily, year-round.[7]

Not that this apostolic outreach was carried out in perfect keeping with the truth Christ had revealed about the dignity of every person; everyone knows the dolorous catalog of medieval sins: brutal imposition of baptism by Frankish overlords earlier in the barbaric period after the fall of the empire; the "power trips" of many rude Crusaders, forgetting they were defending Christian lands against the mighty armed push of a militant Islam and instead going on the offensive to secure lands for themselves; the Inquisitorial counteroffensive against the Cathar heresy in revolt against Church and feudal imperium in the twelfth and thirteenth centuries; the insidious Spanish Inquisition, launched out of resentment and in a power struggle with "unsure elements" in reconquered Spain (reconquered mile by mile from mighty sultans in nearly a half millennium of armed struggle); and, of course, the insensitive imposition of European-Christian cultural forms, accompanied by intolerance of non-Christian experience, by the sixteenth-century colonists.[8]

5. Buddhism, which owes nothing of its universal inspiration to Christianity, lacks, on the other hand, a sense of the personal in God, so that it produces a different and thoroughly non-Western, disincarnating anthropology.

6. "Sorbonne" is a nickname for the University of Paris. A wealthy Parisian merchant, Robert de la Sorbonne, endowed a college, a student residence, and thus unwittingly lent his name to perhaps the greatest of the Christian universities.

7. The Kahbah is the holy shrine of the Black Stone, marking the place of Abraham's sacrifice, where millions of Muslims gather every year at the Hadj, the obligatory pilgrimage. It is important for Christians to be reminded that theirs is not the only claim to catholicity presently working its transforming power on whole peoples. Imagine a theology faculty with Albert of Cologne, teaching a Thomas of Roccasicca (Aquinas), and later this Thomas teaching side by side with John of Fidenza (Bonaventura)!

8. However, many Franciscans and Jesuits of the time were to show remarkable appreciation for "native" cultures, as in the marvelous story of the Paraguayan *reducciones*. Similarly, Muslims, although enjoined by the Prophet to tolerance of peoples of the Book, could be culturally imperialistic: consider the Mogul conquest of India, for instance.

One should be cautious not to become a victim of certain modern propaganda against the old missionary activity. As one approaches modern times, one finds—in the fascinating stories of Père Ricci's efforts to convert the Imperial Court of China, with his respect for Chinese civilization and willingness to adapt to Chinese forms; in the story of the Jesuit *reducciones* in Paraguay; in the sensitivity shown to Huron ways of life by the Jesuit martyrs of Canada; and in the resistance of the Franciscans in Mexico to the power-hungry excesses of the conquering soldiers—material for a nuanced story with more than one side. The spread of the messages of universal truth from, necessarily, limited cultural bases—from the Greek, for *philosophia*; from

As apostolic outreach is central to this universal message, why did European Christendom eventually split, and largely along national lines? The gradual reshaping of Western Christendom into nation-states is a long and complex process. The seeds were sown in the revival of commerce in the twelfth century, which introduced a more urban and mobile class into the soil-rooted feudal system, ultimately weakening the well-anchored internationalism at the top of the feudal hierarchy, and replacing it by a greater sense of rootless, mobile money power, while the merchants and bankers themselves were rooted in the new cities, most often married from among the local bourgeoisie, and developed a fierce loyalty to their city. The Hansa cities and the Italian city-states grew strong. The national states were at first built by feudal expansion. An intermediary stage saw the development of absolute national monarchs in the seventeenth century by kings able to play the bourgeoisie off against the nobles, and a last great effort by international imperia: the Austro-Hungarian, the Russian, the British, and the Prussian. These gave way to modern industrial nation-states in the nineteenth and twentieth centuries. With the old affinities of crown and cathedral swept away, only a set of personal-interest relations and a very personal religiosity was left. (A residual question: to what extent did the floating international character of a money economy provoke a tribal reaction in the form of the extreme nationalism of the early twentieth century?)

This is a vast story.[9] Just the fact that a national France was emerging in the twelfth century while a united Germany and Italy were not hammered together (by an iron chancellor and a tough Garibaldi, respectively) until six hundred years later shows, too, it was a most uneven process, marked by huge cultural differences even among peoples as close together geographically as "the Europeans."[10]

---

the Hindu, for Buddhism; from Arabic, for Islam; from European, for Catholicism and Protestantism; from German idealistic philosophy, for Communism—to many different cultures sets up huge tensions that are never eradicated completely.

9. In today's moment of intense internationalization under the impulse of that new and most powerful "catholicism," the secular HTX, it behooves us to study the phenomenon of other-than-planetary structures, and especially ethnos and nations with new application, as we watch the recrudescence of ethnic rivalries within the sphere of the collapsed Soviet empire and the attempted domestication of such impulses in the emerging European Community. Watch out for the faltering Communist regime of China as it inflames Chinese nationalism to bolster itself: troubles in Hong Kong and with Taiwan are on the horizon. It will be fascinating to observe the other two vigorous rival *catholicae*—Christianity and Islam—interact with the new planetary-scale institutions.

10. Even today, crossing the border from a very Allemanisch part of Switzerland, into a very French Burgundy, can be a shock. The only greater one I have experienced is crossing from El Paso, Texas, to Ciudad Juarez, where one seems to change planets. The marked cultural differences between Germanic north Frenchmen and the very Mediterranean *provençaux*, or between the Arabic Sicilians and the Lombard north Italians, remain startling. The Lutherans of Lübeck and the Catholics of Bavaria seem in different worlds.

Meanwhile, the Church was caught up in constant tension between papal centralism, the power of local synods of bishops, not to speak of the powerful prince-archbishops who amassed great feudal estates, and the stay-at-home outlook of lower clergy. Mixed in with this, as a kind of overlay, were the new religious congregations, especially the powerful city-based Dominicans and Franciscans, who exploded during the thirteenth century, and later, in the sixteenth and seventeenth, the remarkable Jesuits, who went as far as Huronia (in Canada) and China. They were singularly international, and like the monastic orders before them, largely independent of the bishops. The Jesuits were both mixed up in, and destroyed temporarily by, the national rivalry between Spain and Portugal that led to the division of Latin America by the pope.

The nation-state, it is safe to say, arose as the result of *essentially non-Catholic elements* in society, that is, remnants of an old tribalism (responsible for the growth, out of dialects, of new national languages, that most powerful incarnation of the spirit of a *Volk,* hence the substitution of a much more local sense of *Volk* for the Catholic sense of being the one people of God); the ambition of feudal houses and the quest for consolidated political power; and the desire on the part of the rising "bourgeoisie" and even the more enlightened princes to secure trading advantages.[11] At the very time the internationalism of Catholicism was being effective, the sense of nationhood was growing in some places, down underneath as the tribes stopped wandering and became settled agriculturalists and villagers. The failure to develop a viable international political regime in cooperation with, but not dominated by, the papacy, and the "captivity" of the papacy by the French (including even the outrageous removal of its seat to Avignon for fifty years, from 1309 to 1362); the disruption of international life by the decimation of whole countrysides through the Black Death in the fourteenth century;[12] and the Hundred Years' War between England and France all contributed to the weakening of a sense of the Catholic center as the stronger states developed, on an as yet modest geographical scale, the nucleus of the great modern national regimes.[13]

11. These factors were present to some extent all along, of course, but simply at some point were being attenuated as uniting international, feudal Europe moved away from tribalism, then once again began to grow more dominant (especially in France in those most vigorously Catholic centuries, the late eleventh through the first half of the thirteenth). The very success of burgeoning medieval civilization began to push religious motivation to the background, as life became more distracting. As Toynbee says (speaking generally), "Spiritual and secular ideals are at variance. Souls are deaf to the call of the Spirit in times of secular prosperity" (*A Study of History,* vol. 7[b] [London: Oxford University Press, 1954], 425). In religion, socially speaking, nothing fails like success.

12. There were actually a number of outbreaks of bubonic plague during the fourteenth century, leading to (in some areas) more than 75 percent depopulation between the initial occurrences in Europe in A.D. 1348 and the end of the fourteenth century.

13. One should not indulge in fantasies about a politically strong papacy having been capable of serving as the organizing agent for a politically united Europe. Had

I am raising these issues because, when we come to assess the situation of the Church in today's planetary HTX, we shall need to have some understanding of the national and ethnic forces still at work despite the HTX overlay. Meanwhile, all can now see in retrospect that the splitting of Christendom; the religious wars of the seventeenth century and the revolutionary wars in Napoléon's time; the great nationalistic war of 1914 and its aftermath; and the atheist ideological war of 1939, brought on by Stalinist Communism, Hitlerian National Socialism, and big-capital liberalism (with forces of genuine Christian democracy still at work, too, thank God) were, one after another, unmitigated disasters for Christianity and Europe.

Still, before we talk about disintegration, let us consider the ways this incarnational religion found to reinforce throughout medieval Europe the sense of the presence of God, which to some extent has survived all the disintegration. There are lessons in this for today's Catholic international community building.

LIVING INCARNATIONALLY IN THE MIDDLE AGES

A central element in the revelation of the Incarnation is the vision that each of "the saints" has a unique place in the Mystical Body of Christ, a *missio* no other can fulfill. Paradoxically, this revelation of the absolute worth of each person founds a sort of individualism that degenerates into the egoistic individualism of post-Enlightenment man. That happens as the Christian sense that every person owes obedience to his Source, God, and love to all those with whom he is providentially thrown into relation is weakened. The Christian sense of a web of relations can be seen startlingly, Balthasar points out, in each of the "archetypal" personalities of the Gospels: in Peter's role of office; in Paul's charismatic role, showing the spontaneity of the Holy Spirit; in John's face as the archetype of love, so clearly in that most favored of His loved ones; and in the simple maiden the Father chose to be the vessel of the Incarnation itself, Mary.[14]

In medieval men's devotion to this new Eve we see their intuitive grasp of this divinization of the saints permitted by God's associating us with the Incarnation, and in this divinization the weaving of the broadest web of relationships. This divinization begins with Mary's submission to the divine will as she trustingly utters to the divine messenger, "Thy will be done!"[15] Without this free, human act of obedience, the Incarnation would

---

it happened, it would have been an aberration, totally out of keeping with the role Christ gave His Church. Already the existence of the papal states, *perhaps* a temporary, necessary protection during feudal times, was a serious enough aberration, leading popes into the gravest of temptations.

14. Balthasar, *The Glory of the Lord: A Theological Aesthetics*, trans. Erasmo Leiva-Merikakis, ed. Joseph Fessio and John Riches (San Francisco: Ignatius Press, 1983–), 350–65.

15. Christians, too, have the sense of being *muslim*, that is, freely submitted, past tense of the verb *islam*, which means "to submit."

not have been possible. The whole of history hangs in the balance, as the Maid of Nazareth—who tells the angel she does not understand—nevertheless decides to submit to God's will. Mary is granted the unique gift—shared only with Eve—of being innocent, without stain of sin and hence not pulled one way by her passions, another by her intellect. Unlike Eve, she chooses to cooperate with God's grace and takes full advantage of her state of integrity. Never does she revolt, despite a difficult life, not even at the foot of the cross. That is why she shines now forever with the brightness of the Morning Star ("Seat of wisdom, Tower of David, Morning Star . . ." intones the medieval litany, still heard in Catholic prayer today). True freedom arising from true obedience to God. In contrast, our common mother, Eve, left behind her an immense heritage of death, division, and destruction, the viper's brood.[16]

The Enlightenment idealist philosopher Hegel could see only as a deficiency, if not something incoherent, the medieval desire to represent the divine to the senses. He could make nothing of such archetypes, and he even spurned pilgrimages to holy places, above all to the Holy Sepulchre ("the empty tomb," as he called it). He could not understand the desire to possess relics of Christ and the saints, and to want to consume Christ in the Sacred Host (that very "failure of imagination," decried a century after Hegel, by another good son of the Enlightenment, the Universalist Arnold Toynbee).

Both miss the point of what a Catholic understands and experiences. Without a grasp of this Catholic theo-anthropo-ontology, the medieval endeavors are incomprehensible, and the Catholic tradition dead: God not only can create a material reality (which neither Hegel nor Toynbee would deny), but also can sanctify it progressively, that is, perfect it, allowing the divine image to penetrate it and shine forth from it in ever less inadequate icons,[17] which become nodes of relationship. And because each such person

16. Pairs of contrasting archetypal persons are to be found throughout the Scriptures: for example, Adam/Jesus, Eve/Mary, and Peter/Judas (both deny Christ and repent, but the one goes on to martyrdom and sanctity, while the other kills himself). Whereas the Hebrew prophetic tradition and the New Testament reject Levantine dualism on the level of the divine, the struggle of good and evil, and of light and dark on the level of the angels and man, is clearly central. There is no doubt of the ultimate victory of those forces that come from the infinite, all-good Creator. Even modern-day Gnostics are dissatisfied with this second place given evil!

17. The fathers of the Church found this explanation for Genesis's use of the two terms: we are made in His image, which we can do nothing about; but for that image to become fully similar, our free cooperation with His transforming grace, making us Christlike, is required.

It took from the first moment of Creation until the creation of man, as Teilhard de Chardin puts it, to develop "His body"—the material cosmos—to the point where it could support an image of Himself, and it took from the time of that image, Adam's revolt against its artist until the time of Christ, to prepare a people. From that people comes a virgin vessel for the production of the perfect icon, the adequate "likeness"—adequate because Jesus Christ is God Himself, truly among us in history. Oh unsurpassable, oh perfect likeness, that created "fragment," the man Jesus of Nazareth! Imitation of Him

also acts in the world in keeping with the *missio* accorded him, he is instrumental in the Holy Spirit's achieving a degree of Christification of more general human affairs, at least a minute and perhaps rather local sanctification of society.[18] Through this reshaping of human minds and wills, the cosmos itself is sanctified, because those minds can embrace it in thought and love, and because they are the summit of the "nature" that Christ has sanctified by taking it on and offering it on the cross, all and entire, for the repair of the damage wrought by our sins.[19]

Catholic spirituality does not conceive of the material being *aufgehoben* (lifted up into a new synthesis) but rather illumined and animated from within by the Holy Spirit, its differences and distinctiveness preserved and treasured as a web of relationships continues to be woven. Unlike Hegel's *Geist*, the clearly transcendent Holy Spirit carries out an always mysterious and surprising divine plan through the illumination of each human spirit, in its particular (and never "overcome") mission. Obedient like Mary, we respond without always understanding God's game. Meanwhile, for Christian ontology, matter (nature) remains what it is, the underlying structures being as God created them, full of intelligibility (today understood better in its developmental form, an understanding that sees great stability in the midst of an unfolding, complexifying reality). The individual person, loved into existence by God, is ever thereafter irreducible: a Mother Teresa is valuable, not just when she goes to heaven to become part of the resurrected and purified community gathered around the throne of the Lord. She is effective now, as an icon of Christ, with her own concrete essence, capable of being an archetype (she *is* of the Franciscan genus!) who radiates peace from every wrinkle on her face.[20] Her work is unlike the human work

---

by us moves us personally too from being imago toward becoming *similitudo*, as a Christlike order of obedient love is introduced into each converted human heart, with acceptance of our destiny as imago, and the call to become *similitudo*.

18. Yes, it makes sense to speak of a family as holy, or a religious community, without forgetting that not all individuals within these communities achieve the same degree of holiness, and some are even obdurate in revolt. One can even imagine a Christian manufacturing company, where everyone is treated with the kind of consideration and respect due children of God, a company subject to HTX efficiency pressures but aware that it will succeed only because its people succeed.

19. The "enlightened" Hegel deformed the Christian conception, with, at its center, a Christian sense of freedom, which includes the possibility of revolt at any moment. Hegel deformed it into a liberal, progressive spiritualization. Conceiving the material as "mere" nature, it is being transformed into *Geist* (translatable as both "spirit" and "mind"), which turns out to be, in Hegel's imagination, a rational, universal ordering of society. Nature is not *perfecta* (as Thomas says) but *aufgehoben*, changed essentially in a higher synthesis. This being raised to spirit as Hegel conceives of it has a tendency to reduce ever more the surd of natural distinctions, for him the irrational accidental (that is, not source of different *missiones* but the "left over"—junk left behind by luminous rationalization). A clash in fundamental ontology separates the Hegelian Protestant and the incarnational Catholic, resulting in two distinct anthropological visions.

20. That is why hundreds of thousands press just to get near her, and that is how through the Christlike work of her hands, she manages to bring solace and hope to

that Hegel sees creating liberal state-institutional structures in the good bourgeois-model Prussian state: it is an immediate, concrete, "subjective" person-to-person love.[21] Socialist "social workers" often look askance at Mother Teresa's lack of interest in structures.

It is why, too, the hope of the resurrection, as Catholics understand it, is not centered in some vague melding of all our personalities into the Godhead, but in a heavenly city, a society of saints, in which each retains a concrete role, each is caught up in a unique weave of relationships with the others who abide there. In this way we shall see Christ radiated. And, in the same way, through this body of all the faithful gathered around Jesus we shall see the Incomprehensible Holy Source, "the Father," as reflected in the words that end the Canon in the Liturgy of the Eucharist, "through Him, and in Him and with Him." Nothing that constitutes a positive accomplishment in any of us will be lost. This material will, rather, be gathered together (*legein*, the word for "to gather," from which comes "Logos") like the grains of wheat that furnish the bread of the Eucharist, each "dying to self," being crushed into the flour, but each making an essential contribution to the whole. In God's plan it will be less a crushing than an ordering of the pieces into a four-dimensional, ever unfolding symphony in which all that is positive and worth keeping will be allowed the space-time for unending, loving, *inter-active* harmonious development. No individual person gets lorded over, none is sacrificed to future generations, and all appreciate one another fully. As Mother Angelica said, "In heaven all will be good friends." This is not utopian (u-topos, which means "without a place"), for it has a place: in heaven, not by a fantasy of man but through God's loving plan. This place has a forecourt here, where the *communio sanctorum* has already begun its life.

Sacred realities are transmitted through physical beauty, as the sculptor seeks to capture the Virgin's tenderness toward the Child in a statue, or the master mason tries to express to us the peace and radiance of the heavenly Jerusalem through the élan and light of the cathedral. Whereas some Protestant Reformers suspected a priestly plot in the emphasis on the sacraments, the Catholic sees in them an effective way to make visible and tangible the efficacious healing and uplifting presence of Christ in the soul. A passage in which Gilson explains Saint Bonaventure's sense of this transforming power communicates the experience beautifully:

> It happens just as in the order of corporeal organisms, where the introduction of a new form better organizes the matter and prepares it for the reception of a higher form. Grace invests the soul from the beginning with the three theological virtues (faith, hope and charity), and if the human will responds, it conducts it from state

---

thousands. She is "a channel of His peace" (as Francis, who, after Jesus Himself, is her role model, prayed, "Make me a channel of your peace!").

21. That is why, I suppose, she insists on each of the houses of the Missionaries of Charity remaining small, five or six sisters or brothers, and why she insists that the work of all the missionaries be direct, hands-on help to the poor.

to ever more perfect state, to the extent that spiritual matter allows itself to become more docile to its influence and more worthy of its action. There is no spectacle as beautiful as that of God recreating in us by an unrelenting generosity and liberality the work of creation destroyed by a concupiscent will, returning to Himself that soul which was turned towards itself, now willing Himself in it, finding Himself in it, reflecting Himself in it as in a mirror, in that nature purified of its passions, freed of its deforming fault, master of its thoughts and entirely oriented towards its divine object.[22]

The whole conception and experience of a community of saints forming one Body in Christ—each soul is molded to its role, each member having a role in a hierarchy of functions, none losing its identity, helping one another, from top to bottom of the hierarchy and from bottom to top—grounds an anthropology that celebrates body as well as mind, and reflects a kind of incarnate community that is not dissolved by bourgeois individualism, with its overly rationalist notion of in-spiriting.

STRENGTHS AND EXCESSES IN MEDIEVAL "INCARNATIONAL" SPIRITUALITY

As in all things human, there were obvious excesses in the medieval search for the physical presence, sometimes "on the cheap," which could degenerate into hero worship, directed not at rock stars and baseball greats, as today, but at the Lord Himself and the saintly heroes who present distinctive faces of Christ to each generation. When one reads of the physical battles between the monks of Conques and a neighboring abbey over possession of the relic of Ste-Foy, going so far as the capture of the saint's bones, we feel that something is not quite balanced. The elements of superstitious magic attaching to some aspects of the cult of relics are distortions. But one should not, because of it, swing to the opposite extreme, neglecting to see what is in fact touching (if the pun may be forgiven) in this desire to be physically near to the person who permeated a place and a time with the peace and the light of Christ and brought it to one little corner of the world. All things considered, this is a more uplifting hero worship than a pilgrimage to Elvis's Graceland!

Obviously, as we saw in considering the struggle with the iconoclasts, the ideal should be to avoid bogging down in the material to the point of failing to pass through it to the vision of the transcending Father. At the heart of Christian experience is the proper role of mediation. It will always prove difficult to maintain the balance between the materiality of the representation or the Incarnation, and that which the Incarnation is supposed to reveal, which transcends its here-and-now materiality of presentation. There is something to Hegel's charge that, in such things as the cult of relics, medieval man strove to get a tangible hold on God that

22. Étienne Gilson, *La philosophie de Saint-Bonaventure*, 366, translation mine. In English, *The Philosophy of Saint Bonaventure*, trans. Étienne Gilson, Illtyd Trethowan, and Frank J. Sheed (Paterson, N.J.: St. Anthony Guild Press, 1965).

is not our lot in this life.[23] There are excesses of literalism in some of the most sublime medieval spirituality. For instance, some of the stories of Saint Catherine of Siena's marriage to Christ and her drinking His precious blood from the wound in His side are capable of bringing out the Protestant in even the most devout contemporary Catholic. These forms of imagination are all the more disturbing when they are found in the midst of a great sanctity and a powerful spiritual influence: Saint Catherine's influence on the conversion of sinners all about her is well established.[24]

While treasuring the body, medieval man enjoyed an understanding of the need for the material order to be disciplined by the higher order of the spirit, the body becoming forced to submit to the intellectual will. Hence the emphasis on fasting and penance, practices of ascesis, in order to control the unruly passions that tend to bog down in the nearest materially desirable object, and to order the will by building up strong habits ("virtues"), enlightened by the Word of God, to fulfil the Lord's mission. The lives of the monks in the populous monastic orders were filled with such discipline, but then every layman was likewise expected to observe considerable periods of fasting and abstinence from meat.[25]

23. It is ridiculous to want to go on pilgrimage to the holy places, snorts Hegel. Not at all, replies the Catholic, these are holy places, here in this world, because they were sanctified by the real presence of Jesus Christ, present historically, in that time, in these places, or by saints who radiated a face of Christ incarnationally. Christ did not take flesh of the Virgin Mary to transform it into spirit, but through the indwelling of His Holy Spirit in this matter, to sanctify flesh to make it an offering and an instrument for definitively overcoming death. Matter is always *in-formed,* structured, manifesting an intelligible "whatness" and a unique "thatness," a singular hold on time and space, which flows (as causal lines) from before and out beyond the here-and-now space-time limits of this material thing. In sum, Catholic philosophy does not foresee the destruction of the higher forms of individuality/personality, but their ordering in a lasting, fruitful society, in which, in their materiality, purified of destructive and irrelevant elements, and spiritually ordered to one another, they will endure forever.

24. When extraordinary graces are given to a frail human being, there is no reason not to suppose that the God-exalted can mix with the psychological, the unusual spiritual sensitivity of the person being perhaps not only a strength but also a potential psychological weakness. Who is to know what, in all that is reported of Saint Catherine (after Jeanne d'Arc arguably the most troubling of great medieval saints), comes from her and what from her Dominican friends, and what in the things she did report reflects genuine visions (gifts of Christ) and what are imaginings, fired by those experiences, but carried beyond what God Himself authored? While the canonization of the Church declares the ultimate holiness of Saint Catherine, no Christian is obliged to the least degree to accept any of her private revelations. The great Spanish mystic San Juan de la Cruz warns against attaching too much importance to visions and the like, cautioning against human and diabolical distortion (on San Juan, see *BT*, chapter 8). God works with human nature in all its foibles and brokenness.

25. Without debate, the Church, outside of strict monastic orders, has since the 1960s seemed to forget about ascetic practices. (For instance, whereas canon law still requires abstinence from meat on Fridays, its allowing substitution of a good work or other penance has been misread as simple abolition of any special Friday observance as a way of participating in the sufferings of the crucified. And only a minority observe the still recommended Lenten fast.) Within the lay spiritual prelature, Opus Dei, where there

Second, medieval man ordered the whole day and the entire year about a heavenly axis. *Sapientia est ordinare,* declared Thomas, following the insight of Aristotle: wisdom is placing things in their proper order. It is a right set of priorities within the hierarchy of things that has to be sought and properly lived, the life of society being arranged according to divine priorities.

Medieval man was exemplary in respecting the sense of "the things that are God's": Sundays and feasts were as strictly observed as Shabbat is by Orthodox Jews today; life was punctuated with liturgy, celebration, and festival, with time preserved for family life and for enjoying friends, as it still is in village life today. There were so many holy days observed that medieval man, unlike nineteenth-century industrialized workers, enjoyed the equivalent of a five-day week. Moreover, the whole year was ordered to the liturgical calendar, which combines the primitive religious sense of the seasons as they had been incorporated into the Roman calendar, and combined with other pagan festivals, recalling God's creative work and the cycle of life and death and remembering the greatest of His saints.[26] The Christian family today still finds Christmas and Easter moments of gathering the clan. And while Thanksgiving was instituted by civil order (Abraham Lincoln was its author in the United States), it serves, like Succoth for the Jews, as a harvest festival.

To this ordering of the year one should add the ordering of the day: morning and evening prayers; the *Angelus*[27] (inspired by the muezzin calling from their minarets, observed by both Crusaders and the faithful in Dar-el-Islam: Spain, Sicily, Anatolia, and so on); the church bells calling to a prayer recalling our redemption, at sunrise, noon, and sunset;[28] prayer before and after each meal; vespers; and for religious, the canonical hours.

Finally, the whole order of one's life: the sacraments appropriate to moments of passage, administered by the *communio* of God, to consecrate

is still found emphasis on "mortification" and "self-denial," there is also to be found an old-fashioned emphasis on building up the virtues. There has occurred a quiet shift in anthropological faith that requires explicit examination.

26. This consecration of certain days to individual saints (or groups of saints, such as the North American Jesuit martyrs) is a wonderful incarnational symbol.

27. Every Catholic schoolchild knows the evocative late-nineteenth-century painting of Millet showing two peasants, heads bowed in prayer, at sunset, as the Angelus is sounded from a steeple visible on the horizon. The destiny enjoyed by the original painting, when it was owned in our family, is a good symbol of the secularization that overtook France at the end of the last century: just after the turn of the century, my wife's great-uncle, Achille Fanien, a good "Radical," devoid, so far as I know, of the least pious sentiment, sold Millet's *Angelus* to the Louvre for a sum sufficient to buy a splendid hunting lodge in the Brie.

28. Still rung in Catholic Europe, and from the belfry of our College Church in Toronto. To the bells, the faithful respond: "The angel of the Lord declared unto Mary that she would become the mother of God. . . . Behold the handmaid of the Lord, Be it done to me according to thy word. . . . And the Word was made flesh and dwelt amongst us." Like the muezzin's call to prayer, this is a prayer of submission (Islam) to the will of God.

it to its divine end.[29] The day was punctuated by prayer. Yet, the most wonderful medieval invention in this regard was the presence not just of family, friends, and neighbors, but the community of saints invoked at baptism, confirmation, first communion, marriage, holy orders, and extreme unction, welding the Catholic into that living Body of Christ and transcending the limits of the moments of an individual life, a catholicity in time even more than in space.

But space too was transformed, the village huddled around the church, its steeple, pointing toward heaven, raised far above all other human constructions, except, in some instances, the fortified castle on the hill (a reminder that social life was not completely transformed by Christianity into a heavenly Jerusalem). Around the church gathered the beloved dead, the cemetery a daily reminder of that communion of saints in time.[30] A better representation of the heavenly Jerusalem perhaps was the great abbey church, serving as a constant reminder of a more evangelical, purer community, more completely devoted to the interior life. To it flocked thousands seeking spiritual—and material—solace. Finally, the gravity-defying flight of the vaults of the cathedral, that miracle of engineering that transformed stone into prayers, in whose glowing windows were recounted all the events of the *sacra historia* and the marvelous lives of the saints, gathering all the space of the cathedral city under its protection. All roads led to the cathedral town, reminiscent of the way all clerical orders led upward to the fullness of Christ's priesthood, present in the successor to the apostles, the bishop, through whom, seated on His *cathedra*, the throne of His apostolic dignity, the redemptive path led onward toward heaven.[31]

In this well-ordered time-space, everything and everyone came together in the universal prayer of the Church, the Mass. Every Sunday and holy day saw a pilgrimage of the entire village and countryside to this holy space, the church, representative of the heavenly Jerusalem, the place of Christ's redemptive act. That is why, of course, the Mass is much more than a prayer: it is the reenactment of the redemptive event, and the centerpiece of Christ's dwelling with us, the Emmanuel act par excellence, the holy sacrifice, the ultimate sign of sanctification, the most sacred incarnate re-presencing of Christ in our midst.

29. The sacraments were first clearly delineated as seven—baptism, confirmation, Eucharist, confession and penance (reconciliation), matrimony, holy orders, and extreme unction—in 1139 by Otto von Bamberg, taken up by Peter Lombard and settled once and for all by the Council of Trent.

30. Contrast with the sprawling modern cemetery, marginalized to the outskirts of town, with a tiny ugly chapel hidden in it somewhere, looking more like a sort of park for recreation than hallowed ground.

31. The cathedral town could afford to build its great church because it has already begun to prosper as an important commercial center. In our great secularized cities to-day, it is the cluster of Babylon towers—the bank buildings—that replace the cathedral. Their lobbies are built to impress, as one approaches the holy of holies; the vaults are not great soaring ogival arches but the place where the gold is stored.

For someone who rejects the central Christian claim of the Incarnation, it is hard not to see in the Mass an anachronistic remnant of an ancient rite of "consuming the god." For the Christian it is just the reverse, of course: he sees all pagan sacrifice, and especially all rites of consuming the god, to be forerunners, responding to a natural predisposition implanted by the Creator in man, a profound need to reach out to God and for the gap between the divine and human to be closed, along with an impulse in us to reach upward, to become "like gods," a notion not lacking in the religions. Christ Himself, when He first suggested the Eucharist, in which God reached down to us in utter humility, heard many of His disciples call it a "hard saying" (John 6:60). We shall see the difficulties confronting Christians in conceiving of it when we consider, in the next chapter, the Reform's struggles with this central issue of the incarnational religion.[32]

If we glance back over the religious life of those centuries we can easily discern, then, the essence of Catholic practice in prayer, penance, and sacraments, particularly the Mass: prayer, especially in community, as a way of opening one's mind to God's presence; penance, necessary for the kind of self-discipline needed for the interior life, and as a way of acknowledging one's sinful state; and the Sacrament, as the incarnated presencing of Christ in His Mystical Body, with manifestation of the forgiveness of sins at the heart of the matter. Because together these things enhanced a sense of community, there occurred an enormous flowering of individual and corporate works of mercy, vast religious orders devoted to the care of the sick, pilgrims, and orphans; alms-giving; unstinting generosity in the

---

32. Medieval man's hieratic sense of the holiness of the moment of Communion was so great that people were disinclined to frequent Communion, preferring instead to prepare carefully through penance and fasting for the great feasts and then to commune only on special days. (Many communed only once a year—a practice still common in some Orthodox churches.) This suggests that theirs was a great sense of their unworthiness, of the tarnish of sin, of the need for stringent purification of the soul through hard penance, and, more positively, of the appropriateness of approaching the altar table with utmost reverence, after a good preparation. (Much of this sense of unworthiness and of the hieratic splendor of the eucharistic presence is being lost in the contemporary Church, in the present phase of "Protestantization." You do not have to be an Orthodox critic to see that this is happening. In many Canadian churches one can see the congregation enjoying a social bee before the start of Mass, where twenty years ago all would have been plunged in reverential silent prayer in the presence of the Holy Eucharist. Emphasis has shifted from celebrating the holy redemptive act to the "people of God" celebrating itself as social community.) Still, in the eleventh century Pope Gregory VII had recommended daily Communion "as a remarkable means to fortify oneself in the practice of chastity" (Henri Daniel-Rops, *Cathedral and Crusade: Studies of the Medieval Church, 1050–1350,* trans. John Warrington [Garden City, N.Y.: Doubleday, 1963], 78). Saint Peter Damian had preached in favor of the practice. But they were not followed. The Fourth Lateran Council in 1215 promulgated the obligation that remains in effect today: annual confession and Communion. Easter, Pentecost, and Christmas were the great days for Communion. "It was only in the fourteenth century, and above all after the publication of *The Imitation of Christ* that the sacrament came widely to be seen as 'a *viaticum* which gives strength to the soul for its daily combat'" (ibid.).

maintenance of monasteries and the construction of the great cathedrals; and, in general, during the best periods, an apparently high degree of community solidarity.

Such in any event was the ideal that has been preserved for us. Much evidence of vast enthusiasm does in fact exist: the crusades; the pilgrimages; the abbey churches and cathedrals; the lovely parish churches by the thousands; the hostels and hospitals; the explosion of the Cistercians, whose sober priories continue to bless hidden valleys all over Europe; the mendicants, whose great barns of Franciscan and Dominican churches are found in the thriving cities; the confraternities for spiritual perfection; and the Guilds, including those guilds of learning, the universities.

But brutality and barbarisms were by no means rooted out (will they ever be?)—this was a rough Germanic and Slavic folk slowly being civilized— and as Saint Dominic's descriptions of the laxity he found in Provence and Toulouse at the time of the Cathari (late twelfth century) makes plain, there is no room here, as I warned, for imagining a perfect Christian society: education was spreading fast but was still sparse; and we simply do not know how much of all this ordinary people understood and accepted, as most, being illiterate, low-productivity peasants, left no record of their thoughts.

Because, like so many other cultures, the Christian civilization of the Middle Ages lived fairly closed in on itself—its contacts with Islam, except for its profiting from the great philosophers and physicians, were largely hostile, and its forays into Nordic and Slav tribes were experienced as advance of the old Christian civilization into barbarous lands—it tended to develop so tight a weave between its theology and its civil society that deviations in doctrine were looked on as threats to the civil order, and indeed often the "heretics" did challenge the civic authority of the rulers. Given the rigidity of that feudal order, with the rank and place of everyone being carefully defined and upward mobility being highly restricted, deviation was indeed a great destabilizer, as the ultimate Protestant diremption amply proved. This invited uptight defensive measures, which included a rigid enforcement of conformity to accepted religious orthodoxy, "thought control."

The situation was worsened by dominance of that somewhat static concept of truth we discussed in the last chapter. That set the scene for the most sinister of the legacies of the Middle Ages, the effort at thought control that bears the forever sinister name of the Holy Inquisition. Before completing this brief overview of the Middle Ages, we should see what lesson is to be learned from that response, so unacceptable to post-Enlightenment man. As we have learned in our own time of ideological world wars, philosophical inadequacies mixed with social problems can have deadly results.

HERESY IN THE MIDDLE AGES AND THE INQUISITION

It is our will that all the peoples who are ruled by the administration of our clemency shall practise that religion which the divine Peter the apostle transmitted to the Romans. We command that those persons who follow this rule shall embrace the name of Catholic Christians. The rest, however, whom we judge demented and insane, shall sustain the infamy of heretical dogmas, their meeting places shall not receive the name of churches, and they shall be smitten first by divine vengeance and secondly by the retribution of our own initiative, which we shall assume in accord with divine judgement.[33]

Before you condemn those intolerant medieval tyrants, be informed that this not very Christian edict was formulated in 380 by a barbarian become emperor, Theodosius, who clearly shows some of the excess zeal of the recent convert, and, I dare say, little sense of what Jesus Christ came to reveal to us!

I have been pointing out that unitary societies are the lot of most of mankind throughout history. They have become looked on as terrifying by only "post-Enlightenment" men enjoying the freedom experienced in that modern invention—to this day enjoyed by perhaps 20 percent of mankind—pluralistic, secularized democratic society, made possible by the wealth generated by industrialization.[34] The majority still live in either tribal or ideologically based totalitarian (a fifth of mankind in Communist China) or traditionalist Muslim, Hindu, or Buddhist societies.[35] Many societies well on the way to modernization, and many traditionalist ones, are ruled by military dictators.

The Europe of the Middle Ages was emerging from the tribal life of the Germanic and Slavic peoples, with (up to the *limes,* roughly the Rhine-Danube line) a strong underlay of old *Romanitas* that had been somewhat submerged during the austere Dark Ages but had proved a sleeping giant during the developments of the Renaissance of the twelfth century.[36]

At the time of the founding of a more centralized Inquisition in the thirteenth century, the Church had existed more than a millennium without experiencing the need for any such procedure as the Inquisition. That is perhaps not so positive a consideration as first seems. Until Constantine,

33. *The Theodosian Code,* 16.1.2 (February 28, 380).

34. Recent waves of "voting" should not be confused for the complex nature of this type of society. "Democracy" alone is far more than mere "voting"—a key reason that concerns for the health of democracies are still being raised today.

35. Hindu and Buddhist societies have a reputation for relative "openness"—of this I have no direct experience and little knowledge. The murderous tensions in the Indian subcontinent between Muslims, Hindus, and Sikhs and in Sri Lanka between Tamils and the Ceylonese majority cause a healthy skepticism about those lands. Is it possible those folk too have been touched by original sin? One hears, on the other hand, good things about toleration in certain Buddhist lands, such as Thailand. The introduction of murderous Western ideologies into countries like Vietnam and Cambodia has led to the utmost intolerance.

36. The title of Haskins's classic, *The Renaissance of the Twelfth Century* (Cambridge: Harvard University Press, 1927), provides good insight into the remarkable developments of that century. Consider the renewed force of the Roman sense of law in the canon-law reforms of that period as just one evidence. One should also not underestimate the extent to which the feudal societies of Europe saw the importance of the reign of law, with the Roman respect for law reinforced by the Christian sense of conscience rooted in the giving of the divine law.

the Church had no power. After the barbarian invasions, the coherence of tribal society kept local order. Only with the emergence of a more capitalistic and modern society in the twelfth century does the problem of maintaining societal coherence on a broader scale arise. Europe was still strongly under the influence of a gradually weakening feudal system retaining a high degree of religious and intellectual unity. Still, the leaders could feel their power being mightily challenged on the one hand by the newly emerging cities, ruled by *les bourgeois,* and, on the other, by efforts of houses like the Capetians to centralize power in their royal hands.[37] Nothing breeds extremism like insecurity. Europe was not during these "Catholic centuries" at any time a model for "open" and tolerant society as we now experience it in a few democracies. The Jewish minority can attest to that.[38] To be fair, in the thirteenth-century university there was an atmosphere of open debate that much later centuries—the sixteenth to eighteenth, for instance—could envy. And not everywhere and all the time were the Jews molested—in fact, it seems the bishops generally tried to protect them against crowds working out their frustrations on the "scapegoats." On another front, while there existed from the twelfth century onward a high level of enlightened debate within the cathedral schools and universities, and while the rapidly increasing urban population enjoyed freedom of movement (as witnessed by the international character of the universities), and although scholars drew freely on Islamic and Jewish thought, the society as a whole felt threatened by growing groups of heretics who often questioned the foundations of medieval society. They found especially menacing certain radical thinkers who, like Siger of Brabant, drawing on those foreign sources, wandered far from the orthodox center.[39]

Whether a group like the Cathari, whom the Catholics of twelfth-century France and Italy clearly thought constituted a mortal danger to society, really were such a threat is difficult to judge. They certainly introduced disorder into southern France and parts of northwestern Italy. But if they were such a menace, how such a danger should have been handled, consonant with evangelical virtues of justice and charity, and with the necessary courage and efficacy (the latter are indispensable political qualities for any society to survive), is a valid issue for speculation.

37. The Capetians were the French royal house, first of the European kingdoms to develop. (The English Plantagenet kingdom was simultaneously operative, but was in reality a parliament of baronies, which would eventually develop as the institution of English parliamentary government.)

38. Theirs was a somewhat precarious existence, despite fairly consistent protection by the hierarchy. Local outbreaks of xenophobia led to occasional pogroms, and, while these were exceptional, the Jews never could know when the rage of frustration might come crashing down on them. The Church condemned violence against Jews, and many bishops effectively defended them. But the Church itself held them suspect, fearing they would undermine the Christian culture.

39. Siger of Brabant, who lived from approximately 1240–1284, was a philosophy master in the Faculty of Arts in Paris and was condemned for propositions drawn heavily from the great Muslim interpreter of Aristotle, the philosopher Ibn-Rashid, called by the Latin name "Averroes."

Fortunately, it is not our task to sit in judgment of the Christian society of that period. We must only understand the phenomenon of the Inquisition well enough to grasp whatever connection there may be between a certain way of conceiving the truth, the Church's defense of the truth, and those means of fighting error that today we—and the Church explicitly—judge repugnant. One thing in all this is sure: no contemporary Christian looks with anything but distress on the instruments of inquiry and extirpation invented toward the end of the twelfth century and into the thirteenth to deal with the perceived threat, nor with the violent way the Cathari were rooted out.[40] But then neither did a Saint Bernard at the time, who consistently preached the need for charitable persuasion, not force. All today would agree with Jacques Maritain, the Catholic philosopher, when he declares that the Inquisition was, despite all efforts to understand why such a thing might have happened, "an offence to God" and a "blight on the Church." The present pope, in calling on all Christians to prepare for the celebration of the two thousandth birthday of Christ, proposes recalling and asking forgiveness for the sins of the past, which "still burden us and remain ever present temptations." Among the "painful chapters" he singles out for mention is "the acquiescence given, especially in certain centuries, to *intolerance and even the use of violence* in the service of truth."[41]

It is true that an accurate historical judgment cannot prescind from careful study of the cultural conditioning of the times, as a result of which many people may have held in good faith that an authentic witness to the truth could include suppressing the opinions of others or at least paying no attention to them. Many factors frequently converged to create assumptions that justified intolerance and fostered an emotional climate from which only great spirits, truly free and filled with God, were in some way able to break free. Yet, the consideration of mitigating factors does not exonerate the Church from the obligation to express profound regret for the weaknesses of so many of her sons and daughters who sullied her face, preventing her from fully mirroring the image of her crucified Lord, the supreme witness of patient love and of humble meekness. From these painful moments of the past a lesson can be drawn for the future, leading all Christians to adhere fully to the sublime principle stated by the Second Vatican Council: "The truth cannot impose itself except by virtue of its own truth, as it wins over the mind with both gentleness and power."[42]

---

40. The movement of the Cathari, it should be understood, was clearly political as well as religious, and their politics were revolutionary. With the most powerful lord of the south of France, the Comte de Toulouse, playing games with the Cathari phenomenon, the unity of France that the Capetians were painfully putting together was seriously threatened. As in Islam and Northern Ireland today, and in Europe in the seventeenth century, the mix of class, political, and religious considerations makes for a powerful stew.

41. John Paul II's Apostolic Letter, *Tertio Millennio Adveniente* (1994), para. 34, 35.

42. Declaration on Religious Freedom, *Dignitatis Humanae* 1, in *Tertio Millennio Adveniente*, para. 35.

Today's Church not only rejects any use of force (or psychological manipulation) to require conformity to Christian practice, but also has endorsed with increasing enthusiasm the Enlightenment principle of "open society," particularly its plank of complete and untrammeled religious freedom. The Second Vatican Council has so opened up the question of how God's truth comes to us as to weaken fatally, it seems to me, any justification that might be advanced today for repressive measures, like those employed in the Middle Ages, and today in the prisons of China.[43]

The need for instruments of thought control constitutes reason enough for any Enlightenment man to suspect the ideal of unitary society, and the notions of truth they presuppose. When later we discuss contemporary understandings of freedom and the concept of liberation, I shall defend the human and religious superiority of open society, whatever its problems and risks—and they are great—as the ideal to be striven for today by Christians, and I shall argue for a concept of truth necessary to make sense of it, without however having to sacrifice on the altar of expediency the quest for wisdom.[44]

There was little sense that people might hold out against society's authorized teaching because of the sincerity of their own lights (why should the Holy Spirit, whom Christ sent to guide and protect His Church, accord private lights to individuals in discord with that Holy Church?)[45] or a notion there could be distinctive valid experiences not shared by all (after all, our common Father created us all alike). There was no notion that "the people of God," as a society guided by the Holy Spirit, could be wrong. And while the *"kaiserliche und königliche apostolische Majistät"* (the correct form of address, for instance, to a Habsburg emperor) was subject to God's law, how could the crowned authority of a rigorous hierarchy be seriously questioned?

Although some great churchmen sympathized with the need for reform, they could not help but see that the heretics' protests were mixed inextricably with grave errors that might cause in the end more damage than the reform would bring good. There were notable exceptions: to his everlasting credit, Pope Innocent III, for instance, repeatedly showed appreciation for the efforts of the humble to return to the simplicity of evangelical life, and worked tirelessly to convert into currents of reform within the Church

43. In our own time, we are witnessing this reality as we watch the efforts of China and the former USSR to reform without democratizing. The startling adoption of democracy in South Korea and then in Central Europe shows how suddenly opposition can bring about radical transformation. Now add to the list the amazingly rapid crumbling of the USSR—and the probabilities that the successor CIS and the old czarist Russian amalgamation will quickly follow.

44. *TA* and *BT* laid the groundwork for this promised argument. I do not believe either volume oversimplifies the problem.

45. A Catholic today is still tempted to think like that when he is told about "outpourings of the Holy Spirit" at evangelical revival meetings. The magisterium of the Church warns him, however, against wanting to put limits on how and where the Holy Spirit will operate. This tension is evident from the earliest Church, in the relations between Paul and the authorities in Jerusalem.

certain pietistic movements of those espousing evangelical poverty. The Poverii and the Franciscans were among the groups he legitimized. But his attitude was not widely shared. (But then, too, it must be said these movements did not deviate in theology nor attack the foundations of civil society the way the dangerous Cathari did.)

The notion that the state was to be the steward of the Church in implementing the demands of a society founded in truth by rooting out evil effects of perversity was a pillar of Roman imperial law: deviation that threatens the fabric of society is lèse-majesté. Add to all this the fact that most people were little instructed, probably upward of 80 percent of ordinary people being illiterate and enjoying no schooling at all, and the fact that the worldly positions of higher clergy were intimately bound up with the glory attaching to their ecclesiastical offices. Remember that tense and complex relationships existed between the worldly power of this higher clergy (some were "prince-archbishops" and "Electors of the Holy Roman Empire") and that of the secular princes.

Gnostics Appear among the Twelfth-Century Heretics

At some times it is not at all difficult to feel trouble in the air. The heretics of the twelfth century were like the later Protestants in striking explicitly at the heart of the established power: they challenged radically and openly the authority of the hierarchy to teach and of the princes to rule. Like the later Protestants, they claimed to be "the pure," possessing a special charism that authorized them to challenge the "corrupt" society (every society always is, to some degree, and this one was slow to reform itself) and its power structures in the name of a superior gnosis, a charism of knowledge, which somehow fed their own moral superiority.[46]

Some form of such "Gnosticism," we earlier suggested, seems to be a perennial temptation of man. It certainly showed itself early in this tradition. In fact, it had become virulent already in Jewish circles around the time of Christ.

As "Gnostic temptation" was a part of the Protestant phenomenon (Eric Voegelin calls the Protestants, flat-out, "Gnostics," a charge I believe exaggerated) and as the mind-set is so perennial, it would be wise to open a brief parenthesis here to recall what form the Gnostics challenging the early church took.[47]

Gnosticism, we saw, was in the air in the Roman-Hellenistic world of the first and second centuries. The kind of speculative reaching out for answers to the questions of man's fate it represents expresses a deep yearning in

46. The Bolsheviks in early-twentieth-century Russia, despite their scoffing at traditional Christian morality, armed as they were with their superior "scientific gnosis," giving them insight into "the iron laws of history," felt themselves *pure*, vis-à-vis the dirty bourgeois capitalists. 'Tis ever thus.

47. Voegelin, *The New Science of Politics* (Chicago: University of Chicago Press, 1952), 134.

the human soul. This natural desire for reassuring answers gives rise to a temptation that crops up repeatedly in some form, as Eric Voegelin has shown, from the moment the human soul becomes aware of itself and "the sense of the Beyond contracts into it": the temptation to invent speculative theories that will validate immediate experience of the divine and ensure control over the soul's future.[48]

This temptation of speculative philosophy is not a disease of the ancients and Protestants only. Voegelin (as do Étienne Gilson and Henri de Lubac) sees in the speculations of the thirteenth-century Franciscan Joachim of Flore, and in modern ideologies like Marxism and Nazism, with their plans for total "structural" transformation of mankind, forms of Gnosticism, the latter, however, thoroughly secularized.[49] When liberalism too aspires to solve all problems through "high-tech," as control over nature, the same temptation is being indulged.

Within Christianity, as within any thoughtful form of life, one can always pick and choose at will elements of the rich tradition and, weaving them with philosophical ideas eclectically gathered from hither and yon in the culture of the time (even Marxist anthropology), spin a consoling message for the elite of cognoscenti gathered in a self-directing, closed sect, or at least a "politically correct" clique.

How does the "orthodoxy" of the majority, what Frend calls, borrowing the term from Neh. 5:8, "the great church," manage to evolve and maintain itself with the whole balanced message of Revelation (presumably) intact against such an ongoing seductive possibility of derailment into imaginative sectarian constructions, risking to proliferate every time an exalted "do-it-yourselfer"—a self-anointed prophet—raises his head?[50] It is almost a miracle to maintain intact a teaching into which is gathered the entire message of the founding vision, the grasp of which is deepened with the experience over time of the whole community living in daily struggle. Today how does the Church keep the complex message intact and well balanced when a liberal society, sounding off through its mass media, is repulsed by every exercise of authority and discipline, and individuals consider themselves free to pick and choose doctrines from the supernatural cafeteria line?

Once the core message is under Gnostic attack, it is inevitable that full-fledged theology will arise. Fire is answered with fire: philosophical speculation is replied to by Christians, who will to remain complete in their orthodoxy but who must also use the instruments of theoretical reflection provided by the philosophy of the time.

---

48. Ibid., chapter 7.

49. Gilson, *Les métamorphoses de la cité de Dieu* (Louvain: Publications Universitaires de Louvain, 1952), and de Lubac, *La postérité spirituelle de Joachim de Flore,* 2 vols. (Paris: Lethielleux, 1978–1980).

50. W. H. C. Frend, *The Rise of Christianity* (London: Darton, Longman, and Todd, 1984), 260 n. 1: "I appointed against them [the malcontents] a great assembly [*ecclesia megalen*]."

The first full-blown theology, which was especially influential on the Eastern fathers, contained elements that, as Daniélou put it, depended, like the Gnostics, more on the philosophy of the time than on the tradition. There is evidence that heterodox Jewish circles were already affected by Gnostic tendencies before the Christian era began—Alexandria was the center where Greek and Hebrew thought met, and the great Jewish eclectic Philo, roughly a contemporary of Jesus, was a perennial source of Gnostic ideas. Origen (who was born in A.D. 185) grew up in an Alexandria still impregnated with Philo's vision. Some see traces of Gnostic influence in certain Johannine formulations, particularly the strong emphasis on light versus darkness.[51]

The person who despairs of the world either wants to refashion "structures" radically according to the insight enjoyed by a privileged elite to whom it has been given to see through the sham of the present world—the reaction of every kind of modern revolutionary—or, as with the ancient Gnostics, they believe that the distant transcendent God has vouchsafed to an elite an ultimate vision of truth, including a triumphant way to the vanquishing of all the evil represented by this created world, through leaving it behind. Every breakaway religious sect, with its rejection of the world and its puritan attitudes of perfection and its claim to infused knowledge from the Spirit, reproduces this feeling.

In contrast, the "orthodox" majority, which is often bound up with the "establishment,"[52] rejects the sentiment that the world is so bad as to be past redemption; it is prepared to live in the world for all its ambiguity and to work patiently for its gradual, evolutionary betterment. They see the Church as open, not just to a chosen few, but to the entire human community, for God wills the fulfillment of all.[53]

In being anti-Gnostic, the orthodox are emphatically not against knowing, or "intellectuality." They recognize that the Way must of course be known, that correct theory guiding practice is essential. What they object to is that the Gnostics seek salvation by knowledge above all else. What impressed many Greek and Roman sophisticates of the late second and early third centuries, a period of considerable expansion of Christianity,

51. Hans Jonas, *The Gnostic Religion: The Message of the Alien God and the Beginnings of Christianity*, 2nd ed. (Boston: Beacon Press, 1963).

52. In the case of the Arian heresy, this was not the case; the barbarian emperors inclined to the heresy and many of the bishops were won over. That was rather exceptional, until the great splits at the time of the Protestant revolt.

53. That is why the mass of Catholics today resist those more extreme liberation theologians who want to change the structures of society in a radical, revolutionary way. It is not always inertia, fear, or indifference on the part of the majority, nor a cowardly comfortableness with the ruling-power circles. It can be, rather, just modesty, a recognition of the inevitable ambiguity of the condition of a sinful humanity, and hence a sense of the need to work patiently for incremental improvement, even in quite bad situations. Differing "natural faiths," conditioned by distinctive temperaments, experience, and teaching, lead to different ways of living out *hope*, as different as a revolutionary and an evolutionary style.

was more the faith's effect on people's conduct than the novelty of its ideas. But the Gnostics were inclined differently: rather than depend on God's redeeming love, they believed that through study of His word and philosophical speculation spun largely from their own very active imaginations they could be sure of the way and secure it for themselves. Clement of Alexandria, bishop and Origen's senior, quotes an early Gnostic: "It is not only baptism which frees (from the power of fate) but Gnosis—knowledge of what we are, why we have come into being, where we are and at what point (in the cosmos) we have been placed, whither we are hastening, from what we have been redeemed, and what is birth and rebirth."[54]

The Gnostics placed God so infinitely beyond this world, He is seen as a principle of pure being protected from contamination through the intermediation of a whole order of heavenly beings, the lowest of which, in the form of "Yahweh," is responsible for bringing about this tawdry world with all its evils. Incarnation, the cross, redemption, and the Resurrection made no sense—the elusive Most High could not compromise Himself by getting this involved in the condemned world. Rather, God's messenger, the Spirit of Light, made His Word available to the predestined few to whom it is given to understand it. Their salvation has nothing to do with improving gradually this world; instead, their souls are transported in a revolutionary, totally transforming way into another sphere. There is no notion of charity in Gnostics.[55]

Helped by this background, let us return now to our Gnostics of the

---

54. Cited by Clement of Alexandria, *Excerpts from Theodotus*, 78. About the same time a thinker in the Ophite sect of Gnostics wrote: "We alone know the necessity of birth and the ways by which man enters into the world. And so, being fully instructed, we alone are able to pass through and beyond decay" (cited from Ephphanius, *Panarion*, 26, in W. H. C. Frend, *The Early Church* [Philadelphia: Fortress Press, 1965], 50).

55. The Old Testament, which Orthodox Christianity sees as God's Word and testimony to His work with people in this world to redeem creation, is for the Gnostics a tale of unenlightenment and sin. For Marcion, a leading Gnostic missionary, the God of the Old Testament was "just," to the extent He struggled against sin; but the God revealed in the New Testament is "good," at least for those who share in the gnosis, as He will take the few beyond evil altogether.

With the conversion of educated Greeks, philosophical speculation became more frequent, with Alexandria ever the center. In the second half of the second century, there occurred "a process of mutual amalgamations," as the God of the Alexandrian Jews approached the God of the Alexandrian Platonists, as Frend, citing Emil Schürer puts it (ibid., 203). With no sense of discipline from apostolic authorities, no sense of the truth being handed down from Christ through His apostles, Gnostics such as Basilides (around A.D. 130), Valentinus (*floruit* A.D. 140–165), and Ptolemy, whose letter to Flora in Rome (around A.D. 170) provides a remarkable record of a Gnostic attitude toward the Old Testament, felt free to borrow from Greek epics, philosophy, and Oriental religions, to dip where they would into the Old Testament, rejecting much of it, and to shape their own version of the New Testament canon (ibid., 201–3). The recent discovery of a library of Gnostic works at Nag Hammadi in Egypt has added greatly to our knowledge of Gnostic teachings (see J. M. Robinson, ed., *The Nag Hammadi Library* [New York: Harper and Row, 1978], for these texts).

twelfth century, who were the occasion of that tragic addendum to ortho-doxy, the Inquisition.

What was this particular Gnostic heresy, and who were these heretics? As far as can be discerned, the Bogomils (in French, "Bougres," which to this day is an insult in French slang), as they were sometimes called, were descendants of the ancient Manichaeans,[56] the old dualistic, Gnostic religion-philosophy having been brought, on the heels of the first Crusades, from Bulgaria (hence the name) and Romania. They were also often called "Albigois"—"Albigenses" in English—because the important city of Albi, in Languedoc, was one of their strongholds.

The Cathari mixed elements of Docetism and Gnosticism with Mani-chaeanism, although their doctrine varied among groups. The Monarchians believed that the Good God created and divided the original chaos, and Satan made Adam and Eve from sea ooze. When a child was born, an angel, persuaded to leave heaven by Satan, gave it a soul. Thus, humans were not guilty of original sin, but of leaving heaven. The Good God sought a faithful angel willing to go to earth and reveal to humanity how they could be set free. Jesus volunteered, thus becoming the son of God. Because He emanated from the Good God, He was spirit, and only appeared to have a body. The Passion and Crucifixion only appeared to happen, and were arranged by Satan. This rendered the Old Testament God, patriarchs, and prophets bad, and made the Incarnation and redemption pointless.

Extravagant (and old hat) as this may all seem, the sect attracted ec-clesiastical and intelligent people along with the uneducated, and had churches and centers throughout France, with bishops and deacons. The Cathari replaced the sacraments with the rite of *consolamentum*, in which the believer was filled by the Spirit, saved, and made "Perfect." The unsaved were reincarnated until they became Perfect. Because everything made by Satan was evil, the Perfect lived under severe laws. They abstained from eating meat or animal products, fasted much, prohibited marriage in order to prevent Satan's angels from entering the world, and approved of suicide. The social implications of these beliefs alone made it imperative for the Church to respond to it.[57]

Such social challenges were most successful in the late twelfth century in regions where the Church hierarchy, including parish priests, were most lax

56. Mani (*vivebat* A.D. 216–276) had attempted a synthesis of Christian doctrine, ideas from Plato, Pythagoras, Zoroaster, and Iranian Mazdæism, and even some Buddhism. A Principle of Good and a Principle of Evil were involved in Creation. The Good, the principle of Light, is responsible for the spiritual nature and the new law, revealed by Christ, who Himself is only a Spirit, come to combat Evil. The other principle, Darkness, is responsible for the old law and the material world, and the body is its representative. The spiritual soul in us seeks the Good; the evil soul, in the form of the body, rules in this world sinfully.

57. This brief description is based on Fernand Hayward, *The Inquisition*, trans. Malachay Carroll (New York: Alba House, 1966). The major source of the entire section on the Inquisition has been Henri Maisonneuve, *Études sur les origines de l'inquisition*, 2nd ed. (Paris: J. Vrin, 1960).

and unedifying. When Saint Bernard combated the numerous and active Cathari in the *Comtés* of Toulouse and Provence, he discovered an appalling scene of laxity and indifference.[58]

The Counterattack

At first, reaction to the new sects was largely under the jurisdiction of the local bishop. Opinions were divided as to how severe punishments should be. Saint Bernard was not alone in preaching the need for free persuasion. Many pleaded for respect for the free nature of belief.

Partly because of abuses at the local level, partly because by the end of the twelfth century heresy had spread so far in northern Italy and southern France as to constitute an affair of state, the papacy intervened by establishing a regular means of inquiry. Through several steps of juridical and political evolution, this grew into an established process, that of the Inquisition. (Ironically, it was founded in an effort to regularize and to avoid local excesses.)

The rise of this institution coincided with the founding, by Dominic de Guzman and Archbishop Foulque of Toulouse in 1207, of a special order of friars dedicated to preaching in the troubled areas, to bring the ordinary people back to the true way, by free persuasion. The Dominicans came quite naturally to play a considerable role in the workings of the new Inquisition. Many of the leading papal legates charged with investigation and ecclesiastical judgment were Dominicans.

The medieval Inquisition was followed later by the Spanish Inquisition, which has its own circumstances and still worse horrors. It too was an element in a vast civil conflict, growing out of the long struggle to free the Iberian Peninsula of Muslim control. Forced conversions led to suspicion of false conversions: Jews and former Muslims who might be working from within Spanish Catholic society to undermine it. (Some modern scholars hypothesize that the *murranos* were sincere new Catholics, but that through their talents, honed through long centuries of surviving as a pressured minority, and their network, and thus having become successful and powerful, they fell victim of envy and greed.)[59]

Common accounts of the Inquisition have often luridly overcolored the details of torture and of clerical corruption and debauchery. The modern

58. Saint Bernard's cries of alarm and tireless efforts should suffice to warn us not to think, because in this "Age of Faith" the great abbeys and cathedrals were constructed and the magnificent *Summae Theologiae* written, that all was well with the Church and with Christian civilization. These were still rude times, barbarous practices were current, and religious indifference infected large areas. Many heretical enterprises, for example the Waldenses, followers of the Lyonnais merchant Valdo, who renounced his wealth to preach a gospel of poverty and simplicity, arose as sincere efforts to clear out poor practices and superstitions.

59. B. Netanyahu, *The Origins of the Inquisition in Fifteenth-Century Spain* (New York: Random House, 1995).

person tends to analyze it in terms of various abnormal psychological problems, without making any attempt to grasp the main point that resides in the truth of what Cecil Roth, the Jewish historian of the Spanish Inquisition, has written:

> Men really did believe (not merely professed to believe) that they were endowed by God with immortal souls. They really did believe in a heaven and a hell, in which they were destined to make reckoning for what they had done during their transient terrestrial existence. They believed, too, that Theophany and Incarnation had put them in possession of the key to the eternal verities and indicated the path to heaven. Thus it was natural for the man of the Middle Ages to "go to any lengths, and to submit himself to any discipline," to save his soul or that of others. The Inquisition was a manifestation of an ideology almost universal in Europe at its start, set up in the form of judicial bodies in many countries. It is all the more tragic because of this sincerity and idealism.[60]

Studying the procedures for ferreting out heretics—the ways they were put to the test, the trial procedures, the widespread application of torture, in violation of the essence of Christian love, and the handing over of "the obstinate" "to the secular arm" (as though that absolved the clerics of what happened: "Hypocrisy!" cries Jacques Maritain) who were then burned alive in the presence of satisfied nobles and clerics—leaves one sickened, and wondering how Christianity, itself persecuted for four hundred years, could have evolved since Constantine to accept such barbarism as normal.[61]

However much the Protestant revolt may have damaged Christendom and opened the way to the further de-Christianization of society, however much the Enlightenment may have favored the growth of atheism, to the extent these processes also contributed to the creation of those sociopolitical "spaces" we enjoy in open society, leading to the growth of the sense, in the more "advanced" societies at least, that torture is always inexcusable, that no force should be applied to change people's ideas, and that the line separating loyal argument from subtle manipulation should be respected, they have advanced certain societies closer to what every Christian believes God intends for His kingdom, to the extent it can be anticipated on this earth.

Jacques Maritain expresses hope that "God has received all the victims of the Inquisition in His Heaven." Meditating on the mystery that God would ever allow such things to happen in the name of His Church, he points out that their sacrifice has helped purchase a treasure of eternal life: the sense of the absolute transcendence of theological faith. It is not a plaything of earthly power, nor is faith communicated or guarded by coercion.[62]

60. Roth, *The Spanish Inquisition* (London and New York: W. W. Norton, 1964), v–vi.
61. Maritain, *On the Church of Christ* (Notre Dame, Ind.: University of Notre Dame Press, 1973), 183.
62. Ibid., 187.

THE FABRIC RENT

The Protestant Revolt and the Origins of Modernity

THE REFORMATION: PERENNIAL CHALLENGE TO THE CATHOLIC TRADITION AND IMPETUS TO MODERNITY

The two largest historical issues raised by that Richter-8 movement of religious, social, and economic upheaval, the Reformation, are the eruption onto the European scene of a new kind of church and the birth and significance of "modernity."

The two are related. Protestant Churches are very modern churches, in competition for souls with the ancient Church they have reformed. Those struggling to be Christian in increasingly post-Christian times, and to participate in evangelizing the most nihilistic epoch European civilization has ever known, the HTX, are faced with the added challenge of cooperating in this task with Christians divided by very different notions of doctrine and ecclesiology.

The scope and complexity of the issues raised by the break with Catholicism are well brought out in this remark by the non-Catholic historian Lawrence E. Brown:

> The medieval Catholic Church, being by its own definition the Church Militant, not the Church Triumphant, was a human institution which, despite its divine guidance, was necessarily subject to the evils and short-comings of all human institutions. It was a vast political government intermeshed with the secular powers of the newly-risen national states. It was immensely wealthy yet immensely costly to operate. It was eternal, yet its eternity could be maintained only by maintaining its transitory earthly interests. That it was corrupt and that its relation to the new centralized kingdoms needed readjustment, everybody admitted. That it had to be destroyed as the only alternative to maintaining the corruption and the archaic political relations is not so certain.[1]

Brown is right that one should acknowledge the difference separating the post-Reformation Catholic Church from the medieval "united Catholic Church of the West."[2] The earlier entity was the only mainline religious

---

1. Brown, *The Might of the West* (Washington, D.C.: Binns, 1963), 495.
2. I am aware that the term *Protestant revolt* grates on Protestant ears. Protestants prefer, understandably, "Reformation." As I shall show, the universal Church badly

show in town—a Church embroiled with feudal society, bearing a load of accumulated corruption. The post-Reform reality was a Catholic Church with much competition from the newly founded churches, caught in the midst of a European civil war (the misnamed Wars of Religion, more accurately, the Thirty Years' War) struggling with modernity. But still a catholic Church in full continuity with the Church of the Apostles, the post-Reform Church was reinvigorated, renouncing nothing of the universality of its claims but diminished badly in its hold on European society.

As the result of the earlier growing apart of the East and the West, the Church had already been changed involuntarily from being the only Church claiming universality (even though confined in its operations to a small part of the earth's surface as yet) to being the Church universal in claim but in competition with another part of the Church also asserting that it represented the orthodox center. But in Protestantism something different occurs: a new *kind* of Church (even a new kind of Christianity, indeed, given the great differences between Protestants, different *kinds* of churches, with different religious characters—compare, for example, Anglicans and Mormons) emerges, in response to a new era. Many challenge the legitimacy and orthodoxy of the very model of an episcopal Church, heretofore unquestioned by East or West, and even declare the Catholic Church with its "sacerdotalism" to be in league with the devil.

Nonetheless, all historians would agree that the post-Reform Catholic Church remains, at the very minimum, an epochal modification of mainline Christianity. But with other powerful institutions challenging its claims, even its legitimacy as Christian, this Church has been an institution on the defensive, until the pontificate of John Paul II. Now it has confronted communism head-on. It has reached out ecumenically, vocations to the priesthood are again growing, and, because of its worldwide presence, so is Church membership, despite declines in Europe and the Americas. The Catholic Church is growing faster than Protestantism, despite the energy of the evangelicals. It is, indeed, growing faster than any religion except Islam, which is carried by a booming birthrate. At the end of this study I shall assess the extent to which it remains, in worldly terms, a force to be reckoned with, and then consider its inner, spiritual strengths and weaknesses, as I seek to appreciate its responses to the challenges of the HTX epoch.

The competition has forced the clarification of the self-understanding of what has come to be called "the magisterium," the teaching Catholic Church. The Catholic Church continues to hold that "outside the Church

---

needed reform, more urgently than usual. Genuine reform came, spurred by the Protestant revolt. But, contrary to the initial intentions of Luther, the Protestant Reform turned into a revolt, a throwing off of Catholic authority as the whole Church had understood it to then. At the risk of annoying Protestants, for reasons of accuracy I shall reserve the term *reform* for what happens within the traditional Catholic structures, and *revolt* for the break therewithal.

there is no salvation," but its notion of degrees of "being in the Church" and of what "the Church" is and how it should teach has become quite nuanced, as we shall see.

The Catholic Church, remarkably, has not succumbed to a "remnant of the pure" mentality, despite post-Reform temptations in that direction. Today it is certainly not withdrawing from the world. As much as ever, it is out to evangelize it. Part of the explanation for this lies in the fact that the Roman Church under Protestant assault in the sixteenth century was at the same time expanding more rapidly than at any time in its history. Consider the paradox: starting at the moment of maximum diremption, and launched on a wave of brutal European imperialism, this vast missionary expansion made the Catholic Church for the first time in history truly a "world church," at least by the nineteenth century. (Already by the end of the sixteenth, the Church was in North and South America, and had a toehold in India, China, and Japan.) In this way it established new centers of strength and renewal available at the moment of decline of European Catholicism. The "Roman Catholic Church" has become effectively less exclusively European, and remains to this day the only religious institution close to being an actual world presence.[3]

The issue facing us is not whether the Church might have been re-formed without fracturing Christendom. That has occurred, introducing into Christianity a radical new epoch, marked by a rise of individualism and rivalry from new kinds of churches. Lessons have been learned on all sides from this dolorous experience of fracturing,[4] and as in our

3. At the 1993 Youth Day in Denver, young people from 120 nations gathered around the pope. The Church's closest old competitor, Islam, has much less world-scale organization, and is not as effectively present in so many parts of the world. In its thinking it certainly does not embrace so full a range of cultures and issues as a Catholicism facing up to all the intellectual challenges of contemporary existence—a claim that will surprise the reader who gets his image of the Catholic Church only from the media. One might add, at the risk of sounding slightly "triumphalist," that this world Church shows its intellectual and cross-cultural vigor at a time when the Orthodox churches are under great stress, both from their recent persecution (and in some instances their disastrous collaboration) by and with totalitarian Marxist regimes, and from their slow response to the intellectual challenges of modernity. Whether the HTX will become coherent enough to generate a planetary-scale religious competitor or will remain in its materialism more an undermining force for Catholicism remains to be seen. I cannot believe that the ragbag of tired, pagan eclecticism of "New Age" will amount to anything but an escapism of the disaffected. (But then I have always underestimated the force of post-Elvis popular music to mold generations. I fear I just do not want to believe in human beings so faintly.) Will Islam resist successfully the secularizing forces of the HTX, and will Catholicism succeed in the "new evangelization" of the HTX? These are questions with which we shall wrestle at the end of this study.

4. When "Enlightenment" liberalism goes too far, attacking the foundation of Christianity through denial of the divinity of Christ, then out with the medieval goes the role of the divine itself in civil society. (I am here assuming "New Age" spiritualities to be deficient in genuine transcendence, as I suggested earlier. The Christian position on this requires more detailed explanation later in this study.) For instance, if, like the historian Arnold Toynbee, that latter-day Enlightener, who sees in Christianity the last and most

time a spirit of ecumenical cooperation grows at last and wonderfully, we can appreciate these lessons more irenically. For instance, the closer intertwined the Church becomes with the ruling earthly power of the time, the more it is in danger of compromising its mission. The Church needs to function politically as "the loyal opposition," not as bedfellow of always compromised worldly powers. The Catholic Church's present alienation from a so thoroughly secularized Europe and North America—the furthest it has been from political power since Constantine—is a protection (Church officers are kept far from "occasions of sin," at least in this arena of worldly power), but at the same time the Church is reduced to depending on the Holy Spirit instead of its own political muscle.[5] Perhaps the power of faith to move mountains, rather than relying on Pope Julius II's troops as at Mantua, is being rediscovered! The authors speaking for the twenty-four participants in the official American Lutheran-Catholic Dialogue, writing of the theological convergence achieved by their dialogues on "justification by faith," put this new state of affairs quite well:

> This convergence on various points have been facilitated by the disappearance of non-theological sources of division. The crowns of princes, the incomes of priests and pastors, the standings of social classes are no longer intertwined, as they were in the sixteenth century, with the conflict over justification. The disestablishment of the churches and their detachment from the struggle for worldly power make it easier to discern and acknowledge agreements between them.[6]

Out of the Catholic-Protestant split came one immense good for the Church: it provoked the most thoroughgoing reform of the Catholic Church ever in its history, a work crowned by the long labors of the Council of Trent, held from 1545 to 1563. Although it remains with "monarchical" structures for its governance (believing these come from Jesus Himself), it

---

serious veil obscuring our view of God, "the idolatry of man" (Arnold Toynbee, *A Study of History*, vol. 7[a] [London: Oxford University Press, 1954], 467–68), and as many of the eighteenth-century philosophers did, one would reduce Jesus to a kind of *bhodisattva*, a kind of representation of the deity, without being the divinity itself, then the authority of Jesus' preaching is undermined, and the sense of the divinizing he can affect is lost. Such a view of Jesus inevitably transforms the Church from continued prophetic presence in our midst to fabricator of idolatrous myths. A sacramental religion then gets deformed, as has been tendency in "mainline liberal Protestant social gospel" and in "liberation-theology" traditions, into a social work, rather than eucharistically centered, sanctifying Church. The sense of the divine is frittered away, contemplation dissolves in action, and the Holy Spirit gets downgraded to the spirit of reason operating naturally in man.

5. But the opportunity for temptation continues to exist where various concordats are in effect, such as Italy, and where Church officials are close to government. One need not be "constitutionally" empowered to have, nevertheless, the opportunity to exercise power. And, as always, the mere availability of exercise does not imply that corruption has occurred. None of these remarks is intended to encourage the idea that the Church should not speak out in the democratic arena. In his 1993 visit to Spain, Pope John Paul II chided the Spanish bishops for being too timid in letting their views be known.

6. H. George Anderson, T. Austin Murphy, and Joseph A. Burgess, eds., *Justification by Faith: Lutherans and Catholics in Dialogue* (Minneapolis: Augsburg Publishing House, 1985), 7:68.

has emerged from modernity less resistant than ever to efforts of ongoing reform from within.[7]

Reform, Revolution, Individualism, and Freedom of Conscience

In studying this vast process of revolt and reform, I am primarily interested in the positive contribution the saints, who have lived and continue to live their lives in the Protestant traditions, have to offer the entire Christian fellowship.[8] All Christians deplore the fracturing of Christ's Church. I acknowledge, as does the magisterium of the Church, and as do the participants in both the Anglican–Roman Catholic Dialogue and the Lutheran-Catholic Dialogue, that blame for this is to be found on all sides,[9] and that assigning blame is anyway not fruitful. It is better not to get stuck in "complexes" and, rather, obedient to God's will, move on together from here.

This said, the Catholic has to admit he sees a central, insidious element implied, not by raising questions about the adequacy of traditional formulations of doctrine or by criticizing corruption in the Church, but by revolting against the traditional, foundational authority structure of what until then had been simply Christ's Church, His only Church: There is the inescapable implication on the part of those who break away that "we are the remnant, the Pure who will from now on be the Church." This gives tremendous impetus to a kind of Gnostic individualism. When the will to stick with the great mass of the unwashed brethren herded by their often not-so-holy shepherds erodes, and one comes to believe the Church as it is irreformable, and so "we must save the ship" by breaking off a part that will still float and thus, through a purer and more direct openness to the Holy Spirit correct a millennium and a half of abuse, there occurs a revolutionary shift in the sense of where the true authority resides: now it is in *my* conscience, directly the recipient of the Holy Spirit's inspiratio, *Hier stehe ich, ich kann nicht anders!* (Luther's cry, "Here I stand, I cannot do otherwise!"). Luther becomes for his followers thereafter the mouthpiece for the Holy Spirit, *the center of a new magisterium,* the father of all fathers of the Church, for it is he who would interpret them. He becomes the

7. The prefect of the Sacred Congregation for the Doctrine of the Faith, the official charged with looking after the orthodoxy of what is being taught throughout the Church, Joseph Cardinal Ratzinger, raised eyebrows with a radical speech on the need for ongoing serious reform ("Reform from the Beginnings," *30 Days* [November 1990]: 62–69).

8. Pope John Paul II, citing the Second Vatican Council (*Unitatis Reintegratio,* 4), and his predecessor, Pope Paul VI (Homily, October 18, 1964), gives homage to Protestant martyrs to the truth: "All Christian Communities have martyrs for the Christian faith. Despite the tragedy of our divisions, these brothers and sisters have preserved an attachment to Christ and to the Father so radical and absolute as to lead even to the shredding of blood" (*Ut Unum Sint,* Encyclical Letter on Christian Unity [1995]: para. 83).

9. This is very well brought out, graciously and generously, in the concise, lucid history of the controversy over justification by faith, in Anderson, Murphy, and Burgess, *Justification by Faith,* 7:25–38.

center of the new tradition of interpretation of Holy Scripture (which, of course, becomes "the true" interpretation). It then seems to be the Holy Spirit authorizing his condemnations of the pope, his excoriation of the faithful bishops, his enlistment of princely power to make the effects of these claims socially effective.

One might even say, with only slight exaggeration, that this *discovery* of the primordiality of the individual conscience has become now a perennial element of the tension individual-community in the West. (Individualism has to this day penetrated very little the Orthodox, Muslim, tribal, Confucian, Buddhist, and Hindu worlds.) The Catholic Church passed through the whole period of the Protestant revolt, the Enlightenment of the eighteenth century, and the era of totalitarian dictatorships in the twentieth century before finding the stomach to defend individual conscience explicitly in the decree of the Second Vatican Council, *Dignitatis humanae*, which was the decree most fought over by the council fathers. And that decree is quick to emphasize the responsibility of the individual to see to it that his conscience is rightly formed, through humble receptivity of the Word of God handed down by the magisterium!

To understand the reasons for such hesitation, one must look honestly, not just at the great good of open society—which I shall defend as an important part of my overall natural faith—but at the evil fruits of an exaggerated "bourgeois" (because it is a phenomenon of the city) individualism.[10] That kind of free-willing liberty requires the wealth generated by capitalism and industrialization to pay for the luxury it represents. No society living "at the margins" can afford the fooling around that follows unrestrained liberty abused, and the secularism that results from drawing the masses into self-directed search for worldly success.

None of these longer-range results were what the great Reformers wanted. Consider, too, the evil fruits of the fracturing of Protestantism into hundreds of sects, the confusion this introduces at the heart of Christianity, and the infection of Catholicism from the individualistic-efficient milieu, weakening its communitarian effectiveness and encouraging massive dissent to vital teachings among those who call themselves "Catholics," and conservatives deem "cafeteria Catholics."

Against the background of all those worries, is it not astonishing that under Pope Wojtyla, who learned his lessons about the value of freedom under first Nazi then Communist persecution, the Church has become the most vigorous and visible champion of human rights? Given the lateness of the Church's conversion to a modern idea of freedom of conscience, one can forgive those who remain a bit skeptical about the depth of the

---

10. It is easy to underestimate what an innovation, what a radical change it is for man to live predominately in cities, as we do in the HTX world. For a million years man lived in closest harmony with nature; for less than a century, one now sees a significant part of mankind living in the highly artificial arrangements of the city, where light pollution even keeps you from seeing the stars! The implications of all this are explored in *HTX: Learning to Survive in Virtual Reality* (submitted for publication).

Church's conviction. But I can say that from within the Church tolerance of dissent has in fact reached proportions worrisome to all those who care about orthodoxy.

The Main Subtraditions after the Reform

A first step in understanding what has come of this diremption launched by the Reform is to grasp something of the contrasts in the essences of the main subtraditions that have emerged within European Christianity as a result. Basically, they are three. First, the "pure" Congregationalist Protestantism of the Anabaptist sects and their offshoots (a spirit alive among those who today call themselves "evangelicals," and who generally consider themselves the true inheritors of the spirit of the Reform). Second, the "moderate" mixed forms of "mainline" Protestantism, concentrating on Lutheranism. And third, the "Catholic-Apostolic-Episcopal" model of "Roman Catholics" and "High Anglicans," which they share with the Orthodox, as this has emerged from the fray.

I cannot here do justice to the many innovative refinements of these models that have been produced in the last four hundred years, an endless task and we would lose the forest to view altogether. I especially regret not having space to study the great Calvinist movement, with its various streams. But many of the issues raised by this powerful spirit will be dealt with at least briefly in my discussion of the pure Congregationalist model.

The Pure and "the Doctrine on which the Church Stands or Falls"

At its ideologically purest (in the sense of most logically consistent, once one grants the most basic Protestant principles) the Protestant vision is perfectly coherent. The Reformers wanted to return to fundamentals, to cut underneath a vast overgrowth of medieval pious practices that they experienced as more obscuring than usefully orchestrating the essential Christian Revelation and as efforts to earn heaven through busy work (a tendency traditionally called "Pelagianism"). They wanted to emphasize humble, grateful acknowledgment of our absolute dependence on the redemptive act of Jesus Christ, lived out in obedience to His Word.

One of the great attractions of present-day evangelicals is their concentration on what is indeed the center, and in this concentrated emphasis they are true to the Reform tradition: Jesus Christ as our savior, the fruit of the redemption being made available through being born again in the Holy Spirit when we accept the grace coming to us from the cross, the grace to believe and embrace Him in utter gratitude. This call to put *justification by faith* at the center, with emphasis on the utter gratuitousness of God's gift, and the understanding that love and moral purity flow as the fruit (not the meritorious means) of this glorification of God as the great reconciler, is indeed a moving reaffirmation of what is most vital in the Christian faith. It is a rebuke to the perennial temptation of fallen human nature to want to control, by thinking we can earn God's favor. Nothing we can do on our own can heal the infinite rift opened by Adam and Eve's rejection of God.

Whole communities of Protestants have offered, and continue to offer, heroic witness in their efforts to live their lives focused on that vision. When, since Luther, "justification by faith alone" has been explained as the criterion for authenticity in the life and works of Christians, Catholics, while resisting the idea that there be just one criterion, have for the most part found themselves agreeing. As the fathers of the Council of Trent declared, "nothing prior to justification, whether faith or works, truly merits (*promeretur*) the grace of justification."[11] Although the various reformed traditions differed among themselves on many things, on this central doctrine of justification by faith alone they were united.[12]

Not that they thought good works are to be spurned—Luther made that clear in his *Treatise on Good Works*. The Ten Commandments set out a program of works we are expected to follow. But faith alone motivates us to do this, and only through it are our works good in the first place. "Faith must be the foreman behind this work, without faith no one is able to do this work."[13]

Righteousness is "a trust of the heart in God through Christ," on account of which "God overlooks sins."[14] Luther was so confident we could rely on God, he could allow himself to say in his commentary on Galatians: "This is the reason why our theology is certain: it snatches us away from ourselves and places us outside ourselves, so that we do not depend on our own strength, conscience, experience, person, or works, but depend on that which is outside ourselves, that is, on the promise and truth of God, which cannot deceive."[15]

As an antidote to "the gloomy conscience," this is effective! The Council of Trent had to respond, and the fathers took up justification in the council's 1546 session. No other doctrinal issue received such care. Many drafts were produced, and remarkable personal initiatives were taken, especially by Cardinal Seripando. In essence, the council fathers responded as follows: Christ "merited justification for us by his holy passion on the wood of the

---

11. DS 1532. "Whether faith" means that it is not our act of faith that merits justification, but the gift of Christ's salvific act that even makes possible our act of faith itself—the Holy Spirit produces that act in us, even our cooperation with it!

12. Jean Calvin, Reply to Sadeleto (Barth/Niese), 1:469.dd. The Swiss theologian Heinrich Bullinger summed up the doctrine in the title of a treatise he wrote in 1554: *The Grace of God That Justifies Us for the Sake of Christ through Faith Alone, without Good Works, while Faith Meanwhile Abounds in Good Works.*

13. Luther, *Gute Werke* (WA 6:275).

14. Jaroslav Pelikan, *Reformation of Church and Dogma* (Chicago: University of Chicago Press, 1984), 489. I am following this Lutheran historian in this discussion. For Luther, justification is essentially the forgiveness of sins, which is God's work alone. This is accomplished by imputation, when for the sake of Christ "God reckons imperfect righteousness as perfect righteousness and sin as not sin, even though it really is sin" (Luther, Galatians [1535] 3:6 [WA 40/1:367–68]).

15. Ibid., 590.

cross and rendered satisfaction for us to God the Father."[16] Pelagianism, which "says that man can be justified before God by his own works," is, therefore, always to be condemned. But salvation is not to be reduced to the forgiveness of sins, as it appeared to be in Luther's system. Sin cannot be forgiven without grace, righteousness cannot be attained except through Christ, the council affirmed, but at the same time, it is attained not from Christ alone but through the cooperation of our own wills (which cooperation itself is an effect of His grace!).[17]

The Trent canon then asks the causes of justification. If faith is the "cause" of justification, we must define faith carefully. (I would suggest, too, that "cause" needs to be carefully defined in this context, which it was not.) The final draft described faith as "believing to be true what has been divinely revealed and promised." The decree distinguishes between "historical faith," the content of what has been passed down; "miraculous faith," the faith that can move mountains; and "evangelical faith," "faith working through love," which is not only trust, as the Lutherans say, but also "the beginning and foundation of the entire spiritual edifice," comprehending all the other virtues and being inseparable from them.[18] For not by faith alone but "more by hope and love than by faith," those who are justified *take hold* of the righteousness of Christ.[19] "Faith is the beginning of human salvation, the foundation and root of all justification." But in an appendix to the main document the fathers condemned anyone who says "that the sinner is justified by faith alone, as though nothing else were required to cooperate." The decree included the statement of the Epistle of James that "a man is justified by works and not by faith alone."[20] The council unequivocally asserted that our works are meritorious only through God's grace, but was equally careful to restore the sense of the need of free cooperation, obedience to God's law, and merit granted by God to our works. Works are obviously critical in an anthropology of incarnation. Not that the Reformers

16. Council of Trent, VI, Canon X (Alberigo-Jedin, 679).

17. Pelikan, *Reformation of Church and Dogma*, 280–81. Catholics consider it important, for preserving a place for free will, to emphasize this cooperation, while acknowledging the importance of the Protestant insistence that our wonderful contribution, while really our doing, is made possible entirely by grace. We have to accept the grace, but our being able to is itself a grace: danger here of an infinite regress? Carl Peter, commenting on the position of the Council of Trent, explains our "cooperation" this way: our contribution is not exercising our destructive freedom to block the grace that imparts faith (see his article in Anderson, Murphy, and Burgess, *Justification by Faith,* vol. 7).

18. Council of Trent, Act 23, vi, 1546 (CT 5:264), cited in Pelikan, *Reformation of Church and Dogma,* 286.

19. A Presbyterian evangelical friend who worked with me in preparing this chapter, comments at this point: "Here is a conflict: above, faith comprehends all the other virtues, yet here, it's more hope and love, rather than faith. I would want to explore this 'taking hold' . . . perhaps there is a lot of slack in this notion too, though the Reformed are rather consistent in relating 'taking hold' to faith (as the empty hands of the soul which receive). Here there is room for some good phenomenology, some of which I think is in Ricoeur's *Freedom and Nature: The Voluntary and the Involuntary.*"

20. James 2:24, Ap. Council of Trent, Act 31, xii, 1546.

would disagree, but they shifted the emphasis to sanctification, though in the Protestant *ordo salutis*, regeneration is considered "logically" prior to justification, since only a spiritually living person can "do/have faith." The point for the Reformer, again, has to do with guarding the grounds of justification, of merit, of grace . . . as (God in) Christ alone. "Cooperation" is seen by the Protestant to water down the focus. (Cooperation is a valid point in the big picture, but, comments an evangelical friend who wishes to remain anonymous, "misplaced with regard to justification *per se*.")[21]

Commenting on this, my friend notes:

> I agree with the Council's recalling what James says about the need for works: I dislike a doctrine which contradicts scripture, yet it would seem two different senses of justification are at stake here. Of course we should be more concerned about the implications of that time-split for justification (and other doctrines), but seemingly James has a different point in mind than Paul . . . something like final justification vs. initial justification. If so, then any doctrine resting entirely on one or the other is only partial. But how to formulate a "comprehensive" notion . . . my sense is that this has been circumscribed in two different ways by the Catholic Church and the Reform, but not yet adequately formulated "in itself."[22]

Although the participants in the contemporary American Lutheran-Catholic Dialogue acknowledge that the great medieval doctors were in fact clear in rejecting "works righteousness"[23] (but "some later theologians were less careful than Scotus [and Thomas before him] in maintaining that predestination, as the entire effect of God's decree, is not based on foreseen merits"), and that the fathers of the reforming Council of Trent were also clear about this,[24] it must be said, in the words of my evangelical friend, "the Reformed mind and heart is extremely jealous to guard the glory of Christ on this point and would see any shift towards us—ourselves as the grounds, even co-operating grounds of justification—as jeopardizing the focus on Christ's glory. Here too there is a Marian element: 'My soul doth magnify the Lord and my spirit doth exalt in God my Savior (alone?)' . . . that's our passion too."[25] Catholics now see Pelagian excesses on the part of the sixteenth-century hawkers of indulgences, and Catholic teaching and Catholic spiritual sensibility today completely embrace this truth.

Despite this assurance from Catholics, one can still find Protestant doubts, as in the letter of 1957 that Karl Barth permitted the young Hans

21. Council of Trent, VI, Canon X (Alberigo-Jedin, 679). My friend points out that the Catechism of the Catholic Church in para. 1993 says: "justification establishes cooperation between God's grace and man's freedom." He finds this an intriguing way of saying what needs saying.

22. Private correspondence, March 1996.

23. Anderson, Murphy, and Burgess, *Justification by Faith*, 7:20–21.

24. "In its doctrinal as well as in its reform decrees, the Council of Trent recognized that the Reformation critique of the state of the church was at least partially justified. In particular, its reaffirmation of the primacy of grace in the role of justification and salvation assured that the anti-Pelagian intention of the classical Augustinian tradition not be lost" (ibid., 36).

25. Private correspondence, March 1996.

Küng to publish in his volume *Justification: The Doctrine of Karl Barth and a Catholic Reflection:*

> If what you have presented in Part Two of this book is actually the teaching of the Roman Catholic Church, then I must certainly admit that the Roman Catholic teaching would be most strikingly in accord with mine! Of course, the problem is whether what you have presented here really represents the teaching of your Church. This you will have to take up and fight out with biblical, historical, and dogmatic experts among your coreligionists.[26]

We understand this hesitation to believe the Catholics could actually embrace the central doctrine of the Reformers, "If this article stands, the church stands; if it falls the church falls,"[27] as Luther wrote. But they do. I even believe many Catholic theologians and authorities would consider it a good thing that the Reformed tradition keeps Christians' attention on this, not because, as the Reform claims, it is *the* pillar of our faith but because it is one of several absolutely essential parts of its core. With agreement on this essential doctrine, one of the main reasons for our being separate indeed falls. This brings to mind the words of the recent Catholic theologian Karl Rahner:

> Especially in a controversial theology there is the danger that an overly neurotic anxiety might destroy some of the unity that is there, though we might not yet be one "essentially" or "in the deepest sense." Such an anxiety produces every peculiar endeavor . . . to prove a mutual lack of consensus by means of more and more refined formulations and nuances, where our ancestors in the sixteenth century would have maintained a lack of unity with less subtle formulations which everyone could easily see and express, or they would have then united.[28]

So we need to look below the doctrinal surface to understand better why, other than historical inertia, the separation continues. What I see emerging to view is *an important difference in anthropologies,* which involves, among other dimensions we shall explore, the distinctive Protestant and Catholic beliefs regarding the damage wrought by original sin, and behind that a different attitude toward the body. Catholics reject the Lutheran extreme, that our wills became like Satan's, that we came to prefer evil to good. Rather, Catholics hold, the steady control of our reasonable will (reason) over our impulses (passions) was weakened, but man was not essentially perverted. Hence, there remains in place after the disaster of the Fall a goodwill able to cooperate with God's grace in achieving the works of salvation, works that change the world.

For Protestants, "total depravity" does not mean that we are as bad as we might be, but that there is no pristine area of humanity within us untouched by sin. Protestants cite Rom. 3 and, among other texts, Rom. 7: there is in me "no good thing." If this means simply that fallen man is utterly dependent

---

26. Küng, *Justification* (New York: Thomas Nelson, 1964), xx.
27. Exposition of Ps. 130:4, 1538 (WA 40/3:352, 3).
28. Küng, *Justification,* xxiii. Küng closes his preface with this quote.

on God's redemptive grace even for his part of free cooperation with it, then Catholics agree.

But good works are needed because redeemed man is called upon to be God's instrument in "bringing the Kingdom"; Christ, after all, taught us to pray: "thy kingdom come, thy will be done on earth as it is in heaven." The condition for this making Christ present in the world is *an incarnation of His will in our bodies:* by cooperating with His grace, we can be formed by Him, through slow, hard, disciplined work, into more adequate instruments of His presencing. Protestants and Catholics alike today distinguish clearly "justification" from "sanctification."[29] And all agree that our sanctification begins with the forgiveness of all sins through God's totally gratuitous act, that through subsequent sinning we can "backslide," and that God further extends His forgiveness, and helps us back up onto the difficult road to personal sanctity. But Catholics more clearly expound and insist more on the incarnational, bodily aspect of developing "virtue" through our cooperation with God's continuing infusion of grace. Catholic sensibilities stress the corporate working together through the sacramental gifts in this building up of the body of Christ. The Protestant instinct is more immediate, disincarnate: I am swept away by the Spirit, what really counts is what happens deep in the soul, the rebirth.[30] (Paradoxically, Protestants typically form stronger church communities. Catholics are brought together more about the sacrificial table of the Eucharist, and less as a social gathering. However, there is nothing in Protestantism quite as communal as monastic orders and even some of the more worldly religious orders. Since the Second Vatican Council there has been renewed emphasis on "the people of God," priests stand at the door like Protestant ministers greeting the people, and coffee and donuts in the church hall become a sacramental of sociality. I

29. My friend does not find this clearly enough expressed in the Catechism. Para. 1992 says: "Justification has been merited for us by the Passion of Christ. . . . Justification is conferred in Baptism." I would agree: we must be clear that the origin of all is Christ's offering Himself for the sins of all men on the cross. That Christ chooses to confer the fruits of justification to the individual through the instrument He founded, baptism, poses no problem to the Catholic. That para. 1995 asserts "justification entails the sanctification of his whole being" does seem to obscure a bit the distinction between justification, Christ's divine act, and sanctification, which requires the cooperation of our works. And the first line of para. 1987 does seem to equate justification with "cleansing us from our sins," which is, I would agree, the proper sense of "sanctification," which means "cleanse." My friend is especially troubled by the phrase that justification is "through faith and baptism." Tongue in cheek, he invokes "luurrking saaaccerdootalism . . . you get my tone?" Catholics would sin against the glory if they allowed the "sacrament of faith," as the Catechism calls baptism (para. 1992), in any way to obscure that this form of conferring is possible only because of Christ's act on the cross and that it is He who commands baptism. But no Protestant would not want to disobey the urgent command of Christ, "Go ye therefore and baptize all nations."

30. My friend comments: "Luther tended to subsume sanctification into justification, and this does as you say, minimize the co-operation of our wills. The Reformed more clearly distinguish sanctification/justification, but tend to become intellectual about the 'doing'" (private correspondence).

would attribute this to a deliberate effort to combat the individualism that ravages modern urban life.)

Most Protestants today would not be unhappy with the formulation I have just offered as "the Catholic incarnational" version, provided the Catholic acknowledges, as I do, that grace must illumine and inflame my nonperverted will to inspire me to obedience, always remembering, "Not I live but Christ lives in me." That inflaming, will-inspiring grace is, at first, not the infused grace of sanctification, but the imputation to us (not in us) of the righteousness of Christ-faith itself. But I consider Catholic incarnationalism vital for achieving the kind of community that I shall argue is needed to resist the extremes of modern individualism, and that is something much deeper than church social gatherings.[31]

More at Work in the Break than a Dispute over Justification: How Deep Lies the Fault?

I thought it important to bring the core doctrinal issue forward from the start, so as not to degrade the Reform to merely a social, economic, and political phenomenon. It was, and remains, seriously and essentially spiritual. But when the break with the Catholic Church, helped along by intransigence on both sides, happened, it implied something more than what is included in this central doctrinal dispute: that there is something in the nature of Catholicism as it developed, presumably from early on, that necessitates Protestants' different understanding of the faith and of the nature of the Church, and hence their continued separation from the "Rome" that had corrupted the true doctrine at its core.[32] If you accept that, then the Protestants had to found new Churches (as the Catholics see it) or return to the pure primitive Church (as Protestants see it). That implication, which too often finds expression still in our own time in open "antipapist" teaching in some Protestant Churches, makes Catholics defensive, undermining desire on their part to examine seriously the question whether indeed the Catholic Church has persisted in ignoring real difficulties embedded in its understanding of the Christian Revelation.

The intrepid, genuine appropriator, striving to be faithful to the truth, must struggle to rise to the challenge, seeking to face whether indeed there is still something at work here dividing Christians that is much more

31. My friend says at this point: "Why are we different on this point? Word vs. (sacramental) sign focus? Christ vs. Church focus? I wouldn't be surprised if it will come down to something like this, to the effect that, yes, it's both . . . we both (badly!!) need each other, not just 'they' need to become like 'us'" (ibid.).

32. By what point was the Catholic Church already essentially corrupted? And if the date would have to be set as early as I suspect, perhaps already in the second century, where we find fathers like Irenaeus sounding awfully "Roman Catholic," what would my Protestant friends make of the delay of almost a millennium and a half until the Reform, during which, presumably, the Holy Spirit leaves the vast mass of Catholics erring behind a wrong and corrupt leadership?

serious than mere differences of "spiritualities," or of doctrine, perhaps even more radical than the two anthropologies. If there is, would this not then mean that the most mature, united Christianity would have to make a larger place than the Catholic Church has up until now to accommodate better certain truths, underplayed in the complex dynamics of real everyday living out of Catholicism, perhaps also undertaking serious correctives of extremes pointed out by Protestants or discovered in the light of the whole modern experience? For instance, what has Protestant Church organization achieved that merits serious consideration today by all Christians? At the same time, we must ask what difficulties there are in Protestant angles on certain essential doctrines and in Protestant Church life, some aspects of which might be aided by return to Catholic experience. Has Protestantism perhaps thrown out elements that are essential?

All traditions within Christianity must struggle together to face the absolutely radical question being raised by the colossal revolution of the HTX. Loving critique of the difference between the traditions can serve as caution signs for all Christians, pushing our reflection deeper, and offer a contribution to the ecumenical search for Christian unity, and for evangelization of the entire planetary-HTX world.

As the goal of the present volume excludes my expending several hundred pages working through the immense story of the Reform, from the background to the break, through the whole course of the evolution of modernity, tracing its many streams, I shall focus on what I believe to be the most significant Protestant claims in their *contemporary* form as they have matured as a result of four centuries' experience and reflection, and in the way they challenge all Christians today. Some claims have dropped to a position of lesser significance.[33]

Two examples of significant changes along the course of Protestantism's evolution follow. Not explicitly espoused by the great Reformers, and without their wanting it, nationalism has become an issue; and so has unending "nuclear fission," the angels being as unable to keep track of how many distinct Protestant Churches there are as they are of how many different religious orders of women exist in the Catholic Church! No Reformer set out to destroy the Church universal. None wanted to push the national

33. For instance, it may be important in assessing the thrust of Calvinism to know that its founder maintained what would strike the Catholic as a rigid, predestinarian stand, but today many descendants of Calvinism weaken it, though some—a small minority I think—stand by it. (The Lutheran-Catholic dialoguers seem content to consider "predestination" simply acknowledgment that God chooses us, and we are called to respond, sidestepping the issue of whether all are called but only some respond.) "The priority of God's redeeming will over every human action in bringing about ultimate salvation is recognized in both our traditions by the classic doctrine of predestination" (Anderson, Murphy, and Burgess, *Justification by Faith*, 7:72). In reading quite a number of autobiographical accounts of Presbyterians who have become Catholics, I have not seen one who even mentions predestination. So I conclude that a strong form of predestination is not one of the ineluctable central dividing issues between most Protestants and Catholics today.

state to the fore. None foresaw the proliferation of unaffiliated churches. But through their attack on the papacy, center of unity, and through allying themselves with the political forces that would allow their initiatives to succeed, the Reformers in effect founded national or regional churches closely tied to those nationalistic and regional forces that split the West, in much the same way as medieval Christendom was tied, for better or for worse, to the feudal system.

Today's Protestant thinkers are not inclined to defend narrow nationalism (Ulster is an exception). Many Protestant Churches are trying, and with some success, as missionary churches, to break out of national limits.[34] The Catholic Church has had to fight local tendencies, too, but its strong monarchical structure has given it advantages in this, while also proving successful in minimizing schisms. The self-conscious strong center has allowed toleration of a rather daunting spread of spiritualities and, paradoxically, more patience with local infidelities than Protestantism, where the more serious are quick to split away or to expel groups showing deviance. It is interesting how individualism leads to a more stifling conformism demanded by the group.[35] Perhaps Catholics' longer experience showed them two millennia ago that a Church of the pure would soon reduce to two members: Jesus and Mary. And perhaps a deeper community is built on a more enfleshed sacramental system, less "friendly" perhaps, but more consistently rooted in the shared Body and Blood of Christ. As "Latin-European" as "Roman Catholicism" may be, the Church also enfolds Oriental rites, the great Byzantine liturgy, and peculiarly American forms of Catholicism. But at its most American, and apple pie as it is, this local form of Catholicism is not as utterly "made in the USA" as are American evangelicals (greater individualism, entrepreneurial and inventive "marketing," unabashed use of wildly amplified contemporary music, often unrestrained crowd manipulation). But I grant, as they implant in, for instance, Latin America, evangelical churches take on more of a local caste.

That brings up, then, another concern, present from the beginnings of the Church but becoming especially urgent when reform goes over into open rebellion, a perennial problem for every form of Christian church: how should the Church restrain unorthodoxy, and, especially, how is this to be done in those "open societies" where freedom of conscience is allied with extreme individualism?

34. The Anglican Communion, for one, is present in large parts of Africa, India, and all of North America. While Catholicism is de facto better situated than any separated Christian church for reasserting the genuine universality of the Christian community, most Protestant Churches, through their missionary outreach, acknowledge in act as well as theory this need for the Church to be "catholic." Their membership in the World Council of Churches, too, is a gesture in that direction, as well as the generosity shown by many in hard ecumenical work. Every local church, whether Protestant, Orthodox, or Catholic, is tempted to parochialism.

35. I have seen up close, in the case of an evangelical fellowship allied with an international chain of them, how quickly the higher leadership turfed them out over differences that would strike a Catholic as minor.

Almost from the start Luther plainly had to worry about this, seeing in the *Schwärmer* heretics upon whose heads he finally called down, with a fury worthy of the Spanish Inquisitors at their worst, the power of the state.[36] In an epoch when "evangelical" Christianity is propagating a kind of religion that Catholics and most "mainline" Protestants see as an oversimplifying distortion of the tradition, the question remains whether "free church" ecclesiology can avoid an atomization of Christianity: one deals with dissension or unorthodoxy by turfing out the offenders quickly. This seems to me to bring in its wake inevitably serious distortion of the truth of Christianity, as purely local churches yield to the temptation to tailor the gospel to fit too closely the limited vision of a provincial congregation, which becomes rigid in its demands of conformity, without the corrective of the whole Church operating effectively through the center, and the careful organisms it has provided for vetting positions.

In the final chapters, as I explore Catholicism in its present form I shall suggest that the Catholic Church worldwide embraces a far broader spectrum of distinctive spiritualities than the evangelical traditions, not compromising essential core truth and at the same time avoiding atomization. That there may be much going on in some of these Catholic subtraditions that distracts too much from the essentials, and that this policy of tolerance leaves many individuals who are in dissent against essential Catholic doctrines in positions of minor authority—teaching in Catholic schools, even seminaries, and functioning as parish priests—is a serious problem that I shall also consider. If "truth is symphonic," some dissonances can be tolerated. At what point the impurities ruin the concert altogether is a constantly disputed pragmatic point. I have sympathy for my evangelical friend when he comments:

> I'm wondering just how "effective" Rome has been in creating more than a veneer of unity/conformity, etc., that is, there certainly are lots of differences of the wrong

36. *Schwärmer* means, literally, the swarmers—"enthusiasts" is the usual, rather overly polite, translation; it was Luther who launched the term against the Anabaptists and Zwinglians. Various Protestant groups persecuted one another as heretics. The Hutterite Chronicle of 1527 records the first martyrdom of a Protestant killed by a Protestant—that of Felix Mantz, on January 25, 1527, martyred because of his belief in the need for rebaptism. Protestants, like Catholics, were appalled at the Anabaptist notion that all previous infant baptisms, that is, the quasi-totality of baptisms, in the words of the Hutterite Chronicle, "are in fact no baptism" (see the excerpt from the G. H. Williams, ed., *Chronicles in Spiritual and Anabaptist Writers* [Philadelphia: Westminster, 1957], 42). A while later a group of ten Anabaptists under Ullmann were seized in Swabia on the way to refuge in Moravia, beheaded, and their women drowned (ibid., 44 n. 96.) Ulrich Zwingli himself backed persecution of Anabaptists (ibid., 45). Every revolution resists the inevitable *dépassement par la gauche,* for, having broken with the traditional source of legitimacy, the revolution itself is then open to challenge. Whenever it "compromises" with "reality," it is accused of being "impure." Evolutionary reform, like that of the Franciscans in the late twelfth century, can goad legitimate authority into change without opening the Pandora's box by challenging the very ground of its authority.

sort in the Roman Catholic Church, as you too admit (and the bishop of Lincoln! more power to him!!).[37] Mind you, I think I prefer the kind of diversity (good and bad) in the Catholic Church than amongst Protestants, but I doubt whether one form or the other is in fact actually more effective in promoting real unity in Spirit and Truth. Maybe I just want to think more about all this.

If this Catholic-tolerant unity is acceptable, this should challenge evangelicals to take a new look at their ecclesiology, founded in an underemphasis on a true coherent broad community because of embracing a "purism" and a subjectivism that, the Catholic would say, comes from an individualism fostered by both *sola fide* and *sola scriptura* principles essential to Protestantism, as well as to a loss of the sense of mystery.[38] At the same time, the Catholic Church, both locally and at its center, has to be vigilant not to slip into the extremes of too much of the inessential, risking finally a sense of "anything goes."

From Reform to Revolt

Few in the Church at the start of the sixteenth century denied that the *ecclesia semper reformanda*[39] was in urgent need of a housecleaning more thoroughgoing than the periodic reforms of the past. The "medieval system" had grown really old. The network of cozy relationships, in place for centuries as a result of a slowly evolving feudal system; habits of corruption in the power structures of society, which will always settle in where, with certain institutional arrangements in place for a long time, there has been a failure to address growing problems with arrangements favoring certain groups; and general spiritual slackness, in part due to the prosperity enjoyed by the ruling class and the nouveau riche among the bourgeois, and perhaps because the ignorance of the illiterate masses had

37. My friend is referring to that bishop's recent action in announcing Catholics in his diocese must resign from the Masons, Planned Parenthood, and Catholics for Choice or find themselves automatically excommunicated.

38. *Sola fide* means "faith alone," and *sola scriptura* means "*Scriptura* alone," two principles we shall explore anon, and I shall explain then why I believe they demand such "purism." Is there a danger in the "enthusiasm" that goes along with intense personal prayer to a Christ (or in the case of Catholic charismatics, Mary, too), of fantasizing a personal intimacy with Jesus that begins to obscure the hieratic mystery of the glorious transcendent majesty of the divine that is incarnate in Him? The Orthodox already complain of the Romans, with their simplified form of the Eucharist, that it lacks a sense of mystery. Perhaps the evangelicals go even further in this direction. Recall that both Saint John of the Cross and Saint Teresa of Avila warned contemplatives to be wary of substituting their imaginations for true gifts of divine presencing, and Saint John recalled that "one act of charity is more precious in God's sight than all the visions, and communications possible . . ." (*The Ascent of Mount Carmel* [London: Baker, 1928], bk. 1, chap. 22, para. 19).

39. The belief that the Church is always in need of reform is now Catholic doctrine. At the end of the Middle Ages the sense of development of doctrine and of evolution institutional structures was not as strong as it is now, given the better appropriation into Catholic understanding of a historicity that avoids at the same time historical relativism.

reached grave proportions, especially in contrast with the growing learning of the "clerks."[40] As the Church became a dominant social institution, the essential of what it is meant to serve slipped ever further down the real agenda. Venality distorted certain secondary doctrines in a Pelagian direction, the money-raising through indulgences being the worst, but the greed for revenues from ecclesiastical offices being itself disgusting.[41] The degree of corruption and its all-pervasiveness is one reason supporters of the Protestant revolt claim that the situation had indeed gotten to the point where no internal reform could suffice. But it is not, as we shall see, the main reason. That is the accusation of long-standing doctrinal corruption. Together, revolt was the only way forward, the protesters came to feel, a return to the true path of the Church, leaving Rome and those bishops who refused to reform to the devil.

The Nationalistic Diremption of Europe and Freedom of Conscience

Philosophers of history generally—Spengler, Toynbee, Voegelin, Lawrence Brown, for instance (in this Hegel is the big exception)—tend not to look kindly on the rending of Europe's fabric by a religious revolt that fed and was fed by nationalism. Protestantism's dissolving the international bond maintained by Catholicism accelerated a process that otherwise was probably moving toward crisis anyway. For my part, I do not see how without using nationalist as well as certain class forces the Protestant revolutionaries could have escaped the fate of earlier heresiarchs who threatened medieval institutions: brutal, successful suppression. (In Spain, a nationalism, manipulated by a tough aristocracy, forged through centuries of struggle with the Muslims, succeeded in suppressing Protestantism.)

Since in this chapter we are interested in the Reform in the context of the foundations of modernity, I would like to suggest that nationalism, for all the disasters it was to bring in its wake, was a necessary step on the road to the freedom of conscience enjoyed today in a handful of democracies. Rare as it may be as an effective civil good, is nationalism not a very great good

40. This was an inevitable result, judges Voegelin, of the Church's becoming, after Constantine, instead of a small group of the very convinced willing to witness with their blood, a mass, popular Church, where the heavy weight of the mob tends to pull everything down to a low common denominator (*The New Science of Politics* [Chicago: University of Chicago Press, 1952], 123). Now, with the barbarians partly digested, a new elite, not of potential martyrs but of well-educated clerics and bourgeois traders, causes the gap between the Church as spiritual and as worldly to grow.

41. The Lutheran-Catholic Dialogue admitted that some Protestant elements were pretty greedy too in wanting to get their hands on Church wealth: "Deterioration of the relationships between Lutherans and Catholics was powerfully abetted by nontheological factors. In the reformation lands princes and the rising middle classes profited from the expropriation of monastic and church property and were resistent to any reconciliation which would endanger their political and financial advantages" (31).

indeed in the belief of all who have had the (perhaps ephemeral) privilege of experiencing it, despite the distortion of legitimate patriotism though nationalism? Was not this swelling of a sense of national identity a step on the way to democracy, as the people must begin to feel themselves to be a reality? And is not modern Catholic social teaching right to see in a civic order granting responsibility to all the citizens, and hence effective freedom of conscience, a fruit of Christianity that Christ wants as part of the development of His Kingdom? Although it might have been difficult to achieve while retaining the monopoly of a monarchical Church, and too international a sense of the people as the universal "people of God," could it not now be the case, paradoxically, that the best chance of retaining such a free civic order lies in strengthening Christianity within the democratic nations, and might that not be impossible without an increased love of Christians for one another, as they learn to work together to evangelize a frighteningly nihilistic, hedonist society? Because we enjoy open society, might Christian unity not be reachieved with little danger from the reunited Christian Church of forcible stifling of conscience?

Whereas pure tribalism seems to impede development of a sense of self,[42] nationalism—a celebration of difference at a higher level of culture than the purely tribal (nationalism presupposes civilization)—is somewhere between internationalism[43] and the extremist forms of narrow, implicit "we against them" particularity of the tribe.[44] Modern nationalism has gone hand in hand with the development of the increasing "self-standing" (*Selbst-ständig*) individual of bourgeois, entrepreneurial society,[45] the classic "liberal" who remains, not without good reason, the bane of some Catholic authors today.[46] With emerging nationalism still a great danger today, and

42. To the extent the tribe "lives at the margins" economically, it cannot afford the sort of "fooling around" that comes with the exercise of free conscience in wealthy democratic societies. With only slight exaggeration, one could say a college student in Toronto is called on to make more decisions about his life and his "person" in a month than a tribesman in his lifetime. See my explanation of why "authenticity" is impossible under those circumstances in *TA*, 2, 3, 6, 11–14.

43. Internationalism is part of the consciousness of Catholicism and socialism (and to some extent, Islam).

44. In the worst cases when it does not, then the destructiveness of tribal exclusivity, married to the military power of modern industrialized national states, can produce the carnage of a World War I. The disintegration back into the tribalism of an unconsolidated Yugoslavia and the crude systematic destruction in Rwanda in our time show how horrible this belated-development tribalism can be too.

45. The relationship is not a simple one. But could Louis XIV have achieved the outrageous manifestation of *la gloire du Roi Soleil* without Colbert's purse, which came some from military exploit but most from brilliant reorganization of *les manufactures royales* and a generally astute, very modern administration, through all of which the bourgeoisie was profiting and growing?

46. For example, see some of David Schindler's recent articles: "Religious Freedom, Truth, and American Liberalism: Another Look at John Courtney Murray," *Communio* 21 (winter 1994): 696–741; "Christological Aesthetics and *Evangelium Vitae:* Toward

with liberalism degenerating into opportunism, we must not forget that one of the most seductive idols for a people to worship is that rich set of goods, the national culture, that most frequently gets mixed up with some genetic similarity, producing the volatile, emotional reality of "race," a perverse distortion of genuine community.

In the midst of these complex and ambiguous developments, in the eighteenth century there emerged a sense of "human rights," which developed only in the West. Clearly, this would never have happened without Christianity, with the revelation of God's absolute love of each person. Then Christendom has made use of the Roman sense of the rule of law to help bring this into the structured living of everyday social existence. This sense of a communal civic order was absorbed into the medieval consciousness and the medieval polity. But without the breakup of the feudal structures, the modern democratic national state obviously could not have come into existence. "Open society" in its present form as "liberal society" has its problems, some of which are beginning to appear perhaps terminal for the equilibrium needed for it to function, and with devastating side effects on religion. But the political and ideological freedom of open societies has provided an extraordinary window of opportunity for growth of "the self."[47] Early progress toward democracy came in "Protestantizing" and industrializing England and Holland. The Protestant American revolutionaries' leap into democracy and the deist strivings of the Jacobins created experiments in democratic government that were slowly to spread as monarchies and empires weakened. But from the start such development of self-consciousness was accompanied by degeneration into egoism.

The Protestant emphasis on individual interpretation of Scripture played a role in enhancing the sense of the individual's importance, but at what price: the fracturing of the sense of the unity of truth.[48]

If the movement inward of the Christian "spiritualists," the mystical movements of the fourteenth and fifteenth centuries, and the nominalism

---

a Definition of Liberalism," *Communio* 22 (summer 1995): 193–224. Versions of both articles are in Schindler, *Heart of the World, Center of the Church: Christological Aesthetics, Liberalism, and Liberation* (Grand Rapids, Mich.: Eerdmans, 1996). The "self-standing," "free" individual tends to downplay his dependence on God; he gives himself his own mission, and that sense of mission degenerates, without a receptivity to God's will, into an opportunism serving self and the self-centered family.

47. The modern sense of "self" is explored in my *TA*, and further developed in the context of a description of the dynamics of the HTX in *HTX: Learning to Survive in Virtual Reality*.

48. The need for truth to be lived by a community and for the sacred texts to be interpreted authoritatively from out of the ancient, collective experience of the continuous community is a major point, a point critical to overcoming the fracturing of modern society, founded in humility. It carries the resultant temptation, in desperation to achieve unity through blind ideological commitment. We shall return to this.

of Occam with its stress on fideism had not helped destroy the fabric of the Church by weakening the mediating role of the hierarchy—a situation crowned and consolidated by the Protestant revolt—it is doubtful that a space of secularization would have been cleared for "modern times" with its capitalism, liberalism, and industrialization.[49]

If one is convinced that a political economy that allows a high degree of effective freedom of conscience[50] is an important good for humanity,[51] then it is inevitable that one will view with sympathy the developments that made such democratic regimes possible. But progress in human affairs, both personal and social, always has a cost. One heavy price paid for open society weighs mightily in the Christian's consciousness: with secularization, accompanied by large-scale urbanization, and social and geographical mobility, hence isolation and individualism, Christians, after passing through a phase of nationalism, have now lost much of their effective sense of being a people. And with this, the mystical sense of being "the people of God," along with the loss of much of the religious sense that once animated a European life much closer to nature.[52]

As we turn to examine now the major doctrinal and ecclesial innovations the Protestant break brought into Christianity, we shall see how they both encourage and suffer from the extreme individualism the bourgeois, capitalist society was generating. The real question is whether an intact Catholicism can still provide effective antidotes to the resultant extremes of "liberal individualism," with its destructive dimensions. Can

49. A similar situation with the same purported need to break up "medieval structures" is often ascribed to the Islamic world: "Islamic Sufi'ism embodied a tendency to secularization to the extent that it stressed inwardness (*batiniyya*) in religiosity and questioned the mediating role of *Ulema* (the Islamic 'clergy'). Tizini puts forward the interesting thesis that had the heretical Islamic philosophy and Islamic Sufi'ism been able to win the upper hand in Islamic history and had *Ulema* been less successful in combating them, they might have contributed considerably to the industrial development of Islamic society which was at that time undoubtedly socio-economically developed" (Bassam Tibi, "Islam and Secularization," in *Islam and Civilization*, ed. Mourad Wahba [Cairo: Ain Shams University Press, 1982], 70).

50. Not to speak of a very high standard of living, and they are related!

51. Perhaps, as Père Teilhard de Chardin would say, "a necessary step in the evolution of the noosphere." Luther, on the other hand, complained of "fellowships, fraternities, intercessions, merits, anniversaries, memorials; and such like pieces of business are bought and sold, and contracts and bargains are made about them" (*Babylonian Captivity of the Church* [1520], Op. Lat., vol. 16).

52. Toronto, with roughly the same population as the Île-de-France at the time of construction of the great gothic churches, built in twenty years twenty soaring office towers—especially monuments the banks built for themselves—in contrast to the forty enormous cathedrals and abbey churches plus four hundred lesser churches built in forty years' time from the end of the twelfth into the thirteenth centuries. The cost of one of these, Notre Dame de Chartres, has recently been estimated in contemporary U.S. dollars as about $100 million collected in twenty money-raising campaigns. The twenty Toronto towers, all commercial ventures, were built with borrowed money, repaid by rents.

224   The Catholic Tradition

communitarian elements deeply embedded in a Catholic anthropology reassert themselves to give more flesh once again to "the people of God"?

HOW RADICAL THE BREAK?

Now that we have anticipated something of the large-scale social effect the Protestant break was to help along, let us turn back to the break itself, and observe both its dynamics and the doctrinal and ecclesiological "stuff" out of which the movement is made, with an eye to picking out the anthropological differences separating Protestantism and Catholicism.

The Compromises of Martin Luther

We shall consider first not the pure sects, but the mighty, and more compromising, ecclesial work of Martin Luther. We shall see how his decisions, that "the Roman Church" could not be reformed adequately from within, sets up what I shall call "a Protestant logic" that pushes him quite far in the direction of the position that was leaped into from the start by the pure Congregationalist Anabaptist sects.

In *The Appeal to the German Nobility* of 1520, Luther invited the civil authority to reform the Church (shades of Constantine). The main implications were clear, and the results, for Christian, and indeed Occidental, unity disastrous:

> The Romanists have, with great adroitness, drawn three walls around themselves, with which they have hitherto protected themselves so that no one could reform them, and whereby all Christendom has suffered terribly. First, if pressed by the temporal power, they have affirmed and maintained that the temporal power has no jurisdiction over them, but, on the contrary, that the spiritual power is above the temporal. Secondly, if it were proposed to admonish them with the Scriptures, they objected that no one may interpret the Scriptures but the Pope. Thirdly, if they are threatened with a council, they invented the notion that no one may call a council but the Pope.[53]

Luther had become convinced that state intervention was necessary if the Church was to be thoroughly reformed, given the situation he faced. His argument for doing so, however, not only challenged the foundations of papal and episcopal prerogative, and denied the superiority of the spiritual over the temporal power, but implied an undermining of princely power as well. All baptized men are equal, he argued, and all are priests with Christ. "We are all consecrated priests by baptism." As Peter says: "Ye are a royal priesthood, a holy nation" (1 Pet. 2:9); and in the Book of Revelation: "and hast made us unto our God (by thy blood) kings and priests" (5:10). So what is different about the priest or bishop?

The bishop's consecration is just as if in the name of the whole congregation he took one person out of the community, each member of which has

---

53. Luther, *Appeal to the German Nobility,* in *Werke* (Weimar), 11:405.

equal power, and commanded him to exercise this power for the rest; just as if ten brothers, coheirs as king's sons, were to choose one from among them to rule over their inheritance, they would all of them still remain kings and have equal power, although one of them is appointed to govern.[54]

The model in Luther's mind here tends toward the Congregational, with implications for state power of a democratic sort: the power of Christ is vested in all Christians, who together designate their bishop, to whom is delegated the task of picking those who will serve as ministers, using for the congregation the priestly power all possess. Luther makes the point quite clear:

> And to put the matter more plainly, if a little company of pious Christian laymen were taken prisoners and carried away to a desert, and had not among them a priest consecrated by a bishop, and were there to agree to elect one of them, and were to order him to baptize, to celebrate the Mass, to absolve and to preach, this man would as truly be a priest, as if all the bishops and all the popes had consecrated him. That is why, in cases of necessity, every man can baptize and absolve, which would not be possible if all were not priests. This great grace and virtue of baptism they [the papists] have annulled and made us forget by their ecclesiastical law.[55]

Luther adds that "a priest should be nothing in Christendom but a functionary; as long as he holds his office, he has precedence; if he is deprived of it, he is a peasant or citizen like the rest."[56] There is then no indelible character to priesthood, no special charism—that is a pure invention of the Romanists.

Here is where the princes should have had their thinking caps on: "For if a thing is common to all, no man may take it to himself without the wish and the command of the community."[57] Luther is writing in the context of the priesthood, of course, but he says nothing about limiting the principle to the spiritual order.

In the next paragraph Luther has a sentence that ought to have made kingdoms and principalities not just put on thinking caps but also breastplates and helmets: "It follows, then, that between layman and priests, princes and bishops, or as they call it, between 'spiritual' and 'temporal' persons, the only real difference is one of office and function, and not of estate." As to the right and obligation of the "temporal" power to punish the "spiritual," Luther is categorical, although he did soften this stand when he began later to resent princely incursions into the affairs of the Reformed church.[58] "For as much as the temporal power has been ordained by God for the punishment of the bad and the protection of the good, we must

54. Ibid., 407.
55. Ibid., 407–8.
56. Ibid.
57. Ibid.
58. "Some have seen a tension between Melanchthon's *Instruktion für die Visitatoren* (1527) and Luther's comments, which may reveal his distrust of secular in spiritual affairs" (*Encyclopaedia Britannica,* 1967 ed., s.v. "Luther").

let it do its duty throughout the whole Christian body, without respect of persons, whether it strike popes, bishops, priests, monks, nuns, or whoever it may be."[59]

The tendency inherent in the Protestant position toward Congregationalist ecclesiology and democratic political theory is obvious: governance of the Church by the priesthood of all believers and governance of the state by "We, the people" make ready bedfellows. In both realms, this implies that the primary channel of the Holy Spirit's guidance is the individual conscience, and is my interpretation of the Bible. The influence on ecclesiological understanding of democratic political impulses, including a socialist interpretation of "equality," mixing up the issue of the equal dignity of every person given in the creation with the quite distinct, revealed reality of the utter freedom of God in according His grace, remains a central challenge to thinking Christians to this day. Indeed, as we shall see below, it is one of the gravest sources of misunderstanding not only between Protestants and Catholics, and among Protestants themselves, but also menacing orthodox Catholicism from within.

THE NATURE OF MINISTRY AND THE AUTHORITY OF THE CHURCH

The question of the nature and source of ministerial authority in the Church is at the heart of what we have identified as the great separation in Western Christianity between Congregationalist Protestant and those of more "Catholic-apostolic" conviction, whether "high Anglican" or "Roman," who share convictions close to those of the Orthodox.

The independence ensured the Church through a nonpopular and nonstate source of authority has always stood it in good stead, both in locking horns with state power and in dealing with heresy. In our time, with the rise of totalitarian regimes, democratic peoples have come to recognize as central the problem of limiting the power of the state (not to forget that Hitler came to power legally, through democratic processes!). This is a wider issue than the struggle of the bourgeoisie to make a place for itself alongside the landed aristocracy, who had claimed for themselves a natural, and divinely ordained, superiority of estate. (The democrats' effective denial of this "God-given estate" carries over easily into denial of a God-given estate of those ordained to office in the Church, which we see Luther flirting with from the start. [The Catholic Church, as we have seen, continues to believe that Jesus Christ did institute a special "estate," presiding over the Eucharist and teaching and governing with divine authority, for the apostles, the successors they chose—we see them in Scripture doing it—and the "presbyters" whom the apostles and their successors also chose and to whom they delegated aspects of their special divine authority.]) Before rejecting this strong claim, one should ask what

59. Luther, *Appeal to the German Nobility,* 412.

other institution but the Church has ever been able to stand up not just to a caste and class within the state, but to the state itself?[60]

Two Notions of Ministry Mirror Two Anthropologies

Behind Luther's complex discussion is visible the emergence of the different spirits of what was destined to become two distinctive ways of living Christianity, those two anthropologies to which we have become alerted: the Catholic is corporate, hierarchical, liturgical-symbolic, mystical, and highly incarnational-sacramental; the Protestant more individualistic, Congregationalist, and centered more in written symbol, "the Word," hence puritanical (playing down the body) and iconoclastic. It is only an apparent paradox that the more sensual of the two, the Catholic, will prove less given to outbursts of "enthusiasm" than the more repressively puritanical. It emphasizes celibacy, understood nuptially—the priest and the religious married to Christ;[61] it is still "universalist" in thrust, the vast pretensions of which, anchored in a firm hierarchical structure, finally arm it to resist the state; as Voegelin contends, the Protestant, Gnostic in tendency (that is, intended for the knowing pure "remnant"), who nevertheless tend either to try to form the state (for example, the withdrawn Mennonites with their autonomous separate communities, Calvin with his Republic of Geneva, the Puritans with their "New England," the Quakers with Pennsylvania and the City of Brotherly Love), or failing that, to get more in bed with the princes. The Catholic, emphasizing tradition after flirting, as some of the Protestants did, with the power of the emerging national states and later resisting imitation of the new democracies, ends by fighting the ideological totalitarian regimes and discovering the merit of being more independent of all state power than ever since Constantine. The Protestant, moved more by the inspiration of the moment, and hence more immediately susceptible to the changes demanded by galloping "modernization," although with a deep tendency to democracy, generally resists the totalitarians. (Some "corporatist" Catholics were tempted by that element in the fascism of Mussolini and Franco.)[62] The "conservative drag" of a well-consolidated

60. In the recent crumbling of Communist power, many commentators have acknowledged that the degree of performance in throwing off the yoke—starting with Poland, then Czechoslovakia and Hungary, with Bulgaria and Romania at the bottom of the list—followed exactly the strength and real independence preserved by the respective churches. Even within the former Yugoslav confederation, one could see the superiority of Slovenia and Croatia over Serbia and Macedonia, whose Orthodox churches played a more subservient role than the fiercely independent Catholic churches of the northwestern republics. It is paradoxical that the great revolutionary Luther should have played around with weakening this independence of the Church vis-à-vis the state. But the power realities of the time account for it.

61. The celibate who does not succeed in opening him or herself to the grace that brings joy risks drying up, becoming worse than a puritan, a frustrated old maid!

62. In Germany segments of the Lutheran and Catholic churches, because of fear of Stalin, were soft on Hitler at first. Hitler hated Christianity and the churches. But

and deep-rooted Catholicism kept it too long in complicity with the declin-ing feudal structures in those cultures slow to modernize, both in Europe and in Latin America, but also makes it less willing to give in to the winds of the moment, and less tempted to tailor its teachings and forms to immediate popular demand. This both inflamed the atheism of the popular and radical movements and contributed to resisting their extremes, as one sees in the French Revolution. The flexibility of the new Protestant Churches gives an advantage to their prophets in the short run: they can tailor the message to the public, but with quickly changing winds, these often find the forms they have created outmoded and unstylish quite quickly (as with "mainline" "social-gospel" Protestantism today), and so lack staying power. On the other hand, the Catholic Church plows along more faithful to its millennial course, with some feudal elements of course, but others reaching back to the fathers and to the apostolic beginnings,[63] offering an exotic and intriguing alternative to the latest "mode." In fairness, I hasten to add that the profound spirituality of the most faithful Protestants guards them from the extremes of modishness, the best can also "plow along" through stormy seas and shifting winds, keeping their course fastened on Jesus Christ, just as "trendy Catholics" can let themselves be too influenced by the latest ideological fashions.

Ministry, Word, and Office

Before anything else is said about Luther's stand on ministry, the point so well put by the contemporary Lutheran theologian John Reumann should be considered: "Lutheranism is accustomed to discuss the ministry in light of the word, not to defend a divine order of ministers, as central."[64] This statement strikes me as a bit peculiar. For as my friend commented on this, " 'the Word' specifies 'offices'; perhaps the point is that 'valid ministry' is 'office' according to (i.e., in continuity, conformity with) the Word, rather than historical continuity as the key point." Reumann goes on to suggest that it is peculiarly Catholic (East and West) to emphasize ministerial office, apostolic succession, hierarchy, and validity of orders. Lutheran theologians worry about these things more when engaged in ecumenical dialogue with Catholics than in the everyday life of their communities. For Lutherans and most Protestants, the issue, rather than the nature of office,

---

had the Catholics been more resolute democrats, they might have mounted the strong resistance to Hitler that was needed.

63. The Orthodox can legitimately plead this same conservatism. Where the Eastern Churches proved deficient in the recent history of the East Bloc was in their tradition of a too cozy relationship with the state power. Perhaps now that they will emerge from this awful period of totalitarian oppression and misuse, they will find a new spiritual vigor.

64. John Reumann, "Ordained Minister and Layman in Lutheranism," in *Eucharist and Ministry*, vol. 4 of *Lutherans and Catholics in Dialogue* (New York: USA National Committee of the Lutheran World Federation, 1970; and Washington, D.C.: U.S. Catholic Conference, 1970), 230. Reumann is active in the American Lutheran-Catholic Dialogue.

is how well a given ministry serves the gospel.[65] When the Catholic insists that the validity of the sacraments depends on the validity of the ordination to office, and not the personal holiness of the priest, he may neglect the importance, emphasized by Balthasar, of the minister's personal holiness in radiating the presence of Christ in the Sacrament. Overfunctionalizing the office can amount to a kind of "disincarnating," too. Perhaps there is evidence here of "modernism" (in Heidegger's sense of "technology") within the Catholic Church, an overmechanization of sacramental office. The issue of anti-incarnationalism is a large one. There may be a problem inherent to the post-Resurrection state in which we participate, a "new body" while yet living in the "old body" at the same time. We shall return to this.[66]

Ambiguities in Luther's Position on Ministry

I have been emphasizing the potential for Congregationalism in some of Luther's statements. But his position over his lifetime on the status of the ordained ministry was not without ambiguity. While the ministry of all the Church is to spread the Good News and witness to it by living the gospel, it is, Luther believed, the special ministry of those called as ordained ministers of the congregation to preach and administer the sacraments. In *The Appeal to the German Nobility*, the call to these special ministers was said to come from the whole baptized people. In other texts, Luther upheld the divine institution of the minister's office, without emphasizing or elaborating on this.[67]

Some Lutheran theologians today speak of an unresolved tension in their tradition between the universal priesthood and the divinely instituted office. We shall see later how Catholic teaching seeks to reconcile them. Philipp Melanchthon, the most influential Lutheran Reformer after Luther

---

65. This question, of course, needs to be confronted by all Christians. The Catholic Church could well afford to reexamine how well its priests are being formed "to serve the gospel" without weakening in any way the sense of apostolic succession and the fullness of priesthood residing in the bishop. It is important not only that the Eucharist be performed, but also how the priest presides at it, with what effectiveness in leading the people "to gather about the altar," what and how he preaches. Above all, what holiness he incarnates and radiates are vital to the incarnated communal life that is the Church. As the documents of Vatican II show, and the recent speech of Cardinal Ratzinger, alluded to above, reiterates, the Church must not, and has no intention of, settling down comfortably in a given institutional form, no matter how solid its credentials as divine in its basic apostolic foundations. The life of the gospel, as charismatic, obliges a constant evolution in forms, and renewed efforts of personal formation. Office must be filled with grace. But the life of the gospel also demands acceptance by the Protestants of what is clearly mandated by Christ, and soft-pedalled (but not denied by all): the unique authority and power given Peter and the apostles. An evangelical Protestant friend pointed out to me in this regard, "Our ministers are ordained, a self-conscious tie to 'apostolic succession' . . . we don't ignore it, we just understand it differently."

66. This question was posed by my evangelical friend.

67. Reumann, "Ordained Minister and Layman in Lutheranism," 232–33.

himself, was a layman who, paradoxically (but not so unusually), seemed to hold priesthood in more awe than the priest Martin Luther.[68]

Neither the Catholic nor the Congregationalist Position Is Ambiguous

The Catholic Church position in these matters is unambiguous. The Church explicitly accepts the Pauline teaching on the priesthood of all believers.[69] It is "scriptural," after all. In virtue of baptism, every believer can in turn, in case of necessity, baptize; the marrying couple administer the Sacrament to one another; and all participate in celebrating the sacrifice of the Mass.[70] On the difference, yet interrelationship, between the common priesthood and the ministerial or hierarchical priesthood, *Lumen Gentium*, a key document of the Second Vatican Council, states:

> Each of them is, in its own special way, a participation in the one priesthood of Christ. The ministerial priest by the sacred power he enjoys molds and rules the priestly people. Acting in the person of Christ, he brings about the Eucharistic Sacrifice, and offers it to God in the name of all the people. For their part the faithful join in the offering of the Eucharist by virtue of their royal priesthood. They likewise

68. Ibid. According to Reumann, Luther, despite what some historians have claimed, did not change his thinking much once the position of 1520 had been hammered out. The Apology of the Augsburg Confessions once states "we have no objection to calling it a sacrament" (*Apology of the Augsburg Confessions*, 13.10). Luther and the Lutheran tradition consistently restrict ordination to nothing more than the community's way of signaling that a person has been selected—called by God and confirmed by the Church—for an office of public ministry. (This being selected, as a way of being called by God, and confirmed by the Church is not intended to be some mere democratic election; but, Protestant friends have granted, it can rather easily degenerate into conceding, as one put it, "too much to the spirit of the world.") Ordination does not make him a priest, for baptism does that for all believers. He is singled out by function, the minister—be he presbyter or bishop (that distinction being merely human)—being of no different intrinsic status from the layman.

This position, seen by the Confessions as median between the Catholic hierarchical position and the *Schwärmer* (Anabaptist) denial of any special office of ministry, has not been without criticism from within Lutheran ranks. To continue with Reumann: "Some have felt that Luther's daring reemphasis on universal priesthood and the position in the writing of 1520–25 were stultified by later events, and the 'real reformation position' was never carried through with regard to ministry. Others have felt that the 'true Lutheran emphasis' was on the divinely instituted office of ministry and that this aspect needed further development. For such reasons, the ministry in the Lutheran church—precisely because it never was an article on which the church stands or falls but is in so many aspects a matter of human ordinance—could be subject to trends and change in ensuing centuries, with a variety of forms which in the eyes of some were almost an embarrassment—the embarrassment of freedom" ("Ordained Minister and Layman in Lutheranism," 241).

69. Curiously, most Catholics seem quite unaware of this. This teaching is emphasized in the Second Vatican Council document *Lumen Gentium*, 10.

70. Ibid. The layman, however, cannot administer the sacrament of penance or *preside* at the Eucharist, nor confirm, nor ordain priests. These require the empowering by ordination, coming from the apostles, in which alone resides the fullness of the priesthood of Christ.

exercise that priesthood by receiving the sacraments, by prayer and thanksgiving, by the witness of a holy life, and by self-denial and active charity.[71]

What tension there is between the priesthood of the people and divinely instituted office is fairly clearly outlined, removing much of the ambiguity found in the Lutheran tradition. There is little ambiguity in the pure Congregationalist model, as followed by most denominations. Catholics and Lutherans both find this low level of tension in Congregationalism unfortunate, the differentiation of missions within the Mystical Body, and the need always to reconcile them being taken as a sign of life.[72] The Congregationalists reduce the sense of the hieratic to a minimum, but the tension of the paradox is preserved in the divine-human natures of Christ Himself.

IMPLICATIONS FOR CHURCH AND STATE

These indications offer some help in understanding in a preliminary way how the Church-state questions intertwine with the issue of the nature of the priesthood.

Luther's backing of the princes in putting down peasant revolts is a rather infamous incident of the Protestant Reform. But did not his own thinking encourage those further revolts, and was he not retreating in the face of the anarchy he came to fear, just as he was later appalled at the atomization of the Church that he saw, to his sadness, happening in his lifetime?

So it would not be unfair to say Luther recoiled personally at the implications of the revolutionary position of 1520, and I think we can see why. Luther did not hesitate to participate in the invention of mechanisms for clarifying such authority issues in the Church, but he seems to have taken fright at the implications for the civil order of doing so. How clearly did this brilliant man glimpse the future?

Diminution of Church Leads Not Just to Democracy but First to Divine Right of Kings

The inevitable diminution of Church power relative to state power led in the seventeenth century to development of that notion of "the divine right of kings" mentioned a moment ago. It is a concept utterly foreign to the Middle Ages, when pope and king alike were considered strictly bound by God's law, and kings were constrained by popes and bishops, as well as by powerful vassals, but especially by the firm belief that God's law is

71. Ibid.
72. Evangelical friends tell me that not all ambiguity is absent: once the congregation, through the elders, has designated a minister and until they dismiss him, he is recognized as enjoying a certain authority as he leads the service, preaches, and administers the congregation's affairs.

above all. Medieval emperors and kings were emphatically not considered "absolute monarchs." (When one sees how frequently and egregiously the crusading nobles would go back on their sworn oaths, we are reminded that this constraint was no more perfect in their lives than in our own. But at least they would sometimes be prepared to admit they had sinned, confess and do penance, and at least they were being told that their power was not unrestrained.)

Because of the development of monarchical power in post-Reformation Europe, especially in France, where cardinal-chancellors such as Mazarin and Richelieu would not hesitate to use the weakening of the Church by Protestant power (and, for that matter, Turkish power) to strengthen their "most Catholic" kings, radical liberal revolutions became tempting as the means to dismantle an abusive system in favor of parliaments and elected executives. Interestingly, these often yielded much of their power to dictators such as Cromwell and Napoléon and Lenin and to repressive bureaucracies.

The most infamous of these revolutions, that of 1789, was a ferocious enemy of religion, as was that of 1917. Everywhere the Jacobin revolution spread; it did so on the wings of "Enlightenment," itself the offspring of circles of dispossessed intellectuals patronized by a strengthening and frustrated bourgeois class. In the Jeffersonian state the role of religion, already a volatilized Protestantism, was likewise much reduced. Today in every democratic republic, the remaining church hierarchies exercise little restraining influence on the elected governments and the self-perpetuating bureaucracies that rule the state.[73]

73. The anticlerics join the antireligious in breathing a sigh of *all the better!* But some serious students of the process of secularization are not so sure this is entirely a good thing. An example is the liberal Protestant theologian Wilfred Cantwell Smith, a respected student of Islam's struggles with secularization. He is visibly worried about societies that think that undoing the old faith is enough: "No society can survive that does not have some ideal, some faith, some motivation." As he points out, "liberal secularism itself is a faith, a positive conviction. It has its own foundations, moral and intellectual; its own martyrs and heroes and ideals; its own history; and its own institutions. Some expect it to appear of itself as soon as religious faith is circumscribed or dropped. This is glib" (*Islam in Modern History,* 210).

What can happen is that with the collapse of the "Muslim" state, one is left with a vacuum, a flat, ideal-less, disoriented society. The Western liberal secularism, after all, grew out of Christianity, slowly, step-by-step. Many of the best elements of Enlightenment, whether its authors would ever admit this or not, are owed to the Christian revelation of the unique dignity of man. (Without the Incarnation and the sense of man's adopted divine Sonship, indeed with its central, unmitigated sense of absolute submission to God's will [the very meaning of the word *muslim*], Islam has not tended to produce an Enlightenment sense of "human rights." Indeed, there does not exist a single state with a Muslim majority with a good civil-rights record. Probably the least bad is that of the most resolutely secularized state of Muslim ancestry: Turkey, and its record of dealing with the Kurdish minority is terrible.) But even in the best case of the most solidly evolved secular liberalism there is cause to wonder whether its ideals have really succeeded in taking the place altogether of the religious ideals they replaced, or whether there too there has not been left something of a vacuum, being filled by a

We shall have occasion to see many other aspects of the thinking that contributed to the liberal secularism as we now know it. There was obviously more involved than just the weakening of the influence of the churches, including many factors positive for the development of mankind. But for the moment, I want to concentrate on the Protestant challenge, moving on now to contrast the purer sectarian with the "mainline" Protestant position. For, however much its grip on secularized society may be slipping, along with the Catholic, Protestantism—especially evangelicalism—too remains a force and, to the appropriator, as we have seen, intellectually valuable as a relevant questioning of Catholic principles and institutional forms.

Let us then consider the two main sorts of Protestant alternatives on another central issue, core of the sacramental concept of the faith, the nature of the Eucharist.

THE EUCHARIST

A good introduction to the most radical transformation of the notion of the Eucharist effected by the Reform is the prescription for celebrating the "Supper of Fellowship," which the father of the Anabaptists, Conrad Grebel, wrote to Thomas Müntzer in 1524. As one reads this, he can understand Luther's reaction, as a firm believer in the real presence of Christ in the Eucharist:

> If thou wilt abolish the Mass, it cannot be accomplished with German chants, which is thy suggestion perhaps, or comes from Luther. It must be rooted up by the word and command of Christ. For it is not planted by God. The Supper of Fellowship Christ did institute and plant. The words found in Matthew 26, Mark 14, Luke 22 and I Corinthians 11, alone are to be used, no more, no less. The server from out of the congregation should pronounce them from one of the Evangelists or from Paul. They are the words of the instituted meal of fellowship, not words of consecration. Ordinary bread ought to be used, without idols or additions. For [the latter] creates an external reverence and veneration of the bread, and a turning away from the inward. An ordinary drinking vessel ought also to be used. Although it is simply bread, yet if faith and brotherly love precede it, it is to be received with joy, since, when it is used in the Church, it is to show us that we are truly one bread and one body.[74]

Interiority is the key word, with the chosenness of all baptized believers. (No ordained priesthood here, "the server from out of the congregation"

---

mindless hedonism and materialism. Smith fears a worse vacuum in modern Islamic states if the old faith is dismantled too quickly.

A longtime student of the Christian tradition, Smith sees that even at its best the liberal secularist faith, as he calls it, like every faith, has its problems, some of them appearing particularly acute from a Christian standpoint and from the perspective of Muslim faith as well. It is the faith of liberal secularism (ever more transformed by the HTX that it bred), more even than orthodox or mainstream evangelical Protestantism, which challenges the Catholic in Western societies to critical appropriation today, including serious meditation on what is happening to our Western societies as they increasingly embrace la dolce vita as ideal.

74. Williams, *Spiritual and Anabaptist Writers*, 76–77.

pronouncing the words.) This emphasis on "interiority" explains the Anabaptists' insistence on adult baptism. In *enfant* baptism, the child is called, before he can even know any better, through the community. In adult baptism, the individual must first receive the interior call, the Spirit speaking directly to him, so becoming the repository of power. (As we shall see in contemporary evangelicalism this being "born again of the Spirit" is the crucial moment, more important than the act of baptism itself—it is this act of faith alone that is our acceptance of Christ's saving act.) The remnant (even a remnant of one, like the prophet Isaiah) alone can decide if and when he has received this interior anointing, which is not effected by baptism but expressed by it. Grebel was proud that the Anabaptists were so few compared to those poor souls caught up in the foibles and corruption of the feudal structure.

Together with this spiritualized notion of the Eucharist went the transformation of Christology, reminiscent of early controversies, indeed so much so one gets the impression the resolutions of the councils suddenly count for nothing anymore. Luther's famous reply to the treatise on the subject sent by the spiritualist Caspar Schwenckfeld shows how upset he was at the prospect of all these battles having to be fought again. It finishes with these "charitable" words: "The Lord punish Satan in you, and your spirit which has called you, and your course which you are following. May all those who have part with you, Sacramentarians and Eutychians, together with you and your blasphemies, be your destruction."[75] The irenic Schwenckfeld turns the other cheek, trying again to explain his understanding of the nature of Christ and the Lord's Supper. He is able to quote to Luther one of his own formulations of the issue. In *Sermon on John 6:37*, Luther had written: "The bread on the altar is merely a symbol, and is of no value, unless one has already eaten the living, heavenly bread inwardly."[76] For Schwenckfeld, what counts is this inward eating of the heavenly flesh of Christ. On the question of Christ he then affirms: "For, according to the testimony of the Holy Scripture, I know no other Christ than Him who now reigns in the glory of God the Father. In Him dwells all the fullness of God bodily (Colossians 2:9) and is present in the Holy Spirit with grace, with [the chosen believers] as the head of His body and members."[77]

Schwenckfeld expresses horror at Luther's notion that the impure can approach the Sacrament and will find there forgiveness and healing. This is an affair for the elect only, those called by and living in the Spirit. There

75. Ibid., 163 n. 1. Eutyches was the Monophysite Archimandrate of Constantinople, against whom the Council of Chalcedon in A.D. 451 defined Christ as one person with two natures.

76. "An Answer to Luther's Malediction," Caspar Schwenckfeld, April 23, 1544, in Williams, *Spiritual and Anabaptist Writers*, 172. My friend comments: "Here is evidence of the Platonic-like inner/outer split affirmed, rather than 'together with the eating of the bread'" (private correspondence).

77. Ibid., 175.

can be no exteriority, objective efficacy, or objective real presence accessible to the impure.

There is something of the same horror in the idea that the Second Person of the Trinity should have become a creature. Schwenckfeld does not deny Christ's humanity, but his conception of what it is and how it came about avoids qualifying His divinity. In his *Answer to Luther* he puts the mystery in these terms:

> I recognize nothing of creation or creatureliness in Christ but rather a new divine birth and natural Sonship *[Kindschaft]* of God. Wherefore I cannot consider the man Christ with his body and blood to be a creation or a creature. Rather, I believe with Scripture that he is wholly God's only begotten Son and that Christ, the Son of God, his Heavenly Father, the whole person indivisibly *[unzertailig]* God and man was born in time of the Virgin Mary.[78]

Christ, no longer physically present to the community, can dwell only in the hearts of the elect. This helps strengthen the feeling of "us" versus "them" that seems part of Gnostic psychology, for I hold Christ in my heart, He is not objectively available, made so by an objective succession of ordained priests. Dietrich Philips who, along with his brother Obbe, was a founder of the Mennonites in the Netherlands, puts this sense of separation in the strongest terms. The destiny of Cain and Abel "is a clear representation and testimony that from that time on there were two kinds of people, two kinds of children, two kinds of congregations *[Gemeynten]* on earth, namely the people of God and the devil's people."[79] Gone is the Catholic sense that we are all sinners, that we are all impure and constantly in need of the help of the sacraments, and that only at the Second Coming of Christ will the grain be separated from the darnel (Matt. 13:30). Also effaced is the Catholic sense that we here below, members of the Church militant, are none of us pure, none yet freed of all ambiguity resulting from our continued involvement in the earthly city even while aspiring to dwell eventually, purely in the heavenly one.

For Dietrich Philips the Body of Christ in the Sacrament is reduced to keeping His word, which is symbolized by the Supper. "The flesh of Christ shall be eaten and His blood drunk, namely thus, that we accept and obey the Word of God with pure hearts and in pure faith. Why do we eat the flesh of Christ and drink his blood? Because God's word was made flesh, and hence the word of God and the flesh of Christ are one and the same."[80] (Catholics agree to this extent: eating the Body of Christ and not keeping His Word is fruitless; indeed, Christ calls us to eat His Body so that we may be fortified in keeping the Word.) No longer a sign of communion among all Christians, the Sacrament is the symbol of the pure who are born again through keeping the Word. The correct

78. Ibid., 180–81.
79. Philips, "The Church of God," quoted in ibid., 230–31.
80. Philips, *Enchiridion*, 140, quoted in ibid., 243 n. 16.

celebration of the Sacrament, while a "renewing and confirming of brotherly love, unity and fellowship" among the saved, is also given, along with baptism, "that they should distinguish the congregation of God from all other sects, who do not make right scriptural use of the sacramental symbols of the Lord Jesus Christ, although they have the appearance of doing so, and in their hypocrisy confess much about them, and commit and perpetuate shameful sacrilege therewithal."[81] When one speaks in the name of a pure *Gemeynte,* one has no trouble distinguishing the sheep from the goats.

Recall, this is the extreme position within Protestantism, one against which Luther fought. The Catholic always worries, once the strongest sense of the "real presence" is weakened, that one has started down a slippery slope that could end where the Anabaptists already were from the start. As we have seen, some Protestant traditions fight against this, retaining some sense of a corporeal presence of Christ in the bread and wine. In Catholicism and Protestantism both there are many slippery slopes, just as there are faithful elements that resist sliding down them.

THE RADICAL REFORM AND THE LOGIC OF REVOLUTION

A logic of revolt is working here, carrying the radical Reformers beyond the compromises of the more moderate Lutherans. A coherent, radical alternative reading of Christianity is emerging.

What is it about revolutions that seems to demand always a *dépassement par la gauche,* a swinging ever further left? Perhaps this: Once the restraints of traditional society are torn away, so that "radical" groups are free to put into action a "pure" solution, one that would have been rebuffed by intact society as utopian, then a small, cohesive, determined, and exalted group can explore to the hilt the implications of their logic, usually a Gnostic kind of utopianism, and try to live it out in practice at least within the elite group, separated from the vast "rest" of the community, who incarnate the inevitable ambiguities of the whole social reality. The corruption that grows in the dank ground of compromise invites the seriousness turned sometimes fanatic among those seeking purity. Thus a tension ever present in human society.

If the Reformer's starting point is the belief that the Church was corrupted basically from early on, the faithful remnant now being called to renew the Church through interpretation of the Scriptures by means of a different, living tradition from that of the vast majority of Christians,[82] then the whole of previous practice, structures, or belief is up for freewheeling

81. Philips, "The Church of God," quoted in ibid., 234.
82. The Anabaptists particularly cultivated the myth of a continuous tiny underground Church, the remnant of the pure, persecuted by the Catholics throughout the ages, but surviving nonetheless because sustained by the Holy Spirit. Rather, Catholics see Gnosticism as a perennial temptation, with groups bursting anew on the scene from time to time, like the Arians and later the Cathari.

critical review, with no restraint from traditional teaching, not even from the creed, not at least as traditionally interpreted.[83]

Some philosophers of history are severe in their judgments of little bands who think they alone are the inspired ones, moved by the Holy Spirit (or the *Weltgeist*, or by their unique insight into the "iron laws of history," or whatever), justified in setting themselves up against the whole of the tradition and society, seeking to take it in utterly contrary directions. Eric Voegelin, for one, wrote of "magic operations in the dream world" in describing the pretensions of a handful of individuals confronting the collective power of the Protestant and Catholic princes and declaring, in the name of Christ, as once Luther had done, *"Hier stehe ich, ich kann nicht anders!"* ("Here I stand, I cannot do otherwise!") because we alone know this is what the Word of the Lord says.[84] Their sincerity impresses, for the faith radiating from these texts is moving. But at the same time, the enormity of their pretensions can scarcely be overstated.

But, one might object, did not the apostles do exactly the same thing, standing up against all of Judaism and the whole Roman Empire, to lead Jews and pagans alike in a radical new direction? The question is important if we are to understand the reality and the position of the sects vis-à-vis the "mainline" Reform and the traditional Catholic Church.

In the apostolic Church, it is indeed true, a small number spoke in God's name, but they claimed to do so on the basis of the entirety of the traditional Revelation, not against it nor as a radical reform of it, which would have denied the truth of large sections of it. "I have come to fulfill the law, not to abolish it," Christ says, and it is in that spirit His apostles act. (This would not be convincing to a Jew who would see the wholesale abandonment of the dietary laws, for instance, as more than a "reform." Hence the importance of the next issue.)

By what authority do they claim the right to do this? The nature of the apostolic authority is made quite clear—with none of the ambiguities we have seen among the Protestants: the claims as to who Christ was and how He passed on His authority are strong, it is He, Son of God, who personally chose and empowered His apostles. This contrasts to some self-appointed group, sixteen hundred years after the Church had clarified for itself the way in which the apostolic authority is conceived and passed on, surging up to say, "the Holy Spirit has spoken to us, in opposition to the whole authority structure of the Church as it has been known for sixteen hundred years." The Anabaptists were proud to speak against the overwhelming majority of the community of Christians, but they did this not on the basis of a great new event, like the coming of Christ, but

---

83. This extreme position is rejected by most Protestants who accept the creeds as normative, seeking to interpret them in keeping with Holy Scripture. Many do not reject the notion that a certain traditional understanding is at work in all this. And today some favor serious return to the writings of the fathers of the Church, but as yet few would include the medieval doctors.

84. Voegelin, *The New Science of Politics*, 170.

because of their judgment about the corruption they saw in the Church—"the gates of hell are prevailing," as the Anabaptist Schwenckfeld once said. The sectarians resemble more the great prophets of the Old Testament than the apostles.[85] The apostles are different from the prophets, as their teaching and action are founded, more like that of Moses, on the direct divine event; but whereas Moses' witness is to a theophany to which he alone is party, the Christ event is public, squarely in historical time-space. (Luther, ironically, does not hesitate to declare that it is not the Holy Spirit at all but Satan who is moving his more radical opponents.) The Anabaptists say that Christ's promise to stay with His Church, since there was some serious corruption from very early on, must have meant that the Church was destined throughout much of its history to remain a tiny remnant of the pure.[86] The practice of rebaptism shows the sectarians' complete reconstruction of the sense of the sacraments, including the Eucharist.[87] That the Church defended infant baptism, which is now seen by the sectarians as a great evil, means that for the Anabaptists the fathers of the Church were, in effect, false prophets.[88]

But the "in-between" position of the more moderate Protestants does not escape a serious issue of authority in the Church, setting up the tension between what is left of a sense of hierarchy and apostolicity in the Lutheran

85. The various Reformers were seeking a return to the Old Testament as well as to "primitive" (prehierarchical) Christianity—it is why the books present in Septuagint but dropped after Tanakh's canon closed in the first century A.D. were dropped from Protestant Bibles—and the strength of the prophetic (as opposed to the priestly) strain within Protestantism is as strong as the original prophetic strain is within Judaism (fundamentally, inheritors of the priestly strain).

86. There was indeed disruption and corruption from early on, the Catholic admits. (Paul's first letter is scolding the Corinthians for party strife, and Acts shows us the charlatan Simon Magus at work, and the serious dispute between Paul and the other apostles over consorting with Gentiles.) The Catholic notion is not then that the Church is the remnant of the absolutely pure, but rather Christ's promise that the Holy Spirit will guide the Church and the Gates of Hell will not prevail means that the essential truth and the sacramental presence of Christ is ensured in the midst of, and despite, our universal sinfulness and personal mediocrity. Who are these "pure"? "Let him who is without blame cast the first stone!" At the same time, it must always be remembered that every Christian is called to nothing less than perfection, and for those who by their office particularly represent Christ's power in the Church, nothing less than their utmost striving for sanctity will ever do.

87. That is why, of course, Luther himself was so shocked by the notion of rebaptism.

88. To this day, those who are eager to dispute the Church's authority—including many Catholics—are quick to claim, "The Church has changed its teaching." There is an ambiguity here. If the claim is that the essential core of what Christ taught as necessary to salvation has been changed, then indeed the Church is faithless and the promise of Christ not genuine. If, on the other hand, the claim is that the Church's understanding of the message grows with experience of new human situations, indeed it does. Probably the area of greatest change has been its understanding of what the freedom and dignity of the individual entails as regards freedom of conscience: there has been considerable maturing of the Church's teaching and, even more, practice in this area. But the essential sense of the free, loving relationship of individual to God and of individual to individual in and through Christ has not essentially altered.

tradition, on the one hand, and, on the other, Luther's more Congregationalist sense that the Holy Spirit is really speaking through all the priesthood,
that is, all believers. Again, Catholic theologians will agree that the Holy
Spirit speaks through the whole Church, the priesthood of all believers,
but they will be quite unequivocal about the special charism of the bishop
to discern ultimately that *sensus fidelium,* and to pass on the authority of
the apostolic-hierarchical authority as ultimate guardian of the integrity of
its teaching.

HIERARCHICAL PRIESTHOOD, "FAITH AND GOOD WORKS," AND THE QUESTION OF AUTHORITY: DISTINCTIVE ANTHROPOLOGIES

We are seeing quite clearly how the three issues we have been considering
are inseparable: the special charism of the ordained priest to preside at the
Eucharist carries with it participation in the special teaching authority of the
bishop (when the priest preaches, as canon law says he should, he interprets
the Word of God with authority), which becomes a basic determination
point of the structure and nature of the Church. Now see how this relates
to that central dogmatic issue on which the Reformers say the "church
stands or falls: the relationship of 'faith' and 'works.'" In considering this
now more deeply, we shall see better how the distinctive anthropologies,
themselves rooted in a clash of Christologies, work themselves out.

The Foundations in the Contrasting Anthropologies and Christologies

In suggesting that Catholics bring the body into their theology much
more than the Protestants, I have shown that the latter tend to be more
Platonic, looking for faith to operate in the depths of interiority more than
in the Sacrament and the "Mystical Body" understood as visible Church,
which Protestants call "works," and (rightly) remind Catholics that the
goodness of works flows from Christ's merit alone, which, as we saw, is
the position of the Catholic Church, too.

With a nod to the Marxist insistence on the importance of the economic
foundations of society, observers have been tempted since Max Weber
to wonder to what extent this Protestant spiritualistic individualism is
bound up with the distinct experience of the more individualist bourgeois,
who lives more by his wits and who exercises a strong, independent will,
in contrast to the landed aristocrat and peasant, who share a sense of
continuity, of closeness to nature, of the interdependence of the tribe, of the
slower pace of change in the country.[89] To be sure, many of the Anabaptists
were peasants, but often from the fiercely independent class of *Freie Bauer,*

---

89. Paradoxically, the man close to nature, solidly seated in age-old social structures,
while he may be a more "ruminating" critter, is nonetheless so surrounded and supported by these old structures he can count on, he is not forced to be as self-centered,
self-dependent, hence creative and willful as the townsman who more and more lives

who were long at odds with the feudal overlords. Willful, independent men, they also showed great willingness to get up and leave their native soil. A more incarnational anthropology, like that of Catholics, is less shocked by the idea that how the faith is understood and lived out may be affected by such "material" considerations as one's temperament, itself influenced by social class and concrete situation.

We have seen how the greater sense of embodiment works out in the Catholic position on the ministry and the Eucharist. Priestly empowerment comes from Christ through objective, historical apostolic succession, a divine power purportedly bestowed through Christ's chosen human instruments, real flesh-and-blood, sinful individuals, directly, personally chosen, and then taught by Jesus, a founding institutionalized in a strong way, as it is passed on from generation to generation. *Gratia perficit natura*, the supernatural permeates, and gradually, painfully uplifts the resisting (and fallen) natural; the Holy Spirit works through fallen human nature, restoring it. The Catholic receives the Body and Blood of Christ from a priest who was ordained in a line of unbroken succession reaching back seventy-five generations to Christ's own personal choice of the first apostles. The validity of his act of consecration depends not on his personal holiness at the moment, but on the historically Christ-grounded (the penetration of the divine into material history) empowerment of his office, which God has freely chosen to use as His way of being present to us sacramentally. His own personal faith can be weak, so long as he intends to do what the Church means to be done, as incumbent in the act and office. In this case the Mass is valid and genuine and Christ comes to be really present in the Sacrament, because that is what he promised to do. Because this strong sense of the incarnate Word is objectively powerful, it of course opens the way to abuse, but God has by the same token created a most effective way to be present to us sinful and obdurate human beings, as He works with us to mold us to His likeness.

The implications of these differing anthropologies, like those flowing from another crucial clash of anthropologies—that separating Christians generally from the "New Age" hedonists of our HTX times—are many and important. I have barely hinted at them here. In *Being and Truth*, I postponed drawing together the many anthropological hints contained in that study until I could complete my appropriation of the Catholic tradition. Now here I am postponing the anthropology further. I still retain the hope of

---

by his ingenuity and inventiveness in the midst of destabilizing, accelerating change. Great innovators like Zwingli, Luther, Knox, Calvin, and the Mennonite leaders—men of mighty works—distrusted their own works, in this sense: they had to see them as God's doing for them to have any divine authority, hence as effects of faith and grace. The conservative Catholics, inserted in a sacramental, ecclesial, feudal social order, which they experienced as God's work, could effect their own personal saving works within these structures and think of them as inherently salvific because so much part of that order. The routine and solidity did not demand much anguished, critical interior musing.

developing a more detailed and explicit view of man, in the light of such contrasts as Catholic versus Protestant, Christian versus nihilist-hedonistic anthropologies, and after equipping myself better to understand many dimensions of psychopathology that are important for understanding the picture of (fallen and redeemed) human nature, contribute something to the Christian anthropology that is found throughout the work of Henri de Lubac, Hans Urs von Balthasar, Karl Rahner, and the present pope.

A DISINCARNATE ANTHROPOLOGY FAVORS WEAKENED HIERARCHY

Some contemporary Lutheran theologians have pointed out that there is a doubt whether the Augsburg Confessions "have a Biblical basis for teaching only one ecclesiastical office [priesthood of all believers] and concentrating in it the multiplicity of New Testament offices" (see 1 Cor. 12:28 and Eph. 4:11), and wonder whether they perhaps "take too little account of the factors which make necessary the special ministry of the apostles alongside the ministry of all."[90]

The participants in the Lutheran-Catholic Dialogue point out that the term *apostle* is not simple. It seems to mean that in the Gospels, all those sent to preach the gospel were sent as missionaries. In Acts an effort is made to restrict the term to the Twelve, although Paul is twice called an apostle, but in both cases he is mentioned after Barnabas (14:4, and perhaps 14:14). A sustained effort seems to be made in Acts to present all missionary and expansive efforts as subordinate to the Twelve Apostles.[91] Both Mark and Matthew use the term for the Twelve, once each (Mark 6:7 and Matt. 10:12, but both texts, however, seem clearly "apostolic"). John does, too (13:16), but in the farewell discourses it is evident that there is an inner circle, identified as the Twelve (6:70, 20:24). As McCue (to whom I am grateful for these biblical indications) points out, "A theme running through these discourses is that as the Father has sent the Son into the world, so the Son sends His closest followers ([John] 17:18–19). It is through them that others will be brought to the faith; John uses *apostolein* (to send forth) six times. Finally this sending would seem to involve pastoral responsibility (21:15–17)."[92]

Without pretending to trace all evidence for both the strong and the weaker sense of apostolicity in the early Church, I would cite one text favoring the strong, episcopal interpretation. It is in chapter 8 of Ignatius of Antioch's Letter to the Smyrnaeans, dating from the turn of the first

90. Edmund Schlink, *Theology of the Lutheran Confessions*, trans. Paul Köhneke and H. Bouman (Philadelphia: Fortress Press, 1961), 307. In 1 Cor. 12:28, Paul declares: "In the Church, God has given the first place to apostles, the second to prophets, the third to teachers; after them, miracles, and after them, the gift of healing; helpers, good leaders, those with many languages."

91. Cf. Acts 9:26–30, 8:14–17, 6:1–6. Also, cf. James F. McCue, "Apostles and Apostolic Succession in the Patristic Era," in *Lutherans and Catholics in Dialogue*, 4:144.

92. McCue, "Apostles," 147.

century: "Let no man do ought pertaining to the church apart from the bishop. Let that Eucharist be considered valid *(bebaia)* which is under the bishop or him to whom he commits it. It is not lawful *(exon)* apart from the bishop either to baptize, or to hold a love-feast *(agapen)*. But whatsoever he approves, that also is well-pleasing to God, that everything which you do may be secure and valid *(bebaion)*."[93]

Some Catholic theologians engaged in the official dialogue with the Lutherans are open to the Lutheran suggestion that apostolic succession is determined more by faithfulness to apostolic teaching than to a line of episcopal ordination. They hope in this way to encourage the Catholic Church to admit the validity of Lutheran orders, accepting as sufficient a continuity of ordination by priests, as no Catholic bishops (outside of Sweden) would consent to ordain Lutheran ministers.[94]

The more I ponder the Catholic tradition, the clearer it becomes to me that the sense of apostolic succession, and the understanding of the office and authority and special charism of the bishop, and with it, the role of the See of Peter, is the keystone to the Catholic edifice, and hence the cardinal issue separating Protestants and Catholics.[95] It is in keeping with an anthropology that implies that authority should not become so diffuse as to risk losing the integrity of the teaching, which demands a clear line of succession, with those in authority choosing, educating (the Church has stressed more and more long, careful education of future priests, and then bishops are usually chosen from among priests who have gone on to even more advanced study, often in the pontifical universities in Rome—very incarnate!), and ordaining those who are to see to it that the tradition is handed on intact.[96]

A Protestant friend objects: "It seems to me that the Roman Catholic hierarchy has not guaranteed the soundness of its priesthood anymore than the Protestant 'system' has; there is corruption all around. And there is a correction to that corruption in both camps as well, thanks to Christ's pledge to His church, not limited to any particular ecclesiological form. He does not seem to discriminate with regard to which churches he corrects. We all need it, and we all get it."[97]

On the first point, I would respond that it is much clearer in the "Catholic system" that those authorized to teach and to name teachers and presiders at the Sacrament are not self-selecting. With so many breaking away among

93. Chapter 8, in *A New Eusebius,* ed. J. Stevenson (London: 1960), 48.

94. Statement of Catholic participants, *Lutherans and Catholics in Dialogue,* 4:28ff.

95. "Cardinal" means "hinge," and that is just the sense intended here: everything swings on this.

96. Protestantism, like Islam, has had to become much more a religion of the book to retain its identity. Unlike Sunni Islam, however, it can also draw secretly on the substance of a living Catholicism, if only, at times, in modes of opposition, to keep a coherent tradition that goes beyond the letter of Scripture. (See, for instance, how High Anglicanism, in the Oxford revival, drew on Catholic experience for its renewal, and how many mainline Protestant Churches are doing the same today in enriching their liturgy.)

97. Private correspondence, March 1996.

Protestant Churches, succession of authority becomes confused.[98] Clearly, there is a much greater doctrinal consistency throughout the worldwide system of Catholic seminaries, despite some serious deviations here and there, and not forgetting that the evangelical seminaries seem to adhere to a consistent creed. But liberal Protestant seminaries are all over the lot.

Of course, to anyone who is not convinced that the apostolic succession descends from Christ, this very "incarnationalism" gives rise to an objection: "This is precisely how a 'Catholic ideology' has maintained its grip!" But you cannot have it both ways![99] There is a point to all this, and the question of the strictness of that descent and its being limited to bishops is something to which I shall return later.

On the second point, I would agree with my friend that Christ has abandoned no part of His Church, and that the Holy Spirit works in Protestant denominations as in the Catholic Church to achieve that constant reform the need for which Rome explicitly teaches, and "many and mysterious are His ways." Sin and corruption you will have with you all days, until the end of time. But to Catholic eyes, doctrinal purity has been maintained remarkably intact by the Holy Spirit through the instrument of a strong, well-articulated, Christ-founded hierarchy. My evangelical friend points to a consistent orthodoxy among evangelicals in maintaining the creed as understood by the Reform, with a concern even in "paraecclesial" organizations, like the Varsity Christian Fellowship, to see to it that representatives maintain the Reformed body of beliefs.

The fathers of the Second Vatican Council were not willing to go as far as some of the theologians in the Catholic-Lutheran Dialogue as regards the Protestants' maintaining the full sense of the eucharistic ministry. In the *Decree on Ecumenism* we read: "Although we believe [the Western ecclesial communities separated from us] have not preserved the genuine and integral reality of the Eucharistic ministry in its fullness, especially because of a defect of the sacrament of orders, nevertheless when they commemorate the Lord's death and resurrection in the Holy Supper, they profess that it signifies life in communion with Christ and await his coming in glory."[100]

Both Lutherans and Catholics in the dialogue affirmed a special witness to the unity of the Church found in "the traditional episcopal order and discipline of the Church," and "regret that no bishop had been willing in Reformation Germany to ordain priests for evangelical congregations."[101]

---

98. There are exceptions; for instance, in Presbyterianism, the authority structure for ordination is quite clear.

99. Those who, like the Lutherans, Presbyterians, and Anglicans, retain a sense of apostolic succession in priestly ordination will have their own ways of seeing to the maintenance of orthodoxy.

100. Walter M. Abbott, S.J., ed., *The Documents of the Vatican II* (New York: America Press, 1966), 364.

101. "Common Observations on Eucharistic Ministry," in *Lutherans and Catholics in Dialogue*, 4:15. I find it a striking fact that not a single bishop in the German-speaking

All agree, I believe, that in weakening the sense the institution had acquired, Lutherans delivered a mortal blow to Church unity.

Protestants generally do not attach the same importance to unity and coherence "at all costs." Evangelicals especially, when they feel the truth is being compromised, are quick to split. I would venture to say most Protestants see Catholics as paying too high a price of conformism and passivity to retain the Church's unity.[102]

As in all things human, one does pay a price for strong hierarchical control of any institution. Industrial and commercial corporations constantly struggle with the question of centralization versus decentralization and seek to make "participation" meaningful. That the Catholic structure led humanly, and still leads, to "paternalistic authoritarianism," I would not deny. One must constantly struggle within such a structure to allow the experience of subordinates, be they priests or those laymen who have the hands-on experience of running society, truly to percolate up to "flesh out" the teaching.[103] The Church hierarchy in its humanity, like any hierarchy, naturally tends to become a tightly closed and rather insecure club.

But as these are not just issues of organization but of apostolic ministry, grounded on a claim of divine institution, we must return to discuss them theologically, not just administratively, when we consider the situation of the contemporary Church. We shall also return at the end to the whole question of conformism and dogmatic rigidity, and of laxity

---

lands would defect with the Lutherans. It was different in England, where almost the entire Church separated in schism; as the schism turned progressively more Protestant under Elizabeth, the (validly ordained) bishops switched to a form of ordination that deliberately broke the traditionally understood ordinational succession. (Such is the Catholic Church's claim, anyway.) There must be something to it; otherwise, why, in the late nineteenth century, would some Anglican bishops have sought out the newly schismatic "Old Catholic" bishops, after the First Vatican Council, to have themselves validly (but, in the eyes of the Catholic Church, illicitly) reconsecrated? It is upon these bishops and their successors that the argument for valid Anglican orders rests.

102. And many Catholics are dissatisfied with the present situation: those who consider themselves hyper-orthodox feel the bishops allow too much dissent from Church teaching, and the liberal Catholics experience the papal and episcopal teaching authority as oppressive. Ironically, many "conservative" Catholics would complain that the bishops are tolerating too wild a degree of dissent among some theologians and more or less official teachers in the Church, putting at risk the unity of truth to preserve the appearance of the functioning unity of the community. To suggest that the strong hierarchical coherence of the Catholic Church ensures perfect unity, to suggest there are no "sects" within the Church—in the sense of insisting "we are Catholics" and therefore united, while they ignore some essential magisterial teaching—would be deceiving. Each Catholic, every time he sins, in that act weakens "the unity of the Church."

103. This remains true whatever the force of the Church's insisting that, in the eyes of God, all are equally sons, all are redeemed by the Lord's emptying Himself out on the cross, and that the charism and authority of a bishop guarantee him no higher place in heaven or any supplemental protection for him from his own sinning. On the other hand, I have seen many instances where lay people have managed to get themselves heard. Bishops will change their minds!

and lack of exercise of episcopal authority, and of Protestant disunity and disagreement. We shall inquire whether some defensible via media can be found, allowing freedom of research for truth without destroying the patrimony of Revelation and the tradition's profound experience of living out this truth together. In any event, it is clear from history that, when the Protestants struck out at the preeminent position of the hierarchy, the result was an immediate and apparently irremediable atomization of the Church. Even those who, like the Lutheran theologian Reumann, seeing in "an embarrassment of the variety of forms" of ministry and church structure "the embarrassment of freedom," are willing to pay, in exchange for freedom to maneuver, a considerable price in the form of weak ecclesial and authority structures will often admit nevertheless, as he does, that the price in that direction is truly dear. That is why finding a "less costly" medial position is of the utmost ecumenical interest to Protestants and Catholics alike.[104]

Personal Responsibility for the Church

There is a noble dimension to the Protestant vision of every Christian having a personal responsibility for the well-being of Church and society. It comes with a sense of free conscience and the enhanced role of the laity in the Church. Without a doubt, the Second Vatican Council's endorsements of freedom of conscience, the role of the laity, and appreciation of religious pluralism all owe much to the Protestant and, later, democratic experiences.

The question moving the Protestants was certainly not that of finding pragmatically effective forms of institutional organization. The Reformers did not set out in a pragmatic frame of mind at all. Leaders who, like Karlstadt, Müntzer, and Zwingli, reduced the Holy Supper to a mere symbol devoid of any element of mysterious and special divine presencing other than in the soul understood very well the connection between the special priestly power and the strong sense of the Sacrament.[105] They wanted to dismantle the whole hierarchical structure of the Church, but the point was to interiorize radically the life of the Church, doing away with any "magical," that is, properly sacramental sense of the Eucharist. Luther, on the other hand, who believed firmly in the real presence (although he disliked the Thomistic formulation of it as "transubstantiation" and tended to make the presence depend on the disposition of the communicants), insisted on the priestly power of all believers to celebrate together the Eucharist. Even he weakened Catholic teaching on the Mass, however,

104. In his ecumenical encyclical *Ut Unum Sint* (That they be one), Pope John Paul II says he cannot solve by himself the conundrum of exercise of the office of unity while allowing the legitimate distinctiveness of long Orthodox and Protestant traditions. He asks all Christian leaders to help find a solution.

105. See, for example, the suggestions of Father George Tavard in "Roman Catholic Theology and 'Recognition of Ministry,' " *op. cit.*, 301–24; and Prof. Harry McSorley's two articles in the same volume.

balking at the notion of "sacrifice" as too priestly,[106] and by softening the sense of the priest's special charism to consecrate.

He thus took a step toward making the communion more a gathering than an event of high mystery, a real participation in the objective event of Calvary. This was a step away from "works" toward a purely interior faith, and with it evidence of a shifting anthropology.

Paradoxically, such "interiorization" leads, as the Church democratizes, to more, rather than less, arbitrariness. For when the Holy Spirit is thought to work only in the subjectivity of individuals, or, better, in moving the whole congregation, the lack of objectivity of office, and the weakening of the authority of those with the formation, the time, and the special charism that comes with office, favors the emotionalism of the crowd. The incredibly rapid and extreme atomization of Protestant Churches is the result. The Catholic believes other ways have to be found to increase the average Christian's sense of responsibility for the Church than destruction of guiding power of ordained, sacramental office.

---

106. The Lutheran theologians in the American Lutheran-Catholic Dialogue accept the notion of the Eucharist as sacrifice (see volume 3). Both sides have shown the most generous willingness to move beyond traditional positions. The problem lies here: all admit that what happened in Jerusalem on Calvary once and for all was the unique historic event. The problem is how to understand the reenactment at each Mass as a representation of that unique sacrifice. Conceived only as a "remembrance" and hence a symbol is too weak. Moreover, with the great mystery of Christ's real presence here and now corporeally in the bread and wine goes the sense that His being here to allow His being offered up here and now again in sacrificial atonement for our sins reconnects us, standing about the altar, mysteriously with that event, which itself is here re-presented. As this is an experience of a unique kind of time-space relation, unique to eucharistic presence, it is most difficult to express in language suitable for a different kind of time-space relationships.

9

THE CHALLENGES OF MODERNITY

THE PRESENT SITUATION: THE CRISIS OF THE CHRISTIANS' "REMNANT MENTALITY" IN CONTEMPORARY EUROPE AND AMERICA

The Christian vision is radical, cosmic, and eschatological: the mission of the Son of God made man, Jesus Christ, is nothing less than the transformation of the whole of creation. This is to be accomplished through His Mystical Body, of which He is the head and we—"the saints" past, present, and future—the members.

With such a heroic vision to offer, why then does the Mother Church experience painfully the reality of legions of baptized Catholics drifting away from her, often becoming even bitterly anti-Catholic? Something seems to have gone badly awry in the course of the Christianization of the world.

Modernity has stolen the revealed Christian eschatological vision, deforming it into secularized, progressivist ideological politics. The power of the Christian "myth" has been deformed and then diverted into killing machines. Christian love has been parodied by "human-rights" liberalism.

Because of this secularizing course of events, it would be wise, in introducing a discussion of the Christian's situation in postmodern times, first to clarify Catholic teaching regarding the installation of "the Kingdom," a subject not devoid of ambiguity.[1] Unclarity in the tradition has contributed to the lamented state of affairs. An appropriator's own attitude in regard both to what the "Kingdom of God" means for this world and to the distortions introduced by that postmodernity in which he works will affect the whole cast of his analysis of "the Church in the modern world."[2] A liberation theologian and a neo-Thomist will have very different notions about this.

---

1. For an excellent study of the evolution of the notion leading to the modern ideologies, see Étienne Gilson, *Les métamorphoses de la cité de Dieu* (Louvain: Publications Universitaires de Louvain, 1952).

2. *Gaudium et Spes* ("Joy and hope") is the title given to the most innovative of the Second Vatican Council's most important declarations, a rather optimistic read of the world situation in which the Church is to evangelize.

In critically plumbing the depths of our beliefs, we should face the harsh fact that our sweeping overviews of the situation are vast constructs wobbling on a jelly of shifting conceptualized data. A certain humility about these sweeping generalizations, helped by honest critical appropriation, might at least reduce the ardor with which we are prepared to kill for them.

As we approach our own time, "that *now*," that "acceptable hour, the hour of your salvation" (2 Cor. 6:2), Christians, trying to clarify what is expected of them in terms of action in this world, ought to get clear about this strategic question: is it that 1) the transformation of the world Christ came to announce is to be achieved only apocalyptically, at the Parousia, with the Second Coming of the Son of Man and His definitive defeat of Satan (which would mean one expects little of the present world, and that he had best see to his own sanctification and that of the "remnant"—at least the little part of it he can touch); or that 2) the coming of the Kingdom is an ongoing mission, a work of extending Christ's Mystical Body over time and space through conversion of individuals, the purification of hearts, and through the re-formation of social structures by those of goodwill until they reflect the will of God? The second option entails assuming political responsibility, within the limits of one's possibilities. Or, as I believe, a third possibility, a mysterious (and murky) combination of both, a "mixed supernatural economy": We are to work to make this world reflect better the Kingdom, although this world is not the Kingdom, which is transcendent and supernatural and will be definitively installed, forever, by Christ at the Second Coming. At that time He will take up all the good man has accomplished and offer it, perfected, to the Father. The holiness of the Church evident in this world provides already in this life an experience of the transcending Kingdom. (The mediocrity of many Christians makes it more difficult to appreciate this.)

The remnant mentality always goes together with a dominant negative assessment of the contemporary situation. Every sociopolitical situation in every culture provides plenty of negatives if one is temperamentally driven to accentuating the negative. In our situation liberal progressivists, on the other hand, can easily be Pollyannaish about the spiritual and human challenges with which the planetary-HTX situation confronts us. Those of my persuasion—believers in "a supernatural mixed economy"—struggle for balance in viewing catastrophes of sin in the midst of triumphs of grace, ever alert to the fact that we misread both in many situations. One struggles to avoid believing that his own motives, which are never entirely pure, and God's ends perfectly coincide![3]

3. Christians can avoid believing in the inevitable steady spreading of the Kingdom just by keeping their eyes on the facts. They need never confuse its spread with re-creation of Paradise on earth. Redemption is worked mysteriously deep in souls, but still conversion should (and indeed does) produce good works, which always have social benefits. Typical of this conviction is the view (which is that emerging from recent

Scripture gives ample evidence that the apostles, believing Christ would return imminently, awaited a sudden Parousia ready to burst upon them, and so they worked urgently *now:* When Saint Paul cried, "Now is the acceptable hour, *now* is the hour of your salvation!" (2 Cor. 6:2), he meant Christ is around the corner. Five centuries later, as great a Church father as Augustine, disillusioned by his own adventures with a disgustingly decadent, late-Roman civilization, was tempted to a virtual monastic withdrawal from the world. Recall the *Confessions'*[4] rejection even of science as a vanity of dangerous curiosity,[5] which he lumps together with the circus: watching gladiators kill one another and studying the course of the stars are equally distractions from contemplating God, which alone can deepen our love for Him directly.[6] Later, however, the experienced and wise old Bishop Augustine had learned of the need to work with the world, and to understand it.[7]

---

magisterial documents) of a long struggle, uneven, not always progressing, sometimes indeed in parts of the world going into serious decline (a flourishing Christian North Africa has been lost to Islam for more than a millennium!), but nevertheless quietly, mysteriously working to transform the world. This transformation, however, is not destined, short of the Parousia, to conquer the evil forces definitively. Indeed, the evil forces can be counted on to redouble their efforts as the Kingdom advances, and hence the struggle will only intensify. The stranglehold of sin was broken by the cross, but the deforming reality of sin in our midst will be eradicated in a great purification only by the triumphant Christ when he returns. To believers in this uneven but nonetheless hopeful evolution, with struggle-to-the-end, inevitable progress is simply a form of Gnostic error.

4. *Confessions* was written not long after Augustine's conversion, do recall. When one reflects on the long slide into barbarism, beginning from the end of the Augustinian era and continuing until the start of the eleventh century—again a millennium—it is a recognition of the power of the Holy Spirit to see that Christian hope kept those struggling against an overwhelming flood of rough savages always fresh, always creative. Benedict of Norcia, Augustine of Canterbury, the Irish monks, Saints Cyril and Methodius can all be emblems of this second-spring attitude.

5. Curiosity, says Balthasar, was Adam and Eve's sin: knowledge without love (*Bernanos: An Ecclesial Experience*, trans. Erasmo Leiva-Merikakis [San Francisco: Ignatius Press, 1996], 139–40). Recall Pascal's words, *"La vérité sans la charité est un idole."*

6. "Because of this morbid curiosity, monstrous sights are exhibited in the circus. Because of it men proceed to search out the secrets of nature, things beyond our end, to know, which profits us nothing, and of which men desire nothing but the knowing. Such curiosity is also the motive when things are investigated by the magic arts and with the same purpose of perverted science" (*Confessions*, bk. 10, chap. 35). The problem raised by Augustine, it must be said in all fairness to him remains: the magic of technical control and the pride of atheist scientists stand alongside the contemporary Church's enthusiastic embrace of the legitimacy of scientific investigation and the search for sound management of human affairs as indeed a responsibility for Christians. Recall the whole tenor of the key document of the Second Vatican Council, *Gaudium et Spes*, and consider the work of the Pontifical Scientific Council, on which learned atheists seem pleased to sit.

7. This is a theme well documented throughout the grand book of Van der Meersch, *Augustine the Bishop: The Life and Work of a Father of the Church* (London: Sheed and Ward, 1961).

Those who, like Teilhard de Chardin, understand the Christian's mission to be part of a gradual and struggling transformation of the world reject an attitude of settling down to be "a remnant" in a secularizing world "going to the devil." In this they are one with the magisterium, vigorously led by the present pontiff, with his call for "a new evangelization" that is to transform the world: Christ, the mediating creative principle, will never cease being a leaven in the world until all has been *trans-formed* in and by His Kingdom of love. This entails, of course, that with each new generation, a fresh educational initiative is required to *in-form* the newly born members of Christ's Body, preparing them for their special *missio* in carrying out the overall work of the Mystical Body; the "handing on" is neither automatic, nor is the triumph of the Holy Spirit guaranteed in any one sector or any one epoch. To start with, it is not guaranteed in any one free soul. That work, after all, is in every respect an affair of the ultimate mystery: *freedoms*—God's and man's—encountering one another, in a cosmic dialectic, a colossal crash of love and hate.

As Teilhard reminds us, the "great option" of human freedom remains: to produce a false transformation of the world through mediocre "collectivization," "the great Molloch,"[8] or to allow Christ to unite mankind in His Church through love. Teilhard understood this very well to require an arduous transformation, with suffering, especially the suffering of death integral to it. Nothing in all this is inevitable.[9]

Some theologians, like Balthasar (who was not generally a fan of Teilhardian optimism), point out how much Christianity has already bettered the world,[10] showing how so much of the "Enlightenment" ideals of human

8. The dangers of this wrong form of "catholicism" is the theme of a rather frightening book by an evangelical Protestant, Philip C. Bom, *The Coming Century of Commonism: The Beauty and the Beast of Global Governance* (Virginia Beach: Policy Books, 1992). Itself all too apocalyptic, the work nevertheless points to the scary alternative foreseen a half century ago by Teilhard, and offers some interesting facts that show the direction the world, driven by high technology, may be going. For Bom, a "politicized" Catholic Church is part of the problem.

9. Teilhard also saw that at the Parousia it happens ultimately only through one great, final reordering, purifying, free gift of Christ, in which the entire cosmos dies to the old order to be reborn in *"la grande Métamorphose."* Saint Ambrose stated: *"Resurrexit in Eo mundus, resurrexit in Eo coelum, resurrexit in Eo terra"* (*De excessu fratris sui*, 1.2 [Patrologia Latina 16, 1354]). For an analysis of Teilhard's position on this see Henri de Lubac, *La pensée religieuse du Père Teilhard de Chardin* (Paris: Aubier, 1966), 188–90.

10. "Christianized lands have an infinitely better record of respect within the family for the freedom and dignity of individuals, and most particularly of women, than other cultures. What 'Westerner' still believes that the *Pater Familias* has right of life or death over every member of the household, as was the case in the Roman Empire? Where, in the Christian world, is a mere dismissal sufficient to get rid of a wife one no longer needs? Who still thinks families can impose marriages on their offspring as was still true in the Middle Ages, until the Church called for new rites, grounded on the free commitment of the spouses to one another? Who still believes that family loyalty is an excuse for every crime against outsiders or even public good?" (Janine Langan, "Building the Civilization of Love," keynote address to the Second Pan-American Congress of the Family, Toronto, May 1996).

rights and the dignity of man have been "taken away" in secularized forms and propagated successfully to the whole Western world, now spreading to the rest of mankind.

But if Jesus Himself can wonder "whether when the Son of Man returns will He find any faith left on earth?" (Luke 18:8), a Catholic today, allowing himself to become depressed by the patent de-Christianization in Western societies since the onslaught of modernity, with all the trivialization and brutality this brings in its wake—60 million dead and displaced alone in the titanic struggle between the fascist, communist, and liberal ideologies in this century—can understandably fall into the "remnant" mood. Worrying that active Christians constitute still a minority among the 5.5 billion people on this planet,[11] and seeing the incredibly powerful HTX spreading to ever larger populations the hope of material prosperity on the basis of a liberal individualism of superficial spirituality, he deplores the resultant trivialization of human existence, with its cult of ugliness (and death). All this descent into studied hedonism, leading to bestiality, strikes any Christian as diabolical. Then texts like "Many are called but few are chosen" (Matt. 20:16) and the 144,000 elect of the Apocalypse spring front and center despite what Paul, Newman, Teilhard, the council, or the present pope have taught that can feed one's hope for all mankind.

But then they should recall that no society, in its mediocrity, has ever been superbly supportive of profound interior life of holiness. Even in the close-to-nature, stable existence of tribal village life there is much that is brutish, much that inhibits development of the fullest possible human and cosmic awareness. The "Christian" Middle Ages certainly supported a life of Christian piety much more than urban HTX existence, but why could its structures not contain within serious reform the brutality of the onslaught of the brilliant and proud monk Martin Luther? The great deficiencies of earlier cultures admitted, still the present HTX-deformed cultures,[12] so violent in their radicalness and unprecedented dynamism that favors a practical atheism, face the evangelizer with disoriented individuals, poorly

11. Nominal Christians constitute about a quarter of mankind, no insignificant *leaven*, potentially. But no one has a measure of how many Christians are actively, apostolically, struggling to live a Christian witness. One thing is sure: in absolute numbers there are more Christians today, nominal or really trying, than ever before, and probably the percentage of mankind actively seeking to live Christianly is greater than ever before. And remember, not only is two thousand years a short time in the million years man has been around, but the two hundred years since the start of industrialization is but a second for Christians to learn how to evangelize such an explosive society.

12. In *HTX: Learning to Survive in Virtual Reality*, I argue that the HTX, interacting dialectically with civilizations, and through them the cultures at the base of the various civilizations, deforms both civilizations and cultures: de-forms, not only in the sense of changing the form, but also so often twisting it into a parody of itself, the way Jerome Kern de-formed the spirituality of black slave Americans into a vehicle for a superficial version of the Marxist class-struggle anthropology: "You and me, we sweat and strain, bodies all achin' and wracked with pain, . . ." instead of "Where were you when they crucified my Lord?"

supported by community, grasping for some kind of control of their lives. This produces a difficult dynamic for Christian living including the following negative dimensions.

First, HTX life is too *distracting:* a lifestyle unprecedentedly complex, offering the average person more opportunity (one of the deadly temptations of the rich, against which already Pascal warns—*divertissement*)[13] than any other culture ever, and provoking him to constantly interrupting leaps from one thing to another, rendering sustained reflection difficult, and pushing everyone to activism. Because of the unprecedented rapidity and pluralism of this society, one never knows where one is, or who one is. Discovery of self and communion with God require silence and quiet order. In the midst of the pressing crowds, Jesus was forever slipping away to solitude to pray.[14]

Second, urban life is exceptionally *individualistic,* the Enlightenment liberal's dream. The "nuclear family" replaces the extended family, and a casual, sexually lax "living together," helped by high-tech contraception, erodes even that. And with its pluralism, urban living encourages voluntarism, "I have a right to my opinions; no one is going to tell me what to do."

Contemporary education does not support the ongoing search for the common good. And the arts—once encouragements for those seeking beauty and truth—have increasingly been transformed into expressions of the whimsy of will and particular vision, "iconoclastic," the antithesis of the desire for "universality," that is, for the catholic.[15]

Third, evil seductions are allowed an increasingly unhampered course. Indeed, some forms are publicly, methodically glorified. No society since the Christianization of Europe—not even "Restoration" England—has allowed the flaunting of perversions and humanly degrading sins as freely as the present. Drugs are everywhere. Hundreds of billions of dollars in

13. While it is a wonderful good always to have more opportunities to explore, these riches of opportunity hide the need to face hard realities, to see we are responsible for the consequences of our decisions, and to be aware always that we do not have excellent control of our environment—that we are not God. The poor man is reminded of our dependency every day of his life.

14. One evidence our hope is not misplaced: Christianity has never ceased creating new institutional forms, in response to the challenges of every age. The anonymity of the big city and the mad rush of high-tech society are no exception: new Christian institutions are demanded and are forthcoming—whole new kinds of communities—as we shall see later in our more upbeat conclusion.

15. A hypothesis worth exploring: is contemporary art, while perhaps not dead, as Hegel declared, nevertheless, in its individualism and nihilism, *essentially* anti-catholic? Consider most of the films, television productions, and novels, not to speak of the likes of Mapplethorpe's photography of sadomasochistic acts and sad little girls showing their private parts—with crowds lined up for blocks to get in to admire. Everyone can produce his own list of such "liberating" art efforts, which in fact celebrate the degradation of humankind. Is there enough of an appreciative community to support Christian art?

the hands of Mafia organizations form a force of systematic corruption of unprecedented proportions.

Fourth, the sense of the sacredness of life is being lost under the onslaught of the *convenient* (hallmark of what the revolutionaries of '68 despised under the term *la société de consummation*): unwanted babies in the womb and "useless" old people in chronic-care homes are suddenly dispensable, and healing doctors are being transformed into legal "terminators."[16] Doctor-assisted suicide is being touted as the designer way to go.

Rather than presenting a thumbnail-sketch history of the development of the "modernity" that has brought us to this—an immensely complex issue, demanding a book as large as the one the Reform would merit—I shall draw on work done elsewhere for my "HTX" book,[17] which will help adopt a thematic approach. I shall address the key challenges with which modernity confronts the believing Catholic Christian, some of which I have just been hinting at. But at the same time I shall point out the strengths of modern development. This wide-sweeping analysis, for all its generality, will help us see more richly the essence of the Catholic tradition, as the community of Christians seeks to regroup and rearm itself in the midst of this explosive global development.

I agree with Balthasar, despite dreary description of the challenges just offered, that the Christian should welcome as a grace the radicalness and the totality of these modern developments.[18] The élan of science and technical

16. What a recent minister of health in the socialist government of Ontario called "legitimate health alternatives," as she announced new abortion clinics in a time of extreme budgetary constraint. A "pro-life" (imagine a society in which such a no-menclature exists and makes sense!) physician from Holland tells me there were approximately twenty-five thousand illegal, involuntary "terminations" effected on the elderly in his country last year; and that now when a physician approaches a sick old person with a needle "to help you sleep," the poor souls are terrified. Recently, the Dutch Parliament, while refusing to legalize murder of the old, also sent a signal that the homicide laws will not be enforced in these instances. This is nothing less than a breakdown of law.

17. My research group, after composing a long list of some forty factors, agreed to the following condensation of the *essential ingredients* of the HTX that must be included in any adequate discussion of the epoch. I list them here, although not able to go into the questions of their meaning and interrelationships (which is the task of the forthcoming book *HTX: Learning to Survive in Virtual Reality*), because this offers a hint of the kinds of considerations in the background of my selection of factors to consider in their impact on the Catholic tradition: *ideas* (product, plan, what do you want to do and control?); thought of the whole, temporally (eschatological, progress) and spatially (global and gigantic); centralization/decentralization (in bureaucracy); management, manufacturing, and marketing techniques; creativity versus imitation; *investment capital; personnel* (staff, workers, customers, citizens); mobility—interethnic; education versus manipulating "public opinion"; population explosion; family and personal breakdown; social-welfare net; *materials and energy* concentrations; and *information* (needed about all of the above, and key to "managing").

18. See Balthasar's early powerful book *Die Gottesfrage des heutigen Menschen* (The God question and modern man [London: Burns and Oates, 1958], 24–25) (Vienna and Munich: Herold, 1952).

power; the emergence of new, largely urban lifestyles, often clothed in noble humanist terms, and indeed offering undreamed-of opportunities to innumerable persons; and the development of new anthropological dimensions, especially those of economics and of depth psychology, touch every aspect of life, both positively and negatively. All this demands of theists a redoubling of efforts to plunge more deeply into the essence of Revelation. For the Christian, that means recuperating more completely what Balthasar calls the "form" of the revelation in Jesus Christ. To do this the Christian must probe the depths of what the great saints have shared with us of their experience, including those recent and present saints who have lived within the emerging HTX. With this light, Christians must then seek with the saints to enter into the fresh ways God reveals His glory in our new planetary setting.

I shall first offer in this chapter a preliminary survey of the challenges I have come to see as particularly important, trying to show how they imply one another, as aspects of the form of this epoch. Then in subsequent chapters I shall go into them more deeply, seeking to illumine the *fundamentum* with the light the long wisdom of the tradition brings. These are the issues I have seen as essential:[19]

1. the problem on the surface of the Christian's worry: the drift, now a rush, toward atheism;

2. the effects of techno-science: why these developments contributed to secularization and the spread of practical atheism;

3. the challenge of a creative Christian response to the new techno-culture: I shall examine some achievements and problems brought on by the pioneering efforts of Pierre Teilhard de Chardin, still after all this time the most provocative and courageous Christian mystic of modernity, valuable, despite serious problems in his thought, as an entry into this fundamental dimension of the epoch;

4. a possibility of a certain kind of individualism occurs as a mass phenomenon with the discovery of how to produce and distribute wealth widely, and with it a new notion of "liberation." Christians need to go to the core of the Christian notion of freedom in order to respond to an attack on all forms of "authority," without which recovery of an authentic sense of *communio* is hopeless; and

5. the question of a spirituality of affluence and of the proper spiritual nourishment of the peoples in an era that the emerging world system is rendering more effectively ecumenical, and offering the real possibility of feeding the poor, materially as well as spiritually.

19. I know of no principle founding a "transcendental deduction" of these dimensions, nor even any scientifically defensible method already worked out for coming to grips with something so vast, so complex, and so rapidly developing as "modernity." One can survey only one's own experience, and then propose for criticism the bit he has been able to see of the key issues, hoping this will provoke others to add to the list.

Beyond all these looms:

6. the challenge of peace, for not only is the very physical existence of mankind now at risk, but also peace must be pursued as the end of man even as we are swept up in the frenetic pace of modern life. This deeper peace must be related to the "peace" issues in the narrower sense; and finally,

7. we shall swing full circle back to the foundations, reflecting on a challenge arising from the weakening of societal cohesion and the encounter of cultures: the drastic challenge of pluralism with the tendency to relativize truth.[20] This is intimately related to both the practical and the theoretical atheism we shall consider first.

The present chapter's provision of background necessary for understanding what the issues are will help us see where to direct additional reflection in order to discern what needs to be done if the Christian community is to respond to the realities of the planetary epoch. Then, in the final chapters, I shall address these questions in the context of my own appropriation of the Catholic tradition, with emphasis on the contrast of two anthropologies at work in our epoch: this time not the Protestant-Christian and the Catholic-Christian but, at a still more basic level, an atheist versus a Christian anthropology as I am beginning to see it. Out of this will come suggestions for future reflection by the entire Christian community.

THE ATHEIST CHALLENGE

The Anti-Religious Nature of the Subjectivist Turn

In his work of 1,150 pages, *God in Exile: Modern Atheism,* Cornelio Fabro, S.J., distinguishes the kinds of atheism and the issues raised by its modern forms, as he reconstructs the history of the phenomenon since the seventeenth century.[21] The subtitle of the book reveals where he finds its roots: in the subjectivist turn taken principally by Descartes. Fabro is, of course, examining philosophical atheism, not the broader, and, perhaps more significant, development of "silent atheism," the spread among European populations of indifference to Christian institutions and worship, and the diminution of prayer.

It would be hopeless to paraphrase here what Fabro has done so well—and pointless. For a full background to the question, I recommend his work. I shall, rather, concentrate on the main effects of the long drift toward atheism. It is impossible to disentangle the moral from the intellectual factors in a process that led to misunderstanding of what is meant by "God."[22]

20. This question is at the root of *BT, TA,* and this book.

21. Fabro, *God in Exile,* trans. and ed. Arthur Gibson (Westminster, Md.: Newman Press, 1968).

22. That misunderstanding causes many, become through formal education more sophisticated, to dispense with what they then see to be either rather puerile or at least

The "subjectivist turn" engineered by Descartes and his followers was not intended to undermine knowledge of God. Quite the contrary, they wanted, in the midst of the skepticism and cynicism brought on by the bloody religious wars, to found more solidly the whole structure of thought, including knowledge of God. Nor has this exploration of subjectivity been without its positive fruits. In *Being and Truth* and in *HTX: Learning to Survive in Virtual Reality*, I have attempted to show the origins in the subjectivist turn of the discovery of historicity—the sense of Being's[23] coming to be in the revelations and dissimulations it achieves through human interpretation. I have done this to show that historicity is an essential breakthrough, and to integrate it into a philosophy of being that respects as well the reality in themselves of things (their *esse*, in the Thomistic sense) and the demands of all objectivity that modern philosophy has failed to recuperate adequately.[24]

In previous chapters I have offered some hints of how the old order, founded in a belief in objective truth, gradually broke down, finally reaching the point of the great civil wars (the Religious or the Thirty Years' War) in the seventeenth century. The sight of a divided, warring Christendom and the rising voluntarism of an individualistic new class brought on the de-Christianization of whole countrysides. There followed the inward turn in search of a new foundation for thought in the subject. We must now see what this subjectivist turn contributed, in the long run, to the loss of the sense of God and of that most perfect "form" of His self-revelation, Jesus Christ.

Christian experience is emphatically not exclusively subjective. To see this requires an effort to understand what Christians have learned, as a result of Revelation, about *experience*. It is this that Descartes' revolution distorted.

The Catholic Christian claims that God is present in the world to the whole man, as much to external experience—objectively—in His creation of nature, in His rapport with the Prophets and the prophetic people, Israel, and in the historical fact of Jesus Christ, continued in the institutional reality of the Church, as in the depths of consciousness.[25] And even there, He is not most profoundly present to the philosopher reflecting on his own cognitive

---

uninspiring notions. But some who do have a grasp of more sophisticated notions of God also disbelieve because of their adherence, at a profound level, to the new anthropology. We shall have to see what has fed its development.

23. In Heidegger's sense of *Sein*. See *BT*, chap. 9.

24. No more than I can sum up Fabro here, I cannot provide a pithy condensation of that effort, however much it would be of use. I must refer the reader to those two volumes, and restrain myself here to a few remarks about pluralism and the skepticism that is "historical relativism."

25. Balthasar's treatment of this in *Herrlichkeit: Eine Theologische Ästhetik*, vol. 1 (Einsiedeln: Johannes, 1961–1965), and in the seven volumes of *Theodramatik* (Einsiedeln: Johannes, 1973–1983) is among the best. The classic text is Jean Mouroux, *L'Expérience chrétienne* (Paris: Aubier, 1954). For a recent survey of some different approaches to experience, see Donald L. Gelpi, S.J., *The Turn to Experience in Contemporary Theology* (New York: Paulist Press, 1994).

and volitional activities but to the man of prayer who gives himself over to the divine call and the gift of the divine presencing, something to which a Descartes seems rather oblivious. (That is why Blaise Pascal, Descartes' contemporary, was so critical of him for his failure to distinguish aspects of the interior life. Descartes proceeded with what Pascal calls l'esprit de géometrie, ignoring l'esprit de finesse. Pascal would remind Descartes, "Le coeur a ses raisons que l'esprit ne connaît point" ["The heart has its reasons which the mind does not know at all"].)[26]

Once one understands that experience is not just my reaching out to grasp and control a "given" but more profoundly should be a free response to a call from an Other who is not basically for control but to be appreciated, the Other retaining its integrity, then the activistic, controlling demand of the Cartesian search for total possession appears as the dangerous idol it is.[27] True experience as re-sponse is an encounter of freedoms, it is re-sponse to a call that proposes a challenge to the one being called. Once this is understood, one sees that the controlling impulse of Cartesianism is perfectly antireligious.

The Protestant revolt against philosophy is partly to blame for all this subjectivism's having opened the floodgates to fallen man's basic temptation to control. Luther's mistrust of "sinful" reason drove him to posit a "positive revelation," God's inexplicable revealing of mysteries reason cannot relate to. Obedience becomes submission to the brute fact of justification, rather than obedience as audire, listening in order to understand (fides querens intellectum). Catholics, since the fathers of the Church, have always espoused "philosophy," and claimed Christianity to be the true pursuit of wisdom, based in a proper use of reason. Like Luther, the fathers understood this "proper use of reason" to include an openness to the light of grace and revelation, the dependence upon which Luther insisted. They believed, however, that such grace was operative in the thought of the great pagan philosophers when their philosophical reflections produced beautiful truths, including a valid objectivistic theory of knowledge.[28]

Descartes, the philosopher turned inward, did not rediscover Augustinianism. For, helped by the Protestant revolt against reason, the Cartesians truncated and thus falsified what Augustine found in the depths of the soul. They substituted a narrow, rationalistic notion of the spirit for the true life of the soul, a mutilated experience that does not correspond with the totality of what is available to the spirit opened to God's grace.[29]

26. In BT, I explore the dimensions of "the interior life" (see chap. 7, especially paras. J, K, L, and M).

27. See Balthasar, "Christian Experience?" in New Elucidations, trans. Mary Theresilde Skerry (San Francisco: Ignatius Press, 1986), 20–45.

28. For an excellent summary of the history of Catholic thinking on "Christian philosophy," and the Protestant ruining of it, see Balthasar, Explorations in Theology II: Spouse of the Word (San Francisco: Ignatius Press, 1991), 333–63.

29. Not all Cartesians are equally guilty: those in the Cartesian tradition like Malebranche and Leibnitz sought to recuperate a richer life of the soul than, at the extreme,

As we look over that history from Descartes to Kant, Hegel, Marx, and Nietzsche, it becomes clear that what the philosophers were seeking, in looking for an absolute ground to save "reason" from the wreck of the Protestant attack, was something very different from the uncertainties of a love affair with a personal God. This God in creating us allows us the possibility of some control, indeed a limited control of our environment is necessary for survival although never complete—we do end by dying, after all—but this loving God is interested in something much deeper than our material prosperity in a given environment: He draws us out of ourselves, asking the surrender of our narrowing egoism, so that we may be opened to the ever transcending divine freedom, the ever new, ever surprising origin of all environments, and the way to our transcending even the all-englobing environment of the physical universe, a Way that is Life and Truth itself. Eric Voegelin would say, employing Augustine's term, that *libido dominandi* is the driving force of those modern philosophical Gnostics seeking the impossible possession of absolute certainty, because they seek the impossible security that comes from complete control of their surroundings. No wonder this *épopée* ends, with Feuerbach, Schopenhauer, Nietzsche, and Marx, in the exaltation of will, with *"Wille zum Willen,"* "will for the sake of will," as Heidegger labels the denouement of this "end of metaphysics." The Christian nightmare seems to be lived out: human will consumes itself by making itself, in the manner of Narcissus, its own object, having failed, as Christ would have it, to allow itself to be consumed by love for the great Other.

Another *pensée* of Pascal comes to mind, the one I mentioned in connection with Balthasar's condemnation of curiosity as the original sin, which I used to introduce *Being and Truth: La vérité sans la charité est une idole* ("Truth without love is an idol"). The hubris that consists in desiring to discover the foundation of all meaning within one's own psyche has led readily to the construction of great "gnostic dream fantasies," as Voegelin terms the political ideologies of our time. At minimum 60 million human beings have been sacrificed to the vain dream of establishing by human will the Kingdom of God on earth. The Thousand Year Reich and the Soviet Empire both lie in ruins. *The narcissistic voluntarism that produced them is still coursing through modern cultures.*

The Wealth Machine Brings Hedonism and Individualism

Just as important for explaining modern atheism as the unfolding of the inner logic of subjectivism are the dynamics set in motion by the rapid construction of the great wealth machine, through the effect of the

---

the "empiricists" like John Locke and David Hume who, for all their empiricism, were inspired by Descartes' subjectivist turn. Much detailed analysis of these developments is required to show this, as Étienne Gilson and I have done in *Modern Philosophy* (New York: Random House, 1963). See chaps. 6, 7, 9, 10, 11, 12, 13, 15, and 16.

spread of the money society and industrialization. The sense of the power to control led to spectacular innovation, some of which—the invention of machines and the discovery of ways to organize production—helped produce gradual understanding of the fructifying power of capital. At the same time this had a destructive effect on the social structures that supported the old religion. The old structures exuded a sense of dependence on nature and on nature's God. Unfortunately, they also bred resentment among the disfavored classes toward the supposedly natural superiority of their feudal masters who were scarcely divine in their abuse of their monopoly of wealth. The rise of the bourgeoisie and the development of the attitudes and institutions supporting science and industrialization began to challenge everything about the old order. As we have seen, this began as early as the twelfth century. By the seventeenth the pent-up resentment was directed also at the old religion, especially because of the Church's continuing compromises with the feudal order, weakening social underpinnings of belief in God. Many rejected "God" when what they were trying to get free of were oppressive human structures protecting, as the Marxists were to say, "vested interests" on the part of people not above using "God" to their own ends of control. In all religious traditions the divine and the practices bringing God objectively into people's lives are interwoven with the ambiguous realities of everyday ambition. The scientistic attitudes, rooted in Gnostic hubris, bred in the universities and among the intelligentsia, served as a weapon against very real social structures. Some atheist thinkers, such as Feuerbach, Marx, and Nietzsche, have considered it their fundamental *moral* imperative to do away with all vestiges of a mentality of dependence on God so that mankind can at last face nobly its personal responsibilities: "Save yourselves! Give yourselves grace," Nietzsche shouts in *Morgenröte* ("Dawn").

For this to be possible, new ways of thinking and a whole new anthropology were being evolved. Fabro describes both the new ways of thinking that issued from monism and those with an immanentist basis, Marxism and Hegelianism being the most influential examples of each. We shall consider the form Marxism has given to the first, and the anthropology it has bred, when we look at the phenomenon of "liberation."[30] But in many ways scientism—the effort to substitute philosophies like "logical positivism" inspired by the rise of science—is likely to be the most enduring result of the atheist development so far as it is rooted in philosophy. I suggest we

---

30. The "monism," exemplified by Marx's materialism, seeks to reduce everything logically to one principle—matter—the complexification of which is to explain everything. The idealist Hegel, on the other hand, seeks to retain a hierarchy of principles but to demonstrate rationally their necessary unity as they are all seen to be effects of *Geist* (spirit, mind—no English word can translate Hegel's rich notion), exteriorizing itself in creation and returning to fullest self-understanding through a history that leads to the triumph of reason and bourgeois good sense. On Hegel and Marx, see Étienne Gilson, Thomas Langan, and Armand Maurer, *Recent Philosophy* (New York: Random House, 1965), chap. 1.

start there, reflecting for a moment on the rise of a scientistic attitude,[31] and seeking to get at least a first glimpse of its significance for the faith traditions.

TECHNO-SCIENCE, THE RAPID GROWTH OF SECULARIZATION, AND PRACTICAL ATHEISM

Neither in its origins nor in its intrinsic method is modern science the least "atheistic." The pioneers of modern science, from the Augustinian-inspired Franciscan physicists of the thirteenth century to the pious Jesuit and Protestant scientists of the seventeenth century, were committed followers of Jesus. The hubris of a Galileo Galilei, who, incidentally, considered himself a faithful son of the Church, was rather the exception. Sir Isaac Newton considered his work in physics ancillary to his theological speculation. And despite the growth of atheism among many nineteenth-century scientists of the likes of Darwin and Freud, we find even today twelve Nobel Prize winners signing a manifesto in 1983 declaring they could see no incompatibility between science and knowledge of God.[32]

The sad story of Galileo's collision with the Church is often used as evidence of Catholicism's "inherent" suspicion of science. This is utterly unfair. Galileo's work was supported by leading churchmen—prominent among them the brilliant Jesuit Robert Cardinal Bellarmine. The problem arose toward the end of the famous scientist's life when he began pontificating about reinterpreting the Bible in the light of his discoveries. As in the Reformation, a clash of egos occurred, both sides behaving intemperately. But this did not carry over into either an official or an unofficial antiscience attitude on the part of the Church.[33] Long after Galileo had languished those last two years of his life in house arrest in his villa, the Jesuits were founding, from Italy to the Philippines, their colleges, renowned as centers of scientific formation. (Descartes himself was a celebrated graduate of the Jesuit college of La Flèche.)

The objectivism assumed by the methods of modern science[34] logically ought to fight against that immanentism—the search in the depths of consciousness for the foundations of reality—that Fabro has shown to be an implicit enemy of theism. Why then did the development of modern science and its complex bedfellow, technology, contribute, as it appears, to

31. Not to be confused with a *scientific* attitude, to which it is very much opposed.

32. "We are of the view that scientists must possess a sharpened moral sensibility, and we wish to put an end to the traditional differences between belief and science. It is obvious that the Church can play a positive role in the pursuit of such a goal, and we particularly acknowledge that the Catholic Church finds itself in the unique position to give the world order an orientation" (quoted in *Fidélité*, no. 5 [May 19, 1983]).

33. In Descartes' case, it was his radical philosophy, not his science, that caused his troubles with the French state.

34. Most recently the philosophical debates about the status of quantum mechanics raises anew epistemological issues that may permit idealism to reenter the picture, but it is not a voluntaristic idealism. On this see Sven Ortoli and Jean-Pierre Pharabod, *Le cantique des quantiques* (Paris: Éditions la Decouverte, 1984).

the spread of "secularization" and with it (but not as a necessary result) atheism, both in turn encouraging the nourishing of the reductionist attitude in philosophy we are calling "scientism"?[35] Several factors can be identified, as follows.

First, physical science concentrates methodically on deliberately delineated and partially isolated material subsystems.[36] Such intense analytical focus on matters subject to repeated experiment and careful measure has been successful in revealing structures far below the surface and beyond the horizons of casual daily observation. The discovery at a profound level of widely repeated structures and "elements" can give the impression that the ultimate reality itself is, somehow, made up of a few isolable building blocks, from the mere combination of which all else is derived. Such a supposition is a philosophical hypothesis, not a scientifically established or establishable principle. If that were how being itself is composed, then by isolation and analysis of the elements all could be explained (and once explained, controlled)[37] with no possibility that higher form, introducing complex order, involves a reality different in nature from elementary particles and their most fundamental relations.[38]

Second, science, through its discoveries, provided materials for certain new philosophical models, such as mechanistic models of the universe (a revised post-Newtonian version of an old Greek model) and the evolutionary hypotheses, by which the totality of intercosmic being could be conceived of materialistically, while integrating into the model a more sophisticated sense of time-as-becoming than classical philosophy possessed. The variety of ontologies underlying the materialistic philosophies of Auguste Comte, Karl Marx, and Herbert Spencer and the pragmatism of C. S. Pierce, William

35. Of which the "positivism" and the "dialectical materialism" and the "natural selection by survival of the fittest evolutionism" of the nineteenth century are just so many subspecies. "Reductionism" is the effort to explain the world too simply by "reducing" all its complexities to too few principles.

36. The sweeping and fundamental theories of particle physics are something else, posing new and exciting philosophical challenges. For now, let us focus on "classical science," as it affected the whole civilization. See note 39 below.

37. For an enthusiastic support of such reductionism, read "Two Cheers for Reductionism," in *Dreams of a Final Theory*, by Steven Weinberg (New York: Pantheon Books, 1992). Weinberg is a Nobel Prize–winning particle physicist.

38. It is overlooked that the intelligent human controller, once he supposedly knows exactly all the elements, must transcend them in order to decide what he wants to make out of them, and that evolved human intelligence was not available to do the order at every critical step up to a higher plateau of complexity along the vast corridor of evolution! Such a Gnostic reductionism has remained popular even after it has been subject to thoroughgoing critique and discredited among many philosophers and scientists, including some greats, such as Einstein and Niels Bohr and David Bohm, and probably some of the Nobel Prize laureates who signed the 1983 manifesto.

Weinberg, too, shows, from the contemporary physicist's experience, how puerile positivism is, even for those who, like him, adopt a reductionist approach (cf. ibid., 174–84). Theories are often developed by intuitive leap, and while they demand at least indirect experimental verification, they are embraced often for their beauty, the verification often taking a long time to become very solid.

James, and John Dewey furnish examples of how such conceptual possibilities were exploited.[39]

Third, science and technology can develop to some small degree independently of one another, but advances in each help the other. Most important, neither science nor technology unfolds lucidly in a Platonic heaven: they are the work of human beings, pressured by actual social and spiritual circumstances, including the institutional arrangements in which they are caught up, and by what their peers are going to think of them.

One area in which technological advance, breeding new methods of organization and management, produced radical changes in the human situation was industrialization. Whole peoples have been uprooted from traditional agrarian forms of life, a rhythmic existence with nature, and plunged into the voluntaristic setting of the city, or have been molded to the demands of industrialized agriculture. Industrialization has supported a population explosion that reversed the demographic rapport between youth and old age.[40] It has accelerated also a concatenation of growth in the economy and in other processes, the pace of change disorienting many people. The symptoms: rising rates of chemical addiction, divorce, juvenile criminality, and mental breakdown. But the resulting wealth has also lengthened life expectancy, spread education, and helped free many people from old servitudes.

One change all by itself diminished Church influence over the lives of people: the move from the country or village parish, where the pastor knew everybody and could mobilize often stifling social pressure for conformity, to the massive, anonymous city parish, where clergy who know 20 percent of parishioners are exceptional. High-tech media of mass communications, financially supported by a consumer society whose values they inevitably represent, are the new preachers. The most spectacular symbol confronting the villager formerly was the sermon based on the ideal of the Gospel of

39. For a sketch of these thinkers' positions, see Gilson, Langan, and Maurer, *Recent Philosophy*. Paradoxically, the most recent developments of physics, since the Einsteinian breakthrough on relativity and the work of Planck and Heisenberg on indeterminacy, favor the advance of antimechanical, open models like that of David Bohm's "implicate order," more compatible with belief in ongoing "input" into the experienced cosmos. Such models do not demand assent to a "transcendent Source," but, unlike positivist models, they are not closed to it.

Popular philosophy, and some of what is taught in university philosophy courses (and lower-level science courses, when they lapse into poor philosophizing) remains, for the most part, a century behind these events, stuck largely in the aftermath of eighteenth-century mechanism and Darwinian evolutionism, still motivated by the same kind of resentments and social distortions and *libido dominandi* that have fed all along the atmosphere favorable to "popular atheism." See the devastating attack on positivism in Voegelin, *The New Science of Politics* (Chicago: University of Chicago Press, 1952), chaps. 1–3.

40. There are now no more children in many countries than there are people to help acculturate them (an important factor in the "youth revolution" that exploded in 1968).

Jesus; now there is no clear ideal in the midst of the overwhelming on-slaught of printed and broadcast symbols (the call to hedonism is unworthy of being considered an "ideal"). In the process, on this level the religious character of daily life has been destroyed. Neither science nor technology can be blamed for this, but a certain use of the possibilities they have opened up and a partial failure of innovativeness by Christians have produced the obvious result. The unidealistic gospel of hedonism, preached twenty-four hours a day by some of the most highly paid talents in the society, is bound to have an impact.

Another spectacular change brought on by the tandem growth of science, technology, industrialization has been the evolution and expansion of the academy, affecting the mind-set of those who "do" science, and who pass on the tradition by educating and acculturating the young to the religion of scientism. Why the academy grew, from the Enlightenment on, into a privileged breeding ground of atheism is yet another subject worthy of a book.[41]

Fourth, improved technology has made creation of a world system possible, the "HTX." The resulting intimate encounter of cultures has encouraged the rise of new anthropologies. Developmental anthropology, sociology, economics, political science, and depth psychology have all con-tributed to sweeping new notions about human being. These endeavors all grew to maturity in the academy. The new anthropologies, largely products of the nineteenth century, have tended to be for the most part materialist in their assumptions. (The exceptions are the development of personalism [E. Mounier and followers] and the distinction of the *Geis-teswissenschaften* from the *Naturwissenschaften*—the sciences of mind/spirit from the natural sciences—by Wilhelm Dilthey and followers, prominently including Edmund Husserl, the father of phenomenology.)[42] The materialist

41. A central theme of such a book should be the hubris of the brightest, with a reflection on how the religious orders of the twelfth and thirteenth centuries were able to attract so many of the best minds to a humble life of prayer. One chapter of such a book should be a sociological analysis of an intellectual class with more than its fair share of *Ressentimentsmenschen*, or men of resentment, as Max Scheler called negative people. Humility is a virtue often in short supply around the academy, and, without that virtue, religion cannot flourish—not even in the Church. While somewhat extreme, Paul Johnson's recent book, *Intellectuals* (London: Weidenfeld and Nicholson, 1988), detailing the failed lives of some of the great names in modern intellectual life, points out some of the character problems leading to atheism. My hunch is that such a study would demonstrate that many of the most creative figures in science and industry showed a selfless devotion to the objects of their science, and would stand out among the drab pettiness of the academy the way already an Aquinas and a Bonaventure overwhelm with brightness the world of the four hundred or so logic professors at the Sorbonne.

42. Thinkers faithful to the traditional Christian conviction that we are both body and soul, matter and spirit, have been understandably defensive in the face of the materialist anthropologies, to the point of largely ignoring the valuable understanding that has been contributed by these new perspectives. Much Christian anthropology to this day gives little place, for instance, to evolutionary aspects of the human being, to the pathological, to social-class reality, and often even historical creativeness.

contributions—the very old and those from the new materialism—are so pervasive, they seep into everyone's mentality, whether they are aware of them or not.[43]

When one looks back over the various reinforcing dimensions of this development of scientific, technological, industrial, urban, mass-planetary society, especially with an eye to the factors within it that are favorable to producing popular practical atheism, the task confronting apostolic Christians appears in its just proportions: *overwhelming*. Here is an unprecedented social phenomenon, developed over three hundred years, but with roots reaching back millennia: that "HTX" that possesses several new ways of thinking, prominently positivist, experimental, analytic thought, and materialist, determinist, dialectic à la Marx, but also, more encouragingly for Christians, phenomenology in many schools; new models of being, drawn from scientific discoveries, with emphasis on cosmogenesis; a totally new form of social existence—industrialized, urbanized living, bringing with it unparalleled anonymity and voluntarism; new means of celebrating itself through the overwhelming symbolization endeavor of the mass media, with the global result of developing an interweaving system of institutions and mind-sets we call "the world system."[44]

This is why the "strategic question for Catholics" posed at the start of this chapter is so important, providing a context for the Catholic's understanding of mission: Can such a weave of planetary-scale systems be Christianized, as the present Holy Father believes it must? Or, as many others think, is Christianity, in the face of such a massive development,

43. In recent years, more Christians have begun to study the new anthropologies seriously. They can often be carried away uncritically in their enthusiasm for what they discover. A distressing number are influenced by the underlying materialism, in the forms of Marxist or Freudian determinism or sociologism. They seem oblivious to the serious contradictions separating such thought systems from the main tradition of Christian understanding of man, and from the elements of freedom and spirit that are presumed by the genuine gospel message. This collision of anthropologies— atheist, materialist, and determinist versus Christian, spirit/matter (freedom of love)— has yet to be faced adequately. Some individuals strongly influenced by materialist anthropologies teach in Catholic faculties and seminaries, alongside "conservative" colleagues who pass by the last two hundred years of development in the human sciences. The individualism of the modern academy ensures that they rarely exchange insights from their respective natural faiths. Better thinking out of a more adequate Christian anthropology, able to absorb new insights from the sciences without yielding any of the truth revealed about the origin, nature, and destiny of man would permit a more effective contrast, and hence a healthier dialogue.

44. For an analysis of the elements and dynamics of the world system, see *TA*, chap. 6. As for the HTX, this unprecedented phenomenon, while absorbing and transforming other civilizations into itself, is not itself a civilization, for it forms no "city," no dwelling place for man; nor is it a culture, but a spawner of many cultural forms. This was discussed in my paper for the Havel Seminar in Political Philosophy, "Ethnicity and Oecumenism: National Identity and the New World Order," Prague, September 1992.

confined to the nostalgias of the past, and the individual to taking refuge in tight little communities of believers?[45]

To deal with such an immense challenge requires a fresh, creative set of initiatives as radical and sweeping as the HTX reality confronting us. Where is one to turn to hear a firm voice speaking from within the Church, addressing this challenge of modernity, especially its core in the great sweep of techno-science, at a level as fundamental and as informed as the reality demands?

As the Church entered this century, locked in a titanic (and largely defensive) struggle with "modernism," it needed someone of exceptional creative scope, solid in the faith but at the same time sympathetic to the new discoveries, especially the fundamental ones in the physical and biological sciences that were changing our ways of viewing our own nature. The Catholic intellectual world, despite the innovativeness and appreciation of the "new" shown by (a then little understood) John Henry Newman and a young Maurice Blondel ("the grand Newman" and "the grand Blondel," as Balthasar calls them), remained with a narrow, nondevelopmental model of humanity and of doctrine, cramping understanding of Christianity as Life. It was in this setting that a passionate young Jesuit, reflecting in the midst of the trenches of the Great War, said one must love the world, and find it beautiful, as condition for transcending (not *ignoring*) it, allowing the *en haut*—its transcendent Creator—to lift one above it so as to renounce it (as we must in death), to move into his being.

As Henri Cardinal de Lubac said, now that much of what Teilhard de Chardin was the first to grasp so clearly has become common knowledge, many fail to appreciate how great was his contribution in achieving the breakthrough to a more dynamic kind of thinking. At the same time, appreciation of what he still has to teach us is retarded by false notions of what he believed, despite four books by his close friend, de Lubac; a two-volume study by his Jesuit superior, René d'Ouince; and numerous

---

45. Are we to "sanctify the workplace," as the Blessed José-Marie Escriva, the founder of Opus Dei, preached (and that means a "workplace" with worldwide institutions), or shall we more and more live among ourselves, battening down the hatches, living a private family life and pursuing our own personal spiritual development until this planet-embracing phenomenon destroys itself, as have all earlier social formations? The fact that such a collapse could bring nuclear Armageddon, or some other form of cataclysm of world dimensions this time, should be borne in mind were we rather optimistically to assume it will leave in its wake a more fertile field for evangelization. (Did the catastrophe of the two world wars improve the planet for evangelization?)

I shall leave to the last chapters the task of finding the perspective that will allow the best defense of the hopeful position of the magisterium, which I struggle every day to share. Because of the particular form of my own Christian faith, I seek, like the present pope and the fathers of the Second Vatican Council, engagement of the world rather than retreat to the quasi-monastic closed community. (I am not referring to genuine monasteries, nourished by evangelical world-converting prayer, but to the kind of pursuit of "the interior life" that risks being too self-serving, the spirit one might fear in "spiritual survival communities.")

other solid expositions.[46] I now introduce into this discussion of modernity the most creative effort yet by any Christian to think through implications of the discoveries of modern science in the light of his own Christian faith. This work encourages hope that a Christian appropriation of the modern world, in what modernity offers that is true, is fruitful. (Every new truth is to be treated with reverence, he reminds the Christian.) He, too, believed Armageddon is all too possible, but in Christian hope foresaw another possibility, provided human beings respond to grace, in cooperation with what he believes God has revealed of His plan of love for mankind and through mankind, for His beautiful cosmos.

DISCOVERING CHRIST AND THE NEW WAYS OF SCIENCE: THE EXPLORATION OF PIERRE TEILHARD DE CHARDIN, A GRAND RESPONSE WITH ITS OWN PROBLEMS

The Modern Discovery of Time and of Man's Co-responsibility for Creation

It took me thirty years, from the first reading by the young Gilsonian Thomist who was to become your author of the then newly published and much ballyhooed work of Pierre Teilhard de Chardin, to begin to appreciate the significance of his accomplishment. What he undertook was so pioneering, enormous, and hazardous, it is no wonder many Catholic intellectuals still fail to understand what he was doing. (The fact that New Age has expropriated deformed versions of his vision has not helped.) There is little choice if Christianity is going to appropriate the sciences but to pass where Père Teilhard has pioneered. The dangers of the path as he has hewn it are many. And some of the discoveries of science he banks on turn out to be less sure than they seemed. Translating insights coming from "universes of discourse" very different from traditional Catholic theology is always perilous. As great and audacious a thinker as Balthasar, while softening his stand over time, remained to the end suspicious that Teilhard had, for instance, too much naturalized the process of redemption in an effort to synthesize it with his understanding of evolution. (We shall see Cardinal de Lubac's defense of Teilhard against this grave charge.) But, as there is to date no other Catholic thinker who has faced the central challenges of the scientific and technological revolutions so resolutely,[47] with a will to recuperate the full sense of the Catholic tradition, I believe

46. See de Lubac references below; René d'Ouince, *Un prophète en procès: Teilhard de Chardin dans l'Église and dans son temps,* 2 vols. (Paris: Aubier-Montaigne, 1970).

47. There are other Catholic thinkers of note who either, as in the case of the philosopher Maurice Blondel, respected by Teilhard, saw the need quite early—by the turn of the century—to absorb the reality of cosmo-genesis into the Christian synthesis, or who, like the Benedictine physicist Stanley Jaki and the Jesuit theologian Bernard Lonergan, have explored the compatibility of genuine science and Christian faith. In concentrating on Teilhard, the most significant of the pioneers, I do not here mean to imply that anything short of the most serious hearing needs to be given the more recent thinkers, the Jakis and Lonergans who have continued the struggle to appropriate the truths of science.

all efforts to appropriate modernity should pass by way of a preliminary critical encounter with Teilhard's vision.[48]

Without a doubt Teilhard was catholic in intent, sweeping out from his mystical reflection illumined by the light of faith to envelop the whole of cosmic space, the whole of that *Monde* on which he once said his Mass,[49] and the whole of time, from the beginnings of "cosmo-genesis" to eschatological fulfillment in the ingathering of all in Christ. He also remained Catholic in intent to the end,[50] because of his resolve to pursue this vast evolution in thought in perfect union with the teachings of the Church. That is why he humbly submitted to its authority and discipline, especially trying in his case, as the human agents of the Church restricted his ability to engage in the free give-and-take required by the scientific field. This will to be catholic and Catholic meant not only that he had to recuperate all essential truth transmitted by the traditions, both of Revelation and of science, but also that he was determined to remain, however trying, in perfect union with, as dissidents like to put it today, the "hierarchical, institutional Church." (As Cardinal de Lubac never tired of saying, "for Teilhard there was no other church than the 'institutional church.'" His obedience to it was at the cost of great personal suffering, as he was forbidden for a good part of his life to publish his "dangerous" works.) Teilhard believed the Church to be divine and human in its "Christic" unity, papal and episcopal in its authority; it is God's chosen way to salvation, even when its local human agents for the moment lack vision, as they seemed to in forbidding Teilhard to publish his works. "The Christian organism [meaning the church, the Body of Christ]," he wrote one day in the middle of his struggles with certain narrow theologians, "is more important to save than my personal and immediate success."[51]

48. If Catholic intellectuals had heeded de Lubac and D'Ouince by generally appropriating the Teilhardian accomplishments, understanding and defending what was right in his vision, his work might not have fallen victim to a distorting misuse by New Age.

49. See Teilhard, "La messe sur le monde," in *Hymne de l'univers* (Paris: Seuil, 1961), a truly magnificent eucharistic-cosmic poem.

50. Among the many texts cited by his intimate friend, de Lubac (who surely knew his mind on this), I shall cite only one: "to be Catholic is the only way to be Christian fully and to the hilt" (*jusqu'au bout*, which also means "to the end") (Teilhard, *Oeuvres* [Paris: Seuil, 1956–1971], 10:197, cited in de Lubac, *Teilhard posthume: Réflexions et souvenirs* [Paris: Fayard, 1977], 50).

51. Note of June 1925, regarding his forced departure from the Institut Catholique de Paris, quoted in de Lubac, *Teilhard posthume*, 36. Teilhard, like Bernanos, refused to think in terms of "injustice." Bernanos's was an attitude similar to the great critic-novelist who always insisted that his concern was with deepening his acceptance of God's will, not looking for reasons to burn with resentment against others. "I do not disdain others. Far from disdaining them, I would like to understand them better, because to understand is already to love. What separates human beings one from another, what makes them into enemies, probably has no profound basis in reality. The differences our experience and our judgments eagerly feed on are, in fact, insubstantial. They would vanish like dreams if we could manage to look on them with truly liberated eyes, because the worst of our

Much misunderstanding has arisen over the question of who precisely was Teilhard de Chardin—philosopher, scientist, or theologian?[52] The answer is: all three, but none, however, in an outstanding way. He was not a great philosopher. He did not push as far as he might the implications, ontological and epistemological, of his best insights. He was a capable theologian, despite his protest to the contrary (as de Lubac makes clear).[53] He was a serious, working, well-informed paleontologist, but by no means one of the greats of his period, and capable, along with most of his peers, of making serious misjudgments about early man. His propensity to soar, even in a work such as *The Phenomenon of Man*, which he intended to be "phenomenological and scientific," beyond what experimental data could adequately support, while perhaps justified in theological speculation, is not something the natural scientist and experimenter appreciate.

In what then lies the greatness of his vision? Cardinal de Lubac puts it well: "Neither metaphysician by vocation nor theologian by profession, Father Teilhard de Chardin was a mystic, a real one. He was one of those 'souls who see, with a naturally free view, the innumerable connections between conventions.' There was living in him the feeling that the many evolutions that seem to divide the world are, in the final analysis, the 'accomplishment of a single great mystery.' "[54] My summary here, building on de Lubac's interpretation, will emphasize the mystical vision.[55]

---

misfortunes is not being able to give another anything but such an impoverished image of ourselves" (*Lettre aux anglais* [Paris: Gallimard, 1946], 98, cited in Balthasar, *Bernanos: An Ecclesial Experience*, trans. Erasmo Leiva-Merikakis [San Francisco: Ignatius Press, 1996], 169). The fact that the others hampered Teilhard's efforts to give an adequate "image of himself" is not relevant to Bernanos's point, for they always hamper anyone from expressing himself as adequately as possible.

52. Because Teilhard's accomplishment is still so widely misunderstood, one risks not being taken seriously himself if one purports that Teilhard still has important things to teach us. I am putting forth a still more demanding thesis: I believe Catholic thinkers determined to live intellectually in the contemporary world still need to read Teilhard de Chardin in the spirit in which de Lubac did. For the model, see *La pensée religieuse du Père Teilhard de Chardin* (Paris: Aubier, 1962). This not only will help clear up widespread misunderstandings, nor will it not only defend Teilhard's orthodoxy in general, but it will also show what a personal appropriation the pioneer has to offer that remains essential to Christian wisdom. (De Lubac, who wrote in all four books about Teilhard, went on when he was old to write a more apologetic work, to correct the misinterpretations of Teilhard that had been promulgated in the twenty years since his death [*Teilhard posthume*].) This shows how important de Lubac, one of the most ample spirits of the twentieth century, considered Teilhard's accomplishment. Appropriating Teilhard, as with any other thinker, does not mean necessarily agreeing with him. De Lubac has three chapters of criticisms in *La pensée religieuse*, and Balthasar, who read Teilhard seriously, remained, as I mentioned, quite critical, especially of his eschatology (*Theodramatik*, 4:137–47).

53. De Lubac, *La pensée religieuse*, 115–16.

54. Ibid., 120. The quote from Teilhard is from *Le coeur de la matière* (Paris: Seuil, 1976).

55. *BT*, chap. 6, follows important aspects of Teilhard's evolutionary interpretation in some detail. Those interested are invited to consult that chapter. Suffice it to say here that Teilhard accepts as true the discovery, reinforced in the nineteenth century, that the

In approaching Teilhard's work, we should heed his own warning to a friend in 1929, "The somewhat risky or systematic points of my 'doctrine' are for me, in the final analysis, only secondary points; it is much less ideas than a spirit that I wanted to spread."[56] "Spirit," like the much abused "spirit of Vatican II," is to be taken for what it is—a sweeping hypothesis for interpretation. What Teilhard struggled to collate was, in his words, nothing less than the *en haut* of divine transcendence, well grasped and guarded by the tradition, that which "descends" toward us in its initiatives, with the *en avant*, the sense of the evolutionary—prolonging that thrust "from below"—culminating in social progress for which modernity now knows itself in some sense *responsible*.[57] It is a tremendous undertaking to face the central challenge of modernity: the challenge of time, understood as creative, with human liberty at the point, attempting to integrate the "hominization" that appears empirically for the first time in the becoming of humanity, with the transcendent truth about God and His creativity. Seeing this both from below and from *en avant*—from the Alpha and to the Omega—mediated to us through the Christ, who is both Logos from all eternity and incarnate in history in Jesus, makes possible a courageous beginning of a new modern scientific era of thought along the way of the temporal unfolding of salvation and our struggle to understand it. It is vital to remain modest about the claims of enterprises of such immodest dimensions.

---

universe is unfolding in time, a great cosmic process of progressive "complexification," "centering" (we see this, for instance, in the way a cell has a nucleus, and a higher animal a central nervous system, and at the top of the social hierarchy an apex that exercises control, and so on), "interiorization," accompanied by increasing command over an ever wider environment. Matter is in-formed by spirit in varying degrees, from the minimal disposition of atoms to bind with only certain other atoms, to the spiritualization of matter in man able to survive disintegration in death of its material support. Teilhard inquires profoundly into the sense of this development. His mature work, *The Phenomenon of Man* (trans. Bernard Wall [New York: Harper, 1959]) attracted wide attention in the scientific community for its ability to work through the evidence of biological evolution and to find there many signs of the sense of what is unfolding before, and in us. No one can deny that his "demonstration" there has many holes, as do the sweeping, synthesizing efforts of all students of the vast development of the cosmos. Those who wisely remain critics of all evolutionists' efforts to provide canvasses smudging over embarrassing gaps in data are right to characterize the Teilhardian synthesis as more a poem than a demonstration. But they could still profit from trying to see how the big, sound discoveries of the new sciences can be brought together with the lights of the Christian traditions to raise our sights and feed our understanding, provided we do not get carried away and begin ignoring the very tentative nature of the large pictures we then draw. Teilhard raises valid questions that demand our continued reflection.

56. Letter of January 2, 1929, cited in de Lubac, *La pensée religieuse*, 20. Just as invoking the "spirit of Vatican II" in a way that ignores aspects of the letter of the conciliar documents, so invoking the "spirit of cosmic becoming," most authorize no ignoring of any well-verified givens about the cosmos.

57. *En haut* means "on high," while *en avant* means "forward march!"

Creation, while founded in an eternal decision lying outside the process itself, is *as process,* hence finite not a single isolated moment of fiat but a complex becoming, not necessarily smooth or without discontinuities, not without its tentative aspects, many of them dead ends, a movement spread out in time-space, and still going on undiminished,[58] many essential aspects of which are just now beginning to become known to us, *as we learn to look.*[59]

The process has produced, as the highest complexity yet reached, the brain of man, a complexification accompanied, at each higher level of organization, by increasing self-reference. It reaches in us that degree of reflection that permits objectification of the world and hence self-direction over against it.[60]

The extremes of subjectivism can be avoided if one never forgets, as Teilhard keeps insisting, that at each level the individual remains part of the world, dependent on it (the idealists methodically underestimate this!), and reaches out (with various degrees of reach, depending on the species' complexity and interiority) to embrace it. If we are not only the highest result of the process but also *an intended result,*[61] we can then see the reason for the trials and errors as the process feels its way along, pushed from below toward ever greater complexity and "centrification," and attracted from above, as the various constituent elements reach out for completion in a transcending other.[62]

When the level of reflection is attained, the reaching out of every "monad" changes radically. Here the greatest *discontinuity* of all within evolution shows itself. For it becomes the work of consciousness and

58. The huge number of atoms, molecules, cells, stars, living beings, and so on, is needed, Teilhard explains, to let "the law of great number" and chance operate, either by developing regular determinisms (physio-chemical laws) through statistic uniformization, or, on the contrary, by creating improbable combinations through long, repeated trials ("La centrologie," in Teilhard, *Oeuvres,* 7:130).

59. *"Voir et faire voir,"* "see and make to see": that is the goal Teilhard declared for *The Phenomenon of Man.* It is very hard for man to empty himself of ego enough to see anything!

60. Here Teilhard absorbs into his scientific vision a basic thrust of modern thought since the subjectivist turn taken by Descartes. But, as we shall see, he does not fall victim to that *subjectivism* we have seen to be a major contributor to modern atheism.

61. Here he anticipated a half century earlier the "cosmic anthropic principle" that today is all the rage.

62. "Working on the unorganized Great Numbers, the personalizing action of the Omega can only act, especially in the beginnings, by lying in wait [*guettant*] and grabbing the favorable instances as they happen by, sporadically engendered by chance" ("La centrologie," in Teilhard, *Oeuvres,* 7:231). I have doubts whether this suggestion suffices to overcome the kind of objection latent in Fred Hoyle's calculation that the odds the 120 proteins required for the DNA could have evolved randomly within the rather narrow "window" we now believe they had to achieve this—probably less than 200 million years—are 1 in $10^{40,000}$. For details, see *BT,* chap. 7. Not since Darwin developed the theory of evolution by natural selection through survival of the fittest have the mysteries of the mechanisms of evolution seemed so elusive. I imagine that Teilhard if he were active today would back off some of the assumptions that were widely accepted in his time.

socialization—the cooperation of individual centers in a free social endeavor—rather than, as at the molecular level, the mere absorption into the monad's structure, according to its own principle of organization ("form" or "soul"), of vast numbers of atoms.

Socialization is a process of creating "organisms" from many independently directed "molecules," the individual monadic persons. These then become hierarchically ordered into ever larger conscious structures, becoming in the process less individualistic, but, if brute "collectivism" is avoided, not only not losing their personhood but also enhancing it through union with the personal other, in "hyper-personalization"—*communio*.[63] (The extreme individualism that accompanies subjectivism and voluntarism is thus avoided; instead, the love of persons is mutually enriching.)

A key to the entire Teilhardian vision lies in this principle: Throughout the process, a struggle between the "egoistic" forces of disaggregation and destruction, and the "loving" forces of unity, order and construction, goes on. At each higher level, intensified in power and concentration, the struggle continues, becoming at the level of consciousness, because of the degree of "freedom" reached, a moral strife.

Despite his extensive reconstructions of the evolutionary past, for Teilhard the great question is less one of what has been, of how we got where we are, than of the future. He asks, with an intensity, a gravitas exceeded not even by Nietzsche struggling to image the *Übermensch*, where do we go from here, and how is man to be transcended?[64] If there were nothing above that process of evolution of which we are the summit, then horrible consequences would follow: we would be conscious of being trapped in a physical universe destined to fall victim to entropy, a world without hope.[65] Our projects would come ultimately and inevitably to absolutely naught.[66] Second, there would be nothing to direct our own strivings, which would end up devoted not to achieving *le plus être*, more being, but only *le bien*

63. To my knowledge not a term used by Teilhard, but this is what hyper-personalization means. De Lubac, Balthasar, and the present pope favor the ancient term *communio*.

64. The courage, illumined by Revelation and by science, to peer into the future with utmost seriousness (that is what "gravitas" means) was one of Teilhard's great graces, exceeded by no one in our time, as far as I can see. Like Heidegger, he grasped the fundamental ek-sistential truth, "The past is announced out of the future" (this is a typically Heideggerian pun in German, *"Das Gewesene kunftet zu uns aus der Zukunft"* from the late essay "Zeit und Sein").

65. According to the second law of thermodynamics all transformations expend energy, with the result being a long range of energy gradients declining until equilibrium is reached, at which point nothing more can happen. Evolutionary complexification goes against entropy. The great debate is whether this is a local phenomenon in a vast universe sliding toward zero-temperature gradients, or the result of some mysterious "input" from beyond, unexplained by the laws of thermodynamics. For more on this, see *BT*, chaps. 6, 7.

66. This realization led Nietzsche to invent his strange doctrine of "the eternal return of the like." On this see my commentary in Gilson, Langan, and Maurer, *Recent Philosophy*, 90–91.

être, a happiness that sinks inevitably into something like the triviality of consumerist lifestyles.[67]

Teilhard's Vision

The "way out" revealed by the incarnation of the Word in Christ lies in recognizing that the summit of evolution is the person, that the way beyond is a *voie de personalisation*. The motion forward is not to be sought in the lowest elements but in the attraction that has been exercised by a "supreme pole of personalization," which is how, within the tradition of Revelation, God has always been understood.

Without hope of rejoining through an interior life and love such a supreme personal principle, there would not be the hope necessary for us to continue our task. Without any hope, *"l'humanité ferait grève"* ("mankind would go on strike"). Only such a personalizing being can render lovable the whole process of evolution.

The arbitrary reductionism of empiricism and scientism, the notion that all understanding must be built up "materialistically" from below, from the elements, with nothing being added "from on high" to each level of greater syntheses,[68] assumes that the unifying, intentional reaching out and ingathering achieved by "form," "soul," "ego," is for nothing in the process. But as all our human experience shows, it is precisely the higher principle that makes possible the higher organization. Is it not the higher organizing principle constituted by the bird's brain that allows its gathering of and ordering of sticks to form a nest? A push from below responds to a pull from above, on the part of that which orders the elements in the more complex and powerful whole.

At each level of increasing complexity the corresponding principle of unity produces the higher, more complex entity, centering larger structures of molecules, capable, because of this superior centered concentration of capabilities, of more extensive and higher quality activity. At the same time *union differentiates:* not only is the higher unity distinctive, but the elements that make it up (cells, for instance) retain their identity as well. You cannot withdraw atoms from a simple molecule without deforming it, but cells can be extracted from a mammalian bloodstream without destroying it while the cells still retain their complex integrity. This remains true when one reaches the high level of the *"eu-centrique"*[69] (literally, centered on its own well-being) self-reflective entity, where distinctiveness is signaled by the term *personalization*.

Here the "creative differentiation," which has gone on at every level, becomes clear to us, as we can personally experience this high degree of

67. Teilhard, "La fin de l'espèce," in *Oeuvres*, 5:395.

68. For the complex way in which such "positivism" developed in the context of absolute idealism see *Recent Philosophy*, chaps. 1, 2, 9, 17. See also Eric Voegelin, *From Enlightenment to Revolution*, ed. John Hallowell (Durham: Duke University Press, 1975).

69. Teilhard, "La centrologie," in *Oeuvres*, 7:115.

reflective *"eu-centrism"* in ourselves with all the distinctiveness we know we possess. But we also experience with it the next level of union, as from personal center to personal center we reach out, either in clever manipulation of the other, or in self-offering love. That next step in the process is what Teilhard meant by "superpersonalization,"[70] where "two become one flesh." Each personal center, without losing its identity as an "ego," a self, is able to reach out in knowledge and love to the others; whether it is a question of a pair of lovers, a team, or, better yet, the mystic absorbed by divine contemplation, a similar psychological result occurs.

Not that the first trials *(ébauches)*, in the form of the emerging "noosphere," are yet filled with love.[71] For that matter, even the planetary-scale network of relationships of intelligence, of communications, industrialization, emerging world government,[72] showing this evolved creature actively "reaching out" on a scale unprecedented in all of evolution, while opening new vistas for love, is not woven only, not even primarily, of self-offering acts.[73]

Nonetheless, for all the vast scope of these planetary structures, the individual is not totally undifferentiated and lost. On the contrary, instead of tending to be confused with one another, the reflected centers intensify their ego precisely to the extent they press closer to one another *(se resserrent entre eux)*. They hyper-center themselves more and more, to the degree they grow nearer to one another in converging upon the Omega.[74]

This convergence shows the distinction of individual and personal to be critical. What makes a center individual is its distinction from the other

70. Ibid., 122–23.

71. Out of the layer of life surrounding the planet—the "biosphere"—has emerged this further superimposition, the "noosphere" (from *nous*, the Greek term for, roughly, "mind"), a growing network of information exchange and appreciative relationships between conscious centers.

72. In *BT*, chaps. 6 and 7, I have detailed this development, with emphasis on the essential role of information, the form of information itself becoming more sophisticated at every step of the process.

73. This planetary weaving of relationships is a fact that Teilhard saw with startling clarity, a fact the significance of which he was one of the first to grasp. Some kind of planetary "kingdom of this world" of unprecedented form is emerging, and it has become a massive reality of our human incarnation. Whether this relates to the unifying of all things in Christ, and if so, how, is another issue, one of extreme importance. All the calls of the Second Vatican Council and of the present pontiff for a "new evangelization" of the world, accompanied by detailed description of the new ekistic realities, suggests that the eschatological transformation is a transformation of human hearts that are caught up in these worldly relationships. I understand Balthasar's hesitations about Teilhard's eschatology, about which I shall show my own hesitations in a moment, but Teilhard is right to have raised the question forcefully of how the revelation of the eschatological kingdom relates to the dynamic drawing together of mankind in what is now taking the complex form of the HTX. For some rather early reflections of Balthasar on this theme see *The God Question and Modern Man* (Burns and Oates edition), 138.

74. By the Omega, Teilhard means the ultimate unity toward which the whole process of personalization is attracted. What this is and how he argues for its necessity we shall consider in a moment.

centers that are its neighbors. What makes it personal is its being itself, which includes its own particular relations with others, its interpersonal bonds,[75] which contribute to making each of us who we are. As we are pressed closer together, instinctively we seek to increase our ego through separatism, through deliberately increasing isolation—which, drawing a shell about our center, moves against evolution and only impoverishes us. The laws of union show us the true and legitimate "egoism" consists, on the contrary, in uniting ourselves to the others (providing this is from center to center, by love): for only then do we succeed in realizing ourselves fully, without losing anything (and, on the contrary, attaining the maximum of what is true) of that which makes us incommunicable. Individuality declines, and personality increases as the Omega point is approached, and finally all individuality is lost in the Omega, but the supreme centralization with distinct multiple centers—many persons—is achieved.[76]

As the personal increases in quantity (there are now 5.5 billion conscious centers on this planet) as well as quality, we could well worry that quantity may prevail, and "the closing circle of the noosphere"—affective relationships—will see us "sink into a blind collectivism," what Teilhard calls "the great Molloch." At this stage, without the explicit role of Christ being fully effective, we are still fragmentary persons, mere "*ébauches*" (trial efforts) of what persons are meant to be. Only the Whole is fully personal, but that is attained in the only form in which it really exists, in the Omega, "the Universal,"[77] which becomes manifest in history in Jesus

75. Teilhard wrote to a friend in 1917: "I believe my vocation has never seemed as stripped of all that is surplus nor clearer: personalize the world in God" (cited in de Lubac, *La pensée religieuse*, 204).

76. Teilhard, "La centrologie," in *Oeuvres*, 7:105–34. I have explored the phenomenological and ontological foundation of such claims about love and personalization in *BT*, chaps. 7 (para. G) and 8 (para. C). Compare Teilhard's sense of personalization with Balthasar's view of personhood centered in the *missio* granted by the Holy Spirit to each individual to play a unique role in the realization of the Mystical Body, so that it can be said that in only Christ do we find supreme personhood among men, with our particular "person-ness" (to coin a term) being a given participation in the person of Christ, a participation in his cosmic and redemptive *missio* (cf. *Theodramatik*, 2:2:136–259). The dying Bernanos had discovered that his will was Christ's will all along, willed from eternity, and that our struggle is to let Christ live fully in us, removing the obstacles we place in His way. "We want everything he wants, but we don't know that we want it. We don't know ourselves, sin makes us live at the surface of ourselves. We will again go back into ourselves only to die, and it is there he awaits us" (*Agenda* [notes from Bernanos's dying days, for January 26, 1948], cited in Balthasar, *Bernanos*, 184). It seems to me that one needs to supplement Teilhard's global vision with this precision from Balthasar about the indispensable particular *missio* granted each person in Christ, a precision with which, I believe, Teilhard would be in agreement, and one must relate the fact that our *missio* involves a role in this world, in our HTX epoch, but that this role is to be played so that in the end everything obscuring of Christ's will is stripped away, so that nothing but His will remains in the end.

77. Teilhard, "La centrologie," in *Oeuvres*, 7:124–25. Balthasar would put it: "Christ is catholic" (*In the Fullness of Faith* [San Francisco: Ignatius Press, 1988], 27). Alpha and Omega applied to Christ is not Teilhard's invention but is in Rev. 1:8, 21:6, 22:13.

Christic.[78] If mankind pulls together only on its own, faceless collectivization will block the way to authentic superpersonalization.

One needs all the Teilhardian optimism one can muster to read these passages about the tightening noosphere without shivering. It so happens I was reviewing them the day following a fourteen-hour "telethon" broadcast from Europe and America to forty countries, watched by more than 1 billion people, to raise money for relief of the hungry in Africa. In fact, $14 million was pledged. This event would seem to confirm Teilhard's observation of what is happening. Just look at the ambiguities. The artists participating, who donated their high-priced time with generosity and joy, were some of the greats of rock. They concertedly advanced a sense of the "family of man," but a family *without a Father*. A cult of ugliness, frenzy, and arbitrariness was, paradoxically, placed in the service of "human solidarity." The passion poured into the final song celebrating "us," titled "We are the World," showed a desperate need to fill the vacuum left by loss of God-consciousness through an adoration of us, the People, *das Volk* idolized by Hitler, but now not just this *Volk*, *das Deutsche*, but catholic humankind, a more dangerous because truer idol, apparently much riper now for collectivization than even in the Weimar time, because of the intensified display of mindless, personless individualism gathered into the Faceless Crowd, the super Ego, much more ready for collectivization than for superpersonalization through love. Yet, for all the dramatic inappropriateness of the form of expression, elements of superpersonalization nevertheless may have been present: the concern and hard work were obviously genuine, poured out by many (almost all of whom were from countries whose culture is still strongly influenced by at least a millennium of Christianity); the whole effort, after all, was a sign of compassion and love. We cannot judge any heart, not even the purity of our own motives. But signs that could be read by the eyes of hope were not absent that extraordinary day.

The paradox of the whole affair would have intrigued Teilhard: the huge anonymous mass weaving and screaming, the performers pushing the undignified, animal pulsation, not quite to the limit, but far beyond what the Victorians would have thought possible, rejoining the Brüghelian peasants of the seventeenth century and meeting them with an inner-city rawness, all devoted, paradoxically, to a work of compassion, brought forward without even the most distant reference to the reason we are not just members of a species, but "brothers and sisters," which is hardly the same thing.

78. Balthasar agrees on this central principle, drawing on the same source: the letters of Saint Paul. Only Christ, as the Logos, second person of the Blessed Trinity, is, among us as Jesus, fully, unrestrictedly infinitely Person, and our incomplete participations in personhood come from the creative principle acting through the Logos (*Theodramatik*, 2:2:186ff). Balthasar backs up this startling notion of personhood by a thorough analysis of the origin of the concept, showing that basically our modern sense of the person derives from the New Testament and the further developments of the Christological debates of the patristic centuries of the Church.

Teilhard never pretended that "personalization" is a simple affair. He knew that the cross of Christ stood at the center of the process. As we shall discover in our concluding chapters, the whole question of how modern people will live out their freedom, how the struggle of individualism/collectivism versus a mature personalization will go forward from here, is vast and pressing. (For the Christian, this is the question of how life led eucharistically in Christ through the Church can be communicated and made credible to the masses of people, as Christians allow the Holy Spirit to lead them to holy lives in the midst of the booming HTX, the Being of which demands that they learn to manage their time!) This central issue of personalization creates the most painful situations. The clash of old tribalistic nationalisms in Bosnia and Chechnya and Kurdistan is a strong reminder of how catastrophic the false solutions can be.

Teilhard saw the process of personalization as a dialectic.[79] But dialectic is, first of all, hard, perhaps impossible to measure: high-spiritual life forms elude measure.[80] Second, dialectic as Teilhard understands it, in no way ensures progress. Things remain subject, in their internal scaffolding and their interactions, to the laws of thermodynamics and of statistics. So long as they are not fully personal they remain "reversible": all living things certainly will die; and they remain *"caduc"*—incomplete—and in the final analysis, all subpersonal beings come to nothing (the second law of thermodynamics). With reflection and personalization, the human particles become capable not only of undergoing action distinctly but also of participating in the consistency, essentially personal, of Omega. So, for them (as for a body traversing the frontier between the magnetic fields of two planets) a reversal of equilibrium occurs. "To the extent it is personalized, the grain of consciousness becomes free of its phyletic material support. Detached from its matrix of complexity, which falls back towards the multiple, the reflected center can at last, definitively unified on itself, rejoin the ultimate pole of all convergence."[81]

There you have the Teilhardian formula for personal immortality. Does abuse of personal freedom—the refusal to reflect, to love oneself and one's neighbor—destroy immortality, as he has described it? The *eu-centric* fraction of the universe is being "Omegalized" grain by grain through death, as reflective centers find fulfillment, while waiting for the moment when the same phenomenon will occur globally and simultaneously, when the whole noosphere, at the critical point of organization and centralism

79. That is, a back-and-forth exchange that leads to a higher whole, a synthesis, that begins, on a more demanding level, a further give-and-take.

80. For instance—this example is my own, not Teilhard's—is the Church's neglect (to date) of the media of mass communication (measure the *Catholic Register*'s influence against the *New York Times*, or Mother Angelica's Eternal Word Television Network against CNN) a reflection of its rejection of the notion that the Good News of redemption can be broadcast by manipulative means, or is it just a failure of imagination and nerve on the part of Catholics?

81. Teilhard, *The Phenomenon of Man*, rev. ed. (London: Collins, 1977).

will become unified in the Omega, through Christ's intervention at the Parousia. (Does Teilhard emphasize enough the element of judgment, the purification of the elements for the final synthesis, and perhaps the purging away altogether of some?)

"Only the reflected kernels [*noyaux réfléchis*], as they alone are capable of adhering to the Omega, represent the irreversible fraction of the spiritualized Universe."[82] Nothing in Teilhard's thought is more perplexing or more important than the notion of this all-attracting Omega point. What is it, how does it function, and how do we come to know it?

In a late essay, Teilhard points out that given the transcendent nature of the Omega (both above the kind of being that we experience immediately because we are a limited kind of existence and out ahead [*avant*] of the evolutionary process, attracting it as the ultimate point of unification toward which we yearn), it is to be expected that we cannot know it all at once.[83] We rise to it, from knowledge of what we know best toward the illusive ultimate, returning toward the familiar again in the light of the glimpse of the ultimate, coming as a result of these hints of the transcendent to see new aspects of the familiar; then with this new insight we turn again our gaze toward the ultimate point in which all are gathered up in a total meaning. This is the "dialectic," movement from familiar to less familiar and back, that Teilhard sees passing through four moments (*temps):* 1) from the human phenomenon to the transcendent God; 2) from evolutionary creation to expectation of a revelation; 3) from the Christian phenomenon to faith in the Incarnation; and 4) from the living Church to the Christ-Omega.

Teilhard knows this is not the order in which mankind came to embrace each of these aspects, but rather is the come-and-go or "oscillating spark" that characterizes his thought, seeking to fix the steps of his procedure in seeking God. This "apologetic" (as he sometimes calls this "dialectic") may be motivated throughout by faith, but it is important to see its inherent logic, which, he believes, is an eminently reasonable one.

First, ahead in the ascending complexification accompanied by increasing consciousness lies the convergence of human consciousness in a whole, a humanity that would appear to have beyond it no further evolution. At the same time, the process seems irreversible: a humanity "conscious fully of its struggles and of the value of its achievements" can settle for nothing inferior and cannot tolerate, anymore than the reflective individual, the thought of this struggle and accomplishment ending in death. Teilhard sums up a proof for the existence of God:

> In virtue of the process which carries him along, Man sees himself skidding [*se voit dériver*] towards a final position where:
> (a) organically, he can go no further (even collectively) in complexity, and thus in consciousness;

82. It is not hard to see that Teilhard is describing, in his own terms, that ingathering in Christ of all finite spirits the tradition calls *communio sanctorum.*
83. Teilhard, "Esquisse d'une dialectique de l'esprit," in *Oeuvres,* 7:147–58.

(b) psychically, he cannot accept to reverse;

(c) and cosmically, he cannot stay where he is, since, in our "entropic" universe, to cease to advance is to fall back.

What does this mean if not, having arrived at this ultra-critical point of maturation, the curve of the human phenomenon pierces the cosmic phenomenal system, and postulates the existence out ahead and beyond it [*en avant et au-delà*] of some "extra-cosmic" pole where is to be found integrally collected and definitely consolidated, all the incommunicable reflectivity [*réfléchi*] successively formed in the Universe (and especially on Earth) in the course of evolution?

Seen while ascending, from our side of things, the summit of the evolutive cone (the Omega point) is glimpsed on the horizon as a center [*foyer*] of convergence that is simply immanent: Humanity completely reflected on itself. But, upon examination, it turns out that this center, in order to hold together, supposes behind it, deeper than it, a transcendent core—a divine core.[84]

Second, with this "postulate," we return to the humano-cosmic phenomenon, which takes on a different aspect. Instead of a spontaneous, autonomous, ascending movement, this flux is now understood to be "a tide provoked by the action of a supreme star": the Multiple is unified because it is attracted. This attraction is exercised more abundantly and obviously on those beings most able to be attracted: reflective, conscious beings, where the *"Moteur en avant"* is experienced less as a brute force than as the first *"psychique Moteur,"* addressing itself to the most human in us: intelligence, heart, and liberty. This being so, has this *"psychique Moteur"* not made available to us up to now some hidden message—*des paroles cachées*?[85]

Third, this is where, in the midst of the human phenomenon, the question of Christ arises. It is a fact of history that with Jesus "a phylum of religious thought appeared in the human mass the presence of which has not ceased to influence, ever more broadly and profoundly, the developments of the noosphere." Indeed, it is true that no single fact of human history has had so great an impact on the development of the noosphere.[86]

Nowhere outside this current of consciousness has the idea of God and the gesture of adoration taken on such clarity, richness, coherence, and suppleness. This has been nourished by the conviction of responding to an inspiration, a revelation. At the origin of this mystic "vortex," endowed with such remarkable vitality, is it not appropriate to recognize the creative flux at its maximum intensity—the spark surging between God and the universe through the medium of a personal milieu? Precisely the Word that we were in a position to expect?

For Teilhard this is the most crucial of two decisive options. The first might seem, on the lower level of the dialectic, the refusal to perceive

84. Ibid., 151–52.

85. Ibid., 153.

86. Consider the extent to which our techno-scientific planetary civilization is an offspring of Christian civilization, and compare this with the failure of either Buddhism or Islam (to take two great religions) to move mankind very far toward the planetary unification we now see the high-tech world system achieving.

the organic value of "the social fact" that then closes off access to the ultrahuman dimension of evolution. If one is not prepared to face the novelty of full human love, vision of the way beyond the human is blocked. The present option of the emerging noosphere, if it leads to a refusal of "the Christian fact," will "seal hermetically the vault of the universe" that had opened a bit. But if we accept in the living thought of the Church the reflection of divine thought adapted to our state of evolution, then the "movement of our spirit can take up anew its forward march."[87] As a result of the perspective gained from accepting the gospel message as the Word of God, in the Omega, to which we turn our gaze, we access now more than a "center of consistency which we perceive," or "first psychic Motor"; it is more than a Being who speaks: it is *un Verbe qui s'incarne,* a Logos in the process of incarnating itself.[88]

If the universe is progressively lifted toward unity, this is not only through the effect of some external force, but also because the Transcendent has made itself partially immanent to the world. This is what Revelation teaches us. Teilhard draws our attention to the radical change that here occurs in our way of relating to the evidence. Up to this point it has been rational; consciousness reaching to embrace in evidence the object.[89] But what stands revealed the moment one accepts the evidence for a divine address is a change from *connaissance* to *reconnaissance*—from cognition to recognition.[90] This is that whole complex play of two beings who open themselves and give themselves to one another, re-sponding that under the influence of grace emerges as theological faith founded in mutual love. Finally, such a process reflects that complete giving of self that flows from the Holy Spirit of God in the inner life of the Trinity.

Fourth, once the Incarnation is recognized, we can return to the better-known phenomenon, that of the living, teaching Church among us and see it for what it is: "germ of super-vitalization deposited in the midst of the noosphere by the historic apparition of Jesus Christ, a more interior cone at the core of the *masse montante du Monde,* the gradually arising mass of the World, and converging concentrically towards the same summit."[91] If the world could not reach our level of reflected intelligence without the

87. Ibid.

88. Teilhard, *Oeuvres,* 7:155.

89. Balthasar repeatedly points out that all the great natural religions of mankind work like that: our God-given human reasons strain to transcend toward God. Like Teilhard, Balthasar is generally quite positive about the beautiful results thus attained. But with Revelation something altogether different happens: the Source descends (Teilhard's favorite term) toward us, comes down into the sphere of our human existence, pulling us up into an intimacy we could never imagine by reason alone.

90. Ibid., 154. As Balthasar points out, to God as *"Wort"* corresponds our *Antwort,* literally "a word-over-against," a *re-spondeo.* Heidegger, who never mentions the interpersonal nature of this relationship, nevertheless at least speaks of a movement from *Denken* to *Danken,* from thinking to thanking. For an exploration of the ontology of commitment see *BT,* chap. 7, para. M.

91. Teilhard, *Oeuvres,* 7:155.

divine impulse, so too "the Christic summit" could not form itself without the existence of a human-cosmic summit.

But when this happens, God, reflecting Himself personally through an organized summa of thinking monads, in order to guarantee a certain result and to fix precise laws for their hesitant activity, bends over the mirror of the Earth-become-intelligent in order to print on it the first traits of His Beauty.[92]

In an early short work, "Note sur le Christ-Universel," Teilhard explains that the key to this "Christianization" of the world lies in recognizing just how centered in the spirit of man is the whole work of the Cosmos. Speaking of the Fall, he makes this telling remark: for the universe to be able to be affected *en bloc* by an accident that happened in a few souls, it must be that its cohesion, *"in unitate materiae et in unitate spiritus,"* is much greater than we ordinarily think.[93] The world, in order to satisfy the dogmatic givens, can no longer be "an agglomeration of juxtaposed things: it must be recognized as a great All *[Tout]*, bonded together and evolving organically." The importance of this "centering" of the cosmos in the human person, to use later terminology, becomes clear in the next paragraph.

All progress, be it in organic life, or in scientific consciousness, or in aesthetic faculties, or in social consciousness, is then Christian-izable right down into its object (because all progress, *in se*, is organically integrated in the spirit that is suspended from Christ, and this reflects in the way spirit-directed work affects the objective world).[94]

In another text, *Science et Christ, ou analyse et synthèse*, Teilhard offers a hint of how the Christ, through the preaching and example of His incarnation in Jesus, concretely leads the processes of spiritualization.

> Jesus preaches to us purity, charity, abnegation. But what is the specific effect of purity, if not the concentration and sublimation of the many powers of the soul, the unification of Man *per se [en soi]*? What does charity in its turn effectuate *[opère]*, if not the fusion of the many individuals into one body, and one soul, the unification of Men among themselves *[entre eux]*? What, finally, does Christian abnegation represent, if not the deconcentration of each man in favor of a more perfect and more loved Being, the unification of all in one *[de tout en un]*?[95]

This work of elevation and unification is "mortifying and painful" not just for us, but also for the Incarnation of the Word Himself, to the point of being symbolized by a cross. Preparation for his entry into history commenced with the beginning of Creation, and this long and necessary development was pointed toward the moment when, out of the matter He had penetrated from the beginning of the whole cosmic process, that human soul would be chosen that, coming into the world through the womb of Mary, would be there in the midst of material creation to lift it up.

92. Teilhard, "Un front humain spirituel," in *La Table Ronde* (June 1955), cited in de Lubac, *La pensée religieuse*, 261.
93. Teilhard, "Note sur le Christ-universel," in *Oeuvres*, 9:41.
94. Ibid.
95. Ibid., 60.

"Nothing less was needed than the terrible and anonymous labors of primitive Man, and the long Egyptian beauty, and the troubled [*inquiet*] expectation of Israel, and the slowly distilled perfume of the oriental mystics, and the hundred times refined wisdom of the Greeks for this branch of Jesse and flower of Humanity to blossom."[96] After this phase of *kenosis*—emptying out (into matter)—began a second phase of crucifixion, the one we know and understand best, that of human "sympathy."

> To conquer human life, to dominate it by his own life, it was not enough for Christ to be merely juxtaposed to it. It was necessary that he assimilate it, taste of it, tame it in his own depths. Christ experienced, first of all, the individual human heart, "the heart that is our torture and our joy." But he was not only a man, this man—at the same time, because of his divinity, he is "total Man" . . . he who brings together, in the depths of his consciousness, the consciousness of all men. In this way, he had to pass by way of an experience of the universal. Try to reunite in a single ocean the mass of passions, expectations, fears, troubles, happiness, of which each man represents a drop. It is into this immense sea that Christ plunged, to the point of absorbing it by all his pores, altogether. It is in this tumultuous sea that he floundered [*dérivée*] in his powerful heart, until he had tamed the waves and the tides to the rhythm of his own life.[97]

This is the meaning of the Agony in the Garden of Olives when Christ, in His humanity, found insupportable the weight that, through His divinity, He had to grasp. But He freely submitted to the entire burden, unto death.

What is the meaning of that death, that ignominious and glorious Passion on the cross of the Omega become flesh? We can make no sense of it until we first struggle to understand the phenomenon of death in general. For Teilhard, it is first of all a sign of incompleteness, a failure in the process of Being, which results from the higher organizing principle (in living beings, the soul) being unable to dominate sufficiently the elements out of which the thing is composed, and from the revolt of the elements that always are prepared to pursue their own course independently of the higher principle that curtails and tames their operation. Death "introduces itself into the World as the worst of weaknesses and the worst of enemies." (Balthasar, in this same spirit, shows how it seals the ultimate fate even of every merely human love.)[98]

Yet, despite this basic negativity, death has an unexpected utility in the processes of "creative union." Normally, to die is for a being to fall back into the Multiple. But it can also serve for its reorganization as it passes under domination by a higher soul, as when bread is broken down in the

96. Ibid., 88. We do not meditate enough on the fact that these long-prepared currents actually do meet in the human soul of this Nazarene, Jesus, at this place and moment in history, when the Father sends the Word to be incarnate. From there, they are sent forward into history through His physical continuation through the apostles on whom He founds His Church, taken up by those great saints, the fathers of the Church, who continue Jesus Christ's work of "distillation" of the nectar of all previous culture.

97. Ibid., 90–91.

98. Ibid., 91; see *Love Alone: The Way of Revelation*, ed. Alexander Dru (London: Sheed and Ward), chap. 4.

stomach so that its useful materials can become part of the human body. "Why would there not be dissociations in the course of which the elements would never cease to be dominated by a unity that undoes them only to reform them?" In the case of the definitive union with God in the Omega one sees that the world must, in order to be divinized, lose its visible form, in each of us and in its totality.[99] That, from the Christian viewpoint, is the vivifying function of human death, in virtue of the death of Jesus.

Now, for death to fulfill its positive function, it is necessary that the intelligent monads who are facing it learn how to accept it with humility: they must be willing to forego obstreperous elements of ego to serve in the larger whole; with love, they must positively reach out to embrace the Other, and, "above all, with immense confidence." "It was necessary that we surmount, intellectually and vitally, the horror that destruction inspires in us." In taking on Himself individual death, Christ achieved this conversion of our views and our fears. Now we can lead completely different lives, existences not devoted to avoiding death and suppressing the thought of it, but remembering it and preparing for it. At the same time, Christ joins God to man: through Christ's conquering of death, "the World penetrated into God," a God who so loves His creation that He is willing to be intimately involved in it, and through Christ, His Son, to suffer with it, and to glory in its transformation through the Resurrection.[100]

The Resurrection is a "tremendous" (Teilhard uses the English word) cosmic event. In and through it, Christ's whole cosmic role changes. Before, the Christ was *partout*, everywhere, like a soul that *péniblement*, gradually and with difficulty, gathers up embryonic elements. But now, He emerges from the world, after having been baptized in it, to reign over all the universe as a consciousness and an activity that are masters of themselves: *"Descendit et ascendit ut impleret omnia"*—Teilhard quotes the Letter to the Ephesians (4:10), "he descended and ascended in order to fill everything."

99. Teilhard was perfectly aware that this is not merely natural, but rather a supernatural process. The following 1923 text from "La messe sur le monde" makes that absolutely clear: "If your kingdom, my God, were of this world, it would suffice, to hold on to You, that I give myself over to the powers which cause us to suffer and die in the process of making us grow palpably, we ourselves or what is dearer to us than ourselves. But, because the goal towards which the Earth moves is beyond, not only each individual thing, but also the ensemble of things, because the work of the world consists, not in engendering in itself some supreme reality, but in consuming itself through union with a pre-existent Being, it turns out that in order to arrive at the flaming center of the universe, it is not enough for man to live more and more *pour soi*, nor even to give his life to some earthly cause, however grand. The world cannot rejoin you, O Lord, except by a kind of inversion, a turning inside out, an 'ex-centration' in which succumbs for a while not only the success of individuals but the very appearance of our human advantage as well. In order that my being can be decidedly annexed to yours, not only the monad in me has to die, but also the world itself, that is to say that I pass by the tearing apart phase [*phase déchirante*] of a diminution which will be compensated by nothing that is tangible" (ibid., 42–44).

100. Ibid.

How is the influence of this universal Christ transmitted to us, personally and concretely? By the Eucharist. The Host is first and foremost the fragment of matter where, thanks to transubstantiation, the Presence of the Incarnate Word *s'accroche*—literally, "clings"—among us, that is to say, in the human zone of the universe. In the Host is fixed literally Christ's center of personal energy, rather like our own bodies, when we consider them the local center of our own spiritual radiating.[101] It must be said that the initial Body, *Le Corps Primaire* of Christ, is limited to the species of bread and wine. But Christ, because He is above all Omega, that is, "universal 'form' of the World," could find His equilibrium and His organic plenitude only by assimilating mystically everything about Him. The Host is like a burning hearth from which a flame spreads out, the Host of bread envelops itself ever more intimately, through the mediation of the embodied persons who consume it, with an infinitely greater Host, which is the universe itself, the universe gradually absorbed by the Mystical Body. The world is the definitive and real Host into which descends, little by little, Christ, until the consummation of His age. One word and one operation fill up the universality of things and this from the beginning until the end: " '*Hoc est Corpus Meum.*' Nothing is at work in creation, immediately or from far off origins, except that which will achieve the consecration of the Universe."[102] Rightly understood, this truth, adds Teilhard, is the best foundation and the greatest attraction for our efforts toward the good and toward progress.

The Flesh of Christ is fed by the entire universe. Nothing that has proved itself constructive energy is lost; nothing is *impuissant*, impotent, and condemned in the world, except those destructive energies of that which turns its back on the unification of the spirit. At the same time, Teilhard insists:

> the sanctification of souls, however personal it may be, remains essentially collective. We are spiritualized, borne along by the spiritualization of all. We unite ourselves with Christ by communing with all. We shall be saved by an election which has chosen All. And the beatific vision will be less an individual vision than a specific act of the Mystical Body, the Divine revealing itself to each of us through the eyes of Christ.[103]

As de Lubac points out, the central question for Teilhard is understanding how the *en avant* of a humanity progressing, through "socialization,"

101. Even though, adds Teilhard in an aside, our own flesh may not be ours any more than any other matter, by which I take it he means that, while in one sense "I" am "my" body, in another sense I do not control it very much, cannot keep control of it, did not make it, submit to the flow of atoms into and out of the molecules and the molecules into and out of the cells and the cells into and out of "my" body, so like all matter in the final analysis it eludes me. Christ, on the other hand, as Incarnate Word of God alone "owns" the matter of His Body and, because He is the Logos through whom all things are made, can "radiate" from this localized center to the entire cosmos. That is why He can be eucharistically present in this bread or that, anywhere in the cosmos He elects, and as He elects.

102. Teilhard, *Oeuvres*, 9:94.

103. Ibid., 105 n.

toward the "fabrication of one *Humanité*, relates to the *en haut* of our incorporation, each of us individual souls to be saved, into the Mystical Body of Christ, through the gift of grace from on high." We have seen that Teilhard regarded with horror a mankind producing itself as a globe-spanning tyrannical unity without God and hence without love.[104] The production of "superhominization," of the "ultrahuman," must be understood as "transhuman," as arising out of Christ's gracious, post-Resurrection attraction. Let us consider some of Teilhard's visionary hints of how these "two antagonistic poles"—Christ and Antichrist—might unfold in humanity's future.

The "axis" (a favorite Teilhardian term) along which such a reflection is to be situated is absolutely clear: *"Vie—donc réflexion—donc prévision—donc exigence de survie."*[105] Human life *(vie)* cannot continue without survival *(survie)* or without "superlife" *(sur-vie)*, once we recognize the extent to which all the sense of what we do reposes *en avant* in its contribution to the building of the human city. But then we confront the scientific fact of the inevitable destruction of humanity as it exists in this world. Faced with utter ultimate senselessness, mankind would, as we saw Teilhard put it dramatically, *"ferait grève,"* "go on strike," and evolution, lacking all incentive, would come to a halt.[106] One way or another, we must be able to "escape the *caducité*—the ultimate sterility—of the planet that bears us.[107] *"Caduc"* is a wonderfully expressive word, which means outmoded and hence leading to nothing more. Something greater, more complex, more centered than humanity is glimpsed *(se profile à nos yeux)* beyond the spirit of the Earth. Somehow the world must *finir, sans périr*—finish without perishing. Not man collectivized who perishes, but super-personalized, "under the influence of a unique and superior soul," Man who finishes.[108]

The question then is how to grow closer in such a way as to liberate ourselves—the real question of liberation theology à la Teilhard. The liberating relationship of center to center is love. But how is it possible "to love a multitude"? Is that not a contradiction in terms? The antinomy is resolved once we realize that "in a center of our centers it appears possible to encounter one another."[109]

What makes the pure collectivism monstrous is that, multiple by nature, it has neither thought, nor heart, nor face to which, through the depths of

104. Teilhard, "L'Atomisme de l'esprit," in *Oeuvres*, 7:29, cited in de Lubac, *La pensée religieuse*, 311.

105. Teilhard, "L'Atomisme de l'esprit," in *Oeuvres*, 7:50.

106. One wonders what Père Teilhard would say about the declining population among the most "advanced" today, that fruit of frivolous individualism and hedonism, which has condemned to death, barring conversion, whole peoples—the most "sophisticated" and best-educated people on earth.

107. Ibid., 51.

108. Ibid.

109. Ibid.

our being, we can grasp on to one another *(nous accrocher)*.[110] "Society" can very well smother us in its innumerable arms: it would not know how to bring us close together *(rapprocher)* by the marrow of ourselves. Arrested on the level of the collective, humanity, so much exalted since the last two centuries, has started to show itself to be that horrible Molloch that Teilhard predicted. We can neither love it nor love one another in it. This is why it mechanizes us, instead of completing us. But, on the contrary, when in each element of the human myriad, the warm light of a same common soul blazes up, then in this personalizing *foyer*, itself a supreme personality, each parcel, in its effort to complete itself, discovers itself precipitated onto all the others *(se trouve precipitée sur tous les autres)*. Neutralized by the great numbers, a formidable affinity is lying dormant in the human mass. No longer canceled out but rather this time *multiplied by the plurality of spiritual particles*, we see now that in the rays of Omega it will have to wake up one day.[111]

Perhaps the most accessible way to understand Teilhard's vision is through its ethical implications. The challenges to man-become-reflective are the questions: Why am I living? For what am I working so hard? (The question that professed resolute atheist Simone de Beauvoir asked at the end of her life: *"La liberté, pour quoi faire?"*—"Freedom? What for?!") When we realize that not "in the final analysis" but "in the final synthesis" everything positive is destined to be lovingly preserved, our perspective on everything changes. Suffering and evil begin to make some sense; they are the price of the work: if there is to be a space for freedom, there will be failure and perversity, and in the struggle to build there will be pain. Inequality loses something of its push to resentment when we know that we are all part of one great personal whole, each making a unique and indispensable contribution, all destined to participate in the accomplishments of all. The monotony and pettiness of many of our daily tasks are seen in a different light when we realize that they are necessary to the construction "of the great tower" reaching up to God through the Omega convergence point.[112] The dilemmas of individual versus society are much softened when we realize that our individual personalities are to contribute to the triumph of the Superperson in whom we all will have our life and being throughout eternity.

Teilhard is not succumbing to a kind of facile optimism, as though saying, "Not to worry, Christ will see to it that everything comes out in the end." No one was more aware of the ravages of evil, of the scandal of

---

110. Ibid., 54. A sign of this is the extent to which the lie appears essential in the great collectivized faceless regimes, such as the Nazi or Communist.

111. Ibid., 54.

112. "The least action, as humble and monotonous as it may be, is discovered to be a means of cooperating in the universal Great Work" (ibid., 61). The allusion to the Tower of Babel is to remind us that this great construction, built by Christ Himself and by us co-operating with Him, unlike the first will be in the praise of God and not to the self-glorification of man.

the *gachi*, mindless waste of lives; Teilhard never forgot that the way to the resurrection is a *via dolorosa*, and that life is a struggle. His own, marked by the scandal of his condemnation to silence by that Church in whom he saw salvation, was filled with suffering, with personal experience of the *gachi*. But joy and hope lie precisely in the fact that we can struggle, and struggle meaningfully: *"Avoir à lutter, pouvoir lutter, pour toute sa vie, pour créer ce qu'on aime!"* ("To have to struggle, to be able to struggle, in order to create what one loves!").[113]

Thus, we are able to steer between the classical Scylla and Charybdis of individualism versus collectivism, between escaping from the world through turning our back on the material versus a despairing sinking into materialism. The key is to recognize that the spiritual emerges from the material, attracted by the cooperative work leading to convergence in the Omega. Neither individualism nor collectivism, but cooperation, an *agir* that is *communio*, a cooperation that is in-corporation. Instead of either *enlisement*, getting stuck in the material, or *extenuation*, fleeing from it, the Christian attitude is *detachment* by going through *(traverser)* matter or sublimation, emergence from matter. This is the profound meaning of the Agony in the Garden that Christ, in His humanity, found insupportable.[114]

Teilhard's challenge to modernity can be summed up in one sentence: "Now we can lead completely different lives, existences not devoted to avoiding death and suppressing the thought of it, but remembering it and preparing for it." (Paradoxically, the materialists who avoid the thought of death end up being the ones who drive "the civilization of death," the ones most prone to convert healing doctors into agents of euthanasia.)

De Lubac quotes a sentence from Teilhard's report to his father-general four years before his death, as a good summation and proof that Teilhard remained thoroughly orthodox to the end. There he speaks of his "three convictions": the "unique value of man as the forefront of Life *[en flèche de la Vie]*; the axial position of Catholicism in the converging sheaf *[faisceau convergent]* of human activities; finally, the essential consuming function taken on by the Christ at the center and at the summit of Creation."[115]

When I suggested that we find here a theology of liberation, I was being literal. Christianity—and no one has understood this better since Saint Paul and Saint Augustine than Teilhard—is entirely about liberation.[116] But Revelation affirms there is only one way to genuine freedom, and

---

113. Ibid., 56.
114. Ibid., 63.
115. De Lubac, *Teilhard posthume*, 57.
116. The documents of the Second Vatican Council, not without Teilhardian influence, make this clear. A number of great theologians of midcentury, before the outbreak of a Marxist-inspired "liberation theology" after the council, had already begun emphasizing this Paulinian sense of liberation: de Lubac, Congar, and Balthasar spring to mind. De Lubac, as I said earlier, was quite sympathetic to Teilhard's explorations. Balthasar, however, is more than reticent. He concludes his brief summary of Teilhard's thought with the criticism that Teilhard has so emphasized the Incarnation as to downplay the Trinitarian aspect of redemption. One can see the effect of this, for instance, in his failure

that is the Way of Christ, "for this I was sent into the world," and that "sending"[117] is about achieving freedom through *communio* in the Source of all our being, realizing our individual destinies, but together as one people of God. This audacious synthesis cannot be accommodated to orthodox Catholic tradition without difficulty. De Lubac is himself cautious about deficiencies in Teilhard's thought.[118] Part of the problem stems from the fact that this visionary was always experimenting, trying to work into words his vision of the future development of mankind, and sometimes he got carried away.

But the worst misunderstanding propagated about him, that he saw the natural process of the cosmo-genesis and the anthropo-genesis leading *inevitably* to the Christo-genesis—which would confuse the natural and supernatural orders—is patently untrue. De Lubac was at pains in all four books to demonstrate that such was never that thinker's position—Teilhard was clear about this: God ordained the becoming of the cosmos and the summit reached in the becoming of man as a *preparation* for the descent of Christ into history, itself an unimaginable, absolutely free, divine event, coming to us from on high, and by complete surprise.

Another common mistake is the notion that he imagined mankind melting into the divinity, something rather like the notion in Oriental religions. Again, clearly not so. Consider for instance this text, presented by de Lubac: "A person can give himself, as person, only so long as he remains a unity conscious of itself, that is to say distinct. What is more, this gift that he makes of himself has as a direct result to reinforce what he has that is most incommunicable, that is to say to super-personalize him."[119]

A third misunderstanding is the accusation that once Christ is incarnate and resurrected, the Christification of the cosmos is ensured through the progressive spread of the Mystical Body of Christ in history. Again, Teilhard is clear in his orthodox affirmations that the Parousia will be a supernatural, all-transforming event, for which whatever happens in the meantime, all that is accomplished by the Holy Spirit through the Church is preparation but in no way a substitute for that event. Do not forget, with the arrival on the scene of human reflection, and more intensely with the coming of Christ, the possibility of progress is offered man, but given his freedom, there is no necessity that he accept his chance. He can always refuse God.[120]

---

to make much sense of the cross as *Versöhnung*—reconciliation, and forgiveness of sins. Another serious effect of this is to downplay the Marian aspect of redemption that brings out the role of man and woman—this despite Teilhard's lifelong personal devotion to Mary. Worst of all, the element of apocalyptic *descensus* is missing: the vertical element of God's reaching down at this moment in history is sacrificed to the sense of the final gathering-up at the end of time (*Theodramatik*, 4:147).

117. *Apostolein*—the Book of Hebrews calls Christ "the Great Apostle."

118. See the criticisms and questions in de Lubac, *La pensée religieuse*, chap. 19.

119. Teilhard, "Esquisse d'un univers personnel," in *Oeuvres*, 6:84f, cited in de Lubac, *Teilhard posthume*, 67.

120. De Lubac, *Teilhard posthume*, 80, explains this well.

It is with the liberty of lending himself to the effort or of refusing, "the formidable faculty of measuring or criticizing Life," that man re-sponds. Teilhard repeatedly warns us to be on guard against the possibility of being "lost in the exterior darkness (*les ténèbres extérieures*)." Even if scientific research and the work of man were in some sense to conquer the world, that world is "a prison in which the soul suffocates." "Every energy is equally a power for Good or for Evil." The only real progress is that which "descends from above," that of the communion of saints and of charity. It is the progress of the "Divine Milieu": purity, faith, fidelity, charity, meekness, and hope. "True progress is not registered, is not realized in any of the material creations that we try to substitute for ourselves to survive us on earth: it is pursued in souls, veritable sparks where is concentrated the interior flame of the world and where it incarnates itself, and it (the world) goes with them (the souls) [*il s'en va avec elles*]."[121]

> Immense will be the powers disengaged in Humanity by the internal play of its cohesion. Again it could be that tomorrow, as yesterday and today, that energy will work in a discordant fashion. . . . Refusal or acceptance of the Omega? . . . a Conflict can break out. . . . the noosphere would then cleave into two zones, respectively attracted toward two antagonistic poles of adoration. . . . One last time a ramification.[122]

Balthasar devotes a section of the eschatological volume with which he ends *Theodramatik* to Teilhard's position. There he sums up his basic complaint: Teilhard's "overloaded [*überbelastet*] Christology." "The one sided Christological accent does not allow the Trinitarian Gestalt of the work of saving the world to come to the fore."[123] The one-sided incarnational theory lets the theology of the cross, as the Trinitarian work of reconciliation, get watered down, so that despite the accent on freedom, the reality of sin does not get its full New Testament depth. (Balthasar is critical of Teilhard's reinterpretation of original sin as simply the inevitable effect of the finitude of all material creation, rather than the act of revolt and ingratitude the

121. Teilhard, "L'Hominisation," in *Oeuvres*, 3:106; Teilhard, "Le milieu divin," in *Oeuvres*, 4:187–92 (this warning is repeated in other works throughout his life; see the list in de Lubac, *Teilhard posthume*, 80 n. 10); Teilhard, "La grande monade," in *Oeuvres*, 12:75; Teilhard, "L'Énergie spirituelle de la souffrance," in *Oeuvres*, 5:255; Teilhard, "Le milieu divin," in *Oeuvres*, 4:147–87. "The religion of science thought it had found a faith, a hope. It is dead from having failed to find charity" (Teilhard, "La mystique de la science," in *Oeuvres*, 6:215; see also 222); Teilhard, "Genèse d'une pensée" (letter of January 6, 1917, cited in de Lubac, *Teilhard posthume*, 85).

122. *Le phénomène humain* (Paris: Seuil, 1963), 321–22. De Lubac comments on the astonishing comparisons that can be made between the thought of Teilhard and that of several of the Greek fathers of the Church, but especially "that astonishing genius" Maximus the Confessor, and sends us to the important early work of Balthasar on Maximus, *The Cosmic Liturgy*, now available in English translation (San Francisco: Ignatius Press, 1991). See de Lubac, *Teilhard posthume*, 93. He further points out the many points of similarity between Teilhard's thought and that of the great Russian thinker of the nineteenth century, Vladimir Soloviev (ibid., 95).

123. Balthasar, *Theodramatik*, 4:147.

tradition has always understood it to be, hence showing that it was not God's work that turned mankind so self-destructive and perverse.) "The pathos of becoming so overwhelms that of Being, that differences—even that between the sexes—risk getting lost."[124]

Despite the serious pitfalls of this new Christian synthesis, even our brief reflection on Teilhard's response to the challenge of modernism introduces us to what I believe to be the modern challenge par excellence, that of *forging an adequate notion of freedom and then finding ways to live freely in wisdom*. To be truly Christian, such a way of life would have to avoid breeding individualism, which is the fault of the ways of life emerging prominently in our society. So, with Teilhard's modern Christian vision to help us understand it, we return to the challenge of formulating a mature understanding of Christian liberty.

LIBERAL INDIVIDUALISM, "LIBERATION," AND THE CRISIS OF AUTHORITY

"The Gospel of Jesus Christ is a message of freedom and a force for liberation." This in the first pages of the "Instruction on Certain Aspects of the 'Theology of Liberation'" issued in 1984 by the Sacred Congregation for the Doctrine of the Faith over the signature of Josef Cardinal Ratzinger. It is significant that the Church has renewed its expression of this central dimension of the faith—freedom—by responding explicitly and positively to a theme of the atheist Enlightenment, with its emphasis on liberty and human rights. But because "liberty" and "liberation" are such basic notions, they of course mean something somewhat different in each philosophy. Distinctive versions of the notion lie at the heart of different anthropologies. Since the Cartesians' subjectivist turn in the seventeenth century, the philosophic sense of the term has not ceased to become ever more pivotal, its meaning constantly evolving. A clash of notions of freedom lies at the heart of the great Kulturkampf of modern times.

The Church's anthropology differs mightily, on the one side from existentialist (and hedonist) libertarianism, and on the other from Marxist-Freudian determinism. The extreme individualism of liberalism cannot harmonize with a Christian view of "personal" man, created for *communio*. Nor can the social determinism of the Marxists, which they present as a necessary step to liberty, but conceived as precisely that collectivism that Teilhard so dreaded. The Church is nevertheless obliged to concern itself with elements of both liberal and Marxist visions as they currently command the planetary horizon. Can partial truths from both find a place in an adequate teaching on *communio*? (At the deepest level they are not so different: liberalism and Marxism rejoin at the level of materialism and practical atheism; liberals and Marxists meet at the foot of the altar of power where they go to sacrifice personhood to worldly success.)

124. Ibid.

The first Vatican text on "liberation" displays the distinctiveness of the Christian understanding, which it does not derive from modern philosophy but from biblical Revelation, where it is a central notion: "The Truth will make you free!" (John 8:32). From what do we need freeing, if not our own self-imposed bondage: sin? Sin is not a Freudian notion—indeed, the moderns hate it:

> Liberation is first and foremost liberation from the radical slavery of sin. Its end and its goal is the freedom of the children of God, which is the gift of grace. As a logical consequence, it calls for freedom from many different kinds of slavery in the cultural, economic, social and political spheres, all of which derive ultimately from sin and so often prevent people from living in a manner befitting their dignity.[125]

In this understanding of liberty, the sense of individual responsibility is retained, while the reality of social structures and the need to change them, so strongly emphasized by the Marxists, is also acknowledged.[126] The Barque of Peter thus sails resolutely between the Charybdis of individualism (which is well symbolized by the whirlpool) and the Scylla of collectivism (the monolithic state is the great rock jutting into the sea, interfering with the normal currents of life). And the social goal is implied as the salvation of the entire people whom God has chosen, a sense of salvation of all together that would have pleased Teilhard, and is attractive to socialists with good hearts.[127]

"Les philosophes" of the eighteenth century, eager to dismantle the remaining oppressive structures of feudalism, observed that every form of distinctiveness separating humans has been used by someone at some time to exact unjust advantage: hence the insistence of the French revolutionaries on *égalité,* and the socialists' devotion to leveling out the society.

The road to socialist liberation lies in denying the legitimacy of *any* difference, and *a fortiori* the legitimacy of hierarchy—only the dispossessed can throw off their chains and achieve real liberty, through power.

Such a position obscures the Pauline revelation that each person has a unique participation in the personhood of Christ, and hence an indispensable role to play, which no other can fill. In one extremely important

125. "Instruction on Certain Aspects of the 'Theology of Liberation,'" issued by Rome over the signature of Joseph Cardinal Ratzinger, 1984. This was followed in 1986 by a second document, also issued by the Congregation for the Doctrine of the Faith, "Christian Freedom and Liberation."

126. "Sin is always a personal act, since it is an act of freedom of an individual person and not properly of a group or community. . . . But every sin has repercussions on the entire ecclesial body and the whole human family" (Pope John Paul II, Apostolic Exhortation, *Reconciliatio et Poenitentia,* December 2, 1984, para. 16).

127. Balthasar praises the modern sense of the solidarity of all mankind, a kind of socialist instinct he sees as enduring and hopeful. Of Charles Peguy he says, "The most French of all Frenchmen was yet a socialist, and though he did not introduce the doctrine and ideology of socialism into the Church, he brought to her that spark through which socialism has become an essential expression of the anthropological age" (*The God Question and Modern Man,* 138).

sense, for Paul, all are equal, in that God loves each person absolutely. In another sense, none are equal, as each is unique and thus incomparable. If we are all equal parts of a faceless man, as the socialists believe, the sense of individual responsibility is destroyed: only the party can decide. Within the party apparatus (the *Nomenklatura*), each can be replaced by another, and masses can be sacrificed for a future good—we are just cannon fodder for the revolution; I get my personhood from the party, and, as Rudolph Hess screamed in introducing Hitler at the Fifth Party Day in Nuremberg, *"Die Partei aber ist Hitler, und Hitler ist Deutschland! Adolf Hitler, Sieg Heil!"*[128] Such abusive authoritarianism has had the effect, paradoxically, of destroying in present society respect for any kind of legitimate authority. (Lost altogether is the old root sense of *auctoritas,* which meant "a guarantee, helpful influence, weighty recommendation, advice, exhortation, etc., and derivatively an expressed authentic view, and hence a command.")[129] For such liberationists, every form of authority is tyranny in disguise, although they seem to have little fear of the most frightening tyranny of all, that of the Faceless Crowd, manipulated by the Leader. Paradoxically, one authority is admitted after all: the dictatorship of the proletariat that will dismantle all structures. Marxists would arrive at the goal—the self-standing individual, completely responsible for himself—through a period of dictatorship by the all-powerful elite who disinterestedly (the effects of original sin apparently being suspended in the unique case of the *Nomenklatura*) pursue the interests of the masses. All those movements we have mentioned as responsible for the growth of post-Renaissance individualism have been reinforcing this modern sense of the individual's "self-standing" while paradoxically being more and more swallowed up in the currents of the crowd: urbanization, with its anonymous lifestyles (no social pressure to behave if no one knows you—yet self-chosen "peer groups" exercise a relentless pressure!); the invention of printing, then electronic media, making possible mass education, but also mindless mass literature and "the media's" manipulation of "public opinion"; the Protestant emphasis on freedom of individual conscience, in one sense a good development, when it increases a sense of stewardship for church and state, but that, contrary to the Reformers' intentions, can, in combination with other factors, lead to the diminishing of the sense of the need of guidance from the Church community in forming one's conscience in truth; the money-based economy, in which unprecedented productive forces are released and the individual enjoys the freedom of the market, but where also everything gets leveled to a common denominator, *price,* the great "desacralizer"; science's bolstering of the sense of the autonomy of reason, but a degenerated reason, leaving many areas of meaning to the arbitrary; and, finally, the rise of an appreciation for human creativity, but degenerating often into the mere play

128. The scene is preserved in the party's unforgettable documentary film of 1935, *Triumph of the Will.*
129. See Balthasar, *Love Alone,* 47 n. 3.

of whimsy without regard for devotion to beauty and truth as "Other" than the artist.

When you pull them together and see how they work synergistically to produce the notion of the free-standing individual, who often is manipulated by the media, poorly trained in brainwashing bureaucratic schools, battered by market forces (for example, out of a job), running around after the latest changes in "mode"—sartorial, artistic (from Ninja Turtles to heavy metal), and moral—we realize that he is not in fact so free after all.

Liberalism's bleak caricature of the past, mispresented as a dark age of concatenated networks of oppressive social relations designed to hold in check the mass of people to the advantage of a small elite, passes over the protections offered ordinary people by feudal law, by the Church's moral teaching and its interventions on behalf of the oppressed, the power of guilds, and so on. Nevertheless, distorting as it is, it does contain an element of truth. In the best of the modern democracies there is better protection for the rights of the individual than ever before, so long as the respect for the rule of law continues to hold up.[130] Still, modern man feels himself increasingly fated to bob helplessly on the surface of huge economic waves and propaganda for "lifestyles."

The Second Vatican Council accepted the Enlightenment language of God-given "rights of man," and also acknowledged the validity of the socialist insight that without adequate production of wealth and its just distribution, political freedom is impossible.[131] The fathers pointed out that people often lack the material means necessary even to find out what is going on. This implied that the past organization of society left much to be desired. The central conciliar document, the Pastoral Constitution *Gaudium et Spes*, suggests that there is truth to the Marxist insistence on the evil of structures. This has encouraged some of the postconciliar liberation theologians' emphasis on "sinful structures," which had the merit of drawing attention to injustice on the "structural" level, but at the cost of somewhat weakening the sense of the individual responsibility of each sinner.

The council fathers struck a good balance between "structure" and the ineffable dignity and responsibility of the individual. Consider the following, which begins with a Teilhardian note:

> Every day human interdependence grows more tightly drawn and spreads by degrees throughout the whole world. As a result, the common good, that is, the sum of those conditions of social life which allows social groups and their individual

130. A precious heritage of a struggle since Magna Carta to flesh out and extend protection of the law to common rights. But evidence of the erosion of this sense, starting with a dangerous "taking for granted," and advanced by lawyers' and judges' rendering the law ridiculous, and the exaggeration of the whole idea of "rights," and the separation of rights and responsibilities, is mounting. If everyone has "got my rights," and no one has a sense of "my responsibilities," *El Caudillo* ("the Leader") cannot be far behind, to restore order "on the cheap."

131. *Gaudium et Spes*, para. 26.

members relatively thorough and ready access to their own fulfillment, today takes on an increasingly universal complexion and consequently involves rights and duties with respect to the whole human race. Every social group must take account of the needs and legitimate aspirations of other groups, and even of the general welfare of the entire human family.

At the same time, however, there is a growing awareness of the exalted dignity proper to the human person, since he stands above all things, and his rights and duties are universal and inviolable. Therefore, there must be made available to all men everything necessary for leading a life truly human, such as food, clothing, and shelter; the right to choose a state of life freely and to found a family, the right to education, to employment, to a good reputation, to respect, to appropriate information, to activity in accord with the upright norm of one's own conscience, to protection of privacy and to rightful freedom in matters religious too.[132]

As we probe the phenomenon of the modern sense of freedom further, seeking, in the footsteps of Teilhard, de Lubac, and Ratzinger to situate correctly an adequate Christian notion of freedom, it may help bring the discussion down out of the stratosphere to reflect for a moment on two of the groups most talked about today as requiring "liberation": the poor, especially the masses of poor in the Third World, and that entire half of mankind some are energetically promoting as perennial victims par excellence, women. Both are themes situated at the very heart of the modern discussion. Both can serve to alert us to tensions within the Catholic tradition between strongly different accents: not two distinct anthropologies, but differences in emphasis within the one crowning belief about man, the person born to be free as God has revealed to him His created nature.

For the first group, the poor, the issue is centrally one of economic and social development, of providing the material and minimal political means to lead a fully human life. This has become a central preoccupation of the liberal world's agenda in recent times, and increasingly a theme Church teaching has been happy to emphasize.

The question of the role of women raised to a white-hot heat by Marxist-Freudian–inspired feminists raises basic issues about human nature, forcing the Christian to plunge to the depths of the tradition's wisdom. "Male and female He created them," and the mankind Christ came to save is redeemed in their nature, man and woman.

Liberating the Poor

Wealth in the low-productivity agricultural and trading society in which Jesus lived (a form of "production and distribution" in which probably a majority of mankind still lives) was not acquired, as it is today in industrialized societies, by expanding a productive machine but by "cornering control" of scarce resources, above all arable land, pasture, and forest.

---

132. Ibid. What some of these rights mean—such as a right to employment—is much discussed, and indeed some Catholics, while totally in agreement that all should work for the common good, are more than a little disturbed by the philosophical sense of some of these claims. But at least the effort to balance group and individual is there.

The essentially exploitative situation in low-productivity countries is one reason Jesus warned the rich that their status carries the gravest danger for their salvation.[133]

It does not follow from this biblical antiwealth attitude, however, that the Church wants society to remain in poverty. Before modern industrial society discovered how to produce great wealth, everyone shared a general resignation to mass poverty. Christ showed not just compassion but also predilection for the poor; love for Him necessarily entails sharing what one has with those who suffer. This kind of "preferential option for the poor" you will have with you always. But with industrialization, "new things" are upon us. Hence, Pope Leo XIII, responding at the end of the nineteenth century to the socialist challenge, in the first of the Church's great "social encyclicals," *Rerum Novarum* ("New Things"), emphasizes that the Church expects all—now that industrialization makes this conceivable— to work to *eliminate* economic misery: "It must not be supposed that the solicitude of the Church is so preoccupied with the spiritual concerns of her children as to neglect their temporal and earthly interests. Her desire is that the poor, for example, should rise above poverty and wretchedness, and better their condition in life, and for that she makes a strong endeavor."[134]

The 1967 encyclical of Pope Paul VI, *Populorum Progressio,* states: "The Church has never failed to foster the human progress of the nations to which she brings faith in Christ." That will remain the official teaching of the Church. In moving its concern for political and economic development issues closer to the top of its agenda, the Church shares the modern understanding[135] that our freedom is exercised in situation, and that situations are always social as well as individual, and that every human situation has a definite material underpinning. This obliges the popes and bishops to engage in direct debate with the Enlightenment social commentators,

133. Although that reason no longer applies in the non-zero-sum game of industrialized society, where increasing wealth is produced and personal fortunes are often a legitimate reward for ideas and enterprise and daring, and do not *have* to come at the expense of someone else, the other danger of wealth has, if anything, increased: that of preoccupation, indeed *fascination,* with the power and possessions wealth brings. The power that comes with wealth, like all power, is a source of temptation; it weakens one's sense of dependence on God and on neighbor, and the struggle to attain and retain it, and the time taken up enjoying and defending its "perks," are a monumental distraction. The inevitable business of the rich man—most North Americans are in the upper 2 percent of mankind in real income—fritters away his most precious resource: his time, needed to contemplate God and to become an effective apostle, time for his family and friends.

134. *Rerum Novarum,* para. 42.

135. I am tempted to say "discovery," for I believe the strong sense of man's "situatedness" is part of the modern discovery of historicity. The Church avoids, however, any taint of historical relativism—a modern form of skepticism. *BT* works hard to found a theory of truth within a phenomenological-situational anthropology that allows for principles and lasting truths.

and to give a more historical sense to the biblical injunction to "heed the signs of the times" (Matt. 16:3) than just the eschatological sense obviously intended by the biblical text.

Three terms dominate those discussions. They need to be carefully defined. They are *oppression, oppressive institutions or economies,* and *injustice.* I shall offer a preliminary clarification of what these terms might mean.

"Oppression" Can Be Perceived Only in the Light of Justice

Oppression: It is easy to feel that anyone who possesses significantly greater wealth or power than another is an "oppressor" of the less fortunate. *Rerum Novarum* states: "avarice is the most evident form of moral underdevelopment."[136] The same encyclical goes on to speak of "a type of capitalism that has been the source of excessive suffering, injustices and fratricidal conflicts whose effects still persist," and while industrialization itself is not to blame "the woeful system which accompanied it" is to be condemned.[137]

One of the accomplishments of the Enlightenment has been the deliberate construction by nonutopians like Thomas Jefferson and James Madison of the new democracies equipped with rationally conceived systems designed to protect practically against man's sinfulness: systems under law of "checks and balances" in government to protect the weak, including every form of minority, for all are acknowledged to have, as Jefferson wrote in the *Declaration of Independence*, "rights we hold to be self evident."

There is a curious side to this issue of oppression. Most people who have been acculturated into a given system tend normally to look upon it, not so much as oppressive as "natural," meaning inevitable. "That's life," they shrug, accepting as normal those conditions that people in more fortunate circumstances would consider intolerable. It takes special circumstances to lift sights above the "ordinary" and so put the taken-for-granted "natural" structures in question.[138] It has long been recognized that revolutions usually follow periods of increased prosperity.

But the moral issue in a given concrete case is whether there is in fact oppression, whatever the ruling impression and the passivity of the sufferers. In determining that, the key question must be what in the circumstances is concretely, in a realizable way, changeable, for the real question of justice

136. *Rerum Novarum*, para. 19. Pope Pius XI had already written of "the international imperialism of money" (*Quadragesimo Anno*, 1931). In my view this is the most socialist inspired of all the social encyclicals.

137. *Rerum Novarum*, para. 26.

138. This is the point brilliantly developed by the Brazilian Carlos Freire, who sparked much research showing both that reading does begin to "lift sights," and ways in which it can be used more deliberately to get the young to question the "taken for granted."

arises only when something can feasibly be done about what anyone can see is an undesirable situation.[139]

"Oppressive" and "Just" Institutions and Structures, and Structures and Personal Responsibility

Christ loved the vulnerable. They recall to the powerful their own essential but well-disguised vulnerability. But no economically vulnerable person wants to be dependent uniquely on the continued goodwill of society, over which he has almost no leverage and he has reason to doubt in the good faith of the mass of individuals making it up, especially the powerful, given man's sinfulness. All but a few (the "opted out") desire to participate actively in building this world, and then share fairly in the benefits, to ensure as far as possible a solid situation with a degree of independence. Witness as an example the participation rate of women in the workforce, which from the time access became a real possibility has grown steadily, reaching 50 percent in some industrialized societies, with women motivated both by the desire to play in the larger game and by the desire either to ensure a certain economic independence for themselves or to improve the material situation of their families.[140]

I believe there is some point in thinking, as Church documents increasingly do, in terms of "bad structures." The Soviet system as it was imposed

139. Consider an important example. From *Rerum Novarum* on, the popes have insisted in all social encyclicals that "workers must receive their due." Just wages were defined as income sufficient to permit a family "to live decently." "Equity demands that public authority show proper concern for the worker so that from what he contributes to the common good he may receive what will enable him, housed, clothed, and secure, to live his life without hardship" (ibid., para. 51). Just what that is in a given society and epoch must of course be spelled out concretely in each instance, but it can be taken in a general way to mean, as a minimum, that workers shall have enough of the basic life necessities, and then adjusted according to the real possibilities of the society, a certain level of education that the society can provide to all, and in due course, as it is invented, health care, and so on. The popes recognize that it may not always be possible even to provide the bare essentials, but Pope Leo XIII warns employers that they must never greedily profit from the misery of others. If the business is not prospering, the employer should himself live modestly, using all available capital to improve it, so that all may achieve an acceptable minimum together.

140. Who is responsible for realizing the ideal of a just society? The tendency in recent Church teaching is to suggest the elite are responsible. Bad structures, dominated by a selfish elite, keep most people from being able to help themselves. In the poorest and most oppressive societies, this can be obvious, especially when masses of people have little education, the enterprising have no access to capital, and a tight group maintains a monopoly by military force. But not too much emphasis is put in the social encyclicals on the co-responsibility of workers for the health of their enterprises, although it is mentioned. What needs to be said more clearly is that the contribution of every ablebodied person is required to build a society that can meet all essential needs and provide the kind of education and health care that modern high-technology society makes possible, indeed at the same time requires, if it is to maintain the unimaginably high living standards achieved in the First World.

from above by force, without "checks and balances," was a set of "bad structures," as are those of the "mercantilist" elite states of the poorest Latin American lands, when compared to those "in the North" of genuine legislative democracies, coupled with partly entrepreneurial, partly social-welfare economies. To the extent these provide both some openness of opportunity and a "safety net" for those less able to compete, they are good structures. It is sensible to speak of a "bad structure" when almost all the capital of a country, like Guatemala, is controlled by a few hundred families.

But, as the Church also emphasizes, one should be careful not to imply that structures are independent of those who elect to keep them in place, and hence are somehow beyond personal responsibility.[141] There is nothing inherent in the "structures" in Colombia to keep a powerful patriarch from sharing more equitably between family and hired managers opportunities in the enterprises he controls, letting the best advance according to ability, and lending capital to associated entrepreneurs. He may need conversion to rise above the local mentality and recognize his possibilities. But it is not the structure that is to blame for his hardness of heart.

A social "structure" results from a consistent concatenation of wills reinforcing one another, which is maintained through the agents' going along, largely unthinkingly, with a set of little-questioned notions and habits—including roles—into which the incoming young and the "co-opted" are acculturated:[142] a social mind-set. Each person remains morally responsible for what he does within the group. Group mindlessness is no more excusable than personal mindlessness, and can only feed from it. Throughout the Gospels, Christ is shown with little patience for those who do not hear and do not see, especially when it is His own disciples![143] The possibility that always remains of personal awakening grounds the very possibility of conversion.

We have happened here onto a central issue for Christian anthropology: because Christian faith is inseparable from hope and charity, Christians not only should be slow to despair of self or others, but also are called to reject any anthropology, like the Marxist or any other determinism, that suggests that an individual's "alienation" into a class, race, sex, or tradition is so destructive of freedom as to render conversion an irrelevant concept. Despite Christian anti-individualism, there is a kind of "methodological individualism" built into the Christian understanding of humanity: God's grace can work in every individual soul, and at any time; love is a miraculous and inexhaustible source of freedom for the individual who responds,

141. The "Instruction Concerning Some Aspects of Liberation Theology," issued by the Sacred Congregation for the Faith over Cardinal Ratzinger's signature, points this out clearly.

142. This is explored at some length in *BT*, chap. 4, para. G and chap. 6, para. 2.

143. It must be said, however, that Heidegger's convincing analyses of the structures of everyday "inauthenticity" in *Sein und Zeit* stand, along with Bernanos's analysis of "imbeciles," as a warning of how deeply into the individual subject the forces of everyday mediocrity penetrate.

lifting him above mindlessness and the failures of natural justice to deliver liberation. God addresses us through others, but when we are open to Him, He speaks also directly to the individual's heart. This sense of individual responsibility is reflected in the social encyclicals.[144]

Paradoxically, this emphasis on individual responsibility can work against exaggerated individualism. Individual responsibility is properly understood to be an answering for self and society: the *authentic* individual discovers himself to be formed by a community,[145] for which he bears coresponsibility with others. One is influenced, but not determined, by a milieu (including the ultimate, "divine milieu," as explained by Teilhard). Grace gratefully received, as it calls one beyond himself, always tends to raise one above the limits of a social milieu, toward the divine milieu, a life in God.[146]

Those who lay more emphasis on structures are leery of "substituting charity" for fundamental reworking of structures. But if charity is what Christians believe it to be, the power of that God who is love working through and uplifting and transforming us, then it must be the creative source both of the motivation to work at altering structures and of the inspiration to know how to alter them in ways that correspond to the true nature of man.

Liberating Women

The other groups about whom the question of liberation has swirled are oppressed racial minorities and a purportedly oppressed majority, women. The Church, like all right-thinking persons, condemns racial prejudice and injustice perpetrated by ethnic majorities against smaller groups. This is not

144. This sense of love as liberating of the individual is so strong that Christian anthropology has been hesitant to face as squarely as it should the full charge of unfreedom to be found in psychopathological damage. Rightly impressed by the gospel's depictions of Christ driving out evil spirits from suffering souls, Christians instinctively turn toward prayer of healing, without often paying enough attention to the *nature* involved in damaged souls, and what God has already given us to work on that (damaged) nature; a nature that indeed grace can heal, but always in ways that respect the givenness of the natural reality, and the disponibility of graces already given in "natural" abilities.

145. Hardly a new discovery, nor a Christian one. This is what Aristotle meant when he termed man *zoon politikon*, a man of the city. I tried to show what this entails existentially in my 1985 opusculum, *Self Discovery* (San Francisco: Golden Phoenix Press).

146. Working for social justice is an inevitable and immediate fruit of this effective redemptive love. Immersion in political action cannot be, however, the beginning and end of the way to loving justice, for we must first and constantly cultivate that interior life that alone is the soil in which the Christlike vine can grow, and good political order and economic fairness are fruits, but profound, indeed total sharing in *communio* is the end. A sign that one's personal interior life in Christ is genuine should be exquisite concern for those immediately around us. Escapism into the vast abstraction of planetary "causes" is a warning sign. Nothing, I believe, can do more in the short and long run for liberation of the poor from bondage to bad structures than such response to our true neighbors, those we can reach and help immediately.

a difficult theoretical issue, except for understanding the psychopathology that leads to such destructive behavior. But racism is not crazy only; subtler forms are morally evil, a sinful giving in to a cowardice and insecurity that feeds every form of "us versus them" mentality. The problem lies there, in practice: how to expunge such hatred, often subtle, from our hearts, where it festers as a result of resentment at our own failures.[147] This failure of love is really self-hate, a refusal to be humble and accept ourselves as God loves us.

There are difficult theoretical issues surrounding women's liberation. It is urgent in developing an adequate notion of Christian freedom to discuss this tangle of issues. Divine revelation used the whole reality of our humanity as a language to express the ineffable divine reality, and so has woven symbolism drawn from the elementary relationships between man and woman to express the *mysterion* of God's own Triune being,[148] and God's incarnate "spousal" relationship with His people. The "feminist" issues, especially those regarding the accusation of patriarchal contamination of theology, if not to say the very expression of Revelation itself, and male domination of the hierarchy, have become a major concern at the present moment, at least in the West. Scientism has placed into question everything that formerly was taken for granted about our being, especially all the old assumptions about maleness and femaleness.

It is one thing to acknowledge, as the Second Vatican Council teaches, that there is a genuine issue of women's liberation from social inequities, problems associated with the status of women in a given society, but it is another to discern concretely and correctly, in one society or another, in what this oppression consists.[149] That depends in every case also on one's understanding of how women and men ought to relate.

It is very questionable to be guided in this by only "common sense,"

---

147. While I shall not pause to address it here, I have been working in my draft of *Human Being* on the challenge of understanding and properly situating ethnicity, for it is an explosive issue in the present planetary situation. I gave a paper at the Prague Seminar in Political Philosophy, in September 1992, "Ethnicity and Oecumenism: National Identity and the New World Order," cited earlier.

148. This works both ways: what God teaches us about the Trinity throws light on the deepest level of our humanity, as only the Author of our nature knows it. Balthasar, who always seeks within the Trinitarian life of the Source of all created Being the "template" for the great structures of the world—for example, time in a kind of prototime rooted in the activity of procession and return within the Trinity—also seeks there the deepest sense of the male-female relationship, as they are revealed in the Scriptures. In the unfolding revelation, God has woven an exquisite tapestry of relationships: the primordial Source is Father in His totally solicitous loving gift of all He possesses to the Word, who in His complete obedient acceptance is like the Bride, but who in turn is Son, for He then gives it all back to the Father and, in the Father's creation of the world through the Son, to us. We, in turn, are (to be) like Mary in our *fiat!*—our obedient acceptance—but we are likewise all brothers of Jesus Christ in passing on what we have received through apostolic action, and so on. These themes are woven throughout Balthasar's work. For an example, see "Women Priests?" in *New Elucidations*.

149. *Gaudium et Spes*, para. 9, p. 219; para. 29, p. 245; para. 34, p. 251; para. 27, p. 243.

as much of the taken-for-granted foundations in habitual mind-sets of our own culture are exactly what is being questioned. By seeking to be centered in the *catholica*, with a will to all-inclusiveness, back in time and out to the furthest reaches of human society today, the Christian stands a chance of developing a less rigidly ideological notion of how a genuine liberation of women[150] can be pursued.

Historical evidence of feminine consciousness of woman's difference and her place vis-à-vis man can be found from the first texts of antiquity sufficiently developed to reflect personal differences. The dramatic upsurge in consciousness of feminist issues to the point of becoming one of the highest items on the social agenda in America, accompanied by certain more or less Marxist class-hatred and "oppression" twists given to it, are, on the other hand, very recent, intensifying since the turn of this century. This is a fruit of modernity, rooted in the great modern struggle, not just to achieve *liberté* and *égalité* (with *fraternité* taking some strange twists) but to forge an anthropology that can found an adequate notion of human freedom.

In the present chapter I shall limit myself to pointing out the implications of this debate for "human nature," but I shall return in the next and again in the concluding chapters to integrate the whole liberationist dimension critically into my appropriation and resulting anthropological understanding.

It is not hard to understand why issues of women's liberation follow fast on the heels of the raising of questions of liberating "the proletariat," or, less Marxistically put, upon the rise of consciousness of the need for addressing structural issues of poverty. The Industrial Revolution has suddenly opened to much larger numbers of men what since the beginning of time had been limited to a small elite, with the opening of vocational possibilities for women following only a few generations later.

An understandable temporal "optical illusion" accounts for some of the present confusion. To any individual who has become conscious that a new dawn is creating opportunities, but is himself forced to wait for the benefits of this evolution to reach him personally, progress will seem agonizingly slow. But for most of the million or so years of man's existence vocational opportunity was next to nil for individuals "to make something of themselves" in the tribe living at the margins. The brutal toughs who initially emerged as the aristocratic lords were exceptional individuals, wily and hard as iron. The entire democratization of opportunities has been very recent and breathlessly rapid once industrialization made possible the production of wealth.

Our First World society has in the period of less than two centuries become almost totally different from traditional agricultural or pastoral

---

150. And men . . . there cannot be the one without the other, even if men need liberation from their own sins alone, as some extreme feminists seem to suggest. The situation is more tense in North America than in Europe because, I believe, we are more inclined than Europeans to concentrate too exclusively on the local cultural dimensions of these debates.

society. Most people in the OECD lands now enjoy some education—the first time in history that masses of people have been encouraged to think for themselves.[151] After stagnating for hundreds of years in the handful of careers that made up the fabric of rural life, thousands of new kinds of careers, undreamed of even a decade ago, have been created, many of them interesting, scads not requiring a man's physical force. As though it were not disorienting enough to turn topsy-turvy vocations and workplace roles, to move from country to city, and for vast new populations and incredible numbers of educated people to explode onto the scene, now suddenly the most fundamental changes in sexual relations and the reproductive processes are occurring.

In the midst of this unprecedented HTX revolution an adequate sorting out of the changing roles of men and women, lay and cleric, old and young, upper, middle, and lower classes, rich nations and poor, or what have you, is scarcely to be expected.

Fortunately, despite all the changes, many fundamentals remain clear: children still need the loving, sustained attention of both a father and a mother; households still need to be made into homes; many men still are masculine yet can be caring; and many women remain feminine, while being in all ways strong. Whatever the aspects of this masculinity and femininity that may be biologically determined, whatever is, on the other hand, acculturated, these differences remain with us in fact, some for now, some forever, some even being able, it is to be hoped, to survive extreme biological reengineering. However, in radical "feminist" circles, even to suggest that there are "masculine" and "feminine" qualities, and that men and women both need to cultivate some of the characteristic qualities of the other sex without losing their sexual distinctiveness, is thought to be capitulation to mindless stereotyping. Meanwhile—interestingly— biological research turns up almost monthly new evidence of how deeply into the composure of the body, indeed to the cells, the male and female differences go.

On the track of this roaring express of change, the quixotic Catholic stands agitating a little red lantern marked "human nature." Quixotic I may be, but I plead not guilty to any charge of thoughtlessly embracing the notion of an unchanging human nature.[152] I do not ignore the radicalness of what might be called the evolutionist claim: if human will and intelligence are the summits reached by the evolutionary surge of vital power that is cosmic evolution, then the only limits to human-becoming are what we have not yet tried or succeeded in doing. When we heroically experiment, we often find out the hard way what will not, for now at least,

---

151. The OECD refers to the twenty-six rich industrialized nations.

152. *BT*, chap. 4, para. D, all of chapter 6 (see esp. para. F), and chapter 7 explore and develop a notion of human nature, without falling into the trap of assuming an eternal form devoid of development. (Balthasar terms our natures "open" [*The God Question and Modern Man* [Burns and Oates edition], 20.)

endure. We use our intelligence to limit the damage of our experiments through the extrapolations we call "good planning." Much of what Neanderthal conservatives call "nature" is only the past—custom, allowed to seem ineluctable because alternatives have not yet been invented and tried out.

Two enormous consequences follow from such a voluntaristic position. First, any persons or groups perceiving a traditional position or role to be inherently "inferior," by whatever criteria may impress them, are going to consider themselves free to muster whatever power they can to change the situation. None need ever remain subordinate if they can break out of dependence, now understood only in terms of power struggle. (The loving subordination of man to God, of children to parents, of disciple to teacher, and of individuals to a good social order is ignored.)

Second, any aspect of the reproductive process one finds frustrating, including the bearing and raising of children, can be manipulated, to see what can be changed or not, to meet one's convenience: for example, "This is *my* body; these will be *my* (genetically engineered) children."[153] It is up to me to make of them what I can, so long as technicians continue to discover ways to rearrange nature and society.

Defenders of "natural law" are horrified by many recent experiments. They are quick to point out the evidence for every sort of ineluctable limit and ineffaceable distinction between kinds of things and degrees of superiority of activity that they believe are being ignored. They seek to establish on the basis of "the given" what are actions appropriate to the natures found in a particular situation, and what are acts ill-founded in distorted views or mere illusions.

The problem is that many defenders of "natural law" tend to take as given what turns out to be only temporary (although perhaps long enduring; man, after all, was "naturally" hunter and gatherer for hundreds of thousands of years before agriculture was invented, and was either nomad or agriculturalist for centuries until civilization came into being and the first cities sprang up. Much of what has been considered "natural" in agricultural and even preindustrial urban society is now relativized by events in the HTX).

As the contemporary debates roar ahead on many fronts, it becomes ever more obvious that proponents of "natures" need to be clear about all of the following. First, their time frames. If the evolution of the cosmos is acknowledged, "natures" are not eternal Platonic forms but, in the case of living things, structured stabilities genetically transmitted in certain environments during certain periods of natural history, subject to

153. The parallel with *"hoc est corpus meum,"* and Christ's sharing of His Body and Blood with all His children, is meaningful: Christ, as God incarnate, truly possesses His Body and gives it up, "in a death he freely chose." The receptive, antivoluntarist Christian does not believe his body ultimately is his to dispose of as he will, but a gift that is more a loan!

gradual mutation.[154] Upholders of "natures" need to explore the kinds of permanence displayed in nature. Second, spell out carefully the evidence for claims about presently existing objective structures guiding behavior. Third, distinguish the acculturated from the genetically determined, the alterable from the unalterable among genetic factors. And fourth, become as clear as possible about why what can be tampered with in many instances ought or ought not be. Defenders of natures must show convincingly why and how the higher law overrides mere convenience, and show the reasonableness in everyday experience of following basic moral principle.

There is much recoupable from ordinary experience, much still embedded in the much maligned common sense that is the operative wisdom of a given culture to support a superior law of love,[155] where the child, for instance, is not seen as my plaything, what every yuppie should have two of, a "right" that pushes one to every kind of reproductive manipulation so as to get the coveted child. But the reasons for this will have to be patiently spelled out.

A word of wisdom: when the "givens" have been changing so fast, it is vital to find the balance, *le juste milieu,* between the kind of call for patience that is an excuse for tolerating old traditional ways because one does not want to rethink them, and the call for such radical and rapid change that one risks losing important goods that do not have to be sacrificed and creating avoidable abuses.

In sum, then, it is fruitless to enter with intellectual seriousness into any aspect of the liberationist debates until one has begun to clarify an essential anthropology. In these introductory remarks I have offered a few hints of the spirit in which this should be undertaken, respecting modern discoveries but not forgetting the depth of common wisdom and above all centering itself in the most precious of all lights, that offered by the Divine Word itself. When I return in the next chapter to discuss the place of women (and laymen) in the Church, all these considerations will be at work.

PLURALISM AND THE CONCEPT OF TRUTH

With the intimate contact of cultures, Christians have come to appreciate other traditions as something better than just outer darkness waiting for the gospel's light to dispel their error. But today's Western university students tend to be something quite different from open-minded ecumenists: my

154. See *BT,* chap. 4, para. D. This is an issue central to the present volume's steps toward a Christian anthropology.

155. Much in "common sense" is still operative because it has stood the test of time and is consistently confirmed by much of ordinary experience. It is not because some of what "everyone knows" turns out later to be proved false that most of it is unfounded; it is not because invocation of common sense is not a reason for failing to pursue more critical investigation that the treasure of common experience does not need to be preserved, if nothing else in order to be inquired into. On "common sense" and "natural faith," see *BT,* chap. 2.

experience suggests that indeed many are unabashed cultural relativists. That is a form of skepticism. Under the onslaught of what I have called above "scientism," but in a form that emphasizes "paradigm shifts," and uprooted as many of them are from centuries-old milieus to be plunged into the new adventure of a life of urban wealth, they have lost more contact with their own foundations probably than any large group in history.[156] This alienation from roots causes disorientation, low self-esteem, and extreme insecurity. The project of universal truth, binding on all, is dissolved into a vague universalism of politically correct good sentiments that seeks agreement at the lowest common denominator, while being oblivious to how the whole package is being manipulated to serve certain special agendas. Indeed, anyone holding that something beyond vague humanistic, politically correct platitudes may be universally true is treated as a "cultural imperialist" aiming for thought control.

For many, if there is one tradition not in fact equal to all the others, it is the hyper-imperialistic Christian culture, a tool of the Europeans seeking to destroy the precious heritages of all the others. (So the Columbus celebrations became an excuse for an unrestrained outburst against Spanish [read: Catholic] cultural imperialism.) The other great universalist faiths, Islam and Marxism, come in for various degrees of criticism, too. Believing Muslims, for example, are lumped together as "fundamentalists," and communists, well, they deserve what they get, just as do Christians and Muslims who at various periods and in certain cultures have (and some still do) indeed used religion as a tool of political domination.

That is why it is vital to show the difference between a strong living-faith tradition that believes in the dignity and freedom of all and an abusive ideological manipulation that parasitically draws on a true faith for ends having nothing to do with love. The Christian faces the challenge of showing how one can accord the other the freedom that is his due while holding that one's own tradition "has the words of eternal life."

The Crisis of Truth: The Need for a New Concept

Tradition and Authenticity and *Being and Truth* both respond to the challenge of modernity by taking an ecumenical (but not relativist) view and argue for a certain way of searching for ecumenical wisdom. All individuals and cultures enjoy some of the same kinds of human experiences, but also each individual has experiences of his own, and each tradition presents the fruits of experiences foreign to those not in the given tradition. This being so, the search for wisdom demands not only building on the common foundations, which make communication possible, but also respect for the differences. We must undertake the patient (and loving) grind of learning

---

156. *Paradigm shifts* is the term used by the late Thomas Kuhn in his much discussed book *The Structure of Scientific Revolutions* to express the leaps in underlying *Weltanschauungen* that make visible a lack of continuity in scientific traditions.

from one another's distinctive experiences. While I loathe skepticism disguised as historical relativism, one of the most insidious Big Lies of our time, easy New Age–style eclecticism is no answer.[157] Any watering down of the truth claims expressed in the orthodox dogmatic formulations of any of the great traditions is mischievous.

But this simple awareness raises a serious problem. The coexistence of comprehensive universalisms appears to undermine the claims to some kind of ultimacy of any tradition, including those of Revelation. See the practical consequence for anyone the least bit "liberal": if other traditions are firmly believed by their adepts to be sufficient unto salvation, does not Christian proselytizing imply that at the core they are wrong and Christianity exclusively right?

The sense of the collision of the truth claims of the great traditions leads many modern Christians to an attitude—not very "apostolic," to say the least—such as this: "If anyone should happen to ask about Jesus, answer. But if they find their lives made meaningful by studying *Talmud*, or by following the *Sha'aria*, or pursuing 'social justice' through spreading Marxist revolution, leave them alone. All ways proposed by the great traditions are good ways to human fulfillment, even if I may believe Christianity is the best way. After all, have not other traditions formed holy persons?"[158]

The Christian cannot get off the hook quite as easily as just shouting "relativism!" Since he believes Christ to be the Incarnate Word of God, he should accept and understand Christ's command that the gospel be preached to all nations. He also referred to Himself as a "sign of contradiction" and as a sword dividing father and son. The "Good News" is held from the earliest days of the Church to be an expression of the divine will binding on all, and hence, the central point of reference for man's questing after being. That is why Saint Paul called Christ a *skandalon* for the Jews, which we translate as "stumbling block," and a folly or a madness for the "nations" (especially the Greek philosophers, roughly today's scientists), but for those who have been called, Christ is nothing less than "power" (*dunamis*) and "wisdom" (*sophia*) itself (1 Cor. 1:24).

To doubt that the Source of the universe could possibly want to unite all humanity into a single fellowship, brought into harmony along a single, ultimate salvific way under His leadership, is to undermine the "scandalous" claims about Jesus Christ. If one believes the Abrahamic claim of

157. An eclecticism is a grab bag of ideas, lacking coherence because one has failed to penetrate to principle, and on a sound ontological (being) and epistemological (knowledge) foundation, begin the task of translating the symbols coming from different traditions. Such a translation, of course, involves hard judgments about what is compatible, and why; where truth claims are irreconcilable, making clear why, and then, in the light of principle, showing why one is true and the other at least partially if not wholly false.

158. Indeed they have! A friend puts a case for the existence of holy atheists, a state in life for which he ardently strives.

God's Fatherhood, it would follow that it must be possible for a tradition to express truths formulated in a perennially valid manner, hence, despite all the problems of translation, in a culture-transcending manner. And these translatable truths, because they are true and accessible, would be able to bring light to the experiences of all, and hence give their ultimate sense to every good insight preserved in every tradition that has led a people along its way.[159]

To be able to reconcile the sense that the Principle of Being is at work in every good creative impulse in every tradition with the truth that the "Form" of God's fullest revelation is Jesus Christ, into which God desires the diffuse good be gathered "organically," there must be a will to investigate more deeply in three areas where modern philosophy has shown little inclination to dwell. First, to develop criteria for discerning the perennially essential in all human accomplishment from that which was good for its time and place.[160] Second, to bring mutually exclusive universal claims into more direct, honest, and respectful confrontation.[161] And third, to study in a more positive spirit how truths formulated in language reflective of the experience of a given epoch and culture can be transmitted and translated for people in different epochs and foreign traditions.[162]

Being and Truth strives for progress on all three fronts. An adequate ecumenical concept of truth able to embrace the perennial in the traditions of Revelation, and to reach out to the more philosophical ways of spirituality, like the Hindu, Buddhist, and Confucian, needs, for a Christian, to be founded in a conception of the salvation of the world. And it must have integrated into it the truths discovered by science.

159. It is a red herring dragged across the way of Christian universalism to imply that Christians then believe that God, once He has established His preferred way, cannot save people in other traditions who do not convert to Christianity. After all, many, through no fault of their own, still have no or only vague and distorted notions of what Christianity is. On the contrary, Christian teaching gratefully acknowledges that His grace is everywhere operative and salvific. No one should attempt to put limits on God's love. But acknowledging this central truth should not, on the other hand, occasion raising an obstacle to affirming God's plan for the final, collective redemption of humanity, which the God of love will not accomplish in a way that demeans anyone or any accomplishment of any tradition, so far as they are good and true. In the constructive aspects of all cultures the Church expressly sees the same Spirit of truth at work, and prays for all such accomplishments to be synthesized and preserved "in the Kingdom of God," as God Himself has commanded.

160. Not many philosophers, other than committed Christians, are interested in disengaging from the flux of history the fruits that show the permanence of a human nature.

161. Lip service to ecumenical dialogue is easy; patient, respectful, indeed loving exchange of perspectives and experiences is difficult and rare, and desperately called for; it can happen between only those who believe in Truth.

162. Relativist faiths, which dominate much of modern discussion of "interpretation" (hermeneutics) offer no incentive to look for that in experience that reveals otherness and permanence in people and things, without which translation becomes a dream, another fanciful exercise without profound meaning.

I have introduced Teilhard's accomplishment as a hint of some of the dimensions of the question of the truth foundation for a modern synthesis. To sketch out this challenge to Christians more adequately much work remains to be done in the concluding chapters. There, with a deepened sense of ecumenism, we shall address again the question of Christ's call "that they be one," trying to understand its meaning in the light of contemporary planetary consciousness.

In further preparation for that effort, I shall now approach a particular aspect of the question of ecumenical wisdom, an issue of "cultural relativism" par excellence: problems arising from the Eurocentrism of our own tradition. This question of "cultural optics" will thrust deeper into the relativism debate.

The "Crisis of Colonialism": Can Christianity Grow beyond Its European Past?

The objection that Christianity brings with it a large baggage of European culture that "contaminates" traditional cultures when it overwhelms them has substance. After a millennium of evolution in Europe—a civilization it largely formed out of Slavic, Germanic, and Celtic cultures— the Renaissance Christian cultures that the colonizers brought with them did indeed change drastically the cultures of the conquered peoples. This began a process that was eventually to produce new Christian-influenced national cultures that fed modernism, and interacting ultimately generated the immense transforming effect of the HTX. Every culture is an ambiguous, exceedingly complex mix of factors hard to disentangle and difficult to evaluate. In some respects, colonial-induced changes to indigenous American or African or Polynesian cultures were positive: new skills were acquired, a new morality was developed, in some instances the new bondage to the colonial overlords was a lighter burden than, for instance, that laid on the suppressed tribes by the brutal Aztec imperialists of preconquest Mexico. Above all, as the Indian people of Jalisco interpret the phenomenon in their traditional dance of the Aztec and Conquistadors that I saw performed before the beautiful platteresque church of Nuestra Señora de Sapopa, they brought the Good News of Jesus Christ.[163]

But there was great suffering involved as well: whole peoples lost their independence, became disoriented, were often treated by the cruder conquering elements as inherently inferior, exploited, and eradicated, and many of their old customs were snuffed out.

Recently, as intellectuals in many formally colonized lands have tried to recuperate the indigenous culture, some have turned in the process

---

163. It is not fashionable in the university even to try to imagine what that might have meant to a people accustomed to human sacrifices to terrifying gods, or oppressed mercilessly by their mighty Aztec overlords, or to see what it still means to a people who fill their lovely church near Guadalajara from six in the morning until eight at night at hourly Masses.

against Christianity because of the nonindigenous, European expressions it brought with it. With our present planetary awareness, and with our own civilization de-Christianizing so much under the impact of an accelerating development of the HTX, the West also is faced with distinguishing in Christian culture those elements of essential truth that ought to be preserved from more time-bound cultural expressions. Many of these are now inadequate to express what is known of the underlying reality. Some may have expressed realities that no longer exist. To what extent the truths to be preserved should retain their "European" expression has to be examined.

As ours has evolved from a "traditional society" and has become more self-conscious and critical, our appropriative efforts lack the automaticity that comes from well-settled "commonsense" categories and the *Sittlichkeit*, as Hegel called it, of old customary ways: practically everything now requires explicit, critical examination.

Part of this process of self-discovery should be a new determination to retain, because they are good in our Occidental, First World setting, many features of Western civilization that may not be appropriate to propagate to people of other cultures.[164] But those aspects of "Western" life that are direct developments out of Christianity putting into practice God's will, these the Christian should preach to all the world. The absolute dignity of every human life is one of these, whatever hesitations many Catholic thinkers may have about some "rights" language. There may be other goods discovered in the unfolding of Western culture that, while not flowing directly from Revelation, are still recognized by us as desirable for humanity, and that we would want to bring to all people. These are issues to be debated case by case and with sensitivity to the fact that our Western perspective on these matters is different.

The issue of cultural differentiation has arisen because of the discovery of historicity. Before the rise of modern historical sensitivity, the stronger nation typically ran roughshod over the ones it conquered, converting them to its ways by force, without the least bad conscience. But already by the sixteenth century, missionaries were to be found who pleaded for the need to respect the native cultures, a plea that fell mostly on deaf ears with the power-hungry *"conquistadores."*[165] Today, the "world community" (whatever that means) pushes cries of desolation over every invasion or occupation that the media manage to call to the attention of (largely Western) public opinion.

The roots of the discovery of the importance of history and of historically unfolded differences lie in the eschatology of Abrahamic revelation. Out of it was formed a tradition convinced that God intended the Chosen People

164. Many, because of their soil, climates, and cultures, will continue to prove resistant, for instance, to industrialization; and tribal cultures find the transition directly to something like Western democracy impossible.

165. The cases of Las Casas in Mexico, of the Jesuits of the Paraguayan reductions, and of the Jesuits among the Hurons, as outlined in great cultural detail in *The Jesuit Relations*, their official reports to the Society of Jesus, are getting to be well known.

to work toward an end, a goal that Christ revealed to be the mission to bring the Good News of redemption to all the world: it gave birth to the sense of something to remember, namely, God's great deeds. As Voegelin shows in *Israel and Revelation*, this experience at Sinai of a Leader God was indeed the "breakthrough" to a sense of history.[166]

Positively, there has thus arisen an ever more sensitive appreciation of the growth of culture. The need to preserve all genuine accomplishments of these creative impulses has resulted in everything from museums and history departments to efforts to restore endangered species and to promote "multiculturalism" in society. It has also given rise to the sense that life is a struggle to survive. Those struggling have always known this, but philosophy of life as survival of the fittest has not always been center stage. We shall have to situate the contemporary Church's apostolic responsibility in a society of increasingly self-conscious cultural and economic *competition* that has now become planetary.

166. Eric Voegelin, *Israel and Revelation,* vol. 1 of *Order and History* (Baton Rouge: Louisiana State University Press, 1974). This brilliant study establishes solidly the claim that "history began at Sinai." The mating in modern times of eschatological yearning with the dynamism of imperial conquest has brought about intimacy of cultures that in turn raised the question of cultural relativism with new acuteness.

THE CHURCH'S RESPONSE TO MODERNITY

"LIBERALIZING" THE CHURCH FROM WITHIN: "OPENING" OR "DISMANTLING"?

The modern agenda has been preoccupied with freedom, which has only intensified since the Enlightenment. The issue has existed, of course, if not clearly recognized, since the Fall; the Hebrews experienced the mighty liberating arm of their God as He led them from Pharaoh's bondage; and Jesus Christ revealed God as the "truth that makes you free" (John 8:32). With the Enlightenment struggle to get free from the remaining vestiges of the feudal structures and from a Catholic Church accused, not without reason, of abuse of power, there developed an individualistic ("Stand on your own two feet!") and libertarian ("Realize your desires!") sense of freedom. This inadequate sense of freedom has damaged the seriousness of liberal Protestantism. Consider this unflattering description by a Protestant scholar:

> It might be said that mid-twentieth century mainline liberal Protestantism gradually diluted and emulsified itself into culture. It took the strategy of de-emphasizing the specificity of its Protestant faith in order to stress Christianity's co-relation and commonality with so-called universal truths and human aspirations, especially those that could be defined and defended broadly within the culture as justifications for the extension of the individual's human rights and civil liberties.[1]

Rights without concomitant emphasis on responsibilities lead to a litigious society without focus. A society cannot be built out of millions of tiny, autonomous gods. Vigen Gurion's severe, but, in my opinion, justified criticism of "liberal Protestantism" as diluting religion into culture stands as a warning to Catholics. Conservatives worry that the Catholic Church, especially since the Second Vatican Council, is striding resolutely down the path of a rapidly disappearing "mainline" Protestantism. If it continues, they warn, the Church, having lost its distinctiveness—its claim to divine authority—will follow those unhappy humanists into irrelevance. (The supernatural is no longer required to support a vague universal humanism.)

---

1. Vigen Gurion, "Is Christian Ethics Any Longer Possible?" ms. submitted to *Communio* (fall 1990).

The magisterium's efforts to address these issues,[2] the Church's present process of *aggiornamento*, looked at sociologically, can fairly be labeled a serious push for "liberalization," manifesting itself both in an evolution of internal structures and attitudes and in an accelerated "looking outward," aspects of which we shall examine in the next chapters:

1. the hierarchy has been moving toward greater lay participation, which brings internal changes (and new dangers);
2. the Church has been called on to reexamine the role of women;
3. there has been a concerted movement toward other Christians and indeed all persons of good faith;
4. the liturgy has been rendered more "participative" (Catholic liturgies are now more involving, and they are more accessible to non-Catholics than were the Latin Tridentine masses of old);[3] and finally,
5. the Church has been forced to broaden its explicit moral teaching to comment on matters either rarely insisted on in the past (for example, artificial contraception was a lesser concern) or simply unheard of (for instance, nuclear war, all the new possibilities of genetic manipulation, artificial insemination, and so on—the list is long), and to go into more detail than ever before, in order to wrestle with new challenges coming from a radically changed situation, driven by the HTX.

One result: the Church has emerged as a world moral leader in the area of human rights and is calling the world to new directions in social, political, and economic thinking. Two recent social encyclicals, *Centesimos Annus* and *Sollicitudo Rei Socialis*, offer a way forward for a world stunned by the collapse of communism and worried by the increasing anomie of capitalist materialism.[4]

The fathers of the Second Vatican Council (and later the two documents on liberation issued by the Congregation for the Doctrine of the Faith)[5]

2. It did not begin yesterday. When I read back over Pope Leo XIII's pioneering encyclical of one hundred years ago, *Rerum Novarum* ("New Things"), I am astonished at its farsightedness in regard to these questions of freedom.

3. "Latin Tridentine" is a reference to the form given the Mass in the sixteenth century after the great reform Council of Trent, and unchanged until after the Second Vatican Council.

4. Zbigniew Brzezinski, director of the National Security Council under President Carter, expressed his admiration for the world moral leadership of Pope John Paul II and the encyclical *Centesimus Annus* (marking the hundred years since *Rerum Novarum*): "I think it addresses the fundamental issues that are confronting humanity." He says he explores similar issues in his much remarked-upon book, *Out of Control: Global Turmoil on the Eve of the Twenty-First Century* (New York: Scribner, 1993) (interview in *Catholic World Report* [August–September 1993]: 50).

5. As regards the "liberation theology" that so influenced Latin America, one should acknowledge that its authors were addressing a serious social, political, and moral

recuperate in the light of new modern experience a fuller sense of the Christian redemption that has always been at the heart of the Church's life to the extent it is holy. The fathers understood that explaining the Christian message as authentic liberation would have to be accompanied by progress in making the Church institution more effectively a house of freedom and human fulfillment. They viewed the modern discovery of the full self-standing of the responsible individual as a gain, and they understood that the task now is to learn to live in society as individuals more self-aware, more in control of nature, and more deliberately forging of their own destinies than ever before in history.

The Church's new emphasis on "freedom of individual conscience" has troubled conservatives, even though the fathers accompanied it by a stern reminder of the responsibility to form one's conscience rightly. Seeing the liberties with the liturgy taken by some priests, the extremes of the more Marxist-influenced liberation theology, and disobedience of certain Church moral teaching, many conservatives have reacted by redoubling efforts to get the law enforced.

I recall a text of the famous theologian Msgr. Romano Guardini, commenting long before the council on Christ's attack against the Pharisees and their rigid sense of "the Law," that could serve as a warning to those who fear the necessary postconciliar "openness."

> From the moment there are believing souls, knowing the existence of a pure doctrine, and of an authority charged with defending it, the danger of "orthodoxy" arises, that mentality which makes out as though keeping doctrine pure is already salvation and which does violence to the dignity of conscience through love for doctrinal purity. The moment there is a precise rule of salvation, a cult and a discipline, the danger arises of believing that an exact conformism is already holiness in the eyes of God. From the moment there is a hierarchy of functions and powers, of traditions and rights, the danger arises of seeing in the authority and in obedience the Kingdom of God itself. The moment one applies to holy things norms which classify them as good and bad, the danger arises of interfering with God's liberty in the name of those norms and to englobe in laws what comes only from His grace. . . . However noble a thought, the moment it enters into a human heart it provokes contradiction, insincerity and evil. What comes from God is no exception. Discipline in faith and prayer, tradition and custom are certainly good; but they awaken in the human heart and spirit dangerous possibilities. From the moment in the domain of holy truth, a categorie "yes" or "no" is pronounced, from the moment there are objective forms of cult, a discipline and an authority, the danger arises of "the Law" and "the Pharisee," the danger of taking the shell for the kernel, the danger of an opposition between what one thinks and what one says, the danger, in the name of the established and recognized order, of interfering with the liberty of God, in a word the danger of all that of which Christ accuses the Pharisees. That history of The Law is a grand lesson. The Sacred, issued from God, became an

---

situation in old Catholic lands, one of antiquated mercantilist economies (incorrectly termed *savage capitalism* by Church documents) dominated by "the Old Families" who constituted a landed aristocracy somewhat like that which was destroyed in the South after the American Civil War. The Church owed it to the dispossessed to help them move forward.

instrument of sin. From the moment one believes in an explicit revelation, in a rule of conduct descended from heaven, that same possibility awakens. It is good that the faithful (Christian) know this, so that during the Second Covenant, he will be spared what happened to the First.[6]

Sobered by these warnings—to the left of the "fate" of liberal Protestantism, and to the right about the danger of Catholic Pharisaic ideology—let us ask timorously whether the Church's response to the contemporary challenge of liberation is yet adequate. On the other hand, is there the possibility, as some conservatives suggest, that the Church has been swept along by all this modern "activism" to become itself too Pelagian in its teaching, too optimistic about this world,[7] inadvertently, in word and reform, playing down the central religious sense that it is always and everywhere the Father, through Jesus Christ, working all things in grace through us, which alone liberates? Can one reconcile the Balthasarian sense (well grounded biblically) that *Love Alone is the Way of Revelation*[8] (that is, what is revealed in Jesus Christ is simply that God is love, hence all is love, and nothing else matters but the realization of that love) with the Teilhardian sense that this love is effectively at work building the everyday world (that is, the transformation of resistant matter, which is a struggle to realize the Truth in a concrete way, in action, in a transforming, working kind of realization of freedom in social and natural structures)? In this Teilhardian understanding, the whole cosmos is the Body of Christ still being realized, and is offered up for our sins, as Saint Paul tells us in Rom. 8:22: the whole cosmos is groaning in birth to realize its freedom. The struggle to build and consecrate the humankind of the noosphere is that "work of human hands" (Offertory of the Mass) and "gift of the Holy Spirit" molding what God has provided, which is the eucharistic offering itself.

The Church has been the privileged place of reflection and debate on these central divine-human realities since its founding. Now in the last decades it has reemerged, I believe, as mankind's best place of debate about the very nature of human freedom. Once it came to terms with the Enlightenment challenge, this remarkable emergence of the Church as champion of freedom, putting behind it those inadequacies in its conception of truth that could have allowed the Inquisition to exist, has not happened without new strains. Many within the Church, and most without, think its ancient hierarchical structures inappropriate to the new age of self-standing people of all cultures who demand to participate in the institutions that influence their lives.

This helps explain why the council fathers felt pressed to clarify the nature of the Church. Reminding all that it is of supernatural origin and as

6. Romano Guardini, *Le Seigneur* (Paris: Alsatia, 1943), 1:192–93.
7. A criticism some have launched against *Gaudium et Spes*, one for which I have a certain sympathy. I personally find *Centesimus Annus* a more balanced view of the situation.
8. *Love Alone: The Way of Revelation*, ed. Alexander Dru (London: Sheed and Ward), is a little book summing up the heart of his thought.

the supreme witness among men of the divine, it remains a mystery—how impossible to penetrate God's motives or understand His methods! (Rom. 11:33)—that the Church, "open to all" seeks what no merely human social construction could ever hope to achieve: the fullest human development of every man and woman, through their participation in its life. However, as divine it is nevertheless not meant to be a democracy. All its members enjoy, by virtue of baptism, the priesthood of all believers, so all are "laity," all are absolutely equal from the beginning in dignity of being and office, born to a royal priesthood.[9] All are called to special services according to their charism. One among these kinds of service, and only one, is reserved for males: the service of representing the Eternal Priest, Jesus Christ, in the Eucharist. The ordained priesthood, because chosen expressly by Jesus to represent Him symbolically in the complex language of the eucharistic offering, is male, because of the male role of Jesus in the complex divine economy. The Church offers authoritative, indeed prophetic teaching, yet like God Himself, whose Son is among us as the head of the Church, is supposed to respect the liberty of the individual conscience.

In addressing this tangle of issues about freedom I am here going into a number of everyday moral issues, some of them basically economic and political matters. There are several reasons I believe I must here reflect on these worldly matters.

First, I am not appropriating an abstract ideational system, nor just the mystical core of Revelation caught in the highest symbols and the divine teaching authority, but rather a tradition that lives down through time only in actual cultures as incarnated by imperfect human beings. Second, as with all other religious traditions, it is then about the lives of real people, and human beings are essentially social, hence either tribal or political. Third, the Church has more and more launched itself into this arena, especially since Leo XIII's encyclical *Rerum Novarum* (1891), thereby showing, as Balthasar says, that it never shies away from "materiality."[10] Fourth, because the profound moral implications of political and economic questions have become central concerns for most Catholics, such issues are important in an appropriation. And finally, there is the issue signaled by the nuance separating Balthasar from Teilhard that I just mentioned: what does the question of the overwhelming creative love of God have to do with the dirty work of building the City of this world, so muddied by ambiguity and replete with manipulation? The mystery of the relation of nature and grace lurks here. In the introduction to *Theo-logik*, Balthasar insists sound theology has to be founded on sound philosophy, a philosophy of Being sensitive to the all-permeating reality of grace.[11] Without contemplation

9. See Balthasar, "Are There Laymen in the Church?" in *New Elucidations*, trans. Mary Theresilde Skerry (San Francisco: Ignatius Press, 1986), 168–86.

10. Balthasar, *In the Fullness of Faith* (San Francisco: Ignatius Press, 1988), 97f.

11. For an English translation of his introduction, see the excerpt in *Communio* 20:4 (winter 1993): 623–37.

of the unfolding complexities of nature, a theology will be hollow. That includes centrally the need to study the unfolding complexities of human history, including the struggles in our own time to achieve "liberation," which take on a new meaning as mankind discovers the possibility of producing a material plenty that can change the foundations of social existence. Balthasar would agree.[12]

THE IMPULSE TO LIBERALIZATION

What may be accepted in one era as normal social and economic organization—perhaps even considered inevitable—can come to be considered intolerable, through changes in the understanding of the human condition. This truth need not imply moral relativism. It can be that some changes in society help those who come later to understand that what was earlier tolerated has been "objectively" (that is, intrinsically) immoral all along, even if everyone, including the philosophers of earlier ages, failed to see it. Slavery comes to mind. Our forefathers cannot be held *subjectively* responsible for their error, so common it was to the time, eluding even the most morally sensitive. The Christian sees the new appreciation of the intrinsic dignity of man to be a fruit of grace spreading throughout mankind's understanding. Slavery, we have now come to understand, violates human nature. That one of the greatest students of human nature, Aristotle, did not see this impresses Christians with just how needed is the grace of Revelation.

In other instances, it is not a question of something being intrinsically immoral because it is against nature, but rather as new possibilities arise, due to the exercise of human ingenuity, the confining character of old structures becomes no longer necessary, hence intolerable. Failure to exploit legitimate, liberating new possibilities can constitute a sin of sloth, perversity, abuse of power, or simply what ethicists call "culpable ignorance" (a hidden sloth).

We should realize that under earlier circumstances it was not just women who lacked opportunity; all were held to a narrow circle of life except a small powerful elite, patrons of almost all "high culture," the Church being about the only source of high culture from among lower classes. This basic historical perspective is vital if we are to understand the nature of the "liberation" pressures that have suddenly overtaken society, and with it the Church. The basic moral issue of *change in opportunity*, which, after all, has a deeper significance than job equalization, needs to be addressed anew.

Liberalization in the rich countries has not made hierarchy unnecessary. The great banking, industrial, and governmental bureaucracies have grown out of the necessity of managing huge enterprises. Much social charity has been taken over from small Church organizations by huge "social-services"

12. This is clearly stated in *The God Question and Modern Man* (New York: Seabury Press, 1967).

bureaucracies and school systems. Today the more competitive institutions are struggling to achieve "flatter" management structures, and there is talk of shifting social work back more to private agencies. "Participation" and "empowerment" are on everyone's lips. Interestingly, the highly competitive new evangelical churches manifest quite "flat" structures, while the Catholic Church remains resolutely hierarchical, struggling to improve "input from below" and better communication of the teaching that, while arising from the faith of all the saints, comes down formulated from the top. The Church retains its strength "decentralized" at the parish and diocesan level and in new energetic movements, but Rome still strengthens its supervision worldwide, while the effort to improve two-way communications continues. We shall examine the anthropological implications of this in a moment, and at length in the concluding chapter.

Once one begins to grasp the rapidity and radicalness of the socioeconomic change that accelerates in the course of the process of industrialization, it is no surprise that "liberation" concerns come most intensely not in the poorest countries, but in the richest. It is the partly liberated, the relatively rich (although they rarely understand that they are), those with their sights raised who begin to chafe at the bit, resenting their position of subordination in a hierarchical power structure.[13]

Love alone can uplift human relationships above the level of power struggle. Saint Paul, as he faced the quarreling in the young Church, recognized the difficulty of getting love to prevail. Only since the eighteenth century have Western intellectuals first conceived of the issue and believed in the possibility, through social structures providing checks and balances, to hold off realistically, through political means, tendencies in human nature to dominate.[14] Since then, the HTX mind has developed management theories and human-resource concepts. Efforts have been made to develop "open" systems permitting a maximum number of people to exercise their talents fully. Healthy competition "on an even playing field" secured by rules has been sought, and with some success, proving a powerful catalyst for the release of creative energies.[15]

13. They often show concern for those even less fortunate than they in the power structure. But in some, this is self-serving, as resentment may have become a prime mover and power their goal, which is to vent "rage" (the word is today "all the rage") or, worse, to wreck. (After all, the unliberated are sinners, too.) Those seeking redress thus run the danger of creating in turn new abuses and hence fresh resentments; they too in their hurry to improve their lot can run roughshod over distinctions in the old power structure that may still have worth.

14. Montesquieu, Locke, Jefferson, Madison, and de Tocqueville are among the geniuses in this.

15. Open society with constitutional checks and balances has produced a tense society in which the conflict of competing interests keeps life at a fever pitch, but in optimal circumstances it does seem to have reduced outbursts of mass violence. (None of the mature democracies has as yet broken down, or started a major war.) The ruinous ideological regimes sprang up out of the carcasses of the dying imperial states: nazism as an outgrowth of the Hohenzollerns' and Habsburgs' defeat in World War I, Leninism

It is in this explosive setting of the First World's experience of democratic, entrepreneurial, techno-creative living that the present challenges to the hierarchical structure of the Church arise. The first admission the Catholic must make when he begins to reflect on this is that the Church has not escaped all "oppression" from within: office holders, not being themselves perfectly charitable, can abuse the power of their position in the hierarchy. That particularly disagreeable form of churchly "professionalism"—"clericalism"—remains a constant problem, made no better by self-appointed lay pseudoclerks. It would be naive not to believe that, even after reforms, so long as hierarchy exists, there will be mediocrity and imperfect love generating abuses.[16] Recognition of pervasive sinfulness is, however, never an excuse, either for abandoning all hierarchy (then no large institution could function) nor for delaying or softening the push for reform.[17] And mediocrity hiding the sanctity of the supernatural institution, the Church, remains the worst scandal in the world.

For sound reform to take place, we must recall what is essential in the structures. Judgment of that which is essential presupposes a correct grasp of the nature—in this case mystical—of the institution.

THE FORM OF AUTHORITY IN THE CHURCH IN THE PRESENT EPOCH

Since the Protestant revolt, the key issue in reform of Church structure, as we saw, has been the nature of the special divine authority Christ conferred on His Church and the form He intends for its exercise. Protestants and Catholics generally agree on this much about that authority: that it is binding, in its essential core even absolute, and that although indeed divine, it is mediated through human beings. Disagreement is about the form of its exercise, even about the very notion of "office" and "ordination." Protestants and Catholics generally agree that this authority resides in the whole Church, but there is disagreement how the *sensus fidelium* is to be formulated and passed on, and how governing authority and sacramental

---

in Romanov Russia, and fascism in Savoian-Garibaldian Italy. It is doubtful, however, whether open society has created conditions in which it is easier for mankind to respond to the solicitations of divine love. And whether in the long term its flexibility will successfully contain its instabilities remains to be seen.

16. At the same time, it must be recognized that in the most "horizontal" of societies, individuals are found who learn to manipulate the potential power of the group, and turn this ability to selfish advantage.

17. Reform should come by instituting more checks and balances, some of which can perfectly well be compatible with the Church's divine "from-the-top-down" authority (in fact, a surprising number exist: consult the recently revised *Codex Legis Canoniocae*), by intensifying efforts to allow the divine love to show through in the formation of the personnel of the Church, and by vigilantly finding leaders who strive to realize the Church's true potential. God's greatest gifts to His Church are holy priests, bishops, religious (that is, members of religious orders, such as the Cistercians), and exemplary lay saints.

ministry are to be carried out. Recently, with the rise of feminism and an enhanced consciousness of the importance of the laity, the question of who should have access to positions of authority, however defined, has become more burning than ever within the Churches.

The Catholic conviction that the papal and episcopal structure of the Church is willed by Christ gives direction to, and admittedly puts limits on, projects of reform. Thus, those Catholics who are orthodox in their acceptance of a certain dogma about the institutional form are convinced that God Himself does not want the Church to evolve into a Congregationalist body. This is a large claim, so important for grasping the essence of the Catholic tradition, we should seek (as promised earlier) to understand *the theology of love* it is intended to incarnate, and the *anthropology* it implies.

The Church constitutes the principal ongoing prophetic presence of God in history, the central work of His love, transcending history as it glorifies the Father and is with Him, in Christ, forever in the heavenly Kingdom. But that body contains distinctive parts, an infinite dignity inhering in each person, because each is the irreplaceable object of God's love. Yet, in the relationships between those called and given unique gifts, there is a certain hierarchy of service, basically established by Christ. There is an order the heart of which Karl Barth, the Protestant theologian, captures precisely: "Since the Church is a visible continuation of Christ's presence, ordination in the apostolic succession is the appropriate means of entering her official ministry. The office gives authority to the spoken word so that hearers can allow it to judge them, rather than make themselves judges."[18] Barth wondered whether Protestantism had not on this point "diluted the Catholic idea of God's presence."

In Catholic understanding, human freedom is the ability to open ever more fully onto reality (because there *is* a reality that transcends, and does not depend on, human acts, but that we are equipped by our nature to come to know, and need to know to prosper), so human acts depend for their goodness on their respecting that truth. Freedom of conscience is a condition necessary to carry out one's personal responsibility to search for and act on the truth, thereby enhancing one's own being; constructive conscience is correctly informed conscience. "Hear the Word of God and keep it!" Our open revolt against reality works against God's will, made evident to us in His revealed Word and in the structures of nature. The lies we weave in an attempt to justify our unreal behavior make us all the more dependent upon ongoing divine help to be healed of our craziness and to come to know the truth: the Word of God is the indispensable illumination of the essential way, and His grace the indispensable healing balsam. So the question of how the authoritative teaching by which this Word comes to us whole and entire—"catholic"—and how the sacramental system brings that needed healing, how it is humanly, incarnationally dispensed,

18. Karl Barth, "Roman Catholicism," reprinted in his *Theology and Church: Early Theological Writings* (London: SCM, 1962), 313f.

is understood to be, along with our daily bread, the question of sustenance of life.

The children of modernity attack the foundations of this realistic incarnational anthropology from many directions. Once one is convinced that the human intelligence and will is the highest factor operating in an evolving universe,[19] then emphasis is put on our creativity. There is nothing above or beyond it, no word that comes down from on high to direct or to check it if some of our impulses should be misdirected. The correction of meanings can take place only through the play of symbols, and it gets ever less clear in what this self-correction consists. We are encouraged to experiment and let the chips fall where they may. Even the sense that evolving nature will somehow clean out the mistakes is muted. The very notion of "sin" is banished, and sensitivity to the possibility of "perversion" is much diminished.

There is no area of modern experience where the clash of anthropologies can be felt more intensely than in that of "the New Morality," with its preoccupation, if not to say obsession, with issues of sexuality. We shall look into these in the following chapter, after setting the scene here for a better grasp of the conflict over authority. "The teaching of the Church" in these areas of intimate human behavior, in collision with the "Brave New World," is coming to a head in an ever more obvious Kulturkampf.

Because the Christian believes in the transcending reality's loving guidance of our freedom to human fulfillment, he is disposed to receiving direction. (The very thought is horrifying to the classical liberal!) The Book of the Acts of the Apostles shows the chosen apostles at work, acting authoritatively, designating officials, deciding disputed cases, interpreting, if not overriding, the Law as laid down in the Scriptures, even convening at Jerusalem a council to decide the issues separating Jew and Greek within the apostolic Church.

There is a great deal of objectivity claimed by Christians. A flesh-and-blood Christ designated particular men, endowing them with a commanded authority, and they acted, putting into place real intersubjective institutional structures, which endure, and they were involved in the writing of what became canonical works with a particular and great, indeed divine, authority. All this goes against the grain of modern subjectivity.

In developing a Catholic anthropology one should beware not to underemphasize the extent to which these apostles have not been dumb

19. Saint Paul, in the first chapter of Romans, declares that such a distortion cannot be sincere. His position is simple, and follows ineluctably from an experience he calls "faith," the freeing knowledge that dissolves him from the delusions of his sins: since we are made by God, with all creation, we know Him in His creation. What then is with these atheists? They make foolishness with their philosophy because of their sins: they use reason to build fanciful structures to justify their self-imposed blindness. And who are these atheists? Chapter 2 makes it clear: everyone who has ever sinned; that is, all of us! Yes, every Catholic, in the moment he yields to sin, is rejecting and hence in some way, momentarily, partially, denying God.

instruments, but, to the contrary, most responsive, cocreative, coloving instruments, operating in and cocreating Christian cultures. Balthasar puts it this way: never is the artist more himself than when he is seized with the idea he wants to execute. The genuine, dynamic sense of *receptivity* has to be learned all over again by a modern world seemingly incapable of *hearing* anything in the midst of its frantic cries.

Earlier in this work we followed the evolution of episcopal office and the gradual strengthening of the sense of the primacy of the Petrine See. These are subject to further evolution, in interaction with our HTX times. The council, the present holy father, and his spokesman on matters of doctrine, Cardinal Ratzinger, have all made it clear there must be structural response to modern developments, especially the Protestants' development of the participatory model of the Church. Its positive features are gladly acknowledged by the Catholic Church. Let us return for a moment to the strengths of this alternative model, and then reflect on the anthropology it implies.

Every Christian is called to full participation in Christ's Mystical Body, maturing to share responsibility for what becomes of the Body, becoming instruments of His love. It is in that sense that we are all, as Balthasar reminds us, from peasant to pope, "the laity," the broad foundation of the Church.[20] While Catholics and Protestants agree on this, Catholics in considering the passing on of evangelizing activity emphasize more the passing down, through the tradition, from generation to generation, which requires continuity. Protestants emphasize more the directness of Christ's love working "in me," and immediate accessibility to His Word in Holy Scripture. This difference in emphasis, with a distinctive sense of historical time operative in the Catholics' greater emphasis on tradition, more inclined to want to recuperate the riches deposited in the work of the fathers and doctors of the Church, feeds divergence on how to give concrete human expression in ongoing Church life to that headship of Christ in the Mystical Body to which all again agree. In the Congregationalist conception, the whole body elects its spokesman. He or she does not represent or symbolize Christ in any special way, but rather leads the entire congregation in being Christlike, speaking only in the name of all. The central task of this person is to elicit from the body a consensus in matters where the prophetic presence of the Church needs to be seen in a more explicit way. Guidance in dogma and morals comes mainly from Scripture, but as Congregationalists generally recognize, some collective interpretation and witness to the world is required, to which task the Congregational structure is felt to be adequate.

The individual member is less tempted to shift responsibility. He cannot excuse his own inactivity by crying, "The bishop should do something," or excuse his lack of sanctity by insisting the priests should be especially holy. This merit of encouraging assumption of full responsibility and hence

---

20. Balthasar, "Are There Laymen in the Church?" in *New Elucidations.*

maximum participation should be the heart of every democracy. It goes well with what is best in modern views of man, the good bourgeois sense that we must stand on our own feet.

But it is just this that becomes dangerous for the unity of the truth and the cohesion of the church, for behind that individualism is an emphasis on human will as ultimate creative principle, which is in danger of dulling the sense of "the heart" as ultimate receptivity. The Catholic's tendency to voluntarism needs to be tempered by an objective authority with solid roots in the tradition and a profound sense of obedience to God's commands, which can confront us and our egoism. Congregationalist churches remain coherent so long as faith is lively and commitment to God's Word total. When pressures and distractions from the surrounding world mount, then Congregationalists either must group together in what tends to be an exclusivist way, little tolerant of variations in interpretation, like many evangelicals and the rural Anabaptist remnants (such as the Amish) or see their congregations "emulsified" into the surrounding society. When the authority of interpretation of the Word of God lies in the whole community directly, it must become extremely jealous, which tends to breed extreme caution about theological creativity. This is a source of the relative poverty of theological reflection in evangelical churches. The paradox is that the strong authority structure of the Catholic Church permits more experimentation than one finds in the strictest evangelical circles.

Catholics (joined by the Orthodox, the Anglicans, and even many Protestants, such as the Lutherans and the Presbyterians), while agreeing all have received a call, emphasize the distinctiveness of the different gifts and particular calls, bound up with the circumstances, and not our doing, the particular graces of each personality in his situation are vocations from God to various services with special responsibilities for and contributions to the whole body. Catholics insist the headship of Peter and the apostles is one of those calls, passed down through the charism of a continuity of authority. Each of us witnesses in our own way to the continuing presence of Christ. But when occasion arises to state definitively and for the whole people of God the sense of that witness, the responsibility for formulation of such authoritative expression falls to the pope and bishops, however much the way to it may have been prepared by theologians, the reflections and actions of laypeople with particular artistic and spiritual gifts, and the belief and practice of the entire membership of the Church.[21]

21. It is a consolation to the Catholic to be able to draw on the learning and wisdom of the Church, as fruit of erudite persons able to spend most of their lives in study and prayer. The sheer human expertise collected at the Second Vatican Council alone is without parallel in world history. The *Catechism of the Catholic Church* drew on the help of more than five thousand bishops and experts, and the final draft incorporated twenty-five thousand suggestions! Even such a small thing as the functioning of the Papal Academy of Science, to which the most distinguished atheist scientists are pleased to be asked to give their assistance, is a reassuring sign. No Protestant Church can offer anything like that.

Why in the divine redemptive economy may such a structure have been ordained, as Catholics believe it was? Consider the anthropological implications of a strong papacy. As we are incarnate beings, not only has the Source of the cosmos sent His Son, who is its form, into our midst as an objective human being to whom we can relate, but also His Church enjoys a visible head, a particularly striking human representation of Christ's headship. This is a mercy most sensitive to the limited reality of human being.

The alternative would be a "headless" church that would make decisions by consensus of opinion among the bishops.[22] However, the essential point is not to be found in this human "table-of-organization" approach. The vision of the Church is spiritual, and not concerned with economics or politics or administrative convenience. "Peter, feed my sheep!" The responsibility of the whole Church starts there; we are all in service of Peter's mission, which is Christ's mission, preserving the integrity of the faith, without which the sheep cannot be properly fed.[23]

Many Protestants, who dearly love Christ and His Church, continue to believe that "papism" and "sacerdotalism" were the worst developments ever to damage the Church. The Orthodox still look at Rome with utmost suspicion. This mystery of differences in the faith of Christians is a reality that continues to trouble Christ's Church and hampers its representing Him to a vast, secularizing world.

But the bishop of Rome by no means rules alone. He is the head of the college of brother bishops, each of whom also rules either a territory (diocese) or has responsibility for a definite mission,[24] and with the same personal, Christ-given responsibility for the whole Church. As the Church

22. Something like this is the model underlying the loose grouping of "auto-cephalous" Eastern Churches. The ecumenical patriarch, with little real authority, does not exercise much of a central role. So see what has happened: since the great schism, the Orthodox have not managed to hold a single ecumenical council. The separate Churches drift far apart. The present uproar between Moscow and Constantinople is serious. But the Catholic must at the same time hasten to acknowledge joyfully that the Orthodox Churches retain a wonderful unity of doctrine and practice. Indeed, the Vatican Council acknowledges this to be the work of the Holy Spirit. I would add the retention of a strong episcopal order is one of the great gifts of the Holy Spirit to the Eastern Churches.

23. Since the pope, while bishop of Rome, represents, not only Rome but also the Church universal of all times and places, the location of the papacy or nationality of the pope is of no consequence to the idea of the See of Peter. Despite this, there are good reasons for designating the See of Rome as the symbol of united Christianity, and the pope as its particular representative. Avery Dulles suggests the following: the lack of a compelling reason to make a change; Peter's and Paul's ministries in Rome; the internationality of the ministry of the See of Rome, unmatched by any other see or branch of Christianity, with an administration made for that endeavor; its claim (not accepted by all) to have the fullness of the Catholic faith, that is, to ignore no part of Revelation and doctrine; and the recent movement toward recognition in the Lutheran and Anglican Churches of the need for this representative role in the Christian world along with the self-government in which many Protestants and Catholics are involved.

24. "Personal prelature" (see Opus Dei, Chapter 15), or "military vicariate" (chaplaincy), and so on.

at last achieves a factual planetary presence, the flexibility and clarity of the episcopal structure is a source of strength, again even looked at only humanly. Once more, this is however not the point. The local bishop is the unequivocal, objective head of the local community. All that was said about the advantages of a clear center and an authoritative voice in Peter can be repeated on the local level.[25]

The fact that, canonically and in actual practice, the bishop once named is so untouchable would tend humanly to make for a conservative, perhaps even unresponsive, leadership, not as easily swayed by local and passing political interests as an elected leader. Catholic bishops, in my experience, are far less "political" than Protestant ministers, who must continually reflect the congregations who choose them and maintain them in office.

Many conservative North American Catholics lament that their bishops are nevertheless still too influenced by the currents of public sentiment, and that they should be "tougher in maintaining discipline." The human failings of this bishop or that, or of a whole crowd of them in a given society, to exercise the independence of mind that goes with the actual authority of office is an affair of human frailty, of sin, just as is the abuse of a bishop who exercises supernatural authority in a brutish, authoritarian way. When holy bishops allow the light of the Holy Spirit to shine forth from them, and thus are "faces of Christ," listening, lovingly responding, objectively, firmly and discreetly incarnating God's authority for us, the sacramental reality of the Church becomes palpable for those who care to look.

Christ's sovereign choice of authorities for His Church is a clear reminder of our objective position. He chose humble fishermen and a tax collector. As children of God, the bishop and I are equal. We have both been consecrated priest, king, and prophet. As particularly called, ordained apostle, holding the apostolic teaching and consecrating office, the bishop is a channel of God's Word and power in the way that I am too, but also in a way that I am not: I do not possess the fullness of authority and divinely bestowed teaching and consecrating power he possesses. God loves us absolutely, but He does not designate us for the same roles. I owe the bishop obedience. The bishop should listen to me, if I talk sensibly, but my authority in his regard is deontic only, that is, it depends on the quality of my witness.

Is this in any way humiliating? It certainly galls the post-Enlightenment egalitarian to the core. But it is intended to be at least humbling, which is not the same as humiliating. It is a concrete reminder that we are not God.[26]

25. When you consider a modern Church like that of Toronto, with its nearly 2 million Catholics, its 240 parishes, and university, hospitals, social agencies of every kind, seeking to hold together ethnic communities from almost every great nation on earth, the point is not hard to see.

26. The emotion that surges up in me spontaneously when I think about the bishops is not some small-time resentment but gratitude (and relief!) for the burden they agreed to take on in humbly replying to the demanding call God sent to them. All this generosity on my part is somewhat spoiled by a bit of the conservative Catholics' annoyance at certain bishops' overcaution—they can let some pretty intolerable heresy go on for a

An objection is heard from the lay ranks: does the episcopal structure as it stands not guarantee a cleric-dominated Church?[27] Of course it does. Despite all the calls for enhanced lay participation, and an increasingly visible lay role, the Catholic Church remains led by its bishops and priests. But is that a bad thing?

De jure, canonically, the layman enjoys no authority *of office*, and given the lack of any effective "supervision" *(episkopein)* over laymen's carrying out evangelizing duties, beyond the little bit some bishops will exercise over official catechists, this is as it should be. The cleric, on the other hand, should be a Christian who comes forward to religious life and office in response to a special call from God. The bishop exercises care in discerning among vocations. Admitted to ordination are only those who have received theological education (today, fairly extensive education), whose lives have been observed, and who are willing to make special promises of obedience to the bishop. On top of that, more and more in the Roman Church it is being recognized that the priest should be a special witness to Christ by living the religious counsels—poverty, chastity, and obedience—more fully.[28] The

---

long time—and by what I would see as some other bishops trying to be just a little too "with it." But, overall, in the spirit of the ironic Jew who asks God, "Couldn't you choose some other people for a while?" I am relieved he did not choose me for such supreme office in His Church! Those married men and those feminists crying to share the "power" of the bishops seem to me to lack all understanding not only of the Church but also of the simple human realities of what these men face. (If those demanding *power* are truly now called by God, as they claim, the first thing they will do is abandon all talk of "power.") Does it matter much, either to the image of the Church as people of God or to the effectiveness with which it functions, by what machinery bishops are chosen? The way of choosing bishops has changed several times in the long history of the Church. Today the details of how men are chosen for ordination to priesthood and consecration as bishops differ in various parts of the Church, although the ultimate authority of the pope in this matter is universally accepted. (Well, almost. An element of the people of Chur-Zürich, jealous of an old Swiss tradition, are angry that the pope appointed Msgr. Haas bishop when his name was not one of the three the canons had put forward.) Were the pope and bishops to allow it, there is no reason a kind of diocesan synod on the Anglican model could not nominate episcopal candidates, in lieu of the present procedure of widespread, confidential consultation, often with considerable input at critical moments from the pope's representative in the country. These are matters of governance about which one can discuss endlessly.

27. I have had occasion to talk at some length with a retired Anglican primate about the actual workings of the synodal structure. While the archbishop insisted the bishop remains in synod, a majority of one on matters of great importance, synodal democracy (the estates' [that is, clergy and laity] representatives within synod are all elected) appears to me to invite a degree of politicization altogether undesirable in the Church. But that is just one man's opinion. I do recall the comment of a wise old canon, a university professor of theology and active in dialogue with "the Romans": "Coming under the pope's authority might introduce some badly needed discipline into the Anglican Church of Canada."

28. Balthasar, in a long and difficult book on the Christian state of life, points out that while the religious counsels belong first to the lay state of monastic existence, they should be lived in their appropriate form by nonreligious, and in exemplary form by all priests who represent Jesus Christ as they preside at the Eucharist. For the family person

cleric is then especially chosen and prepared and is supposed to live in a way that shows he is meant to be a particular kind of channel of God's grace and authority, official and objective.[29]

The inconsistency between priests' act of generosity in promising themselves in special devotion to Christ and then living in some instances (and in some societies massively) a life of luxury is obvious.[30] Personal insecurity leading to a know-it-all attitude is something found in all walks of life, and is especially strong among "professionals," to the point of meriting an "-ism" of its own. But the contrast with what should be the exquisite public charity of the priest is Pharisaic, and can be the source of intense suffering: a "suffering at the hands of the Church," splendidly brought out by Bernanos, which he links with the supreme suffering of Christ in His loneliness on the cross.[31] These are mysteries that lie at the heart of God's will to bring salvation through a Church of sinners. "Clericalism" is not a monopoly of the ordained. Anyone who has dealt with an officious lay theologian announcing, "You would not understand, as you have no degrees," will know what I mean.

THE ISSUE OF MALE DOMINATION OF THE HIERARCHY

More radical than the Protestant claim that Catholic hierarchical structure leads to demotion of the layperson to "second-class citizen" is the feminist claim that male domination of the hierarchy led not only to women suffering an inferior place in the Church, but even to a distortion in the way the prophetic message of Christ has been transmitted. Some feminists go even further, claiming that the Revelation of God as "Father" is a patriarchal distortion at the Hebrew root of the tradition, obscuring aspects of the

---

"poverty" would not exclude property but would demand "detachment"; chastity, not abstinence from sex with one's wife always, but at certain periods, according to circumstances, and always with all other persons; and obedience, not to a religious superior but to the Church authorities—pope, bishop, and pastor (see *The Christian State of Life*, trans. Mary Frances McCarthy [San Francisco: Ignatius Press, 1983]). The discipline of celibacy for priests is being strengthened at the very moment the secular press is calling for its relaxation. The Church thus gives witness that sex is not the center of human existence.

29. The clergy's remoteness from secular life can be a problem. But clerical striving for more lay participation, and the education of laymen to responsibility in organized apostolic activity, can largely solve that problem. The more intensely laymen and clerics work together day by day, the better their mutual education of one another. Unduly sycophantic and insecure laypeople contribute to the "clericalism" of the priest. Between mature adults, lay and cleric, there need be no intractable obstacle.

30. The same must be said of Christian lay folk, but the same abuse is always more shocking in the priest, because of his charism of office and his better preparation.

31. A major theme in Bernanos's work on Jeanne d'Arc, *Jeanne Relapse et Sainte*. See Balthasar's sympathetic reflection on this in *Bernanos: An Ecclesial Existence*, trans. Erasmo Leiva-Merikakis (San Francisco: Ignatius Press, 1996), 281, and the distinction between suffering for the Church and suffering through the Church, that is, at the hands of the Church.

divine presence. The feminist charge has obliged the Christian community to think searchingly about the "sexual" imagery that plays an important part in Revelation. What emerges is a complex picture, in no way justifying oversimplified charges of "patriarchy," but at the same time, there may have been a tendency on the part of some to interpret the Revelation so as to fuel male preference in practice beyond anything theologically, indeed morally, justifiable.

Throughout the million years of human existence there has been an almost total identification of brute power with maleness. Matriarchal rule is in fact rare, and while found in some cultures, it has existed in no civilization.[32] So there is nothing surprising about the fact that from the beginnings of monotheistic spirituality, the Source has revealed that it exercises infinite power—the unfolding of the universe attests to that— but with solicitude. The God-given image in the Abrahamic tradition that best expresses this combination of absolute power with loving care is not that of warrior (Yahweh, Lord of Hosts) but of Father.[33] Jesus, who alone knows the Father, calls Him, intimately, "Abba," the closest English term being *Papa*.

Anyone who has difficulty with the very concept of a loving father, and who sees in it a "put-down of women," as though the only way loving fatherhood can be advanced is at the expense of motherhood, may well be speaking out of a devastating personal experience with an unloving, abusive human father. I hesitate to be so psychological and personal, but when people are blocked from appreciating elementary experiences, it is usually as the result of a concrete devastating experience they have suffered, for which one should have compassion, but compassion does not require acquiescing to distorted judgment.

But there is a rejoinder that makes a good point: cannot a woman, after all, a mother for instance, also temper power with love? Indeed, would not "mother" be a better image of this love? Could it not be appropriate to think of God sometimes as "our Mother who art in heaven"? Did not the great goddesses of certain traditions show just these "loving, nurturing" qualities we should like to see in the loving Father too?

The Christian tradition teaches that, of course, women are called just as much as men to learn to exercise power with love. For that matter, there is no role so powerful in its lasting effect of molding personalities as that of mother. So, of course, the image of mother can and has been used as well by Revelation to express tender solicitude. The image of God showing toward us a mother's love is in fact quite old in this tradition. God is a mother who would not abandon her child (Isa. 49:21) and hence, too, all the feminine

32. Matricentric rule is also rare, but more common than matriarchy. Other societies have maintained inheritance through the female—as, in a way, Judaism does today with its focus upon the mother of the child—but operated a patriarchy in practice.

33. For example, Ps. 68:5, Prov. 3:12, Isa. 9:16, and Jer. 31:9: "For I have become a Father to Israel."

imagery in Isaiah (29:43, 25:55, 63:8). Great mystics have conceived God in this way. In the twelfth century, the influential mystic Julian of Norwich deliberately developed this kind of maternal imagery of God. Saint Paul speaks of his activity among the Thessalonians as "like a mother feeding and looking after her own children" (1 Thess. 2:8).

Above all there is the role for which was chosen the most perfect and most exalted (and most powerful) of all human beings, save only the Lord Himself: Mary. In giving His mother to us as our Mother, in making her the center of His Church, incarnating the holiness that is the Church, putting her thus at the heart of His own Mystical Body, Christ elevated the maid from Nazareth to the most exalted position occupied by any child of Adam and Eve. Sin came to us through one woman, and salvation from another, so the Church interprets "the great sign" of Revelation: "A great sign appeared in heaven, a woman, adorned with the sun, standing on the moon, and with the twelve stars on her head for a crown. She was pregnant and in labor" (12:1).[34] She brings forth the Son who conquers the dragon. God may have made the first woman from the rib of "the Man," so that they would be inextricably bound to one another, and not merely extrinsically related by sameness of nature; but after that all men who have ever existed, including Jesus Himself, are born of woman. That woman is, of course, symbol of the Church's obedient acceptance of God's loving creative initiative, but she is portrayed not as a passive bystander, but as the one upon the freedom of whose loving *"Fiat!"* the success of God's plan is dependent, and ever after as the human coworker, the medium for realizing God's work.

Moreover, "Holy Mother the Church" is so called because it is the Marian Church. This is intended to invoke just such a feeling of solicitude and forgiving, subordinating power and authority, an image intended to counterbalance whatever may remain harsh in the familiar paternity of God. God, in His humbling Incarnation, dwells with us in the Spirit, who, in the words of the Jesuit poet Gerard Manley Hopkins, "over the bent world broods, with warm breast and ah! bright wings!" He dwells with us incarnate as mother, in Holy Mother the Church. Devotion to Mary, in her role as intercessor through the power bestowed upon her by her divine Son, not only elevates the feminine principle to the highest exaltation, but also does so in a way that reminds us that in and through and with Jesus Christ all mankind has been exalted.

The Old Testament writings reflect the historical situations of the Hebrews, so they are not devoid of passages that show the inferior position in which women were held in that society. Yet, we are shown powerful women and women in key salvational roles even in those harsh times. If the male-female aspects of the imagery in the tradition is singularly complex, so too is the picture of the position of women that emerges from a study of the history of the Church. Something wondrous happened in the male-dominated Church evolving in what was always a male-dominated society

---

34. It was in this form that Saint Bernadette of Lourdes saw the "Immaculata."

commanded by a small elite (in which elite, incidentally, powerful women played not inconsiderable roles): the sense of compassion, tenderness, love, forgiveness, nurturing, and education—qualities one easily thinks of as "feminine"—permeate the Church's thinking and preaching. The males who put the greatest imprint on the central tradition were amply endowed with these feminine qualities. Furthermore, women have had much say, some indirectly, the way Monica speaks to us through Augustine, but others as influential spiritual leaders, like Julian of Norwich, Catherine of Siena, Teresa of Avila, and *"la petite Thérèse,"* that other great Carmelite nun, "the Little Flower of Lisieux," to whom Balthasar devoted a profound book. Great women in the Church—from the female friends of Paul; Helena, the mother of Constantine; Saint Macrina, the brilliant sister of Saint Basil, who pays great homage to her wisdom and intellect in his famous *Dialogue with Macrina;* Clare, Francis of Assisi's closest friend; through to the great Teresas (of Avila, Lisieux, and Calcutta)—have had a molding influence on the tradition.

"Balance," in these matters, is very much in the eye of the perceiver. "Balance" is never perfect in human affairs, and I do not imply that anything approaching perfect fairness as regards male-female relationships has prevailed, anymore than in parent-children, cleric-lay, bishop-priest, pope-bishop relationships, or that they ever will be achieved, in the Church or in society at large. It should by this point no longer be necessary to add that recognizing this imperfection is never an excuse for going along with any given concrete injustice.

Moreover, none of the evidence of these inevitably subjectively experienced tensions provides support for or against any present issue regarding claims of injustice to men or women. One certainly cannot expect to speak adequately to the burning issue of the ordination of women by fishing in the troubled waters of these endlessly varied and complex historical relationships. In any event—and this is the stated position of the hierarchy—the challenge within the Church remains that of achieving relationships that encourage the fullest development of all men and women, and love and harmony between them.

Some argue that such fullness of development cannot be achieved so long as women are excluded from orders. That is one argument being advanced for women's ordination, but there are others. Let us consider them, and then I shall seek to place the issue in as adequate a Christian anthropological and theological context as I can.

One argument put forward is that there is no good reason women should not become priestesses. In the past, women were shut out of positions of authority in many hierarchies because the men could not countenance sharing their power with them. Now that that is changing in all other hierarchies, why not in the Church?

A second argument is the one alluded to already: that women cannot enjoy the benefits of full development as Christians so long as they are excluded from the hierarchy. The response to this second argument offered by opponents of women's ordination suggests at the same time some reason the tradition has until our own time embraced hierarchy. To suggest that women cannot achieve fullness of membership in the Church or cannot properly mature so long as they are not admitted to the priesthood is to imply the same regarding the status of every layperson, male and female, suggesting that no one but priests are full Catholics. (As there is about one priest for every 2,100 Catholics, that would mean the other 2,099 are second-class—patently absurd.) We have seen that this is an elementary theological and anthropological misunderstanding, as though the call to serve at the altar is what fulfills a human being. The host of canonized saints who were laymen is just one evidence that this is not borne out by the witness of history. Sanctity, not ministry in service of the sacraments, is our end. Baptism, which introduces one to the priesthood of all believers, is admission to the fullest possible participation in the Mystical Body of Christ. The sacraments themselves, and, of course, the sacramental ministry, is only a means. When in heaven perfect union with the Father through Christ is attained, even the magnificent gift of the Eucharist will no longer have meaning. The Christian's call is to be a saint, not a priest.

The argument that those who believe themselves called to ordained priesthood cannot be fulfilled until they obtain ordination should, if one is going to be logical, be extended to advocate that the priesthood of all believers be interpreted in the Congregational model; not admission of the women to the hierarchy, but dismantling the hierarchy altogether, for all in justice should enjoy full participation in Christ. Even if some women join the ranks of men called to ordination, the nonordained remain hierarchically "dominated" by clerics, some of whom would then be women, if one thinks in these power terms.

But for others who argue in favor of women's ordination, this is all beside the point. For them, the only real question is vocation: are some women indeed genuinely called to the priesthood? Some are persuaded that they are, and churches within the episcopal-hierarchical Anglican communion have been pressed to recognize such vocations by ordaining women.

But there is a hierarchical principle that answers this with an argument that is circular, so long as one rejects the legitimacy of Christ's giving authority to the apostles and their successors: the genuineness of calls to ordination is ultimately decided by the authority who ordains, to whom that properly divine power of discernment has been given. Even Paul, who of all apostles is the only one to have claimed an exceptional direct call from the Risen Lord, and who was clearly hesitant about submitting to the Church authority—the other apostles and especially Peter and James— nevertheless finally (however reluctantly, and not without at least one recorded grumbling qualification) did so submit. At the heart of the or- thodox tradition's conception of the Church lies the belief that only God, working through the apostles He has already called, discerns the genuine- ness of any prophesy or charism. If and when the pope and bishops in communion with Him decide that certain women are genuinely called to ordination, only then will those calls be recognizable by the whole Church as coming from God.

Is it not conceivable that God may have called some women to the priesthood to move His Church to a more radical rethinking of women's place in it? That is not for me to judge. Perhaps He has moved certain Anglican bishops to be pioneers in this. But that is not the only way of looking at this seriously divisive development. Those firmly opposed to women's ordination, including some bishops within the Anglican communion, see this whole development, on the contrary, as weakening the Church, and hence as merely humanly inspired—or worse. The uproar has renewed doubts in Anglican ranks about the validity of Anglican orders altogether.[35] For the Catholic, only the voice of the bishops in universal council under the pope can ultimately decide an issue that requires such a reversal of the tradition that on this issue has been unequivocal for two thousand years. If they were ever to do it (and I am next to certain they never will), I am confident they will act, unlike those parts of the Anglican communion that have moved unilaterally and with little regard for the unity of the whole Church,[36] in such a way as not to throw yet another obstacle in the way of reunion with the Orthodox.

The issue of women's ordination has been turned inside out for the last thirty years and was becoming a source of bitterness when the pope stepped in, declaring in June 1994 that he has no power to change what Christ decided. Despite some suggesting that despite the firmness of this declaration later popes may reexamine the issue, continuing the discussion openly has become tantamount to publicly dissenting from the papal authority.

The same pope insists that the Church do everything else possible to make sure that women enjoy their full place in the Church. In fact much is being done; the whole Church is moving to strengthen women's roles. A deliberate effort is being made to enhance the participation of women in all

35. Several Anglican and Episcopalian bishops have requested reordination in the Catholic Church, and hundreds of priests in England have requested to come over to Rome.

36. Those who are filled with resentment at what they are convinced is an immense injustice against women tend to exult at the Anglican revolution, seeing it as a long-overdue first step. That will perhaps explain the attitude of the presiding bishop of the Episcopal Church who, as he watched the first woman bishop ever, Mrs. Barbara Harris, place the miter on her head, shouted rather odd "encouragements," like "Go for it, Barbara!" I must admit that as I witnessed the historic scene on television, I felt the movement toward Catholic-Anglican union was being dealt a large setback. Since then the revolt of priests of the Church of England to the decision to ordain women has led to clarification. As Bishop Graham Leonard, retired bishop of London, who has become a Catholic, explains, it is the blow to Church unity caused by such a unilateral reversal of central tradition that calls the sense of responsibility of the Church of England into question (interview in *Catholic World Report* [June 1993]). The three other bishops who are leaving the Church of England said that the issue raised the question of who has the responsibility for such a fundamental change in the tradition, and that could be only the center, Rome.

Church organisms, in every function save only the ordained ministry with its *alter Christus* symbolism.

In civil society, a society not much based in relationships of charity, although it should be, there is validity in the argument "without power, one is not heard." But this kind of argument has no place in the Church, where the only kind of "listening" that is worth having is loving listening, not "you had better hear now, brother, or else!" A husband listens to his wife and a wife her husband in Christian love, not in response to threats. Bishops listen to priests and priests to their bishops, clergy to their laity and laity to their clergy, in loving receptivity. Any other kind of listening is of no value in building the Kingdom of God. (In fact, it does not lead very far in the secular world either, it so happens.) To the extent power rules within the Church, to that extent it is sinfully human and not fulfilling its mission of love and redemption. The recipient of authoritarian abuse may suffer submissively, always conscious of what Christ submitted to because of our sin, and hence straining to hear behind the superior's abusive voice the Word of the God whom he is serving. There is no place in the Church for revolution. That is the "anthropological bottom line" in this whole discussion.

One cannot develop adequately the argument sustaining the tradition without developing fully a theology of the drama of God's interaction with man in the history of redemption, including a thorough examination of the role of each of the key *dramatis personae*. This begins with the revealed inter-Trinitarian relations of the Father, who as Source of all gives all to the Son, who in His obedient receptivity is like a feminine principle, but because He is the Logos of the Father, through whom all that is passed on in Creation is authoritatively given forth, He is revealed as Son, not Daughter; and the Holy Spirit, the creative, governing, and inspiring principle of the world, who is that perfect reciprocal, all-giving and giving-back love of the Father and the Son. It took Balthasar seven volumes of the centerpiece *Theodramatik*, of his seventeen-volume unnamed theological trilogy, to explore the implications of these roles. I despair of summing up here the understanding of the Church as Marian that Balthasar develops there, with the subordinate male role of the Petrine office: it is Mary who is the Church in its perfect holiness, not the bumbling Peter. Yet, she does not demand a part in the apostolic authority, which is a service entirely devoted to achieving that sanctity of which she is the perfect realization. (To get an idea of the depth and beauty of this theology of interpersonal drama, see the two concise and clear essays "Are There Lay People in the Church?" and "Women Priests?" in *New Elucidations*.)[37]

It is insufficient to wade into the discussion over ordaining women agitating something as simple as the issue of the appropriateness of a man to incarnate the symbol: the priest represents, as head of the community, Christ Himself, who in His Incarnation, came into the world as a man, with all that this connotes in the relationship of paternity and filiality, and

---

37. Balthasar, *New Elucidations*, 168–97.

of bridegroom and bride. There are two problems with this. The first we have already considered: there is much more to God's Revelation about the internal life of the Trinity, about the "external economics" of the redemption, about restoration of what Adam and Eve ruined, about our femininity in receiving the Word of God, and so on, than can be dealt with in a few slogans.

The second problem lies in a certain collision of symbolisms. In this age of liberation and of recognition and defense of human rights, the access of women to office has itself become a symbol as well as an effective realization of the equal dignity of all human beings. Hence the tension: that between, on the one hand, the maleness of the Petrine and episcopal—sacerdotal— office, deliberate on Christ's part because of its place in the dense and carefully balanced weave of symbols through which God reveals Himself, and, on the other, the access of women to the highest offices, which puts into action that truth of the equal dignity of all persons.

Catholics can explain that no one has a "right" to ordination and that the refusal to ordain women is no more intended to suggest unworthiness than the maintenance of a celibate clergy suggests that married people are somehow intrinsically inferior. But most of the world will have trouble really believing this. Unjust discrimination against women has been so widespread in the past that many will continue to suspect antifeminism as the motivation behind the refusal of ordination.

To accuse the pope of what is tantamount to letting an "injustice" fester is not only unfair but also implies a primitive misunderstanding of religion. There is in the precise issue of women's ordination no "injustice," that is, no failure to render what is due. God does not owe us anything, least of all selection to particular offices of service in His Church. No person, male or female, has a *right* to ordination, ever.

Many genuinely religious people who desire a change recognize this, of course, and do not argue in terms of rights. They ask, rather, as God gives the great gift of ordination to unworthy human beings, why must this be limited to unworthy men?

This can be answered only by continuing the important struggle to master the rich sense of what has been revealed by God of the ultimate mystery of His Trinitarian life and the relations He has undertaken with His people in this dense weave of symbols, based in that fundamental reality, the distinctiveness of the male and the female. There remains much work to do to develop an adequate theology of the body, making deeper sense of that maleness and femaleness God created, ordaining that the two should become one flesh. (The several volumes of the pope's Wednesday reflections over several years in the early eighties provide a beginning).[38] There is no responsible shortcut here: everyone concerned with the basic

---

38. Pope John Paul II, *Original Unity of Man and Woman: Catechesis on the Book of Genesis* (Boston: St. Paul Editions, 1981); Pope John Paul II, *Theology of Marriage and Celibacy* (Boston: St. Paul Editions, 1983).

anthropological and liturgical-sacramental issues owes it to himself and to the Church to begin to breathe in this atmosphere of God's own self-revelation in the Word and in the teaching of the Church, in a Marian attitude of obedient receptivity.

The Christian should never assume that contemporary man has now at last gotten it all right as regards the best possible male-female relationships. The relentless and no-holds-barred Faustian probing of modern man has revealed much about the human reality we either did not know before or downplayed. At the same time the new dynamics in the HTX have not produced an avalanche of happiness: promiscuity, broken marriages, children raised by one parent or shuffled between two, children dumped in day cares or given over to nannies while daddy and mommy frenetically pursue their careers, unprecedented sterility, dying populations, ghastly sexually transmitted diseases, a raw exploitation of women for male sexual gratification, a promotion of homosexuality, male insecurity, and female hardness. The Church has bowed to feminist pressure by removing "to love, honor and obey" from the marriage formula, despite the clear Scriptural base for it. (Poor Saint Paul is getting treated as a Neanderthal man.) But the family needs a head, for after the most loyal efforts to arrive at decisions jointly, there are some intractable problems where time for discussion runs out and someone has to cut the Gordian knot. Husband and wife can assign areas of ultimate responsibility, but for the ambiguous cases there needs to be an authority *ex officio*. The present pope in his teaching has—astonishingly—obscured this.[39] Each of us has

39. The "serious differences in tone between John Paul and earlier documents on marriage" led the reporter of a student discussion group on "male and female" to wonder "whether he glosses over it in hope that it will be reinterpreted (at the very least), or forgotten, or whether there is no problem integrating the previous documents with his thought. . . . Nowhere does John Paul mention the term 'male primacy.' John Paul makes the case that the author of Ephesians describes familial authority in terms of 'mutual subjection.' He emphasizes that the domination of man over woman is the result of original sin, . . . and goes on to say that the perfection of humanity consists in the mutual 'sincere gift of self,' or 'mutual subjection.' . . . He even goes so far as to contrast the one-sided subjection of the Church to Christ to the mutual subjection of the spouses. . . . Again, in the *Theology of Marriage and Celibacy* he argues that the submission of woman to man signifies the 'experiencing of love' " (study paper, drafted by Teresa Olsen Pierre, unpublished, Toronto, June 1993). An evangelical Protestant, reading this, commented: "This interpretation of Eph 5:21 is wide-spread and I think wrong: that verse serves rather as a 'heading' for the 3 classes of submission to follow: husband-wife, parent-child, master-slave. In the latter two cases it is especially clear (and should be in the first as well) that it is not a matter of mutual submission (in the symmetrical sense), that is, to each other (just look at the verbs used). It is, however, clear that there is submission to God called for in all cases, though with different applications!" (private correspondence, 1993). One Catholic theologian, commenting on this discussion paper, suggested that the pope does not mean to undercut what is clearly established in Scripture—the man is the head of the family—but he wants us to see that any authority exercised lovingly calls for mature adults to work everything out together, to the extent this is possible. Where agreement honestly cannot be reached, as can be the case in unclear matters, especially when time demands a decision be made,

to learn in concrete human situations about obedience and about loving exercise of authority. Humility—another name for realism—demands that we acknowledge there is much we do not understand about our sexual makeup, and about the interaction between the sexes in different societies across thousands of years, and about the dynamics of personality generally, including how authority is to be exercised. In all these relations, sin weaves its mysterious and terrible lines. As Bernanos warns, the psychological is not what is ultimate, either in our relations with God, or in our relations with one another.[40] It is rather the sacramental, it is in the Church's power to forgive sins, amazingly given to it by Christ, that we must seek to plunge into the mystery of forgiveness, fruit of the cross, and without which human existence slips into hell. A Christian anthropology must be a sacramental anthropology, for this is the form of the God-made-man who dwells among us, trans-forming us into His Mystical Body.

DOES THIS AGE OF LIBERTY CALL FOR A NEW STRUCTURE TO THE CHURCH?

Let us now draw a few conclusions about the form of the Church from this discussion of "liberalizing" it.

Where possible, throughout "postmodern" society, hierarchical relationships should be replaced by associations between equals, partnerships should be established, as Pope John Paul eloquently pleads in his encyclical on the nature of work, *Laborem Exercens*,[41] and in his Wednesday lectures on marriage. This is happening: the pope himself emphasizes the mutual devotion of husband and wife, rather than the husband's headship; co-operatives are being created, and a more democratic governing style is being introduced in many kinds of organizations. Even in Catholic religious orders, the governing style is much less authoritarian than it was even thirty years ago.

Still, in many areas of society, hierarchy will remain inevitable. A hard fact: no human, unless beaten down by vicissitudes of life to assume a serflike mentality, or transformed by love to complete humility, can accept subordination to God or human without a trace of resentment. That resentment, when directed against God who is unfailingly just, shows our sinful, destructive pride.[42] When directed against a human, it is most often likely to be a mixed phenomenon: partly justified, as man normally sees

---

ultimate authority has been divinely designated: it resides in the husband. Fortunately, time has not run out on this discussion; the understanding of every kind of authority and of all aspects of male-female relations will certainly continue . . . until the Second Coming!

40. See Balthasar, *Bernanos*, 419–42.

41. See esp. paras. 11, 12, 13.

42. Max Scheler's brilliant phenomenological analysis of resentment as a driving force in everyday life has never been surpassed. The work is titled simply *Resentment*.

things, to the extent we have been victims of injustice,[43] and partly pride, for we are easily envious of superiority, whether of office or of talent, and we bridle when our evil instincts are curbed, however gently and justifiably.

Feminists and most Protestants reading what I have suggested in this chapter may well react by saying, "We have heard much about authority in this discussion and little about the purported central theme of freedom. How do you expect freedom to flourish and human beings to become mature self-responsible adults in an authoritarian system? Cannot our poor Catholic author see that the Church is being overwhelmed by events? The old structures cannot contain the new reality of an age of effective freedom. The Church is losing millions of adherents because, rather like the centralist Soviet state, it cannot respond fast enough to what the times objectively demand." The feminist can even be "triumphant" about this, for it is obviously true, up to a point: the Church has lost millions in the most advanced countries, and therefore it is indeed proving in some way inadequate to its task. In my view, there remains, to be sure, some of that "superfluous scaffolding" of which Cardinal Ratzinger spoke. But on the other hand, impressive innovations in the form of new channels of communications and new movements, new forms of effective *communio*, have been forthcoming, but still they are not enough.

The Christian community as a whole, and the Catholic Church as bravely as any, has been seeking to adapt. While differences between the pre– and post–Vatican II Church should not be exaggerated, as though "pre–Vatican II" means "Dark Ages," there has been an unprecedentedly rapid evolution these last two decades both in the way the Church works interiorly and in the way it relates to the rest of the world. But, as the Church knows itself bound by divine mandate to remain the same in its very essence, this has led to the most sustained effort the Church has ever made in two thousand years to think through what divine Revelation has to tell us about the being of the Church, and how it fits with the actual world of today. That gave birth to the two foundational documents of the Second Vatican Council, *Lumen Gentium* (the Sacred Constitution on the Nature of the Church) and *Gaudium et Spes*, as well as important ancillary statements.

But still the question keeps coming back: are the changes that have been introduced into the Church in recent times radical enough to respond to the actual challenges? This question cannot be answered in sweeping generalities. The only way to begin developing a responsible sense of the adequacy of the Church's response to these revolutionary HTX times is through a detailed overview of the reality of the present Church, in situation. It seemed hubristic to undertake this, but I did not see how this personal appropriation of the tradition could be complete without the

43. Georges Bernanos refused to think in terms of injustice to himself, for ultimately all, including all of life's trials, come from the all-just and loving God. The issue is how I react to pain inflicted by others, if cooperating with God's grace; like Christ Himself suffering the Passion, I shall grow in holiness.

attempt. So with the help of many friends in various parts of the Church, I gathered the materials and sifted through as best I could, striving for some sort of balance. The result is the long concluding chapter of the present work. In closing the present chapter I shall anticipate slightly, borrowing something of the conclusion of the whole study.

In my view, both the demands made upon the Church by our time and her responses are fundamental. The changes that have been made already go far beyond tinkering or cosmetics. *Ab interior,* emphasis has shifted from legalistic observance of pious practices to efforts to make practice a reflection of commitment, of a deepening love of God.[44] A shift has occurred from a rather passive obedience to authority to hearing the Word of God in what the bishop or priest is preaching and responding to it in conscience, with a deepened sense of personal responsibility to act.

This is reflected in the "feel" of day-to-day operations. Authorities are more open to participation than ever before. Parish and diocesan councils have been founded in many places, laymen and laywomen have been added to some of the high commissions of the curia in the Vatican, and synods of bishops have been meeting in Rome every two years, and lately have begun (as yet cautious) association of selected laypeople to their work. The liturgical reforms have increased participation by all the people in the celebrations. Laymen and laywomen have been educated in theology and now hold posts in seminaries, chancery offices, and in the bureaucracy of bishops' conferences. The Catholic universities have become predominantly lay and participatory in their governing structures. There is much more variety and experimentation in liturgy and institutional structures, including secular institutes[45] and to new forms of communities. Migration and ease of travel and communication have reinforced the sense of the Church's effective catholicity. New Catholic publications, like *Communio* and *Concilium, Catholic World Report* and *Inside the Vatican,* but also old ones, like the *Tablet,* the *Register* and diocesan newspapers, have become more international in their perspective and concerns.

Ab exterior, in the Church's relationship to the world, the change has taken the form of a new ecumenism, accompanied by an effort to appreciate and value cultural differences and see the hand of God in the positive and constructive aspects of all religious traditions. Within Christianity, there has been the greatest upsurge of cooperation between the Churches since the Protestant reform. Much bitterness from the past has been put to rest by all sides, who are united in attesting to the exceptional fruits of the Holy Spirit in this period. Since the council, the Church has consolidated the new attitudes. This has had the effect, among other things, of its becoming

44. This, of course, was what was always intended but sometimes was obscured by an overdose of formalistic practice backed by too ready threats of condemnations to hell.

45. Religious orders whose members work in the world, in appearance like laypeople.

far less zealous in reaching out for converts than in even the recent past. In some quarters, internal turmoil has led to sufficient self-doubt to make it hard to present a clear picture to those outside. In many other cases, the effort to learn and love other traditions and distinctive cultures has caused missionary activity to give way in some places to development aid. This has not consoled those with a strong sense of the Church as mission; they tremble to see the message of Jesus Christ as Lord and Savior put under a bushel when it should be proclaimed to every creature, as the "evangelicals" unflinchingly do.

Just that one important example reminds us that no human structure can possibly respond adequately to all the needs for guidance, spiritual succor, and definitive insight into what is happening. Our governments are having tremendous difficulty keeping up with the needs of society. The U.N. Security Council has proved inadequate to the world task the nations thrust upon it. Even the international banks, with their much narrower mandate, have shown an ability to lose contact with reality. Some of the greatest have teetered on the brink of insolvency.

In its humanity, the Church manifests its limits: patent, often shocking inadequacies in every era, starting with apostolic times (apostles arguing, three parties near schism in Corinth, magicians, and so on, which Luke candidly records for all generations, and Paul's epistles echo as well). But in the Church's struggle with and through this broken humanity the believer recognizes the signs of its divinity: the believer is one who is convinced that the Church continues to offer in the midst of ever new temptations to heresy sound guidance in the main lines of life's direction, the fathers and great doctors and mystics—the saints—surge up out of the midst of mediocre priests and sisters and laymen; despite heresies, schisms, and degrading battles at councils, the saints illumine, under the Spirit's guidance, the true Way, and the magisterium stays faithful to Scripture and the saints. In its sacraments and prayer life, one is helped by graces and admitted to intimacy with Christ, and through these to communion with God, beginning with insight into His will that, far from leaving one "in the dark," is usually uncomfortably clear as to what is demanded of us. The "sayings may be hard," but they are clear.

That, many find, is precisely "authoritarian," but no, replies the orthodox believer, that is divine authority, and what is demanded is ennobling, favoring the development of a spiritual, interior life, and it is uplifting for society and for the whole of mankind, because it is of God.[46] As Saint

---

46. One can experience the two poles of the Church's reality in the very act of communion with fellow Christians. There is, on the one hand, ample opportunity to taste the bitterness of our sinfulness: there is no lack of hypocrisy, perfidy, and mediocrity all about in the Church, and easily discoverable in oneself, which discourages through bad example and through a sense of self-defeat. The pride and hurt in us is always on the lookout for scandal, is quick to anger and slow to understand compassionately, and

Anselm said, it is not in sinning we exercise our freedom, rather, we abuse it; we exercise it in embracing the reality of God.[47]

Many of those struggling to follow the Way that is Christ are separated from the Catholic Church, and so are deprived of some of what the Lord offers them, especially the full eucharistic life. But we are one with them in the same Lord, and from both sides there is a Spirit-driven desire to draw closer. Often one finds less hatred separating one from serious Protestants or *serious* atheists than from some practicing Catholics one knows quite well, who leave the impression of extending their confusion about themselves to the Church of Christ itself and their all too human resentment to fellow Catholics who, like them, are struggling to live the Christian life.

This brings us quite naturally to yet another basic issue in the question of "opening up" the Church: the challenge of ecumenism. The question is, of course, much larger than inter-Christian relations, with the attendant issue of appropriate structures for the Christian Church in an ecumenical age. It brings us back to the overriding issue of pursuing wisdom in an ecumenical age, the subject of *Tradition and Authenticity*. For all Christians together are in the process of opening toward our brothers and sisters in Abraham—the Jews and the Muslims—and finally, toward all religious people pursuing different ways toward God, many of them age-old.

Being and Truth discussed the development of a concept of truth adequate to the demands of the present planetary situation. In the following chapter, as we discuss "the New Morality" and draw out more implications for the clash of anthropologies, we shall see just how critical the conflicts can be. Then in Chapter 12 we shall confront the ecumenical truth question directly. In developing a concept of truth adequate to embrace the reality of such conflicts of tradition, we rejoin the spirit of the great Ecumenical Council in responding to the challenge of the times. The question we

---

dams up what should be floods of God's generosity moving through us and toward one another.

But at the same time, in the best Christians with whom one is thrown in communion by virtue of Church membership, including those great saints of old who continue to live with us down through the centuries, continuing to play a vital role in the everyday Church—among other things, they are daily invoked and their intercession requested—one comes to know intimately many "faces of Christ." In a way, contact with one person who is trying to live out the Truth in daily life, showing forth in a thousand small ways the love of Christ, through those corporeal works of mercy Balthasar calls the "center of gravity" of Christian love in action, makes up for and largely effaces the discouragement coming from all the lukewarm, the confused, the self-liars—especially all of that in ourselves!—and gives one courage to open to God's grace in struggling to root out evil in one's own life.

47. *Nec libertas nec pars libertatis est potestas peccandi* (Anselm, *De libertate arbitrii*, Opera, ed. Schmitt, 1.208.11). Augustine says, *Multo quippe liberius erit arbitrium quod omnino non poterit servire peccato* (Enchiridion 105, PL 40:281). In the same spirit, Saint Thomas says, "There is a greater freedom in the angels who cannot sin than in us who can" (*ST,* Iæ 62, 8 *ad* 3). These quotes are in Balthasar, *Theodramatik*, 2:2:183 n. 20. His commentary on Christ's human freedom, while being unable to sin, is most interesting.

have been examining will continue to haunt us. How far can the Church go in recasting structures and in fashioning its expression of essential truths without deforming them to accommodate the often quite different experience of others?

THE "NEW ANTHROPOLOGY"
AND THE "NEW MORALITY"

An area where we can see the inroads modernity has made into the mentality of Catholics, and where the Church's guidance is being most vigorously challenged—even systematically ignored by many Catholics—is the moral sphere. I am not thinking of only the much publicized sexual morality, obsessively harped on by the mass media.[1] I find even more worrisome self-styled "Christians" ignoring Christianity's teaching about ways one should relate to the world fundamentally. Many Catholics have accommodated uncritically to practical atheism, adopting a materialist, consumerist lifestyle while still attending Mass regularly.

One's attitude to any aspect of daily life, including sex, is based in one's response to the all-orienting moral challenges of honesty, starting with honesty toward oneself. Honesty implies a willingness to deal seriously with these questions: Who am I really? What am I supposed to be doing here in this world? What are the problems with my character? How does my body fit into this? Such seriousness (*gravitas*) requires a love for truth. And one's response to the challenge of developing the courage and discipline to abandon hypocrisy and live out in the midst of a hostile world, what one believes, *inevitably* demands sacrifice.

"Sacrifice?" asks in shock a self-indulgent population. "Whatever for?" The Catholic who joins this skeptical chorus has little understood the clash of anthropologies, the Kulturkampf between what Pope John Paul II has termed "a Gospel of life and a culture of death."[2] Because of a mindlessness the Catholic may have settled into, he probably fails to see

1. The obsession with sex of journalists who have embraced "the other anthropology" is partly responsible for this. Typical: during a three-hour review of the Church's teaching for the American bishops in Philadelphia during his first visit, the pope included one line on contraception: "Regarding artificial contraception, I maintain the position of my predecessors." If he had said nothing, it would have been interpreted as a sign of a change of position, that a softening was in the wind. The *Globe and Mail*'s story was headed, "Pope Blasts Birth Control," and the whole review was distorted to reflect the journalist's own obsession.

2. Encyclical letter, *Evangelium Vitae*.

that the two do not mix very well. He has not considered why an anthropology of life demands sacrifice, and that sacrifice is about becoming holy.

The present chapter seeks to highlight this clash of anthropologies, one that knows from Revelation that true life is unending, the other, despairing of any meaning beyond death, looking for gratification now. One anthropology envisions a life that flowers in the resurrection of a glorified body worth sacrificing for; the other, a materialist anthropology, fails to draw out the implications of man's transcending spirituality, depends excessively on what is below man, suffering death as the final end of all. Life then becomes about avoiding death as long as possible. Such a life is not lived out into an ever open future, and so pain can in no way be redemptive. There is nothing lasting to invest in. Redemption becomes an empty concept. There is no past to atone for, because the past too is swallowed up in the nothingness of death. One must struggle within this short existence to make sense out of it in terms of man's own creation of symbol systems, and this within the narrow sphere between birth and final dissolution.

Catholic teachers at all levels need to get a surer grasp on the philosophical implications of the Church's vision to be able to give effective, concrete guidance on how to live *counterculturally* in a world in which distractions make it harder than ever to develop any semblance of an interior life. A death-ridden culture has to be noisy to keep our minds off the ultimate meaninglessness. It inevitably becomes trivial.

The challenge to Christians is not just theoretical. The Church is creating new social and institutional structures to bring Christians, dispersed in the anonymity of the city and suffering from family breakdown, closer to one another, so that they may create new families to realize human life as social life: Christians must instruct, support, and inspire each other to their task of developing the interior life required if they are to evangelize a hostile world and to raise children with good and generous hearts capable of resisting and leading, allowing the Holy Spirit to sanctify them so that they become the eucharistic presence of Christ in this world. That the HTX as yet has no satisfactory name gives some measure of how new and how vast are the processes roaring forward, pulling us in their wake, with no sense of where they are going. In an effort to get an intellectual hold on what is happening, previous popes have composed social encyclicals over the last century; the council fathers worked through fourteen drafts of the pivotal document *Gaudium et Spes: The Church in the Modern World;* the present pope has issued a series of encyclicals with a vast redemptive vision for the end of the millennium, from *Redemptoris Hominis* to *The Gospel of Life;* and synods and bishops' conferences have added their voices in recent decades, discussing the problems of modern economies and modern politics. This, "the Church's social teaching," as it is familiarly called, is a substantial start in understanding how the modern world is to be sanctified. But vast as this corpus has become, it is only a beginning.[3]

When critics come crashing down on one or another aspect of the Church's teaching in the area of sexual morality, they rarely try to understand the thrust and sense of the large vision that underlies this or that aspect.[4] They make no effort to see the Church's position as something positive, preferring to distort it as some kind of repressive "Puritanism,"[5] often as an almost criminal perversity leading to destruction of the planet through overpopulation.[6]

The Church possesses no explicit divine revelation about all the details of sexual conduct, beyond clear biblical condemnation of fornication, adultery, homosexuality, and "coveting others' wives"; there is no revealed blueprint on how to build a just society in the epoch of the HTX. Christ came to reveal a way of redemption, from which moral principles, long reasoned about in many cultures, receive essential new illumination. But He was neither a Kung Fu-tse, a Lao-tse, or a Gautama: He did not teach explicit, detailed ethics for twenty-five years. In His brief public ministry, yes, He hammered home some principles: the revelation of the inviolability of marriage, for instance; the explicit, revealed condemnation of fornication and adultery are as old as the Pentateuch, and are explicitly strengthened by Jesus and by the epistles of His apostles, but Jesus simply tells the woman taken in adultery, "Go and sin no more" (John 8:3). These are not the matters emphasized in the New Testament records. Rather, Jesus attacked at every occasion hypocrisy, making the Pharisees its very symbol. He praised the poor in heart. He bid His followers have courage, trusting in Him, "Be not afraid!" (words chosen by the present pope to begin

3. In building up a picture of the HTX with no less than twenty-four essential dimensions—eighteen "software" and six "hardware" (genera of tools) in dialectic relationships to existing nature, culture, and civilizations—I have become astonished at the complexity and dynamism of the planetary social reality.

4. From the *Toronto Globe and Mail*: "Can nothing be done about Pope John Paul II? Can he not take early retirement? The latest in a string of his retrograde actions has been his resistance to a European Union effort to end discrimination against homosexuals. The pontiff was clearly goaded by the resolution of the European Parliament on Feb. 8 calling for recognition of homosexual families and marriages—or 'registered partnerships . . .' calling for same-sex couples to have the right to adopt children. . . ." (Linda Hossie, March 4, 1994).

5. Linda Hossie contends that the Church's answer to all problems is abstinence!

6. As though Vatican teaching influences the Muslim world, India, or Indonesia— the fastest growing parts of the world! These critics never pause to admit that nobody really has any easy answers to the problems of population and family planning that have recently emerged because of the HTX, where high-tech medicine and agriculture result in population explosion in some parts of the world. They do not emphasize that meantime whole peoples—those with the bulk of the technical and managerial expertise—are dying out as the laboratories churn out chemical abortifacients and hormone manipulators. On the average, each of the First World nations, if current rates of reproduction continue, can expect to see from one-quarter to one-third of its population disappear in each of the coming generations! At present world population growth is flat. We shall discuss this issue, so vital to all of mankind, later.

his first public pronouncement). He preached compassion for the poor. Revelation founds the sense of the dignity and nobility of the person, those "little ones" who are to be united to one another in Christ, and through Him, in the Father; and Revelation has illumined the sacramental, which includes the sacred nature of marriage, elevated to a new status by Christ, a transforming light on the human incarnational situation at the most basic level.

But as we now seek a glimpse into the foundational principles of the Christian anthropology through consideration of how we are our (mortal) bodies, how that life is a gift, and therefore how we are to treat each other respectfully in the light of the end willed by the creating Source, we should be aware at the same time of the accusation that the Christian tradition nurtures as well a dark element, one coming not from God but from man, a Platonic suspicion of the body, which allegedly influences Christian views on sexuality. Some claim that actually imbedded in the New Testament, especially in Paul's letters, is a fear of sex and of the potentially tyrannical family (which is where the sexual life produces the new generations, and where their character is formed, which can become a bastion for settling down in this world for the long haul, dangerous to the Christian sense of absolute dependence on God).

The Church's sexual teaching has changed considerably over time. A recent historical study of Catholic sexual morality shows the strong Stoic input at the beginning, and the changes in emphases, some of them quite startling, over the centuries.[7] Today, in the midst of a tidal wave of self-gratification, new discoveries in biology and in psychology, the Church is seeking to explain a concept of relationships between men and women that would ideally make the family a haven of stability and love with, installed at its core, respect for the great and mysterious gift of our selves, including the body that I am and that is destined to glorious resurrection. Such an elevated belief does not favor maximizing sensual pleasure, which is a means and an expression of good things, but not an end in itself. Countercultural indeed, but the underlying, spiritual Christian anthropology has been countercultural since Roman times.

FOUNDING CATHOLIC MORAL TEACHING IN A BETTER GRASP OF CHRISTIAN ANTHROPOLOGY

A Quixotic Way into the Debates over Sexual Morality: A Christian Defense of Modesty

I am going to propose as a way into the heart of these anthropological matters a route about as popular as preaching obedience and humility. But so long as Christianity is challenging the reigning culture, I might as

---

7. Marcel Bernos, Charles de la Roncière, Jean Guyon, and Philippe Lecrivain, *Le fruit défendu: Les chrétiens et la sexualité de l'antiquité à nos jours* (Paris: Centurion, 1985). The authors are all Catholic historians; each wrote on the period in which he is expert.

well begin with a reflection that gives the feel of the Christian sense of the body as sacred. I shall invoke an experience of *modesty*, a virtue Christians share with many other traditions, but one that is definitely not "in" for the yuppie set.

Fresh from a morning on the beach in Cannes, I undertake the defense of this "Victorian," "Puritanical," "repressive" virtue, for somewhat selfish reasons: as a way of trying to make more explicit for myself underlying convictions that throw light on the basic Christian understanding of human nature. I believe a meditation on modesty can clarify something about the Christian conception of responsible freedom we have been exploring in these chapters, right in the midst of the contemporary (still somewhat restricted) freedom to take off your clothes in public.

The underlying Christian attitude is not "sex is dirty,"[8] but rather a recognition that the sexual drive, a creation of the loving God, is fundamental and hence powerful, and so like all other drives, indeed all forces of nature, all power, needs to be dealt with carefully. Overtones of sex (in the narrow sense of physical attraction) can be found mixed in with many human activities, with all sorts of pleasure seeking, but especially with our drives to power and domination. Sexual attraction is often exercising its magnetism in the midst of our relations of friendship, where it needs to be watched like the proverbial hawk. The drive to possess, even to dominate, and the drive to reproduce are closely related to our greatest need: to be loved and to love; those egocentric drives easily become perversions of the love-need and can destroy love. The ease with which we can fall into painful obsessions and can contribute to breaking up families ought to make any thoughtful person cautious about provoking overt sexual response in inappropriate circumstances.

As these are truisms one wonders why they are so disregarded in the present society. Even if it is a selfish society, even if transcendence is played down, you would think that by now more people would see the disaster of mutual exploitation by "consenting adults." But when pleasure takes a prime position in society, the dignity of the persons used for gratification and the destructiveness of the game of mutual exploitation are obscured.

It is in this dramatic context we must situate Dame Modesty. It is a good virtue to reflect on precisely because it is so affected by context. Holding hands in one situation can be more provocative than seeing a nude body

---

8. In its present teaching the Church has moved far from the Neoplatonic tendency to see the ending of virginity as a kind of defilement. Celibacy, practiced along with poverty and obedience, as a total gift of self to Christ's Church, is still held up as a higher call to witness to sanctity than marriage, but emphasis now in the magisterial documents is put on marriage and parenthood as roads to perfection. Not all the old suspicions of the strong passions of the body are gone, nor, as I shall suggest, should they be. A more developed theology of marriage and the family is evolving. The present pope has blessed with his name the network of theological institutes devoted to reflecting and teaching on marriage and family—the John Paul II Institute for Marriage and Family has branches in Rome, Washington, and many other places.

in another. Obviously, intention, signaled by the manipulation of signs in context, is key (but it is not everything). Hence the relativity governed by context as to the intention of certain conduct *to mean modesty* or not.

Intention is not, however, everything. At the limits, even in this affective and culturally relative order, one approaches a kind of fixed objectivity. It is not always impossible, but it is surely more difficult, for naked people to signal the intention of "modesty": "Please respect my body (nude for justifiable reasons) as the 'temple of the Holy Spirit' rather than as a 'turn-on.' " Physicians, quite accustomed to seeing bodies, take the precaution of keeping patients of the opposite sex covered by sheets maximally when conducting tactile examinations. When certain "liberated" European families run around the house naked, I would think they usually mean to signal a set of attitudes to sexuality probably less cautious than the Christian! When Christian missionaries convince tropical peoples to cover their more sexually stimulating parts, they are deliberately teaching them a new degree of reticence toward their sexuality. Such "inhibitions" are part of a set in a pedagogy about the inviolability of the person, based on the absolute dignity of each, an independence requiring self-restraint on all sides. Such "inhibitions" are read negatively by modernists, who proclaim that they themselves sympathize more with "those natural people": unlike the "puritans," we are "unafraid" of sex; the missionaries are imposing their "hang-ups" on a system of customs that works quite well, if not to say better.

This problem of deliberately changing tropical modesty is more difficult because of the cross-cultural contexts with their different sets of symbols signaling intentions. Missionaries are aware that bare-breasted African women can be pure. But consider this: polygamy often is found in tropical tribal settings, along with a whole range of different sexual attitudes woven into the distinctive culture. Missionaries can, of course, wade into such situations insensitively. It should be noted, however, with what ease the missionaries have been able to convince people in many tropical societies to adopt a more Northern standard of modesty in dress. Why has clothing so often proved attractive? Does it introduce an added degree of distance necessary for founding more social independence than one often finds in certain tribal settings? Even though it may have produced this result in many societies, given the horrible AIDS epidemic in some African countries, one can deduce that this Christianization has not reduced promiscuity enough to prevent a social disaster. And missionaries are still finding it difficult in some African situations to discourage polygamy, which goes directly against a Christian understanding of the dignity of the individual, expressed in the equality of male and female in the founding and governance of a family.

Why One Should Be Cautious about "Passions"

These few thoughts on modesty do nothing to counter the charge that Christians are a bit afraid of sex. I am trying to show why they well ought to be! Christianity, like Judaism before it, has always held sex in respectful awe, but also, I would quickly add, has feared lust for power, acquisitiveness, and indeed every appetite, and all the "capital sins" that "kill the soul." When any of these drives escapes the control of properly informed and loving reason, these passions-become-obsessive do prove destructive of the higher good: they compromise the integrity of the person and the charity of human relations, disordering society.[9] The Christian Church simply reiterates the teachings of most of the great pagan philosophers in this. Thoughtful people—even philosophers—have transmitted to cultivated society their hard experience how easy it is for passions to ruin people's lives. Nietzsche wrote eloquent pages defending genuine purity against the suppressed passions of puritans, and he scorned greed in every form.

This cautious attitude does not so much flow from a dogma about the damage done to our nature by original sin as the other way around: experience with the fragility of human beings, with our propensity for getting stupidly in trouble prepares us to believe there is a difficulty about our basic makeup. A good Creator could not have wanted us to be so perverse. The virtue of modesty exhibits realistic recognition of the need for caution on the part of "fallen man."

In marriage, too, Christians should, of course, seek to foster a cautious attitude toward sex, just as they seek to be cautious about the acquisition of material things or the search for power, or toward addictive substances— an attitude of avoiding excesses that can lead to obsession. The atheist humanist anthropology seems to accept obsession as a difficult fact of life, dangerous and fascinating. Christian anthropology treats it with horror, in Saint Paul's word, as a slavery from which Christ has come to free us. Pope John Paul II became the butt of jokes for once saying that a married man can treat his own wife like a whore. The grotesque insensitivity of the present age was apparent in the media people's inability to see how right he is.

It is not that Christians are under no circumstances to become rich, or never to take pleasure in gourmet foods, or to enjoy sexual relations. But the danger of *"dis-traction"* from the goal God has set for us and the need for discipline to hold open the interior space within which grace can be received are ever at the center of concern. In ancient Platonic-Aristotelian and Stoic philosophic traditions, which influenced the fathers, order to the one end is understood to demand self-control through virtue.[10] Failure to

9. This book is already too long, otherwise I would pause here to offer some evidence for these declarations. The reader who, understandably, may balk at these fatwas can find considerable evidence in *BT*, 226–29, and in *Human Being* (in progress).

10. An up-to-date Christian anthropology can justifiably still use both Aristotle's categories of "faculties"—distinct "faculties" or capability centers in the human makeup (building muscles is one thing, acquiring piano techniques is another, and learning to reason as one does in physics is another)—and their notion, experientially verifiable, of building distinctive good and bad habits (virtues and vices) in these faculties. Neurophysiology has been teaching us much about some of the mechanisms of this. Cf. *BT*, 37, 38, 77, 98, 161, 171, 195–98. *Human Being* explores the virtues.

develop character opens one to the traumas that follow thoughtless, bad decisions. The exercise of character receptive to the inflowing of God's love is the foundation of a dignified human life.

A Contemporary Angle onto the Anthropological Debate: The Church's Attack on the Contraceptive Mentality

Sexual desire, while like most desires self-centered, can be the beginning of a close relationship that may blossom into genuine love, perhaps leading to marriage and the wonder of bringing new humans into the world, and helping educate them to develop their own character. But sex can just as easily sidetrack love: the desire for the other as an object for fulfillment of one's own desire (for example, for control) is the opposite of that unselfish solicitude for the welfare of the other that constitutes the mystery of love: being diffusive of itself, reaching out to help the other grow.[11] Functionalizing another human being is the beginning of all evil.

The present uproar about contraception provides a good way to see this. Married Christians should worry when intercourse gets too far from its reproductive goal, just as getting overconcerned about the gustatorial quality of what we eat can quickly reach unreasonable, *gourmand* extremes, or starting to enjoy pushing people around when one is in a responsible position. Using people is much more serious than abusive use of things.

But the Church does not hesitate to accept the obvious, and indeed celebrates the fact that we use the act of intercourse to express and embody the unstinting gift the couple make to one another in the conjugal relationship. That is a legitimate use of a kind of object for justifiable self-expression. That is a good and beautiful thing, and the pleasure that accompanies (just as pleasure accompanies laying a splendidly prepared meal before one's beloved) is God's gift through nature. But that does not authorize seeking out the "kinkiest" titillations that obscure the loving communication and move far from the basic nature of the act. (After the excesses of a gourmet dinner, and before the Tums kick in, we can lose sight altogether that eating is also about nourishing rather than damaging the body.) To the extent sex is allowed to become a fascination in itself, the sex act ceases to serve as a communication of love because it has slipped into being an end in itself.

From the perspective of such a belief in the dignity of the person it is easy to understand the Church's attack on what Catholics call "the contraceptive mentality," which in our time has taken on HTX dimensions. The use of chemical and mechanical contraceptive devices to avoid having children, uncoupling completely the act of intercourse from reproduction, truncates the man-woman sexual relationship. Far from issuing in the fruitfulness and maturity of family life, sex is perverted into something one plays with, it runs the risk of fostering little worlds of two-headed egoism, and it invites manipulation.

11. For more on this, see *BT*, chapter 7, G.1, "Eros and Benevolentia."

The Church does not condemn birth control. In the much maligned encyclical letter *Humanae Vitae*, Pope Paul VI recognized there are many circumstances in which families are required to limit the number of children. In those cases, the pontiff, acknowledging the good of married couples continuing to express their relationship through the conjugal act, expressed the legitimacy of the use of the means of birth control that nature has made available.[12]

Many have felt that Pope Paul VI got too engaged on the prudential level, taking Church teaching into technical details of family planning and involving the magisterium in arguments about what is "natural" and what is not. Many criticisms have been raised against "natural family planning," even by some who entirely espouse the Church's attitude about "the contraceptive mentality." I do not mean just technical questions about the safety of one or another method, but concerns about just how technical is the mentality needed to carry out a disciplined program of "natural family planning." (Proponents reply, technical, yes, and not to be used to avoid new life where it can prudently be welcomed, but less artificial, less brutal, because making maximum use of the possibilities nature has provided, without interfering violently in the very nature of the act. Choosing the time nature provides is not an interruption or destruction of the very act itself.)

Others have argued that the Church has failed to take seriously enough the gravity of the population explosion. In many countries, all among the poorest, populations are growing at a rate far in excess of the proved ability of economies to produce sufficient surplus to permit adequate social capital investment. It helps Kenya with its 4 percent annual increase in population—the highest in the world—not in the least that there are large tracts of underutilized land in other parts of Africa or that populations are stabilizing in Europe and North America. (Fifty-one countries—40 percent of world population—now have *declining* populations.) Population growth

---

12. "If there are serious motives to space out births, which derive from the physical or psychological conditions of husband and wife, or from external conditions, the Church teaches that it is then licit to take into account the natural rhythms immanent in the generative functions, for the use of marriage in the infecund periods only, and in this way to regulate birth without offending the moral principles which have been recalled earlier" (*Humanae Vitae*, para. 16). At the start of the encyclical, Pope Paul VI acknowledges the demographic pressures, and adds, "working and lodging conditions, as well as increased exigencies in the economic field and in that of education, often make the proper education of an elevated number of children difficult today." He then mentions the changing status of women, and as well an appreciation for the conjugal act as expressive of the love of husband and wife: "A change is also seen both in the manner of considering the person of woman and her place in society, and in the value to be attributed to conjugal love in marriage, and also in the appreciation to be made of the meaning of conjugal acts in relation to that love" (para. 2). While other problems are explained as pressures leading to the sense of a need to control births, none of them offers grounds for destroying the nature of the act by artificial means that alter the act. Cf. also *Gaudium et Spes*, para. 50, 2, where the decision that the parents alone before God must take regarding the number of children is mentioned in a context of consideration of the social situation of the times and the proper education of the children.

rates in excess of 2 percent a year are a disaster for poor countries, a guarantee of remaining in grinding poverty. At the same time the disappearance of the European peoples caused by their contracepting is also a disaster at the opposite end of the scale: the loss of the old Christian cultures is serious for the Church and for the world.

A Colombian intellectual, not an active Catholic, expressed the view to me that the Church's attack on the contraceptive mentality was exactly right for "the North," where all the peoples are dying out, but that adjustments have to be made in the South because the destabilizing effect of 3 percent a year population growth rates (which Colombia had in the 1950s—now it is about 1.5 percent) has proved devastating. In the view of many Christian observers of the scene in underdeveloped countries, while horrors such as abortion and sterilization are evils to be avoided at all costs, artificial birth-control methods, in the face of the reality of rampant *"machismo,"* poor education, conditions making the discipline needed to follow the rhythm or the Billings method of birth control most difficult, has to be tolerated as the lesser evil.

I have consulted a number of persons active in teaching natural-family-planning methods in the poor barrios of Mexico, Guatemala, India, China, and elsewhere, and they contend that the disciplined application of these "natural" methods becomes the occasion of loving cooperation between spouses, and that with proper education, it can be made to work, fostering a stronger bond. One of India's best-known experts on natural family planning tells me that success rates vary widely in different milieus. She has been trying to identify the sociological conditions under which it works best.[13] It is significant that the Family Council of the Municipality of Shanghai has adopted the Billings method as the preferred form of birth control.[14]

The popes, and most bishops even in the South, continue to oppose vigorously all artificial birth control. From many papal and episcopal statements it seems clear that they consider rampant population growth to be more an effect than a cause of poverty, and that efforts should be made to stop the

13. Verbal communication from Dr. K. Dorairaj, Executive Director, Natural Family Planning Association of India.

14. In one Latin American country I was told (although I have not been able to verify this) the hierarchy has agreed to tacitly tolerate artificial birth-control programs but neither abortion nor sterilization, while the Communists, favoring destabilization, opposed birth-control programs. This alleged grudging acceptance by the hierarchy does not, presumably, imply an ecclesiastical pragmatism, but perhaps reluctant acceptance of a lesser evil. But that is just speculation. The program, along with social progress generally and urbanization, has resulted in a reported drop in population growth rates in Colombia from more than 3 percent in the 1950s to, supposedly, under 2 percent now. No one is really sure of the figures either. A recent census of greater Bogotá turned up approximately 1 million fewer people than was generally expected: 5.5 million rather than 6.5 million. No satisfactory explanation of this surprising phenomenon has been forthcoming. But the very imprecision gives an idea of the chaos one faces in many poorer countries.

social and political evils leading to poor development rather than resorting to evil means to stem population growth. If their assumption is that with increased and better distribution of wealth, birthrates drop because people are less dependent on progeny for their old age and thus control themselves, I would agree. But if they mean to imply that this is done without massive recourse to artificial birth control, the evidence—however much one may regret it—points the other way. The experience in the North suggests, rather, that people succumb more to the contraceptive mentality and to the use of artificial means of birth control as they become more urban, wealthier, and begin limiting their families.

There is a popular misunderstanding, cultivated by the mass media of misinformation, that the "ban on contraception" is some sort of "Church law": an arbitrary decision of the hierarchy, as though the Church ever acts capriciously in grave matters of moral or dogmatic teaching. In fact, the position is squarely founded on Catholic moral philosophy. It is argued that artificial birth control is in all circumstances intrinsically evil because, by a positive act of intervention these chemical and mechanical means frustrate the primary end of the sex act, separating out the secondary end.[15] The act is thus degraded, and that is always wrong. Were one to eat for pleasure some "food" deliberately chosen because it has no nutritive value, or eat and then deliberately vomit, as bulimics do, this would be a degradation of eating as such. So long as this sense of the need always to respect the primary end of an act remains a moral conviction—and I see no way around the principle—how can the Church reasonably act otherwise than to teach this? Just keeping mum, as the Colombian hierarchy allegedly did at one point, implying grudging acceptance of the lesser-evil argument, is an unsatisfactory response.

The philosophical argument will rage on.[16] There are Catholic theologians, orthodox in all matters of dogma, who remain unconvinced that the

15. It is often asked how one distinguishes the primary from the secondary end in this case. Clearly, in the kind of mammal we are it is only through copulation new life comes to be: clearly that is what the drive is there for, to entice men to reproduce. Now we can and do use this capability, and many others, to symbolize how we feel about another. Making a fist is basically a useful way of pounding on something, but it can also be used as a symbol to warn someone. The principle that no human (that is, voluntary) act should be undertaken without love does not mean that artificially destroying the basic natural end in order to use copulation only as a symbol (and a gratification) is justified, any more than signaling unhappiness by eating minimally and then vomiting is justified.

16. The argument here *is* philosophical. It does not require Revelation to see that perverting acts by turning them away from their primary end is, as a distortion of reality, evil. And, it is rather technical, all of this discussion about first and second ends of acts, and "consequentialism," with debate over the morality of choosing the lesser evil. The poor little old layperson is left a bit high and dry. Imagine the case of a tired-out woman with seven children and a sexually active husband who has no intention of abstaining, and who does not trust the Billings method to be safe enough, or simply refuses to acquire the necessary discipline: is she in mortal sin by giving in to his insistence that they use some form of artificial contraception that she may well abhor? These are the kinds of pastoral problems confessors are faced with.

blanket condemnation of artificial birth control as evil in all circumstances is justified.[17] Some argue as follows: Normally, the sex act should be an expression of conjugal love between spouses, open to procreation. When, however, it is morally required to avoid conception, because of the number of children or for health reasons, then birth control is allowed, for under those circumstances it is licit to use the sex act to express conjugal commitment, and the enjoyment of the act is something natural and good. The use of something like the Billings method is less intrusive, but it could result, for many women, in the need to avoid the act at the moment when it is most pleasurable and natural for her, at the moment of fertility. The question of the relative efficacy of the different methods is a technical, medical question, presently much disputed. The basic moral issue is that of the acceptability of contraception as such, whether by measuring fertility and avoiding the act during fertility, or some other more interruptive or chemical means.

As more experience is gained with interruptive or chemical (anti-implantation) means of contraception, it appears that couples who give in to them tend to be letting themselves be taken over by a "contraceptive mentality," which can include both decisions to have tiny families, or no children at all when they could well afford to, and to become less aware that each sex act has a sacred dimension. The "spontaneity" without need for discipline (a "spontaneity" purchased at the price of ingesting hormones, surgical intervention, and installation of unpleasant and even sometimes dangerous mechanical devices) contributes to a social atmosphere of sexual libertinism that is bearing the fruits we now see. It is more difficult for parents to insist on their teenage children's chastity when they themselves have reduced the sex in their bedroom to something without reference to reproduction.[18]

17. For instance, Michael Novak, *Confessions of a Catholic* (San Francisco: Harper and Row, 1983). Novak offers an excellent discussion of the right and proper mode of dissent within the Church, an issue raised below. Interestingly, after dissenting on the blanket condemnation of artificial contraception by the 1968 encyclical *Humanae Vitae*, and after reiterating his stand in the book just mentioned in 1983, Novak has recently changed his mind, becoming convinced, in the light of further experience and the ravages of the "contraceptive mentality" on society that the profound intuition at the base of Pope Paul VI's teaching is correct. (This last in an article he published in *Crisis* in 1989.)

18. The more natural methods are praised by their advocates for encouraging a great deal of loving cooperation between father and mother, both of whom need to be involved in the method. Three problems: it is the mother who, as usual, assumes the greatest sacrifice, for it is she who must give up intercourse at the period nature most wants it. And, claim some observers not unsympathetic to the project, advocates often seem to become rather obsessed with the subject, as keeping on top of the situation does become a constant routine. Finally, I have known two women (hardly an adequate sociological survey) who while devoted to earlier, less reliable versions of natural family planning, managed to have, respectively, seven and nine children, and then turned rather bitterly feminist. The HTX has so altered the situation of mankind: HTX medicine vastly improving the survival rate of children, HTX society encouraging late marriages, HTX economic attitudes encouraging the sacrifice of children to higher material standards, HTX birth-control methods bringing their own complications, and

How Authoritative Is the Church's Teaching in Such Issues?

No matter how trying, even in some situations tragic, the complexities of reproductive issues can be for couples, the birth-control question should not be blown out of proportion as though it is somehow the center of the Church's moral teaching. I have taken this much time with it not only because of its serious pragmatic consequences for married couples, but also because it brings out the sense of a Catholic anthropology, illustrating the Christian call for willingness to sacrifice goods to higher ends. Everyone, of course, daily makes sacrifices: the yuppie sweating through a workout may not feel like doing it this day, but, disciplined, he sacrifices his present desire to sit and read the paper to the greater good of keeping up his health. Because the Christian is so strongly focused on our one end, all other goals in life being ordered to it, and because he is so motivated by the love streaming through him from that end who is also Source of all life, he is willing to sacrifice everything—even the present life—for the sake of this love. Put this way, and when you think of the sacrifice of family life itself made by members of religious orders and priests, you might think that sacrificing the ability to have intercourse at times would be unproblematic. But back to the ambiguities of everyday life: both parents (like every monk and nun) are sinners, and their particular weaknesses of character have a wonderful way of grating on one another. Consider, for instance, the common situation of one of the partners being unwilling to accept the discipline the other believes they should embrace.

The resulting pastoral concerns have raised more intensely than in any other area of Church teaching the issue of the status of papal and episcopal authority when teaching on the prudential level, with its inevitable heavy "philosophical" input . . . Revelation provides no ready blueprints.

According to some, the contraception issue falls into the category of infallible teaching on a matter of morals. If that were so, there would be for orthodox Catholics no need for further discussion about the degree of authority.

Rome has never advanced such a thesis. Most theologians do not believe that the teaching on contraception is intended to be put forward as infallible. My understanding of mainstream orthodox consensus on the point is this: No pope has engaged the infallible teaching authority of the Church, guaranteed by the Spirit, for the moral teaching that artificial methods of birth control are evil.[19] However, as this has been the consistent teaching

---

so on. Every honest person must acknowledge that each married couple struggles in juggling all the resultant issues.

19. Pope Paul VI in introducing *Humanae Vitae* simply states that Christ "constituted His apostles guardians and authentic interpreters of all moral law, not only, that is, of the law of the Gospel, but also of the natural law" (para. 4). He also mentions that the special advisory commission convoked by John XXIII and continued by him to help in the preparation of this teaching split on some questions. (It is well known that a majority favored avoiding an outright condemnation of artificial birth control.) "The conclusions at which the commission arrived could not, nevertheless, be considered

of all recent popes and most bishops, Catholics are bound in prudence and loyalty to obey the teaching. A couple of bishops conferences at the time of the promulgation of *Humanae Vitae* issued statements that were widely interpreted as opening the door to the possibility of "prudent dissent" on the birth-control issue. One of these (the Austrian Conference) has subsequently clarified its position, leaving no place for such dissent, while the other rather notorious statement (the Canadian) has never been redressed.

But this way of considering the matter is itself deficient in Christian charity. The Catholic who loves the Church as God incarnate working to uplift sinful mankind will be eager to hear the Church's teaching in every sector of life, no matter how difficult our present circumstances in this world may make its active reception. He will view with compassion the difficulties everyone, from pope to a couple of young people just starting their family, has in formulating and applying every manner to divinely illumined truth to ambiguous, sinful situations.

HUMAN NATURE AS TRUTH SEEKING

The Virtues Necessary for Pursuing Truth

The recent encyclical *Veritatis Splendor* is a warning about letting rationalizing weaken our sense of absolute moral truth. "Renunciation of the world," as a kind of running away from the effort to deal with the world, is rejected by the pope. We are neither to flee it nor "rationalize" about it. We are called not just "to deal with it" but to carry out Christ's call to sanctify it, right in the workplace.

In a Church struggling to help us come to grips with the difficult issues of the day, there is latitude for the individual's prudential judgment, without which our finite freedom could not be exercised, and the body of Christians, like the child Jesus returning to Nazareth to be submissive to His parents, would not "grow in wisdom, age and grace before God and man" (Luke 2:51–52). As one approaches the prudential level of concrete decision making, debates are fed by differences of temperament, motivating distinctive spiritualities, by different experiences in life, and attitudes about just how the Christian is to come to terms with living in this new, only partially tested, world of the HTX. Just how deep the differences run, how close they cut to first principle, is not always clear.

---

by us definitive, nor dispense us from a personal examination of this serious question, and this also because, within the commission itself, no full concordance of judgments, concerning the moral norms had been reached, and above all because certain criteria of solutions had emerged which departed from the moral teaching on marriage proposed with constant firmness by the teaching authority of the Church" (para. 6). As a friend of mine commented, "When I retain advisors, that does not remove me from my responsibility, having carefully considered their advice, to make a decision." As the pope put it, "Having attentively sifted the documentation laid before us, after mature reflection and assiduous prayers, we now intend, by virtue of the mandate entrusted to us by Christ, to give our reply to these questions" (ibid.).

Even wanting to find the truth is a grace and so is being able to face up to the challenges with which reality confronts us. The Scripture—through prophets, angels, and the Lord Himself—repeats seventy-seven times the call "Be not afraid!" and seventeen times "Be not anxious!"[20] In the Mass we pray, just before communion, "Save us from all anxiety."

The "truth seeker" is not merely a passive receiver of data, but a respondent and cocreator of what then subsequently is given, a reality partly shaped by man, and so our attitudes are vital. Of course, the truth is shaped on a basis of nature, with nature quite able to exact a toll if, for whatever psychological reason, we ignore her structures. *Honesty* is as important in pursuing creative goals, in respecting the integrity of an emerging work of art or of institutional reform, as in scrupulous empirical observation of phenomena of nature in a scientific experiment.[21]

The ground condition for even making an issue of such honesty is what Christ, in the Sermon on the Mount, called "purity of heart" (Matt. 5:8), echoing Ps. 24:3–4:

> Who may go to the mountain of the Lord?
> Who may stand in his holy place?
> One who has clean hands and a pure heart,
> who has not set his mind on what is false
> or sworn deceitfully.

We are told by Saint Paul upon what the carrying out of the divine-human life of our personhood depends.[22] Catholic philosophy will later call these "habits" the qualities of the pure heart. They are three, all unheard of before this revelation, but now become pillars of Western and Eastern Christian thinking: *faith, hope, and charity* (1 Cor. 13:13).

A Christian anthropology and, based on it, a Christian morality cannot be understood without contemplative penetration into the life of the soul understood as faith, hope, and charity. The last, charity, is, as Saint Thomas said, the very "form" of all the virtues, the condition for the possibility of all good character, hence the key to the essence of man made in the image of that God who is love, the hinge of all efforts to attain truth. That is why, at the end of this volume, when we sum up what it is to be a Christian, consolidating our modest discoveries of the outlines of a Christian anthropology, we shall finish with a meditation on these three aspects of the supernatural life of the soul.

Institutional Support for the One Seeking Social Truth

In all the moral issues we have been considering, the role of Church as community is evident. It is urgent for the Church to provide institutional

---

20. Christof Gaspari, "Füchtet euch nicht!" *Vision 2000*, no. 3 (1996): 4.

21. The epistemology and ontology of *BT* has been worked out in an effort to clarify the dialectical, moral conditions in which such honesty can be exercised.

22. The theology of this personhood is extensively and profoundly developed in Balthasar's *Theodramatik*, "Die Personen in Christus," esp. 2:2:185ff.

support for the kind of "lifestyle" that is compatible with the principles of Christian teaching, that is, institutional forms founded in, and animated by, faith, hope, and charity, able to survive in the midst of the HTX revolution.

No society has ever left individuals so much to "hack it all on their own" as the present HTX. In one respect, this is a sign of maturity: the first society in which the majority of individuals are not "surviving at the (economic) margins" is able to afford the luxury of much experimentation and of probing by individual initiative.

The individual and the family need institutional support, however, to encourage the self-discipline necessary for prayer, contemplation, and serious study—all that is involved in the cultivation of the interior life. Young people must be brought into contact with potential marriage partners who share their faith, and they need help, where families are absent, in raising their children. Religious congregations, "secular institutes,"[23] and the priestly life provide considerable structure for those who make that all-out commitment to the religious way of life. But those pursuing the equally challenging vocation of marriage require formation and encouragement far beyond what they presently receive.

New movements like Communione e Liberazione, the charismatic communities, and Opus Dei have understood that need and are trying to supply it through community.[24] Something of the thoroughness of formation undertaken by such organizations should characterize the atmosphere and programs of all Catholic schools. Every parish should have organizations that assemble Catholics who are serious about cultivating their spiritual lives: prayer groups, family spiritual-formation groups, Bible- and doctrine-study groups, and so on. It is through the pursuit of the spiritual life in supportive community (family being the most basic) that the moral formation occurs.[25]

To the natural understanding of the fact that our personalities are formed through intersubjective interaction comes the supernatural revelation that we are meant by the Creator to fulfill ourselves, as His image, in interpersonal loving intimacy. Basically, that is the first and last word of this anthropology, illumined by the *Gospel of Life*.

23. A new form of religious life in which the members, while taking the vows of poverty, chastity, and obedience, continue to work in the world at regular jobs and professions.

24. These and other movements are described in Chapter 15.

25. On the family as an effective Christian community, T. Langan, "Bolstering the Domestic Church," *Communio* 9:2 (summer 1982), 100–109.

THE CHURCH'S OPENNESS
TO OTHER "WAYS"

The Challenge and Perils of Ecumenism

The last chapter ended on a note of "togetherness." "As the Father and I are one, so you are to be one" is the message of Saint John's gospel. Enter, the ecumenical challenge.

No serious Christian doubts that movement toward Christian unity and eventually the union of all mankind in one family of belief is God's will. "There will be but one flock and one shepherd" (John 10:10) prophesied he who was no mere prophet. But the commission with which Christians are sent into the world by Christ, "the Supreme Apostle" (Heb. 3:1), precludes any easy "New Age"–style syncretism—no Catholicism based on an ill-conceived liberal humanism will do: "Full authority in heaven and on earth has been committed to me. Go forth, therefore, and make of all nations my disciples; baptize them in the name of the Father and of the Son and of the Holy Spirit, and teach them to observe all the commands I gave you. And know that I am with you always; yes, to the end of time" (Matt. 28:18–20). "All authority . . . baptize . . . make disciples . . . teach to observe *all commands*. . . .": All very illiberal! Along with the commission that ends Saint Matthew's gospel, we find Christ adding, in Saint John's version, after declaring that He is the (sole and unique) gate to the sheepfold and the good shepherd, "And there are other sheep who are not of this fold, and these I have to lead as well. [Then the prophesy:] They too will listen to my voice, and there will be but one flock and one shepherd" (John 10:16). Again, at the last supper Jesus prays, "Father, that they be one!" (John 17:21). Those texts sound the opposite of a note of wishy-washy "pluralism." The Truth is one, and it is the key to life; there is one Way, and that is Jesus; there is but one genuine life, *communio* in Christ.

Accepting then that Christians are called to evangelize, I want to consider in this chapter the challenge of evangelizing in the new HTX era, which is one of vastly heightened self-consciousness in the midst of a strong feeling for the pluralism of traditions and cultures. In a time of growing appreciation for this distinctiveness of "the nations" and the multiplicity of ways to God (the traditions), what does the Church's conception of itself as the *communio* of all mankind tell us about the proper, nonsyncretistic Catholic ways of ecumenism?[1]

As the world advances toward a secular HTX *oecumene,* with old cultures and whole civilizations tending, through the travails of often bloody struggle, to be washed out in a new homogenization, and as the Church finds itself advancing (now with help from the HTX) toward a true world presence, how should the Church of Christ open out toward those who are "not of the fold"? What kind of "kingdom" does this revelation and this social anthropology call for, here on earth while awaiting the Parousia, when Christ will install the definitive Kingdom, and how are we in the Church to work with the Holy Spirit concretely to realize it? Are we, in responding to the call for one humanity centered in Christ, in danger of indulging in planetary-dreaming utopia? Are we serious about being instruments of the Holy Spirit actually converting what Teilhard de Chardin warned could become "the great Molloch," an HTX-collectivized mankind?

While the HTX is still a fairly loose weave of planetary-scale institutions and has no sharply focused center (the mother civilization is European American, and it is emulsifying the cultures nourishing that civilization as well), it has already a formidable power of cultural deformation: "The HTX eats cultures for lunch and civilizations for dinner!" as one wag in my HTX research group put it.

As I show in *HTX: Learning to Survive in Virtual Reality,* if it is true that much of what we call "contemporary cultures" are in fact social phenomena of a new kind, in some respects inimical to what has previously been understood to be "culture," the question then confronts us: does not Christianity need to be rooted in cultures, and through them in nature? If so, can old Christian cultures be revitalized, or are we confronted with the task of cooperating in the formation of quite new forms of Christian culture? Can the preparation in this world for Christ's Kingdom advance without moving down from the planetary weave of "the Web" to the heart of the individual and the nuclear family, through whatever replaces tribe, class, nation? Can "movements" produce their own social reality with something of the good one could earlier expect out of high cultures? What role could a proper ecumenism—cross-cultural and cross-civilizational— play in cultural revitalization?

A range of positions is conceivable as one strives to imagine the unification of mankind, moving on a spectrum from "minimal engagement" in a worldwide internet, disincarnate social interaction (I balk at calling that kind of social interaction a culture), to a maximum institutional

---

1. On the notion of the Church as *communio,* see the never surpassed reflection with which Balthasar launched an initiative to work toward that communion, "Communio— A Program," *International Theological Review: Communio* 1:1 (1973): 3–11.

unification, culminating in a huge worldwide government. Elements of this idea are emerging in various planetary-scale regulatory agencies, and could mold people in new ways. How would a world Church function in each case?

What I shall term *Christian Minimalists,* while acknowledging the social interdependence of men, would consider unrealistic any project of unifying humanity beyond a superficial exchange of technical information and goods; they believe that nothing more is possible than some kind of basic arrangement among nations that, accepting cultural differences as irreducible, simply strives to keep the peace. Meanwhile, within differing traditions individuals may pursue a "deeper" life according to distinctive visions of human nature. "Ecumenism" would be reduced in that case to polite discussions with neighbors, avoiding hard differences, in the interest of keeping the peace. Catholics who adopt this position would then seek to hold intact within a Church—many of whose bishops are seen as less than perfectly orthodox—small Christian communities to which those individuals moved by God's grace would be most welcome, but without any realistic expectations that nominal (and, worse, dissident) Catholics would by this means gradually come together.

The minimalists despair of serious ecumenical dialogue even with fellow Catholics of different theological tendencies, not to speak of "the unfaithful." The *"maximalists"* strike the minimalists as naive. They are indeed radical. Observing the constant warring not just between nations but between individuals, within families, within (even the best) Christian communities, between races and groups of all kinds (including the Christian sects), the maximalist in fact believes nothing short of personal conversion will do: hearts must be changed. But their Christian hope leads them also to believe, because such personal conversion makes one an instrument in God's plan of redemption of all mankind, that everything is possible to God, even the building of a worldwide people. We are called to cooperate with the Holy Spirit to work for lasting peace—we all agree on that—but peace will be attained only in full *communio* in Christ. In the interim one can enjoy local stretches of what is really a cease-fire. This work of conversion must go on urgently ("Now is the acceptable hour!") at every level, within this world, here and now, even though its ultimate accomplishment, and hence true and lasting peace, will be achieved only at the Parousia.

The need for salvation and the cardinal role of the Church in it is not a question of Church as concept nor as something that acts only on the innermost recesses of the soul, but is rather a reality of the Church as people of God, a planetary-scale institution working for "the salvation of the world" in ways that affect what goes on in the world: an objective existential, social, institutional, history-changing actuality concretely molding human existence. Here are the words of the council: "The Church, or, in other words, the Kingdom of Christ now present in mystery, *grows visibly in the world* through the *power* of God."[2]

Armed with its mission of unity and peace, the Church now understands well that it must have no intention of imposing truth on anyone, for that goes against its revelation of living truth as a love relationship. Respect for the variety of ways in which people seek the truth and for the multiplicity of cultures has to be the starting point of evangelization, a respect the Church has had to learn over time. What is distorted in every individual and every culture must be purified, for every error and, worse, every sin, breeds disorder. But today the Church accentuates the positive. All, insofar as they seek the truth and strive to live up to what they have discovered of it, are recipients of God's grace, and, therefore, the Holy Spirit operates "beyond the frontiers of Christ's Mystical Body."[3] How clear this is in the first encyclical of Pope John Paul II, *Redemptor Hominis,* his "inaugural lecture," as he called it: "Does it not happen sometimes that the firmness of belief of members of non-Christian religions—also an effect of the Spirit of Truth operating beyond the frontiers of the Mystical Body—ought to put to shame Christians, so often given to doubting truths revealed by God and announced by the Church, so inclined to relax the principles of morality and to open the doors to a permissive morality."[4]

But how can the Church hold there is one Truth, one Way to that truth, one life, yet be "liberal" in its respect for "other ways"? Why does it continue to evangelize?

Everyone who has loved any truth desires to share that knowledge with everyone. Sharing Jesus Christ encountered as living truth is the Christian's joy and his most sacred responsibility, and so he *should* work tirelessly to offer this ultimate treasure to all mankind. Consequently, every true Christian (like every devoted Muslim I have ever met) is an evangelist.[5]

2. *Lumen Gentium,* 3; emphasis added. I intend, in what follows, to develop the importance of this *objectivity.*

3. Ibid., 16.

4. *Redemptor Hominis,* para. 6. The pope's linking of truth and moral practice should be noted, an entirely "Pauline" position. There is no truth without love, and no love without being on the True Way. Recall Pascal: *La vérité sans la charité est une idole.* Balthasar says that "Catholic truths have such vitality that, on occasion, they can unfold their authentic content even under considerable limitations, like strong plants in poor soil" (*In the Fullness of Faith* [San Francisco: Ignatius Press, 1988], 128). He cites H.-E. Jaeger's three-volume collection of spiritual texts from the reform traditions, *Zeugnis für die Einheit. Geistliche Texte aus den Kirchen der Reformation: Luthertum, Calvinismus, Anglikanismus* (1970–1972).

5. My Jewish friends have trouble with this, just as the Christian has difficulty understanding why, preoccupied with being Jewish though many may be, and eager to tell friends about the joys of Jewish life, they seem to do little to bring anyone to the faith—they hate "proselytizing." This may be because they have suffered too much historically from every manner of pressure from uncharitable and too often even murderous Christian neighbors.

But the Christian, knowing true love can be in short supply, should be ever aware of this about "proselytizing": it is one thing to be an evangelist, but it is something else to be an oppressive manipulator, or a bore. In their personal insecurity, in their lack of love, many Christians are either totally nonevangelizing or else intolerable proselytizers, pushing an inevitably defective (because not really loving) Christianity, to which, alas, they nevertheless manage to win converts.[6]

The Catholic Church is able to distinguish between its enjoying, in the truth of Jesus Christ, the fullness of God's Revelation and the false idea of having a *monopoly on truth,* as though no one in any other tradition knows anything valid or discovers something Catholics do not know. The text I quoted from *Redemptor Hominis* reminds us of this fact. It rejects explicitly any thought that God works uniquely through the structures of the Catholic Church,[7] which is a silly idea, as though God, having created His Church as the fullest expression of His providential love, could work only through His prime instrument, and somehow could no longer work on hearts through whatever is available in a given milieu at a given time. The document of the Second Vatican Council on relations with non-Christian religions, after passing in review great and positive things of each of the major non-Abrahamic religions, has this to say: "The Catholic Church rejects nothing which is true and holy in these religions. She looks with sincere respect on those ways of conduct and of life, those rules and teachings which, though differing in many particulars from what she holds and sets forth, nevertheless often reflect a ray of that Truth which enlightens all men."[8] By saying Christ Himself is "that Truth which enlightens all men," the council fathers are saying that a reflection of Christ, the Logos of God, is found in each great religion to the extent it is true.

At the same time, it holds that God wills for all that they come to enjoy maximum participation in the whole truth, which would entail enjoying *to the full* the life—the sacramental life—in Christ that the Church alone, continuing His Incarnation in history, can bring. For that reason, the fathers immediately add: "Indeed, she proclaims and must ever proclaim Christ, the way, the truth, and the life (John 14:6), in whom men find the fullness of

6. The sick preaching to the sick. How else do sects spread? There is plenty of pathology out there waiting to be exploited, by everything from skinheads and scientologists and tarot-card readers to certain oppressive "born-again Christians."

7. See, for instance, Balthasar, *Love Alone: The Way of Revelation,* ed. Alexander Dru (London: Sheed and Ward), 106–7. The key conciliar document, *Unitatis Reintegratio,* the *Decree on Ecumenism* of the Second Vatican Council, and the *Decree on the Church's Missionary Activity, Ad Gentes,* and on *Relations to Non-Christian Religions, Nostra Aetate* should also be consulted. The stale jokes, like "Shush! The Catholics think they are the only ones here in heaven" should cease, as they are a not-so-funny way of spreading anti-Catholic hatred based on a lie, the falsehood that the Church believes Christians can learn nothing with time and from non-Christians.

8. *Nostra Aetate,* para. 2.

religious life and in whom God has reconciled all things to Himself (2 Cor. 5:18–19)."[9]

In the context of an HTX ecumenical age, what does this kind of "total truth" do to "ecumenical dialogue"? In the next sentence, the fathers point the way: "The Church therefore has this exhortation for her sons: prudently and lovingly, through dialogue and collaboration with the followers of other religions, and in witness of Christian faith and life, acknowledge, preserve and promote the spiritual and moral goods found among these men, as well as the values in their society and culture."[10]

If one is sincere about this, would not the distinctive goods of all the traditions, in order to be preserved and promoted, demand on the part of the Church, destined to be the common home of all mankind, some accommodation, not compromises with the God-given truth of Revelation, but corrections of excesses and neglects in its own traditions and in various forms of Christian cultures (none of which are the pure work of the sinless) so that, "prudently," Holy Mother Church will have "to collaborate," extending her understanding and modifying her structures, sometimes dramatically, to accommodate all?[11]

Second, the ecumenical dialoguer's *orientation* is Christ's teaching and

9. Karl Rahner's famous term *anonymous Christian* overstates the Church's teaching here, at least as some have interpreted it. I believe Rahner himself did not mean to weaken the sense of evangelical *missio:* the full Good News about Jesus Christ is something all deserve to hear, and need to embrace. He meant to point out only that the good working in all peoples is the Holy Spirit—the one Holy Spirit of Jesus Christ—whether they, or we, recognize Him for who He is or not.

10. *Nostra Aetate,* para. 2.

11. For a Catholic consciousness, this is a difficult matter. I must confess, in all candor, that I believe Christian theology at its best, in the works of a de Lubac, a Rahner, a Barth, a Ratzinger, or a Balthasar, is so much more complex, rich, thought provoking, and sweeping in vision than even the greatest Muslim theology (to take a most challenging instance). In studying Muslim theology I can see it contains many precious treasures, fruits of prayer, and genuine inspiration. But Christian thought can more readily accommodate the monotheistic beauties of Islam, than can Islamic thought ever penetrate the complex and subtle Trinitarian Revelation that nourishes Christianity and shocks the Muslim in his most central conviction of the absolute Unicity of Allah. A Muslim who may be the least bit open to the claim that Christian doctrine of the Trinity in no way softens faith that God is One is already (in Muslim eyes) playing with fire. Likewise, while there are many wonderful rays of truth shining from the rich treasures of the Talmud (plunged as it is in the Word of God in the Old Testament and nourished by a life of profound prayer and ritual and intense discussion) as well as insights of enormous depth in, for instance, Buber (see Balthasar's grand book of appropriation of Buber's thought, showing more appreciation than almost any Orthodox Jews), again, the Trinitarian theology can make a place for these but Jewish thought must basically ignore the Christ. At the same time, I doubt that Christian good sense would allow any committed Christian to get any more involved with cabala-type mysticism than with alchemy, or tarot. There are limits to what one should waste time trying to understand. There are byways in the mystical life that it is not profitable to follow. Reading tarot cards, I believe, *pace* the great Balthasar, who lapsed a little on this, is one of these. The treasures of Talmud are one thing, cabala another.

mighty works, His sacraments, and the structure that, through His Holy Spirit, gives direction and form to His Church.

THE PROBLEM OF "THE HERMENEUTIC CIRCLE OF INTERPRETATION"

There is a fundamental epistemological problem raised by ecumenical dialogue.[12] However appreciative of other traditions one tries to be, the obvious fact that everyone approaches the other necessarily from the perspective of his own natural faith is one facet of what the philosophers call the problem of "the hermeneutic circle of interpretation," and it presents an *aporia* (an apparently unsolvable difficulty): how do we then open ourselves to the other lovingly, that is, in his otherness, when we must, in order to understand him ourselves, integrate what is different in his experience into our own "horizons of interpretation" on the basis of what we believe true? The criteria are drawn from our own natural faith. Does this not in effect reduce my approach to that "otherness" to what I can understand, in effect reducing that "otherness" to "sameness"?

Sobered by my effort at appropriating the Catholic tradition—I have discovered how little my *fundamental* position has changed in the course of a sustained consideration of objections to it—I am more aware than ever of the practical force of this interpretative dilemma. As Thomas Kuhn said about scientific theories, a "conversion" would be needed if "anomalies" are not to be either incorporated (procrustean style: just cut off their legs) or ignored.

In the introduction of the present appropriation, you will recall I suggested, as in *Tradition and Authenticity,* the methodological importance, in searching in other traditions for elements of truth, of distinguishing two phases, easily separated in theory but difficult to keep apart in practice. In the first stage, it is important to remember that in approaching "the other," whether one is dealing with a person or with the formulations of a foreign tradition, the appropriator first makes his best effort to understand, *in the others' own terms,* and tries to enter sympathetically into their own horizons of interpretation, accepting provisionally their predispositions as they reveal them in their expression, their own "language."

Much ink has been spilled over the very possibility of empathetically infiltrating others' worlds, through *sympathetic*[13] learning of their "language." There is no way to settle these disputes theoretically. Common sense suggests we are right in affirming different degrees of ability, for instance, of historians or art critics in reconstructing the horizons of others

---

12. "Epistemology" is the study of knowledge. In *TA* and again in *BT* the question of interpretative perspective was examined as a general issue in the search for truth. Here is the briefest résumé of those reflections, needed to deal with the issues of ecumenism.

13. The Greek root words mean "to suffer with," where suffering means receiving, or in other words, being receptive to the otherness of the other. Empathy cannot be profound without sympathy.

in distant times and cultures, just as some individuals seem better able to "decenter" from themselves and thus penetrate the friend's world, "to see things from his perspective," and hence to be *sympathique*. The proper attitude is not just a matter of sophisticated education, it is moral. Such empathy is a manifestation of love; empathetic people are, as we say, "less self-centered." A nondefensive attitude is required.

This may be helped, when the "other" appears menacing to us, by the decision to hold off integrating what we are learning into the larger picture of truth as we understand it. At the very least, in even the most hostile circumstances, one can adopt a "let's see what makes this guy tick" attitude.[14]

In the second phase, the critical moment of *judging the truth* of what the other puts forward involves integrating what has been learned of what the other has expressed in terms of his world, into the totality of the appropriator's own wisdom. If one admits there really is something new to learn from the other, this logically requires adjustment in some of the assumptions of one's own natural faith to accommodate realities that previously found no place there.

This is not so difficult when it is just a question of complementarity. But when conflicting claims have to be reconciled, or failing that, adjudicated,[15] and when interests clash, it is difficult. Something has to give, and we must struggle to be honest on the basis of what a change or a rejection of truth claims is being made. Often what is demanded is a deeper examination of principle. Every experience needs to have its meaning tested in the fabric of the fullest reality one can reach. Growing beyond defensiveness requires a well-founded confidence in truth, a clear sense that reality can be reached and that things can be known as they are in themselves. It requires confidence in others, for much knowledge comes to us not from personal experience, but rather from the *witness* of the other.[16]

In my epistemological studies I have sought to avoid naïveté about the psychic limits to sinful man's sympathy. The mysterious blocks to love thrown up by psychically damaged ego and pride make all progress toward wisdom, personal and intersubjective, painful and sacrificial. To reach truth we have to immolate some prized fantasies! One needs to forgive and accept the other when he aggressively invades one's being. Each of us needs to give up on parts of himself—the poorly grounded parts. For this we require

14. An example: I have been amazed at the ability of the best Israeli experts on the Palestinian and Arab opponents to understand their point of view. This is a strategic force for Israel. I have had the impression in speaking with them that their ability is rooted in a genuine respect for these opponents, even though they pose a serious danger to Israel.

15. I use that term with its overtone of getting a third, arm's-length party involved to bring out the need to be fair when *interests* clash.

16. See Balthasar's eye-opening essay on why we cannot experience God, but only He experiences us, and how He reaches us through the witness of lives of Christians ("Experience God?" in *New Elucidations*, trans. Mary Theresilde Skerry [San Francisco: Ignatius Press, 1986], 11–19).

redemptive grace: the Catholic faith teaches—contra Nietzsche—that we cannot save ourselves from ourselves; we cannot uncover and undo our own refuges from reality. Divine grace of forgiveness and healing is the key, often mediated by other people.

THE NEED FOR REDEMPTION: WHY THE CHURCH REMAINS MISSIONARY

In Pope John Paul II's "inaugural lecture," the encyclical *Redemptor Hominis*, the pontiff, as he meditates on the significance for these ecumenical times of the central Christian truth, raises explicitly the question with which we began this chapter: if our belief about the Redeemer is true, every Christian stands under the obligation of spreading the Good News that the Incarnation has happened.

A first problem for the Christian as missionary, the pope points out, is communicating the very sense of "redemption," starting with awakening the realization that we need saving, each individually, every society, and mankind as a whole. In a later encyclical, *Dominum et Vivificatem*, the pope wrote that only the Holy Spirit reveals sin to us. That is a notion not fully understood outside of Judaism and Christianity. It is rejected energetically by the secularists in our own society. It clashes with the centrality of "freedom" in its deformed versions in contemporary anthropology ("Save yourself!" exclaims Nietzsche in *Morgenröte*).

The clash of anthropologies is quite relevant here: the secularist is hostile to the notion of need of divine redemption because his natural faith is rooted either in the essentially antireligious conviction of human self-sufficiency or in despair of human existence's having any sense at all. As usual, Nietzsche has affirmed autonomy most boldly: having raised the question of why anyone should live in the humiliating condition of being in need of the love and grace of God, he exhorts: "Love yourself through grace, then you are no longer in need of your God, and you can act the whole drama of Fall and Redemption to its end in yourself."[17] This is uplifting, a defiance on the part of the life force in the face of every form of skeptical determinism!

For Christian belief, the heart of the issue is the mystery of evil in its most disturbing forms: the pathological, where past trauma has destroyed some of the ability for free self-direction we normally possess; and worse, the mystery of sheer perversity, deliberate revolt against reality, and with the destruction that follows—hatred (because love, with its openness to the Other, always reveals the shoddiness of the structure of lies we have built to protect our wrong course of action); and the desire (which only a spiritual being like man could ever harbor) for annihilation, especially self-destruction (the lie consumes the liar).

Confronted with the crippling reality of evil, the anthropologist should pose these central questions: how and under what circumstances can good

17. Nietzsche, *Morgenröte*, in *Werke* (Munich: Carl Hauser, 1962), para. 79.

vanquish the downward spiral into nothingness of a person or even an entire society committed to a bad course of action? Where might one find the possible *healing* good that can save us from ourselves, and in what does it consist?

The Christian witness is that love alone, which is the primordial creative life force of the universe (not a blind "life force" à la Nietzsche), can make right the depredations of sinful destructiveness. But the dilemma is getting this love unlocked in every damaged human being and flowing to give life again in the society. Because God has granted a sovereign freedom to those made in His image and likeness, a struggle ensues for souls. This is signaled most starkly by the event of what seemed the ultimate victory of evil over good: the Crucifixion and death of the just man, Jesus, the fruit of monstrous acts of refusal of love, acts of fear, pride, self-blinding. And how was this ultimate victory of death, this total emptying out unto despair of Jesus of Nazareth overcome? Uniquely *supernaturally*, that is, by *a new creation*, through the power of God manifest in His "harrowing of hell" and His raising this Jesus from the dead, "lifted up," "re-created," with a glorified body and everlasting life, at "the right hand of the Father." There is no other way; there is no natural triumph of good over evil. The perverse use of freedom destroys finite good. Left to itself, such perversity can erode all good, sowing a terminal disorder. New creation, fresh originative activity, is necessary to rebuild order in hearts, in society where disorder has been allowed to reign. Prayer, the first sign of a finite freedom's seeing the need for help and being humbly open to the divine Doctor's ministrations, is already a manifestation of the first steps of such a healing.

Blaise Pascal tries to awaken his contemporaries by showing the artifices by which we run away from the hard truth of the groundlessness of our existence.[18] *Divertissement*—distraction (especially, today, workaholism and entertainment, the largest industry in the most developed countries)—is the lowest form of escape; the will to power and the quest of technology for control of the environment is the highest. All are perversions of legitimate strivings. Pascal's ingenuity in cajoling his readers into facing up to the essential lack of power of the human situation and the groundlessness of our science (when it pretends really to know absolutely how it stands with being)[19] owes some of its effectiveness not just to the depth of his own spiritual life but to his quality as a scientist and a member of the power elite during one of the periods of spectacular intellectual advance in France. Perhaps the most devastating moment in the Pascalian "demonstration" is

18. Pascal anticipates in the seventeenth century, in those magnificent fragments we call *Les pensées*, Heidegger's phenomenology of the ambiguity and "averageness" of inauthentic daily existence (*Sein und Zeit*, pt. 1). Pascal was himself a brilliant mathematician and scientist, but his openness to divine grace as the source of life kept him from any illusion about control.

19. That hubris has, of course, grown stronger with the more recent spectacular successes of science. For a good example of this see Stephen Weinberg, *Dreams of a Final Theory* (New York: Pantheon Books, 1992).

when, having shown our need for love, he points out that of ourselves we never really love nor are we ever really loved: we are loved *for* our charm, our prestige, our power, which when they fade allow the underlying infidelity of the "lover" to show through nakedly.[20]

The unique "argument" a Christian can give in support of his claim that only from the transcendent divine Source does love come is a "demonstration" (*monstrare* means "to show forth") by allowing Christ's love to flow through him. I offer my demonstration forthwith ("let those who have eyes to see, see" [Mark 8:18]):[21] Mother Teresa of Calcutta. That tiny old lady is worth more than all the philosophical "demonstrations for the existence of God." The most effective missionary is not the person who only preaches the Word, but the one who demonstrates it through his superhuman giving of self. Charles de Foucault lived with his beloved Berbers in Morocco and died a martyr's death at their hands in order to be a presence of Christ in their midst, without the slightest hope, or perhaps even thought, of proselytizing.[22] Pope John Paul II in his first encyclical says that in approaching others "with a profound esteem for them as human beings, for their intelligence, their will, their conscience, and their liberty," the evangelical message is conveyed, "even without having to have recourse to words, by the simple way one acts in their regard." He adds, "This attitude seems to correspond to the particular needs of our time."[23]

The apostle must always remember that it is not just the Christians who are Christlike. When the non-Christian saint—a Gandhi, a Buber, a Sakharov[24] (all of whom have been "canonized" by popular acclaim, despite their warts, which all saints have, of course)—gives of himself in service to

20. The Pascalian character of chapter 4, "The Failures of Love," in Balthasar's *Love Alone,* is striking. (Balthasar acknowledged Pascal's influence.) The reader is urged to savor this little masterpiece of Balthasar, the most wonderful reflection on love as the creative force I have ever read.

21. The "third way" (the way of love) is unique in that either the form of Christian Revelation is seen as that of the glorification of divine love, or it is not seen in that way at all. In this respect, Rousselot's theory in *Les yeux de la foi* is entirely correct: "either one sees, or he does not see, but to see the glory of love requires at least a beginning of supernatural love" (Balthasar, *Love Alone,* 50).

22. Terribly ineffective, in the eyes of this world. I have even heard Mother Teresa criticized because she did not address the underlying political and economic inequities built into the "structures" in India. All she aspired to was to be a loving presence to this dying man here, and that little orphan there. She had no pretense of being able to change the structures of India with its billion people.

I recently learned from a friend who was president of the North American network of the Compagnons of the Missionaries of Charity that he received a handwritten fax from Mother canceling the twenty-five-year-old worldwide organization because, having prayed over it, she saw no point in wasting time and money on big meetings. "Compagnons, stay home and help the poor in your community" (telephone communication, Mr. F. W. Hill, Regina, Sask., September 15, 1993).

23. *Redemptor Hominis,* para. 12.

24. See Joseph Cardinal Ratzinger's glowing praise of his successor (as well as his vigorous defense of freedom of conscience) in his inaugural lecture as he assumed the Russian's place in the Institut de France (*Crisis* [May 1993]: 36–37).

his brothers and sisters, it is the power of the divine love that is shining forth through him, even though all the implications of the redemptive reality are not made explicit, and may even be seriously obscured by the limits of the particular saint's ideology.[25]

Suppose a non-Christian sees the need of some kind of redemption, and concedes that somehow or other it must come from the very ground of our being, as an expression of the end and fulfillment of that existence. Suppose further that he believes this ground transcends the field of my own initiative—that it founds the very possibility of my will. With all that, it may yet not be obvious to him that the transcending initiative for this redemption should somehow also situate itself within history, concretely, involving direct initiatives on its part with human agents—prophets and finally an actual human "Redeemer." He may be put off by all such a notion entails of the Source's condescending to work within the limits of persons and history. A vaguer healing source working we know not how seems less problematic. That a man, Jesus of Nazareth, could offer Himself as "the perfect sacrifice" to overcome the ultimate disaster of human sinfulness—our alienation from the Source and End—is likely to strike the non-Christian as an enormity, perhaps even, as with Muslims, a blasphemy. How does one even begin to touch on such things in ecumenical dialogue with non-Christians?

The key Christian notion that has to be confronted in ecumenical dialogue is that of the need not for appeasing an angry God (this is not the ancient "scapegoat" motif recycled) but of covering over the stain of sin, the need for propitiation, in the sense of the Hebrew *kipper* (which means "cover") as in Yom Kippur, the Day of Atonement.[26] The revelation that the divine Son Himself elected to make this reparation for us, because only He could bear to us the divine love needed to renew the relationship, is the cornerstone of Christianity. To be sure, the ill-tempered gods of the nations required appeasement or entreaty. But Yahweh had revealed Himself as merciful and just.

Yahweh passed before (Moses) and proclaimed "YHWH, YHWH, a God of tenderness and compassion, slow to anger, rich in kindness and faithfulness; for thousands He maintains His kindness, forgives faults, transgressions, sins; yet He lets nothing go unchecked, punishing the father's fault in the sons and grandsons, to the third and fourth generation" (Exod. 34:6–8).

Already clearly in the Old Testament, it is God who carries out the work of "wiping clean," through His forgiveness, and it is God who empowers

25. For a more detailed discussion of the dynamics of sincere actions within traditions that contain grave, ingenuine elements in their belief systems, see *TA,* chaps. 4 and 5. Marxism, for instance, leads to ingenuineness, despite the good intentions of some who devoted themselves to the cause, because of its failure to acknowledge the full human reality. Indeed, the Marxist class-struggle anthropology is essentially false, and so it leads eventually to the destruction of vital, genuine possibilities.

26. Jerome Quinn, "Propitiation," *Lutherans and Catholics in Dialogue,* 1–3:41–42.

His priest to ask for this.[27] That is a beginning in our common root for Judeo-Christian and Christian-Muslim dialogue. In 1 John 2:2 and 4:10 the noun *hilasmos,* entreating, is applied to Jesus: "but if anyone does sin, we have an advocate with the Father, Jesus Christ, the righteous and He is the propitiation *[hilasmos]* for *[peri]* our sins and not for ours only but also for the sins of the whole world." While the death of Jesus is the starting point for this affirmation, as Dodd points out, it is wide enough to cover the whole life and work of Jesus.[28]

WHY DOES GOD SO DESIRE THE UNITY OF MANKIND, AND WHAT KIND OF UNITY?

At this point, a related issue has to be faced, one that is particularly actual in this time of global HTX unification and standardization: the questions of why God so desires the unity of mankind, what is meant by this, and how the Creator intends that it be achieved. The search for such unity, more than the admittedly vital effort for peaceful coexistence, is the Christian's reason for seeking ecumenical discussion in the first place.

Not everyone agrees that mankind should be one. There are among us full-blooded pluralists, indeed libertarian individualists, who approach every manner of social unification with caution, but then, paradoxically, alienate their freedom into anonymity and group manipulation. We earlier agreed there is reason to fear Teilhard's "great Molloch," some form of collectivization—an enslaving unification of all mankind.

To start with, mankind is already in a meaningful sense one. We are all intelligent creatures enjoying free will, and as such able to affect one another, intimates, and massive but also sometimes relatively small groups of humans enjoy "leverage": they have potential effect on vast numbers of their fellows. (It takes only a small number to destroy mankind through nuclear holocaust.) The only limit to this kind of unification, based in common human nature, is man's ability, in a given era, to conquer time and space. Indeed, see where we are now: discoveries made by lonely individuals come to affect the entire destiny of humankind. Japanese attitudes, driving certain decisions, affect what my daughter must do, as an engineering manager in an IBM factory in Quebec, and this *within weeks.* Given this reality, would it not follow that if the Creator God cares for His children, He will of necessity desire for them a harmony in which those with power to affect others will work lovingly for their development and not their domination and destruction?

But to achieve that—to attain global harmony and justice—is there only one acceptable way? Is, as Christians believe, mankind to be gathered into a universal Church under the headship of the divine Son, Jesus Christ?

27. Ibid.
28. C. H. Dodd, *The Johannine Epistles* (New York: Harper and Row, 1946), 27.

If what is envisioned in such an ingathering is understood in a genuine Christian way, much resistance to it might disappear. Union of all in Christ means realization of a community of love among all persons, a society of utmost concern, one for another. No one would be against that in theory, but many would doubt sincerely that there is any chance of its realization, other than by a final colossal, all-purifying miracle at the Second Coming! Such a love-in would demand no "imperialistic" structures, no destruction of national cultures, no vision of international government, nothing "utopian" at all. Clearly, this is not an HTX vision. But is it not only a wonderful dream?

The image the media daily present of an imperialistic Church, headed by an "authoritarian" and "conservative" pope—a *Polish* pope—seeking to impose a retarded morality on his reluctant flock, does not feed belief in the vision of the Church as a universal gathering of love.

If the Church were to attempt "to impose a morality," as the Inquisitors once did, then to the extent it imposes anything, it is not realizing the called-for community of love. The Church is obliged to let the light of Christ's teaching shine on everyday life, to be sure. But it is not called by God to govern society, but rather to inspire it. We have seen that in the past the Church has sometimes allowed itself to become too intimately bound up with governance. But that fact does not constitute a valid objection to its efforts to propagate a community of love, by being an effective teacher of love. Past and present failures to love *by Christians* is the greatest obstacle to the realization of God's plan. To be sure, there are the catastrophic failures of man's structures, which oblige the Church, as institution, to supply temporarily for the cares of state, as in Barbarian times, in Marcos's Philippines, as it did in communist Poland, in the barrios of São Paulo, and in Zaire now. Then it looks good in contrast to secular failures. But these should be considered anomalous, undesirable yet unavoidable situations.

As Western society has grown further away from the central Christian vision, Christian moral teaching becomes necessarily more detailed and at the same time increasingly incomprehensible and even horrifying to secularists, particularly when they know it only in the distorted versions from the media. The media present as restrictions what the Church, in her wisdom, knows are liberations and admonitions against ways leading to death of spirit and body. The Church has to turn not just to ancient great traditions of spirituality, as it does in dialogue with Jews and Hindus and Muslims, but toward the new secularism especially, which it does in struggling to come to terms with the challenges of "the New Morality" and the "other" anthropology.

HOW CAN THE TRADITION CHANGE, YET HAVE AN ESSENCE? HOW CAN TRUTH BE "ETERNAL," YET UNFOLD IN HISTORY?

THE LASTING ESSENTIAL CLAIMS

With the challenges of a relativistic modernity fresh in mind, I shall continue along my contra-cultural way with the "unity" theme, returning now to the challenge with which we began, that of finding the "essence" of the tradition. I have assumed there is one Catholic tradition that envelops many Catholic traditions (or, if you prefer, "subtraditions"). If that is so, the core tradition must have an "essence" (so too must the subtraditions, whose particular essences then fit into the main tradition as parts). Each tradition must be "something" distinguishable, with its own form of unity, or there would be no sense in talking about it; some reality must account for that unity, a principle able to demonstrate its flexibility, adapting to changing surroundings while remaining faithful to its core being. How does such a dynamic "form" work?

In many explicit traditions the sociohistorical effective continuity of an institution responsible for teaching the vision has much to do with the continued coherence; so too do "canonical documents," works that express the group's understanding of the vision that have been "canonized" in some way by the institution's acceptance of them as definitive, and its using them in its ongoing teaching, passing on the vision from generation to generation.

In the case of a tradition that claims to mediate Revelation, the challenge is not just to trace the mean vector of the path followed by a living community amid the twists and turns of its development, as the community's life adjusts to the realities of new epochs and situations. Given the nature of the extraordinary claims made by that tradition, we face the added challenge (for which we have in earlier chapters prepared the way) of understanding how the Church achieves *definitive symbolization* (as the tradition claims that it does), including its explicit understanding of itself as a definite, institutional structure unchanging in its essence, corresponding faithfully two millennia later to what its divine-human Founder instituted. One can make no sense of the essence of a tradition of Revelation without facing the question of the whole mode of "dogmatic" teaching unique to it, as regards both the unique kind of content of that teaching and the way the tradition receives that truth, formulates it, passes it on, and how that truth is lived through one changing epoch after another, a revelation that is not first and foremost theoretical but meant to form the faithful's everyday existence.

The very idea of definitive formulation of truth is so under assault from the creeping pragmatism of a democratic era and the skepticism that has grown since the Christian civil wars of the seventeenth century, one might be tempted just to ignore this basic claim, especially when one sees the enormity of the whole claim—that not just some truths but *the* truth can be found, in some sense, "once and for all." But if the appropriator is scientifically considering traditions of Revelation as they actually present themselves, and not simply contemptuously dismissing them, he has to try to show such an absolutist claim can still make some sort of sense in postmodern times.

Let us be clear right from the start that making complete, rational sense out of what is, after all, the profoundest of mysteries—the meaning of our life in Him who is *the* Truth—is impossible. By "rational" I mean sure to be a satisfactory explanation for all and sundry, however little experience they may have of a life of faith. The magnificent Augustine, a spirit never exceeded, struggled his whole life with just this question—what is that Truth and how do I live in it? The little I shall accomplish in this chapter barely sketches the outline of the issues. And even that requires some technical philosophical discussion, at once off-putting for most readers and insufficient for professional philosophers. But as this book aims to show what we are up against in appropriating a vast tradition, the question of the unity of meaning threading throughout the history of the tradition has to be raised.

Since first writing this, I happened on the following remark of Edouard Cardinal Gagnon, relating what the pope had said to him about truth. It puts us on warning that we are confronting here what I might call a personalized notion of Truth:

> The Pope told me, "Error makes its way because truth is not taught. We must teach the truth, repeat it, not attacking the ones who teach errors, because that would never end—they are so numerous. We have to teach the truth." He told me that truth has a grace attached to it. Anytime we speak the truth, we conform to what Christ teaches and what is being taught by the Church. Every time we stand up for the truth, there is an internal grace from God that accompanies that truth. The truth may not immediately enter into the mind and heart of those to whom we talk, but the grace of God is there and at the time they need it, God will open their heart and they will accept it. He said that error does not have grace accompanying it. It might have all the external means, but it does not have the grace of God accompanying it. This encouraged me very much.[1]

1. Edouard Cardinal Gagnon, talk at the "Church Teaches Forum," Louisville, Ky., July 1, 1989.

A confidence in truth like that, because one has experienced it as a personal relationship to the living God, witnesses to my point: we are not here dealing with a merely theoretical concept about the verification of propositions but with a claim about experience of the life of God in His Church.

From the earliest fathers it has been clear in the Catholic tradition that the truth the Church is sent forth *(apostolein)* to proclaim is the truth about that Jesus Christ who claimed that He Himself *is* the Truth, and who called His disciples to find Truth by following in His Way. (Truth and method [from Greek, *meta ton hodon,* which means "along the way"] are joined, and the living out of this truth is *"the* life," which Jesus, too, claimed to be. Hence the *vital* importance of keeping whole and entire that concrete, purportedly objective reality that He is.) Clearly, what is claimed here is that the Truth is first and foremost the (adequate!) manifestation of a *divine-human Person.*[2] The showing forth of that finite human form is God's response to man's endless searching for the source, beyond his own meaning-creation, of meaning itself, as Being. (That is why Balthasar declares "there is only one dogma." Every facet of the creed reflects an aspect of the one truth: The Son of God came into history to save us by His cross and Resurrection, a redemption that in-forms us. That is the whole and complete revelation of the sense, the origin and the end, the Alpha and the Omega, of all that is, and the way we are to follow from that beginning to the end.)[3]

So all discursive efforts to speak about this living Word must be intent on invoking the sense of this reality of the Whole of Being dwelling among us in a "Fragment," Jesus of Nazareth, male, not female, Jew, not Greek, born then, not now, who is yet (paradoxically) the perfect Symbol and Image of God, the form of forms, who leaves us wanting nothing else. That is the root sense of the *katholou,* the universality claimed since Pentecost day: it is not just the mission to all peoples but the sacred trust of passing on the whole *(katholou)* truth incarnate in Jesus Christ—"passing on" then the living (eucharistic) presence of the divine Person, to which all particular truths, even those of all science and technology, are to be referred in judgment.

---

2. "What is truth?" the Procurator of Judaea once asked the Truth incarnate . . . who did not answer, but went on "to bear witness to the truth, for this I was born, for this I came into the world," and that by voluntarily allowing himself to be crucified! Strange notion of truth? All fundamental notions of truth are strange, for they lie at the root of philosophical-theological understanding. The Greeks termed what we call in English "truth," *aletheia: a* means "negative," while *lethe* means "the veil," in terms of "unveiling." Heidegger seized on this to claim they understood Being to shine forth, to presence and manifest itself. Friedlander, the great Greek scholar, may have finally convinced him that the Greeks themselves did not really have this sense. The Hebrew word *AMN,* from which we derive "Amen," has the sense of standing firm, remaining faithful—very much the sense of truth, from *treu* in German, which means "faithful." The German word *Wahrheit* has the root meaning "to preserve," not too far from this sense of keeping to what you have. The fathers and doctors of the Church that lives the truth that Jesus Christ is the Truth, the Way, and the Life obviously would have to develop richly this "transcendental predicate of being," "truth." *BT* is wholly devoted to exploration of being as truth, and truth as reality appreciated.

3. Balthasar, *In the Fullness of Faith* (San Francisco: Ignatius Press, 1988), 103.

We recall the famous formula of Vincent of Llerins, in the fourth century, that the mark of the church is its passing on "all that has always and everywhere been taught as always the same," because it is a passing on of Jesus Christ Himself.

But what to make of the historic fact that the whole *(katholou)* teaching of the orthodox tradition is historically part of a larger family of traditions— the other revealed religions that do not embrace every essential dimension of the catholic truth? This Christian part of the larger family transcends and envelops the rest, for this "fragment" is the whole truth. Allow me to explain this paradox.

Starting with the Abrahamic root and continuing parallel to Christianity, as the different branches of Judaism and Islam, the family of traditions also includes lesser branches off each main branch: for example, Shia and Sufi branches of Islam, with, of course, Christian subtraditions that stand in tension with the truth as it is formulated and passed on by the Catholic Church. (These, says Balthasar, live from the vibrancy of aspects of the whole truth.)[4] Most Protestant subtraditions, as we have seen, strenuously deny dogmatic elements considered part of the essential truth of Christ by the Catholic Church. That is why the Church, from earliest days, called sects "heresies," from the Greek word "to choose"—they make a selection.

If one were to map the set of traditions of theistic revelation, he might think of them as a series of concentric circles, the larger outer circle enfolding all theists, and the smallest inner circle, "Roman Catholics" of orthodox belief, who are convinced that the Catholic Church's teaching alone has a place for all the truths of the larger more diffuse circles, and thus hands on the whole truth about God as revealed in Jesus Christ. Or he might imagine a temple solidly anchored on the temple mount formed of theistic belief: Within the generous walls of the courtyard are all those who embrace "Abrahamic theism." The temple itself is "Christianity." The sanctuary, to which priests are admitted, "Catholicism," or perhaps "the apostolic-episcopal church," and the altar, the most restricted space, before which stands the (male, celibate!) bishop presiding at the Eucharist, "Roman Catholicism." Within each precinct there is an enduring element of truth, unchanged since the moment it first came to be grasped by a group of human beings, forming a tradition, and in the case of what is most solidly consolidated, an institution, each time more rigorously articulated: the people of Israel, the Church, the papal-episcopal magisterium at the heart of the Church, and the pope standing as the vicar whom Christ—the Absolute Center—chose to represent the whole truth of Himself in its unity, down through history.

Consider in succinct recapitulation, the truths held within each precinct. The first circle of belief, the temple mount, embracing a creating God who is Father, has been held by "the people of God" since that folk first appear in history institutionally as a federation of Hebrew tribes under the

4. Ibid., 128.

leadership of prophets and "judges" proclaiming a revelation of this God, and consistently through more than a millennium insisting that His mighty deeds of leading them to freedom be remembered. The central revelation, that God is Providence, has essentially not changed in its core meaning since at least the time of King David's court.[5] The origins of a sense of "the leader God" probably does go back to Abrahamic times, fifteen hundred years or so before Christ. Something experienced by those tribes convinced them that this God was leading them where He wanted them to go—a notion unprecedented in the history of peoples. Jews, Christians, and Muslims are all gathered within the vast walls of such theistic belief—that is, significantly, now *half of mankind,* found in every corner of the world, continuing to live under the influence of an experience of being led in freedom toward a divinely ordained destiny. Such theism calls, then, for the living out of a cluster of truths expressing fundamental experiences of this God and of His creation, most essentially that creation is "good," and that it is destined to be "fulfilled." This prophetic vision has been grasped, celebrated liturgically, forming modes of prayer, taught methodically, the founding events remembered, and forming Scriptures, and thus passed from generation to generation to be incarnated through social action, in great struggle with infidelity, punished by social disaster, and this for at least three and half millennia, mankind's longest enduring and most widely accepted tradition.[6]

Lest we misplace the challenge of "dogmatic formulation," and with it the claim of "infallibility," thinking it somehow a Roman Catholic "problem," one should remember that this truth claim of a "faithful God" who "leads His people out of bondage" has been unwaveringly *and dogmatically* formulated since the earliest known texts of the Old Testament, and has been consistently appropriated by the New Testament and Qur'an alike. It is shared by every sector of Judaism, Christianity, and Islam. All three have been vigilant in keeping the vision intact.

The great inner structure—the magnificent Christian temple building itself, into which is gathered the bundle of subtraditions we call loosely "the Christian church"—is built out of faith in Jesus Christ, its "cornerstone" (Eph. 2:20). All Christians know Him as the most perfect theophany of this caring God, come to redeem all mankind and remaining with us through His Spirit in the Church. Again, here is a set of dogmatically formulated truth claims held unwaveringly, and hence put forward as absolutely true, not just by Catholics but by all Christians worthy of the name. Many Protestants dislike the word, but in fact they believe the Church is *infallible* in passing on this truth. With this revelation comes a glimpse into the

5. "Providence" means God is a center of reflective, free, and loving initiative who can enter into a dialogic relationship with man, for whom He has benevolent plans, and whom He guides along the path of history for the fulfillment of those plans.

6. This is important to remember, as the nihilistic Western media work constantly to diminish the presence of revealed theism in the world.

Trinitarian inner life of God, which is missed by Jews and Muslims.[7] These glimpses have become more explicitly formulated in the New Testament writings, and rendered more precise in certain essential respects by the great creeds, starting with the very early "Symbolon of the Apostles," and attaining a definitive creedal summit in the formulations of Nicaea and Chalcedon, again embraced unflinchingly by all "true Christians." As the formulation of the creeds, exceeding biblical language, is a work of the Church, and as Protestants accept the creeds as true teaching about God, this ecclesial work has been accepted in effect as infallible and hence definitive.

While many Christians accept the creeds whole and entire, not all who call themselves Christians accept as essential all the things said in them about Jesus, the Holy Spirit, and the Church—or they give an essentially different interpretation of some of the elements. From the start of this work I have examined the historical record assuming, as a Catholic, that all elements of those creeds are indispensable parts of the "orthodox" tradition. Some of the elements in the Nicaean creed about Jesus and the Church were clearly distinguished and adequately formulated only after several centuries, but they are all well founded in Scripture and in the writings of the earliest fathers, although some language not in Scripture is employed.

Once the essential facets of what Balthasar points out is "the one dogma" are found more precisely and definitively formulated, these formulations are forever to be honored in any theological working out of the expression of the essence of Christianity, remaining a signpost and a kind of binding guide and warning of limits beyond which lies error. (I shall return to the huge problems of "interpretation" that keep this question of "fidelity" from being a simple one!)

To the inner priestly sanctuary enter only those Christians who accept a certain notion of how the Risen Jesus has elected to continue God's work of guiding His people, how He lives among us, and unifying us in the full "eucharistic" sense of the Mystical Body, a revelation about the Church the Catholic believes founds ordained ministry based in apostolic-episcopal authority. This is essential to the Catholic tradition, not only because this claim about the structure of the Church, fulfilling the express will of Jesus Christ, goes back, Catholics claim, to the beginning of the community, but also because this very personal sacramental sense of how the truth is lived out and kept whole and entire is *existentially* the very essence of the tradition. It displays the very economy of the Incarnation itself at work. These ministers of His saving sacraments, through which He is physically, miraculously present, assuring, with divine power, forgiveness of sins and

---

7. Even though this is more than hinted at in the Old Testament and by some of the profoundest Sufi mystics. At creation the *Ruach* (spirit, breath) of Yahweh moves over the waters; in the Book of Wisdom, the Logos, God's daughter, is that *sophia* through which all creation comes to be. For the hints of the Trinity in Islam, see Robert Caspar, *Cours de mystique musulmane* (Rome: Pontificio Instituto di Studi Arabi e d'Islamistica, 1968).

the daily miracle of the eucharistic sacrifice, gather us about them as we all continue Christ's incarnation in the midst of a sinful but redeemed world.

We have seen that it took some time for the implications of the mystery of this sacramental ecclesiology to be unfolded and clarified to the point where a definitive formulating could make sense. This understanding was accompanied by changes in the precise ways in which the governing structures are humanly grasped and arranged. The core of the teaching, the notion of *apostolic office* and *ordination* as the communication of divine power and authority coming from Christ through the Holy Spirit, has not changed since the primitive Church. The articulation of offices has not altered much since the second or third century and may well have been understood in the apostolic church in a way close to what emerges in due course into the full light of historical record. Balthasar makes the point that it is dogma that develops while the basic structure of the Church remains stable.[8] Details of the way these responsibilities are carried out day by day change, and we have seen no less an authority than Cardinal Ratzinger remind us of the urgency of reform of these actual operating apparatuses, but the essential institutional form is now set forever.

The Catholic Church and the Orthodox Churches accept all of this, with almost no uncertainty as to what it entails, and a core of Protestant Churches subscribes more or less to some version of it, but with ambiguities—the Anglicans and Lutherans especially. But all other Protestants reject it, the "Congregationalist" ecclesiology they have developed implying profound differences in the sense of the way the Holy Spirit continues Christ's presence, less centered in the celebration of the sacraments and more on preaching the biblical Word, and with emphasis on the equality of priesthood of all the believers and rejection of a vicarious representation of "headship" to the Body of Christ, which is Christ Himself.

But to continue our survey within the edifice of the tradition: to the altar come the bishops and their delegated ordained priests, but gathered around the papal *cathedra*—the throne of Peter that is raised, as is the altar, at the back of the sanctuary—are only those who others call "Romans," or "Uniates," and who call themselves (or should, if they understand their own tradition), not "Roman Catholics" but, simply, "Catholics."[9]

8. Balthasar, *Love Alone: The Way of Revelation*, ed. Alexander Dru (London: Sheed and Ward), 50.

9. It is distressing to see even Catholic bishops falling into the habit of speaking of the "Roman Catholic Church." There is only the Catholic Church, presided over by the successor of Peter, as we have seen. Anglo-Catholics and the Orthodox are free to call themselves what they want, but Catholics should be "consequent" in their own naming of the Church. Recently, Remi Brague, an orthodox Catholic himself, has argued a case for the essential *"Romanité"* of Europe, and then on the basis of this sense of "Rome" he develops a "Rome" that honors and looks back to draw constantly on its Greek and Old Testament roots, goes toward the future never thinking it has a definitive possession of the truth, and so Brague sees this "Roman" quality of the Church as a symbol of an attitude toward the Truth it possesses. There is a good point to this, but I persist in

The primacy of Peter, understood the Roman way, gives the clearest possible icon of the headship of Christ, the pope as his vicar standing as the head of the human hierarchy of the Church on earth, and thus giving a focus to its authority, a rock upon which crash futilely the waves of superficial change, thereby underscoring the divine nature of all episcopal authority. So goes the teaching of "the Roman Catholics."[10]

Because of the diremption of Christianity by the Eastern Schism and especially by the Protestant revolt, I have found it necessary to spend so much effort developing and defending the Catholic position on the structures for the exercise of authority that this emphasis risks distracting from the real center of the Church's life: the sacramental, scriptural, traditional life in Jesus Christ present in the *communio sanctorum*. It also risks causing us to forget that Jesus Christ Himself invites every person to join Him at the heart of His Church. In the penultimate chapter I shall try to redress the balance, and get the focus back on the essence of the essence: every person living a life of love in Jesus Christ.

But before leaving this discussion of the authority structure, it would be wise to consider just how dogmatically formulated these Catholic teachings about structure, about popes and bishops, are, which will offer a better understanding of just how fixed they may be. Today, they are quite clearly defined, but that became true only recently: The Council of Trent responding to the Protestant revolt consolidated expression of the magisterial authority. But it was only the First Vatican Council in 1870, in response to an increasing relativism in the nineteenth century, which raised explicitly the question of how the infallibility guaranteed to the Church was to be expressed. This kind of exercise of living, "magisterial"-defining authority by the Catholic Church, with its pretension of formulating dogmatically "in later days" what it claims to have been the teaching of the apostolic Church since the beginning, upsets Protestants. But, Catholics argue, is not this (daring) exercise of teaching authority, of the ability to formulate even in our own time what has always been and will always be the truth about Jesus Christ and His Church, not precisely a mark of the Church's divinity and a blow against every form of relativism? What strikes many Protestants as the arrogance of the Catholic hierarchy is lived by many

---

thinking that the qualification "Roman" on Catholicism risks weakening the sense of the absolute universality (Brague, *Europe, la voie romaine?* [Paris: Criterion, 1992]).

10. Is this to say the only essential element separating "Catholics" from all the Eastern Orthodox and Anglo-Catholics and perhaps Lutherans is the notion of the "presidency" of the Church by the successor of Peter? We have seen that the American Lutheran theologians in dialogue with Catholics and the Anglicans of the Anglican Roman Catholic International Commission are even ready to accept a certain primacy of Rome, if it is understood in a way to which they can agree. If that were so, it would indeed not be a giant gap remaining for all within the sanctuary to be unequivocally one. Unfortunately, other matters remain: Lutherans do not consider marriage a sacrament, for instance, and both communions will remarry divorced persons. And now the challenge of women priests has reared its head.

Catholics in gratitude and obedience, and by the "hierarchs" themselves as a constant reminder of their own obedience, which we all—pope, bishop, and layman—owe to the Holy Spirit.

GIVEN "HISTORICITY," HOW IS IT POSSIBLE TO FORMULATE LASTING TRUTHS?

Supposedly, then, the definitively formulated essential core remains intelligible across the great span of epochs and cultures.[11] This is at the heart of the claim about the Church's "infallibility" that is so misunderstood, partly because of the word, and especially because the First Vatican Council, wishing to clarify the effective seat of this guarantee, emphasized the role of Peter in speaking for Christ.

But there remains a basic epistemological reason causing many people of goodwill to doubt the very possibility of such "unchanging meaning" in any "tradition of discourse." Let us separate the claim of endurance of such fidelity until the end of the world, which demands faith and hope, from the contention that the age-old formulations can and have retained their basic meaning, which is subject to historical verification, or at least rational argument over the implications it raises about the very nature of *interpretation.*

Earlier I explained why I am not disturbed by the charge that dogmatic formulation "closes the theophanic space."[12] If it does, that implies that the meaning somehow manages to stay the same to the exclusion of some new meaning. This is the philosophical issue that I want to examine now: flying in the face of postmodern historical relativism, I ask, is it possible for the same claim to be made with the same understanding as to what it means *essentially,* down through a vast suite of cultural changes and despite ongoing elaboration of the understanding of the claim (and its translation into many languages)?

Obviously, this critical issue is central not just to this tradition but to "the truth question" itself. It is a challenge, not just for the dogmatic tradition of Catholicism but for any explicit tradition—scientific, philosophic, associational, revelational, artistic—that would pretend to pass on truth. I have elaborated on this in *Tradition and Authenticity* as regards the different kinds of truth in the various genera of explicit tradition, and on a more basic ontological-epistemological level in *Being and Truth,* which explores

11. One element of the essence of the tradition is belief in Christ's promise that the Church will persist in the truth until the end of the world—"and the gates of hell will not prevail against it" (Matt. 16:18). Properly understood, one must see that if this tradition is basically true, *that must be so* (for all it says, basically, is that the Church, both when it is understood as Christ's Mystical Body and when it is expressed as His "bride," is so intimately united with Him as to be guaranteed by Him).

12. Eric Voegelin, *The Ecumenic Age,* vol. 4 of *Order and History* (Baton Rouge: Louisiana State University Press, 1974), 48, 56–57. See my earlier discussion of this in Chapter 3.

the debate between relativists and those who believe lasting truths can be formulated.[13] Here I confine myself to reflection on this kind of revelational truth only, with emphasis on the unique form the faith and love dimension takes in Christianity. This form opens, I believe, new depths of understanding of what Truth is.

The basic problem of intersubjective truth already exists on the level of everyday communication: how can I express, from the depths of my own personal little world, complex truths with any hope that you will receive them interpretatively into your own quite different little world without hopelessly deforming my meaning? Your loving receptivity to that to which I am trying to witness is vital to the communication's succeeding.

THE HERMENEUTIC QUESTION AGAIN: THE OBJECTIVITY OF INTENTIONALITY

No communication of any kind, no meaningful agreement could occur were it not for the *objectivity* of *intentionality*.[14] The structuralist linguist, sounding much more subjective than objective, would at once emphasize how a sign, such as "Son of God," makes sense only within a system of signs—a given language at a certain phase in its evolution. That language implies a whole set of "horizons of interpretation"[15] deployed intersubjectively by those communicating in terms of which what is meant by "God" and by "divine sonship" gets its meaning in relation to all the other relevant notions sedimented into the collective *natural faith*[16] of those who participate in the linguistic group. These horizons provide context. When we attempt to spell out what we mean by "Son of God" or whatever, we have to do so by mustering other linguistic signs, all of which get their sense from one another and refer beyond themselves to further signs, in terms of which they can get spelled out further, and so on, ad infinitum, the whole set of meanings constantly evolving historically.

Basically what the linguists are saying, for all its flavor of relativism and idealism, is correct. But, unfortunately, many (the whole field being influenced by the "transcendental idealism" of Immanuel Kant, who

13. See especially *TA*, chap. 3, and *BT*, 326–27.

14. This "technical" term from phenomenology points to the fact that every bit of knowledge is about an ob-ject, that is, a content thrown *(jactus)* over against *(ob)* the sub-ject; I never just see, I see something, this tree, that person; I never just wish, I wish to have a birthday party, and so on. Every "noetic" act in-tends—tends toward—its object, and every act of consciousness shows the forming activity of consciousness.

15. The subject opens a time-space "world" within which meaning can occur, brings to it from his past knowledge many meanings, some assumptions, others coming from past experience that has been taken up into the mind. The deployment of these resources now to understand the object confronting me is "interpretation."

16. "Natural faith" is the overall context, one's basic convictions about how it stands with the world, which operates in the horizons of interpretation in which we enfold every object as we judge what it is and means (see *TA*, 23–24, and *BT*, 7–12).

lived from 1724 to 1804) do not pursue sufficiently the other side of the issue,[17] the objective *realistic:* how thought is nurtured in experience of realities that thrust themselves upon us. These realities come both from the exterior surrounding world, through perceptual experience in which is revealed something of the real form of the thing, and from interior experience, knowledge of ourselves and of the imagination and reflection and matters of emotion, which can provide "revelations of the heart." This presencing and self-giving of the thing, the emotion, or even the concept, which has, after all, an intelligibility, guides our search for signs that can capture and express what is experienced.[18] This objectivity and structured form of what offers itself to the knower has been downplayed in modern thought,[19] in favor of emphasizing the human creative molding of signs and the fact that we learn most of what we know through handed-down signs.

The fact that we are confronted by radically different kinds of objects emerging from a variety of experiences (a real tree is quite different from a fantasy about a party I would love to throw) complicates our understanding of how truth is lived. The danger of trying to force other ways of understanding into the mold furnished by one of them—for example, some scientific methodology—is real. Each kind of knowing has to be reflectively examined to understand how and with what degrees of certitude different kinds of evidence motivate judgments of objectivity ("I really do want that party! But the party may never exist!"); and then one has to attend to the accuracy of expressions to retain and communicate what is intended.[20]

The signs of language are meant to express the thoughts (and emotions) that arise from the experiences, including the internal experience of reflection on and emotive reactions to external experiences. The relationship between thoughts and the linguistic devices of different kinds of language that

17. Throughout *BT,* I have shown how one must constantly swing back and forth (dialectically) between the subjective, idealist, voluntarist side of the knower to the objective, realistic, in-itself side of the known; underweighting either obscures the full reality of the human interaction with the world (see *BT,* esp. chaps. 2 and 4).

18. To be sure the subject—the whole human being, body and soul—is active in this knowing, deploying the mysterious light of understanding (of *intellectus,* which means "the ability to 'read in' the thing or the feeling its form"). But this act of loving reception of the object as other is a receiving of what is not the subject, but lies over against (*ob-jacere*) the subject, challenging him to open up his world.

19. Two hundred pages of *BT* are devoted to recuperating some sense of the other's (person or thing) ability to presence "as it is in itself"—*pace* Kant and the deconstructionists, whom the *Truth and Tradition* project tries never to lose sight of, because I am always trying to drive back into their cages those who are so skeptical about the other's ability to presence and reveal its distinctive reality. A society that loses its anchors in reality is bound to sink into a subjectivist nihilism.

20. *TA* offers a lengthy discussion of the distinctive *kinds* of truth claims characteristic of the four genera of explicit tradition, and the long survey of "Kinds of Objects, Kinds of Truth," which is *BT,* chapter 4, is a phenomenological presentation of evidence for objectivity in knowledge.

express them is as complex as the human reality itself.[21] Words incarnate thoughts, but not exhaustively (just as our thoughts never capture completely the reality they express), and words do so more discursively than the greater spirituality (Gilson's term for unity of sense) of the thoughts. On the other hand, the distinctions the symbols assist us in making and in keeping straight and their relative fixity as a given system of signs aid thought's analysis.[22]

The point requiring emphasis is that the verbally incarnate thoughts capture and transmit cogitated experiences, and so speak of things, actions, and situations revealed in those experiences that themselves are neither linguistic nor merely thought about, but rather are known and spoken of *as existing*. Most of our thoughts are judgments about things and people (including about ourselves, our feelings, and reactions), our experiences constitute relationships with things and people and reflectively with ourselves. Even when I think about my own emotion, I distinguish me, the center of awareness and initiative (the ego) and that about which I am aware, say, this spate of fear. If language did not refer beyond itself to things, actions, and situations experienced, there could be no communication and no translation. Nor would we ever learn anything about the world beyond our imaginations, or, for that matter, even about my imagination as distinguished from me, the ego. But we experience learning, communication, and successful translation every day, although the struggle to learn what is true about the other and the limits to successful communication and translation are painfully obvious.

In *Being and Truth*, evidence for objectivity in our judgments about many things of everyday experience is mustered phenomenologically. But the case at hand, an expression of a divine revelation, is much more difficult than knowledge of trees and monetary systems and why my wife is in such a good humor. How, in the case of something such as Christ's reality as divine Son, which is scarcely for us an object of immediate experience, can we possibly know what is meant and that we are talking today of the same reality as that which the drafters of the Nicaean creed had in mind?

Take, for example, the claim that we translate into English today in these words: that Jesus was "begotten not made, one in being with the Father."[23]

21. I shall not tarry here to argue that thought is not reducible to the language in which it is expressed. I prefer instead to send the interested reader to the extended argument in Étienne Gilson, *Linguistics and Philosophy* (Notre Dame, Ind.: University of Notre Dame Press, 1987).

22. If not fixity, then at least evolving less rapidly than fleeting experiences of fast-changing things and situations.

23. Until recently, the *homoousios* was translated as "one in substance with the Father." The change in translation reflects widespread doubts about the wisdom of associating the formulation of the dogma with the "substance metaphysics" of the medieval Aristotelians, the same disquiet that hovers about the term *transubstantiation*, regarding the Eucharist. The interesting fact is that we can both understand what this means in terms of the old Aristotelian metaphysics and recognize that a deeper sense is buried in the term *ousios*, then try to capture that with the term *being*, and all the while

On one level, the sense is quite clear, even though the mystery expressed is impenetrable: what is being asserted is that the Son is distinct from the Father, standing in a relationship of the begotten to the begetter, yet they are both equally God, the same God, because they enjoy the same being—a being within which each has a distinctive role *(prosopon)*.[24] I believe I have caught at least the surface meaning of what the creed is here asserting. But how do I know that I have interpreted correctly what is meant by the claim? How can I be sure that my understanding, despite a millennium and a half separating us from the fathers of the ancient ecumenical council and the translation from fourth-century Greek into twentieth-century English, is faithful to what was intended?

Behind all those questions looms the bottom-line issue: on what basis do we know not just what is meant by the assertion, but that what is being asserted is true? The two questions go together, for the grounds of my assurance that I am interpreting the words of the creed as they were intended cannot be separated from the question of the grounds of my knowledge that what the expression conveys is true or a fantasy, for the being involved has to come to me in some definite way that is entirely relevant to what the expression means.

In the case at hand we can safely answer, "I know the declaration is true because it has been revealed to us." How? By whom? When? Who constitutes this "us," and, again, what guarantee is there that we have the meaning right?

It is recorded in the New Testament that the underlying reality has been revealed by Jesus, and confirmed by the events surrounding the annunciation of His conception, birth, public life and preaching, His "mighty works," His Crucifixion, Resurrection from the dead and Ascension into heaven, witnessed and testified to by the apostles, recorded in those writings, and authenticated by the life of the Church.[25] The fidelity of the Church[25] to the preaching of Christ Risen and in sacramental practice, which it-self witnesses to Christ's divinity through the institution of the sacra-ments, and the witness of Holy Scripture, mediate to us the Good News of what happened.

---

recognize that none of this suffices to capture the mystery, which cannot be contained but only correctly indicated by our linguistic symbols, whatever they are.

24. *Prosopon* is the term the fathers chose from Greek theater, Latin *persona*, the mask worn by an actor, to express this distinction.

25. "Look not on our sins but on the faith of your Church" (words from the canon of the Mass). In discerning the authenticity of the orthodox teaching, one must recognize and turn away from our infidelities and learn to recognize in the faithfulness of the saints and the steadiness of the magisterial teaching that continuity with the originating reality, the mighty words and acts of Jesus Christ. That steadfastness of the teaching is verifiable from the historical documentation. In an earlier version of the present work I included a long paraphrase from the works of Saint Irenaeus, first bishop of Lyons at the beginning of the second century, because they show how the teachings are the same in a striking way.

In one sense we know of these things the same way we know of the events of Napoléon's life—because we are told of them by those who witnessed them, both through documents and through traditions handed down in the teaching of the Church.[26] But what is claimed about Christ is so demanding it causes any critical person to examine carefully the nature of the witness offered. The content of what is being held up as true and the way the reality founding this truth is communicated to us cannot be separated. It is rather like a friend telling me of a mutual acquaintance, "Look, trust me, I know Adrien very well and I assure you he is capable of fuzzing the truth when the going gets tough." My acceptance of the truth of the assertion is bound up with my confidence in the one speaking. The willingness of the apostles to give up their lives in testimony to the truth of what they preached is then important, but it proves either that they were, to the last man, deluded fanatics, or men who had been privileged to have witnessed genuinely divine events so extraordinary they would die for them. When we place the reported events, the entire life of Christ and the epic of the early Church in the context of the millennial unfolding of the messianic expectation, when we see what was prophesied, then see that it does all add up to something much like the anticipated fulfillment, but that the enormity of the event leaps beyond anything anticipated, all this feeds our confidence in the truth of what is being reported in the relevant symbols.

Consider just one example of this prophesy: Mary, humble maid of Galilee, prophetically declared "all generations will call me blessed." Humanly, at the time this was recorded it was utter folly. Who is this little Jewish girl to say that! But look what has happened: for two thousands years, all generations have called her "blessed," even the Muslims. It is just as startling that the carpenter's son would calmly declare that His infant church with a couple of hundred hangers-on would last until the end of time, and here it is, mankind's longest enduring institution plunging ahead through the heavy seas of modernity.

One's overall assessment of the interaction of all these factors constitutes an act of faith—of confidence—as it does in the assessment of any complex historical event, indeed any event, even one that just happened yesterday. Our understanding of a happening has to be assembled from many factors of differing kinds, including often many witnesses of different degrees of credibility. *Natural faith* comes into play in every judgment, providing context, hence ultimate meaning. But the more complex and constructed the object, the larger the element of faith throughout the process of construction.

That there may be "supernatural" elements involved in the judgment about Jesus is not the point. But then why has the tradition always taught that only with the outpouring of supernatural grace from the Source that is infinite love itself can the *adequate response* come from man, the response

26. Legends of Napoléon perhaps play a lesser role here, because so much was written about him during his time and immediately after.

of that divine love flowing through us and returning to the Father as the Son's adoration? That very love has moved us to love in our turn.[27]

We possess a record, historically well founded, of at least a millennium of intensifying anticipation of the coming of a Messiah. I am not saying everything reported in the Old Testament obviously happened historically exactly as reported. That would be ridiculous. But that it stands as a record of prophesy of a coming intervention of God and of the people's anticipation, while their lives as a people do not live up to what their "chosenness" demands, is there for all to see: in this it is a historical record recoupable without the need for supernatural faith. Then, in the New Testament we possess another record of extraordinary events in and around the life of Jesus of Nazareth, which show not only that His followers believed He was the awaited one, but also that He claimed a relationship to God far more exalted than anything that had been conceived of before, indeed "beyond belief."[28] He calls us into a special love relationship to Himself and through Him to the Father, Source of all being. The object of our knowledge in this instance reveals itself as a person calling to an interpersonal relationship of trust and love, showing us that only through His redemptive act—the love act par excellence—can we be invited into that relationship. Our accepting all this in confidence is the very act of accepting His self-gift, which is a grace.

We can see something analogous in more common experience. Only if another freely invites me into the inner sanctum of his soul is the possibility opened of my knowing him and therefore loving him as he really is, which is a gift from him, a natural grace, creating the possibility of my response, which I am then free to give or not.

If something as mysterious, fundamental, and transcendent-immanent as the Incarnation of God in Jesus Christ were to happen, one would scarcely expect the event to be expressible in one neat formula, or, for that matter, any number of neat, or poetic, or exalted formulas! And any formula you would expect, as Augustine shows, to elicit many possible responses, some

27. Balthasar, *Love Alone*, 62–63. We are not called upon by Napoléon to respond to his remarkable life by loving him. The challenge in knowing Christ is that His witness is such a call; the only response that can fully embrace the reality He shows forth is response to His call to give ourselves to the Father through Him. No truth is affirmed without engagement of will. But in this case what the object demands is total self-gift. That is the great obstacle to accepting such an extraordinary claim.

28. There is no good reason to believe His followers simply made up these claims and projected them onto Jesus; it is far more reasonable to conclude that He Himself made such claims about Himself. Recall our glance through Mark's gospel. It is extravagant to think Mark simply made all of that up, rather than that Jesus not only made claims of divinity about Himself, but also worked astonishing acts that helped His followers accept these enormous claims. The critic determined to believe no one could possibly do most of the things falls back on simply asserting the followers must have been duped and are guilty of posthumous projection of delusions onto the figure of the dead Jesus. But that assertion too is an act of faith. "Because I have never seen anything like these 'mighty acts' they could not have happened" is not the soundest principle.

of them compatible, complementing one another in enriching our grasp of the sense of the expression, others in tension, some perhaps ultimately found to be false.[29] Indeed, as we peruse the *preparatio evangelica* from the Old Kingdom burial hymn of the Pharaoh,[30] called "My Son, My Beloved," through the anointing of David as Messiah and Son of God, through the prophesies of Isaiah to the formulations in the complex prologue to Saint John's gospel and throughout the great discourses of Christ in that gospel, then contrast these with the more sparse (and sober) declarations in the synoptics (recall, we examined those of Mark in detail) and finally see Paul rivaling John for richness of expressions and scope of vision in his efforts to communicate "who is this Jesus," we begin to get some idea of the richness of this vast effort at expressing the ineffable, the *mysterion* (Eph. 1:9),[31] of the Incarnation.

When we go on to follow the fathers of the Church through the first four centuries as they seek to plumb the depths of all this, we see that they did not do this only through meditating on Scripture. Rather, out of the liturgical and eucharistic experience of the living Church, and in struggle against initiatives found inadequate, some even condemned as heretical, they become aware of the immense inheritance, enriched it and passed it on to the fathers of Nicaea and Chalcedon, who had all this wisdom at their disposal as they faced the christological crises. Confronted by the need for more precise formulation, in answer to challenges of the Arians and others whose teaching they found erroneous, they could draw in their conciliar debates on the whole living tradition of the Church, and then advance it through the forging of extrabiblical expressions for the truths they were clarifying.

While the council fathers were willing to go beyond Scripture to find their formulation, one can nevertheless multiply evidence of the Scriptural well-foundedness of that formulation, "begotten not made, one in *ousios* [being/substance] with the Father." That previous body of "canonized" formulation plays an important role both of furnishing symbols and, more negatively, in controlling the limits of the possible. The prologue to John's gospel, for instance, says "the Word was with God in the beginning, and the Word was God, and through Him all things were made" and that "the Word was made flesh and dwelt among us." And later Jesus says "To have seen me is to have seen the Father—I am in the Father and the Father is in me" (14:9–10). Paul tells us in Ephesians that the Father "has made Him the ruler of everything" (1:23) and that we are "created, chosen from the beginning, in Jesus Christ" (2:10), which says much the same as John's prologue.

29. Recall Augustine's reflection on various senses of "In the beginning God created the heavens and the earth" (*Confessions*, book 12).

30. Voegelin, *Israel and Revelation*, vol. 1 of *Order and History* (Baton Rouge: Louisiana State University Press, 1974), 85–87.

31. *Mysterion* is the word seized on by Paul to express the unfathomable depths of being revealed in the Christ.

See then how the creedal formulation simply renders more precise the relationship, in a way that seems to me, whether one consults the Greek originals or considers it in careful translation, totally in harmony with what Scripture is striving to communicate, but adding a kind of definitive clarity that can scarcely be surpassed—again bearing in mind that the fathers are striving to express the ineffable. It is quite wonderful that in grappling with such a mystery a position can be, so to speak, so well "staked out": the Son depends on the Father, as that which is begotten depends on the begetter, but this dependency is not a relationship of inferiority. An analogy drawn from human experience helps: a son owes his parents respect and gratitude for bringing him into the world—without them he would not be—but as a human being, in terms of inherent preciousness and dignity, from the instance of conception the baby is equal to the father and the mother.

To sum up then: That is how we know these things, the Revelation is mediated to us by the teaching of the Church—its saints striving in their lives to be faithful to the witness of the apostles; both Christ Himself and the Church are the source of the symbols that constitute the New Testament and for the canonization of the texts that become Holy Scripture. It faithfully preaches this "Good News," and further generates the symbols needed for clarification through the reflections of the fathers. All subsequent theological efforts are guided by this treasury, with the Church authority discerning, guaranteeing, and guiding right interpretation.

But lest I leave you with the impression that the real object of our faith is the Church itself, recall our starting question, about the objective referent of this creedal expression. It is about a concrete human being, Jesus of Nazareth, who lived at a given moment and place in history. What is claimed is that there exists a real, objective relationship of this historical person to God, understood, in the context of the creed as creator, with emphasis here on His "Fatherhood," that is as Source, begetter of the Logos. Through this Word all that is made is made. It is this Logos that has taken flesh, being born of a woman, to become the historic man Jesus.[32]

THE WITNESSED EVIDENCE: OF THE MOST UNFORTUNATE OF MEN?

We have seen that witness on the part of the apostles and the evangelists and epistle writers reporting for them, of what Jesus said about Himself, backed up by His "mighty deeds," especially His Resurrection from the dead, is crucial here, and that Christians believe sufficient to found Jesus' credibility regarding the most demanding of claims. It is upon that credibility that the claims about the interior life of God and the relation of Father and Son (and of course also Holy Spirit) are based: Jesus indeed taught "with authority"; it is Jesus who would then, by the Resurrection, be established

32. The humanity—the Flesh and Blood—of Jesus is created through His own divinity, through the Logos.

as Son of God, who instructs us on the interior life of God and the nature of these relationships. Paul saw that with total clarity:

> If there is no resurrection of the dead, Christ Himself cannot have been raised, and if Christ has not been raised then our preaching is useless and your believing it is useless; indeed we are shown up as witnesses who have committed perjury before God, because we swore in evidence before God that He raised Christ to life. If our hope in Christ has been for this life only, we are the most unfortunate of men. (1 Cor. 15:14f)

Are the Christians "the most unfortunate of men"? Does it, as the tradition teaches, require a special gift of supernatural grace to respond to God's invitation to see the divinity in the glory of Jesus Christ, born, living, crucified for our sins, and raised up from the dead? If it turns out to be just the effect of mass hysteria, what we Christians believe to be that grace to accept the witness, the claim, "the most unfortunate of men," given the immensity of the Christian claims and their impact on the whole of history, is indeed just that: "most unfortunate." But not just for Christians! Pity the poor Occident. The impact of Islam, of Judaism, of Buddhism, of all the Hindu religions is also "unfortunate" to the extent they too are dupes of false claims, and in the case of the other Abrahamic branches, supposedly "supernatural" claims at that.

What the reflection of the present appropriation has brought to the fore is the personal nature of truth. Encounters with reality constantly mold who we are. And who we are is at the base of the whole truth we can know.[33] Authenticity is at the heart of the search. The time has come, in our following along the way, to reflect on what it is to be a self, a true self, a *person* responding to a particular call.

UNITY IN THE MIDST OF CHANGE: THE CHALLENGE OF DOGMATIC FORMULATION

If nothing can ever be discovered as lastingly true, and if such discovery were not able to be expressed in terms that reflect the permanent character of what has been discovered, then indeed man would be delivered up to a morass of historical relativism: every expression would reflect only the peculiar conditions of those forging it, such pronouncements would tell us more about the speakers than about that which they are seeking to express, and all would be change, with only the larger contexts moving slower than narrower ones, and hence provisionally supplying a context of meaning for them. There can be no ultimate context. Such a relativism leads to pure pragmatism: expressions of "truth" enjoy their "truth" only so long as they work, that is, succeed in building mythologies that are for the moment able to mobilize some masses of men to march in a given direction.

---

33. Balthasar makes the point that in every act of knowledge the whole person is engaged and the whole of truth (*das Gesamtwahrheitliche*) is implied (*The God Question and Modern Man* [New York: Seabury Press, 1967]).

Karl Rahner sought throughout his intellectual life to establish a theological hermeneutics that would acknowledge historicity, yet save the project of lasting truth, providing a more adequate understanding of the role of dogmatic formulation.[34] In wrestling with the same problem, not only as regards religious dogma but also (and this was Rahner's concern, too) in an effort to found science, morality, and the convictions of ordinary good sense, I strove in *Being and Truth* to bring out, as strongly as I could, the evidence for the presencing, the self-giving of real things, other persons, and the objective relations that bind things and persons. I emphasized the mediating role played by objective givenness in our communication, especially the evidence of persons and things having permanent natures.[35] Such a position goes against so much of the relativism of modern thought, I was required to muster carefully the phenomenological evidence for such a position. That is why *Being and Truth* is a long book. I cannot hope to sum up that evidence here.

But I would like, before giving up here, to make two points that might be overlooked in a technical consideration of interpretation. First, for enduring expression of lasting truth to be possible, continuity of human nature is required. *Being and Truth* examined the sense of the claim, that we are the same basically as those prophets of the Old Testament and as that Jesus whose teaching we must seek to grasp. Second, those prophets and that Jesus in communicating lasting truths drew on the simplest, most accessible things and situations of perennial, everyday life in order to get their message across in a way that remains accessible. The claim that the Author of all creation, who knows us as we can never know ourselves, can find means to express in enduring fashion the eternal truths we need to know for our lives to have meaning is entailed in the belief that the Source of our lives is a providence. Anyone who has attempted to follow Christ by listening to His gospel knows that the problem is not at all trying to figure out what He expects of us. It is, if anything, too clear! (Mark Twain said somewhere, "My problem is not with the parts of the Bible I don't understand!") The problem is a moral one: how to find the courage to let His love transform us. We have to give up our narrow little program based in achieving a false security.

Take as an example the carefully formulated teaching the disciples of Christ found "the hardest saying": the eucharistic injunction, "Unless you eat my body and drink my blood, you will not have life everlasting." While the mystery of the real presence of Christ in the Eucharist introduces us into the heart of the Incarnation itself, and holds a key to what the economy of this ultimate act of love reveals about the triune Godhead, an uneducated

34. For a brief and clear exposition of Rahner's accomplishment in this regard, see Mary Hines, *The Transformation of Dogma* (New York: Paulist Press, 1989).

35. Permanent does not mean that any finite nature lasts forever, either as individual of a certain kind, or even as species. Rather, it points to the evidence that things enjoy different ranges of stability, remaining for a while this or that kind of thing, knowable as such.

person can, in any culture and any epoch, grasp the core of what Christ wants us to know about His great gift of Himself. Nourishment, food and drink, as sustainer of life, everyone understands. That supernatural life must be nourished by God's giving Himself some way is not hard to see. That we are to find our everlasting life by entering into the person of the Word who has come into history to share our destiny is difficult, but one can sort of understand what is meant. That Christ should find a way of incarnating this participation within His community in a manner that would rally our participation, make it palpable in historical, sacramental continuity with Him through ordination of the priests who were to make His sacrifice daily present, and in a way that becomes "our daily bread," is, on one level, something quite simple, a simplicity that stuns us. It is so direct, *it reorders our sense of what is real!* Just as one would expect God to do, if ever He undertook to teach us. The key to our beginning to grasp this is faith, *fides,* as con-*fide*nce: willingness to accept the gift, to believe that God would so love us that He would accord us such a participation in His own life. We pull back from this because we know that to make room for it in our lives, we shall have to do away with all the little addictions that accord us a false sense of security. But courage is a moral, not an intellectual, problem. Our problem is not *interpretation,* it is *generosity,* namely, finding a bit of it in ourselves to begin the reception of so great a generosity it threatens the pseudoreality of our ego constructions.

I am not suggesting that there is no need for the profoundest theological penetration of which we are capable of these "simple" mysteries. But, as I attempt in the last chapter an overview of the actual reality of the Church as a divine-human presence in the world of our time, we shall see that there are no easy answers to the question of practical wisdom: how to balance the intellectual and moral dimensions of our lives. It would be well, against the background of what has just been touched on, to recall a word of wisdom from the great Thomist theologian Marc-Dominique Chenu, which I quoted earlier.

> The scientific function is necessary for the spiritual and temporal architecture of a Christendom: thus it triumphed in the thirteenth century; but it can only achieve solid results if it remains evangelical, always bearing the Word of God as a message, assiduously frequenting the ancient witnesses, resisting the temptation to objectify the mystery in an unconscious scientism, conserving the free intimacy of the faith in the midst of the most rigorous explanations.[36]

Even in science the truth engages the whole person. If gift of self is condition for realization of our personhood and the attainment of truth, we should probe more deeply into the anthropological question "what is the self?" and become clearer yet about the relationship of self to the call to personhood. With this we shall begin the next chapter.

36. M.-D. Chenu, *La théologie au douzième siècle* (Paris: J. Vrin, 1957), 249.

AUTHENTICITY AND CHRISTIC MAN

THE CHRISTIAN SENSE OF SELF AND THE PROJECT OF AUTHENTICITY

From Autonomy to Mission

Tradition and Authenticity spelled out what it means to be an *autos*, a self. It showed how the self's search to become more properly and responsibly itself requires, today, development of methods of formal, critical "appropriation."[1] But when I wrote that book, I had not proceeded terribly far in the present methodical appropriating of one of the two traditions that has most formed my natural faith.

In confessing that this appropriation has not caused me to change my mind fundamentally about my Catholic faith (I never expected that it would), in effect, I testified to the depth of those "first loves" that, anchored deep in the self, mold our entire lives. Recall Saint Augustine: "Show me a man's loves and I'll show you the man!" The Catholic Church has certainly formed me to the core; I am as happy to be a Catholic as I am unhappy with my infidelity and those of fellow Catholics to the divine call; and I remain grateful, and struggling to learn to love better that Jesus Christ the Church announces to me, to deepen this most vital of all interpersonal relationships. Given this reality, when faced with negative aspects of the Church's life in complex, ambiguous situations, what is more natural than still to want to put the best face possible on a Church one loves? But respect for truth is served by writing down such rationalizations and asking those who do not agree to hammer at the dishonesty fed by insecurity. Authenticity cannot be reached without the loving help of others.

These several years of reflecting methodically on my most beloved tradition have, however, changed me. The project has not proved fruitless. This hard work not only has produced a deepening of my understanding of what the tradition centrally claims, but also has led me, for the first time in my life, to face up explicitly to the main thrust of what is claimed. Doing so has altered my understanding of what it is to be a self. *Tradition and Authenticity* did not develop well the reality of self as *person*, and person

1. Compare with my early article, "The Problem of the Self," *The Review of Metaphysics* 15:1 (September 1961): 19–33.

as call to a mission, and hence the reality of person as relational, and the relational as self-transcending. The present appropriation has led me to reflect on personhood's ground in love, and it has driven home that love is not first and foremost an idea but an ontological reality, an illumination and energy one receives from another person and, with difficulty, passes on in the events of being. The Catholic tradition is centered neither in the vision that it has produced, nor in the institution that continues it, but in the real presence of Jesus Christ. My sense of the faith as a living reality centered in the reality of Christ, a *communio sanctorum*, in which "things happen" between persons, living and dead, has strengthened. The effort to communicate this living reality to the reader risks annoying him by being perhaps too personal, too existential. *Being and Truth,* which profited from my work on earlier drafts of the present work, proposes some of the same insights, but less personally.

I understand better now that man is a nature intended from the first moment of creation to be called into fulfillment *super-naturally,* by a second higher creation, due to God's *dramatic* reaching down from His supreme transcendence to intervene into the history of fallen man. Both reflection on the Incarnation and a recuperation of the lived experience of the eucharistic Church that is Christ continuing to incarnate through a titanic struggle against evil and a reflection on the being-implications of that mysterious reality have inevitably reverberated on every aspect of my understanding of human nature.

I am beginning to see more clearly our social and historical character in the way I believe God intends it to function in His Kingdom, as revealed in the living tradition of the *catholica.* Human beings are meant to be in this world but not "of this world," a world destined to entropy. While fulfillment of God's Kingdom will be achieved only eschatologically and supernaturally, nevertheless the nature-transforming effects of the Kingdom, mysteriously already in our midst through our acts of response, begin to be felt on the struggle against evil in this world, the beginning traces of the Kingdom that will have no end. In heaven its finite subjects will be called to advance in perfection forever.

What are the implications for the project of authenticity—of becoming more fully and responsibly one's self,[2] hence of realizing our freedom—of what has been learned here about ourselves as "Christic persons" bound to one another in that unique eucharistic community of love, the Church? What light does this understanding of the Church as divine call issued to all throw on the ambiguous sociological reality of the Church, the flawed, indeed in daily experience often exasperating, community in which the Christian is called to live out his earthly existence?

These questions about concrete existence in the real Church of the objective Christ suggest two parts to the conclusion of the present immodest

2. One must understand "the self" to be the reflective, willing center of an essentially social being. See *TA,* chap. 1.

volume: First, a concluding reflection on the ideal of what God has revealed He intends redeemed man to be, with emphasis on the concrete nature of one's *missio*, that personal call to be the person God intends each of us to be. And second, with this ideal as criterion, a survey of the actual ambiguous communitarian reality: how does the present Church measure up? Obviously, only God can judge. But every evening in his personal examination of conscience the Christian is asked to assess his progress and to target faults for attention. The Holy Father has asked the Church in preparation for the coming of the third millennium to make an examination of conscience.[3] So, with the help of friends in different positions and various movements in the Church, I have sought to make a modest contribution in that direction, by sharing what I have been able to glimpse of this singularly complex human-divine incarnate reality as the pilgrim progresses through this *lacrimae valle*.

The revelation of the supernatural in Jesus Christ calls us to look beyond ordinary experience, which, due to our finitude, is myopic and, because of sin, distorted: everyday experiences could cause us to lose hope in man. In contrast to the individuals in all other natural species, man is not intended primarily to be sacrificed to the survival of the species.[4] The astonishing good news is that we are each created, neither inherently egocentric nor species-centric, but Christo-centric. The human person should be characterized less centrally by *auto-nomia* (rule by the self) than by *missio*, the realization of the place in Christ's gathering together all mankind to which this unique self alone has been called; less by that natural *formation*, the base that has been molded throughout the long natural and cultural history that leads to him, than by *re-formation, metanoia, con-version*—a supernatural response to a supernatural call of love, trans-forming and uplifting nature and culture, creative of "a new man" (2 Cor. 5:17; Gal. 6:15) and a "New City," citizen of the City of God.[5]

It is this revelation of our personhood that has directed Western man's attention to the uniqueness and sacredness of the person from whence alone stems the Occidental doctrine of "the dignity of the person" and "the rights of man." (The *United Nations Declaration of Human Rights* is a document squarely founded in Christian anthropology, a code in fact

3. Encyclical, *Tertio Millennio Adveniente*.

4. The Christian tradition's exaltation of virginity is then antipagan; it is meant to be a sign that mere species survival is not the ultimate end, but only a condition for mankind's fulfillment. The extreme witness of giving one's life says, "I am not the supreme principle, nor is my family, nor even humankind."

5. If we reject the destiny God has planned for us, does that mean a part of His plan comes to nought? While the loss of one human soul is in the eyes of God a tragedy, He knows from all eternity how to build His Kingdom around such efforts to frustrate it; the believer is confident that His design is not ultimately frustrated. Whether, as Balthasar says in one of his last books, *Was dürfen wir hoffen?* (Dare we hope "that all men will be saved"?: With a short discourse on hell, trans. David Kipp and Lothar Krauth [San Francisco: Ignatius Press, 1988]. God may find a way in fact to get every person in the end freely to accept His love, or He has fashioned the design knowing who would absent Himself; we know that His plan is not ultimately frustrated.

written with strong Christian leadership, the Catholic philosopher Jacques Maritain playing a leading role.)

From Appropriation to Expropriation

The ontologically appropriate movement of the maturing self is then not finally appropriation *(Aneignung)*—my subsuming critically all reality into my conscious self—but expropriation *(Enteignung)* of my self by Christ into His divine personhood. I die to my ego, I am brought out of the bastions of my carefully nourished illusions, I am taught to abandon the illusion of control, in order that I may "put on Christ" (Gal. 3:27). "If any man comes to me and does not hate his own father and mother and wife and children and brothers and sisters, yes, and even his own life, he cannot be my disciple" (Luke 14:26). In the words of Saint Bonaventure, "To possess God is to be possessed by God."[6] And in the words of Balthasar:

> Such a "following after" *[Nachfolge]* requires according to the Gospel a "leaving all," "a hating all" [refusing to make an idol of anything, even one's own nation and culture, even one's citizenship as a "child of the West"], above all not out of one's own Ego *(the* sin of Adam), in order to find all again in the unique Act *[Tun]* of the Father's will: God, whom one obeys, one's fellow men, whom one serves, and one's self, which one encounters first in such obedience and service.[7]

"The World," home of the self-starter yuppie, of the self-made man, of the Führer (Mr. Superself), the First Party secretary "servant of the Iron Laws of History," and of the Iron Lady,[8] proponent of liberalism, does not choose to understand this, any more than Adam did. Even someone born, baptized, and raised Christian can, as I did, take a lifetime to start to grasp the great mystery of our true personhood, that it is rooted more in Christ than in nature, that what we are is revealed more by Christ's suffering on the cross to redeem us than it is by DNA and pathological traits of character. We are so sunk into our egocentric pursuit of natural and worldly success, and so distracted by frenetic activity, we are blind and deaf to the quiet call of the supernature born in us through "the mystery of the water and the Spirit."

The radical ontological claim unveiled by this revelation is uncompromising; it radiates the absoluteness of divinity: every phase and every entity

---

6. Cited without reference in *The Church's Confession of Faith* (San Francisco: Ignatius Press, 1987), 206.

7. Balthasar, *Theodramatik*, 2:2:248. Note the movement here is from expropriation out of a false, sinful, egocentric self into the personhood in Christ, where we discover the true self He has appropriated.

8. The Iron Lady, who here serves as a symbol of materialistic liberalism, was not, in the person of Margaret Thatcher, a person without Christian concerns for the good of society. I have read some profound reflections by Lady Thatcher. But economic liberalism by itself cannot, as I believe she would agree, produce a happy society.

of the creation is expressly willed by the Father (Ephesians speaks of His *telematos* [1:9]).[9] Only human moral evil goes against His will.[10]

If the genuine way to attain true selfhood ("authenticity") is to discern what it is the Father wants one to do, really what He wants one *to be*, where do I find out concretely what is expected of me? The will of the Father for each of us is made known by the Son's continuing incarnation as head of the Church that, through His Holy Spirit, and this in a way a feeble human being like you and me can relate to, and through this means know clearly what is expected of each as *homo ecclesiasticus*.[11] The life in me, with the beginnings of which the freedom of my parents had something to do, and with the fulfillment of which my decisions have much to do, is a gift of the "grace" that is creation and hence nature itself, a genetic inheritance reaching back to the origins of life, and is bestowed on me for a purpose in the exact concrete form in which it comes. I am born, genetically predisposed, into a situation in history.[12] My freedom consists in actualizing as fully as possible the potentialities of my specific nature and particular capabilities in the precise situations in which I am called to play out my life. This demands working with God's grace to reform morally unacceptable deficient elements in my inheritance and social situation. This can be achieved only supernaturally, through revelation to me of what it is the Father sent the Son to restore (rescuing nature from the distortions and obfuscations introduced by sin, freeing it from its self-imposed bondage, raising it above itself).

A first prerequisite is to know the divine instructions: I must cooperate with God's grace to exercise the supernatural virtues—faith, hope, and charity. These provide the structured force of my supernatural character, the form of my new life. They inform the concrete exercise of those acts of following Christ along the way designated by Him.

This may still sound vague until we consider the other aspect, how through the living teaching and sacramental direction of the Church God tells us what He expects of us. Natural ethics is thus subsumed into a supernatural "love life," based on a revealed supernatural understanding of man, which shows that God intends His redeemed nature to be fulfilled

9. *Telematos* invokes an end or plan. In the same phrase we are told that the Father makes known to us in Jesus Christ the *mysterion* of His will, as a plan for the fullness (*pleromatos*) of the times (Eph. 1:10) according to the "economy" of His plan, with all "to be headed up" (*anakephalaiosasthai*) in Christ.

10. By "evil" is meant here not the *malum* of finitude nor physical evil due to defects in nature. For elaboration on this, see my article on the suffering of the cosmos, "Das Leiden des Kosmos," *Internationale katholische Zeitschrift Communio* 6/88 (November 1988): 500–508. The Bible hints that without the disorder introduced by the revolt of man, the sufferings brought on by finitude would have been much reduced, just as in the eschaton "the lion will lie down with the lamb."

11. Balthasar, *Love Alone: The Way of Revelation*, ed. Alexander Dru (London: Sheed and Ward), 97.

12. On our "situatedness," see *BT*, 27–29.

only beyond *(supra)* itself, eucharistically, through that unique mode of sacramental incorporation into Christ through His Church—by discovering and reenacting what has already been fulfilled in Christ, which His Church teaches us and to which it directs us. "To join in doing what has already been done in its fullness, and to realize and fulfill what has already been realized and fulfilled, is the fundamental law of Christian ethics, and even of Christian knowledge; for it is only then that what is in itself manifest is made manifest to us."[13]

If we were to say that human action then should be more *imitatio* than *creatio,* we would not mean that Christ expects, in our cooperation, no new contribution on our part, but what we achieve is never utterly new, for everything is to be rediscovered as always already having been in the infinite Source, through the Logos. Time is permeated by eternity both originating all possibility and breaking into history. A Marc Chagall would be the first to admit that his overpowering biblical canvasses in Nice are only un-covering *(a-letheia)*[14] shallow depths of what is hidden in God. There remains no natural ethics untouched by the light of Revelation. Everything, the whole cosmos, is transformed by "the new creation." In a moment we shall consider what this might mean concretely. We cannot get off the hook of our personal responsibility by staying with the contemplation of abstract form!

The philosophers had already discovered that man transcends himself, that his consciousness and his desire reach out beyond and above the sensibly experiential, yearning for fulfillment in that "something higher" that the philosophers were not sure he could attain adequately. For neither Plato, Aristotle, the Stoa, nor Plotinus could this "Beyond" personally respond to man and his profound yearnings. The Idea of the Good, and the Unmoved Mover, Self-thinking Thought, and the Ineffable One were in no love relationship with man. Yet, as man reaches out straining to transcend himself, that is what he seeks, *a chance to respond,* to be loved and to love.[15]

So what then does this "following the Way" by practicing the three supernatural virtues as foundation of the character of the *homo ecclesiasticus* mean concretely, operationally, in everyday life?

13. Ibid., 95.

14. The Greek word for truth captures this sense of transcendence perfectly, taking away the *lethe,* the veil, of forgetfulness ("Do this in remembrance of me"), which allows the true reality of something or someone to shine forth (an appearing in German is an *Erscheinung; scheinen* means "to shine, to appear").

15. In one of the great moments of American corporate history, Patrick Haggerty, the then young president of the still young Texas Instruments, and a serious Catholic, stood up before a group of cynical security analysts in New York City, seeking investment funds, and told them, "Man needs three things: to love, to be loved, and to be able to create. Any institution that offers him the setting in which these are possible will succeed" (anecdote recounted to me by Bryan Smith, who was vice president of the company and a close friend of Patrick Haggerty).

THE FOUNDATIONS: THE SUPERNATURAL VIRTUES OF FAITH, HOPE, AND CHARITY

Although God is working in the world, ruling over the "having become" (*essentia, das Gewesene*) of nature and my own human nature and inherited temperament and culture, there still remains, even after the redemptive act of the cross, the enormous difficulty[16] that our efforts on our own to be gods has disastrously distorted that nature and introduced twisted elements into every culture, and, worse yet, killed a part of the vital two-way relationship, the mutual intercourse of self-giving between the infinite freedom and the free finite persons Scripture calls *agape,* love. From the moment of the Fall, our essences have become *ambiguous.* We have broken the interpersonal relationship from the finite end, cutting ourselves off from the ontological possibility of our true fulfillment. We cannot by our initiative restore the lifeline,[17] for our offense is limitless, the effects of it reaching down into the very processes of nature, and rendering all our cultures and civilizations skewered. The initiative for restoration of the generous relationship can come again unilaterally only from the offended infinite Source,[18] and only on His terms, for they require His new creation, "When you send forth your spirit they are created and you give new life to the face of the earth" (Ps. 104:30). Consequently, since the Fall, we have been no longer able to fulfill our nature, which then became, for that reason, in Paul's terrifying but, as regards the essential, exact word, *dead.*

Dead? Is that not a bit extreme? How can a Christian maintain such a claim in the face of the immense vitality of the great civilizations, especially the modern HTX? It is not extreme if one understands what life really, ultimately is, as the Source of all vitality, who is Life itself, has revealed it in Jesus. A certain painful, diminished, natural, biological, and often perverse cultural existence (but with its glories, to be sure, God never abandoned man, neither nature nor culture became completely perverted— beautiful temples emerged among the slaves) continued after the Fall, but with no known destiny. All the greatest empires have fallen into dust, their temples into ruins. We now know that without the new creation all the achievements of man will end in the zero temperature gradients of cosmic entropy, reduced to everlasting silence. If we cannot reach beyond this disturbed natural and often hateful war-filled cultural life, then all our works, individually and collectively, are destined to end in death, leaving not a trace. We have now ingeniously created means of hastening the end of human life through the effect of nuclear winter.

---

16. It would be more than a difficulty—a tragedy—if God knew no way to undo its effects.

17. Balthasar, *Love Alone,* 62.

18. A Christian cannot defend unequivocally any culture, and emphatically not the "Christian West," for all its Christian-inspired benefacts for mankind. God, working through the teaching Church that He (painfully) guides must show the way to criticism and *re-form* of this, the as yet most "Christian" civilization.

The great blessing of man is also his curse, he alone of all species can grasp time, he alone can "make use of time," he alone can waste it, only he knows the futility of the material cosmos—if he cares to face the facts, as self-styled "tragic men" from Aeschylus to Nietzsche have done. When first uttered, twenty-five hundred years before the contemporary discoveries of thermodynamics, that word—that the world would end—was prophetic; the Greeks did not learn of it until Christianity brought the good news that man was not destined to end in shadowy underworld existence; the cosmos, the Greek philosophers believed, would continue endless circling. Only in our time has science established that the truth is worse than the tragedians and philosophers thought. As the prophesy to the Hebrews had already established, there will remain, in the language of the second law of thermodynamics "no information." So "Eat, drink and be merry, for tomorrow you will dissolve in entropy!"

Enter, just when we need it desperately, *the supernatural virtue of hope.* The atheist may consider it pie-in-the-sky optimism. The Christian believes hope to be the effect of the always-creating God in us, lifting our sights above the depressing battlefield toward the coming glorious victory of His Kingdom, constantly reminding us of His sacrificial triumph over death.

Obviously, there can be no hope of everlasting life unless one believes the witness to Christ's victory. So hope is supported by the supernatural virtue of faith, the human response to the most generous of all divine gifts, letting God work in us to get us to drop our fears and welcome His invitation. The life of God in us must be allowed to take the *form* that Paul invokes in Ephesians: "For He has made known to us in all wisdom and insight the mystery of his will, according to his purpose that he set forth in Christ *as a plan for the fullness of time,* to unite all things in him, things in heaven and things on earth" (1:9–10).

This life of God in us that reveals the *mysterion* is not experienced first and foremost as knowledge or theory, for it is grace flowing through us into loving personal interaction that builds the Kingdom—"the center of gravity of which are the corporal works of mercy."[19] We experience it first in the love of parents drawing out (e-ducating) our own personhood, our ability to re-spond to their love. That is why there can be no faith and hope without love: properly understood, this is an *ontological* impossibility. Faith is rooted in that experience of being loved by others, a love pure enough to show a face of Christ to the one loved. A theoretical knowledge of a Jesus Christ formed out of pieces of Bible and tradition is not that knowing Christ in the true biblical sense: that occurs only in letting oneself be penetrated by the effects of concrete acts of love. The *appearance* of faith may be there in the man who cries "Lord! Lord!" "But only he loves me who does the will of my Father," "Only love can recognize love," *"Glaubhaft ist nur die Liebe"* ("only love can be believed").[20]

19. Ibid., 99.
20. Ibid., 62, 68. "Only Love Can Be Believed" was the original title of *Love Alone.*

Talk of separating "faith" and "good works" is based then on an ontological misunderstanding: acts of love are the acting out of faith, they are the practical manifestation of that insight and wisdom that are granted in faith. Faith without good works would be really only a hypocritical protestation that one believes, were it not for the damage of original sin, which weakens the connection between mind and heart. We can actually believe (up to a point, and even then only out of an experience of love) yet lack the courage to open our hearts[21] to the full reality of the life trying to flow through that enlightenment of the mind (*sophia*, in the word of Ephesians)—our every addiction is an obstacle to Him and contradicts His love;[22] such an unfulfilled faith will die.

Saint Paul never termed faith, hope, and charity *virtues*; such a classification stems from medieval theology, building on an Aristotelian "faculties" analysis of human nature. The exercise of each faculty (such as the intellect or the will) is made surer through reinforcing repetition of appropriate acts, building the good habits, the "virtues."[23] In Paul's vision the emphasis is not on power flowing from something we do, by repeated action or otherwise, but on the reception of the grace of God that takes the form of these participations in the divine life Paul terms *pistis* (faith); *elpis*, "in this hope we are saved" (Rom. 8:24), "our adoption as sons and the redemption of our bodies"; and *agape*, "faith working through love" (Gal. 5:6). This recalls the effects of the sacraments: the *ex opere operato* points to the divine origin of the efficacy, but the human agent, the minister, must freely act, as instrument, with the intention of cooperating with what God wants to effect, but with that efficacy not being dependent on the holiness of the instrument, the always sinful priest.

Similarly, our reception of the grace of faith, hope, and charity is not due to some preexisting merit in us, but the effective reception does require our cooperation, and for that we must know concretely what is expected of us. While faith, hope, and charity are all manifestations of the same grace of God operating in us, Paul does distinguish them, even going so far as to say "the greatest of these is love."[24] When Saint Thomas characterizes love as the form of the other virtues *(caritas forma virtutem)* he captures this sense.

IF WE ARE "EXPROPRIATED" BY GOD, IS THERE ANY ROLE LEFT FOR "APPROPRIATION"? HOW CONCRETE IS THE REVELATION OF GOD'S WILL? "CHRISTIAN PHILOSOPHY" REVISITED

If through faith, hope, and charity God "expropriates us"—*enteignet*

---

21. This is the most mysterious thing about us. Why, when God is offering us this life, are we so afraid to accept it, especially when we know we have everything to gain, and will lose everything by trying to hang on desperately to our little *redoute d'ego*?

22. On the way we stop grace by hanging onto our securities, see Gerald May, M.D., *Addiction and Grace* (San Francisco: Harper and Row, 1991); Balthasar, *Love Alone*, 68.

23. The word *virtue* comes from the Latin *virtu*, from *vir*-man: they give power.

24. "So faith, hope, and love abide, these three; but the greatest of these is love" (1 Cor. 13:13).

uns—into Himself, how can there remain any role for something as activist-like as pursuit of authenticity through "critical appropriation"?

It is not to save face for my project that I want to show that for the believing Christian the role of appropriation of the traditions is an essential aspect of a still valid pursuit of "authenticity in search for ecumenical wisdom." Supernature does not eradicate nature, rather it builds on and trans-forms it.[25] Our rational nature, though damaged, remains a grace of the "first dispensation," the creation of the cosmos. Natural (and partly sin-obscured) reason is illumined by the light of faith. Thus, the Christian knows that the Way lies in his listening to "every word that comes from the mouth of God" (Matt. 4:4) and in following His commandments, "the greatest" being to love God with all one's heart and one's neighbor as oneself. Love of self then, rather than remaining egoistic stubbornness, requires struggling for authenticity; it demands in our self-conscious era appropriation of the traditions that have made us concretely who we are.[26] A dialectical situation here reveals itself: successful appropriation requires expropriation into God; only He can enlighten us about ourselves definitively. But the knowledge appropriation brings helps us find the way to that expropriation and move along it, just as, dialectically, steps in surrendering to the expropriation—acts of conversion—bring the light for more penetrating appropriation of what constitutes us.

Just how full—and detailed and concrete—is that Word into which we are expropriated? The tradition responds without ambiguity: in the ongoing teaching of the Church, which is the intellectual dimension of its eucharistic life in Christ, the Word is full and entire. Consequently, for the Christian, appropriation is not a lonely, egocentric exercise. (Already *Tradition and Authenticity* had shown that the critical task of appropriating the traditions relevant in our vast planetary situation exceeds the capacity of any individual, or even small research group.) If one lives in the Church, the task goes forward in loving receptivity of the whole and entire Word of God, as it unfolds from the oldest patriarchal materials retained in Genesis to the most recent teaching of the Church. This teaching calls on the united efforts of all the bishops, theologians, and scholars working cooperatively in the Church. (The CIA may be a much larger think tank, but it does not have roots in almost every society and every class, and it fails to return to the roots of three millennia ago, nor is it necessarily always the work of the Holy Spirit!) When the Christian approaches the tradition and the Church with love and docility, seeking to understand all that it is given to one to understand, he is supported by a unique, communally lived *sophia*, the *communio sanctorum*, an incarnational, human reality become instrument of the Holy Spirit.

25. Saint Thomas, *ST* 1.1, 8 *ad* 2.
26. This I show in *TA*. For a briefer version, see the three essays I published as *Self-Discovery* (San Francisco: Golden Phoenix Press, 1985).

This ongoing communal appropriation calls for a sustained effort of study, prayer, contemplation, dialogue, spiritual direction, and social action. Those who undertake it are henceforth conscious that their freedom is not engaged in the form of an imperial sitting in judgment on the whole tradition (as happens in egocentric appropriation, never advocated by *Truth and Authenticity!*), but in a freeing recognition of the poverty of one's own limited personal wisdom,[27] and in obedience (which is to say "listening") to the symphonic truth gathered in Jesus Christ. The Christian's being conformed to Christ is an ontological process, a progressive trans-formation of his being. (This is not just transformation of his *Sein*—the *Mitsein* world of his interpretation, but of his *esse,* as he comes to live more and more in Christ through His eucharistic Body. He is changing in the very kind of person he is; he acts differently; he is "a different man" after each conversion; everyone can see this reality radiating from the saint.)

When I discuss matters of Church teaching with some of my Catholic students, I am amazed with what nonchalance they will announce, "The archbishop said *X*, and I really don't agree at all," when it is some difficult matter over which the archbishop has agonized, consulted his moral theologians, and prayed for guidance in the light of the Church's teaching in which he has spent a lifetime immersing himself. Of course, "he does have the right to his opinion. . . ." That he may enjoy a charism of discernment, and has been handed in ordination the authority to discern, they have never heard.

The poverty that must be at the root of our willingness to receive—dependently to accept God's love and hence to receive the gift of faith, of con-fidence—should manifest itself concretely in confidence in the Church of Christ speaking through the magisterium. Does the Holy Spirit guide the Church or not? If He does, that guidance has to be effective through human means, which includes visible signs of unity: an authority capable of speaking out even when a truth is "unpopular."

Because we ourselves are not instant saints, and so our social, national, traditional, and personal histories include many complex, "insistent" (in Heidegger's sense—"stubborn" might be a good equivalent),[28] and destructive elements, the critical process of appropriation is not only a receptive listening to the good and the constructive, but also a struggle to address our own complexes, which paralyze our desire to listen and incite us to indulge in fantasies. We have to seek healing of traumas, undo bad habits, see beyond limiting ideologies, learn to be discerning (better, to allow the Spirit to discern through us, in all humility and service). Every act of sin, even long forgiven, leaves its mortgage on our ability to see—as Plato put

27. See the development of Saint Ignatius's attitude of intellectual poverty by Peter Henrici, S.J., "The Spiritual Dimension and Its Form of Reason," *International Catholic Review: Communio* 20:4 (winter 1993): 638–51.

28. Elements that function rather like the popularized notion of the psychological "complex," blocking our access, our receptivity to experiences of the new.

it, every sin constitutes "a disturbance in the soul," for it is a bad *re-sponse*, a wrong commitment, and hence breeds an *in-sistenz* to justify itself, which blocks the liberation of new *ek-sistenz*. Even after conversion, skeins of tangled thinking have to be untangled. The Christian's appropriative task is personal in the transcending sense of allowing the person of Jesus Christ to come in and "penetrate into a realm where everything is an obstacle to him and contradicts his love." "A human spiritual-subject *[Geistesubjekte]* will be at the same time de-privatized, socialized, made into a Space and a bearer of the community." Just how far this potential *reach [Ausgriff]* will become actual, how far then *en Christoi* and in analogy to Jesus he will provide, in his own person, "a freedom giving Space *[Spielraum]* for others" depends both on how far the person's call and mission reaches and on how actively he seizes onto it and carries it through.[29]

A final question about the project of appropriation: if one is so fortunate as to be open to an inexhaustible tradition of faith, grounded in the Infinite God become man, why would he want to divert his limited time of study and contemplation to appropriation of other traditions, not so fully formed to the divine will?

There are four levels to my answer. First, pragmatic: as *Tradition and Authenticity* pointed out, either we of differing traditions are going to learn lovingly to appreciate one another, or there will be war. Second, God will "gather into the barn" of the Kingdom all the truth discovered and expressed in the experience of all the great traditions. The people who live out their lives in the "other" traditions are our "neighbors," whom we are to love. We are not called on to love them in the abstract, but as they are, that is, formed by "the already having been" of their traditions. Intimate, appreciative knowledge of "the other" is expropriative: it helps pull us free from the cocoon we have woven about ourselves, and to give ourselves to them in loving attention and just appreciation.

Saint Thomas Aquinas, according to Brother Reginald, asked at the end of his life that all his works be burned, because next to the glories of God seen mystically, they were "mere straw." Brother Reginald disobeyed Brother Thomas, in the process, I believe, doing God's will. For I do not think God sees as "straw" all that He has accomplished through us in the form of the glories of human discovery and culture. Here, on the contrary, is good grain that in the final judgment He will separate from the remaining chaff.

Remembering Père Teilhard de Chardin, I would put in a special word here for those grand new traditions of natural and psychological sciences that have opened to the gaze of man fresh vistas of cosmos, life, and soul. In

---

29. Balthasar, *Love Alone*, 68; Balthasar, *Theodramatik*, 2:2:249. Elsewhere Balthasar suggests that while response to the call of "ordinary sanctity" requires that the whole field of one's life become con-formed to God's will, there are in the distinctive missions God grants different intensities and depths of penetration. The great saints are special gifts to the Church, special charismatic in-breakings of the Holy Spirit to help the Church show Christ in new circumstances (*Thérèse de Lisieux: Histoire d'une mission* [Paris: Apostolat des Éditions, 1973], introduction).

the process, they have prepared the way for those technical and managerial accomplishments that allow mankind to embrace, construct, and manage ever larger systems, an essential part of the spread of the noosphere, uniting mankind. Teilhard was convinced that this expansion of knowledge and control is in fulfillment of God's will, indeed is the divine creative impulse working itself out through the cooperation of that created finite human freedom that is essential to this achievement.[30]

Is Teilhard correct to believe this? Is it better that I am able to phone my friend Joseph in Vienna and arrange a meeting of our forum to discuss efforts to help the Church in the newly freed lands in Central Europe, and then climb aboard a 747 and be whisked there in seven hours, than the situation confronting Saint Thomas: a note from the superior-general in Rome summoning him would entail three weeks' travel, and then Brother Thomas would set off for a perilous, and not very comfortable, month's journey on the back of an ass. That speed, of course, does not make me more knowledgeable when I get to Vienna, certainly not more profound or saintly than Brother Thomas! But I do know the situation of our planet far better than he did and basic things about the state of the cosmos of which this great man could not dream. And HTX data-processing capabilities permit me easy access to the voluminous legacy of the sainted doctor himself. On another front, our better knowledge of psychopathology holds hope not only of managing illness better but also of enhanced understanding of our human nature, when we bind it together with the wonderful "straw" Thomas gathered into his barn. Yes, it is better to know than not to know whatever is good: that is an elementary corollary of natural faith in Being. But the Christian at once adds: "provided we allow the Holy Spirit to illumine our wisdom as we seek to integrate its meaning, and provided we avoid the distractions of idle curiosity." Only thus is Thomas's straw revealed to be wheat, and that wheat can be milled to become the flour of a wise Eucharist humbly offered by the contemplating, teaching, praying community.

With the power brought by HTX developments in knowledge come, as always, new dangers. But the fact that with each breakthrough in understanding and managing energy come new possibilities for manipulating, not to speak of slaughtering larger numbers of people more efficiently, in no way negates the beauty of our cooperating in allowing God's creation to support nearly 6 billion people with an ever lengthening life expectancy, and ever richer cultural possibilities for the masses. Their ability to read opens new worlds to them; that many choose to read trash is typical of the tragic abuse of all God's gifts. That democracy places undreamed possibilities in the hands of the average citizen, who may then turn to "Elvis-the-pelvis" worship and so throw most of the opportunities on the

---

30. Balthasar basically agrees. See his highly appreciative view of how modernity has freed man to encounter God as a drama of freedoms, without the confusion of divinized nature in *The God Question and Modern Man* (New York: Seabury Press, 1967).

increasing mountain of garbage, and in the meantime not even bother to vote, takes nothing away from the accomplishment of modern government in at least giving him the chance to make something more of himself.

That brings me to a fourth reason we should appropriate other traditions: Islam is missionary, communism is (or was) missionary, any tradition with a strong love for its truth coupled with an eschatological sense will be "apostolic," in the sense of seeing itself as sent forth by the source of truth to propagate it. Now, we have learned much about how the truth about Jesus Christ is to be spread: not by the sword, not through skillful manipulation of the weak, but as between friends who thoroughly respect one another's mature freedom. That overworked word *dialogue* is here for once appropriate: in sharing the word (logos) it has been given to each of us to see, we move forward together toward *the Word* itself. In dia-logue about Christ I not only must know well my Lord but also must have a sympathetic, penetrating understanding and appreciation of the other's experience, so that I can meet and join with him where he really is, see the Lord working in him, show Him working in me, so we can go forward together in search of the truth.

APPROPRIATION, AUTHENTICITY, AND *ECCLESIA SEMPER REFORMANDA*

In appropriative interaction with other traditions and in constantly deepening encounter with one's own ongoing experience of the Church we must be open to reform—personal, scientific, and institutional. Such realities as new depths of encounter with what once were distant traditions, a growing sense of the possibility of "liberation," and a heightened feminine consciousness are all experiences growing out of new social relations in which we now find ourselves. The fluidity and rapidity of change and unprecedented pluralism of contemporary society make the liberal mentality extremely suspicious of "old structures" as such and of all dogmatic formulation,[31] and of any authority that would dare say to anyone that what they want is wrong.

These demands of the times that we change impinge on us not just individually but as Church. I return to Joseph Cardinal Ratzinger's remarkable speech delivered in the summer of 1990, "Reform from the Beginning." It invokes such a living relationship with the infinite God who overcomes all boundaries, and at the same time so wonderfully situates reform *in us*, that the issue of "dogmatism" we have been exploring gets put in its proper place.[32]

31. On this see Matthew L. Lamb, "Inculturation and Western Culture: The Dialogical Experience between Gospel and Culture," *International Catholic Review: Communio* 21:1 (spring 1994): 137–40.

32. Ratzinger, "Reform from the Beginning," *Thirty Days in the Life of the Church and the World* (November 1990): 62–69. Cardinal Ratzinger, as secretary of the Sacred

The cardinal begins in a way that reminds us how sensitive one must be to changes in language, and that we in Europe and North America live indeed in a liberal society. He will not speak, he declares, of the "Church," because people immediately become defensive when they hear the word, but of "community." He then comments almost in passing, "Might the problem be that until now, the type of reform which could make the Church a community experience worth living has not yet been discovered?" Consider the source, as you contemplate the radical implications of the question, call to mind the inroads of evangelical sects in many "Catholic" countries, and remember the question when we listen to what he will say about this need for radical reform at the end of the article. He clearly intends to take up what we have found to be the most significant challenge of Protestantism: the effort to live the Church as a true community as congregationalism does.

After reviewing what our liberal contemporaries want of the Church—that it be "an oasis of liberty" where one could "savor the taste of liberty, of being free: that emergence from the cavern of which Gregory the Great speaks with Plato in mind"—and after showing why the Church cannot be a democracy that would make of it purely our human work, and because in a democracy every majority suffers eventually in being replaced by a new majority, he passes to a description of the authentic *reformatio* that must always occur in the Church as a realization of true freedom.

It does not consist in always being able to remodel "our" Church as we like; it is not based in our power to reinvent it, but in the fact that we keep clearing away what we have constructed to make for the purest light that comes from above and that is an explosion of purest liberty. Saint Bonaventure was like Michelangelo in seeing our task to be that of the sculptor, liberating the image that is deep in the stone by removing what is superfluous: it is an *ablatio*, so that the *nobilis forma* emerges. Only when we allow to be removed the dross in ourselves that clogs the Church's arteries will the image of God in us shine forth most purely. To be sure, the Church will always need new human support structures to be able to address every historical epoch and operate in it for the benefit of those faced with the new conditions.

These ecclesiastical institutions with their juridical features are not negative but on the contrary are simply necessary, indispensable to a certain

---

Congregation for the Doctrine of the Faith, is responsible to the pope for the maintenance of the integrity of the Church's teaching. When he speaks, therefore, it is with an important authority. I am convinced the Rimini speech was intended by the cardinal to be a major statement. This speech, typical of how this devoted man thinks, may also help put straight the record about him personally. Some, resentful of his exercise of authority, have engaged in a campaign of *disinformation* about a gentle servant of the servants of God whom I have had the privilege to know. I have also had the privilege to know well some of his closest collaborators, all of whom share an unbounded love and admiration for him. Given his position, the calumny from which he suffers damages the Church itself, most unjustly.

degree. But they grow old, and they risk presenting themselves as the most essential aspect, and so attention is turned from what is really essential. That is why they must always be removed, like scaffolding that has become superfluous.[33]

Along only this path will occur *con-gregatio*, a community that does not pit one against another, but rather, because each "self" gives itself, "entrusting oneself in that faith that is part of loving, becomes reciprocal receiving of all that is good and pure." Cardinal Ratzinger brings this out by contrasting the attitudes of the "activist" and the "admirer." Because the activist gives overall priority to his own activity, his horizon of feasibility is limited to what he already has: he has difficulty seeing what is bigger than him, for that would set a limit to his activity. Having built his own prison, he then rails loudly against it. "It is only that which has no limits that is of sufficient scope for our nature." That is what the "admirer" sees, that reality is greater than he, and that he is beholden to it, but at the same time that transcending reality is the full field of our real liberty.

The fundamental liberation the Church can bring is that of standing on the horizon of the eternal, going beyond the limits of our knowledge and power.[34] Faith itself, therefore, in all its greatness and fullness, is always the essential reform we need; faith is the starting point for putting constantly to the test the institutions we ourselves created. This means that the Church must be *the bridge of faith* and that—especially in the associative, unifying aspects—the Church cannot become an end unto itself.[35]

Cardinal Ratzinger denounces the tendency to ecclesiastical activism, as though the Church always has

> to do something, and everyone should be on some Church committee. It can happen that a person is continually active in ecclesiastical associations but he may not be a Christian at all. It can also happen that a person simply lives by the Word and the sacrament and puts the love that comes from faith into practice, without ever sitting on an ecclesiastical committee. . . . We do not need a more human Church but a more divine one; only then will it be truly human.
>
> Liberty in the Church is not achieved when the largest possible majority imposes its will on the smallest possible minority, but only when no one imposes his will on anyone and that everyone acknowledges they are bound to the word and will of the one God, who is our Lord and our liberty.[36]

The atmosphere in the Church becomes restrictive and suffocating when its ministers forget that the sacrament is not a distribution of power, but the expropriation of myself for Him in whose likeness I must speak and

33. Ibid., 65.
34. "When men cease to believe in God, he observed, they do not then believe in nothing; they will then begin to believe in anything" (Michael O'Brien, "Chesterton and Paganism," *The Chesterton Review* 16:3–4 (November 1990): 191.
35. Ratzinger, "Reform from the Beginning," 66.
36. Ibid., 67.

act.[37] When increasing responsibility corresponds with increasing self-expropriation, no one is anyone's slave; only then is the Lord the Master. "Now the Lord is that Spirit: and where the Spirit of the Lord is, there is liberty" (2 Cor. 3:17).

As was admitted, institutional apparatus is inevitable, but we should be aware: the more apparatus we build, even the most modern and most attentive to the Spirit, the less space there is for the Spirit, for the Lord, and even less for liberty. This is an inherent paradox of the human condition. "From this point of view, I think we will have to examine our conscience unreservedly at all levels within the Church—it would restore a sense of liberty in all of us, a completely new feeling of being at home."

Cardinal Ratzinger is, of course, not saying we should construct no new structures. On the contrary, faith helping us toward the transcendent inspires new initiatives in every epoch, but the structures must never become the essential factor. "The Church does not exist to keep us busy, or to keep itself alive but it exists to provide access for all of us to eternal life."[38]

But what does this liberating and purifying *ablatio* that is effectuated in us by the grace of faith add up to on the personal level? How is this life in God experienced? How does it bring the "precious form" to shine out through the dust of the form overlayed by Adam?

The key is in the forgiveness of sins. "It is certainly not by chance that, in the three decisive steps of the Church's formation according to the Gospels, the remission of sins plays a vital role." First, the nucleus of the authority handed Peter is to open or close, "to admit, to pardon, to welcome home" (Matt. 16:19). Again at the Last Supper that inaugurates the new community, from the Body of Christ and in the Body of Christ. This is possible because the Lord shed His Blood "for many for the remission of sins" (Matt. 26:28).

Finally, the Resurrected Christ in His first appearance to the Eleven founds the communion of His peace in the form of His gift to them of the power of pardon (John 20:19–23). "The Church is not a community of people 'who do not need doctors' but a community of converted sinners who live in the grace of pardon and who transmit it in turn to others."

Pardon in the New Testament is not magical—it is not pretending to forget, or acting as though nothing happened. Rather, it is a totally real process of change the Sculptor is effecting. Removing guilt means something is stripped away; the advent of pardon is manifest in us when penitence steps in. In this sense, pardon is both an active and a passive process; God's powerful life-giving Word within us spurs us to accept the pain of change, and thus we actively become transformed. Pardon and penitence, grace

37. That the sacrament empowers us is not denied, but it dispenses the power that comes with Christ's total emptying out of Himself in powerlessness.

38. Ibid. The expression used by the founder of a vibrant new monastic order speaking of one of the more successful charismatic communities says it well: "*Quel dommage!* I knew the founder, a saint. But now, they are losing themselves in their works [*Ils se perdent dans leurs oeuvres*]!"

and one's own personal conversion, are but two facets of one and the same event.

Ratzinger sees in this a key to Christian anthropology: "This fusion of activity and passivity expresses the essential form human existence takes. Indeed all our creating has its origin in our own creation, in our participation in the life-giving activity of God."[39] Perhaps the cardinal should add that our creating always grows out of "the already having been" of our culture, of our previous creating. The obscuring elements of that heritage always need rectification, and the enabling elements God builds on, even on what remains good and serviceable in the old structures of the Church.

Pardon is only possible where guilt is admitted. Efforts to build morality without sin and guilt, and hence where there is no need for pardon and expiation, fail, and the laws of morality are experienced as prisons, precisely because all sense of responsibility is destroyed. Where the law comes forth from the living, loving Source of all reality, and pardon is seen as a restoration of reality, and expiation is understood as a making right what was twisted and deformed, purification and self-transcending growth become possible.

Because pardon concerns a person in his most intimate heart it is the nucleus of community renewal.[40] If the dust and dirt obliterating God's image in me is removed, I will then truly become as any other who is also that image; I will become like Christ, and we all will. "I am snatched from my isolation and gathered into a new subjective community; my 'I' is inserted within the 'I' of Christ and so it is united with that of all my brothers. Only from the profundity of the individual's renewal is the Church born, a community that unites and sustains in life and death."

> The Church: it is not just a small group of activists who gather in a certain place to launch community life. Neither is it merely that broad category of people who get together on Sundays to celebrate the Eucharist. And the Church is more than the Pope, bishops and priests, those who are vested with the ministry of the sacraments. All the people we mentioned are part of the Church, but the spectrum of the community we join through faith goes beyond that, even beyond death. All the saints are part of it, from Abel and Abraham and all the testimonies of hope the Old Testament recounts, to Mary, the Mother of God, and His apostles, to Thomas à Becket and Thomas More, right up to Maxmilian Kolbe, to Edith Stein and Piergiorgio Frassati. The people we do not know are part of it, whose faith is known only to God; all men in all places and of all time are part of it, men whose hopeful loving hearts are open to Christ, "the author and finisher of our faith" (Heb. 12:2). It is not the occasional majorities which form here and there in the Church who decide its or our direction. We are oriented by the saints, for they are the real, determinant majority. We hold to them. They translate the divine into the human, eternity into time. They are our masters of humanity and they do not abandon us in times of suffering and solitude but walk by our sides even at the moment of death.[41]

39. Ibid., 68.

40. This brings to mind the vigorous renewal community Communauté Emmanuel, which has only one rule: "Don't criticize!"

41. Ibid., 69.

This is a "congregationalism" that has nothing to do with majority votes, or the limits of a local community: in the *communio sanctorum*, we are led steadfastly by the example and the prayers in heaven of the saints of all ages—they are the realization of Christ's Body.

Biological life ends in death. The individual is for the sake of the species, and the species is for the sake of . . . what? It too starts and ends in nothingness. A vision that can make no sense of death and of its handmaid, pain, and render both precious fails us in the crunch. It fails at the precise moment the decisive question of existence arrives. Of course, everything possible must be done to alleviate suffering, but without pain there can be no purification: rectification is always painful, and so is transition to a higher state. United to the sufferings of Christ, pain becomes full of meaning. "It makes me happy to suffer for you," Paul says to the Colossians, "and in my own body to do what I can to make up all that has still to be undergone by Christ for the sake of His body, the Church" (Col. 1:24).

We must ourselves be filled with a faith such as this! The Church will grow as a communion on the path to and within the true life, and then it will be renewed day by day. Then it will become the great house of many mansions; then the many gifts of the Spirit can work within it. Then we shall see "how good and how pleasant it is for the brethren to live in unity. . . . As the dew of Hermon, and as the dew that descended on the mountains of Zion; for there the Lord commanded the blessing, even life for evermore" (Ps. 133:1, 3).[42]

---

42. Ibid.

THE CHURCH IN THE WORLD OF TODAY

Seeking to Dwell in the Center

Because this tradition is about God's Revelation and about His redemptive eucharistic presence among us, it would have been suitable to end this appropriation on a mystical note. But what is most startling about the Revelation is the Good News that this divine presence not only reveals itself to be love but also for our sakes has become a human presence: in coming into history in Jesus, God continues to walk with us in the sacramental form of that Mystical Body that is the Church, thereby, through His Holy Spirit, divinizing the full spectrum of human characteristics. But that entails a titanic wrestling of freedoms as God in Christ works concretely to free us of the sinful elements in our persons and cultures.

Because of the stubbornness of our sin-induced faults, it is, even for God, hard, purifying work gradually to reform us from dimmed imago to saintly *similitudo Dei,* something like Adam and Eve before the Fall. That is why appropriation demands close attention to the human, the historical, including the sociological and historical reality of the actual Catholic Church in the (still sinful) world in our time. This sociological, cultural reality is part of the manifestation, after all, of the present form— for which we are coresponsible—of the perennial struggle of divine good and divinized human good against diabolical and human evil, both in the individual and in social structures.

A Christian society can exist effectively only through Christian cultures. The Church's efforts in this time of dynamic HTX social transformation to sustain, purify, and reinvigorate Christian cultures is a central aspect of the life of the tradition. The personal and intersubjective social reality of that actual real Church called to forgive sins and to heal "the sick" (Matt. 9:12; Luke 9:2) is, to the extent it is a faithful eucharistic development, God's main visible instrument for the divinization of men (but, of course, not His only instrument, during the time He is working to draw all men within that Church). It is for that concrete divine-human body, the Church, that we, the present inhabitants of the earth, share, with the angels and the entire communion of saints, a stewardship, in a continuing struggle to overcome sin and the effects of sin, and to draw all men into full union in Christ. The nurturing of Christian cultures is an essential aspect of this mystical-social endeavor, an indispensable part of ongoing reform of the Church.

Our concern in this closing chapter then is focused on the present moment, the present state of the Church and of Christian culture. "Now is the favorable time, this is the day of salvation" (2 Cor. 6:2). In his widely read book *The Catholic Moment*,[1] the then Lutheran pastor Richard John Neuhaus raised the question whether, with the collapse of communism and growing dissatisfaction in many Western circles with the tawdry effects of atheist, secular, hedonistic humanism, the Catholic Church did not represent a privileged alternative. He showed that the Church, consolidating through the two Vatican councils its understanding of its ecumenical responsibility to all humanity, and enjoying the strong leadership of Pope John Paul II and Joseph Cardinal Ratzinger, finds itself with a unique opportunity to give guidance to world society in general, and to help in particular the United States—the leader of the industrialized world—find its way. (One person at least was convinced by the argument: Lutheran pastor Richard John Neuhaus is now, since the book's publication, Father Neuhaus, priest of the Catholic Archdiocese of New York!)

One might add that if the Church is what it claims to be, then every moment in history must be considered "a Catholic moment": the Holy Spirit is always at work, however inauspicious the moment may appear to limited human observers.[2] The Spirit is always doing *what we will let Him* in order to spread the saving Word destined for all mankind.

There is no justification for taking a triumphalistic view of the Church's present situation, nor did the then pastor Neuhaus intend that. If anyone needs a bath of reality, he can find most of the negative aspects brought together powerfully by one of the fathers of the recent "charismatic-pentecostal renewal" in the Church, Ralph Martin, analyzing the immense growth of Pentecostal churches throughout the world, and showing up moral weaknesses and tepidity in that "Church of the Catholic Moment." In *The Catholic Church at the End of an Age*,[3] Martin speaks of "the third reform," claiming that the truth of Pentecostalism, in centering attention

---

1. Neuhaus, *The Catholic Moment* (San Francisco: Harper and Row, 1987).

2. Humanly, the odds did not look good for that little band taking on the Roman Empire out to crush them; or for the beleaguered bishops struggling with hoards of newly arrived barbarians in the sixth to ninth centuries, the Church at times threatened to be buried by Arianism; or for the Avignon popes during the three-way split over the papacy; or for a Pope Leo XIII assuming the mantle of a moribund bourgeois Catholic Church in the face of an atheist industrializing world.

3. Martin, *The Catholic Church at the End of an Age: What Is the Spirit Saying?* (San Francisco: Ignatius Press, 1994).

on a personal relationship with Jesus Christ and on renewal in the Spirit with a fresh awareness of the necessity for and abundance of His gifts, constitutes a "third reform," and calls the Church to pay attention to the clear announcement of this reform by the council and by Pope Paul VI and Pope John Paul II. The clarity of the conception of "the new evangelization" and its immense implications for renewal in the Church, Martin makes clear, present an enormous challenge for Catholics.

One of the limits we oppose to the Holy Spirit is our self-servingly narrow human perspective, restraining our ability to grasp the real situation of the Church at any one moment. But that is no excuse for not continuing to try, with God's help, to improve our *estimate of the situation* (the military term is appropriate), because of the responsibility Christ has handed us for guiding His Church, cooperatively (which means prayerfully) with the Holy Spirit.[4] "Intelligence" is crucial.[5] God expects us to develop all the natural and supernatural gifts He has given us to fulfill our "field" responsibilities— and that includes (however humble and always inconclusive) planning and organizing. Only God can renew us, but He gives us individual missions of cooperation, using too the natural gifts He has generously provided.

Neuhaus describes how difficult such an "estimate of the situation" is: of all the Churches, the Roman Catholic (as he calls it, to emphasize the importance of the strong center in the Roman pontiff) "is by far the most diverse of churches. With its discrete orders of ministry, its monastic communities, its myriad works of mercy, its multifarious national and cultural traditions, its political and ideological inclusiveness, and even its different patterns of theological reflection, the Roman Catholic Church is the paradigmatic instance of the unity in diversity that other churches should emulate and to which the world aspires."[6] That is the ancient and beautiful reality I shall attempt to glimpse in the contemporary form of its development, struggling to achieve a balance of attention to its more damaging concrete limits[7] and the hope inspired by its more radiant successes.

4. The Church, as divine, cannot lose the war; but in many lost battles along the way, entire continents can be lost from basic Christian formation for millennia. Consider the loss of Christian Africa to Islam.

5. In this case, "High Command," being divine, enjoys a strategic overview reaching to the Parousia. But the commander in chief can reveal only aspects of His view to corps commanders too egotistic to listen, and He leaves much leeway for tactical initiatives to the field commanders of every age. For He knows that winning demands that each lower soldier mature. "Be as cunning as serpents and as harmless as doves," was Christ's own command (Matt. 10:16), and "fight the good fight," the exhortation of one of His most formidable field commanders (1 Tim. 6:12).

6. Neuhaus, *The Catholic Moment*, 285.

7. The limits of "one man's opinion" will be obvious in this survey. But I pray that the attempt will stimulate contributions and reactions from others more knowledgeable of one or another aspects of the current reality and life of the Church. Written methodical appropriation is necessary to foster the most serious dialogue. By sending out drafts of this survey to friends in various movements I have been able to see that this works. I thank them now for their generous contributions to making this survey more accurate.

I shall put down my impressions of the present strengths and weaknesses of the Church under three headings: structure, doctrine, and liturgy. That order occurred to me spontaneously. I now see better what lay under the surface: the discussion of structure secures first a view of the Church as institution, which not only is the most visible and overarching framework, but also in one sense precedes doctrine, "operationally," as the community, from Pentecost day, has been the teacher and formulator of Christ's word. Theology first is lived out by the saints, whose existence is ecclesiological and intensely personal (between the solitude of the depths of their souls and the divine solitude), and only then theorized, in reflection on what has been lived. Reflective science follows personal experience and unfolding social reality. Cardinal Ratzinger points out that the Church called itself "the way" before it even got a name, because it is, first of all, action, a way of living.[8] Moreover, as Balthasar says, paradoxically this is what changes least in the Church, the basic structure established by Christ: the priesthood of all the believers taught and shepherded by a consecrating priesthood descended from His chosen apostles, a structure that grows from Christ's will. The institutional changes and innovations down through history and in our time all take place within that unaltered framework established by Christ's commanding action. That continuous authority oversees the ongoing growth in penetration to the depths of the mystery contained in developing doctrine, including the unexpected charismatic "breaking in" of the initiatives and the spirituality of the great saints, as the Church seeks to both evangelize and learn from the secular world of any given time. The "structure" provides a sturdy house, able to remain intact over the millennia, while growing as the Church learns from the ever surprising fresh initiatives of the in-breaking of the Spirit who never confines Himself to working only within the visible authority structures, but who guides the shepherds of the Church so that they are able to allow the Church an orderly growth from the Spirit's fruits. The Spirit, Catholics believe, presides over both development of doctrine and ongoing efforts to adapt liturgical form to its function of making Christ sacramentally present in an effective way to the people of this era—effective in the sense that people are drawn to worship and led into ever deeper prayer, and effective as instrument of personally transforming grace. The sacraments, along with the corporeal and spiritual works of mercy, lie at the heart of the Church's activity, the heart of the theo-drama for the service of which the Church exists, and are the most visible fruits of the Spirit.

I found it personally helpful to try to pull together my impressions and sift them more methodically than one usually does.

8. Joseph Cardinal Ratzinger, "Christian Faith as 'the Way': An Introduction to *Veritatis Splendor*," *International Catholic Review: Communio* 21:2 (summer 1994): 199–200.

Structure
Strengths

The Papacy

A Catholic cannot imagine a world Church, charged with preserving and propagating the whole Truth (the *catholica*) without a strong personal center, visible in Christ's vicar, who represents this very "wholeness in a fragment" and who functions as ultimate guarantor of unity and wholeness (and who, therefore, above all else *should* himself incarnate personal holiness: "Your holiness" should be more than a title! Yet, from Peter's cowardly denial of Christ, through the vagaries of Renaissance pontiffs, to the personal limitations of every pope, we are reminded that the Church achieves perfect holiness only in Mary. The paradox of the Church starts at the top, that it is holy while those who make it up, except for the New Adam and the New Eve, remain sinful). While the authority vested in each of the popes is supernaturally efficacious regardless of their personalities and limited personal sanctity, they are called, as is each of the baptized, to fulfill their role by developing their personhood in Christ. That requires the forgiveness of their sins and the radiation of their personal sanctity, which through their example should become a source of "actual" grace rather than of the highest scandal.

Since the emergence of the strong modern papacy at the end of the nineteenth century, the Church has been blessed with a series of saintly "holinesses," most of whom provided exceptionally strong leadership, rarely equaled in quality of human and spiritual guidance in any other period of the Church's history. This exemplary central leadership continues to constitute one of the strengths of the present Church.

Catholics who dissent from one or another of the directions in which a strong pope is leading the Church will, of course, point out the price that is paid for direction from the center: some diminution of local variety, the danger that comes from an inevitable remoteness of the center from the vast periphery of the largest and most widespread institution on earth,[9] and whatever (again inevitable) one-sidedness manifests itself due to the accents and foibles of the particular leader in power at a given moment.

I have discussed why I am convinced the price is worth it. (Obviously, Catholics believe, the Lord thought so!) Allow me to repeat two. First, the strong center provides a unity, clarity, and quality of teaching, in part because the center *does* listen to the periphery (not perfectly, but much more than any local authority in such a vast Church possibly could—how can Chicago really attend to Madras's problems?)—and that periphery is everywhere in the world, from all areas and social levels, feeding the center,

9. The Catholic Church may have fewer members than the government of China has subjects, and it may be less widespread in some respects than the United Nations, but the depth of its penetration into such a wide variety of societies around the world is still, I submit, unexcelled.

beyond anything found in any other organization on earth. Second, the Catholic Church provides the best antidote to three of the most murderous idols: the old powerful extended family, the tribe, and the nation. There is nothing worse than the many-headed egoism of a tight-knit family that serves only itself. Look at what the "great families" have wrought in many Latin American countries.[10] Similarly, patriotism, love of one's country and culture, easily is twisted into a folk egotism in the form of an ideologically inflamed nationalism.[11] Love of Christ is the best antidote to this poison, as He leads us to our common Father. And in Africa, the Church is the best hope of transforming tribal loyalty into a larger loyalty among Christians, a demanding and urgent task.[12] Secular governments have succeeded more by destroying what is good in the tribe than by transforming it constructively. Despite failures, the Church can still probably do more in this area than development agencies and the IMF and the new evangelical sects.

My emphasis on the center is not meant to deny that there is strength in what is near, and has formed us, in one's family and one's people. Hence, the great importance of the local within this centralized Church. A second strength of the Church has often been noticed by students of administrative structures, the balance of center and local authority, which brings us to our next section.

The Bishops

The position of the bishops is in fact strong. The bishop rules supreme in his diocese, providing again a visible center for the local people. Once Rome, after elaborate (and largely confidential) consultation, has named a bishop, he, as the successor of the apostles, enjoys much autonomy, canonically and in cold political reality. Few are ever removed, no matter how nervous Rome may become about them. This recognizes the reality and strength of local communities, whether tribe or regional political reality or nation— bishops are sometimes given specific ethnic responsibilities. But at the same time, every bishop is explicitly charged with care for the universal Church.

That there are any number of bishops in all parts of the world doing things and even teaching in ways that may make the Roman curia nervous

10. That is why the Church, starting with Christ, has always fought to protect the individual against the family. "Unless a man leave father and mother to follow me. . . ." See the research of the late Rev. Michael Sheehan on the medieval church's protection of the individual against the feudal family ("The European Family and Canon Law," *Community and Change* 6:3, 347–60; and "Theory and Practice: Marriage of the Unfree and the Poor in Medieval Society," *Mediaeval Studies* 50 [1988]: 457–83). What an irony that the Renaissance papacy became the captive of the great Roman families! A perfect perversion of what the papacy is there for!

11. I have developed this in a paper delivered to the Prague Seminar in Political Theory, in September 1992, "Ethnicity and the New World Order."

12. This has been shown by the horrible failure in Burundi and Rwanda. The recently implanted Christianity, mostly Catholic, was not able to overcome the fears and hatred manipulated by evil, power-hungry leaders that produced the unimaginable catastrophe.

is not a priori always a bad thing. The variety of cultures interacting with the one faith is bound to produce tensions and misunderstandings. But when originality reaches extremes, when Rome seriously disagrees with what a bishop is doing or teaching, what can the pope do about it? Whether the Roman authorities simply deem it politically prudent, whether they feel they do not have the power realistically, without paying a price of schism or of bad press, Rome in fact rarely removes a bishop.[13] Just why in one given instance or another Rome acts or more often fails to act, the casual onlooker usually cannot say.

Thus, basically, Rome bides its time. The institution by Paul VI of mandatory retirement at seventy-five has permitted Rome to replace bishops sooner. This is done with the help of papal legates, after confidential, private consultation with more than just local bishops, but almost exclusively, I believe, with those Rome considers "faithful." Since the arrival of John Paul II the attention given to appointing solidly orthodox bishops has, it appears, intensified, although mistakes have been made. Sometimes care is taken to circumnavigate an entire national college of bishops when Rome has come to be dissatisfied with its collective tendencies, especially when the bishops are being steered by a small, cohesive ideological group of senior bureaucrats in the offices of the National Bishops Conference.[14] Such Vatican circumnavigations, such as in Holland, have outraged the functionaries

13. Witness the efforts to bring Seattle's Archbishop Raymond Hunthausen back into line, which included "parachuting" the Rev. Don Wehrle as auxiliary bishop: they failed totally. Witness Rome's action against Evaristo Cardinal Arns, archbishop of the largest diocese in the world, São Paulo: displeased mightily with what was perceived to be an exaggerated liberation theology direction, the pope took the (on the face of it quite a defensible administrative) step of splitting his diocese into four. Basically, the politique of the present papacy seems to be "look to the future": great care in appointing new bishops, and little action against dissenting present holders of sees.

14. Cardinal Ratzinger has repeatedly identified this recent development of strong National Bishops Conferences as a danger to Rome's leadership. A small number of determined bureaucrats in the offices of the National Bishops Conference can control the agenda. Bishops are horribly overworked individuals, and when they constitute a body of dozens to hundreds at a national conference, assembled individual bishops find it difficult to stand up against debates where bishops sympathetic to the bureaucrats' agenda have been coached to speak. For a glimpse of just how deliberate this process has become in Washington (and, I would add, in Ottawa), read Neuhaus's analyses of a talk by Father Brian Hehir, formally of the NCCB in Washington, in which he lays out the whole strategy (*The Catholic Moment*, 277–78). Recently in Canada, two archbishops, Exner of Vancouver and Wall of Winnipeg, went against the Communications Committee of the CCCB, chaired by Bishop O'Meara of Thunder Bay, to testify before the Canadian Radio and Television Commission in favor of a more open attitude toward religious cable channels. The CCCB committee, hostile to Mother Angelica's Eternal Word Television Network, took the astonishing position of favoring exclusivity to one interdenominational channel now operating, "Vision Channel," less than 1 percent of whose programming is Catholic (and is known to permit blatantly anti-Catholic programs to be aired from time to time) on the grounds that this would exclude evangelicals from having a channel of their own. The two archbishops protested that, first, evangelicals should have the freedom to broadcast, and two, other Catholic networks might be formed. The commissioners were perfectly aware that the two archbishops

and those sectors of the Church whose tendencies are markedly different from what they then label "the archconservatism of the pope and Cardinal Ratzinger." In some instances, such as the nomination of the archbishop of Cologne, Cardinal Meissner; of Bishop Haas in Chur-Zürich; and of a priest of Opus Dei to a diocese in Austria, this led to tense situations.[15]

The episcopal office attaches great prestige: again like the pope, this descendent of the apostles is consecrated in an unbroken line of succession reaching back to Jesus Christ Himself, the longest "reigning aristocracy" on earth, and one to which the local shopkeeper's son may be elevated, hence a nonhereditary aristocracy[16]—an aristocracy of ability, not inbred blood, the desired quality being in this case, it is hoped, a disposition to strive seriously toward sanctity and to serve unstintingly the Church.

Some liberals find the bishops to be daunting male authority figures, and grumble that they never listen, while the conservative, strict disciplinarians find them too often indecisive and permissive. Conservatives agree with the liberals on at least this one thing: "the bishops never listen." The poor overworked bishop, a man of service, will reply: "I do nothing all day but listen!" Thank God, most ordinary Catholics ignore the whole issue, and simply respect the bishop—from afar. (In large dioceses, most bishops are in fact regrettably remote figures.)

What I shall claim next as a strength in the Church today will come as a shock to many of my Catholic readers: arguably, never in its history has the Church enjoyed a better college of bishops than at the present

---

were in fact favorable to EWTN (October 1992). The archbishop of Toronto, Aloysius Ambrozic, already embroiled in fights with the CCCB on other fronts, declined to get involved in this fight. One bishop who is member of the committee told a friend of mine that Bishop O'Meara took the stand he did without that bishop's prior knowledge.

15. Rome named seven Peruvian bishops in a row from the ranks of Opus Dei priests.

16. That was one reason the Church has insisted from the early Middle Ages in the Latin rite on celibacy—in much of the Orthodox Church essentially only celibate monks may be consecrated bishop, even though priests may marry. But while celibacy (already recommended by Saint Paul) may have started to spread for practical antifeudal power reasons, the Western Church has progressively deepened its understanding of the mystical nature of the spousal relationship between Christ and His Church and has been tending for a long time to extend the ideal of the theological counsels of religious life (poverty, chastity, obedience) to all the faithful, in forms suitable to the distinctive states of life—chastity for married people obviously does not embrace celibacy but sexual fidelity between spouses and a respect for sexuality as symbolic of the most fundamental relationships between the Creator and His creatures. See the long reflection on this in Balthasar, *The Christian State of Life* (San Francisco: Ignatius Press, 1983). Today, Catholics who are more action oriented, those more attracted by theology of liberation, and those simply less mystical in their approach oppose mandatory priestly celibacy. The present pope, the vast majority of bishops, and those who are attracted to a more mystical, a more contemplative theology, are deepening their appreciation for, and commitment to, priestly celibacy. Because of their reflection on the sexual symbolism employed in God's Revelation of His Trinitarian life and His relations with His Church, these oppose firmly any break with the tradition, solid from the beginning, of ordaining only men to stand *in loco Christi*.

time. Consider the following strengths of the actual body, some three thousand strong:

1. more worldwide and socially varied (class, race, nation) than ever in the Church's (or any institution's) history;
2. as faithful as can be imagined (since Vatican II in the vast U.S. Church of 55 million Catholics)[17] I know of one American bishop and one auxiliary bishop who have been deposed, both because of temptations with women, one African bishop asked to resign his see and to come live in Rome (Msgr. Melingo, who now lives on Via Ottaviano and is popular on talk shows, who became too involved in chasing out evil spirits), and one Canadian auxiliary bishop (there are more than 11 million Catholics in Canada)[18] convicted of sexual relations with females in incidents from twenty-five years earlier when he was a priest at a boarding school, and perhaps three worldwide deposed from office[19] because of heretical teaching, including the African bishop just mentioned who became so enthusiastic about witchcraft;
3. never since Constantine's time have bishops been as remote from personal political power—this may be due to circumstances beyond the Church's control, but I believe all bishops welcome the situation in which their "power" is one of example and persuasion, which, admittedly, in situations like that in Korea under the military dictatorship, Poland under communism, and the Philippines under Marcos, can be quite consequential;
4. never in the history of the Church have the bishops been as well educated as the present pastors;[20]
5. and I find it difficult to imagine a more dedicated, serious, hard-working group of men, earnest in their desire to be open to God's grace.[21]

17. The *1992 Catholic Almanac* gives the figure 55,646,713, or 22.2 percent of the population (Huntington, Ind.: Our Sunday Visitor, 1991), 431. The same almanac states there are 919 million Catholics in the world, 17.5 percent of the population (99).

18. *1991 Statistics Canada*, 11,375,445 (94–95). Approximately two hundred thousand of these are Ukrainian Byzantine-rite Catholics.

19. My sources of information are uncertain here, and there could be more.

20. Highly educated Catholics frequently grumble that their bishops should be better educated, and of course the ideal is never attained. But many of the bishops I have known are among the best all-round educated persons I have encountered, far broader in experience and formation than the average conceited, narrowly specialized university professor.

21. I recall the remark of my *Communio* friend Prof. Kenneth Schmitz, who chaired a weeklong study session for fifty American bishops who had invited Balthasar to lead them on that retreat-study session. He was impressed by their earnestness and devotion, and recalled that they voted unanimously to cancel the half-day of recreation to have one more session with Balthasar. As Schmitz said, when you realize how hard these men work, such devotion is admirable.

This last quality is important, as they are faced with leading a Church that has a better-educated and more actively involved laity than at any time in its history—another structural strength. Of course, active involvement in Church affairs does not guarantee more sanctity. Cardinal Ratzinger reminded us that "one can be active on Church committees all one's life and not even be a Christian"![22] But the Second Vatican Council and subsequently the two popes, Paul VI and John Paul II, have called for serious lay involvement, recognizing that the apostolic mission of the Church, especially the sanctification of home and workplace, and every form of political involvement, is primarily the task of the laity. When I examine in a moment structural weaknesses, I shall return to this issue to ask whether such involvement is yet sufficient and whether it is adequately "overseen"[23] by the Church hierarchy.

The Parishes

One of the most solid parts of the Church structure's foundations are the parishes. A charismatic friend, Michael Keating, in a discussion of "covenant communities" that I shall quote at length later, offered these words of wisdom:

> the great pastoral need of the Church is to transform parishes into genuine "local churches," places of enough real relational and religious cohesion that people involved have a sense of belonging to something meaningful. *The great rise in Catholic Mouvements of a communal nature since Vatican II is a response to the same hunger, and a much needed response.* The ticklish question, as you wisely note, is how to integrate such movements into the life of the Church so that they neither become sectarian and wander off, nor promote divisiveness within the Church.

Absolutely vital to the Church, and to be replaced by no other structure, is the local territorial community. This is where the average Catholic meets His Church. The pastor is for him a principal face of Christ, and he may find many friends through his participation in parish activities. It is here, at the parish level, that the fruits of "the renewal" (of which I shall say more later) need to be felt. A holy pastor, especially when with this essential of holiness goes at least a minimum of gifts of leadership, resulting in a true parish community, is a fruit of the Church's life like nothing else. His can be a parish small in numbers or a large one, the activities can be numerous or restrained to the essential, but in any case the local flock gathered around a holy priest is where most of the life of the Church as social reality is to be found, there and in fervent Catholic families.

Consequently, the formation of parish priests—a task today shared by the seminary and to a lesser extent by parishes themselves to whom the semi-

22. The speech was reported in *Thirty Days in the Life of the Church and the World* (October 1990), and is summarized in Chapter 14.

23. Recall that "overseeing" (*episkopein* in Greek) is the task of the *episkopos*, the bishop. Finding new modes of effective guidance for all the new forms of lay initiative is a present challenge for the Church.

narians are sent in "apprenticeship"—is a work of the Church exceeded by no other in importance for its health.

My emphasis on the pastor's leadership is not meant to downplay the importance of the people's response. It is they who must carry out enthusiastically the actual work of the parish in its every activity, from the central life factor, the liturgy and prayer groups (an increasingly important phenomenon), through all the organized works of mercy (almost every parish has some, including often the huge burden of Catholic education, frequently entirely financed by the parish), to the most mundane tasks of management and repair that must be carried out.

In the urban setting with its many parishes, participation is not as strictly territorial as formerly. The gap between different theological and liturgical tendencies in the Church has brought about some seeking out parishes with a particular spirituality (there are, for instance, "charismatic" parishes, although typically the more exuberant manifestations of charismatic gifts will be confined to a single mass known by all parishioners for just that). There are parishes with more "swinging" Masses and others with a staid liturgy, more respectful of traditional forms. Some will gain fame for continuing (with permission)[24] the Tridentine Mass, or perhaps the new *ordo* but said in Latin. In some large parishes, there will be Masses regularly said in different styles. This is another illustration of a strength, the fact that there is room in the Church for different spiritualities.

In more-Catholic countries the network of parishes forms a dense weave. I recall one day during the communist gloom being shown in the Krakow Seminary a large wall map with all the parishes of Poland indicated. I could not help thinking, "if this is the map of the General Staff, they have the territory well covered!"[25]

New Institutional Forms

The Church has always shown ingenuity in the creation of new institutional forms, evolutions both in the governing structures of the Church (for example, the rise in importance of the great ecumenical councils in the fourth and fifth centuries, and the recent development of National Bishops Conferences) and in the invention of new kinds of communities (monastic communities, lay confraternities, guilds, knights templar and hospitalier, mendicant orders [the Franciscans and Dominicans of the thirteen century], the Jesuits [key in the Counter Reformation], the Saint Vincent de Paul Society [for aiding the poor], Catholic Action, and so on—the list is long).

24. Or without permission, as in the case of the near-schismatic parishes of the Society of St. Pius X.

25. In many large dioceses the potential of this thick net is much reduced by the exaggerated independence of many pastors who pay scant attention to letters from the bishop, often neglecting to read them from the pulpit when requested to do so. Again as with the bishops in relation to the popes, pastors enjoy much de facto independence from the bishop. And also from their own flocks, as bishops are reluctant to move pastors just because a group from a parish is agitating against one.

Today, the tradition is showing its inventiveness as imaginatively as it ever has: not only have the periodic synods of the bishops in Rome sprung up since Vatican II, ensuring a more vigorous input from the periphery, and bishops' conferences achieving the ability for the bishops to speak with a unified national voice, and even, as with CELAM[26] to achieve a regional presence, and not only has lay participation been improved through the creation of diocesan synods and parish councils, but whole new forms of Catholic community have been created, as well as more traditional forms of religious orders springing up with renewed vigor as needed.

I shall examine several of the more prominent among these various innovations, to understand better the needs to which they respond, to examine their distinctive spiritualities and to appreciate what is appropriate in these kinds of responses. (One should not, even by implication, fail to appreciate the continuing contributions of older movements, such as the Saint Vincent de Paul Society, active throughout the world in help for the poor, the Legion of Mary, founded in 1921, vigorous too in helping the poor, in fostering spiritual development of its members, and in apostolic work, especially home visitations [both with members numbering in the hundreds of thousands] or, in America, the Knights of Columbus, not to speak of the venerable orders of various knights hospitalier—the list of long established yet still vigorous organizations is impressive.)

But how to make a fair selection out of the numerous new initiatives, to offer some sense of the Church's vigorous creativity? Twenty "movements" were invited by the Pontifical Council for the Laity to a conference in 1981. In a resultant volume of essays, *Les mouvements dans l'Église*,[27] each is summed up. Twenty-four movements, with little overlap with the previous twenty, are covered by Frédéric Lenoir in his more recent work, *Les communautés nouvelles*. Each deserves a longer chapter than either book can give them. Out of so many my selection is inevitably rather arbitrary, and my treatment much too brief. But within these limits, I shall try to discover a few general lessons about the nature and contribution of these new initiatives. These movements, in the words of Karol Wojtyla, then archbishop of Krakow, are all "forms of self-realization of the Church."[28] Their importance is well summarized by Prof. Stanislas Grygiel, confidant of the present pope.

> The movement of God creating is refracted in history in different movements, each of which bears something of the breath [souffle] by which God animates the human mud and draws from it man—Adam/Eve. The human movements which are not "of that race" are those [like Communism (addition mine)] of solitary individuals which destroy their *being for and by someone*, thereby reducing them to objects exposed to the action of any force whatever. The *ecclesia* of men is born of

26. Conferenca Episcopal Latino Americao, which had held important continental meetings in Medellin and Puebla, and maintains a bureaucracy in Bogotá.

27. *Les mouvements dans l'Église* (Paris: Éditions Lethielleux, 1982).

28. Lenoir, *Les communautés nouvelles* (Paris: Fayard, 1988), 13.

the breath of the Spirit, which transfigures the dust of the earth into man, unifying him in the life of God. For that reason, outside the *ecclesia* there is no liberty.[29]

Professor Grygiel offers us a criterion for assessing the "success" of each movement, not numbers of adherents but the truly Christian nature of the *communio* each achieves.

The status of these movements in the Church poses many problems, which turn about the central mystery of the priesthood of Jesus Christ, found in Him alone, and its relationship to the "common priesthood of all the faithful," and with the "ministerial (or ordained) priesthood," including the issue of distinctive "charisms,"[30] some belonging to the various estates, others visited upon laity, religious, bishops, and popes.

The reality of "charisms" is an elusive subject. Saint Paul not only launched the issue, but also right from the start contributed to making it difficult by noting in different letters distinctive lists of "gifts of the Spirit," yet telling us little about their nature. Bishop Eugenio Corecco assures us of their importance, saying this:

> The charismatic dimension belongs to the essence of the Church, but as such it is different from, and is to be distinguished from the institution. . . . Besides the Word and the Sacraments, the charism is a constitutive element of the Church. While the first two engender the institutional structure through their structural reciprocity (the Word, in effect, concretizes itself in the sacraments, and the symbolic signs are sacraments thanks to the Word), the charism, by its nature, presupposes the existence of the institution.
>
> As a privileged expression of the presence and activity of the Holy Spirit, the charism has as its function to provoke the institution to its proper authenticity and its proper vitality which allows it to be really a support and an expression of the Church's ministry.[31]

Charisms are given both to members of the ministerial priesthood and to laymen who share in the common priesthood. Whether it is a pope, like the present one, who, in addition to his charism of office, through his special personal charisms challenges the Church, or a layman, like Chiara Lubich, prophetic foundress of the vast Focolari movement (which I discuss below), these charisms always challenge the whole Church.

By recalling the eschatological dimension of the Church's existence, the charism sustains the institution in the search for its proper unity—constantly menaced by the always latent *antinomia* (opposition to law) found in every form of power—which in the Church takes the form of dominance by the hierarchy over the laity or of the laity over the hierarchy.[32]

29. Ibid., 130.

30. On this see the long and excellent article by Bishop Eugenio Corecco in ibid., 181–208, which traces the history, from Saint Paul on, of this notion.

31. Ibid., 190.

32. As we saw earlier in the "Congregationalist" form of the Church, and as we see today in the push for a "people of God" Church, and as was seen for centuries in undue power of kings and counts over bishops (ibid., 192).

Among the many forms charisms take, "the evangelical counsels"—living in poverty, obedience, and chastity—represent a fundamental mode. As to the charisms found at the base of the movements, Bishop Corecco declares: "By definition the movements are not individual charisms but rather a form of charism lived in a communitarian fashion, where each one lives the principal and stronger charism of the founder, and participates in it."[33]

One benefit is some breaking down of the clericalism-anticlericalism confrontation that has plagued the Church. Many of these movements see laymen at the head and priests as ordinary members. There is hope they will avoid the recent plague, what Msgr. Nevis calls neoclericalism, "the laicization of clerics and the clericalization of laity,"[34] as one sees in the often officious "lay ministers" buzzing about the parish altars these days.

The variety of spiritualities the movements incarnate provide a prime instance of that desirable pluralism Neuhaus lauds. God created each person as unique participation in the personhood of Jesus Christ. So in a sense there are as many "spiritualities" as there are persons. This does not preclude the fact of types of personalities. And birds of a feather *do* flock together, because they can understand one another and offer loving support of a kind peculiarly suitable to certain personalities and stations in life. It is not easy to understand empathetically the spiritualities of others. But an effort in this direction is essential to pursuing "ecumenical wisdom."

A word of caution before I begin. Recently, the movements have come under fresh attack under the guise of a warning against "sects within the Church."[35] Pointing to the great influence of the founders and leaders, some excesses (now admitted and often corrected by the movements) of authority over the lives of the members, and pressures exercised against leaving, the critics accuse these movements of having all the faults of "sects." Their defenders reply that the movements in question have been docile in submission to episcopal authority, that they remain orthodox in doctrine and have proved extremely fruitful in vocations and in greater religious fervor. It would be useful to reflect on the history of religious orders that also have often tended to live a life within themselves that, while not in tension with the greater life of the Church, could become a bit "in-groupy." With warning of these rumblings, I shall now describe, inevitably superficially, a few of the movements.

The Work of Schoenstatt

I begin with two older movements. One, "the Work of Schoenstatt," founded in 1914, is now mature but still vigorous, although it has tended

---

33. Ibid., 193.

34. Ibid., 139.

35. One of the most virulent, *Les naufragés de l'esprit*, by Thierry Baffoy, Antoine Delestre, and Jean-Paul Sauzet, all three former charismatic-movement leaders, provoked a response from the French Bishops Conference (communiqué of May 17, 1996) defending the movements. See *Inside the Vatican* (August–September 1996): 44–51, for a good résumé of the dispute, and p. 48 box for the full text of the bishops' communiqué.

to remain largely among German-speaking peoples and their immediate descendants in the diaspora, especially in Chile. The other, Opus Dei, was founded in 1928. This is a reminder that "movements" are not new, and even lay movements embracing whole families are not a post–Vatican II phenomenon. Many of the great, old religious orders have inspired something like "third orders," lay movements associated with their charism and spirituality, some reaching back to the seventeenth century.

The "Work of Schoenstatt," which because of its resolutely familial character is usually called "the Family of Schoenstatt," was founded by the charismatic figure Father Josef Kenternich (who lived from 1885 to 1968), and centered locally in the German sanctuary of "Mary and Three Times Admirable Queen of Schoenstatt." Of his influence, a spokesman said this: "[The movement Schoenstatt] can be considered a prolongation of the person of its founder; everything it achieves as a movement of ideas, of charisms and of life, comes finally from its founder, as a privileged instrument in the hands of Mary in order to maintain always unity, in love and filial dependence."[36]

Not just personal charisma, but a gift of the Holy Spirit, a call. Hitler was charismatic . . . Such emphasis on the charism of the founder is recognized, by those who have studied the various movements, as characteristic and legitimate of many of them, as with some of the great religious orders, illustration of the power of certain extraordinary personal missions given individuals for the good of the whole church.

"Schoenstatt is essentially a movement of educators and of moral religious education, 'to engender a unity between theory and practice,' as the Founder said."[37]

Mary is for Schoenstatt the prime educator: "We turn towards Mary as our guide for Christian existence, and recognize with fervor the bond that unites us to her as mother, queen, and educator leading men to Christ, according to the words of Saint Paul: 'It is not I who live, but Christ who lives in me.' "[38] Indeed, I have heard it said that the Marian consciousness of the movement is so strong that even many pious Catholics who hold Mary in the highest place among all saints are somewhat put off by what they see as an exaggeration. I report this, although I cannot pass on its substance, to illustrate how no one of the variety of spiritualities in the Church is attractive to all Catholics, and indeed many are put off by what is foreign to them, often appearing as "exaggerations."

Faith in divine Providence, coupled with a zeal to fulfill God's will in carrying out the mission of His Church, a discernment of that will in the "signs of the times," characterize the *jubilees*—the great reunions—of the Schoenstatt family. "For this we have become more attentive to the action

36. These are the words of the person reporting to the meeting that produced *Les mouvements dans l'Église,* cf. 99.
37. Ibid., 100.
38. Ibid., 103.

of God in our daily lives. Father Kenternich always said that in all the situations of life God opens a door. We have only to pass by that door to do His will, to realize His desire for our active collaboration with Him. For instance, when the father was interned at Dachau for three years (1942–45) 'he entered into contact with young men from many nations, and then realized that God was calling on him to found the international family of Schoenstatt' expanding it beyond its earlier dimensions."

A young Chilean labor lawyer, fifteen years a member of Schoenstatt, appealed to this example when explaining why he is always so hopeful in the midst of the most discouraging situations. "I am not in harmony with reality and at the same time I am terribly inserted in it, I am not in harmony in the sense the reality does not please me and I want to change it, and I am inserted in it in the sense that I am not crushed by it and that, *au contraire,* I believe I can dominate it."[39]

The work of Schoenstatt is totally apostolic, "embracing being and action." Being: change man in the direction of the maturity of Christ, reformulation of "the new man," announced by Saint Paul, a personality intimately free and animated by the fundamental force of love, exempt of all manipulation, life in and through the other, avoiding any trace of individualism or collectivism. That is why Schoenstatt is basically a pedagogical movement. Action: Schoenstatt works in every social milieu to try to prepare the Reign of God, through a better social order.

Today Schoenstatt maintains about one hundred *"Bildungsstätten"*—formation centers—and about twenty-five independent communities with about one hundred thousand participants worldwide, particularly in Europe and Latin America. There are Schoenstatt sisters working in Texas and Wisconsin.[40]

My own lack of personal contact with this vast and venerable movement, beyond a few close friends living in other countries, keeps me, regrettably, from having much more to offer here than this brief acknowledgment of its long and vigorous existence.

Opus Dei

Because I do have friends in Toronto who are members of the "Prelature of the Holy Cross and Opus Dei,"[41] I can say something more about this earlier modern form of apostolic endeavor. It alone of all of the new institutions has been accorded the canonical status of "a personal Prelature of the Catholic Church," which I shall explain below. For that reason, and because of its influence, which is immense and growing (not the least

39. Ibid., 106.

40. *Brockhaus Encyklopädie* (Mannheim: Brockhaus, 1992), 19:493. The sisters have been discovered through detective work by my assistant Antonio Calcagno, whom I thank for much research on the present chapter.

41. The full canonical name is Prelatura Sanctae Crucis et Operis Dei. The new canonical status of a "personal prelature" is explained below.

because this organism is a favorite of the present pope), I am giving it prominence.

Opus Dei was founded in Madrid in 1928 by a priest of the Archdiocese of Saragossa, Father Josémaria Escrivá de Balaguer (who died in 1975 and in May 1992 was pronounced "Blessed"). The basic notion of "the father," as Blessed Josémaria is affectionately called by members of "the Work," was that sanctity, being intended by God as the goal of everyone, needs to be cultivated by laymen there where they are, in the everyday world of home and work. While in the process of acquiring personal sanctity, they are at the same time to help in the sanctification of others and of the workplace itself. For this they need training, support, and expectations, "norms."

Thus, continuous, intense spiritual formation is offered. It is needed as much by lay apostles as it is for priests and religious. (A similar realization motivates Schoenstatt. Both were pioneers in this effort to prepare the laity. This was not well understood at the beginning; indeed, the hostility unfurled against Schoenstatt and the Work may be part of a heritage of suspicion of vigorous works parallel to what is usual in the local churches, which continues in some degree to plague them.)

After a relatively slow start, rendered a calvary by the Spanish civil war,[42] Opus Dei found so many young men and women finally gathering about "the father" the organization began to grow rapidly, starting about the time of the Second World War. By the 1950s the Work had received approval by the Holy See, and had begun to spread widely in the world.

The call from God that the founder was convinced he had received was to establish a radically different kind of structure within the Church. (In the papal document establishing the Work as a "personal Prelature," the words "The Founder *divina ductus inspiratione* ["led by divine inspiration"] appear."[43] Members put emphasis on the Church's acknowledgment of the divine inspiration of the founding, and upon the conferral of its present juridical status, after a long struggle.[44] The prelature constitutes something rather like a worldwide diocese (in the sense that it is a jurisdictional

42. The founder and his tiny band of "sons" were, for months, in daily danger of immediate assassination in a vicious war that saw six thousand Spanish priests and thirteen bishops shot by the Republicans.

43. Apostolic Constitution, *"Ut Sit,"* effective November 28, 1982, opening line.

44. The *épopée* of this struggle to find correct judicial status within the Church is detailed in a large book by Amadeo de Fuenmayor, Valentin Gómez-Iglesias, and José Luis Ilanes, *El Itinerario Juridico del Opus Dei: Historia y Defensa de un Carisma* (Pamplona: Ediciones Universidad de Navarra, 1988). An earlier solution, to acknowledge Opus Dei as a secular institute (Apostolic Constitution, *Provida Mater Ecclesia*, February 2, 1947 [*AAS* 39 (1947): 114–24]) never satisfied Blessed Josémaria, because it did not make clear enough the unique, the new status of the core, the lay members of the Work as laymen purely and simply, married most of them, in no sense religious, although they work to carry out in their lives all the virtues, including the spirit of the "counsels of perfection," chastity, poverty, obedience. There are proper lay forms, applying to all Catholics, for instance, ways of remaining chaste in marriage, which obviously does not mean abstinence from sexual intercourse; remaining poor, which does not mean renouncing the lay responsibility that, in man's fallen state, requires owning in

structure of the Church's organization, and in the sense of being part of the constitutional secular—as opposed to religious—framework),[45] a comparison that becomes somewhat less misleading since the first prelate, Alvaro de Portillo, the engineer ordained priest in 1944 who joined the Work almost from its founding, was ordained a bishop.[46] Don Alvaro died in March 1994, and a new prelate, Don Javier Echevarrià, was elected and consecrated bishop.

The founder once summarized the heart of the inspiration in these terms: From the first anchorites, the world always lured religious to come out of their hermitages to help it. With Opus Dei, "it is now from the world itself apostles rise up, who dare sanctify all the ordinary affairs of men."[47]

The prelate now presides over what has become a worldwide organization in the order of seventy-five thousand members and more than 2 million "cooperators," more loosely affiliated people who assist the Work, which in return provides spiritual direction, retreats, evenings of recollection, and other activities of spiritual formation. The Priestly Society of the Holy Cross, founded by Blessed Josémaria in 1943 and intrinsically united to Opus Dei, includes, as well as the priests incardinated in Opus Dei who are specialized in spiritual formation for laity, many diocesan clergy. They participate for fraternal help in pursuing their own spiritual development, formation, and, just as the laymen, working to sanctify their professional work and ordinary duties. The priestly vocations within the Work are discerned among the lay members, only after they have received a thorough lay spiritual formation.

---

stewardship private property, but rather means being "detached," poor in spirit; and remaining obedient, which takes the lay form of a docility to spiritual direction, but does not relieve one's own responsibility for making decisions in his professional and family life. For a profound theology of the states of Christian life within the unity of the "Christical" center, see Hans Urs von Balthasar, *Christlicher Stand* (The Christian state, trans. M. F. McCarthy [San Francisco: Ignatius Press, 1983]) (Einsiedeln: Johannes Verlag, 1977).

45. Books have been written to explain this new kind of ecclesial entity, the implications of which will have to be worked out over time. I personally have no doubt about its being a significant innovation, such as we have seen from time to time in the Church's history.

46. This category of organization is since Vatican II and the laws promulgated by Pope Paul VI in 1965 *(Motu proprio Ecclesiae Sanctae)* a common legal framework for personal—as opposed to territorial—juridical structures in the Church. This legal framework has now been incorporated into the 1983 Code of Canon Law (canons 294–97). Even if, up to now, Opus Dei is the only institution established explicitly as a personal prelature, there are many other "personal" jurisdictions: military ordinariates and ritual churches or eparchies (Ukrainian, Maronite, and so on) being the more numerous ones. They group persons according to a particular mission rather than by territory. They can be local, national, or worldwide. In the case of the Work, the purpose is a particular pastoral and apostolic task at the service of the universal and the local Church. Prelatures are "secular," in the sense they are not religious orders. Their own prelate is their ordinary (cf. P. Rodriguez, *Particular Churches and Personal Prelatures* [Dublin: Four Courts Press, 1986]).

47. Fuenmayor, Gómez-Iglesias, and Ilanes, *El Itinerario Juridico del Opus Dei,* French trans. *L'itinéraire juridique de l'Opus Dei* (Paris: Desclée, 1991), 399.

The founder thought these priests (there are about two thousand) should be obvious examples of excellence in their chosen lay fields by having first achieved high standing. As a result many of the Opus Dei priests are physicians, engineers, doctors of science, and the like. They are widely acknowledged to form a talented, zealous, and faithful corps of priests.[48] They are expected to form close relations with the diocesan priests where they work, and to consider themselves a part of the local diocesan clergy. This is one reason Opus Dei never starts its apostolates or installs a center in a diocese unless, not just invited by the local ordinary—which is canonically necessary—but enthusiastically welcomed.[49]

All lay members of the Work continue their professional activity, but some (barely 10 percent of the membership)—the "numeraries" (which category includes the priests of Opus Dei as well)—live the celibate life in Opus Dei centers, and devote their time and effort, beyond what the laymen need to earn their living, to the formation of the laity. The "supernumeraries" and the "associates," because of their personal circumstances, remain with their families, but strive, just like the numeraries, to do all they can to sanctify themselves in their respective milieus, following the prescribed "norms" of the Work.[50]

The bond between members and the Work is contractual. They do not take vows as religious do. We saw that even the priests of the prelature began their association with Opus Dei as laymen, and have the same contractual relation, although they also have priestly obligations, including obedience to their ordinary (the prelate). Members of the Priestly Society of the Holy Cross remain at all times under the jurisdiction of their own bishop. All members of Opus Dei freely assume a program of disciplined pursuit of personal perfection, including a regime of spiritual direction, both received and given. One of the "norms" is that members try to receive the sacrament of reconciliation weekly. Most strive to see the same priest,[51] who may also

48. The present pope has been recruiting many bishops from their ranks.

49. The founder's greatest moral supporter in the difficult early days was the cardinal archbishop of Madrid. Once, when things were going so badly, criticisms were become so severe, and one could worry whether Don Josémaria would give up, he received a mysterious phone call at one o'clock in the morning. A voice (which he recognized as that of the bishop), said, "*Ecce Satanas expectivit vos ut cribaret sicut triticum* [Behold, Satan will shake you and sift you as grain is sifted in the threshing (Luke 22:31)]. I pray so much for you. *Et tu confirma filios tuos!* [You confirm your sons!]." And then hung up (S. Bernal, *Msgr. Josemaria Escriva de Balaguer: A Profile of the Founder of Opus Dei* [London and New York: Scepter, 1977]).

50. Dominique Le Tourneau, *L'Opus Dei: Que Sais-Je?* (Paris: Presses Universitaires de France, 1984), 70–71. In English: *What Is Opus Dei?* (Dublin: Mercier Press, 1989), 80.

51. Indeed, the Work endeavors to supply a priest once a week wherever there are members, and will not assign members to a region unless a priest can be available at least weekly. The Work has been criticized by many sympathetic to its aims for being in this way too closed on itself and overly directive. Members reply that they find this form of consistent direction fruitful and submit to it gratefully. Seriousness (critics say "Spanish seriousness") characterizes the Work, whose members consider pursuit of sanctification for oneself and for the world to be the only thing that matters. I recommend, as a good

pursue with them a long course of direction, becoming for them an objective aid to formation of a right conscience. Most members, however, receive spiritual direction from a fellow lay member. Members—both priests and laity—are really specialists in spiritual direction and formation.

I have heard criticisms of this approach from friends involved in charismatic movements. One, himself a person serious about his spiritual life who once opined that the priests of Opus Dei "constitute the finest corps of priests in the Church," nevertheless worries that such heavy direction unwittingly risks "dampening the freedom to grow." As I personally have known well perhaps only four or five members of Opus Dei, I would not presume to pass judgment on that. Whatever signs of "rigidity" or any "narrow mindedness"—and I have seen little—I could discern in that meaninglessly small sample of men, along with perhaps four Opus Dei priests I have met, pales before the bright impression of faith, apostolic zeal, and courage I have seen from them in abundance. I found exemplary fidelity to the Church's teaching and a rather old-fashioned language, traditional, let us say—a guard of doctrinal correctness,[52] a rather stiff liturgy, and a somewhat oversimplified neo-Thomistic anthropology accompanying total devotion to their mission.

Another complaint one hears is about the emphasis placed in Opus Dei spirituality on personal "mortification," growing out of the conviction that because original sin and our own personal vices have disordered us, we must discipline the body by methodically refusing to indulge it, through corporeal penances. Corporeal mortification has been a fact of all saintly lives, and is always looked for in the lives of those presented for beatification. (The founder was known to have mortified himself severely. An excessively Spanish approach to spiritual formation, complain the critics, a mistrust of "the flesh," turned, they allege, into a veritable abhorrence of

---

piece of journalism, Robert Moynihan's "A Contested Beatification," *Catholic World Report* (March 1993): 43.

52. In theological and philosophical discussions with these several priests I have bumped up against a certain rigidity of attitude toward some recent developments in Catholic thinking that I believe important, as the Church wrestles with problems posed by modern developments. One priest, who holds an advanced degree in science, in the course of an argument over whether any good could come of studying what Teilhard de Chardin sought to achieve, acknowledged, when I complained of an uninformed attack by him against Teilhard, that the philosophy and theology training from seminary carries one only so far. For my part I would add that the formation received in Opus Dei seems, from its fruits, rather heavily influenced by Thomistic scholasticism. I have found over the years many Thomists quite closed to what has happened in post-Kantian thought. It would not be fair to expect Opus Dei priests to be accomplished philosophers or theologians, but it is distressing to get the sense, as I have, rightly or wrongly, that thinkers as important as de Lubac and Balthasar are hardly known by those with whom I have spoken, and Teilhard is anathema. One finds the same limits in theological breadth among most parish priests, too, but given the proximity of the Work to the university world, one can hope, in the future, for a more serious discussion with a broader range of efforts to think through today's problems, which points to the need for movement toward a theological tradition more like that of the present Holy Father.

it. But these critics forget, for instance, the urbane Lord Chancellor Thomas More and Cardinal Newman and Pope Paul VI, none of whom was under "Spanish influence.") In three Opus Dei retreats I heard no exaggerated emphasis on "mortification," nor any association of the idea with severe physical chastisement.

As I have sought, from the outside, to learn about and appreciate the spiritualities of different communities, I have discovered that the distinctiveness of those that really do not suit one's own personality tends to come across—given a general lack of charity—always as "distortions." I admit that I too personally pull back before what seems to me strange in each of the more distinctive initiatives, say a certain heavy-handedness in the approach of some members, or the emotionalism in some manifestations of the charismatic movements, and a sense that some feel Christians who have not experienced "baptism in the Spirit" have really not "made it." And I admit to remaining a bit leery—as one must—of the tendency in all successful communities and institutions to become preoccupied with their work[53] and to close in on themselves, and to take a not-always-sinless pride in their accomplishments, starting to act as though they had found the Way rather than a way, despite their protestations of concern for the whole Church. Just as the intense life of a healthy extended family tends to absorb all one's free time, so the life of these groups is demanding. (When I criticized a friend in Opus Dei, who has lived twenty years in Toronto and is president of two companies, for not even knowing the name of the local seminary, nor anything about the travails from which it recently successfully emerged, he shot back, "It is not fair to blame the Work for my personal ignorance and failings!") I suppose when one is offered the grace of finding a movement the spirituality of which fits, one then comes to love this home, and can become insensitive to its particular (and inevitable) limits. Whereas parishes tend to be somewhat haphazard mixed gatherings of peoples, groups (as have the religious orders) can suffer from the "birds of a feather flock together" syndrome.

But most important, groups, just as individuals, must be alert to *pride,* always remembering what happened to the great Society of Jesus. Spiritually, nothing fails like success. No Catholic has to join anything, he is even free to belong in only a casual way to his parish, so long as he fulfills the Church's law regarding practice.[54] On the other hand, given the call from Christ to all "to be perfect as the heavenly Father is perfect," and given the secularization of our world, indeed its hostility to all religion, he who thinks he can "go it alone" with no support from a community of like-minded fellow human beings may well be suffering from pride too and not

---

53. Père Dominique Marie Philippe, founder of La Communauté St.-Jean, commenting on a charismatic community he knows well, *"Ah, ils sont devenus victimes de leurs oeuvres!"* (They have become victims of their good works).

54. Mass on Sunday and holy days of obligation, confession once a year, and communion once during Easter season.

be taking seriously enough the urgent call of the Second Vatican Council to universal holiness.

The more visible movements have drawn unsympathetic fire. Communione e Liberazione, because it is not only big and dynamic but also political, has been viciously attacked. So have some of the larger charismatic communities. Opus Dei is visible enough[55] so that it too draws virulent attacks. There will always be those who, not troubling to come to know what it is really striving to do for the spiritual perfection of all who join, will accuse it of thinking of itself as though it *is* the Church, or as though the rest of the Church is somehow, in contrast, a bit impure. Opus Dei members insist the Work aspires to be a mission within, and open to the whole Church, and only that. It is a vocation, not at all for everyone, and in no sense "elitist." They do not deny the danger, as with any good community, of some degree of self-preoccupation.

If some of the forms, the underlying anthropology and the rhetoric within the Opus Dei traditions strike many, as I suggested, as "old-fashioned," it should be acknowledged that it is always difficult to discern what these questions of style and philosophy reveal about deeper issues.

I do not myself believe that the Work is more at risk in this regard than other groups—we are all different and all limited—nor do I agree that because institutions in various senses "succeed" and become powerful and hence always constitute, as does everything human, a potential temptation, new forms within the Church are to be looked upon with so much suspicion. Only because I remain perplexed by the meanness of the attacks I have personally heard in Toronto and a more diffuse suspicion I have felt in what should be more informed circles, I shall permit myself a most tentative opinion here about the Work.

As Opus Dei members point out, first, the Church has canonically recognized the Work, and its founder has been beatified. Of course, no one thinks this provides immunity to the perennial temptation: the founders of many religious orders were canonized and the rules of all of them canonically regularized. The members of Opus Dei with whom I have spoken about the accusation of being "closed" reply that the very mission of the Work is to reach out, and that no one should mistake a certain privacy connected with one's personal pursuit of spiritual perfection with "closedness." Second, there can be no doubt about the fidelity to the magisterium of its members—

55. Opus Dei has its own international seminary, several universities founded and directed by members of the Work, international student residences at sixty-five universities around the world, hundreds of members' residences, retreat centers, and the various lay catechetical and family-formation initiatives inspired and operated by members, including elementary and high schools. Critics fail to understand that at Opus Dei universities, the prelature takes responsibility only for the teaching of doctrine and spiritual formation. In resolutely avoiding any ownership or any involvement, as prelature, in the operation of the university, it wants it understood that it has no responsibility for what is taught in the nonreligious courses, or for the academic quality of the institution, which is the university's own business as an autonomous institution.

part of what annoys many "progressive Catholics"—or their exemplary zeal, the earnestness with which solid spiritual formation is pursued, which I suppose inevitably gives a bad conscience to the more lukewarm. There remains just one apprehension on my part: a bit of defensiveness when it comes to wrestling theologically with the most challenging problems with which the world confronts the Church. My humble suggestions here would be two: some soul-searching about the philosophical and theological formation of future priests and an effort to be involved in initiatives, like Communio, which seek to improve contact between sectors of the Church.

Communione e Liberazione

Like many movements in the Church, Communione e Liberazione (familiarly, C&L) came into existence from a first unplanned step in 1954 in response to a local need, and then grew to be something wider in scope than was ever originally foreseen, and indeed continues to grow "without any plan."[56]

In the postwar period the powerful student groups (which enjoy a far greater role in the Italian universities than in American colleges) were dominated by the communists. Meanwhile, as the traditional Catholic groups seemed to lack élan, students were exhausting themselves trying to maintain a set of laws that little accorded with their immediate experience. But then, too, their sense of what it is to be a Christian was rarely well developed.

A young priest, Father Luigi Giussani, teaching theology in the diocesan seminary of Milan, became aware of the state of so many students as he talked to them during his trips on the commuter train. So eventually he asked to be sent to a high school, where he might help arouse in the students a sense of living their *ethos* as ground for relating to its *ethic:* the Church should be a place of *encounter,* that welcoming home where one discovers the warmth of Jesus Christ. If the Church is that sacrament by which Christ transforms the world, then the pedagogic challenge is to make the reality of the sacrament become an experience[57] so that it will be grasped as the essential constituent element of the conscience.

So Father Giussani called together some students to experience a "pedagogy of friendship": to verify by experience the ability of Christianity to

---

56. Says Prof. Walter Maffenini of Milan in an interview in *L'Homme Nouveau* (January 3, 1993): 8. This is typical, say those involved in the movements, of how the Holy Spirit works. "We are directed, from day to day, without any plan, as we remain attentive in prayer to the Spirit's in-spiration."

57. As Balthasar explains, while man cannot, by his own initiative and renunciation of self and environment, experience the almighty transcending God, God can experience us, reaching down by His initiatives and putting our response and fidelity to the test (the root sense of experience is testing and controlling); because as Author of our being, He knows us, He can find ways to develop us, through the experience of Jesus Christ, fully Man, and His Church to which we can be experientially formed. On this see the remarkable short article, "Experience God?" in *New Elucidations,* trans. Mary Theresilde Skerry (San Francisco: Ignatius Press, 1986), 11–19.

give sense and value to every aspect of life, and thus to be a response to the question of human existence. Groups of young men and women, Christian and non-Christian, were called together to discuss a particular issue in their lives, striving to recount experience—not their ideological solutions to the problem.[58] At the end of the discussion, the adult present would bring their experiences into the light of a Christian understanding of human nature. This is not enough to convert anyone to Christianity, but as it is in a company—a little society of friends—that experience becomes "*ethos,*" it was a start down the road, and a source of strength.[59] In the company of the Christian "adult," the *whole group* is guided toward its "destiny": *the total realization of the person of each of its members.*[60] What characterizes the company is that one applies to any event of personal and social existence the criterion of truth that the encounter has taught us, in order to see, by this comparison, whether its aptitude to make sense of the totality of existence is confirmed. At the same time, one tries to bring to this depth one's entire existence, by living each event at that depth.[61]

Three "essential dimensions" are stressed: culture, charity, and mission. First, each culture has to be transformed Christianly. Second, this can take place only through love—love of Christ, and because of Him, gift of one's person to others. And third, the mission is transformation of one's milieu, and the spread to the end of the world of the Good News of our salvation. That means to seize the opportunities in everyday life to give Christian witness. One is educated to this aptitude of the Spirit by personal and community prayer, which has its center in the Eucharist, and is prolonged by the recitation of the Hours, penetrating with a Christian feeling the time of each day, opening into the different forms of personal prayer. Preparation of the liturgy takes on a special importance: to learn to sing together and to chant the Psalms signifies a triumph over individualism.[62]

Anyone can see that as such a formula started to work, networks would develop as friends identified social needs and set about finding solutions together. The result: by the late 1970s the movement had grown so large and so effective in Italy (and beyond), it became—always unplanned—a sociopolitical force to be reckoned with. While "the school of community" (which I will discuss below) remains the heart of C&L, the movement has spawned more than three thousand "little enterprises," the "Company of Works," each enjoying autonomy: newspapers, a large publishing house,

58. I am told that diocesan officials in the 1950s were suspicious of this mixing of the sexes.

59. *Les mouvements,* 23.

60. Emphasis added. Again, Balthasar (who was a close friend of Father Giussani) stresses that our personhood comes from Christ, and is a participation in His divine personhood as Logos, so that each of us is called to a unique mission, the fulfillment of which ensures the fullest possible development of the personhood God has destined for us. See, for instance, *Love Alone: The Way of Revelation,* ed. Alexander Dru (London: Sheed and Ward).

61. *Les mouvements,* 23.

62. Ibid., 25.

a radio station, private schools, centers of political initiative, work and social-assistance cooperatives, cultural centers, and musical and artistic associations. Invited by the pope to reach out beyond Italy, missions were implanted, again without plan, in Brazil and Uganda, then in North America, now in Eastern Europe, and even as far away as Japan.

The name Communione e Liberazione came only in 1969, on the heels of a crisis in that period of turmoil, and recognition that the only real liberation is in Christ, a liberation that comes to us through the *communio* that is Christ encountered in His Church. Out of this crisis emerged a strengthened sense of wanting to work for a transformation of society to make it more apt to favor a Christian form of life. So, as the students grew older, religious vocations were discovered and a movement of Christian families grew up. A fraternity of people devoted to the religious counsels but working in the world, the "Fraternity of Communion and Liberation," was founded and was recognized by the Church in 1982.

As always with any movement that expands to attention-grabbing proportions, critics arose. C&L has been accused by some, rather as Opus Dei, of tendencies to develop into a kind of "Catholic Free Masonry." Well, my C&L friends reply, since when is the formation of a network of friends who support and help one another, and who remain open and welcoming to all, in any sense a Free Masonry? Does C&L have rituals of its own, to celebrate itself? Certainly not; the little companies of friends gather in the sacramental-liturgical life of the Church. Second, the Christian friendships formed and service engaged in are meant to be at all times and in all ways not self-serving, never exclusive, but of genuine loving service to the entire community. That makes C&L in fact diametrically opposed to the spirit of a "Free Masonry" that would exist to advance the cause of its members. To be sure, here is another instance of that obvious truth, that every close-knit group of human beings who band together to be of service must be constantly vigilant to purify their love, so as not to become a power group, precisely like some Masonic traditions, despite whatever good intentions may have been there in the beginning, have obviously become. And, or so I have been told, certain C&L groups—perhaps because of the intense political activity in certain parts of it—have a tendency to be less than forthright in response to questions about how they are organized.

When I asked the coordinator of one North American C&L group about this, he expressed astonishment, and then added, "You might be referring to the frustration that many people outside the movement feel when they want to know about how C&L is organized, and they do not want to believe that there is a loose structure in which the person is left totally free to adhere or not."[63]

Recently, I heard it said that C&L groups in Canada tend to listen, perhaps rather passively, to positions taken by the leadership in Italy on political

---

63. Private letter of February 11, 1993. A friend of that leader told me that he has tried repeatedly in vain to learn details of how the fraternity works and what is expected.

issues, the complexity of which leaves ample room for Catholics to disagree. Specifically, I was told one C&L group, following the lead of C&L officials in Italy, virtually unanimously condemned the Persian Gulf initiative of the United Nations. When I asked my C&L friend about this specific instance, he replied,

> To take the example of the Gulf War, no one told me that we had to agree with the judgment of the movement, to go hand out posters, etc. There is an attempt on the part of those who belong to the movement, however, to understand a judgment from the center of the movement, who ultimately is Luigi Giussani. We did not "passively" follow the leadership in Italy on this question. The movement does not ask anyone to agree with a judgment but to try to understand the reasons behind that judgment. We were not mixing faith commitment with partisan politics, as you suggested. We were asked by the center of the movement to take seriously the judgment *by Pope John Paul II* on the war.[64]

C&L came into being partly in response to political needs, and its members have never eschewed political action. Members of C&L have published, others have worked to reform the Christian Democratic Party (one avid member, Prof. Rocco Butiglione, is now secretary general of one of the two factions split from the old party), while other prominent members, university professors, have become leaders in the reform of state industries. While these members engage in these activities on their own, there remains some contact with C&L, the spirit of which flows through these activities. As I already mentioned, Opus Dei also stresses that there are no works of the Work, other than the residential "centers" where numerary members of the Work live, and retreat houses and seminaries. Other activities, such as schools and university residences for which the prelature assures the chaplaincy, are autonomous. But because leading figures in them are members of the Work, and subject to strong direction, this turns out in practice to

64. Ibid. The principle of not mixing faith commitment with partisan politics is situated at that incarnational point where Christians are struggling to let the light of Revelation illumine their concrete action in an ambiguous world. It is almost always prudentially difficult. In the example at hand, I am prepared to argue that the holy father himself may have stepped over the line, taking as he did, in all sincerity and from his well-informed vantage point, a strong position against launching the war, a position with which, I contend, the most faithful of Catholics could in perfect good conscience disagree—while remaining in perfect fidelity to the holy father in basic moral principle, because one disagrees, as I did in this instance, with his prudential application in the event. Remember, the point—as I see it, in all fallibility—became this (however lamentable the actions of great Western governments in trying over the years to control oil supplies in the region, which remained, to be sure, the most basic motivation for the UN intervention). Once Kuwait was invaded, whether Iraq in invading fell into a trap or not, what was "the world," that is, the greater part of it that is grouped under the banner of the UN, to do? This kind of situation is difficult enough without the pope adding this complication: muddying the waters of the freedom of conscience of the individual Catholic, loyal to the magisterium in matters of faith and morals, to form a prudential judgment on such disputed political matters, into the partisan aspects of which the holy father enjoys no special charism, but certainly has the right to speak his own mind.

make of them activities *everyone else* thinks of—not altogether unfairly—as "doings of Opus Dei."

But the political dimensions of C&L should not distract one from appreciation of its central mission: *evangelization,* at the heart of which stands "the School of Community." This is instruction based on three volumes of Father Giussani. One is to help develop the religious sense, starting with the questions "Who am I? What I am doing here?" The second presents Christ as the historic response to the question of man. The third presents the Church as the ongoing point of encounter with Christ.[65] This school in *communio* gathered about Christ has been successful first in Italy, and now in many parts of the world.

As my friend wrote, what is significant is not the figures about the numbers of adherents to C&L in Italy, or Mexico, or Russia, but "the fact that many people (in and) outside Italy have discovered Christ and the Church through the movement, [which is] a sign that the C&L gestures are open to the world and not to a confined situation."

Communio

Concerned by the growing tendency of many theologians to pit an alleged "spirit of the council" against the authentic teachings recorded in the official documents of the Second Vatican Council, several then members of the International Theological Commission, including Hans Urs von Balthasar, Henri de Lubac, and Joseph Ratzinger, founded in 1972 a new initiative, naming it for the true life of the Church, Communio. This was not conceived as yet another "movement," but as a service to the whole thinking and praying Church, an effort to reinforce the spirit of unity and cooperation between all elements of the Church, by drawing on persons of goodwill in every part of it, including, of course, the movements themselves, to strengthen the unifying life flowing from Jesus Christ in the midst of legitimate plurality of spiritualities and "paths."

As an initial instrument in this service, the *International Theological Journal: Communio* was founded. The German edition was the first, but rapidly others, each guided by an autonomous but cooperating editorial board, in French, English, Portuguese, and so on, appeared, until today there are fourteen. Some publish six times a year, others quarterly, some—means lacking—only annually. (The Arabic edition, centered in Beirut, has, for reasons you can imagine, appeared irregularly.)

The struggling journal has become the tail wagging the still rather hypothetical Communio dog. To be sure, an intellectual communion has developed out of the twice-annual coordinating editorial board meetings. Those are taken up largely with rather quick decisions about which issues to discuss in the next year. There has developed a much closer bond between certain students of the thought of Balthasar, with the danger always present of the journal becoming more the paper of the Hans Urs von Balthasar

---

65. Interview with Prof. Walter Maffenin in *L'Homme Nouveau* (January 3, 1993): 8.

Society[66] than an effective channel of communication drawing people from all sectors of the Church closer together. But not much more than that—until May 1992, when another of Communio's founding fathers, Cardinal Ratzinger, gave a weighty formal address at the twentieth-anniversary meeting of the editorial boards in Rome, and piqued the consciences of all by suggesting that Communio had barely begun to fulfill its promise to help the Church transform the culture of our time. His hint, that the moment had come to go further, was sufficient to launch an initiative in North America of Communio study circles.[67]

In just over a year, more than twenty were founded, mostly from readers of the English version of the journal. These are intended to deepen the *communio* in the spirit expressed by the journal, one of fidelity to the magisterium, devotion to achieving greater unity in the Church through sensitive appreciation for and discussion of different spiritualities, different missions, and legitimately different theological tendencies, with supernatural love providing the basis of mutual understanding between the different communities within this vast and far-flung Church. Two years later the first of three annual Communio retreats scheduled for different parts of North America took place.

Lack of communication has always been a basic human problem, since man outgrew the tribal village (where everyone knows everything, especially the most carefully guarded secrets of the elders!). One of the disastrous fruits of original sin is insufficient nonmaleficent interest in what the other is doing, and of just plain mediocrity in the form of poor organization. Ignorance breeds tragedies and in the Church is particularly disgusting because it is God incarnating Himself through the *communio*. Communio is meant to be a service to the whole Church by first living that spirit, and then communicating it to the whole institution.

In the first issue of every new edition there is printed a profound essay on *communio* by Balthasar. It would not be an exaggeration to say that Communio, as a group of friends within the Church, exists to further in every conceivable way, but especially on the intellectual level, exactly what Balthasar wrote there. I cannot sum it up, every sentence carries a weight, but only suggest that anyone wishing to help in this central work of the whole Church should read it.[68]

66. The editors are aware of this danger and resist the temptation by which I, for my part, am attracted, because I too want the world to share in the immense and inspired vision of this great spirit. On any subject about which *Communio* reflects there are always texts of von Balthasar that bring so much to the discussion it would be a shame to neglect them. Other inevitable favorites of *Communio* are de Lubac and Ratzinger. As a member of the editorial board of the North American edition I honestly do not feel apologetic about that.

67. The French edition years ago started such an initiative, which spread rapidly but then, for reasons I do not know, seems to have largely withered away.

68. *International Theological Review: Communio* 1:1, 1ff.

Cursillo

A good example of how the same undertaking within the Church can give birth to quite distinctive initiatives would be to compare Cursillo with the New Catechumenate.

The "Little Courses of Christianity"—known everywhere by their Spanish name, "Cursillos"—began in Majorca in 1949. Six million people in more than sixty nations have now participated in one of these intense special retreats. Thirty national secretariats and more than six hundred diocesan secretariats organize the giving of these Little Courses.

The movement's short-term goal is "to give to the baptized adult the opportunity to hear the Good News of Jesus Christ, to be able to adhere to it in faith, and to experience communally the realities which found Christianity."[69] The long-term goal is stated thus: "to animate the world Christianly, thanks to the birth of Christian groups which, fully inserted in the ecclesial community, engage themselves to live their baptism in an authentic manner, continuous and progressive, thus causing to rise as leaven the dough—the milieu where they live—thanks to ferments of evangelical criteria and the spirit of that very Gospel."[70]

Most Christians have received the gospel message in such little doses they have become vaccinated against the radicalness of the vision and the demands Christ puts on us. To overcome this "taking for granted," Cursillistas proceed in these three actions:

1. The *precursillo*, a time of prayer and sacrifice, discernment, and pre-evangelization of individuals susceptible of profiting from a *cursillo;* a selection and preparation.
2. The *cursillo* itself, a three-day intense presentation of the *kerygma* by a team of priests and laity, the experience of a "true Christian life together."
3. The *post-cursillo* (or *ultreya*), when small groups of six or seven meet weekly to help one another grow in the Christian life, "a veritable catechumenate leading to a maturation of one's life in Christ." Testimony to what one is living through plays a key role in this ongoing process.

The movement does not desire to be a thing apart, but rather an integral aspect of the parish's work of sanctification.

The New Catechumenate

The other vigorous new movement built around the very idea of the need, on the part of those already baptized but poorly instructed in the faith, for a serious catechetical formation, a molding of the whole person

---

69. Ibid., 48.
70. Ibid.

to lead the Christian life, is the New Catechumenate. Of late it has been in the news more than Cursillo, in part because of its vigorous expansion, its exceptional rigor, and because it has attracted the particularly strong backing of the present pope. It has become five hundred thousand strong, is found in thirteen thousand communities in 186 dioceses, and operates twenty-eight Redemptoris Mater seminaries with more than one thousand seminarians.[71]

With a demanding program of catechetical and spiritual preparation lasting years, the Neocatechumenate, while pursuing the same end as Cursillo, does so with a scope and a rigor of step-by-step progression over a long period unparalleled by any other lay formation. This is made possible because the movement first enlists the support of a bishop and a local pastor and then works for years within that parish structure.

During the beginning, "kerygmatic," phase, when the candidates are being prepared for and convinced of the need for catechetical formation in community, volunteer itinerants—an evangelization team consisting of a priest, a layman, and a laywoman (whose travel expenses are paid by the "mature community" from which they come)—visit the parish, setting the times and places for the meetings, which usually occur twice a week and last for two months. Once the kerygmatic phase is complete, a three-day "convivence," rather like a retreat, takes place to help the formation of a community for those who freely choose to continue. Everyone has an opportunity to convey his own experience of the Word.

The second phase, the "pre-catechumenate," sees the community participating every week in a "Celebration of the Word," based on a theme drawn from the *Dictionary of Biblical Theology* and prepared in advance by three or four brothers, and on Saturday nights the Eucharist.[72] Monthly "convivences" give everyone again an opportunity to share their experience of living the Word.

After two years the community enters "the passageway to the catechumenate," in which the "Celebration of the Word" is directed toward study of the major events in salvation history, with the aim of the Word's becoming bread, with emphasis on how the events in daily life relate to Jesus Christ.

The next step, lasting several years, the "catechumenate" proper, stresses intense private prayer, entering into a deeper relationship with God, which should give one the strength for the next phase in this step: evangelization, when the community is called to proclaim the gospel in their neighborhood. One member said of this, "they realize it is more important to appear publicly clothed in the Word than to maintain social appearances hiding one's Christian identity." Now the Celebration of the Word attends to the patriarchs: Noah, Abraham, Isaac, Jacob, and Moses. The renewal of baptismal promises is the last step of this long journey. The community

71. Figures from the article cited in next note.
72. Marietti, *Dictionary of Biblical Theology*, 5th ed. (Monferrato: Casale, 1976).

has passed through the three fundamental stages of Christian life: humility (pre-catechumenate), simplicity (post-baptismal catechumenate) and praise (renewal of baptismal promise).

In a recent report on the movement, Sandro Magister, an Italian journalist noted for his reporting on the Vatican, complains of secrecy—the complaint heard, unfairly I believe, of Opus Dei, too.

> Thirty years have passed since the movement was established yet the voluminous manuals written by the founders, Kiko [Arguelle] and Carmen [Hernandez] remain secret, and no community member is allowed to consult these. Even Curial cardinals had to wage a major battle to examine these texts when the first accusations of heresy were leveled against the Neocatechumenate's strange and confusing theology. Even today, the movement's internal proceedings are kept hidden from outsiders.[73]

I offer this example of the kind of criticism being hurled at this movement, reminiscent of attacks on Opus Dei, but not forgetting that the pope supports both organizations energetically. It is difficult for a Catholic not in a movement to assess either the nature of their spirituality, the human dimensions of their disciplines, or the praises and criticisms one hears. The same can be said of older organizations and even of religious orders. This is just a fact of life in a worldwide Church of great complexity, that variety Richard John Neuhaus finds congenial. The responsibility for supervising them lies with the ecclesiastical authorities; one's own judgment comes into play only if one is thinking about joining a particular community. And it may be valid only for that local community, not the movement as a whole. In any vast movement there are bound to be excesses, as there are among Christians in any event.

I did find a thoughtful, well-informed former member, not an enthusiast of the movement, who found the criticism extreme. As she said, spiritual movements, involving intimate personal relations with God and with members of a community, are the people's own business. The Catechumenate, like others, has been subject to vicious attacks and hence likes to be sure with whom they may be "opening up" when outsiders come snooping around. She found no foundation either to the accusation that their theology is weird, "rather oversimplified if anything" was her reaction. She says the movement has been particularly successful in attracting drug addicts and alcoholics away from disastrous lives. That there may be a tendency to create one dependency to replace another worries her, but she agreed that this is done with the best intentions. These are the kinds of considerations one gets into in discussing the peculiarities of any of the movements.

The Charismatic Movement and the Covenant Communities
A radically different kind of spirituality became accentuated in the Church with the upsurge in the 1970s of the charismatic movement.[74] The

73. "In Kiko's Name," in *L'Espresso* (May 13, 1996), cited in *Inside the Vatican* (August–September 1996): 47–48.

74. This "infusion of the Spirit" began in a prayer meeting in Pittsburgh in 1967. See *Les mouvements*, 94.

emphasis on the gifts of the Holy Spirit that one finds in this multistreamed and vast development results from taking a basic dimension of Christian belief and moving it to center stage, a perennial recurring tendency, as we have seen already among the Montanists in the second century, then with the pietistic movements of the fourteenth century, in the Anabaptists (with whom it took the form of a revolt) in the sixteenth, and again in the last century with the rise of evangelical Protestantism, starting with Rutherford and his Jehovah's Witnesses and then in our own century with the Pentecostal movement in Kansas around 1905. Because of its quite distinctive theological character (not that formal theology has been its strong point), the charismatic movement deserves discussion under doctrine, when in the next section, I discuss doctrinal strengths and weaknesses. But as is always the case, the theological-doctrinal has structural-institutional implications. The charismatic movement has resulted in significant institutional innovations, which I shall mention here, judging them as a sign of strength on the structural level. To understand what has happened ecclesially will require some anticipation of the theological issues.

There are important questions here: why should such a "pentecostal" eruption have occurred once again within the Catholic Church, and why where and as it has, and why was it so long in doing so, and why—this time—have those affected remained for the most part faithful to the Catholic Church? Nothing much happened until the late 1970s,[75] although the phenomenon had been powerful among Protestants for half a century, but when it did finally happen in the Catholic Church, it touched within ten years hundreds of thousands, perhaps millions of Catholics, coming from all parts of the Church, producing everything from an explosive mushrooming of loosely affiliated prayer groups to highly structured "covenant communities."[76]

I asked a friend who has been long involved in one of the pioneer and most important "covenant communities," the "Word of God" in Ann Arbor, Michigan, about the explosive growth of this phenomenon. I quote what Michael Keating responded:

> The Pentecostal movement as a whole is a staggering phenomenon. Reasonable estimates put the number of pentecostals or charismatics, whether independent or gathered into new denominations or members of existing denominations at over one hundred million,[77] and rapidly growing. Latin America is experiencing a pentecostal revolution, mostly at the expense of the Catholic Church. Africa is also seeing tremendous growth among pentecostals, as are parts of Asia. And main Pentecostal denominations, The Assemblies of God for instance, are filled with

75. The important book of a couple who were present that day in Pittsburgh when a praying group received an impulsion of the Spirit published an important statement already in 1969 (Kevin Ranaghan and Dorothy Ranaghan, *Catholic Pentecostals* [New York: Paulist Press]).

76. Ranaghan and Ranaghan, *Catholic Pentecostals*, 95.

77. For an up-to-date analysis of estimated growth and where and why it is happening, consult Ralph Martin, *The Catholic Church at the End of an Age*, chaps. 1 and 2.

former Catholics. There is something about this form of spirituality that is proving extremely attractive to large numbers of people, in both the developed and the developing worlds. What? Why this explosive growth, often among members of existing churches?

Perhaps it has something to do with the increasing alienation people are experiencing as a by-product of modernization. Increasingly alone, atomized and free-floating, finding traditional religious categories not integrated in their lives, people look for an experience that floods their world with meaning. This experience is not, I would argue, the one-time shot of high-powered "release of the Holy Spirit" so much as the experience of belonging to a group within which meaning can be found. The pentecostal movement (including the Catholic charismatic aspect of it) is very much oriented toward groups, however they may be constituted. In fully modernized countries deep soul-loneliness is the great epidemic. In developing countries (e.g., Mexico) modern life has brought rapid urbanization and population growth, leaving vast numbers without a clear social context, uprooted from their traditional life, spiritually wandering. The Church has not been able to keep up with this, and many people are left with virtually no spiritual nourishment. Along comes a pentecostal missionary speaking a simple and powerful gospel message, and establishing a close-knit group (a new church, most probably) that lends meaning and dignity to its members.

In addition to this, the pentecostal message lends itself to the modern experience-oriented quick-results mentality. It is easily packaged and communicated, and it offers those who embrace it a genuine change of life, both internally (experience of God) and externally (membership in a close-knit and affectionate group).[78] This is all the more powerful, because it is evident from the Scriptures that conversion to Christ and entrance into the Church is *supposed* to represent a radical change of life, both internally and externally. The pentecostal formulation is often theologically impoverished and ecclesiologically problematic, but it does represent an attractive and powerful experience (I use the word broadly, not meaning [just] an emotional high) that is the true possession of the Catholic Church (Paul, Augustine, Francis, to name a few out of hundreds of thousands) but that all too often has become close to meaningless in a typical Catholic context.

I have often spoken to former Catholics who experienced "conversion" in a Pentecostal denomination. If I try to express my concern about the theological problems involved, about the unique nature of the Catholic Church, about the importance of the sacraments, they listen with impatience. Then they say, "Look, I go to a Catholic church, I don't know anyone there and it seems like nobody knows anyone else, half the people are asleep, sometimes the priest included, no one really seems to care about their faith, and it all seems a waste of time. I come to the Pentecostal church and the place is alive. People come because they love Jesus, and you can see it on their faces. They're warm and friendly, they welcome newcomers, they have all kinds of activities from bible studies to picnics and softball leagues; I'm growing in the Lord, I'm making all kinds of new friends, I'm getting help with my family, my life is taking on new meaning. And you're telling me I shouldn't stay because of bad theology? That's like telling a drowning man not to grab hold of the life preserver next to him because it isn't made by the right company."[79]

Regarding the sense of the recent outbreak, Keating offered this view: "I think of the Charismatic renewal, rather than being a thing unto its own,

---

78. Someone has suggested that with charismatics it seems that a sudden strong conversion is followed by a gradual deepening, while in the other kinds of movements it is more that a gradual deepening leads to a new level of conversion.

79. Michael Keating, letter to author, April 3, 1993.

and functioning on its own, as an instrument for the renewal of the Church, that is all of the already existing institutions of the Church, for example the religious orders, parishes, base ecclesial communities, apostolic programs, the other movements, programs of social action, etc."[80]

Taken in this way, the phenomenon is basically theological-doctrinal, but with liturgical implications, too. And any student of the contemporary Church will have to come to terms with its profound implications. But it has generated new communities, especially the full-blown "covenant communities," which I shall discuss here. Michael Keating's comments about loneliness show us why they have proved so important.

The leadership of the Catholic Church seems to have sensed almost immediately—certainly by the early 1970s[81]—the importance of this development, its potential, and at the same time a certain danger inherent in a movement stressing the infusion of the Holy Spirit in the individual and within little communities, with its age-old potential of stirring up "prophet versus priest" tensions. "Pseudo-mysticism, illuminism, fundamentalism" is the danger, according to a student of these movements, himself a member of a new community.[82] Almost from the start, certain bishops took an intense interest in the movement, and fairly quickly the Belgian cardinal Leo J. Suenens, sympathetic to the charismatics, became a liaison between them and Rome. Some early worries about "covenant communities," which developed tight authority structures, with mutterings from unsympathetic quarters that they might develop into sects, have required adroit redressing, but the fear of "spin-off" into schismatic or heretical sects has proved thus far largely groundless. Two facts are important here. First, most charismatics are not even in such communities, and second, of those who are, it is clearly admitted that they are exceptionally devoted to the Church: the communities, and the much broader movement beyond them, have been a fertile breeding ground for religious vocations and source of the best evangelizers in a difficult materialistic time.

Charismatics understand their movement as that work of the Holy Spirit through which He is strengthening in the Church our sense of His power and presence. They stress that the gifts of the Holy Spirit are normally poured out in the sacraments, initially in baptism, and in a renewed way in confirmation, and daily in the celebration of the Eucharist, to which Catholic charismatics have the greatest devotion. The Holy Spirit responds

80. Ibid.

81. Cardinal Suenens's book *A New Pentecost?* dates from 1974 (New York: Seabury). Other "classics": René Laurentin, *Catholic Pentecostalism* (Garden City, N.Y.: Doubleday, 1978); Donald Gelpi, *Pentecostalism: A Theological Viewpoint* (New York: Paulist Press, 1971); Heribert Mühlen, *Einübung in die christliche Grunderfahrung,* 2 vols. (Mainz: Mathias-Grünewald, 1976), trans. as *A Charismatic Theology: Initiation in the Spirit* (New York: Paulist Press, 1978); Simon Tugwell, *Did You Receive the Spirit?* (New York: Paulist Press, 1972); and Kevin McDonnell, ed., *The Holy Spirit and Power: The Catholic Charismatic Renewal* (Garden City, N.Y.: Doubleday, 1975).

82. Lenoir, *Les communautés nouvelles,* 13.

to the prayers of any and all the faithful. But He has elected in our time to renew in some in a special way the sense of their baptism, which happens in that "rebirth in the Spirit" that can occur, usually during an episode of intense communal prayer and the "laying on of hands" by a group who themselves have enjoyed this gift.

Theologically, this is an important point, the precise sense of which is disputed among charismatics, as anything so fundamental and sweeping is of course bound to be. Protestant charismatics of the Anabaptist extreme will claim that only in the "baptism in the Spirit" is one "born again": only then does one truly and freely take Jesus Christ as one's savior, and until that happens, the baptism of water and going through the motions means little. This constitutes a repudiation of the "institutional Church," and any sense of sacraments being effective *ex opere operato* is dismissed. Catholic charismatics have a completely different interpretation. They point out that as baptized Christians[83] grow to adulthood, they need to reaffirm their baptism promises, made for them by the Church through their sponsors. One does this in several ways, in confirmation, in prayer, and every time we receive the Eucharist. But also we can be invited to do it with unusual intensity in a privileged moment the Holy Spirit may grant some, that moment of "pouring out [*effusion*, say the French] of the Spirit." This occurs characteristically during intense prayer meetings and with a laying on of hands. Charismatics are quick to add that the laying on of hands on such occasions is not an eighth sacrament or a form of confirmation, but a mere sacramental,[84] a gesture helpful in realizing our faith, like making the sign of the cross, one that has no quality of the *ex opere operato* sort. If the Holy Spirit does grant a special gift sometimes on such occasions, He does not always—in contradistinction to the sacraments, in which, as the Church promises, through the very administrating of the sacraments, He always does infuse grace. Just as prayer, while always the source of a gracious response on God's part, can nevertheless be at one time "dry" and at another the moment of a special grace in the form of a sense that God is near, so too there can be granted a grace of a renewed sense of the great gift of our baptism, which can happen when one is all alone in prayer, or when one

83. Whose baptism they acknowledge as a being born again in the spirit *ex opere operato*, by virtue of the efficacy inherent in the ministering by Christ's Church of His promise. See, for instance, Charles-Eric Hauguel, "L'effusion de l'esprit," in *Quand deux ou trois . . .* (Paris: Éditions de la Maison de l'Emmanuel, 1990), 25–27.

84. "What is the 'effusion of the Spirit'? It is not an eighth sacrament! If some speak of 'Baptism of the Spirit' the expression is improper and leads to confusion. It gives the impression of a second baptism, as though the first were not enough. That is all wrong. It is also not an ancient rite of the Church suddenly rediscovered and made prominent. The effusion of the Spirit is an event [*démarche*] at once personal and communal in view of a deliberate renewal of the life of the Spirit in us, a deepening, a 'reactualization' of the grace of Baptism and Communion" (ibid., 27–28). This collection of essays is a superb introduction to "sensible charismatic life" and to the spirit of Communauté Emmanuel, one of the most remarkable of the European communities of *"le Renouveau"* and *"la ré-évangélisation de l'Europe."*

experiences the group's gesture of laying on of hands. If it occurs more often in community, this is not to be charged to the "power of suggestion" or group hysteria; rather, it is the Spirit's way of showing that the Church is, after all, a family. "Where two or three meet in my name, I shall be there with them," said the Lord (Matt. 18:20).

Such signs can be dramatic. One hears of individuals being "slain in the Spirit," passing out and going limp. Catholics less emotional and somewhat skeptical about charismatics tend to see excess emotionalism and power of suggestion in such phenomena.[85] Catholic charismatics work hard to shift the emphasis, in talking about "religious experience," from "an emotive charge" to "a substantial amelioration in the Christian life of the person." I believe I see evidence of such "substantial amelioration." A charismatic friend describes those fruits: "This manifests itself in a newly intensified desire to pray, a new freedom expressed in the prayer of praise, a new enthusiasm for, and comprehension of the Word of God, the need to be part of a Christian community, new victories over sin, a new desire to serve others, spiritually as well as materially, with a love more practical than theoretical."[86]

Charismatics also stress other gifts of the Holy Spirit that are not the usual fare of most Catholics: healing, prophecy, and speaking in tongues. Again, more "radical" charismatics will make more out of these things, some going so far as to suggest that if one is not receiving such gifts, then one is obviously not "born again," and that is of course bad news. The majority, however, reject such extreme suggestions, and tend to downplay any notion that the outpouring of these gifts endorses some kind of "super Christianity" of the "born again."

These phenomena, because they are strange to the vast majority of practicing Catholics, may tend paradoxically to divide more than they unite the Church. This is worrisome, for a genuine work of the Holy Spirit should above all unite us. The problem is related to the tight unity within the charismatic covenant communities, which produces, without anyone's intending it, a degree of "us versus them." But remember the covenant communities are only one aspect of the charismatic movement. These communities, "especially the Word of God," says Michael Keating,

> were self-conscious attempts to construct a Christian culture. "Word of God" was far more than a prayer or support group, or even a religious movement. It was a kind of sociological experiment. Unlike many fundamentalists whose view of "the world" tends to be black and white, the leaders of the Word of God enjoyed a fairly sophisticated critique of modern life that came from theologians and social scientists with whom all of us are familiar. The emphasis on family life, husband-wife

85. Significantly, so can some evangelicals. One of the reasons the Pastors of the Vineyard movement decided to part ways with the Toronto Airport Vineyard was their perception of abuses of emotion and crowd suggestion, to the point—it was accused—of someone being stationed behind anyone witnessing on the stage waiting for them to be bowled over by the Spirit.

86. *Les mouvements*, 95.

relationship, and "conformity" can sound just plain strange if not seen against the background of a (voluntary) attempt to build a counter-environment within which marriages could be strong, children could grow up healthy, and creative cultural expression of faith could flourish. I have my doubts as to whether or not the attempt was simply too ambitious. . . . The whole movement was very young, lots of mistakes were made, balances between freedom and communal responsibility were often not properly struck, the very energy of the participants to build something they deeply believed in made certain youthful excesses almost inevitable.[87]

These remarks help us understand why those responsible in the Pontifical Council for the Laity stress that every movement must strive to be open to the whole Church, and that the community members should keep their communities welcoming.[88]

Most covenant communities have striven to remain under the close supervision of the Church, and those communities that I know in France are in fact called on by the bishops when they want an especially demanding service carried out. A community like Emmanuel, whose leaders I am privileged to know, would never countenance either an interfering form of direction, a patriarchy, or an extreme like husbands giving spiritual direction to their wives, which apparently did occur in a few American communities earlier on.

Indeed, Emmanuel's attitude to spiritual direction shows the good sense and balance of this group. Each postulant and, later, member is assigned annually an *accompagnateur,* a lay member of the community, whose task it is, meeting monthly, *to listen.* He is not to direct, and he may, if asked a specific question, give his advice in response, but he is instructed otherwise just to listen. It was a friend in Emmanuel who expressed the opinion that Opus Dei's weekly direction and confession strikes him as in danger of invading the member's freedom.[89] The two friends I interrogated both expressed satisfaction with the *accompagnement* they were receiving, and protested they would be unhappy with a paternalistic overdirection too. Having to say what is going on crystallizes a view of one's progress, or lack of it, and an occasional discreet pointer from a well-meaning other, especially when blessed with a charism of office, as in confession, is a precious advantage.

I should mention another family of more or less charismatic institutions, Les Foyers de Charité (founded 1936, and thus anticipating the main

87. Keating, letter to author, April 3, 1993.

88. In the three instances when I went to visit communities—two "covenant communities" and one large charismatic community in Europe—I was made welcome and all my questions were answered with openness and patience.

89. I have asked Opus Dei friends about this, and they replied with two points: The object of the weekly encounter with a priest is to take advantage of the grace Christ has offered in the sacrament of reconciliation. And, second, the role of the spiritual director—usually a fellow lay member of the Work—is also basically to listen: if he is a good director, he will not impose, he will be extremely discreet and respectful of the member's freedom; but there are times when he ought to point out deficiencies, and suggest a way forward.

charismatic movement by forty years), and the educational branch of the same family of institutions, L'Eau Vive. These flow from the extraordinary gifts of the influential stigmatic[90] Marthe Robin, who was bedridden in her farm from age twenty-one until her death in 1981 at age seventy-nine.[91] Her spirituality influenced such later charismatic communities as Emmanuel and Lion de Judah (now Les Béatitudes). But the Foyers were her main work. There were, as of 1988, in addition to a large high school for girls and another for boys in Châteauneuf, twenty-seven Foyers in Europe, fifteen in the Americas, sixteen in Africa, and five in Asia, varying in number from three to fifty, always with a priest at their center, and living communally, devoted to various apostolic tasks, prominently, retreats. "The Foyers are communities of workers sharing their lives, their prayer, their material, intellectual and spiritual goods. They receive *retraitants* of all ages, social milieu, and countries, men, women, single, married, priests and religious."[92] Some operate schools, or dispensaries, or retreat houses, or animate parishes. L'Eau Vive is seeking to renew Catholic education, in the spirit that this statement by one of the leaders captures well:

> Education, to be profound, is founded on authority, which is to be exercised in a paternal manner, as all the great educators, from St. Benedict to St. John Bosco have shown us, and as Marthe Robin saw so well from the first moment when she began to give their orientation to the *Foyers de charité*. That radiating authority, which must never be confused with an arbitrary use of power, will know how at once to fortify, redress, and develop the elements constitutive of a personality, in order to cooperate in the action of grace in souls. It is to be exercised in perfect filial harmony

90. A stigmatic is a mystic who receives the gift of participating physically in the suffering and Passion of Christ. The stigmatic is marked by the wounds of Christ, and generally suffers the Passion of Christ sympathetically, especially on Good Friday. Saint Francis of Assisi was the first recorded stigmatic. Saint Catherine of Siena is another famous stigmata. In modern times, in addition to Marthe Robin, Padre Pio in Italy (stigma started 1916, and he died in 1968), Theresa Neumann (who lived from 1898 to 1962) in Germany, and Rose Ferron (who lived from 1902 to 1936) in America have gained notoriety. Dr. Adrienne von Speyer, Balthasar's close associate, suffered the Passion every year. See Pierre Adnès, "Stigmatics," in *Dictionnaire de spiritualité, ascétiques et mystiques, doctrine et histoire* (Paris: Beauchesne, 1966), 16:1213–26. It should be pointed out that the Church does not hold up as an article of faith any such claims in the order of personal spirituality or revelation. Controversy swirls about every case of stigmatization, and with unimaginable intensity about the case of Theresa Neumann, with great effort to establish the hysterical nature of the phenomenon. See bibliography in ibid., 1223f. The experiences of Marthe Robin seem to have attracted far less negative press.

91. From 1930 on, bedridden in Châteauneuf de Galaure southeast of Lyons and never sleeping or eating, except the Eucharist, Marthe Robin suffered every Thursday to Friday the Passion of Christ (see Lenoir, *Les communautés nouvelles*, 740). As incredible as these physical claims about Robin may seem, they are well documented. See the book of the philosopher, Jean Guitton, *Portrait de Marthe Robin* (Paris: Grasset, 1986), for the life of this most extraordinary person. From her little divan, Marthe gave spiritual direction to hundreds of visitors, and influenced the founding of many movements and institutions.

92. Lenoir, *Les communautés nouvelles*, 76.

with that of the Supreme Pontiff, the common Father, and in profound docility to the Divine Maternity of Mary.[93]

L'Eau Vive has given particular attention to summer camps, where the young are taught to live together in the spirit of a Christian family and are instructed in the faith.[94] (Have they taken a page in this from Schoenstatt's book?)

If it is true in general that each of these new movements deserves at least a book, volumes can and have been written about the charismatic renewal. I have mentioned here a small, arbitrarily chosen cross section, not even scratching the surface (and below, under "Doctrine," not much more will be achieved than just pointing out that this enormous and fascinating phenomenon has become a vital—and not generally well understood—dimension in the life of the contemporary Church).

Focolari

Founded in 1944 by an Italian laywoman, Chiara Lubich, and some friends, Focolari[95] is thoroughly Catholic in origin and in spirit, and resolutely ecumenical in form and intention. In this Focolari anticipated the Second Vatican Council's ecumenical opening of the Church to other religions, and to the world in general. I cite this large, international movement here as an illustration of how Catholics, responding to the call of the Holy Spirit, have been able to make this move of intensified outreach beyond traditional missionary activity. This marks an end to the long period of woundedness that followed the breakup of Christendom and the religious wars of the seventeenth century. It is a movement to restore the sense of *communio* so strongly emphasized in the Vatican documents.[96] In *Les mouvements dans l'Église* it is stressed that one of the signs of an authentic charism in a movement is its ecclesial character, which perforce includes *catholicity:* the movement's concern for the whole truth and for bringing it to all men. Focolari pursues ecumenism in this spirit.

93. *Les mouvements,* 54. I find a harmony here with the stated educational intention of Schoenstatt. Regrettably, I do not have enough personal familiarity with either to draw comparisons of style, which would probably prove interesting—at the least the French-German difference must show!

94. While not charismatic in origin or spirituality, I should mention another interesting initiative, directed toward spiritual development of Catholic families, the Équipes Notre-Dame, founded in 1937, in France, and now consisting of five or six thousand little groups of six or seven families, assisted by a priest, who work at helping one another develop a family spirituality. They also give generously of their time in the family pastoral activity of their dioceses (ibid., 58–63).

95. With the sense of folk who gather about a fire, hence *"foyer."*

96. On the sense of the Church as a *koinonia* or *communio,* we shall see below that the Final Report of the Anglican-Catholic Commission saw its whole work in terms of this mystery of the *communio* of the Church. See especially the brilliant statement penned by Balthasar that has appeared in the first issue of every edition of the *International Theological Journal: Communio* (there are now fourteen such semiautonomous but associated language editions) (for instance, the American edition, 1:1 [1975]).

In those early wartime days of discovery, when five hundred women gathered around Chiara Lubich in a matter of months to pray and work for peace, and the bishop of Trento, approached as the representative of God, approved, a particular spiritual experience riveted their attention: the abandonment of Christ on the cross.[97] The representative at the Rome meeting put it this way:

> Are not the anguished, the lonely, the disgusted, the turned-off, the failure, the weak, like him [the abandoned Christ]? Is not He the image of each division between brothers, between Churches, between the slices of humanity represented by different ideologies? . . . In loving the abandoned Jesus, the Christian finds the motive for never fleeing evils, divisions, but to accept them through Him, to take them on oneself, to bring one's personal remedy to them. And thus Jesus abandoned becomes the key of unity, the secret of all renewal.[98]

With this goes a sense of the presence of Jesus in the Eucharist, in the hierarchy, in each brother, in Mary. If a single word were to express Focolari spirituality, continues our source, it would be *unity*.

The movement grew rapidly to become vast, embracing consecrated men and women, whole families, a movement of priests. Formation centers ("Mariopolis") in several countries, and an ecumenical center in Rome have sprung up. In 1968, with approval of the Catholic and Lutheran bishops, an ecumenical center was founded in Ottmaring, near Augsburg. Later the movement was welcomed by the Anglican primates. The patriarch Athenagoras welcomed the movement to Istanbul, as has his successor, Dimitrios I. Today Buddhists, Muslims, and even nonreligious people have been attracted to the movement "because of the witness of concrete charity and Christian unity given by the movement."[99]

At the present time there are 4 million *Focolarini* in the world. It is spreading particularly fast in Africa. Twenty-seven different branches carry out distinctive initiatives.[100] The movement is very much seen by its members as an extension of the extraordinary charismatic gifts of its foundress, Chiara, whose spiritual writings and personal presence continue to play a great role.

Official Ecumenical Dialogues

In the same spirit of innovation and response to clear impulsion from the Holy Spirit toward the healing of the gaping wound of Christian disunity came initiatives, already discussed in Chapter 12, to establish official

97. To my knowledge there has been no influence of Balthasar on this movement, and certainly not at that early time, yet it is interesting to note that Christ's *kenosis*, especially the ultimate moment of it, His abandonment by even the Father on the cross, is also a central theme in the theology of Balthasar and Adrienne von Speyer.

98. *Les mouvements*, 82. This recovery of the sense of the ultimate *kenosis* by Chiara Lubich and her companions at the very time Balthasar and Adrienne von Speyer were experiencing the same spiritual insight is significant. That it should happen at the end of the terrible war is understandable.

99. Ibid., 86.

100. I am grateful to Maria del Grande, a local Toronto focolarina, for these figures.

structures for high-level theological explorations of ways to move toward definitive healing of the breaches. There are also provisions for serious ongoing Muslim-Christian dialogue,[101] for Jewish-Christian exchange, and there may come to be others with religions like Buddhism, in addition to many local, officially sanctioned initiatives. A good example of the latter: the ashram founded twenty-five years ago in Madras, with the approval and support of the local bishops, directed by the Rev. Ignatius Hirudayam, S.J., devoted to Hindu-Catholic exploration. This has resulted in an approved Catholic liturgy with Hindu aesthetic forms, and strong emphasis on sacred dance. Because of our earlier discussion of these efforts to open out ecumenically, I shall limit myself here to brief mention of two prominent Christian dialogues I happen to know something about, with an update. They are good examples of the Church's institutional innovation in response to new conditions.

First, there is the Anglican–Roman Catholic International Commission. Founded in 1966 by the archbishop of Canterbury, Dr. Michael Ramsey, and Pope Paul VI, this exploration, which has gone on to many sessions, completed its first set of discussions, outlined in the "Final Report," from Windsor, in 1981. The themes of the various sessions are telling: eucharistic doctrine (1971); further elucidation (1979); ministry and ordination (1973); authority in the Church, divided into two sessions—1976 and 1981, with an elucidation between times. The resulting impressive documents are a treasure house of theological insight, won in the context of earnest and loving debate and common work. The spirit of that work is admirably captured in the conclusion to the Common Declaration of 1977, repeated in the preface to the "Final Report":

> To be baptized into Christ is to be baptized into hope—"and hope does not disappoint us because God's love has been poured into our hearts through the Holy Spirit which has been given us" (Rom. 5:5). Christian hope manifests itself in prayer and action—in prudence but also in courage. We pledge ourselves and exhort the faithful of the Roman Catholic Church and of the Anglican Communion to live and work courageously in this hope of reconciliation and unity in our common Lord.[102]

The theologians have placed the whole endeavor under the symbol *koinonia—communio*—pointing out that "the term most aptly expresses the mystery underlying the various New Testament images of the Church."[103]

Remarkable agreement has been forged on many issues grouped under the aforelisted topics, and the reports favorably received at the highest

---

101. On October 21–22, 1991, an official national-level Catholic-Muslim consultation took place in Washington, sponsored by the NCCB, the American Muslim Council, and the Muslim World League. For a discussion of issues, see the Rev. Elias Mallon, "The Challenges in Catholic Muslim Dialogue," *Origins* 21:33 (January 23, 1992): 531–34, an excellent discussion.

102. Anglican–Roman Catholic International Commission, *The Final Report* (London: McAdoo and Clark, 1982), 4.

103. Ibid., 6. Recall the importance of this term, so well explained by Balthasar; see above.

levels of the respective churches. The portion that remains—there is agree-ment to disagree for the moment, but to work further in reducing the remainder—seems small compared to the substantial points of agreement that have been clarified. The accomplishments speak well for the doctrinal clarity, strength, and faithful flexibility of the Church's doctrine, qualities shared on both sides of the table at these long, continuing, strenuous dia-logues. I shall review these accomplishments, and the remaining problems below, under "Doctrine."

Second are the Lutheran-Catholic Dialogues. A recent update summa-rized these dialogues as follows: "The U.S. Lutheran–Roman Catholic dialogue is the oldest of all the dialogues to have continued meeting without interruption, from 1965 to date, and is in many ways the most productive."[104] Publications give an idea of the vast range of subjects cov-ered: *The Status of the Nicene Creed as Dogma of the Church* (1965); *On Baptism for the Remission of Sins* (1966); *The Eucharist as Sacrifice* (1967); *Eucharist and Ministry* (1970); *Papal Primacy and the Universal Church* (1974); *Teaching Authority and Infallibility in the Church* (1980); and *Justification by Faith* (1985).

The dialogue continues to operate "with considerable freedom, without precisely specified or narrow goals. Informal annual meetings of bish-ops and church presidents have helped determine the attention given to important, traditionally divisive issues like infallibility, justification, and Mariology, though the dialogue sets its own agenda and one topic grows out of another."[105]

The overall assessment offered by Braaten, Johnson, and Reumann is, I believe, correct: "Its work is impressive to all, scholarly, detailed, chal-lenging, and probably unequaled as a model of theological dialogue."[106] The international dialogue, which continues in parallel with the North American, "does not duplicate these efforts but frequently builds on them."

To offer my reader a feel for the kind of exchange that is happening, and because it throws light on evolving thinking as regards the structural linchpin of the Church, the papacy, I shall quote at some length from Braaten and the others, evaluating more recent discussion of papal infallibility:

> Lutherans had conceded in Series 6 that under proper conditions the papal office, alongside the episcopal and pastoral offices, could be accepted as a legitimate development in the ordering of the church's ministry. Now Lutherans were being challenged whether they could take an additional step and remove their traditional objections to the dogma of papal infallibility. The Roman Catholic participants softened the interpretation of this dogma to the point that the Lutheran participants responded in an irenic spirit, a far cry from the confessional identification of the papal office as the antichrist.
>
> The dogma of papal infallibility was carefully placed within a comprehensive treatment of the doctrine of authority in the church. With this approach it was

104. J. A. Burgess, ed., *Lutherans in Ecumenic Dialogue: A Reappraisal* (Minneapolis: Augsburg Press, 1990), 25.

105. Ibid., 26. At the present writing, the dialogue, both international, and the American Lutheran-Catholic discussions continue.

106. Ibid.

possible to show that Lutherans and Catholics can walk hand in hand a long way before they reach the point of diverging paths. They can agree on the authority of Jesus Christ, the normative role of Scripture, the apostolic tradition, and the creeds and councils of the church, but they cannot agree on the way in which all of these authorities are bound together in the papal exercise of infallible authority. The Catholic theologians gave Lutherans the impression that Vatican II has nuanced the papal claim to absolute authority: "For Catholics, papal infallibility is now commonly discussed in the context of the infallibility of the Church and in relation to confidence in the faithful transmission of the gospel. As a consequence, the infallibility of the Church takes on greater importance than papal infallibility" (para. 52). Lutherans were assured that "the pope is not an absolute monarch" (para. 53).

Lutherans, for their part, acknowledged that Roman Catholic teaching as presented in this dialogue no longer teaches infallibility in the sense which Lutherans in the past had to reject as contradictory to the gospel.[107] The Lutherans heard the Catholics to be affirming infallibility in largely the same sense in which Lutherans have confessed the indefectability of the church, namely that "the gates of hell shall not prevail against it" (Mt 16:18). . . . The Lutheran rejection of the infallibility claim need not detract from an emerging interest among Lutherans in regaining an effective magisterium . . . nor does the rejection of infallibility imply the rejection of either the papal or episcopal ministries within the church. But effort in regaining an effective magisterium may open up a new appreciation of the role of local pastors, local congregations, and the laity in sharing power and authority in the church (cf. Vatican II's emphasis on the *sensus fidelium*).[108]

While transcribing this, I took pleasure imagining the reactions of my readers at various points along the "conservative-progressive" spectrum. As it is not my intention to enter here into these ecumenical dialogues, I shall not comment, but rather move on in this survey of "structural strengths" after reiterating my judgment that the fact of these intense dialogues is a good thing in the contemporary Church scene structurally as well as doctrinally, and at the same time cautioning that the way forward will not be easy. Two interesting Catholic authorities have pronounced on this recently. The first, Father Max Thurian, is the Swiss Protestant cofounder of Taizé (discussed below), who converted, becoming a Catholic priest in 1987, and in 1992 became a member of the International Theological Commission, chaired by Cardinal Ratzinger. Asked by an interviewer, "Is ecumenism dead?" Father Thurian replied,

No, but the "federal" vision of ecumenism is impossible. The idea of federation has the majority against it, for it corresponds neither to Orthodox ecclesiology nor to the Catholic vision. In point of fact, being impossible to put into practice, this road must be abandoned.
Interviewer: Without any way forward?
Father Max Thurian: We must go back to spiritual ecumenism: insistence on prayer, prayer for unity, joint prayer between Christians of different confessions, and not only during the week of prayer in January, but in a more constant, more frequent manner. In this prayer, in each action, in Bible study, we must do everything

107. I personally would think it less misleading to say something like this: the RC members of the dialogue explained that RC teaching on infallibility was never what Lutherans previously believed it to be, and so on.
108. Ibid., 29.

together. Everything. Except, clearly, what we are obliged to do separately. And while it is necessary to quicken the pace it is also necessary to take time and pay the price. For unity cannot be had cheaply. The Catholic Church cannot have a clearance sale on basic essentials. . . . The Church cannot again bring up the question of faith in the Eucharist, the real presence, the presence of Christ's sacrifice, the Church's sacrifice. She cannot change the nature of the ministry, the continuity of the Apostles. Nor the certainty that the Bishop of Rome presides over the universal Church. Finally, she holds the conviction that Mary, today, intercedes for us; that she is our Mother and that this maternal intercession is essential.[109]

The other comment was contained in an interview with Cardinal Ratzinger.

Interviewer: Ecumenism is going through a difficult period because of the revival of national tensions in Eastern Europe, but also because of your recent reminder of the Pope's primacy, which aroused violent reactions amongst your Protestant and Orthodox partners.
Ratzinger: Exactly. The Letter of the Congregation for the Doctrine of the Faith of last June on "certain aspects of the Church as communion" wished to stress, in a context of resurgent nationalisms, that each local church is at once particular and universal. There is no German Church, or American, or French. There is one Church "communion," supranational, open to the world, to other confessions, to non-Christians. On the question of the primacy of Peter, we have added nothing to traditional Catholic doctrine. We have only wished to emphasize that, for us, Peter's ministry is not a profane administration imposed by the combined local churches, but an interior element of the Church's life, a theological reality willed by God. It is possible that other Christians do not accept this, but it should be clear that we have not wished to add any new dogma or to apply any pressure.
Our letter even gives a hopeful view. It says that a theological reality as essential as the primacy of Peter has been possible to realize in the past according to some very different historical forms. On the path to unity, it cannot therefore escape us that the realization of this principle, as 2,000 years of Christianity have shown, can find new forms. That should be a motive for new conversations and dialogues. Our letter expresses the hope that one day all may be able to recognize, in the concrete exercise of the Roman primacy, the continuation of Peter's ministry and to see its conformity with God's will. It was Luther himself who said: "If one day there is an evangelical Pope, then I shall kiss his feet with joy."[110]

Developments among Religious Orders

Since the springing up of the first monastic communities in the fourth century one of the perennial forms of institutional innovation has been the periodic founding of new religious congregations. Some have had the profoundest imaginable influence on the whole Church, the Benedictines, for instance, being an unexcelled institutionalized force, especially in the early Middle Ages. The "mendicants" (Franciscans and Dominicans) in the High Middle Ages, and the Jesuits in early modern times and again refounded after seventy-five years of suppression in the first half of this century have been powerful molders of the tradition. The staying power of these great congregations is astonishing, especially when contrasted with the many small religious orders that spring up, prosper for a while,

---

109. *The Catholic World Report* 3:1 (January 1993): 32–33.
110. Ibid., 55.

then decline and disappear. Astonishing, too, is the distinctiveness of their collective "personalities," incarnating the missions of their founders.

Many of these communities were founded in response to quite focused needs, local in character, involving every conceivable kind of "corporeal and spiritual work of mercy." Not only contemplation, or even the call to live the "counsels"—poverty, chastity, obedience in most perfect imitation of Christ—but particular missions as well, whether contemplative prayer, missionary outreach, teaching, hospital care, or care of orphans, have motivated these foundations. As Richard Neuhaus points out, no other tradition in the history of mankind has shown such fertility in the creation of varieties of highly devoted groups as the Catholic tradition's swarm of religious congregations of every description. Looked at through the eyes of faith, this appears a wonderful garden filled with blossoms from plants whose seeds were sown and tended by the Holy Spirit. When, damaged by the pests of pride and indifference, certain congregations fade in faithfulness, and then wither rapidly, new vocations to them disappear as if by magic.[111] But new "species" spring up in God's wonderful garden.

Because the Catholic world is so enormous, and the modern world so complex, it is difficult for Catholics to hear the encouraging news that fresh foundations are springing up and prospering, and of some old ones showing signs of revival. I accidentally learned of the Legionaries of Christ; of Mother Angelica's overflowing contemplative monastery in Birmingham (of both sisters and priests), from which she operates a worldwide apostolate of spiritual pamphlets, written by herself (40 million distributed to date), the world's largest religious television cable network (the Eternal Word Television Network, which reaches into 30 million homes), and now a worldwide shortwave-radio broadcasting facility, with the world's four most powerful transmitters—five hundred thousand watts—reaching to every part of the globe; of Bishop Glennon Flavin's new orders of women, one contemplative, the other teaching, in Nebraska; of the Communauté St. Jean founded by Père Dominque Marie Philippe, O.P., in Europe in 1978 and now with more than two hundred young priests; of the 120 priestly vocations of Communauté Emmanuel since its founding in 1975; of the innovative community in Connecticut associating the Franciscan Sisters of the Blessed Eucharist, a monastery of contemplative Benedictines (both growing), Sisters of Notre Dame, several fathers of the Congregation of

111. There are in Toronto, for instance, several once large religious congregations of women the tone of which, in the seventies, turned trendy, even feminist. Result: in just one generation they are on the way to complete disappearance. One, the fifth largest property owner in Ontario, had hardly had a novice a year for some time. During the same period, an Oratory was founded in Toronto, a Trappist Priory moved to the suburbs from Quebec, a convent of cloistered Carmelite nuns near Waterloo is full, the diocesan seminary is doing well, and seven young men have gone off to join the new Mexican foundation, Legionaries of Christ, which is growing so rapidly their three hundred priests are swamped by two thousand seminarians. There is presently talk of founding a diocesan religious order of women.

Saint Basil, and a hundred laypeople, all under the inspiration of a Jesuit chaplain, Father Prokes, S.J.; and the Johannes Gemeinschaft, a secular institute founded by Adrienne von Speyer and Hans Urs von Balthasar, with a female and a male arm, both growing.

As one struggles to form a balanced view of what is going on in the Church in our time, it is important to offset the odor of decaying religious institutions on one's doorstep with the fresh scent of these new blossoms, some still in orchards far away. To this end I shall include a brief encouraging word on several of these.

First, the Legionaries of Christ was founded about fifty years ago by a Mexican seminarian when he was only nineteen years old, Father Marcel Marciel, who is still vigorously in charge today. This is the fastest-growing religious congregation of men in the Church, and a branch of female religious is now also growing rapidly. With its three hundred priests and two thousand seminarians, its future for the moment is secure. With a mission rather like that of Opus Dei of helping in the spiritual formation of the laity so that ordinary working folk and mothers may carry out their missions of sanctifying the home and the workplace, the Legionaries have been the guiding spirits behind many new schools, at least two universities, and flourishing associated lay organizations. Demanding a rigorous and long preparation for its priests,[112] the Legion seems, because it tends toward the heroic, rather to attract than repel. Strict in its fidelity to the magisterium of the Church, and like Opus Dei again rather old-fashioned in its spiritual expression, the Legion attributes its success to precisely this fidelity to faith and vocation. Not surprisingly, it is looked on with the same suspicion, if not to say horror, by "progressive Catholics," as is the Work. The situation is similar with the following religious congregation of women.

The School Sisters of Christ the King was founded by Bishop Glennon Flavin, recently retired bishop of Lincoln, Nebraska. It reminds one of the Legion, and Bishop Flavin is unapologetic about the clarity of the line he takes: completely faithful to the pope and "the true spirit of the Vatican Council," the one published explicitly in the documents.[113] A far more modest affair than the Legion, the bishop recruited young women, largely from the University of Nebraska, through the Newman Center, to which he assigned the most effective priest he could find. Their mission is to teach in the parochial schools (where no tuition is asked, as they are financed through diocesan fund-raising; more than half the Catholic children of the diocese attend the schools). The sisters, who number twenty, with five novices and postulants, wear a full traditional habit, and when I visited them, seemed radiantly happy, young, and enthusiastic. Perhaps other bishops will want to consider following Bishop Flavin's example.

---

112. Father Marciel's book, *The Integral Formation of Catholic Priests* (Rome: CES, 1960), is a wonderful combination of profound spirituality, good sense, and much practical experience. I recommend it to anyone seeking a deeper understanding of priesthood. It is obtainable by writing the Legionaries of Christ, Chester, Conn.

113. In private conversation with the bishop.

The Missionaries of Charity are the next group to discuss. In numbers and world span all of these fade in comparison with Mother Teresa's Missionaries of Charity; the women's branch is by far the largest, but there is also a men's branch, a congregation of priests, and a contemplative order founded by her. So much has been said of this wonderful *floraison* I need only mention them here, and confirm that the self-abnegation, the total poverty, the willingness to tackle the most off-putting tasks that characterize Mother Teresa's orders is, to those who have worked with them (as has one of our daughters), totally edifying, a special favor of God to our time.

The Meridan (Connecticut) Community is encouraging, not only because of the close cooperation between lay and religious, but also because, contrary to the tendency of communities to close in on themselves, here is common work by members of five religious congregations. The community is active in a variety of apostolic work, especially care of the elderly, catechetics, family counseling, but also in an experiment to apply the Church's social teaching on the factory floor. The community has concentrated much contemplation and discussion on the development of a theology of incarnation, with a special effort to animate a Christian sense of sexuality.

There is a positive story to tell about each of the orders or institutes I have mentioned, my list being but a short ad hoc assemblage of things I have heard. These stories need telling, for they witness to the work of the Holy Spirit concretely in the Church today, on the institutional level.

Taizé

On the level of a religious community there exists a most remarkable ecumenical institutional initiative. Like Focolari, Taizé was an ecumenical undertaking from the start, which has found acceptance at the highest level by the pastors of the Reformed and Catholic Churches and came to enjoy a strong Anglican as well as Orthodox participation. It constitutes a unique sign of the times, "a parable of community,"[114] and so merits more careful study than I can give it in this overview.

Distressed by the massacre of the innocents during the war, and remembering his own grandmother's efforts in similarly trying times at the end of the First World War to be a witness to Christian unity,[115] a young (he was born in 1915) layman, the son of a Swiss Protestant, Roger Louis Schutz-Marsauche, known the world over today as Frère Roger, was searching in 1940 for a quiet place to pray when an old woman invited him to stay

114. *Régle de Taizé*, words taken up approvingly by Pope John Paul II upon his visit to Taizé. The sense of this is brilliantly commented on in an article by Marguerite Léna, *"Taizé," Études* (July–August 1992): 111–20, which a brother of Taizé opined is perhaps the most intelligent article ever written on Taizé. (English translation in *The Month* [February 1993].)

115. "To bring out clearly that her own Protestantism was not a refusal but an expectant waiting for the necessary reconciliation, she began to attend the Catholic church while retaining the faith she inherited from her own" (ibid., 112).

in a tiny village in Burgundy, Taizé. Little dreaming that his initiative of solitary prayer in the desert would have the effect of the fourth-century desert fathers in Egypt—to put on the map of the world that hamlet, which would become as famous as the great monastery of Cluny, just ten kilometers away, and without any plan or effort on his part, beyond Frère Roger's desire to be a living witness to reconciliation among Christians and indeed among all men—he soon found himself joined by other young men, both Protestants and Catholics, in his prayer and help to refugees, the poor Jews most prominent among them. After the war the little impromptu ecumenical community, putting its roots back into a pre-Reform monastic tradition, continued, with its mission more and more clearly focused on praying for the unity of the Church.

"Brother Roger has always viewed the reconciliation of Christians not as a goal in itself but in order for Christians to be a leaven of reconciliation in the human family," a young Taizé brother explained to me. "At Taizé and in our meetings with young people in various parts of the world, the young are always asked: how can you become bearers of trust and reconciliation where you live? There is both an inner pilgrimage to the sources of faith and reconciliation and an outer pilgrimage to places of suffering where reconciliation is needed."[116]

Out of nowhere, young people began finding their way to the modest little community, the visitors growing rapidly from a trickle to a flood. Today the ninety brothers receive four or five thousand *a week* during the summer—80,000 in the summer of 1992, for example—initiating them into their quiet life of prayer, incarnated in the most peaceful (Gregorian- and Eastern-inspired) music of Taizé's own fabrication, sung in many languages, as a living instance of the world coming together. The community has also gone out to the young in recent years, with small groups installing themselves where suffering is great, and large gatherings being convoked in some of the most secularized big-city centers. For instance, in December 1990 in Prague, 80,000 young people, and in Vienna in late December 1992, 105,000 young people from every country of Europe, including large numbers of Orthodox from Romania and Russia, prayed together for several days. Despite extreme financial hardship, the people of Prague reached out to the young, housing them in their tiny apartments.

It is not the community's intention to blur important theological distinctions or to suggest one can "short-circuit" the serious matters causing divisions among Christians. But there is a way forward. By living together in community, the brothers can be that "parable" that shows, by doing, how Christians can pray and live together and work together to help young people find the sources of faith, to learn to pray, and to be strengthened to return into their own parishes and communities to be themselves examples of the love that brings pardon and reconciliation. The brothers seek to

116. Letter from Frère Émil, February 2, 1993. I am grateful to him for two careful revisions of this section.

achieve what Frère Roger speaks of as "inner reconciliation," which perhaps can best be understood in his own words, addressed during an ecumenical prayer service in Rome celebrated with Pope John Paul II, in which Roger said this: "Without being a symbol of repudiation for anyone, I have found my own identity as a Christian by reconciling in myself the current of faith of my Protestant origins with the faith of the Catholic Church."[117]

The community believes it is important to respect the denominations of its visitors. Everything is done so that each may receive Communion in his or her own tradition. Blessed bread is offered to those who do not receive Communion. Catholic Mass is celebrated daily, and the Eucharist is preserved in the huge modern Church of the Reconciliation. One of the brothers explains:

> Many of the brothers, without denying their own Christian roots in a Protestant tradition, live reconciled with the Catholic faith. What can be done for them while the churches work towards full reconciliation? Brother Roger has written, "The ecumenical wave will fall back if the day does not soon arrive when these members of different Churches who believe in the real presence of Christ in the Eucharist all meet around the same table."[118]

Several years ago one or two of the brothers came several times to Toronto, to prepare a group of pilgrims to meet the entire Taizé community at a gathering in Dayton, Ohio, the first such meeting in North America, in May 1992.[119] This was my first opportunity to get a personal taste of Taizé spirituality at work. Nothing is more difficult than discerning the character of another's spirituality, for, as Balthasar reminds us, the Spirit is the most elusive and subtle of God's aspects. To appreciate the inner and most personal life of even a close friend is the fruit of years of intimate interaction in many settings, and demands a good spirit, that is, love. And so it is with the social reality of the spirituality of a community, and even though the community's work is something that goes on in a more intersubjective and hence more public mode than the spiritual development of an individual person, it is still the work of the Holy Spirit interacting in sovereign freedom with the finite freedom of the members, all of whom are neither yet perfectly holy nor simple! Close contact and really "working with" the community extensively is necessary before one begins to discern the flavor and depth of a group's spirituality.[120]

117. In J. L. Gonzalez Balado, *The Story of Taizé*, 3rd rev. ed. (Oxford: Mowbray, 1987), 31.

118. *Dynamic of the Provisional* (Oxford: Mowbray, 1981), 56. This is translated from *Dynamique du provisioire* (Presses de Taizé, 1965). Frère Émil's letter, from which I am quoting, dates from March 3, 1993.

119. Attended by about eighteen hundred, from all over the continent, the turnout exceeded expectations, and was considered an excellent beginning to making known the Taizé witness in the United States.

120. When may it be important to attempt to gain such knowledge? First, as common sense would dictate, and canon law has always insisted, if one is attracted to become part of a community, a sufficiently long period of getting to know one

I can report two things about the three Taizé evenings of ecumenical prayer, the *form* and, more personal, the *atmosphere*. In a mostly darkened Anglican church, decorated with Byzantine icons and many candles (all of France is crazy about icons since about fifteen years ago, but Taizé has loved and featured them for forty years), with, at the center, on the floor in the middle and inclined at a forty-five-degree angle, a large reproduction of the Cimabue crucifix, while a locally gathered choir that had prepared[121] for the occasion over several weeks filled the air softly with the mantra-like music, much of it of Gregorian and Eastern influence, but always sung in four-voice harmony, slowly, softly, inducing an atmosphere of peace and reflection. The two brothers in their white habits introduced the service, a short reading from the gospel repeated by laypeople in five or six languages (a reminder of the catholicity of the Church's *missio*), followed by a simple commentary, always devoid of anything possibly divisive of Christians, and completed by prayers of petition, with veneration of the cross for those who wished to come sit or kneel on the floor at the feet of the crucified Christ, while the singing continued, and gradually people filed out, over a period of an hour. Outside, in the narthex, cookies and coffee, the contemporary sacramentals of fellowship, kept a good and happy crowd busy getting to know one another for fully another hour.

I would like to return to the one question I have heard asked about the Taizé spirituality: "Do they avoid the hard issues?" I anticipated a Taizé response to this, which was subsequently corrected by Frère Émil:

> Our mission is not theological discussion—though theology is not neglected—it is about achieving "a parable of reconciliation" through life by disposing ourselves day after day to welcome the entire Mystery of faith. No brother of *Taizé*, it is my impression from talking to them, intends to minimize the seriousness of theological and disciplinary divisions separating the churches. It is not, the brothers explain,

---

another should precede any serious commitment. In the case of religious communities, requiring the lifelong vows taking on the "religious counsels," usually years of strict formation are demanded, and often temporary promises precede by some years permanent vows. This is the case for a brother entering Taizé. With some of the newer and less all absorbing lay-communities, especially when the rule is "casual in, casual out," neither the preparation nor the nature of the promises is necessarily demanding. Again, that depends, and again the more casual approach is nothing new: many of the religious orders founded associate lay groups, such as so-called third orders, in which laypeople associate themselves with the community's mission, making promises demanding a fairly minimal commitment of regular prayer and some form of service. The other circumstance in which one may want to strive to get some feel for different spiritualities is one like the present: the responsible Catholic seeking to gain a broader and more accurate understanding for what is going on in His Church struggles to form a fair impression of vital, important new communities. Because much of this goes on while he remains essentially outside the community, the impressions he gains, however open-minded and sympathetic he tries to be, will be of dubious quality—yet another warning about the present description.

121. Which itself proved a remarkably successful way to get an interchurch group working together.

a question of leveling out any element of the Mystery of Faith. Beyond a simple acceptance of the differences and of peaceful co-existence, this way leads to an interior disposition of welcoming all the treasures of faith that God has put in his people since two thousand years.[122]

"Brother Roger searches constantly, while awaiting the actions of the Holy Spirit re-uniting Christians, to find *'une petite voie intérieure'* ["a small interior path"] open to every Christian, the way of a reconciliation within one, without denying what is legitimate in any tradition, without humiliation for anyone."[123]

Frère Roger, in the words he addressed to John Paul II on the occasion of his visit to Taizé, is ever "attentive to your ministry as universal pastor." In reply, the pope had much to say, but the following paragraph stands out: "I do not forget that in its unique, original and in a certain sense provisional[124] vocation, your community can awaken astonishment and encounter incomprehension and suspicion. But because of your passion for the reconciliation of all Christians in a full communion, because of your love for the Church, you will be able to continue to be open to the will of the Lord."

There then followed a wonderful statement of the spirit of *Taizé's* mission, which the Brothers have taken to heart:

> By listening to the criticisms or suggestions of Christians of different Churches and Christian communities and keeping what is good, by remaining in dialogue with all but not hesitating to express your expectations and your projects, you will not disappoint the young, and you will be instrumental in assuring that the effort desired by Christ never slackens to recover the visible unity of His Body, in the full communion of one and the same faith. You know how much I consider ecumenism a necessity incumbent on me, a pastoral priority in my ministry for which I count on your prayer. By desiring to be yourselves "a parable of community" you will help all whom you meet to be faithful to their church affiliation, the fruit of their education and their choice in conscience, but also to enter more and more deeply into the mystery of communion that the Church is in God's plan. By His gift to His Church, Christ liberates in every Christian forces of love and gives them a universal heart to be creators of justice and peace, able to unite to their contemplation a struggle along the lines of the Gospel for the integral liberation of human beings, of every human being and of the entire human being.[125]

Why are the young so attracted to Taizé? Reflecting on this "spiritual mystery," Marguerite Léna suggests this: "If the young recognize themselves there, it is not because of a more or less deliberate complicity of Taizé with the often rather indeterminate character of the youths' search, on the contrary, it is because of the community's own firm spiritual identity. It can freely open itself to all without diluting itself, and give rise to engagement beyond itself which it pretends neither to govern nor to demand."[126]

---

122. Letter from Frère Émil, March 3, 1993.
123. *Taizé et les jeunes* (Paris: Le Centurion, 1987), 126.
124. The pope means that the brothers would love to see their mission of seeking full communion fulfilled once and for all.
125. Pope John Paul II at Taizé. In Balado, *The Story of Taizé*, 50..
126. Léna, *"Taizé,"* 114.

As a parable can say strong things in familiar words, so Taizé. In the sheet handed the young visitor it is forcefully stated: "You have come to *Taizé* to go to the well-springs of Christ by prayer, and silence. You have come to discover a sense to your life, to regain momentum (élan), to prepare yourself to take responsibility there where you already live." The instruction given is fundamental. Léna offers this opinion:

> One of the strengths of the Community of *Taizé* is to have rediscovered and put to work in fresh modalities, the spiritual inspiration of the baptismal and mystagogic catechesis of the first centuries, in their double character of gradualness in the approach to the Mystery and of a delightful *[savoureuse]* experience of this same mystery. If one means by ideology a discourse which replaces the real by the system which pretends to explain it, mystagogy is the anti-ideology act par excellence: only the one who has had the experience of the living God in the silence of prayer or the grace of the sacrament encounters *[éprouve]* the need to get to the sense of that experience and has the means of doing it; he knows that his discourse will no more exhaust his experience than his experience will equal the Mystery. The young, especially those from the East, saturated with ideology, make no mistake.[127]

L'Arche

Founded in 1964 by the Canadian Catholic philosopher Jean Vanier, L'Arche has grown to a network of some seventy interfaith communities (with a strong Catholic core—some assistants are from non-Christian religions) around the world devoted to the care of the most severely handicapped. Typically, a community of L'Arche consists of ten to twelve persons, half of them handicapped, who share their lives together. This call of Jesus to live with the poorest of the poor has resulted in the spontaneous multiplication of such homes and the appearance, as needed and apparently out of nowhere, of the assistants required and of priests ready to assume spiritual leadership. The story of the spread of L'Arche, like that of many of these new communities, reads like a fairy tale of wondrous happenings. I say this at the risk of sounding a bit jejune because it is true: when one does research in this domain, one cannot help being struck by the sense all these communities have of dependence on the Holy Spirit, and their evidence of the most improbable arrival of resources is marvelous. According to one of the early founders of L'Arche:

> Today we see clearly that our Father in Heaven sends everything that is necessary for the poor to live and to grow up in community. He loves these littlest and most deprived ones so much that He is, as it were, obliged to give us what is needed to sustain them. All of the communities throughout the world experience that Providence which sends us, often at the last minute, marvelous young people. Some stay just a few months, some a few years; others discover that their life has meaning only through and in a total sharing with the poor.[128]

Commenting on their life together praying to the Father in heaven but as adherents of different faiths, a L'Arche spokesman comments: "Our

127. Ibid., 115.
128. Odile Ceyrac, in *Les mouvements*, 33.

ecumenic communities are of a great richness. What a wonder to live and to advance, in a great respect and love, with men and women who do not know Jesus, or who do not know the Church! But it is also a suffering. We wish to live these sufferings and divisions in order that the Body of Christ not be ripped apart. We wish to be in the Church and in the society ferments of unity."[129]

L'Arche has as a principle to work closely with the state wherever they may be, seeking to establish solid institutions for welcoming and caring for the handicapped, and in many wealthier countries their communities are indeed substantially financed by public funds. At the same time, they seek to associate the families of the handicapped closely with their work. L'Arche seeks to be thoroughly professional, utilizing the services of the best medicine and psychiatry to do whatever is possible to help the handicapped advance toward the maximum maturity and autonomy possible. "The poor lead us to Jesus and Jesus leads us to the poor. . . . To lead this life, we need the daily nourishment of the Eucharist. Much time is required for a familiarity, a true confidence to establish itself to the point of convincing the most deprived that they are lovable, that there is somewhere within them a heart which can love and be loved."[130]

Media Innovations

While the Church's failure to stop the most nihilistic forces in the society from assuming solid control of the mass media of communications and entertainment must be counted among the most serious structural weaknesses of the Church today, there are a few signs of hope, just enough to show that Catholics in fact have no excuse for their abandonment of this most important field of cultural and spiritual influence to the Enemy. To think that pioneer Jesuit broadcasters, like St. Louis University, Loyola University of Cincinnati, and Loyola of New Orleans, who came from the beginnings of radio to become broadcasting giants in their communities, have not had the vision to continue. All three stations have long since been sold!

One of the new initiatives we have mentioned already is Mother Angelica's television apostolate, Eternal Word Television Network (EWTN), and now her worldwide shortwave-radio apostolate. The programming on the EWTN offers solid catechesis, the rosary, the Mass. As resources increase, it becomes more varied, more imaginative, and is being aimed somewhat more at the vast secularized public so badly in need of evangelization.

Most effective in this regard has been a Colombian group, Promotores de los Medios de Communicacion (PROMEC), in Bogotá. Disgusted with the nihilism of television, this group set out twenty years ago to produce prime-time entertainment, replete with advertising, but with a subtle Christian message underlying it. They have been so successful that their soap opera,

129. Ibid., 34.
130. Ibid.

Los Pecados d'Ayer (The sins of yesterday), which had run to 450 episodes when I last heard, commanded, at its moment of greatest popularity an audience of 18 million out of a population of 30 million. When *Los Pecados* aired, Colombia stopped. They also produced a popular series about leading Colombian personalities who could be an inspiration for the population. An ironic result of this apostolic initiative: the company became very rich, and so has been able to support cultural magazines and a national news-gathering service. Why this kind of thing can be done in Colombia and nowhere else so far as I have heard remains to me a mystery.

To be sure, when Jean-Marie Cardinal Lustiger became archbishop of Paris one of the first things he did was to expand Radio Notre Dame, which carries imaginative broadcasting twenty-four hours a day. Recently, Radio Maria has sprung up in Italy, with great success, and is now, under the direction of Father Leo Maasberg, opening branches in many countries. Whereas the EWTN is on cable only, Radio Maria occupies frequencies, especially FM, available to the entire public.

Another grand initiative has been the effort to establish a worldwide Catholic monthly news magazine. An initiative originally of Communione et Liberazione, *Thirty Days in the Life of the Church and the World* managed to appear in about five languages, and was excellent until a new young editorial group took it off in a bizarre editorial direction, with obsessions like finding Free Masons under every bed and castigating George Bush as the enemy of mankind for causing the Gulf War. As a result, several editions—prominently the most subscribed, the American—broke away, and reemerged as *Catholic World Report (CWR)*. The work of the Rev. Joseph Fessio, S.J., founder of Ignatius Press, an excellent Catholic publishing house and originator of the American edition of *Thirty Days, CWR* has grown into an excellent magazine. It is packed with interesting information from all over the world, not just about the Church, but about the most important social, cultural, and political happenings. More recently, it has generated a worthy competitor, *Inside the Vatican*.

When one thinks that there are hundreds of millions of practicing Catholics throughout the world, one wonders why as the Church we are not able to do better than the little sect of Christian Scientists, who made the *Christian Science Monitor* a world-respected daily paper. Why cannot we give the world an example of what honest, high-quality journalism is by publishing the best daily in the world simultaneously in a dozen centers, a paper open to the whole world, where disputed issues can be fairly debated, with different viewpoints honestly represented, and of course with an opportunity for the Catholic understanding to be clearly and regularly represented. A failure of imagination and nerve, a failure to respond to the needs of the time!

Some say that starting daily newspapers is too expensive and that, anyway, the new inexpensive technology of the Internet is the way today to broadcast information and to foster discussion. While I believe newspapers will remain influential among the elite, and even a broader public for some time, the Catholic initiatives on the Internet[131] already undertaken point to a brilliant future through this medium.

Concluding Remarks on Strengths of the Church's Contemporary Structure

As I see the picture emerging from this survey of strengths in the Church's structure, what appears is a combination of clear unity at the center, considerable cohesion at the national level, along with variety suitable for a Church operating in every country on earth—enormous fertility and flexibility in the invention of new forms of institution and community. At the same time, we see the great variety of ancient "rites," traditions within the great Tradition that pass on in living form the liturgies and spiritualities impregnated with the juices of old cultures. Even within the one, cohesive, and dominant "Latin rite," predominately European in culture, there is national variety, and a wide variety of movements group people of distinctive kinds of spirituality, while remaining faithful to the one Church. "In my Father's house, there are many mansions" (John 14:2). No Catholic can legitimately complain that the Church fails to offer him what he needs for his spiritual (that is to say *total* personal) development, for, in addition to good parishes, there likely exists a small community probably somewhere in his city that will respond to his own particular human needs.

The problem is communications. Catholics of different rites are isolated from one another, and Latin-rite Catholics tend to forget about their Oriental brothers, rich in traditions. The different groups and communities are hard to learn about. The right hand does not know what the left hand is doing. That is a weakness—lack of coordination and cooperation within the Church. It is both a management problem (the qualities that go into making a spiritual bishop are not those of the hard-bitten big-time manager!) and, worse, the bad fruit of lack of charity among Catholics, hence lack of openness and outreach by the groups, and a preoccupation with one's own concerns, which can be crushing when the majority tradition is as preponderant as the Latin rite.

Weaknesses

While the basic Christ-founded structure remains perennial, the Catholic must at the same time acknowledge that as sinful human beings apply these structures to ever new situations, the divine intention can become obscured. That is why Cardinal Ratzinger calls Catholics to take seriously the constant need for reform of the structures,[132] and it is why the appropriating

131. Recently, EWTN acquired the best of the Catholic Internet services, one that makes essential Catholic documents freely available.

132. "*Communio:* A Program," *Communio* 19:3 (fall 1992): 448. "Every time that the Church has been in a period of crisis and the rusty structures were no longer resisting the maelstrom of universal degeneration, such movements [the new communities] have been the basis for renewal, forces of health." See also his Rimini speech to *Communione*

Catholic should be frankly critical of all the weaknesses he perceives in the everyday Church.

Consider this criticism by a once-apostate[133] eighteen year old who, one year later, thanks to encounter with a *communauté nouvelle* in France, and to his complete stupefaction, converted to Catholicism, of the face of the Church as he saw it at the time he left: "the almost systematic gap between word and act; the lack of quiet reflection in the churches, of interiority in prayers; Catholics' feeble knowledge of their own religion and little determination in their faith; and above all, as Nietzsche had rightly pointed out, the lack of joy in their hope."[134] In contrast, here is what attracted that young man to Mahayana Buddhism: "the lucidity and knowledge of self, true detachment, interior liberation, a true and compassionate love towards every living being."

That, of course, is not a criticism of structures directly, but "feeble knowledge of their religion" on the part of Catholics—which is depressingly the case in Toronto—is in part an institutional failing; so is the failure to teach interior prayer, and so on. I shall be searching in all three sections on weaknesses for elements of a diagnosis of the causes of the syndrome the young convert so devastatingly describes . . . and found his way out of. Ever mindful that, just as he, miraculously, found his youthful way back to Christ and his Church, so an intense life going on in the Church is indeed hidden away under the ugly blanket of mediocrity he describes. So it is with no discomfort, and mindful of Christ's devastating cry in the Apocalypse, "the lukewarm I shall vomit out of my mouth," that I now offset the slightly triumphalist tone of the previous discussion of strengths in the Church's structure with these negative observations.

Strong Center Remote from the Periphery

There is no way a pope, aided by even the best possible curia, and armed with modern means of communication,[135] can avoid not only being remote from all His vast Church, but also being limited in his involvement in his own enormous (and insufficiently healthy) diocese of Rome.

---

e Liberazione, August 1990, republished in *Thirty Days in the Life of the Church and the World* (fall 1990).

133. *Apostate* is an ancient term for a Christian who leaves the Church.

134. Lenoir, *Les communautés nouvelles*, 12.

135. The small and badly overworked curia has never been accused of exceptional absence of the usual foibles of bureaucracy, and even the most charitable, after a lifetime of wrestling with the curia, can write, in the last sentence of a long life of writing, "It is time for this whole Roman Carnival to cease." I was present not ten years ago when a German electronics firm made the presentation of the first computer, a micro, to Cardinal Ratzinger, the prefect of the Sacred Congregation for the Doctrine of the Faith. Of the efficiency (and terror) of this "interior ministry of orthodoxy" Ratzinger once quipped, "Some CIA! There are a billion Catholics and I have a staff of ten, including the secretaries, to assure the teaching stays in the Way of Christ!" (reported from a private conversation).

Those who fear and resent authority—often people who themselves have suffered from abuse by parents or teachers—discern "insensitivity," "lack of knowledge," "little empathy for the local situation," "Eurocentric ignorance of the old Oriental traditions," and "refusal to move with the times" whenever Rome intervenes. All too many loathe those who maintain discipline in the Church. They are more than suspicious of those who declare themselves energetically to be faithful to the papal teaching. Such "resenters" remark the "conservatism" of these and find them too recalcitrant to the problems posed by recent developments in the world. These "liberal" or "progressive" Catholics will complain of the bishop too when he upholds the teaching of parts of orthodox Catholicism that many modern people find particularly inconvenient, or "sexist," or whatever.

In large metropolitan dioceses they can point justifiably to a considerable remoteness on the part of the bishop, a structural problem not satisfactorily overcome by appointing auxiliary bishops. On the other side of this tension about the "remote" authorities stand those "conservatives" who, wanting a strong worldwide Church with clear, demanding teaching absolutely faithful to the tradition, are distrustful, for the most part, of much that is happening socially and morally in the contemporary society. They will complain of "pusillanimous hesitancy" on the part of both pope and bishop to intervene to "clean up messes" and "to impose order and defend the faith."

This tension in the Church is, of course, not so much a structural problem as a clash of ideologies grounded, as William James pointed out long ago, in differences of temperament, producing colliding "natural faiths." The divinely mandated basic structure remains the framework within which the pastors of the Church must continue to deal with the tension, and all persons wherever they are situated on the spectrum of positions. There will be a continued erosion of many individuals, some leaving for the evangelicals, others just dropping out of religious practice altogether, but at the same time attraction of many others.[136] But so long as the center holds firm, and continues to proceed much more positively than negatively, there will be no overt schism. I say "overt," because here and there matters reach the stage where the heresy and the rejection of papal and episcopal authority amounts to an interior schism, unannounced, and hence especially capable of leading the unsuspecting astray. The loss to the evangelicals of Catholics seeking fervor is especially disturbing. (That is one reason I emphasized the strength of the charismatic movement.) But the flow out of the indifferent while the ardent converts flow in brings a certain renewal. But the Church can never be indifferent to the losses to indifference!

To utter any personal opinion in the midst of the tension between the "permissive" types too ready to adapt to the siren call of modernity and the

---

136. At the current time in America at least there are many conversions of thoughtful and well-educated people, as well as spectacular successes in helping the poor, resulting for instance in a 300 percent increase in African American Catholics in the last twenty years, admittedly from a low base, because the Church did not abandon the ghettos.

conservative disciplinarians is to ensure getting oneself classified according to one or the other of these divisive and confusing categories, hauled in inappropriately from secular politics. A considerable effort has been expended to propagate the notion that the present papacy, with the aid of the "Panzer Kardinal," Ratzinger, and the "Christofascists" (Father Matthew Fox's term for Opus Dei and their kind), has been quick to stifle dissent. The *Polish* pope,[137] product of an authoritarian tradition—so the story goes—moved heavily to "restore" the pre–Vatican II Church by "suppressing the new freedoms" gained since John XXIII and Paul VI, ignoring "the spirit of the Council." No sensible person would want to be labeled "conservative" described that way!

Your author personally has little charity for the angry "right-wing" ideologues, crying about "the desolate city"[138] and *Bare Ruined Choirs,* and too ready to see in every effort to think in fresh categories a "sell-out to modernity." At the same time I find adolescent many of the reactions to legitimate teaching authority. While acknowledging the need for expert discussion of difficult points in moral theology and the need to continue development of doctrine in the best Newmanian sense, I embrace the God-given responsibility of the magisterium to oversee the process. But I also see how, given the sinfulness of the men who bear this responsibility, acts of frightened oppression of debate can occur, even flagrantly at certain moments in history.[139] But I believe efforts to misrepresent the actions of the present pope and Cardinal Ratzinger in the several cases in our own time where discipline became notorious are bad-faith distortion, indeed unconscionable mudslinging, which is always a sign of weakness in the slinger's position.

Because several of these cases have been used so effectively to propagate the sense that the structures of the Church are oppressive, I was tempted to examine two of the most notorious. Through a series of accidents, I have been able to follow, almost blow-by-blow, the development, over twenty-two years, of one of the three most notorious causes célèbres, in this case, as with that of Prof. Hans Küng, involving the removal of the license to teach theology from an official Church chair, that is, the authority to teach in the name of the Church. And I know quite a bit, from persons directly involved, about the Küng case, too. After some reflection, I have decided not to recount all that here, because, to make sense of the whole business, it would be necessary to examine in some depth the social psychology of the confronting parties, and then recite the long history of the "to-ing and fro-ing" between Rome and the theologians involved. This would take a chapter of its own, and would be, in the end,

137. It is curious how those who so label John Paul II are oblivious of their racism—or at least cultural bigotry—in so doing.

138. Title of a brilliant and dreadful book of Anne Roach Muggeridge, which leaves the reader shorn of hope.

139. And not so long ago: recall the muzzling of Teilhard de Chardin and the pioneers of *la nouvelle théologie:* de Lubac, Balthasar, and so on.

anecdotal. I believe most readers have ample opportunities in both general political life and the lives of their local churches to observe the complex dynamics and the underlying pathologies that reveal themselves in this kind of situation. The matter is grave, but best explored in the context of a general Christian-inspired anthropology, with a chapter on some forms of sociopathology, both the antiauthority-revolt syndrome and the control syndrome, with much consideration of what lack of love has wrought in the life of the Church.

While I was first drafting these pages, I happened to hear a lecture at St. Michael's College by a young theologian of the Byzantine rite (Ukrainian) Catholic Church on present difficulties in Orthodox-Catholic relations. I was prepared for his lack of any interest in understanding the Vatican's perspective on these issues, but I was still surprised, first, at just how unfair he was in presenting the Catholic Church's understanding of the situation, and second, how ready he seemed to be to see the Russian Orthodox and the Ukrainian Catholics work out an entente, indeed even potentially some kind of cautious union, without Rome, so at the expense of the larger Church. I know this young man quite well, and he is an excellent apostle in many regards, but the painfully obvious way in which his concern for his national church and his national traditions seemed to override any consideration whatever for the universal Church centered in Peter naturally strikes me, as a "Roman Catholic," as against what Christ intended for His Church. I might add, the few Catholic voices who spoke up in the question period were all patently anti-Roman in what they said.

As I was mulling over this event, and coming as it did just after the Taizé people's failure to attract much Protestant interest in Toronto, Balthasar's splendid analysis of what he termed (that is the title of the original) *das antirömische Effekt*[140] ("the anti-Roman effect") came to mind. When I think of all the negative forces ranged against "the Roman Church"—the Orthodox, the Protestants, many clergy in the Eastern Churches united with Rome, and all the antiauthority elements within the Catholic Church, especially those now being carefully nourished by a well-organized "feminist" movement— I hear Christ's sigh, "But when the Son of Man comes will he find any faith on earth?" (Luke 18:8).

Still, it is the same Balthasar who, about the same time he wrote on the chair of Peter, penned the following complaint:

> Is western theology (with a few exceptions, such as that of Louis Bouyer) not becoming more and more alien, in its understanding of tradition, liturgy and ministry, to the venerable Church of the origins, as though the latter no longer seriously counted, and were a negligible quantity in the world's debate? This can only be to the great detriment to those who unthinkingly despise it. Moreover, do we not still much prefer (perhaps for political reasons?) to engage in discussion with the Orthodox Church, passing over the eastern Churches in communion with Rome as though they scarcely existed, although western churchmen are alone responsible

140. In English, *The Office of Peter and the Structure of the Church* (San Francisco: Ignatius Press, 1986).

for their artificial western character (where it does exist)? There is such a thing as genocide among Christians.[141]

In terms of the strength and well-being of the whole Church, the real worry is not with the Orthodox and the Protestants. It is not the age-old controversies between those *ad extra* and the Church that are weakening it but rather the combination of plain, poor understanding of its teaching on the part of so many Catholics—the young convert's complaint—with all forms of "natural" (natural for fallen human nature, that is) suspicion and resentment of all authority, fueled by egalitarian democratic society, that one finds eating away at the Church from within. This is especially dangerous in those who are, on the contrary, well educated—some of the many dissenting theologians and unhappy "feminists."

The problem takes the form of a vicious circle: if one does not understand (or because of pride does not want to understand) as essential to the way Christ is present among us the presence of the *center teaching*, then there will be little docility, poor reception of the teaching, no way of experiencing what that teaching brings, and hence no incentive for becoming more receptive. Without a contemplative deepening in the mystery of the infinite transcendence and majesty of God and of the incomprehensible generosity of the way He chose in His sovereign freedom to transcend the infinite gap, where will the desire to obey Him come from? It is toward providing the spaces for this contemplation that all the structures of the Church should be directed.

When I observe the local scene in Toronto, it appears that a lethal combination of that liberal individualism propagated by the society and a kind of Marxist resentment—"hate the big capitalists, hate the tyrannical patriarchs" ideology—spread by the school system and the mass media, but also carefully nourished and methodically orchestrated by elements in the theology faculties, is offset on the teaching level by very little. The bishop has sparse access, direct or indirect, to the masses. (Many pastors disobediently do not even read aloud his [infrequent] pastoral letters. The weekly diocesan paper, which is firmly controlled by the bishop, and appears as a fairly tame "house organ," is not much of an influence [nor for that matter is the "liberal" *Catholic New Times* weekly], not, certainly, compared to the overwhelming influence of films, magazines, television, and daily newspapers.) But these are nothing compared to the continual insinuating going on in the Catholic schools, hotbeds of the *antirömische Effekt*, and of course the frontal attacks on the Church in the mainline mass media, which in Toronto are totally self-indulgent in their hatred of all religion and particularly the Catholic Church. At the same time the theology faculties are pouring out "lay ministers" formed with strong elements of this rather "Protestantizing" and "politically correct" line and who are bringing it into hospitals, parishes, and service organizations.

141. "*Communio*—A Program," *International Theological Review: Communio*, 1:1 (1975): 9.

Looked at in purely human terms, without making allowances for the wondrous workings of God's grace, one would find here the recipe for disaster. In any instance where a local bishop is not totally faithful and indeed a fearless coteacher with the holy father, things are in an especially bad way, for the pope can do little effectively to circumnavigate the local bishop and reach the people directly, however hard the present pontiff through his pilgrimages and letters has sought to do so. That is why Pope John Paul II has been right in putting great effort into finding new bishops, as vacancies occur, who are not "anti-Roman," and who embrace unstintingly and seek to communicate the magisterial teaching.

But the bishop *has* to find ways to reach the people. The highest priority is, by every means, to strengthen the seminary. The bishop must make absolutely sure that his seminary is loyally forming the new priests in the teaching of the Church, and with love for her. It must be a joyous place. They must be learning the ways of a contemplative prayer life. Allowing university-based theology faculties, safely ensconcing unorthodoxy behind the bastion of "academic freedom," to continue, untrammeled, a work of forming masses of lay ministers and religion teachers for the schools, in theologies that deviate seriously from the Roman understanding of the nature of the Church, the bishop is permitting a disaster to work its way through the whole fabric of the local church. Turning out activist priests who have not acquired the virtues of a profound prayer life is to risk producing the hard ground of disobedience. The problem is that in the liberal society there are too few quietly, clearly, consistently explaining and living the Church's whole vision of itself in a way that brings out its countercultural reality and shows the attractiveness of its message as precisely a *response* to the grave difficulties the society is getting itself into. With too few Catholics seeking to penetrate the dynamic essence of the explosively developing planetary society—the HTX—and such a tiny number of genuinely Catholic schools and insufficient alternative Catholic mass media of communication, what but a miracle can save the local church from deformation?

The failure by bishops to define better the role of "lay ministers," and to supervise first the formation and then the licensing of them and their ongoing activity is especially grave. (Rome has recently been cracking down on the confusing of priestly and lay ministries.) Their spreading activity is confusing the sense of the ordained ministry. This can reach the point where, in the Archdiocese of Quebec, all three finishing seminarians sent out in their last year as ministers in the parishes quit because they could see little distinctive role left for themselves beyond presiding at Mass (on those occasions when it replaces a lay-ministered communion service!) and hearing confessions (when lay therapy groups do not suffice!). Forgive me for exaggerating a bit, but the situation is so grave the seminary professors of the Grand Séminaire de Québec composed an irenic and profound document warning the Quebec bishops that if they did not address the issue, they would have no candidates left for ordination.[142]

The archbishop of a large metropolitan see is inevitably hard-pressed to follow closely many important developments in his diocese. He must depend on subordinates. Moreover, as I pointed out already, the bishop's power is more limited than most imagine. Canon law makes it difficult to remove a titular pastor, for instance, and in Ontario, to take one local example, the bishops have no legal authority over the publicly financed, elected Catholic school boards, indeed the teachers' union has the big say in what will be taught in religion classes! So much autonomy has been won by academic institutions that many a bishop finds himself unable to act against thoroughly unorthodox elements even in theology faculties; and when, finally goaded, one does act, *he* becomes the enemy, and is pilloried by the media, being treated as the Grand Inquisitor.

One solution pioneered by some bishops is to create new institutions and ignore the old, letting them "die on the vine." Cardinal Lustiger, for instance, distrusting the Grand Séminaire de Paris, simply sent his candidates for ordination elsewhere, as far as Louvain. That is surely one way to secure a future, comparable really to the holy father's attention to naming sound bishops. Another possibility is to found private, faithful Catholic schools. Four have sprung up in Toronto in the last few years. Meanwhile, in all of Canada, there does not remain one Catholic college still serious about defending its Catholic character. (One that has done a poor job with the rest has recently begun to show new signs of life.)

The Vastness of the Church Hampers the Sense of Community

One can go to Mass in a large urban parish for twenty years and never get to know well a single soul. As the Mass should be centered on the mystical event occurring on the altar, and not be basically a celebration of community,[143] this is not per se untoward. But the individual Catholic, especially if he is surrounded by a family indifferent to religion or practicing a routine Catholicism, can get to feel very lonely in the faith. A dreary liturgy, accompanied by exhibitionist musicians whining atrocious songs, can be rather more draining than uplifting.[144]

142. I owe this information to the Rev. Marc Ouellette, former rector of the Grand Séminaire de Montréal in private conversation, September 1992.

143. That it should constitute genuine *communio* is of course also true, but not to be confused with just any sense of "fellow-feeling."

144. Recently a friend told me his life story: He grew up in Trinidad an ardent Catholic and there married a young woman as seriously Catholic as himself, but they had felt their faith drain away in the course of six or seven years of attending weekly Mass after immigrating to Toronto, and they ended in the Full Gospel Church, because they felt there a devotion and zeal utterly lacking in their Catholic Masses. A touristic visit to Rome, on a day when the pope spoke to a jammed Saint Peter's Square, awoke a

And how does one "identify" with a local Catholic community of 1.3 million? There is not even a facility where one can gather a fraction of that crowd. When the holy father came to Toronto, Downsview Airport was turned into an assembly field, and the pope looked out from a temporary structure, which appeared for all the world like the Pyramid to the Sun at Teotihaucan, onto a shivering (but happy) crowd of six hundred thousand.

One result is that the average Catholic feels little personal responsibility for what happens to his church in Toronto, even when it is attacked with lies in the media almost every day. Indeed, he is fortunate if his own attitude does not become tainted. Emotionally, he may be more moved by the scandal of a small number of religious caught in acts of sexual abuse at an orphanage in Newfoundland (a story replayed a hundred times by the television news) than in edification before the witness of personal devotion given by the people at Daybreak, the largest L'Arche community,[145] and in the some thirty excellent Catholic social agencies.

It is difficult for Canadian Catholics to feel any solidarity at all with their Lebanese or Palestinian brothers, being squeezed out of existence in their homeland by the Muslims and the exigencies of the Israeli state, or with the Catholics in Bosnia, being slaughtered by atheist Serbs, nothing like the way the small Jewish people feel a sense of responsibility for what happens to Jews anywhere in the world. It is claimed that 250 million Christians are suffering serious persecution throughout the world.[146] The "people of God" is not an ethnic reality, and indeed one of its grave problems is the tendency of many ethnic communities to place their national concerns ahead of the perspective of the world Church.

Two institutional ways of improving on this are, first, the establishment of strong "Catholic Leagues for Civil Rights," on the model of the effective organization in the United States and Canada, which not only fight anti-Catholic bigotry in the media, but also, by demanding equal time, can use those media to present, undistorted, Catholic teaching, and second, the strengthening of worldwide Catholic media. *L'Osservatore Romano*, potentially a most valuable resource, is presently about as exciting as the *Congressional Record*. *Catholic World Report*, the monthly news magazine I mentioned earlier, is a good start, as is the even more recent *Inside the Vatican*. Catholic radio and television, like Radio Maria and the Eternal Word Television Network, should be established in every country that will

---

nostalgia for the faith of their youth. Then a friend, who had never been to an Opus Dei function, suggested he attend an evening of reflection at the Opus Dei center, which he had read about in a pamphlet. There, he recounted, "I heard a priest and a layman preach with the same seriousness and deep faith I experienced at the evangelical temple." He returned to the Church and is now a member of Opus Dei!

145. When my wife asked her Christianity and Culture students at the university if they knew of L'Arche, only one had ever heard of it!

146. Paul Marshall, *Their Blood Cries Out* (Dallas: Word Publishing, 1997).

tolerate it. And a worldwide *daily newspaper,* printed in a dozen centers, could be a strong witness to Him who is the Truth.

Need for Improved Participation and Procedures

Different times, different sensibilities: one should not be defensive about the fact that these are democratic times, for democracy brings immeasurable good to masses of people. Those educated in democracies, just as people formed to any other kind of political economy, are going to have their foibles and special demands. Democratic peoples, for instance, are offended in any sphere of life when authorities are too "dogmatic" and when there appears to be little "participation" in decision making; they demand that administrative procedures be carried out with "due process." It is not because one finds many, especially North American, Catholics going too far in clambering for "democratization" of the Church that the curia and the bishops have any excuse for neglecting the need for and potential of a rightly understood "participation," nor for failing to ensure that "due process" is seen to be respected in disciplinary actions.

The Church has made strides both in promoting participation and in due process. Laity and clergy at all levels, being better educated and formed in democratic society to know how to speak up, are listened to more receptively by bishops and curial officials who themselves, for the most part, are products of democratic society. Structures for regular soundings of views have multiplied at all levels.

But this good institutional development has a downside. Consider this structural warning from Georges Chantraine: "The bishop should be on guard against the bureaucratic cancer which is undermining the body by the parasitical proliferation in a certain Post-conciliar Church of organisms, councils, commissions, sectors, etc.,"[147] a theme echoed by Cardinal Ratzinger in his Rimini speech. And earlier, in the famous interview, published as "The Ratzinger Report," the prefect expressed strong misgivings about episcopal conferences. A reader complaining to the editor of *The Catholic Register* about the Canadian Council of Bishops' intervention in detailed partisan politics over efforts to clean up abuses in the unemployment-insurance scheme, and who found the intervention lacking in credibility, recalled Ratzinger's words:

> The decisive new emphasis on the role of bishops is in reality restrained or actually risks being smothered by the insertion of bishops into episcopal conferences that are ever more organized often with burdensome bureaucratic structures. We must not forget that the episcopal conferences have no theological basis; they do not belong to the structure of the Church, as willed by Christ, that cannot be eliminated. . . . No episcopal conference, as such, has a teaching mission. . . . The national dimension is not an ecclesial dimension. . . ."[148]

147. Chantraine, "Charismes et mouvements dans l'Église," in *Les mouvements,* 153.
148. *The Catholic Register,* March 6, 1993.

Henri Cardinal de Lubac commented on this in his 1971 work *Les églises particulières dans l'Église universelle* (Particular churches in the universal church). After pointing out the advantages of national episcopal conferences, he warns of the problem: intrusion of an anonymous bureaucratism[149] where theologically only the individual bishop has personally full ecclesial (and collegial) responsibility for his diocese (and therein also for the entire Church). The "conferences," which possess no legitimation from the original institution of the Church but (like patriarchates and cardinalates and the sort) are secondary constructions, could theoretically and practically endanger the position and personal authority of each bishop. Thus, there is an inevitable structural dilemma here that will never be simply "solved": Participation demands organs of consultation; pastors and bishops have to assure themselves of channels of "feedback." Too often, however, these consultative bodies become the playthings of activists, creatures of a certain mentality, often noisy and agitated, with agendas not always good for the Church as a whole. The bishop, like the president of a large company or a prime minister, has difficulty finding out what the rank and file are actually doing and thinking. If he gets too absorbed by official commissions and committees of all kinds, he may never find out what is going on in the trenches. The sheer size of our modern institutions imposes these dilemmas of bureaucracy. If IBM could become remote from its customers, the archdiocese of Los Angeles can fail to know the masses of its faithful.

De Lubac reminds us of the essential distinction between decentralization and democratization.[150] He explains that the bishops lose their role of "fatherhood" when the receiving "motherhood" of the Church has been weakened. This is an institutional matter, but it is even more a spiritual question: an attitude of "nonreceipt," of closedness to God's teaching authority, manifested when the masses want to grab authority. In this very context, de Lubac brings in celibacy as a sign of the Church's origin "from above" in the Trinity.[151] (It is significant that almost every antiauthority Catholic is also opposed to priestly celibacy.) He concludes by pointing out that the Church remains the last sanctuary today in the anonymous mass society of persons and personal values where there is more going on than power struggles.[152]

Fortunately, bishops and pastors have for the most part avoided allowing any form of consultation to give the misimpression that the hierarchical teaching and governing authority has been watered down. The Catholic Church is not moving toward an Anglican "synodal" structure that gives

---

149. *Les Églises particulières dans l'Église universelle*, (Paris, 1971), 227. I am following here Balthasar's condensation of several chapters, in *The Theology of Henri de Lubac* (San Francisco: Ignatius Press, 1991), 113–15.

150. *Theology of Henri de Lubac*, 132.

151. Ibid., 198–209.

152. Ibid., 225.

voting rights to lower clergy and laity, thus weakening the position of the bishop. Even the occasional synods of bishops in Rome is purely consultative to the holy father.

Unfortunately, projecting the sense of who is in charge and who is responsible for the integrity of the teaching is not the same as convincing the mass of Catholics actually to live according to that teaching. A certain sense prevails of "Well, the Church has the right to teach what and as it does, but I retain freedom of conscience, either to believe it or not, or even if I do believe it, to sin against the teaching publicly and endemically, while continuing to consider myself a Catholic, and *they* have no right to do anything about it."

This creates an ambiguous situation. There is a widespread lack of respect, a paucity of docile acceptance of what the Church teaches among (if one credits sociological surveys) a majority of European and North American Catholics, a cause of consternation on the part of all who believe in the supernatural nature and mission of the Church. The situation betrays serious structural weaknesses in the face of relentless cultural onslaught (consumerism, libertinism, secularization) in the Church's carrying out its mission, especially a failure to catechize adequately, and continuously, in a way that leads Catholics to pursue an interior life of prayer.[153]

This points in fact to a glaring weakness: the decline in numbers and in the fidelity of Catholic schools, colleges, and universities, a process aided by the decline of so many of the traditional religious orders since the 1960s.

Need for More Cooperation between the Various Movements, Religious Congregations, and Communities

Verily, the right hand does not know what the left hand is doing. On March 31, 1980, Pope John Paul II issued this plea to leaders of the movements: "Each Movement pursues its own objective, with its own methods, in its sector or milieu, it nevertheless remains important to become aware of your *complementarity* and to establish connections *[liens]* between the Movements: not only a mutual esteem, a dialogue, but also a certain joint planning *[concertation]* and even a real *collaboration*."[154]

This has yet to happen on any important scale. Establishing regular communications is time- and energy-consuming, and the people charged with running any institution find themselves absorbed in day-to-day operations. Here is a place for fresh, private initiatives, enlisting people who are not burdened with office. One such initiative, begun six years ago by an Austrian layman, and from the start submitted to *episkopein*[155] by an appropriate bishop of the Pontifical Council for the Laity, brings together

---

153. On this, see the papal exhortation, *Catechesi tradendae*, October 16, 1979.

154. Address to the French leaders of the Apostolate of the Laity, quoted in *Les mouvements*, 14.

155. Recall the meaning of the term: supervision, hence the title *"episcopos,"* or "bishop."

yearly fifteen persons involved in about a dozen important movements to continue personal friendships and to share them (friendship is explicitly what these reunions are about), to exchange information and views about what is going on in their little part of the Church, and to cooperate, personally, if not officially, in some new initiatives of evangelization and education.[156] It is hoped that similar informal cooperation meetings will take place on a regional basis (this has already begun in Vienna, but local church politics makes it more difficult than the international meetings, which began on a basis of personal acquaintances). But this is only the tiniest beginning.

Also, fortunately, we have noted that the movements generally have either been sensitive from the start to place themselves under episcopal direction, or have in due course yielded to suggestions that they do this. I found this statement, penned by one of the persons responsible for La Communauté Chrétienne de Formation (CCF), representative of the best spirit of ecclesial responsibility, and not atypical of the attitude of most of the participants in different movements with whom I have spoken:

> The C.C.F. attaches first importance to openness in the desire to work together in the heart of the Church and with other movements. The C.C.F. takes its place in diverse ecclesiastical organizations, e.g., presence at the Synods in Rome, the Pontifical Council for the Laity, etc. Each community is united to its Bishop, who names a vicar or priest to accompany it; indeed this is the first concern of the C.C.F., to have within it the ministry which it needs to be rooted in the essential: the Eucharist, from which it issues, and to which it will return.[157]

Georges Chantraine, reporting in the same volume on the 1982 Rome meeting of representatives of twenty movements, warns of the danger of converting what should always be "personal and ecclesial prayer" into group prayer. "The danger is that prayer come to celebrate the group, the joy of being together, rather than the glory of God, found in the Church Catholic. Such a group prayer ceases to be personal, for our personhood is found only in Christ, in the *kairos* of the now of our presence in Him and Him in me." Chantraine sounds this warning: "The passage from the ecclesial to the collective, which can be seen happening a little bit everywhere in the liturgy, *a fortiori* the decided substitution of the collective for the ecclesial in diverse groups, ought to be seen, in my view, as one of the causes (or one of the signs) of the weakening of faith in the occidental world."[158]

Need to Strengthen the Episcopacy

In reflecting on the Christian state of life and the structures of the Church, the fathers and doctors of the Church regularly warn of the need for the

156. As a founding member of this group, I can testify that both the horizon-opening and the moral support I have received as a result have strengthened my own apostolic initiatives.

157. *Les mouvements*, 29.

158. Georges Chantraine, "Charismes et mouvements dans l'Église," in ibid., 151.

bishop to incarnate the perfection of holiness. He is to be a man whose life is an exemplary living-out of the counsels of perfection. The same position is reiterated in recent Church documents.[159]

All well and good, but everyone knows that in addition to the example given by the many saintly bishops of the present Church, there is evidence of both unsaintliness and inadequate leadership, as there always has been and always will be. The evangelists warned us by painting the apostles, personally chosen by Jesus, as losers (except John!) until they were filled with the Holy Spirit at Pentecost.

But, one might rejoin, our bishops live after Pentecost. The fathers of the Church and its greatest spiritual figures today continue to insist on the absolute need for saintly bishops. Simply, there is no excuse for any of us, who believe in the Church as Christ's Body, stopping short of everything we—inspired by the Holy Spirit—can possibly imagine to do to ensure that at the top the Church is seen to incarnate that perfection to which Our Lord has explicitly called all of us. There are in the Church of Jesus Christ, at this time as in all times, more than enough truly holy priests who are also men of good education, intelligence, and personal-leadership potential to provide an exemplary episcopate. Failure to achieve an even higher degree of perfection in this regard than is already evident is, basically, the result of neglectful use of structures, brought on in part by some self-serving ambition, but probably more because papal legates do not push their inquiries far and deep enough. I agree with Balthasar, who echoes Dionysius the Pseudo-Areopagite, that nothing less than radiant holiness will do at the hierarchical summit of the Church.

Doctrine
Strengths

Strong, Clear Positions

The fact that there is no other such clear, strong moral leader as the Catholic Church of course ensures its—as Christ had warned—persecution.

159. For a review of the texts of the fathers, and for reiteration of the centrality of priestly holiness in recent statements of the Church, see Balthasar, *The Christian State of Life*, 292–321. It is painful to be reading such documents at the same moment one sees in his morning paper that a Canadian bishop, indicted on two counts of rape and two of molestation, has signed affidavits that these sexual relations, which occurred many years before he was named a bishop but while he had in his care a home for young women, were "consensual situations." It does not help either to be involved in discussions about the alcoholism of a North American archbishop, a problem that was well known in his milieu to exist before the priest was even named auxiliary bishop quite a few years ago, and to see his fellow bishops, cognizant of the gravity of the situation, stall and hem and haw, managing never to do their duty, which was to intervene. And then there is the case of a bishop who recently played extremely loose with the truth in connection with disagreements over religious broadcasting. This bishop told several people in important positions that "the American bishops were critical of Mother Angelica's television network." As people were at pains to show the bishop the untruth of this allegation, he has little excuse for continuing to propagate the lie.

As each day passes, the brazenness of the attacks on this Great Satan of Reaction, and its chief, the Polish pope and the German Panzer Kardinal, increase.[160] To anyone basically skeptical about the possibility of attaining truth in fundamental human matters, and to all (understandably) nervous about ideologies, the very clarity and firmness of Catholic positions appear rather as "rigidity" and "inhumanity."

I hope the present study has shown that, for all their clarity and firmness, the positions taken by the Catholic Church are both subtle and rich in the depth of the ideational background that at once founds and orchestrates them. *Resourcement*,[161] I find, recuperates vast riches from the Old and New Testaments, the fathers and the medieval doctors, and from the creative currents of modern theology and passes this immense accumulation of wisdom, this treasure house of symbols, through the crucible of modern criticism, facing rather than running away from the challenges of the Enlightenment, of the sciences, and of all contemporary philosophy. Indeed, I am convinced no other tradition compares with the central Catholic tradition in its combination of richness and depth of historical resources while at the same time being open to present sociopolitical reality, and none enjoys such institutional cohesion, which allows a (loosely) coordinated research effort and transmission of results through a vast network of papal universities and institutes, seminaries, lay Catholic universities and colleges (250 of them in the United States alone), Catholic primary and secondary schools, and Catholic journals and newspapers.

Obviously, the effectiveness of these institutions depends on the spiritual condition of each: on the faithfulness of the leaders, on the quality of their education, and above all on their personal holiness. At any one time, many of these institutions leave much to be desired. The majority of North American Catholic colleges and universities, for instance, have, by and large, strayed from the path of fidelity, leaving a remnant of faithful, even holy, professors to soldier on. (Recently, I have noticed some awakening of desire to reverse the drift from fidelity.)

Still, many find their way to this treasure house despite "Catholic" colleges and schools that may have forgotten about it. A basic aspect of the intellectual capital of this, the richest of all coherent traditions, is the immense body of splendid documents, to begin with that earliest and most crucial "institutionalized" book, the Holy Bible, in which the living Word who is Jesus Christ is mirrored "unalterable and correct" for all ages.[162] Then there are the 161 volumes of Migne's *Patrologia Graechae* and 161 of

---

160. George Weigel documented the virulence of these attacks in "respectable places" in an extraordinary article in the liberal Jewish journal *Commentary*, "The New Anti-Catholicism" (June 1992).

161. The name by which the great thinkers in the recent tradition labeled, less happily, *la nouvelle théologie*, prefer to call their endeavor. De Lubac, Daniélou, Chenu, Balthasar, Bouyer, Congar, and Ratzinger figure prominently among the gifted spirits in this tradition.

162. Balthasar, *New Elucidations*, 92.

his *Patrologia Latinae*, the various *Opera Omnia* of the modern doctors of the Church, and the endless library of Catholic literature of all sorts. And finally the official modern teaching documents, the social encyclicals of almost every pope since Leo XIII issued, just one hundred years ago, his *Rerum Novarum* down to the centenary encyclical, the long and rich *Centessimus Annus* of Pope John Paul II, encyclicals on many other issues, including, like the three "Trinitarian" encyclicals of John Paul II, fundamental doctrine; and finally those two great monuments, the official teaching documents of the First and Second Vatican Councils and, most recently, *The Catechism of the Catholic Church*, the result of the desire expressed by a general synod of the bishops who hope to clarify for all the Church's basic teaching, developed by the First and Second Vatican Councils.

This last initiative is drawing intense fire from some circles in the Church who fear that its strong focus may be used—if I may quote the auxiliary bishop of London, Ontario, from a newspaper report (*Toronto Star*, November 12, 1992)—"to straight-jacket theological debate." I shall address this criticism in a moment when we come to consider the flip side of the Church's strength in doctrinal formulation. For the moment, while cataloging strengths, I would continue to stress the advantage of the institution's being able to make its teaching clear through an instrument like *The Catechism*. Passed through the fire of criticism by all the bishops throughout the world, who sent twenty-five thousand suggested revisions of the drafts, this rich document—some seven hundred pages—has been more widely participated in and debated than any other in the history of any tradition. (Reflection on that fact alone can reveal something of the uniqueness of the Catholic tradition and of the mystery of the Church that can bring together in such profound and orthodox collaboration hearts and minds from every country in the world, and from every social class.)

The critics, hostile to "Vatican centralism," will point out that "Rome" never lost control of the process, and so in their eyes this "Roman document" will remain more than suspect until the end of time, as the *antirömische Effekt* is not going to disappear. Those who more stress "process in being" and thus the need to reformulate the truth constantly will never be comfortable with those who, while accepting the obvious fact that history moves on and understanding of the mystery develops, stress, first, the eternity of God and His ability to reveal unchanging truths about Himself, and second, the ability of His Holy Spirit to guide the Church in the achievement of dogmatic formulations that attain a definitiveness, making them signposts until the end of time. (*The Catechism*, it should be pointed out, recapitulates the Church's dogmatic formulations, from Holy Scripture to the documents of the Second Vatican Council, but is careful not to give the impression of adding new dogmatic formulation, and adroitly avoiding too much theological elaboration. Indeed, a spirit of openness prevails, in the sense that more thinking is invited rather than discussion being peremptorily shut off.)

Ability to Harmonize Doctrinal Nuances Incarnated in, and Fueling, Distinctive Spiritualities: The Truth Is Symphonic When Pure Hearts Animate Well-Formed Catholic Minds

That there are dangers in the great pluralism of methods and philosophical foundations within Catholic theology, especially today, has been pointed out.[163] But this outburst of theological creativity, responding to the unprecedented progress in the human, psychological, and physical sciences of our time, has at the same time been a boon for the Church. When one acknowledges the richness, indeed the infinity of reality, and the limits of our human perspectives onto it, one has little difficulty accepting a notion of truth such as Balthasar's—"the truth is symphonic"[164]—provided one does not misinterpret it in a way that softens the need to search for the unity (of being, *"analogia entis"*).[165] Within the harmonizing colors of the kaleidoscope, representative of so many fragmented experiences of being and perspectives from personal histories, that unity shines out when the fragments are genuine. Within the Church, which professes "One God, One shepherd and One flock," the imperative to show forth that unity, without ideologically repressing any reality, demands an effort, in the midst of so much theological creativity, for communication always seeking to render visible the *communio*. It is necessary that, in charity and with a sharp critical sense, the Catholic intellectual community carry out its role of helping the magisterium draw good fruits from the cornucopia of insights, theories, and symbols that has been produced. This must not be done, to be sure, in a spirit of eclecticism[166] but of a genuine synthesis of critical appropriation of what has been revealed in and through these diverse currents of thought.[167]

As I have followed efforts to bring about a rapprochement of Teilhard de Chardin and Balthasar, through the intermediation of de Lubac, who admired both; or the efforts to bring together the insights of Balthasar and Rahner, who some like to oppose, for the perennial Catholic wisdom, despite the fact that their followers have valid criticisms to direct against the other thinker; or to take from the vast impulsions somewhat loosely grouped under the etiquette "liberation theology" and discover in them new insights into Christian freedom consonant with the orthodoxy of the tradition, I have been encouraged by the progress I see being made in thus enriching the Catholic wisdom. Where there exists a wellspring of

163. For a good discussion of this issue, see the summer 1983 issue of *Communio* 10:2, especially the articles by Balthasar, Peter Henrici, Remi Brague, and Val Peter.

164. Title of a small book full of wisdom, *Die Wahrheit ist symphonisch: Aspekte des christlichen Pluralismus* (Truth is symphonic: Aspects of Christian pluralism, trans. Graham Harrison [San Francisco: Ignatius Press, 1987]).

165. See Langan, *BT,* chapters 9 and 10.

166. Collecting a loose jumble of ideas is a serious temptation when the resources are so rich. Unifying insights without sacrificing some to ideological facility calls for such a sustained effort of highest quality thinking. Perhaps the Holy Spirit might help!

167. In chapter 10 of *BT,* 354–58, I have described, in a philosophical context, the attitude that needs to undergird the search for the unity of wisdom in the midst of a vast pluralism of experiences.

unity in common faith, animated by that charity that alone makes such a faith possible, the intellectual differences produce fruitful tension rather than schism. Where impurity of heart is present, exacerbating personality clashes, every problem becomes grounds for division. It is this question of good hearts that is most critical, good hearts illumined by well-formed Catholic minds.

Accommodating the Pneumatology of the Charismatics

One of the contributions of the charismatic renewal has been to emphasize prayer as opening to the grace that purifies hearts. Somehow this cleansing influence of the fire of the Holy Spirit has to be brought to permeate the intellectual life of the Church ever more. That is mostly a matter of continuing personal conversion.

But, as I have suggested, the Pentecostal-charismatic spirituality strikes most noncharismatic Catholics as unusually strange, and something very new in the Church, and as somehow "anti-intellectual." "In fact, as regards its origins," reply the scholars Killian McDonnelle and George Montague, "it is most ancient," as they show in their careful review of Scripture and the fathers.[168] And as I have just suggested, openness to the Holy Spirit in intense prayer should improve the intellectual performance of the Church.

As mentioned earlier, confusion begins right at the core, with the notion of the key experience, "effusion of the Holy Spirit," or "Baptism in the Holy Spirit." Orthodox charismatics point out that this does not replace sacramental baptism or confirmation. It is not effective *ex opere operato.* Michael Keating wrote this to me about "the gifts of the Holy Spirit":

> It has always seemed to charismatics that the difficulty about prophecy and speaking in tongues was no difficulty at all, seeing as they are smack in the middle of the Scriptures. The burden of proof lies on those who deny the validity of the gifts. Repeatedly in the Acts of the Apostles, the pattern is the same: the laying on of hands, the descent of the Spirit, and speaking in tongues and prophesying among the recipients. See Acts 10:44–48; 19:6; Mk 16:17. And of course there is the Letter to the Corinthians where Paul is emphatic about the excellence of the gifts, if equally emphatic about avoiding their abuse. He assumes that both tongues and prophecy are a normal part of Corinthian church life. ("Pursue love and strive for the spiritual gifts, and especially that you may prophesy" [1 Cor 14:1].) He even gives personal testimony of a rare kind: "I thank God that I speak in tongues more than all of you" (14:18). The significant thing here for the purpose of arguing in favor of the validity of such gifts is not that Paul spends so much time correcting their abuses. It is that he assumes their use. . . . Abuse does not disallow use, is the old maxim. Why then so much suspicion, especially when the first experience of receiving such gifts is so often accompanied by a deep encounter with God and an undeniable change of life?[169]

There is no doubt about the gifts in the early Church. Prophecy may have come into disrepute, suggests Keating, because of the Montanists,

---

168. Killian McDonnelle and George Montague, *Christian Initiation and Baptism in the Holy Spirit* (Collegeville, Minn.: Liturgical Press, 1991), 25–27.

169. Letter from Keating, January 26, 1993, quoted with permission.

but prophetic figures have emerged throughout the history of the Church. Balthasar agrees, emphasizing the great saints as prophetic prototypes— charismatic, one might say—responding to a need of the time. Indeed, a proper understanding of the prophetic dimension of the tradition is so important—vital in the context here of renewal of Catholic intellectual life— I am going to quote at length Keating's disquisition, a beautiful presentation of a charismatic perspective:

There were prophets under the Old Covenant, as is obvious. It is also evident that the famous prophets whom we know so well were only the best known of a whole group, almost an order, of people who were understood to have the responsibility of hearing the word of the Lord. Moses was in some respects the greatest of the prophets, Saul was "among the prophets" for a brief time, and scattered throughout the historical and prophetic works are references to a dimly seen group of people set apart and pursuing a special task for all Israel. The prophet was also a New Covenant figure, as is shown by the prophet Agabus who warns Paul about going to Jerusalem (Acts 11:28 and 21:10) or by allusion to the daughters of Philip whose "four virgin daughters were prophets" (Acts 21:9). The *Te Deum* refers to the prophets as a kind of order mentioned in the company of apostles and martyrs, and Paul mentions prophets as a position in the Church (e.g. 1 Cor. 12:27ff: "Now you are the body of Christ and individually members of it. And God has appointed in the Church first apostles, second prophets, third teachers . . ."). All this is only to note that the prophet, whoever he is, and prophecy, whatever that is, seem to have played a clear role in the Church as it was first constituted, and there is no intrinsic reason to think that it was not intended to continue. That role changed over time, and I do not think we know much about how and why it changed due to the lack of sources from the first few centuries. The Montanists' abuse made the danger of false prophecy clear, and it has remained clear. At the same time, many of the saints have been prophets, Francis, Vincent Ferrar, Don Bosco come to mind. Such a powerful gift, capable of bringing God's presence and thought so directly into human affairs, so susceptible of abuse whether sincere or malicious, was bound to have, and has had, a chequered history.

In the charismatic movement prophecy is rarely involved in foretelling future events. It is usually oriented toward a group of people gathered in prayer, representing some aspect of truth that God wants to emphasize especially at that time and to that group of people. . . . It has nothing to do with ecstasy or loss of consciousness; it has more to do with the strong sense by someone present that God has something specific He wants to bring to mind, usually involving encouragement, occasionally admonition. There are those who are considered experienced prophets, people who are understood to have the special gift. It would be their special concern to keep an open ear, not only during a time of prayer, but generally.

Prophecy is to be discerned. Is it in keeping with sound doctrine? Are those prophesying people of firm faith and upright lives? Have they shown wisdom and discernment in the exercise of this gift previously? As one sees, such matters are not cut-and-dried, and I have heard some real doozies, especially in the early days of the charismatic movement when anyone might consider himself a new Jeremiah. And there is an undoubted apocalyptic strain running through Pentecostalism, where you can find people predicting the end of the world every three months. This millenarian attitude has had its impact on the Catholic renewal, but Catholics have always been slower to buy into the end of the world scenarios, perhaps because of their long history, and this strain has been ever less significant as the movement gets older (and, one hopes, grows in wisdom). A certain sobriety about the times in which we live, and the need for a firm response, has remained among the communities, but increasingly in the terms that the Holy Father and many other clear-sighted people have been using.[170]

I know that within charismatic communities there is a heightened sense of "discerning": in prayer, charismatics are always discerning together, and with great deference to their leaders, allowing the Holy Spirit to direct them toward right solutions of their problems and to show them their way forward. But then any Catholic should subscribe to the basic necessity of our listening to the Holy Spirit as He directs us in our *missio*. But normally one looks to the ordinary teaching of the Church, the Church mediating the gospel to us; and then some turn to an authorized (and wise) spiritual director for particular help in discerning, and that will usually be an ordained priest, who represents the Church's teaching with an authority granted by the bishop, in whose special charism of office the Catholic would not doubt, a charism that endows him with the Christ-given authority of discernment. I am aware that in saying that I come down on the "priest" side of the perennial "priest versus prophet" tension. This has been an unabashedly Catholic predisposition running throughout this appropriation. "Prophesy" in its more spectacular moments—from what one can guess, anyway—often goes beyond the "safe" bounds of magisterial teachings, but need not, indeed should not, contradict it.[171]

Regarding the gift of healing: the Church has always prayed for the sick; indeed, the New Testament clearly shows an importance attached to divine healing, and the sacrament of "extreme unction" is today renamed "the sacrament of the sick," being administered to the ill who are not necessarily in danger of death. Again, laying hands on the ill and invoking the Holy Spirit, asking him to deploy the infinite healing power of God, should be nothing out of the ordinary.

One also hears about "talking in tongues," that glossolalia that Saint Paul claimed for himself, but the importance of which he rather downplayed (1 Cor. 14:5–12). It seems fairly scarce until the recent explosion of the charismatic movement. One hears tales of individuals breaking into ancient

170. Keating, letter of April 3, 1993.
171. Is even the most authentic prophesy at risk of subtly undermining the authority flowing from the charism of the ordained bishop and priest? I continue to be cautious, as those who uphold the ordinary authority of the Church as Christ-founded structure have always worried in the face of "charismatic outbursts," to use Voegelin's term. But one must admit that charismatic, prophetic saints, like Francis of Assisi, have moved the Church forward. Recall Balthasar's distinction of ordinary from extraordinary sanctity. The latter refers to special gifts of the Holy Spirit meant for the service of the whole Church, the way a Saint Benedict or a Saint Ignatius of Loyola provides answers to the problems of the times, but with lasting implications (*Ste. Thérèse de Lisieux: Histoire d'une mission* [Paris: Apostolat des Éditions, 1973], introduction). So, yes, the reality of prophesy must be admitted, in principle and in fact, but one remains cautious when confronted by concrete claims that this person here is uttering prophetic insights. Wise is the instinct to demand first of all that the established teaching of the Church not be contradicted by it.

languages that they do not know, but that a knowledgeable bystander recognizes (for example, Egyptian has been heard). Not to be exaggerated, reply the sensible charismatics: sometimes "speaking (or singing) in tongues" is nothing but an innocent prayer technique, a kind of mantra chant of praise and glory, sung softly by the prayer group, creating an atmosphere as they express themselves in praise of God in a virtually wordless form. So explained, "tongues" sounds innocent enough. I once or twice heard people in a charismatic chapel sing like that, and it was quite beautiful, staying this side of any obvious emotional excess.

Despite the potentials for misunderstanding we have been considering, I count as a strength in the doctrinal realm both the fact that the charismatic movement generates large numbers of Catholics committed to the orthodox teaching of the Church and the fact that this more "emotional" strain of Catholic religious life[172] has attracted to, and kept in, the Church many persons who might well have joined the hundreds of thousands of others who have left the Church to join a Protestant Pentecostal denomination. Even if some of these persons show signs of pathological excess, it is better they remain attached to the Church, and subject to her wise guidance, than that they become swept up in the freelance atmosphere of the Pentecostals who more often than not harbor a great suspicion for the Catholic Church and vehemently deny central Catholic teachings, the Mass, five of the sacraments, the magisterium, and the role of the Mother of God, among others. But the main point remains: the intense prayer life of the charismatics, to the extent it is part of that essential purification of hearts, is bound to contribute to a healthy intellectual life in the Church, because pure hearts are open to the in-pouring of truth. The charismatic can lead to better intellectual life by opposing a deadening *intellectualism*.

Weaknesses

Dogmatic Clarity Can Lead to Slowness to React
On the negative side stands first and foremost the danger that comes precisely from the chief strength, the Church's evident ability to arrive at clear, "definitive" dogmatic formulation, and hence to take firm stands and to teach definitively. It is the case that in some periods of the Church's history this has restrained theological innovation. Most recently, one has only to consider the difficulties surrounding "modernism" at the start of this century, with the brakes that put on appreciating Cardinal Newman's contributions to understanding the development of doctrine, and the silencing in the 1940s of such lights as de Lubac, Congar, and Teilhard de Chardin. (As recently as 1962, Balthasar was pointedly not invited as a

---

172. This is the way another friend, long in the movement, characterized it, in the context of telling me that the bishop who had been "accompanying" him had moved him away from emphasis on mystical experiences and toward greater seriousness about doctrinal substance.

peritus—theological expert—to the Second Vatican Council. One can only imagine what effect this kind of repression had on more timid souls.)

The Church has often been slow to grasp what was happening in the world around it: for instance, only now, with the council, has freedom of conscience been thoroughly appreciated—an issue that was already burning in the eighteenth century. (To be fair, thinking this through requires developing a much more dynamic and open theory of truth than that handed down since ancient times, a development fraught with perils of relativism, as the "antimodernists" clearly saw.) And the avoidance of coziness with state powers has largely been achieved only after the Church was in fact thrown out of the public sphere by the political power manipulators. Slow in grasping the sense of the great revolution of open society and entrepreneurial industrial society, at last, especially with the recent great encyclical *Centesimus Annus*, the Church's position is actually getting in some ways ahead of the times, as earlier Leo XIII had managed in *Rerum Novarum* to get ahead of a time that was fomenting an erroneous socialist view. But in between these two great social encyclicals, the teachings were often behind events, and the penetration of complex economic matters limited.

Some critics see the Church as once again slow in grasping the full reality of the sexual revolution. Others, on the other hand, see Pope Paul VI as prescient in the encyclical *Humanae Vitae* in anticipating the disaster of that sexual revolution. While searing practical problems remain, with every passing day the warnings and the positive teachings of the much disputed encyclical look more brilliant. Now Pope John Paul has placed the entire teaching about sexual morality in a beautiful and ample anthropological-mystical context in the 1995 magistral encyclical *Evangelium Vitae*.

When one is being critical of the "control mentality" that is never totally absent in the Church, as it is a sinful tendency in all the children of Adam and Eve, one should not forget that the limitations of the Church's vision in the modernist controversy do not invalidate its sound warnings, and that those limitations and abuses of control did not succeed in stopping ultimately the sound innovative influences, like those of Newman and Blondel. Nor did the more recent silencing prevent ultimately the rehabilitation of Teilhard and the move into the mainstream of the Newman- and Blondel-inspired thought of the likes of Yves Congar and Henri Cardinal de Lubac. On the other hand, it should also be recalled that the Eastern Orthodox look generally askance at the "Roman effort to control doctrine," and believe that the personal holiness of the theologians is the real issue, and the only guarantee, and that this holiness, which comes from the Holy Spirit, will ultimately prevail, without the need for censuring, controlling institutional structures.

Preoccupation with the avant-garde theologians and worry about keeping theology orthodox perhaps distracts from the even greater problem: getting the message of the sound core teaching of the Church across to the mass of Catholics. I have no reliable sociological data to offer in proof of the soundness of the doctrinal understanding of masses of Catholics in one country or another. We know that the level of Mass attendance in many Catholic countries is low, and the numbers not bothering with a marriage in the Church are increasing. I can tell you that in Toronto the graduates of our vast, publicly funded Catholic school system are arriving in university often "turned off" by the Church altogether, or with distorted and superficial understanding of what the Church holds.

A part of the difficulty is the very richness of the teaching documents that pour forth from Rome and from bishops' conferences: they are so many, and often so long and complex, and couched in lofty (and often rather soft-pedaled) theological language, the great lines of the teaching have to be dug out. Here the new *Catechism* is a help. But the book is enormous, more than seven hundred pages, and while a wonderful poetic weaving of great texts from the tradition, it is quite demanding for the average layman. (It was expressly intended for the bishops, as guide to their development of local and more accessible catechesis.) While it touches on many aspects of the faith, it is excellent in its highlighting the great essentials.

But still the question haunts us: how is it that with such clear teaching at its disposal, the Church seems to have lost the ability to ensure the most basic orthodoxy of what is being taught in Catholic universities and above all in the seminaries? For an important aspect of the problem of transmitting to the laity the Church's teaching lies right there. The hierarchy seems to have had a much greater control of what its agents taught before that period of general liberalizing in the Western world: the 1960s, which coincided with the council.

I do not look with nostalgia to the earlier period of strict control. It could not and should not have continued that way, reaching the extreme that as an undergraduate in a Jesuit university I had to request written permission from the bishop's delegate to read Descartes. The atmosphere of maintaining strict ideological purity—only Gilsonian neo-Thomism was tolerated in the philosophy department—was unhealthy. But, at the other extreme, anyone with an understanding of the essence of the traditional teaching has got to be worried by the degree of antiauthority, especially anti-Roman and antibishop sentiment, the slide toward relativism, uncritical application of the "historico-critical method" of studying Holy Scripture, softness on many moral issues, the emphasis on "empowering people," as though power were centrally what the Church is about, that has invaded many seminaries and all but a few theology faculties in Europe and the United States.

To keep in perspective the problem of strengthening the orthodoxy of these institutions without stifling genuine efforts to think anew the truths of the tradition, recall that in the sphere of secular education questions are being asked about the effectiveness of democratized education to transmit subtleties to masses of people: the huge bureaucracies and labor unions of the public schools and universities are not the stuff of sensitive formation of souls. The problem is a general one transcending that important aspect we are considering here: religious education and formation.

For now Rome's strategy in bringing order to what has become a bit of a *foire* appears to be to select as bishops priests who themselves are clear and firm in the Church's teachings, and then they choose rectors and directors of studies for the seminaries who reflect the same fidelity. But, while Rome has issued firm guidelines for ensuring the orthodoxy of teaching in universities, this has been largely scoffed at by college administrations and faculty alike. There is no effective plan for guiding university theology faculties and, more generally, colleges back toward orthodoxy.[173] The removal of the license to teach in the name of the Church from the most flagrantly unorthodox professors, such as Hans Küng in Tübingen, Charles Curran in Washington, and the one-year silencing of Leonardo Boff in Brazil (he subsequently left the Church), have produced no positive result that I can see, save only to give clear warning that there does exist a point—one leaving large margins—beyond which one cannot go with impunity and retain an official chair of Catholic theology. This may frighten some theologians into being more "prudent" about what they put into print, but probably produces more burning resentment than it does a purifying of hearts. In any event, there is no visible evidence this kind of thing has done anything to improve the hearing "Roman positions" get in many faculties, colleges, and universities.

To date, efforts to found new Catholic schools and colleges have been rather timid. (No new full-fledged university—an expensive proposition—has been attempted in North America, except the University of Dallas and the "conversion" of Steubenville, although the Legionaries of Christ have started small universities in Mexico, and Opus Dei has expanded its universities in Navarre and Mexico.) One interesting development has been that booming "converted" charismatic college, Franciscan University of Steubenville, Ohio, which, while small (twenty-five hundred students), is growing and is certainly energetic, especially in missionary outreach, and is now working to strengthen its academic credentials. A number of small Catholic liberal-arts colleges have also, at the cost of great personal sacrifice, been founded.

At the request of the pope a network of John Paul II Institutes for Family and Marriage, associated with the Pontifical Lateran University, have been founded. While the name signals the area of specialization, they are in fact new centers of theology in a more basic sense, ensuring a foyer of orthodoxy and of lively theology in many countries.

A new kind of possibility is provoking fresh initiatives: use of the Internet to gather into a more effective focus the resources scattered throughout the

173. The beautiful encyclical *Ex Corde Ecclesiae*, and the well-meaning preaching of the secretariat for Catholic education in Rome, provides no real plan. There is nothing therein that has any hope of improving the lamentable situation of infidelity and just plain ignorance of doctrine afflicting many "Catholic" colleges.

world. The new International Catholic University exists at this writing in cyberspace, but is only just beginning to provide courses for credit and to gather good minds from far and wide, and accumulating intelligence about what is already available.

A more systematic effort to spread *Catechism* study groups, Bible study groups, and to insist on the use of the sermon at every Mass to teach as well as exhort should become a high priority of every bishop.

But when I step back to consider the perennial drama of maintaining orthodoxy while encouraging originality, of remaining faithful to the best lights of the tradition while responding to fresh challenges from a rapidly evolving society, I candidly confess that I believe the problem of achieving rightly and profoundly formed Catholic minds is more a challenge of charity and prayer than anything to do with lack of intelligence or with institutional innovations. All is vain unless individuals are penetrated with the reality of God revealed in Jesus Christ. And that cannot happen without contemplative prayer and a serious participation in the Eucharist. Without a personal love affair with Jesus Christ one will not plunge into the mystery of the infinite transcending Father. Families, schools, and seminaries must raise the young in an atmosphere of contemplative prayer. Everything possible must be done to give them *le goût de prière* (the taste for prayer) and to get them to see that a pure heart is everything. There will be no pure hearts without obedience—listening to God and to the instruments of teaching He has left us—and no obedience without pure hearts. The new *Catechism* contains a long and wonderful section on prayer. The strict "norms" of Opus Dei and the New Catechumenate and the fervor of the charismatics' prayers have much to teach us about building a Catholic culture of prayer. And Taizé is a wonderful "school of prayer."

Some Lacunae in Vatican II's Teaching, Mentioned by Louis Bouyer
But to turn now from the question of orthodoxy of the teaching and the challenge of propagating it to the laity to the question of possible areas of underdevelopment in the teaching itself, consider what the renowned theologian—a convert from Protestantism—Louis Bouyer has to say at the conclusion of his study of the Second Vatican Council. He drew up a list of the things the council did not treat at all, or not very adequately. Several of these offer us clues of possible areas of doctrinal underdevelopment. I shall pause to consider them, and then ask subsequently whether and how thoroughly the new *Catechism of the Catholic Church* addresses these.

The lacuna Bouyer finds "perhaps the most surprising" is that tradition is not even mentioned in the most important document, *Lumen Gentium*.[174] It is treated "very fruitfully and at length" in the *Constitution on Revelation, Dei Verbum*. To understand the Church today one must integrate into the vision of *Lumen Gentium* what is said about this elsewhere. (Here *The Catechism*

---

174. Bouyer, *The Church of God, Body of Christ, and Temple of the Spirit*, trans. Charles Underhill Quinn (Chicago: Franciscan Herald Press, 1982), 171.

responds beautifully, for it does integrate tradition prominently and well into its discussion, almost from the beginning [paras. 81ff].)

A less obvious lack is the scanty treatment of the presbyterate, the priesthood in general including all the hierarchy, in relation to the importance ordinary priests had and continue to have in the Church. "There is no question but what an analogical extension of the problem of collegiality should be envisioned here."[175] As the fathers throw light on the relationship of the bishops to one another and collectively and individually to the pope, so they should have reflected on the relationships between priests, and between ordinary priests and their hierarchical superiors.

The distinction between the hierarchical and the lay priesthood requires further clarification. This is most important in view of the downplaying of hierarchy in the Protestant "Congregationalist" tradition, a model that, in increasingly egalitarian times, attracts democratic peoples. (Bouyer, a convert from Protestantism, is especially sensitive to this.) (Again, *The Catechism* corrects all these points.)

The question of the relationship of the Church to the state, treated in the first draft of *Lumen Gentium*, somehow was forgotten in the subsequent redrafting. Some aspects of the problem are briefly touched on in *Gaudium et Spes*, but there is no adequate treatment of this perennial question. (*The Catechism* addresses the issue in paras. 2244–46.)

Finally, Bouyer expresses astonishment at two realities that are not adequately treated in other conciliar documents. These at first seem in tension, but need to be discussed together, and properly balanced in any treatment of the Church: the Holy Spirit and canon law. "The constitution on the Church practically ignores canon law, and, with the exception of a paragraph that is more pious than doctrinal, completely ignores the Holy Spirit!"[176] (*The Catechism* has a chapter titled "Law and Grace," but it too does not give much emphasis to canon law—"the precepts of the Church"—some of which are cited individually, but codification is not underscored.)

Bouyer accounts for the lacuna as an overreaction to complaints of "legalism" in the Church. He points out that legalism is the abuse of the good and necessary use of law in any large institution. Nothing would do more to revitalize a proper sense of the rule of law than an adequate doctrine of the Spirit, such as that being developed in the most vibrant Orthodox theology today, proceeding from Khomiakov. Bouyer finds this a most serious piece of unfinished doctrinal business.

Today, a vast refashioning of the corpus of canon law, if not the theory of the role of law in the Church, has been completed. In that act the Church has gone far toward reaffirming the centrality of law in the regular functioning of the institution.

Given the importance the charismatic movement assumed in the years following the council, it is a pity that the relationships of the Spirit, the

175. Ibid.
176. Ibid., 172.

ordinary magisterium, and canon law were not explored. Not that the Holy Spirit is ever to be reduced to a variable in the equation, but the role of institution and law as fruits of the Spirit needs emphasis. (The Holy Spirit's role is brought out strongly throughout *The Catechism,* and I have emphasized it in the earlier discussion of the charismatic movement.)

The council, after all, is but one brief, intense moment in the life of the Church, albeit a singularly important one. Bouyer is satisfied that out of the council's deliberations came the reaffirmation of a large number of essential themes, and the recuperation of many that might have slipped from sight. The topics chosen for treatment in subsequent chapters of Bouyer's book show how many and rich those themes are. It would be interesting to know to what extent he was satisfied with *The Catechism*'s effort to integrate these themes and to achieve a good balance.

Dogmatic Clarity Plays into the Pathological Problem of "Hyper-Orthodoxy"

The reasons for and the problems caused by dogmatic formulation enjoying highest ecclesial authority have emerged as an important theme in the present study. I return to them one last time in the present negative context of examining doctrinal weaknesses with emphasis on the damage done the Church by those who misunderstand and abuse the clarity achieved in the Church's dogmatic formulation.

Because, I believe, the "fundamentalist right," as Balthasar once referred to them, cause harm to the life and credibility of the Church, I shall recall for you the quote from Msgr. Romano Guardini[177] on "orthodoxy" that states the problem brilliantly:

> From the moment in the domain of holy truth, a categorical "yes" or "no" is pronounced, from the moment there are objective forms of cult, a discipline and an authority, the danger arises of "The Law" and "the Pharisee," the danger of taking the shell for the kernel, the danger of an opposition between what one thinks and what one says, the danger, in the name of the established and recognized order, of interfering with the liberty of God, in a word the danger of all that of which Christ accuses the Pharisees. That history of The Law is a grand lesson. The Sacred, issued from God, became an instrument of sin. From the moment one believes in an explicit revelation, in a rule of conduct descended from heaven, that same possibility awakens.[178]

The more I observe the dynamics of day-by-day Church life, especially Church politics, the more I am convinced that such pharisaism of the angry, righteous right is an especially damaging blot on the witness of Christ the Church is called to give. Here are those who announce themselves as the most "faithful" showing, often, so little understanding in any depth of that to which they are "faithful" and a patent lack of love in serving it up to others; here is "Truth" made into a club for beating over the head "the

---

177. Romano Guardini's orthodoxy has never been questioned. He is held in the highest esteem by Balthasar, de Lubac, and the present pope.
178. Guardini, *Le Seigneur* (Paris: Alsatia, 1943), 1:192–93.

enemy" (for them largely the enemy within the Church, "the betrayers"). These angry men run the pope's flag up the flagpole, but it is not evident they have absorbed his spirit by obediently reflecting on his encyclicals. There is not a drop of such pharisaism in anything the pope has written. He respects "the Other," he tries to find the kernel of truth in every position, and he is not afraid to break new ground in his thinking, to find fresh expressions to make old truths understandable to our time, "dangerous" those this may be.

Perish the thought that suddenly at the end of an appropriation that I have striven to keep orthodox I have inexplicably become soft on infidelity to the Church's teaching and to "leftish" efforts to undermine fidelity to the holy father and the bishops in the name of "liberty to think." I have tried to show the perennial nature of the problem of maintaining enduring truths of a tradition, which requires at points definitive expressions, while absorbing into the vision new dimensions of being that not only come to light with time (for example, discoveries in science) but even *come to be* as new being, as in the arts, creative new social relations, both fruitful and corrupting, and technological capabilities undreamed of (even by Jules Verne). These new discoveries and new creations can be synthesized with the old truths in their authoritative formulations only through fresh thinking that must always go to the foundations.[179]

But it is when the doctrinal truths are promoted with a surface show of fidelity but in an unloving way that perhaps the most perfect perversion Satan can wish for is achieved. Recall Pascal's mot, which I used as a motto for *Being and Truth: "La vérité sans la charité est une idole."* Why was Our Lord so desperate about His "Pharisees"? Is it not clear why the same persons are so rejecting of the Church's efforts, imperfect to be sure, to reform the liturgy? Legitimate criticism of imperfections should not lead to an atmosphere of schism. Dogmatism in this sense is a perennial pathological problem, an especially corrosive fruit of pride, a failure of love. Abuse of "the letter" is to be found in all traditions that explicitly formulate truth. In Christianity there is a remedy: contemplative prayer, opening one to obedience to the living Word of Jesus Christ until one can say, with Saint Paul, "Not I live but Christ in me" (Gal. 2:20).

The Isolation of the New Communities

When I consider the "weakness flip side" of the strength found in the variety of new communities, with their offering of many distinctive spiritualities, two problems come to mind: communications and the need for mutual enrichment. In a busy world, it is extremely difficult to help people discover which of these resources respond best to their own needs, given the differences in personalities and missions. I stressed earlier the difficulty in getting to know and to appreciate another's spirituality. Still, millions do find their way into what one can only hope are appropriate

179. On the "ultimate structures" of being see *TA,* chapter 9, and *BT,* chapter 10.

communities.[180] Recognizing that people have spiritual needs and that the local church must in some way "meet these" is an exercise of love.

The issue of mutual enrichment has been well raised by the spiritual writer Carlo Carretto, in terms of the need to pray for one another, part of a fraternal effort to come to know one another better—the need for "ecumenism" within the One Holy Catholic Church.

Every sound Catholic community and every good parish priest is devoted to finding ways to do this, to get Catholics praying together and caring for one another, while trying to pass on the faith in its integrity. But no one hears of these beyond the confines of one parish, or unless he bumbles by accident into contact with a community that may have been operating for years, right on his doorstep. Lack of communication means that these success stories do not get widely enough imitated.

The diocese should issue yearly a directory explaining the activities of and places to contact various movements, parish-based organizations, and all other resources—some prayer groups, approved by the bishop, *Retrouvaille* (a service to marriages in trouble), marriage encounter, where catechetical instruction can be found—and see to it that these are distributed throughout all the parishes and movements. Each diocese should post this directory on a "web page" of its own.

The Need for a More Adequately Formulated Catholic Anthropology
At a more theological level, if Catholics are to be more effective in putting forth a view of the human condition that will prove more convincing than the libertarian, egalitarian, antiauthority, consumerist, and high-tech activist vision sweeping everyone along in democratic society, a more adequate Catholic anthropology must be developed.[181] Various areas requiring

180. I have heard so many stories of amazing "coincidences" through which one or another person has been guided to the rendezvous that was best for him, I would be tempted to abandon the whole affair to the Holy Spirit, but for two considerations: that same Holy Spirit, as I understand, has given us our brains and our means of communication and asks us to use both; and second, thousands more have drifted from the Church into spiritual organizations of every sort that are virulently anti-Catholic, which, for someone who believes in the divine mission of the Church, has always got to seem at least a temporary defeat. And as much as I reject the campaign to find elements of cultism in all movements, one should not be cavalier about the danger of enthusiastic members of movements bringing unacceptable pressure both in recruitment and in discouraging those who want to leave.
181. Communities of Catholic thinkers capable of working together sustainedly on such an enormous project actually exist: 1) Communio, which as I mentioned earlier was founded twenty-five years ago by Balthasar, Ratzinger, de Lubac, Wojtyla and others, today groups fourteen semiautonomous theology journals, each national board being responsible to found local Communio circles, capable of such coordinated research and discussion in the service of the Church and in fidelity to the magisterium. 2) While limited to North America, the Fellowship of Catholic Scholars groups academics from many fields who insist on their fidelity to the magisterium. I believe this group is growing beyond its earlier reactive phase, where anger over betrayal hung in the air. 3) The International Catholic University, which will depend heavily on the new

collaborative thinking need to be defined, such as advancing Catholic understanding of cosmic evolution, of human sexuality, of psychopathology and its intimate relations with sin (while clarifying the difference between them), of the anthropological foundations of social life, including the foundations of a modern form of political economy more worthy of human nature than the emerging HTX, a set of intellectual challenges of the first order! The task of integrating insights from so many areas of reality into an enhanced vision of human nature and the human condition with particular reference to the challenges of the planetary HTX epoch is daunting, but drastically needed.

One of the reasons for a certain flagging of Catholic missionary activity in our time is precisely widespread acceptance of an inadequate anthropology. What feeds the idea that Catholic "relief" should be devoted simply to economic development and the aid workers should avoid "proselytizing"—accompanying aid with preaching? To some extent, it is based in a sound Christian insight: one must not "buy" adhesion to the faith, as some missionaries may have done: listen to an hour's harangue for a bag of flour. But for Catholic aid agencies to provide economic aid and at the same time shy away from announcing, joyously, freely, nonmanipulatively, the good news that it is the love of Christ that brings Christians to help is, for no good reason, to diminish the effectiveness of a witness that the recipients deserve. Because it is the truth, the recipients have a right to know this is Christ's love at work, they have a right to know in this way better who this Jesus is, and to be helped to recognize in the aid worker a manifestation of the new man who is the true man.

Of course, simply making progress in understanding the human condition in the light of recently gained insights into body, spirit, and cosmos illumined by the wisdom of the tradition will not somehow automatically protect the Church from liberalism and Marxist-collectivist thinking, nor from the attraction, on the one side, of the materialist, consumerist, careerist society, and on the other, of zealous "evangelical" sects. I would be guilty of that "overemphasis on philosophy" of which the Orthodox accuse "the Western Church" if I thought that; indeed, I would be revealing a pathological denial about the strength of the social forces of the HTX. Corruptions from within and ceding to attractions from without are often more matters of the heart than of the head—that principle, which I stressed here, is central to a sound Christian anthropology. Guardini's warning about how the impure heart receives doctrine in a way that always distorts God's truth expresses this conviction. Many of the distortions in liberal society

---

means of communication, has been founded, and hopes eventually to foster cooperative research with the help of the Internet. 4) A number of cooperative projects have already been undertaken by the International Association of Catholic Colleges and Universities centered in Rome. 5) The Pontifical Academy of Sciences could be enlisted to this end. Meanwhile, as a prod to this effort I am completing *Human Being,* a phenomenological anthropology the Christian inspiration of which is not hidden.

stem from an unwillingness to admit the absurdity of an anthropology of victimhood, the refusal to see that basically, down deep, we are not just full of goodwill—only the "oppressors" being evil. We are all also our own oppressors, as Saint Paul told us.

Properly Inserting the Charismatic Renewal into the Life of the Church

Two developments on the level of popular religion bring out the truth that religion is not basically theoretical but is about prayer and devotion, and Christian religion is about these in the most *personalist* way: the dramatic rise of the charismatic movement and the prominence of private revelations, especially those involving devotion to Mary, including some rather startling purported apparitions of the Virgin. These, along with the drift into evangelicalism of many Catholics—it too being more about the personal heart than the head—is a telling symptom that something is seriously missing in much of everyday Catholicism as it is experienced.

For all the difficult elements in charismatic theology of the spirit and for all the distaste many feel for emotional extremes found among some in that movement, it has brought home the urgency of a life of prayer. This is no monopoly of charismatics, of course, but they bring an element of personal sharing that invites to friendship and gives witness to a personal, heartfelt relationship to Jesus and to His Holy Spirit. To do this without stepping over the line into show is not easy, but it is accomplished when genuine receptivity to grace holds down damaged aspects of personality. No question, such genuine sharing bears fruit in an active life of education, evangelization, and social work. Other movements, like Opus Dei, the New Catechumenate, and the secular institutes, develop a sustained life of prayer in their members, but without the emotionalism so often accompanying charismatic prayer in common.[182] This more traditional kind of interior life and prayer, practiced for a millennium and a half in monasteries, has proved fruitful in good works and evangelization, and indeed has proved able to produce steady and reliable members of the Church. Does the charismatic outburst in recent decades respond to a special need in our activist, noisy world, channeling some of the strong emotions aroused by the HTX anticulture back into fruitful channels?

Has the Church Addressed Adequately the Challenge of Private Revelations?

The other issue in popular piety, private revelations (the Padre Pios and the Marthe Robins of this world), and the apparitions of the Virgin—Lourdes in 1858, Fatima in 1917, and Medjugorje continuing since 1980 being the best known, with others, Ecuador in 1989 and Denver in 1991, and who knows where else—proliferating at a startling rate, all with the

---

182. The "norms" for members of the Work include Mass, rosary, and a half hour of contemplation daily, daily reading of Scripture and a spiritual reading, as well as spiritual direction and confession weekly, evenings of reflection monthly, and a retreat and theological formation workshops annually. These all assume forms charismatics would find cold.

message: pray earnestly, reform your lives or . . . watch out! Are these genuine heavenly initiatives or products of mass hysteria, or are some genuine, while others are not, and how is the simple Catholic to discern?

One thing is sure: their prominence since about a century is a symptom of a certain widespread desperation. As the world slides from secularization into nihilism, those who are convinced that this is devastatingly destructive of all the Catholic tradition stands for are bound, unless they allow the Holy Spirit to renew in them the supernatural virtue of hope, to become more frantic. Fear is the poorest counselor. But there are sound reasons for being afraid about the abyss into which we are sliding. In a recent interview, Cardinal Ratzinger had this to say:

> Even though perverted, the political social terrorism of the 1960s had a certain kind of moral ideal. But today, the terrorism of drug abuse, of the Mafia, of attacks on foreigners, in Germany and elsewhere, no longer has any moral basis. In this era of sovereign subjectivity, people act for the sole pleasure of acting, without any reference other than the satisfaction of "myself." Just as the terrorism that was born of Marxism of yesterday put its finger on the anomalies of our social order, in the same way the nihilistic terrorism of today ought to show us the course to be followed for a reflection on the basis of a new ethical and collective reason.[183]

Is it any wonder that in an incarnational, eucharistic religion, the faithful expect that a personal, incarnate God will not abandon them before the onslaught of radical evil?

No one denies that some reported "supernatural" events are hysterical projections, nor that these can at times attract crowds of gullible people. (The discredited "apparitions of Mary" at Bayside, New York, in the late 1960s are a textbook example. After all the Church has done to condemn them as pathological, I understand there are still believers. But with the archbishop's disavowal at Denver, that "apparition" seems to have faded quickly. Most recently, the Seer Vasoula in Switzerland, an Eastern Orthodox attracting a large following, has been disavowed by the Vatican. It will be interesting to see how long it takes for her influence to subside.) The Church consistently warns against the "Gnostic" tendency of an avid following after apparitions.

Consider this well-put warning by Father Frederick Miller at the first International Pastoral Symposium on Fatima:

> More often than not this form of "religion" has little or nothing in common with Catholicism. It rather witnesses to an ancient heretical tendency called gnosticism. The gnostic is not truly interested in the conversion and faith of the "ordinary" Christian. Rather he desires a secret knowledge (gnosis) not available to the commonplace practitioner of the Catholic Faith. He wants to have knowledge of world events and above all of apocalyptic events.[184]

---

183. *Catholic World Report* (January 1993): 54.

184. In *Fatima Family Messenger* (January–March 1993): 28. Its publication in this source shows that some pastors who are involved in movements founded in apparitions guard their critical, ecclesial good sense.

Some of the private revelations have produced phenomena in the public domain difficult to dismiss as simply effects of mass illusion. For instance, if one adopts the most demanding critical scientific stance, the portrait of Mary (now termed *Nuestra Señora de Guadalupe*)[185] left to the Mexican peasant Juan Diego as though photographed on his *tilma* remains disconcerting for any fair-minded investigator. The *tilma*, a cloak made of cactus fibers with a normal life expectancy of fifteen years, has endured since that day in 1532 when he unfolded it to allow to spill out on the floor before Bishop Zumàrraga the miraculous flowers picked on a barren winter hillside, only to further astound the bishop, his entourage, and himself with the discovery that an image of a lovely young lady shone forth from the rough material. This image is not painted (this is the conclusion of repeated scientific examinations with X-rays and all the modern methods), and microscopic examination reveals in the pupils of the eyes reverse images of figures looking at the Virgin! No one can explain this. (However this image came to exist, there is no more lovely and touching icon of the Virgin anywhere.)[186]

Typical of what has happened after the more credible of these private revelations, long-lasting and public spiritual fruits resulted for Mexico. The story of Juan Diego's incredible influence on the previously resistant Aztecs from the little chapel built at Tepeyac (today engulfed by the monstrous spread of Mexico City) is summed up by Francis Johnston: "The trickle of conversions soon became a river, and the river a flood which is perhaps unprecedented in the history of Christianity. 5,000,000 Catholics were lost to the Church owing to the Reformation in Europe at this time, but their numbers were more than replaced by over 9,000,000 Aztec converts."[187]

It would require a series of volumes to recount all of the extraordinary events that have accompanied the most famous of the Marian apparitions in recent times:[188] the medically authenticated cures at Lourdes;[189] the miracle

185. According to Francis Johnston, *The Wonder of Guadalupe* (Rockford, Ill.: Tan Publishers, 1981), 46–47, Becarra Tanco, who played a dominant role in the apostolic investigations of 1666, the name was a Spanish misunderstanding of the Nahuatl dialect of Aztec in which Our Lady would have addressed Juan Diego, the word being *Tequantlaxopeuh* (pronounced "Tequetalope"), which means "who saves us from the Devourer." Guadalupe—Arabic for "river of wolves"—is a royal monastery erected in 1340 by King Alfonso XI, housing a miraculous statue of Mary, so the mistake is understandable.

186. Johnston, *The Wonder of Guadalupe*, chapter 7. In 1996 the abbot who was keeper of the shrine of Guadalupe was forced to resign after he came under massive criticism for having told a newspaper that the whole story was only a beautiful legend. Skeptics still abound.

187. Johnston, *The Wonder of Guadalupe*, 56.

188. The official history of Lourdes, with all the documentation, requires six volumes! See R. Laurentin, *Histoire authentique* (Paris-Lourdes, 1960–1964). For an excellent summary see Dom B. Billet, O.S.B., "Lourdes," in *Catholicisme*, (Paris: Letouzey et Ané, 1956–), 7:1193–1200.

189. A commission established by the bishop began work July 28, 1858, interrogated Bernadette Soubirous, to whom the Virgin appeared, twice and investigated thirty-two cases of healings. On January 18, 1862, the bishop published his findings that

of the sun, witnessed by seventy thousand people in 1917 at Fatima;[190] the whole story of Mary's purportedly appearing to a group of children daily over a period of thirteen years (and, as I write in 1998, still continuing), attracting more than 30 million pilgrims to Medjugorje, in (of all places) Bosnia. Were one to add to these other more private revelations and details of the lives of holy persons like Padre Pio with the stigmata and Marthe Robin (who died in 1982), the bedridden women who consumed nothing but the Eucharist for the last fifteen years of her life and from whose influence have flowed entire communities and religious congregations, one would end with a vast collection of facts difficult, on the basis of the canons of historical investigation, to deny, and just as difficult to explain scientifically. But a library of such authenticated reports would convince few who refuse to believe in the "supernatural,"[191] and would continue to discomfort those believers who are unhappy with the idea that "heaven" should intervene in this world so heavy-handedly (as though we were

---

the apparitions were authentic, basing his decision on "the sincerity and veracity of Bernadette, the certitude of the healings, and finally the concours," that is, the movement of prayer and conversions that followed. Presently from 2 to a high of 5 million pilgrims in special anniversary years visit Lourdes every year (Billet, "Lourdes," 1196–97). Since 1882 a medical office at Lourdes investigates all claims of cures; more than five thousand have been examined, passing the persons through a thorough medical examination at the time the claim is first made, and revisiting them later; authentic cases are sent to Rome. Over the years Rome has accepted fifty-eight cases as authentically miraculous. All cases of nervous disorder or neurasthenia are ignored (T. F. Casey, "Lourdes," in *The New Catholic Encyclopedia* (New York: McGraw Hill, 1967–1969), 8:1032–33. Most of the miracles concern dramatic organic repair or overnight new growth.

190. The Virgin appeared each thirteenth of the month from May to October 1917 to three shepherd children, ages seven, eight, and ten. The crowds grew each month. On August 13 the prefect of the province kidnapped and held the children for two days, but the Virgin appeared to them on the nineteenth and promised a great miracle for October 13. On that wet and dismal day, the Virgin appeared (only the children saw her), announcing to them that she is "Our Lady of the Rosary." Then the sun shone through and seemed to tremble, rotated violently, and finally fell toward the damp crowd, then repeated the performance twice after a pause, the whole event lasting ten minutes. When the sun dove toward the crowd, all seventy thousand threw themselves into the mud, terrified, praying, and shouting. A journalist who had mocked the events in the morning wrote on October 15 in the Lisbon *O Século* with a changed attitude. Two of the children died in the next two years, as the Virgin had said they would. The eldest, Lucia, lives to this day as a cloistered nun. Over the years she released many prophesies and promises made by the Virgin. One prophesy, the defeat of communism in Russia and its conversion if people would pray for this intention, has been the subject of intense interest over the years. It was not until completion of long investigations, in 1933, that the bishop of Leiria finally declared the visions worthy of credence, but passed over in silence the "Miracle of the Sun." As G. Jacquemet says in his article in *Catholicisme*, on the one hand there is no reason to doubt the authenticity of the firsthand reports that have been recorded, and on the other, the event was observed nowhere else, and there is no obligation on the part of anyone to explain what it is that happened to that crowd (*Catholicisme* 4, col. 1114.) See also H. M. Gillett, "Fatima," in *New Catholic Encyclopedia*, 5:855f.

191. Such things would probably continue to attract little interest, strangely, from the "New Age" adepts of the "paranormal" and the magical.

still in Old Testament circumstances!). I have heard a prominent Catholic sigh, "After all, Christ left us the greatest miracle, that is all that we need, his Church, its sound teaching, and its valid making available his Holy Eucharist, so who needs this kind of thing?"

These private revelations and especially the spectacular purported apparitions divide Catholics as well as bring some together. One faithful Catholic who is not warm to such piety once said to me, "Catholics who hunger after such things must have something wrong in their religious psyches." Protestant Christians certainly do not, in general, have any truck with such "superstitions and magic"[192] (although there have been some notorious conversions, such as Ernst Psichari at Lourdes; the Jew Franz Werfel, who wrote *The Song of Bernadette;* and the Lutheran pastor Wayne Weibel, who has become a leading exponent of the events at Medjugorje while remaining Lutheran).

Proponents of the authenticity in principle of some apparitions would reply, first, that Christ already said that His coming would divide brother from brother, son from father, that any intervention from God sorely tests our pride, and that only the poor in spirit relate properly to these things. (Why have all the most widely accepted—Guadalupe, Lourdes, Fatima, and now Medjugorje—happened to peasants, and only, except for Juan Diego, children?)[193] Those receptive to the possibility readily acknowledge that

192. There are exceptions: the televangelist Rev. Oral Roberts of my hometown, Tulsa, Oklahoma, reported on television having seen a ninety-foot Christ. And evangelicals experience "charismatic" phenomena—spectacular healings, "swoonings in the spirit," prophesying, and so on.

193. A striking feature of Fatima is that the three children could not even have understood the real thrust of the predictions they transmitted from Mary: that the (distant) Great War would end, that Russia would become communist (they had no idea what that was), that, following a great sign to be seen throughout Europe (a huge burst of light in the night was recorded in newspapers—I have seen an extract of the *New York Times*—in the fall of 1938, and never explained astronomically), a second world war would begin, and "Russia would spread its errors throughout the world." Our Lady said, however, that if people would repent and pray and if Russia were to be "consecrated to my sacred heart" (this was finally done by the pope and almost all the bishops of the world in 1982), Russia would be converted. Those who faithfully gathered the first Saturdays of every month to pray for that intention see the events of these last years as a sure sign of the authenticity of the Fatima apparitions.

One of these is a wealthy Dutch benefactor of the Church, recently deceased, who, after perestroika, sent a radio transmitter to Moscow to broadcast the prophesies of Fatima. Gorbachev refused permission, so the transmitter remained in boxes. When the coup against Yeltsin happened, the benefactor's agent remembered the radio and told Yeltsin, who had barricaded himself in the Parliament building. The radio was smuggled in and assembled, and by this means Yeltsin called the population into the streets. The benefactor, Piet Dirksen, showed me the original of the letter from Boris Yeltsin recounting this and thanking him. In return, Piet received permission to have Russian television broadcast, direct from Fatima, the anniversary mass, on October 15, 1991. A friend who was personally moved by his visit to Medjugorje commented: "Our Lady, being human, loves her children, and like any good mother, likes to be with them. See how tender and appreciative she is with the young visionaries!"

every apparition and even the most credible among them attract curiosity seekers, the superstitious, and the mentally deranged, but so does the entire phenomenon of religion, just as does sex, economics, or any other basic reality important to fallen human nature. Those who gain from these loving special favors of heaven are those who can become like little children, and trustingly accept God's graces. Evangelicals believe in faith healing and "prophesy," but like their "colder" "mainstream" Protestant brethren, they refuse all cults of saints, any role for icons, pilgrimages to "holy places," and they downplay the sense of "the real presence" in the Eucharist, certainly the notion of the essential role of an ordained ministry physically linked by a chain of ordination to Jesus Himself, and energetically reject "Mariology," all those things that prime Catholics to expect a more physical relation to Jesus Christ, His Mother and the saints, and to one another in a strong corporate structure. Protestants believe Catholics imagine all these things, thereby further contaminating the spirituality of the faith, as Catholics, they believe, have done almost from the Church's beginning, which is the reason Protestantism has to exist.

The "Mariological" content of many of these apparitions is taken up by Balthasar as an important point about them. In the context of an essay on women priests, he affirms the essential feminine, Marian character of the Church, and he points out how assertedly our Blessed Mother is offering "active testimonies from heaven" to her status as "the Immaculate Conception," chosen by God for a role of free obedience without sin, and hence primary incarnation of His Church.

> She is not allowed to hide herself behind her Son in false humility; she comes uninhibitedly to the fore and manifests her nature: "I am the Immaculate Conception," she insists at Lourdes, and this in connection with the Rosary, which points clearly enough to the divine origin of the Son and of the entire Trinity. The masculine hierarchy was willing enough to recognize the messages of Lourdes and Fatima, and the numerous Marian encyclicals of the Popes have underscored the rightful place of women in the Church's inmost nature.[194]

The impact of all this has been, without doubt, a strengthening of the role of Mary in private piety, with emphasis on the position accorded her by God in the redemptive work of the Church.

Neither the conciliar documents nor *The Catechism* places any emphasis on private revelations. But as I see what is happening in the Church today, I have the impression that they are more significant than their "private" character might seem to call for. This is why Church authorities can scarcely avoid pronouncing on their authenticity. They do this circumspectly. First, the magisterium insists clearly that none of these events nor anything purported to have been said by the appearing Virgin or saint is binding on the faith of anyone. A Catholic is free to disregard and disbelieve in any or all such events and private messages, and he may even deny the

---

194. Balthasar, *New Elucidations*, 195.

likelihood that they would ever occur.[195] Second, if the Church finds the least unorthodoxy in what is being purported, it will act energetically in condemning the phenomenon as spurious. ("The phenomena have no supernatural origin," was the phrase in a report to a bishop about a recent "apparition" in the United States.) Third, in its official teaching and in the whole sphere of theology the Church does not like to dwell on these things. *The Catechism* acknowledges but downplays "private revelation." On the whole matter of private revelations, *The Catechism* has only this to say:

> Through the ages, there have been so-called "private" revelations, some of which have been recognized by the authority of the Church. They do not belong, however, to the deposit of faith. It is not their role to improve or complete Christ's definitive revelation, but to help live more fully by it in a certain period of history. Guided by the magisterium of the Church, the *sensus fidelium* knows how to discern and welcome in these revelations whatever constitutes an authentic call of Christ or his saints to the Church.[196]

The Catechism does affirm that these revelations can be genuine helps from God, but they are not "mainline," and even when pronounced authentic, they may be ignored by faithful Catholics. I have found over the years that in the editorial-board discussions regarding what to publish in *International Theological Review: Communio* none of the learned theologians seemed inclined even to consider the issue of these "private revelations," despite the fact that they have become a major sociological-spiritual reality within Catholic life these last years.[197] Personally, I believe they deserve discussion, and the effect of many of them on even millions of lives deserves both careful observation and serious reflection.

195. Given the infinite power of God and His unceasing ability to surprise us, it would seem odd to deny the very possibility that He could intervene miraculously and obviously in the personal life of any individual. I have found when one opens the subject of intimate personal experiences of divine intervention and even miracles with one's personal acquaintances, a host of extraordinary happenings are recounted, somewhat giddily but often surprisingly credibly. The story of Dirksen's radio is typical. Another comes to mind, told by a tough-minded lady with a Ph.D. in anthropology, a convert, in a context that provoked her to announce, "I have never told this to anyone before." Teaching catechism one Saturday to thirty girls, she discovered they had forgotten to make any provision for lunch. When she asked if anyone had brought something to eat, one said she had a packet of Kentucky Fried Chicken—three pieces. "Well," replied the teacher, half in jest, "let us say the blessing and just do like Jesus with the loaves and fishes." To everyone's stupefaction, all thirty ate to their fill, in awed silence. This story came out because I had recounted how a friend, distributing baskets of grapes to the hungry in Chiapas, Mexico, had lived the same experience. I tell these stories because their existence and recounting make up a part of Catholic life, abominable to rationalists and disliked, as I said, by many practicing Catholics, but a significant current in the tradition, nonetheless.

196. Para. 67. I find it significant when *The Catechism* gives so little space to something many persist in thinking central.

197. Of course, the lives of the great saints are full of wondrous stories, the more legendary and colorful the further one goes back in history. Can anything top the Fioretti collected about the poor Saint Francis in the thirteenth and fourteenth centuries?

One way the Church signals its approval is through canonization of the visionaries: the canonization of Marie Margaret of the Sacred Heart (Paray-la-Moniale, Burgundy) and Bernadette of Lourdes certainly adds credibility to those particular private revelations. (But then one may wonder why Juan Diego of Guadalupe has never been canonized.) In the case of Fatima, Mary purportedly predicted two of the three children would die young (the children reported the prediction at the time), and, low and behold, within a few years they did, while the third, who became Sister Lucy, keeper of the famous "third secret" revealed by Our Lady, lives on into her eighties in a convent at Fatima; no canonizations are thinkable until after her death. But three popes have blessed Fatima with their pontifical presence.

The travails of Medjugorje in the most recent years are telling. The responsible bishop, the bishop of Mostar, was opposed to the authenticity of the apparitions from the start, and with time grew more adamant.[198] The metropolitan Archbishop Franjic of Split has been convinced of their authenticity. Two episcopal commissions charged to investigate have been cool. The pope and Cardinal Ratzinger reportedly both have been cautiously supportive, but only in private and *à titre personel*—there has not been public endorsement from Rome. A number of foreign bishops have gone as pilgrims, again *à titre personel*. Spiritual fruits—conversions, deepening of personal piety, even cures, although that has not been emphasized—have flowed in abundance. Everyone with whom I have spoken who went there skeptical returned at least impressed with the quiet and dignified atmosphere of prayer, devoid of sensationalism, while most were in some way moved. What the future will bring in the way of Church approval of the devotion is at this writing difficult to predict.

In the cases of Lourdes and Fatima, it was a matter of commissions of investigation, accompanied by growing devotion, carefully investigated reports of cures, ever swelling masses of pilgrims, joined by more and more bishops, and finally visits by popes, which are a way of saying, "It is good to be here."[199]

198. Now the poor bishop of Mostar is retired, after having first gone into exile, at his episcopal house in ruins. He was a victim of the civil war in Bosnia. I have yet to hear a proponent of the apparitions uncharitably shout "See!" On the contrary, I was impressed, when I was taken there while at a meeting in Zagreb, to hear the priests of Medjugorje preaching respect for and patience with the bishop, and recalling that he was exercising his proper authority in a difficult situation. Meanwhile, a new bishop has been appointed, who, I hear, is as adamantly opposed to acknowledging the validity of the apparitions as his predecessor. I have recently heard proponents say that the fact Medjugorje has been spared in the war raging all about is a "sign," accompanied (allegedly) by other miraculous signs. But the sites of the most followed apparitions are always filled with signs and rumors of signs. Everyone admits they become focal points for disturbed people. But then they are the poor whom God especially loves.

199. On the occasion of a Communio board meeting in Lisbon, we went to Fatima with Father von Balthasar on one of the great anniversary days, May 15, 1988. That year the cardinal archbishop of Angola presided and preached, the cardinal archbishop of Lisbon and two other cardinals, forty bishops, and four hundred priests concelebrated

I have been asking myself why, when I made an outline for the present overview chapter, spontaneously I listed the question of apparitions and private revelations under "weaknesses." I recognize that three thoughts were troubling me. First, were the Church—that is *us*—doing what Christ expects of us, His Blessed Mother would not have to be intervening so directly and miraculously to advance His Revelation, to stave off the worst, implied in her Son's own sigh, recorded by Saint Luke: "When the Son of Man returns will he find any faith on earth?" Second, aware that even some of the most pious and well-disposed theologians do not like to talk formally and officially of these things, I thought, "Well, whatever one tends to hush must be something less than ideal." And third, I knew the Church's way of approaching and approving of these things is itself complex, even perhaps a bit disquieting. As I just suggested, local bishops are (understandably) suspicious; commissions take forever to say something, and then it is often carefully hedged; finally, popular practice prevails, and perhaps bishops from afar start to come, and maybe even a pope or two. The "priest" has always been suspicious of the "prophet," and well he may be, as most turn out to be false prophets; but then many priests are not such holy servants of God, which gives the prophets work to do!

One last remark on this difficult issue: if the fruits that incontestably have flowed from Medjugorje—to take the most recent notorious example—have at their root only a phenomenon of mass-hysterical pathology, then the best one could say (as a Christian might say of Islam in the authenticity of whose prophesy he does not believe) is "God writes straight with crooked lines": the devotion and the prayer of the pilgrims, and their conversions, are sincere, the work of God's grace, even if the immediate cause of their going *there* were dubious.[200]

---

the mass. In a scene of great dignity and peace, five hundred thousand pilgrims were in attendance. In his homily in Fatima on May 13, 1982, Pope John Paul said this: "If the Church has accepted the message of Fatima, it is above all because that message contains a truth and a call whose basic content is the truth and the call of the Gospel itself: 'Repent and believe in the Gospel' (Mark 1:15)" (*Fatima Family Messenger* [January–March 1993]: 25). That is a key message: so long as such phenomena strengthen in an orthodox way the faith, then, as the pope said, "it is good to be here."

200. On my one visit to Medjugorje, where I was driven by "Medjogorjephil" friends after a family congress in Zagreb, and where I went trying to keep an open mind, I sat around the little camping table in the cramped house trailer serving as temporary parish office with my friends, talking to one of the most active and reflective of the Franciscans. He was telling of his latest exchange with the then bishop, in which, exasperated, the priest replied, "Look, bishop, if you really believe we were able to achieve all this through power of suggestion over these poor kids, why don't you ask two of your cleverest priests to try an experiment at the other end of your diocese with some impressionable shepherd children, and see how many people come and how many evident conversions occur?" I left that meeting with not the slightest doubt about that priest's own belief in the authenticity of the apparitions. I came away impressed by the quiet piety I saw there, the sense of respectful submission to the judgment of the Church, and an absence of jarring fanaticism. And I cannot deny being impressed with the conversions, deep and apparently for life, I know about personally.

Inadequate Communio between Those of Eastern and Western Spirituality

I would like to return to a great sorrow in the Church, to reflect on the weakness it manifests. Recall a text cited earlier from the important manifesto *Communio: A Program*, written by Hans Urs von Balthasar:[201]

> Dialogue can certainly help to bear and resolve tensions between Christians, but only communion will bring an end to them. First among them is the rift between Eastern Church and Western Church. Between them, of course, *communicatio in sacris*, sacramental community, does indeed exist as sign of a deeper unanimity. But is this most important and most intimate communion vividly present to western theology, whether Catholic or Protestant, in its plans and discussions? Or is this western theology (with a few exceptions such as that of Louis Bouyer) not becoming more and more alien, in its understanding of tradition, liturgy and ministry, to the venerable Church of the origins, as though the latter no longer seriously counted, were a negligible quantity in the world's debate. This can only be to the great detriment of those who despise it. Moreover, don't we still much prefer (perhaps for political reasons?) to engage in discussion with the Orthodox Church, passing over the Eastern Churches in communion with Rome as though they scarcely existed, although western churchmen alone are responsible for their artificial western character (where it does exist)? There is such a thing as genocide among Christians.[202]

Balthasar is not given to hyperbole; he would not use such a drastic term as *genocide* if he were not convinced of the extreme gravity of this estrangement. I agree that it has reached such a point even the best thinkers, with few exceptions, are even aware it is a problem. Your author can personally attest to the difficulty he, as a "Latin," has had in even beginning to penetrate the sense and the "feel" of the Eastern spiritualities, those of the "venerable Church" that is our heritage too, indeed, as Balthasar said, "the venerable Church of the origins." Spontaneously, I have even neglected the importance of the rites other than my own dominant Latin rite in appropriating the tradition. I confess that my efforts in this book to appropriate "the other lung" are seriously insufficient, the surface is not even scratched, and this for no want of goodwill. We are as though trapped in the rationalism of the West. The mysticism of the East belongs to a "Levantine civilization" that is truly foreign to us, but, paradoxically forms an essential part of our origins. We are alienated from our own ground, a most dangerous situation for the Church. I further agree with Balthasar that "dialogue" is necessary but insufficient; *communio* is the demand of Jesus Christ Himself, and nothing less will do. I shall continue, despite a lack of

---

201. At the time Balthasar, Ratzinger, de Lubac, and others founded *Communio*, with the intention of working to strengthen the sense of the mystical *koinonia*, community in Christ, that is the Church. Recently, following the initial intention, circles of readers have sprung up, to help in the effort to influence the culture in the light of the gospel and to provide grassroots experience in feedback to the editorial boards. These boards, in turn, mobilize the thinking powers in the Church to tackle profound and difficult issues. Readers interested in joining a local *Communio* circle to contact *Communio*, P.O. Box 4557, Washington, D.C., 20017 or telephone (202) 526-0251.

202. Balthasar, "Communio—A Program" in *International Theological Review: Communio* 1:1 (1977): 9.

living contacts, my efforts to understand and love what, while foreign to me, alienated in this respect from the roots of our Church, is paradoxically also mine, crying out for appropriation. I applaud the efforts being made in many of the communities in France to study Eastern spirituality and to integrate icons and Byzantine music and something of their sense of the sacred space that is the Church into their liturgies.

The crying shame of our isolation from an essential part of our origins drives home a central point of which I have become ever more aware as I completed *Truth and Authenticity* and *Being and Truth:* from the start I saw the necessity of achieving *communio* with the great traditions, for those who live in them are all our brothers, yet I must acknowledge how difficult it is to move toward loving interaction even with a tradition as foundational and as close to one's own as the Eastern churches in union with Rome. Of course, the nearest and most relevant traditions are the most threatening, as we are always insecure about our own central accommodations. I was right, it turns out, to insist in *Tradition and Authenticity* on the need for first deepening one's critical grasp of his own tradition as ground for the security needed to risk earnest dialogue with the other. But openness to the other is already necessary to discover one's self.

Liturgy

Strengths

Orthodox- and Byzantine-rite Catholics complain of the Latin-rite liturgy rather as Roman Catholics complain of a typical Protestant church service: that it is too severe, too summary, lacking in hieratic sense. Since the postconciliar liturgical reform, many Catholics also complain that the new liturgy not only lacks hieratic sense but most often, on Sundays at least, also takes on a feeling closer to a church picnic than a great liturgy at least trying to be worthy of the mystery that is happening on the altar. I shall consider these complaints when we come, in a moment, to discuss liturgical weaknesses in the tradition. But first, there are strengths, believe it or not, in the Catholic Church's liturgies: first, the richness and variety of the great Eastern liturgies of the Uniate churches; but, second, even in the Roman-rite liturgy, which can be made ornate in a most dignified manner, quite sufficiently to awe Protestants at least! On the first, it must be said we have a long way to go in making available those Eastern riches to the entire Church. Solemn procession, blazing candles galore, rich vestments, elaborate incensing, awesome silence at the moment of consecration—I have seen all of these combined in solemn Latin liturgies to provide a most dignified setting. Recall how essential it is that what is visually and audibly happening reflect as far as humanly possible what is (as the eyes of faith can see it) actually, mysteriously happening. We incarnate spirits are affected profoundly by our sensible perceptions, to the extent that we really expect a holy person to look holy and to act *obviously* holy (which does not mean pietistically). To be sure, nothing disgusts us so much as a phony show of being holy, or even just McFriendly, with the fast-food smile and the department store "Hi, deary!" of forced bonhomie. Again, one must make allowances for the differences between people. Just as there are some who are professionally "friendly," there are kind persons who are gruff in manner. I know priests whose theologies are sound and whose lives are examples of self-abnegation who, despite profound devotion to the real presence of Christ in the Eucharist, say their Mass, not inattentively to be sure, but in a somewhat matter-of-fact manner. Just as some people cannot carry a tune, others have no sense of gesture, elocution, and pace. And I can easily imagine a priest who says his Mass with perfect dramatic balance, a show of great reverence, being a self-centered, arrogant, critical egoist in real life.[203]

Yet, liturgy carefully performed, with evidence of the congregation's care and concern to make it lovely, within the limits of their possibilities— provided it is done in a way that makes it clear that what is being celebrated is truly the crucified and Risen Lord and not the community celebrating itself—can successfully set an atmosphere of *adoration*. This can be accomplished within that austere Roman rite. This austerity, abhorrent to the East, actually has some merits. I can think of three. First, the Liturgy of the Word gains in relative importance, becoming almost half (in time) of the Mass, provided, of course, there is sufficient emphasis on the sermon. (The problematic aspect of this will be addressed in "weaknesses" below.) I personally believe this redress of balance in favor of the Word is one of several "Protestantizing" initiatives of the postconciliar Church that actually rights a wrong.[204]

203. Priests are trained in seminary to be careful not to overdramatize. I have noticed that the holiest priests I know do not linger unduly over the words of consecration, nor fall into long lapses of personal meditation during the Mass. This is a protection against contaminating what is in fact the greatest drama on earth with mere theatrics, and touches that are too personal, and would center attention too much on the humble instrument, the priest.

204. If the hieratic sense recalling the awesomeness of the Real Presence has suffered, that, I believe, is the fault of other factors: an inexcusable relaxation of the discipline of confession as preparation for communion, the neglect of all fasting beforehand (supposedly one hour, but increasingly ignored altogether; before, it was no food from awaking until communion); and taking the host in the hand, increasingly from laymen with little or no preparation as "lay ministers." Canonically, "lay ministers of the Eucharist" are supposed to be trained and given a blessing, and are to be used *only when insufficient priests are on hand*. That is widely abused, often as a way of involving as many women as possible in the liturgy, which can sometimes amount to using the liturgy to make a point against the "Roman authorities," when the very purpose of liturgy is to unite around Christ, represented by his vicar on earth. Fortunately, that attitude is often more innocent: we want the women to feel part of the ceremony, now that laymen too are becoming massively involved. So as the law permits woman lectors and eucharistic ministers, once reserved to men of minor or major orders only, they make full use of the opportunity to involve women legitimately. In our archdiocese there has been considerable progress in choosing and preparing lay ministers of the

Second, because the core is reduced to the essential, thought and attention must be given to embellish it. In the Byzantine rite, what is set out and mandated by the *ordo*[205] is so long and elaborate, there is no need or even, really, possibility of thoughtful embellishment. One continues to do simply what one has forever been told. This Eastern approach has a number of strengths: the Mass liturgy is always rich and dignified, a sense of the antiquity and greatness of the tradition is conveyed, and tasteless or otherwise inappropriate innovations are avoided. The catholicity of the liturgical form, which bespeaks the unity of the Church, everywhere and at all times, is ensured. The disadvantages are again the flip side of these strengths: because no personal thought has to be given to provide anything over and beyond the given essentials, local creative participation is minimal, and hence there is no place for expression of the local culture (although long-standing national variants in music and language are to be found in the liturgies of the national churches). Again, with careful thought and good taste both can be accommodated, the dignified showing forth the unity of the Church through time and space, and its inculturation into many societies—appropriate to a world church.[206]

Third, both frequent Sunday liturgies—a practical necessity when large numbers are practicing—and daily Masses become much more feasible. And daily Mass attendance results in an internalization of what is happening, difficult in great feast-day and Sunday liturgies, which inevitably are something of a show, an affair indeed more of the "community" than the more intimate daily Mass.

Regarding the use of the vernacular for the celebration of the Mass and

---

Eucharist. But what a change since the sixties. Before, no lay person except the sacristan would dare touch the golden eucharistic vessels.

I would add, as a result of the increased emphasis on the Eucharist as *communio*—which is good, but often is understood somewhat in the spirit of a social get-together—there has occurred a serious degradation in respectful comportment in Church. Not long ago, non-Catholics were impressed by the silence and adoring respect shown the presence of the Lord in Catholic churches. Now, frequently, the choir's country-western performance (in plain view on the altar) is literally applauded at the end, like any good spectacle, and people stand around visiting in church, like it was Methodist. The positive side of this is that even in big-city parishes some people are actually getting to know one another a bit, a necessary step toward loving one another more than just theoretically. With a little attention, both goals are achievable, and those who wish to stay a few minutes in prayer after receiving the Eucharist might still be able to pray in silence. For instance, save all the greetings for the vestibule, leaving the adoring remnant in peace before the Eucharistic Lord.

205. The *ordo* is the set of liturgical instructions the celebrants are supposed to follow.
206. The catholicity and respect for "the center" is shown by adhering carefully and completely to the *ordo*, avoiding improvisations, especially in the canon of the Mass. Local color is shown by a) use of the vernacular; b) tasteful and liturgically appropriate banners, but in the style of the local art (Eastern churches remain uniformly with the Byzantine icon styles of old); c) local styles in the music, which nevertheless can be respectful and beautiful, as the Missa Criolla from Argentina (by Ariel Ramirez) long ago demonstrated.

the other sacraments, there continues much dispute and considerable un-happiness about the translations. This has made possible the enhancement of the Liturgy of the Word, and it has made everyone more conscious of the sense of the words throughout. The congregation accompanies the celebrant more actively than before. Great care in pronouncing the words can avoid loss of hieratic sense, indeed when the congregation understands better what is being said, the immense power of the words themselves add to the dignity of the service. Loss of the beauty and rhythms of the great Latin texts, forged over centuries, is compensated by the beauty of other languages, if the translations are works of art. I shall discuss the catastrophe of using the translations to drive political agendas as we turn to the weaknesses.

Weaknesses

The invitation to innovation has opened the door to every manner of abuse. I shall not detail them all; it is too depressing. Many of these have with time been corrected. But there are a couple of widespread problems that demand urgent attention.

A distressing recent development in North American churches, of a type completely new, is the playing of self-conscious, indeed *ideological,* language games in response to feminist pressures. I am assured that in Europe this has not happened, or not much, and indeed the extremes of American feminism are looked on there with amusement. Here, however, it is no laughing matter. Ignoring the fact that a serious sexism has arisen, namely, the political correctness of condemning all men as patriarchal oppressors of women, accompanied by a truly sick effort to tarnish the very name of "Father," a scandalous injustice to all fathers who have ever tried to live up to their responsibilities, the notion that the language is discriminatory toward women because in English the male form is also the inclusive form has adroitly been exploited to promulgate a vague sense of guilt and conspiracy and an intense, disruptive, awkward self-consciousness in the use of language. (All totalitarians have been language rebuilders. Have all the lessons of Hitler's and Stalin's "new speak" and of Orwell's *1984* gone unheeded?) So whereas before unconsciously (so it is purported) women were being put down by the language, this wrong is now supposedly made right *by consciously putting men down* through a great show of torturing the language to right the alleged wrong men have committed in skewing the language. Msgr. Robert Sokolowski, remarks in *L'Osservatore Romano* that such a change is not a normal "organic develop-ment of the English language. It is an engineered change, a prosthesis, not a gradual, normal development. It is being forced on the language because of an ideology."[207]

---

207. Robert Sokolowski in *L'Osservatore Romano* (March 3, 1993): 9. It will be crucial that Rome demonstrate the strength of having a Church solid at the center, by its intervention into the decision of the American bishops to proceed to such ideological tampering with the historic and sacred texts.